HUMAN RESOURCE MANAGEMENT

We work with leading authors to develop the strongest
educational materials in Human Resource Management,
bringing cutting-edge thinking and best learning practice to
a global market.

Under a range of well-known imprints, including
FT Prentice Hall, we craft high quality print and electronic
publications which help readers to understand and apply
their content, whether studying or at work.

To find out more about the complete range of our
publishing, please visit us on the World Wide Web at:
www.pearsoneduc.co.uk

Second Edition

HUMAN RESOURCE MANAGEMENT

A Concise Analysis

Eugene McKenna
Nic Beech

 Prentice Hall
FINANCIAL TIMES

An imprint of **Pearson Education**
Harlow, England • London • New York • Boston • San Francisco • Toronto • Sydney • Singapore • Hong Kong
Tokyo • Seoul • Taipei • New Delhi • Cape Town • Madrid • Mexico City • Amsterdam • Munich • Paris • Milan

Pearson Education Limited
Edinburgh Gate
Harlow
Essex CM20 2JE
England

and Associated Companies throughout the world

Visit us on the World Wide Web at:
www.pearsoned.co.uk

First published 2002
Second edition published 2008

© Pearson Education Limited 2002, 2008

ISBN: 978-0-273-69418-2

British Library Cataloguing-in-Publication Data
A catalogue record for this book is available from the British Library

Library of Congress Cataloging-in-Publication Data
A catalog record for this book is available from the Library of Congress

10 9 8 7 6 5 4 3 2 1
12 11 10 09 08

Typeset in 10/12pt Minion by 3
Printed by Ashford Colour Press Ltd, Gosport

The publisher's policy is to use paper manufactured from sustainable forests.

CONTENTS

PREFACE

We are delighted to present a second edition of **Human Resource Management: a concise analysis**. We are grateful to the many students and lecturers who have used the first edition and given us feedback over the past few years. In writing the second edition we have sought to retain key aspects of the principles that stimulated us to write the book – a need to present theory in an accessible way without over-simplifying it, a need to ground the study of HRM in practice and an aim to help readers develop as reflective practitioners.

The concept of reflective practice is particularly important to us. It is one that has recently been stressed by the Chartered Institute for Personnel and Development and we regard it as central to the successful management of people. Getting the right structures and systems in place (such as appraisal, rewards and training) is important, but is only part of the story. The way that systems are put into action and the relationship employees have with their managers is fundamental to how they interpret the meaning of the systems and structures. It is possible for employees to interpret managerial systems as well-intentioned and trustworthy, or conversely as ill-intentioned and exploitative. The interpretation that is made will impact on the commitment and behaviour of the employees, and hence on the performance of the organisation. HRM is fundamentally about trying to create a virtuous cycle in which trust is built up along with commitment and performance. Reflective practice is important as this is the process through which managers weigh up the needs of employees, the theories and practices they could apply in a situation and develop good judgement in order to be able to choose an effective course of action.

Developing such judgement does not happen over night. It can be informed by action-oriented theory and previous practice. It is also informed by self-awareness and a questioning approach. This book seeks to assist readers to develop such judgement by presenting theories and case studies, and also by posing reflective questions and suggested activities. Exercising judgement must incorporate an understanding of ethics because it is people rather than ordinary 'resources' that we are dealing with. Consequently, ethical issues and questions are raised throughout the book. Many people have been exploited by organisations, and sometimes the title 'HRM' has been used to hide practices that have negative outcomes for people. We believe that an ethical approach to reflective practice should challenge exploitation and unfair treatment, and at the same time should overtly be concerned with individual and organisational performance.

The second edition is a significant updating of the first. New and lengthier cases have been introduced and areas of theoretical debate reflect developments in the field. We have paid careful attention to practice and professional standards in order to ensure that the practical aspects of the book are useful. In making such changes it is easy to move away from being 'concise', but we have sought to keep the book accessible and to-the-point. We hope that readers will find it so, and that it will be helpful in stimulating a thoughtful approach to managing people.

Eugene McKenna and Nic Beech, 2008

ACKNOWLEDGEMENTS

We are grateful to the following for permission to reproduce copyright material:

The British Psychological Society for an extract from 'State of the Art: Personality' by Sarah Hampson published by *The Psychologist*, Volume 12, Part 6, June 1999 pages 284–90 copyright © The Psychologist; Chartered Institute of Personnel and Development for a table from the CIPD *Reward Management Annual Survey Report* (2007) copyright © CIPD 2007 used with the permission of the publisher, the Chartered Institute of Personnel and Development, London (www.cipd.co.uk); National Statistics for the tables 'UK Employment by gender', 'UK part-time employment by gender', 'UK part-time employees who did not want a full-time job', 'UK temporary employees by gender' and 'UK temporary employees who did not want a permanent job', and the figures 'UK population: by age' and 'UK population by gender and age' published on www.statistics.gov.uk © Crown copyright material is reproduced with the permission of the Controller of HMSO; and Pearson Education Limited for the table 'Employee participation' from *Contemporary Human Resource Management* 2nd edition by T. Redman and A. Wilkinson published by Pearson Education 2006 copyright © Pearson Education.

In some instances we have been unable to trace the owners of copyright material, and we would appreciate any information that would enable us to do so.

AUTHOR'S DEDICATION

To Alison, Geraldine, Graham, Linda and Rosie

LIST OF CASE EXAMPLES

LIST OF ABBREVIATIONS

16PF	16 personality factors (Cattell's)
ABLE	Aptitude for Business Learning Exercises
ACAS	Advisory, Conciliatory and Arbitration Service
AI	appreciative inquiry
APR	aligning people with roles
ARP	aligning roles with people
ATM	automatic teller machine
BPR	business process re-engineering
BPS	British Psychological Society
CBI	Confederation of British Industry
CEO	chief executive officer
CIPD	Chartered Institute of Personnel and Development
CPD	continuous professional development
CSR	corporate social responsibility
CV	curriculum vitae
DIY	do-it-yourself
EAP	employee assistance programme
EFQM	European Foundation for Quality Management
EI	employee involvement
EOC	Equal Opportunities Commission
ESG	environmental, social and governance
ESRC	Economic and Social Research Council
EU	European Union
EWCs	European Works Councils
HCM	high-commitment management
HR	human resource
HRM	human resource management
HRP	human resource planning
ICT	information and communication technology
IDS	Income Data Services
IiP	Investors in People
IPM	Institute of Personnel Management (now the Chartered Institute of Personnel and Development)
JIT	just in time
LSC	Learning and Skills Council
L Tips	long-term incentives
MBO	management by objectives
MOD	Ministry of Defence
MSF	Manufacturing, Science and Finance (union)
NVQs	National Vocational Qualifications

NTO	national training organisation
OD	organisational development
OECD	Organization for Economic Cooperation and Development
PBR	payment by results
PRP	performance-related pay
QCs	quality circles
SBUs	Strategic Business Units
SCW	skilled contingent worker
SHRD	strategic human resource development
SHRM	strategic human resource management
SME	small and medium sized enterprise
STARs	situations, tasks, actions and results
SWOT	strengths, weaknesses, opportunities and threats
T&G	Transport and General Workers Union
TEC	Training and Enterprise Council
TQM	total quality management
TUC	Trades Union Congress
VDU	visual display unit
WERS	Workplace Employment Relations Survey

Supporting resources
Visit **www.pearsoned.co.uk/mckennabeech** to find valuable online resources.

For instructors
- Complete, downloadable Instructor's Manual
- PowerPoint slides that can be downloaded and used for presentations

Chapter 1

INTRODUCTION AND OVERVIEW

Introduction

Human resource management (HRM) seeks to maximise organisational performance through the adoption of best practice in the management of people. In seeking to understand best practice HRM draws on theoretical foundations from disciplines such as psychology, sociology and industrial relations, and has developed a distinctive body of research over the years. The aim of this book is to conduct an analysis of HRM – the practice, theories and implications from research – in a concise and accessible way. The first chapter seeks to set the scene for such an analysis by introducing some of the key themes that will be revisited in more detail in subsequent chapters, and by showing how they can be integrated in practice.

Having read this chapter, you should:

- understand the general nature of HRM – its aims and practices;

- be aware of the development of HRM and its context;

- have a broad awareness of the various aspects of HRM that will be covered in greater depth in the book;

- be aware of some of the main topics of debate in the subject area.

Human resource management (HRM) can be viewed as an approach to management that considers people as the key resource. It subscribes to the notion that it is important to communicate well with employees, to involve them in what is going on and to foster their commitment and engagement with the organisation. In addition, a strategic approach to the acquisition, management and motivation of people is heavily emphasised.

HRM developed from the practice of personnel management, and so this begs the question: what do we know about the origins of personnel management and its current standing? Before answering this question, a definition of personnel management would be useful. Personnel management assists with the management of people in an organisation. It is concerned with establishing, maintaining and developing systems that provide the framework of employment. These systems operate throughout an employee's membership of the company, starting with the system for entry (recruitment and selection) through the management of the employment relationship (reward, appraisal, development, industrial relations, grievance and discipline), finishing with the termination of the relationship (retirement, resignation, redundancy or dismissal). Ideally this management process is reinforced by the drive for efficiency and equality of opportunity.

Historical development

In the latter part of the 1800s the concept of welfare personnel developed. This was prompted by the humane concerns of certain families involved in business (e.g. Cadbury and Rowntree), and could be referred to as the Quaker tradition. Welfare personnel was concerned with the provision of schemes, considered progressive at that time, dealing with unemployment, sick pay and subsidised housing for employees. The introduction of these schemes could be viewed as a reaction to the harshness of capitalism at that period of British history. The motives of some industrialists adopting welfare schemes were questioned because there was a belief that some practices were intended as an alternative for realistic wages, and as a ploy to keep trade unions at bay.

Welfare personnel continued as a force until the Second World War, and later manifestations of it were the provision of canteens and company outings for workers. Even today it can be recognised that the welfare tradition has some significance in the current practice, for example health schemes and crèches for the children of employees.

The next phase in the development was the emphasis on personnel administration. This amounted to support for management and was basically concerned with recruitment, discipline, time keeping, payment systems, training and keeping personnel records. It came into its own in the period between the First and Second World Wars. The growth in the size of organisations is a factor to consider in connection with this development.

After the Second World War and up to the 1950s personnel management incorporated a wider range of services, including salary administration, basic training and advice on industrial relations, but the main focus was at the tactical rather than the strategic level. Again, increasing organisational size was notable in activating certain changes in industrial relations practices. For example, the movement from collective bargaining at industry level to the level of the company was apparent, resulting in the advent of the industrial relations specialist within personnel management.

The 1960s and 1970s saw a significant increase in the number of staff engaged in personnel work. This could be attributable in part to an increase in the amount of employment legislation. However, the state of the economy had a part to play as well. In conditions of full employment, up to the early 1970s, there was evidence of much recruitment, selection, training and payment system activity in the practice of personnel management. This was prompted to some extent by labour shortages, and was reflected in actions to retain skilled labour and increase the skill levels of the workforce. The approach to training was systematic and planned, heavily influenced by the establishment of the Training Boards, which exacted a training levy from industry and offered grants to companies that conducted training to acceptable standards. In turn this spawned a rapid growth in the number of training specialists within the personnel function. Related activities, such as performance appraisal (e.g. management by objectives) and management development, also assumed importance, as did forecasting manpower needs (manpower planning).

The prevalence of ideas and insights derived from behavioural science ought to be acknowledged as having a part to play as well. Also during this period the strength of the bargaining power of the trade unions at the workplace was conspicuous. The consequence of greater union influence was a substantial increase in the workload of the personnel specialists. The involvement of the personnel function in matters connected with industrial relations issues, and with productivity deals, elevated its concern to some extent to matters of strategic significance to the organisation, at a time when most of its activities could be considered tactical in nature. The emphasis on industrial relations heralded a delicate role for the personnel specialist interacting with both management and workers. This signalled a need to develop negotiation skills and to learn more about various systems of remuneration, and there was a tendency to identify the personnel function with management.

The 1980s saw personnel management entering the entrepreneurial phase, adapting itself to the market economy and enterprise culture. It was not uncommon to find senior personnel executives contributing to the debate within the company about future direction, the relevance of existing business objectives, and improved ways of achieving revised objectives. This era heralded a preoccupation with the management of change, the development of appropriate corporate culture, the acceptance of Japanese industrial relations practices, such as single unions to represent a company's workforce, and Japanese management practices in the form of quality circles and total quality management. A noticeable feature in the practice of industrial relations, in some but not all cases, was the shift in emphasis from workforce collective bargaining to centralised bargaining, and in the process a reduction in the involvement of personnel managers in negotiations at local level.

As the recession in the economy of the early 1980s began to bite, the role of the trade unions began to change. The threat of strike action became less effective as organisations could replace workers relatively easily. This resulted not only from the recession and high unemployment, but also from new legislation introduced at this time. The power of trade unions was reduced with the ending of closed shops, and changes in the rules about industrial action, including balloting and picketing.

The relative weakness in the power of trade unions signalled the need for less elaborate processes in collective bargaining and conflict management. It also culminated in swifter negotiated wage settlements. In addition, organisations were better placed to make changes in work practices that resulted in increased productivity and a reduction in the numbers employed. There were also changes in personnel practices due to the large pool of available labour. For example, the emphasis switched from recruitment (attracting candidates) to selection.

The reduced volume of negotiations based on collective bargaining between unions and personnel specialists, together with the reduction in time devoted to recruitment and selection, provided personnel management with opportunities to manage redundancy programmes and enter negotiations to bring about lower wage settlements in a relatively calm industrial relations climate. Then the first signs of fundamental change to the nature of personnel management appeared on the horizon. Hunt (1984) speculated about the personnel function shifting in its emphasis. It was during the 1980s that the rise in HRM began to attract the attention of personnel practitioners. There was a move away from the traditionally adversarial industrial relations of the 1970s towards an approach that sought to achieve excellence in the organisation through a committed workforce. The reasons for this will be offered later.

The post-entrepreneurial phase for personnel management in the 1990s still saw HRM as the standard bearer, though some would argue that HRM would subsume personnel management. In fact the early 1990s witnessed a change in emphasis. The reaction to individualism and unjustifiable greed of the 1980s made way for the spirit of consent and the value of teamwork. There was concern for core workers who are essential to the operation of the organisation since high commitment is required from these workers. They are expected to be flexible about the hours they work and to work above and beyond their job descriptions. Wages tend to reflect the market rate rather than the rate determined by agreements with trade unions. The number of part-time and fixed-term contract workers as a proportion of the total workforce is increasing.

There was a continuing preoccupation with the value of a strategic approach to human resource management in the context of organisational success. Of course the challenges of the single European market had to be faced, and the significance of the Social Chapter in the practice of human resource management was considered, particularly by companies with European operations. (Amongst the issues covered by the Social Chapter are improved working conditions, equitable remuneration, equal opportunities, labour mobility, union representation, access to information and workers' involvement, and health and safety provisions). In this context, it should be recognised that Europe provides a different socio-technical and economic environment to that of the United States, where HRM took root, and this could influence the type of HRM that is pursued (see Table 1.1).

If one were to consider the application of the principles of HRM in an Asian context, it would be productive to note the following values in the population:

- being polite and courteous;

- not losing face, and placing value on personal relationships;

- hard work and thrift;

- harmony and avoidance of open conflict – strive for consensus;

- group interests predominate over individual interests;

- reciprocation in social relationships;

- discipline and respect for authority (including elders);

- normative system of control rather than a system of control externally imposed;

Table 1.1 Factors influencing HRM in Europe

The following features of the European scene should be recognised:

- pluralism instead of unitarism (explained later, and reflected in the attitudes of trade unions and the nature of their role);
- collectivism and social orientation instead of individualism (the emphasis is on national welfare schemes and group-based systems of work);
- legal framework (e.g. the impact of the Social Chapter, constraints on hiring and firing decisions, changes to laws on employment and remuneration);
- social partnership (e.g. industrial democracy, reasonable employment security, protection of workers' rights (e.g. health and safety, recognition of the role of the workers' representatives (unions)), and the importance of the workforce as a stakeholder);
- social responsibility (concern for the environment, and social obligations (e.g. training));
- importance of community (interaction between industry and the community, the issue of subsidiarity reflected in degrees of local autonomy, community pressure on companies with respect to employment/environment);
- toleration for diversity – cultural diversity (heterogeneity) as opposed to homogeneity (United States) – is prevalent and finds expression in many forms: organisational systems, vocational education, training and skills development, and the internal/external labour market;
- recognition of complexity and ambiguity (e.g., influenced by a long European history and cultural diversity, there is less inclination to go for simple solutions, and there is a recognition of the complexity of the relationship between the various stakeholders in the organisation and the operationalisation of the concept of subsidiarity).

Source: based on Guest, 1994

- trust and mutual help in business relationships;

- family business interests are to be protected;

- centralisation and authoritarianism;

- long-term view, with the guiding hand of government.

It has been noted that HRM is increasingly taking a hold in Asian countries (Huang, 2001).

HRM/personnel activities

In organisations of reasonable size one can expect to find a HRM or personnel function, just as one would expect to find a finance or marketing function. However, in the smaller organisation this level of specialisation may not prevail, and the personnel/HRM function is performed by a manager who handles personnel/HRM matters in conjunction with other duties. In very small organisations personnel activities could be carried out by all managers. Even where personnel/HRM is normally seen as a specialist function it could be carried out by other managers where the amount of work does not warrant employing a specialist. Part of the concept of HRM is that whatever the size of the organisation all managers should be involved. A number of activities can be identified with the personnel/HRM function, though not all the activities listed below may be carried out in some organisations.

HUMAN RESOURCE PLANNING

This process has developed from what was previously called manpower planning. Human resource (HR) planning is concerned with matching the organisational demand for quantity and quality of employees with the available supply. The demand is derived from current and forecast levels of company operations. The supply side consists of human resources available both internally and externally. The internal supply, which has been a target for rationalisation in recent years, consists of the existing workforce and its potential to contribute. The external supply resides in the population outside the organisation and is influenced by demographic trends, developments in education and competitive forces in the labour market within the European Union (EU). The planning exercise outlines the human resource needs of the organisation and provides useful information for a number of activities listed below (e.g. selection, training and rewards).

RECRUITMENT

Prior to recruitment, job analysis is undertaken. This is a process whereby the work to be undertaken by an employee is closely examined, and results in the preparation of a job description. Then a specification is produced of the attributes a suitable candidate will need in order to perform the job. The most appropriate means of recruitment (e.g. newspaper advertisement, employment agency or job centre) is specified with the intention of attracting suitable applications.

SELECTION

A variety of techniques, for example, the application form, interviews, tests and assessment centres, are available to select the best candidate from a pool of applicants. It is likely that a shortlist of applicants will be produced as a first step in the selection process. This may be unnecessary where there are only a small number of job applicants. Some measure, i.e. criteria relating to the ideal candidate, is used to assist in making a selection decision.

PERFORMANCE APPRAISAL

This is a technique, not universally accepted, of assessing the performance of employees against agreed targets. HRM practitioners would be most likely to be involved in designing the procedures, leaving the line managers normally to administer the process. This commonly takes the form of an interview following the completion of forms that facilitate assessment of achievement in the period since the last interview (often one year). Performance can be measured against criteria set previously. The outcome could signal the need for training, or in some cases remuneration.

TRAINING

This is a process concerned with establishing what type of training is required and who should receive it. Training ranges from simple on-the-job instruction to educational and training courses offered by providers external to the organisation. Training, coupled with development, is apparent when organisations plan the progression of key employees through the company, in which case an attempt is made to reconcile organisational needs with individual career development.

REWARDS

This covers a wide area incorporating rates of pay, trade union involvement (where appropriate) and other factors such as the use of job evaluation in the determination of rates of pay, methods for calculating pay (e.g. flat rate, piece-rate or performance-related pay) and fringe benefits.

EMPLOYEE RELATIONS

Under this heading could be considered collective bargaining, grievance procedures and employment legislation. In collective bargaining the HRM/employee relations specialist normally prepares and presents the employer's case in the negotiations with the employees' representative (trade union official). A responsibility of the HRM manager is to monitor the outcome of collective agreements.

With respect to grievance procedures, the HRM manager could be involved in preparing and implementing those procedures and be actively involved in trying to settle disputes that fall outside the collective bargaining process. Disputes within the gambit of collective bargaining could be considered to be group- rather than individual-based matters. The HRM/employee relations specialist is normally involved in discipline cases, and has the function of gathering evidence and preparing the case, and also ensuring the employee is treated fairly.

The HRM specialist is likely to be called on to give advice on matters connected with employment legislation, and is expected to be conversant with the practical issues relating to the applicability of relevant legal provisions.

EMPLOYEE COMMUNICATIONS AND PARTICIPATION

This could amount to taking on board activities in connection with communicating relevant information to employees, and arranging for ways in which employees can participate in the processes of the company (e.g. suggestion schemes). In certain circumstances counselling could become part of the service under this heading. Increasingly, participation also incorporates aspects of Japanese management practices, such as quality circles and teamwork, in which operators take over certain aspects of production control such as quality control. In this way employees are involved in decision making that affects their work.

PERSONNEL RECORDS

A record of the employee is likely to be kept centrally by the personnel/HRM department. This could contain information provided in the original application, with subsequent additions to reflect qualifications and experience gained, achievements and potential. The employee record could provide a useful input to HR decisions. Records are normally computerised and can be used as part of the HR planning process.

The personnel/HRM activities described above, which are expanded in subsequent chapters, can be executed in diverse ways (Needle, 2004) and the personnel/HRM specialist or senior manager with responsibility for HRM/personnel matters:

■ can be involved at the strategic level at which policies are formulated;

■ provides an advisory service for line managers – for example, he or she could set up a performance appraisal system and advise managers on its use;

■ could join forces with a line manager in order to perform a specific function – for example, the line manager and personnel specialist could sit on the same interview panel when interviewing candidates for a job vacancy;

■ may engage in a specified number of activities, leaving line managers with a high level of autonomy for personnel matters close to their area of responsibility (e.g. selecting their own staff).

In practice, particularly in large organisations, HRM activities will often consist of several of the above roles. For example, if a production manager has a vacancy for a charge hand or team leader, there will be a planning exercise to consider the need for the job, the internal supply of labour and the cost of filling the vacancy. If there is a decision to appoint somebody the HRM specialist may support the production manager by providing particular expertise, for instance by drawing up the job specification, preparing the advertisement and advising on the interview process. Normally you would expect the HRM specialist to issue the employment contract. This example indicates a high level of involvement on the part of the HRM function. In some organisations, and often for jobs that are lower in the organisation, the involvement of the HRM specialist is less, and may be confined merely to preparing the advertisement and employment contract. Nowadays external consultants are often used, particularly in the area of recruitment, selection and training. The involvement of the HRM specialist in this field is that of obtaining the services of the consultant and managing the process.

Personnel management versus HRM

Although personnel management shares a platform with HRM on some key issues – a natural concern for people and their needs, together with finding efficient means to select, train, appraise, develop and reward them – there are some points of dissimilarity. Traditional personnel management tended to be parochial, striving to influence line managers, whereas HRM is integrated into the role of line managers, with a strong proactive stance and a bias towards business. Personnel management has a history of placing emphasis on bureaucratic control often in a reactive sense, i.e. control of manpower and personnel systems. To be fair it has had to respond to various bouts of employment legislation over the years and has been forced to develop adeptness in the design and use of administrative systems to cope with statutory and non-statutory matters. Some of this process was positive in a societal sense; for example the efforts against unfair discrimination based on sex or ethnic origin. Other legislation also had an effect on practice. For example, the Equal Pay Act (1970) (amended in 1983) led to a growth in job evaluation in order to establish that people doing the same type of job would be uniformly rewarded. However, some would argue that personnel management represented a highly compartmentalised system, with thinking to match.

By contrast, as the commentary on HRM in the next section will show, HRM makes a determined effort to be a more integrative mechanism in bringing people issues into line with business issues, with a pronounced problem-seeking and problem-solving orientation, and a determination to build collaborative organisational systems where employee development features prominently. The role of top management in setting the agenda for change and development is very much in evidence in HRM. The typical concern here is offering good leadership and vision, with a commitment to creating and sustaining strong cultures that are compatible with evolving business needs. A strong culture is one in which there are clear organisational values and approaches that are held by all the members of the organisation.

There is the general view that HRM must play a critical part in the success of the organisation in order to ensure its own viability (Ulrich, 1998; Ulrich and Brockbank, 2005); that HRM professionals must be able to handle information technology proficiently and use computer-based HRM systems (Carrington, 2007), as well as acting as agents of change by developing competence in managing and implementing change (Whittington *et al.*, 2005); and that they need to become business partners of line managers so that the latter can acquire the competences needed to perform the HRM tasks that are part of their jobs (Heneman *et al.*, 1998; Redman and Wilkinson, 2006). In addition, HRM professionals will increasingly need to utilise 'outsourcers' to reduce costs in connection with running the HRM system and it will be necessary to tap expertise not readily available in the organisation (Mohrman and Lawler, 1997; Dessler, 2005). With reference to the 'knowledge age' and the needs of knowledge-intensive organisations, there is a need for HRM professionals to develop high levels of competence in designing HRM systems that support knowledge sharing (Hislop, 2006).

We have already characterised personnel management as a series of activities related to various aspects of an employee's relationship with the organisation. In addition to these issues, HRM stresses the primacy of business needs. Other points of departure are that HRM embraces individual flexibility and congruency between individual and organisational goals, whereas personnel management is concerned with systems applied to individuals and collectivism.

Distinctive features of HRM

Before looking at the distinctive features of HRM it seems appropriate to identify some of the factors that have led to the creation and popularity of HRM. Forces in the environment have influenced organisations to be responsive. This could be reflected in increased competitiveness, an emphasis on quality in staff and products/services, flexible modes of operation and a willingness to adapt to change. In such circumstances it would not be surprising to find organisation and management structures and systems responding to the new business conditions in the changed environment.

Examples of management and organisational responses would be increased decentralisation to facilitate a better reaction to market conditions, and greater autonomy and accountability for the efficient use of resources. Also, there could be a striving to inject flexibility into the roles employees play in teams (e.g. autonomous groups) and in getting people to adopt a wider range of skills (multi-skilling). A key point here is that these developments allow an increased speed of reaction which is vital if the organisation is to adapt to the changing environmental and market conditions that characterise the current situation. An example of this is the reaction of Hewlett-Packard to the current business environment (see Case example 1.1).

CASE EXAMPLE 1.1

HEWLETT-PACKARD – A DISTINCTIVE APPROACH

Hewlett-Packard, the technology giant, became known for its distinctive approach to management. Dave Packard, co-founder, elucidated the 'HP way': 'Early in the history of the company, while thinking about how a company like this should be managed, I kept getting back to one concept: If we could simply get everybody to agree on what our objectives were and to understand what we were trying to do, then we could turn everybody loose, and they would move along in a common direction' (Packard, 2007). The approach to management incorporated a participative management style with managers being accessible to employees, jobs arranged in teams, and decentralisation of decision making where possible. There was a focus on training to develop 'cross-functional individuals' who could apply their skills to new products and tasks as changes in the business environment demanded. The core elements of the HP way (Kotelnikov, 2007) were:

- defining and agreeing the values;
- setting and agreeing on the objectives;
- empowering employees;

This approach was very successful for Hewlett-Packard, and it grew to be one of the dominant players in its market. The approach was very people-centric and efforts were made to provide employees with job security. More recently, however, changes in the business environment have impacted on Hewlett-Packard. Since 2002 Hewlett-Packard has laid off 30 per cent of its 150 000 employees (Wong, 2006) but it has hired almost the same number. This represents a re-focusing of the workforce. As Chief Executive Mark Hurd said: 'We are trying to get our cost structure right ... the places that the cost is coming out of are not the places where we're adding cost' (Wong, 2006). The refocusing is removing 'back-office staff' and replacing them with people in 'revenue-generating' jobs, such as sales. However, there is another aspect to these changes. Whilst employee numbers are reducing in the US and Western Europe, they are increasing in Asia, Latin America and Eastern Europe where skilled labour is available more cheaply.

This strategy helped to increase revenue by 6 per cent in 2006 and the stock market approved of the strategy with HP's stock price increasing by more than 60 per cent. As a result of the revenue growth HP is seen as the largest technology company in the world (Wong, 2006).

However, HP faces challenges in the future. On the other hand, some question whether it can maintain the 'HP way' with this shift in its employment practices and with its expansion into parts of the world where there are different cultures. On the other hand, the HP way has brought considerable success and the company could jeopardise its long-term future if it does not maintain key practices such as decentralised decision making, team-working and an emphasis of shared objectives so that employees are clear on what they are contributing to the organisational goals.

Questions

1. Do the recent actions of HP in 're-focusing' the workforce represent a contradiction of the 'HP way' or are they compatible with the espoused approach?

2. What are the potential dangers for organisations if they are perceived to be contradicting their stated values?

A major theme running through HRM is the acknowledgement that employees are valued assets of the company, that there should be an interplay between a strategy for human resource and the main strategy for the business, that national culture is influential in shaping HRM practices (Budhwar and Sparrow, 1997), that corporate culture should be managed so as to make it compatible with the requirements of corporate strategy (Beer and Spector, 1985), and that seeking the commitment of employees to the organisation is of far greater value than forcing compliance to the demands of the organisation. The value of commitment is that it binds employees to the organisation. But one has to recognise that commitment to an organisation is not something that springs out of thin air with little prodding. Individuals have attitudes and attachments to their own values as well as values connected with membership of the family, the trade union or professional body, and these could clash with commitment to organisational values. Therefore changes in attitudes and behaviours have to be contemplated.

One can view employee commitment as part of the 'psychological contract'. This is an unwritten contract between management and employees whereby management offers challenging and meaningful tasks and employees reciprocate with loyalty and commitment (Tichy *et al.*, 1982; Rousseau, 2001). In contexts where organisations have cut jobs and imposed cost cutting, the perception of employees can be negative and this can impact on their psychological contract. One should add that commitment on its own, without competence, may be an empty shell. There is further comment on commitment in Chapters 2 and 5.

To elicit commitment, reference is often made to mutuality. This stands for HRM policies that provide mutual goals, mutual influence, mutual respect, mutual rewards and mutual responsibility (Walton, 1985). But mutuality may be a tender creature, as it is not uncommon to find a situation where the employee is short-changed by employers. In a climate of mutuality the cause of commitment is advanced, with the consequence of both improved productivity and the development of people. A method used to foster mutuality is the 'development appraisal' discussed in Chapter 8. The aim of this approach is not to control the employee by judging past behaviour alone, but to offer encouragement by examining how the employee can contribute to organisational goals, and to specify the nature of the individual's development needs in order to achieve these goals.

Another feature of HRM that is often emphasised is the existence of the 'common interests' of management and employees in the profitability of the enterprise, which can lead to the tapping of a substantial reservoir of initiative and commitment within the workforce. The objection raised to this view is that while it sounds good in principle, in practice there will be divergent interests. For example, the organisation could damage goodwill when the wages bill is cut following a cost-minimisation exercise.

The interaction between the HRM system and the corporate planning process is something that receives special attention. Proactive intervention on the part of the HRM system has been advocated here (Bird and Beecher, 1995). The guiding light comes from the strategic direction enumerated in the corporate plan. It is expected that the HRM policies and practices that develop as a result of identifying the human resource needs of corporate strategy can prove useful to managers (Gratton *et al.*, 1999). The following are examples of questions that might be asked with a view to establishing whether key facets of HRM are underpinning business strategy:

■ Has the organisation the right calibre of employee to meet the demands of business strategy (Miles and Snow, 1984)?

■ Are the techniques for selection, appraisal and promotion of people supportive of business strategy?

■ Are managers as committed to HRM issues as they are to issues related to their primary specialism and function?

■ Are the employment systems flexible enough to allow speedy adaption to change?

(There is further discussion of strategic HRM in Chapter 2.)

Other key considerations are as follows (Beer and Spector, 1985):

■ People ought to be considered as social capital capable of development.

■ Participation in decision making is of value, and people's choice of options or alternatives ought to be based on informed judgement.

■ Power should be distributed throughout the organisation, rather than centralised, in order to foster trust and collaboration between people who are credited with a realistic sense of purpose.

■ The interests of all parties with a stake in the organisation (e.g. employees, shareholders, suppliers and customers) should be harmonised.

The message coming across as a result of a serious consideration of the above issues is that properly conceived and applied HRM is beneficial in terms of individual and organisational performance. The performance theme has attracted the interest of a number of academics (e.g. Becker and Gerhart, 1996; Delery and Doty, 1996; Dyer and Reeves, 1995; Guest, 1997), and is expanded later in the section on the interaction between HRM and business strategy.

In the next short case (Case example 1.2) we examine Fedex's approach to HRM. Fedex puts great value on its people and builds its business model on the quality of the service it provides. The intention is to build commitment through listening to employees and paying attention to matters such as training and career progression.

FEDEX'S APPROACH TO HRM

Fedex is the major international package delivery and logistics company. It has become highly successful, growing to be a £15.3 billion business. The approach that has led to this growth has been consistently people-centric. Dominique van den Peereboom is one of the vice-presidents for HRM and he explains the underlying philosophy. 'At Fedex we have one key policy that underpins everything. People, service, profit. We want to focus on people because we believe that only satisfied employees can provide the satisfied customers who will secure our future' (quoted in Roberts, 2006).

This central philosophy is realised through a range of practices. For example, there is a practice of promoting from within where possible. In the European region, 95 per cent of managers started at a junior level. This means that managers are not brought in above current employees and so employees can aspire to staying with Fedex and building a career. These aspirations are made real by the policies on training. Employees who are interested in promotion are enrolled on the 'New Horizon' Programme. They take an initial psychometric test, which helps to identify the competencies they need to develop in order to get a promoted post. They then develop a one- to two-year action plan to develop the competencies. Each employee has access to a £1,550 tuition fund. Once they have gained the competencies that are needed they can apply for the position of team leader. After 18 months' experience they can apply to move up the managerial ladder. This policy has been very successful in achieving a staff turnover rate of 7 per cent, which is very low for the sector. An advantage of a low turnover rate is that the costs of recruiting and inducting new staff are greatly reduced.

Fedex has a positive view of diversity in the workplace. The European hub is at Charles de Gaulle airport in Paris where 1,700 people of 43 different nationalities are employed. The company has recently won the Diversity Award from the Great Place to Work Institute.

At Fedex there is a guarantee of fair treatment. There is a system that enables staff to complain to senior management if they feel that they have not been treated fairly by their manger. If a complaint is raised, the senior manager has to react within three days, meet the employee and evaluate the situation. A decision must be communicated within seven days, and there is a right of appeal. Last year 45 complaints were raised and in 15 per cent of cases the managerial decision was changed. This gives staff confidence in the system. Peereboom believes that the system is revolutionary because it gives power to employees to disagree with their managers.

Another form of communication is the annual opinion survey. In the survey employees review the management. Managers present the feedback from the survey to the employees and agree action plans between them to address any issues that are highlighted. This system has the potential to be abused by employees, but it is not, and Peereboom believes this is because of the strong culture. It may also be related to the fact that the vast majority of managers have been in the position of those filling in the survey and hence have the ability to understand issues and win trust.

Source: based on Roberts, 2006

Question

Fedex is a logistics company, operating on an international basis. To what extent do you think its approach could be taken up by companies in other sectors such as manufacturing, or knowledge-intensive functions?

There are two models of HRM: one is called 'hard' and the other 'soft' (Storey, 1992), but this does not mean one is difficult and the other easy. (The models are used in the context of problem solving and decision making.) A hard problem is one that has a clear definition and an agreed method for working it out, and it will have a definite solution. For example, 2 + 2 = 4 is a hard problem and solution. When one adopts a hard position there is a tendency to view people as a passive resource to be managed and controlled by adopting a rational, quantitative and calculative approach so as to ensure that the labour force is efficiently deployed in order to achieve a competitive advantage (Legge, 1995). Soft problems are less clearly defined, and there are alternative problem-solving methods and potential solutions. An example of a soft problem is how to motivate your subordinates or to suggest the best way to manage people.

In HRM the hard approach is concerned with costs and head counts, and tends to be associated with a unitarist view; that is that the goals of individuals and the organisation converge. (This is akin to the 'Michigan School' of HRM (Fombrun *et al.*, 1984), introduced in Chapter 2 in connection with strategy.) The following is an illustration of one aspect of the hard approach. In HR planning the organisation will need to know its turnover rate. This gives the number of leavers in a given period as a proportion of the number of employees and is calculated by the following formula:

$$\frac{\text{Leavers in year}}{\text{Average number staff in post during year}} \times 100$$

This statistical approach exemplifies the hard approach and naturally is less compatible with ideas derived from behavioural science that are ingrained in the soft approach. The soft approach will be concerned with the complexities behind this simple formula – for example, if there is a high turnover, is this because people are demotivated? If so, what can be done about this situation?

The soft model, which is similar to the 'Harvard School' of HRM (Beer *et al.*, 1984), includes the following features:

■ There is a view that individual needs and organisational needs will not always be the same (i.e. a pluralist view), but the organisation will endeavour to balance the different types of needs.

■ The uniqueness of the human resource must be recognised, and cannot be treated like any other resource. After all, people have feelings and emotions.

- People are creative and responsible and can benefit from involvement in the participative management process.

- A climate of consent features prominently.

- There is a belief that commitment by employees to the organisation is nurtured when the organisation informs them of important matters, such as the mission statement, the values it cherishes and trading prospects. In addition, it is considered wise to involve employees in decisions related to organisational and job design, and allow them to function in self-managing groups.

- There is a recognition of the role of trade unions in representing the collective interests of employees, but at the same time it is important to respect the rights of management to liaise directly with individuals and groups within the organisation.

Objectives of an HRM system

The following list reflects the major items you would expect to find in a set of objectives relating to an HRM system (Armstrong, 1992):

1. The company's objectives are to be achieved through its most valued resource – its workforce.
2. In order to enhance both individual and organisational performance, people are expected to commit themselves to the success of the organisation.
3. A coherent set of personnel or HR policies and practices geared towards effective organisational performance is a necessary prerequisite for the company to make the optimum use of resources.
4. An integration of HRM policies and business objectives should be sought.
5. HRM policies should support the corporate culture, where appropriate, or change the culture for the better where it is deemed inappropriate.
6. An organisational climate that is supportive of individual creativity and in which energetic endeavours should be created and nurtured. This will provide a fertile terrain for the promotion of teamwork, innovation and total quality management.
7. The creation of a flexible organisational system that is responsive and adaptive, and helps the company to meet exacting objectives in a competitive environment.
8. A determination to increase individuals' flexibility in terms of the hours that they work and the functions they carry out.
9. The provision of task and organisational conditions that are supportive of people trying to realise their potential at work.
10. The maintenance and enhancement of both the workforce and the product/service.

Implementation issues

Here we now examine selected issues associated with the implementation of a HRM policy. Because of the selective nature of the examination, certain topics are excluded. For example, although some of the concepts and issues (e.g. commitment, mutuality) discussed earlier have features that relate to the implementation process, it is felt that enough has been said about them in this introductory chapter. The issues that will now be discussed are: *the role of management, the role of values and culture, the use of HRM/personnel management techniques and the HRM–business strategy interaction.*

MANAGEMENT

There seems to be the view that it is important for management to display a strong interest in the continuing profitability of the organisation, with an appropriate vision for the future. The chief executive is said to be an important person when it comes to eliciting the commitment of employees. For example, it is he or she who sets the scene for change, takes responsibility for the change process, and by his or her actions reinforces the existing corporate culture, if appropriate, or reshapes it if not appropriate.

The responsibility for the implementation of HRM policy should rest with all managers who adapt it realistically to local circumstances. Although the HRM function may have been vocal in the setting of the guidelines contained in the HRM policy, it is the responsibility of all managers to implement the policy. The HRM function has the responsibility for monitoring and developing the policy. A stated policy of British Airways is that every manager should be a human resource manager. This emphasises the importance of people management in all managerial roles. An important feature is the management of human resources in a strategic way when managers are pursuing normal commercial and organisational objectives. It seems as if HRM is a frame of mind determining a behavioural perspective on everything a manager does, from policy making to normal everyday decision making (Armstrong, 1992). A valid question to ask at this stage is: to what extent do line managers embrace HRM? Apparently, there is evidence to suggest that HRM is not too popular among line managers because it does not excite them as an approach to managing people that offers instant solutions (Sparrow and Marchington, 1998), and there are fears that their competencies are not necessarily in the people management area (Renwick, 2003).

VALUES AND CULTURE

The culture of an organisation is the collection of values, beliefs, attitudes and behaviours commonly held by the members. The culture is learnt and reinforced through interaction. Culture and its management are explicit features of HRM. Values expounded by top management have significance in gluing together policies and practices with respect to human resources. In this context, respect for people is crucial because without respect how can the necessary commitment be created? Commitment is a reciprocal process (Beer and Spector, 1985). To this would be added trust, and its operationalisation could be seen in the adoption of open management styles, particularly participative management.

Senior management is strategically placed to imprint its values on human resource policies and practices right across the spectrum of activities, ranging from selection practices to reward systems. In the process, considerable influence can be exerted in shaping corporate culture. Training is commonly used to shape cultures. When British Aerospace wanted to introduce autonomous teamworking at one of its production plants it undertook extensive training of all the workforce affected by the changes. The training was not just in the technical skills which would be needed but also in the culture and behaviour that needed to be developed. This necessitated a move from a belief in a hierarchical organisation to an acceptance of organisational roles where greater responsibility and involvement feature prominently.

Commentators who have examined HRM values from an industrial relations point of view refer to the existence of a unitarist perspective (Guest, 1989) in the sense that management and workers share a common interest, and that there is not much need for communication or negotiations between these two camps to be conducted by a representative system associated with the role of trade unions. This can be contrasted with a pluralist system – a voluntary system reinforced by collective bargaining at the local level – where the interests of the employers on one side and employees on the other, including many trade union members, are not seen as identical. The traditional industrial relations system in the United Kingdom and the rest of Europe is most likely to embrace a pluralist perspective, unlike the situation in the United States (although, as stated earlier, union power in the United Kingdom has waned somewhat in recent years). Perhaps a control strategy studded with adversarial industrial relations practice, where conflict of interests occupies a position high on the agenda, is akin to a pluralist perspective, while the unitarist perspective is more compatible with a commitment strategy that in its ideal form reflects mutual interests and respect in interpersonal and management–worker relations, where flexibility exists with respect to the nature of organisational roles, and participative management pervades the area of decision making.

A strong culture underpinning key aspects of organisational functioning (e.g. product quality, a climate of creativity, rapid response to environmental pressures) could be associated with an HRM system (du Gay, 1997; Legge, 1989). To some, this could be construed as a control system reinforced by internal propaganda and persuasion to exact commitment from people, irrespective of whether or not it serves their interests. The natural consequence would be to label HRM as a manipulative process. Supporters of HRM might retort by maintaining that HRM is manipulative, but only in a benign way. They might ask what is wrong with a system that offers realistic personal benefits and job security to those who commit themselves to the company's objectives and values, which encapsulate efficiency, innovation, quality products, customer service, etc. – the hallmarks of a potentially successful organisation. That is fine if the benefits, etc. are realistic and fairly dispensed!

Earlier in this chapter the virtue of flexibility was acknowledged as a key feature of an HRM system. But can the cause of flexibility be served by a potent, all-pervasive culture that requires employees to conform to specified values? Perhaps flexibility could be neutralised in such circumstances! Where a potent culture supports a prompt reaction to familiar events, because the prevailing ethos accommodates such an eventuality, it could be a different story when the organisation faces unfamiliar events (Legge, 1989, 1995). In such circumstances the organisation could benefit from flexibility to confront novelty and uncertainty but is denied it because of the strong culture. A classic example of this was IBM, which had a strong culture and an established way of doing things. IBM's competitor, Apple, was small, flexible and able to try out new ideas and innovate in a highly competitive market. At the time when personal computers were becoming popular, this lack of flexibility led to problems for IBM and the company found it difficult to change. Such a situation also raises the question of the tension between individualism, which flexibility supports, and collectivism, which is promoted by certain features of organisational life. Normally organisations try to tackle this tension, not always successfully, when on the one hand individual competence and achievement are recognised by a reward system, such as performance-related pay for individuals, and on the other hand the value of teamwork is advocated with reference to autonomous work groups. Further discussion of culture can be found in Chapter 5.

HRM/PERSONNEL MANAGEMENT TECHNIQUES

The question to ask about techniques is: are they good enough to select the right calibre and mix of people, to develop individuals and to ensure that working relationships and incentives are of the required standard so that people's services are retained in the implementation of a realistic corporate plan? Coherence in the application of personnel management techniques is something that is continually stressed. A set of techniques that do not fit neatly together is anathema to the serious HRM practitioner. What is not required is the application of isolated techniques that have more to do with practitioners displaying their technical prowess in their chosen field than tackling problems awaiting solution. The preferred action is the purposeful interrelationship and reinforcement of the battery of techniques in the service of the organisation's objectives (Hendry and Pettigrew, 1990; Becker and Huselid, 2000). However, it must be acknowledged that it is no easy matter to develop a consistent and integrated set of HRM management techniques. It requires perseverance, managerial competence and a personnel function tuned in to commercial thinking and sympathetic managerial attitudes and behaviour.

The internal coherence of HRM policies in practice could receive a fundamental challenge from the way the organisation is structured. (There is a discussion of organisation structure in Chapter 3.) In well-developed divisional structures authority can be delegated to business or divisional units with a high level of autonomy. The head office in such a structure might confine itself to overall financial control and setting broad guidelines, leaving the division to implement its own brand of HR or personnel management. Some divisions may adopt a full-blooded HRM approach, but others may not because of an absence of firm guidance from top management at headquarters, in which case there is a lack of consistency in the use of HRM systems.

The role of reward systems is given pride of place in HRM. Reward systems are normally used as a change mechanism to create a more pronounced performance-oriented culture. Also, they can be used to encourage the development of new skills, and can be linked to performance appraisal schemes. A discussion of reward management appears in Chapter 9.

Another technique to consider is training and development because HRM embraces the notion of developing employees and enabling them to make the optimum use of their abilities for their own sake as well as in the interest of the organisation. Given the pivotal role of managers in the implementation of HRM policies, they should be targeted for training in this context. Training and development are considered in Chapter 10.

An example

HRM has been introduced to a New Orleans restaurant business (see Case example 1.3). This is somewhat reminiscent of early welfare approaches referred to above, but also incorporates a focus on training. There was a high turnover of staff, and in a service industry this can have a negative impact of the quality of service experienced by the customer. The new HRM function analysed the specific context of the problem and produced a set of solutions that were not as sophisticated as those in Hewlett Packard but were appropriate to the company's situation.

CASE EXAMPLE 1.3

ACME OYSTER HOUSE – A FOCUS ON TRAINING

The Acme Oyster House company operates four restaurants in New Orleans, employing around 200 people. The company competes in the tourist market with over 3,000 other restaurants and has been suffering from a turnover rate of 120 per cent. In order to address the turnover problem a new HRM function was established.

The first step was to consult the staff. Quarterly meetings were introduced to gain an insight into what staff were thinking. This identified a number of areas that were ripe for change. The overall reward package was standard for the industry, but relatively poor.

Entitlements to sick leave were introduced along with bus passes, paid holidays (which increased annually) and a pension plan. Awards for long service were also introduced.

The greatest emphasis was placed on training. 'Training is going to make the biggest difference to our retention. Employees are more comfortable in a place where they know what is expected of them and how to do it . . . Financing education means you attract and retain career-oriented, future-thinking people' (Tom Payne, HR Director, cited in Pickard, 2004).

There is some evidence that the approach is working as turnover had been cut to 85 per cent within a year and it was expected to fall further (Pickard, 2004). Although there were costs associated with the new approach, these could be offset against the significantly reduced recruitment and selection costs. What is more difficult to quantify, but which is nonetheless perceived, is the enhanced customer experience of being cooked for and served by people who are experienced employees rather than by people who do not yet know the systems, and may well leave in the first few weeks of employment before they have the chance to learn.

Question

Acme Oyster House is a SME – a small and medium sized enterprise. To what extent do you think the principles and practices of HRM are applicable to SMEs?

Although HRM has sometimes been associated with large organisations, the Acme Oyster house example illustrates that HRM practices can translate to smaller organisations. It also illustrates the need to take account of the costs and benefits of changes in the management of people, some of which will be quantifiable, and others of which may be expressed in qualitative terms.

HRM–BUSINESS STRATEGY INTERACTION

Earlier there was reference to the importance of successfully integrating the HRM strategy with the business strategy. It would be a positive advantage if the HRM director or personnel director is involved in decision making with respect to normal business issues at board level. In this way he or she is in a better position to orchestrate the development of HRM strategies related to selection, training and development, rewards and employee relations.

HRM defines itself as strategic, with an emphasis on performance through people. For example, Sisson (1990) sees the strategic aspect of HRM as being to provide a workforce that is flexible, adaptable and cost effective, with one of the means to this end being 'high commitment/involvement management'. Similarly, Beer *et al.* (1984) link commitment with competence and cost effectiveness. Storey (1995) encapsulates this view by saying that 'Human resource management is a distinctive approach to employee management which seeks to achieve competitive advantage through the strategic deployment of a highly committed and capable workforce using an integrated array of cultural, structural and personnel techniques.'

The nature of the practices employed to achieve commitment and performance is a matter of debate. Singh (1996) emphasises selection, performance management, appraisal, collective bargaining and joint consultation as the basis for seeking to achieve the desired HRM outcomes of strategic integration, commitment, quality, flexibility and cost effectiveness. These HRM outcomes, it is hoped, will lead in turn to overall performance outcomes of organisational effectiveness, congruence between objectives and performance, employees' well-being and harmonious employer–employee relations (Walton, 1985). Lawler (1986) presented the policies and outcomes as an exchange. The policies include participation, career flexibility, individual rights and performance-based rewards. They are designed to develop a highly skilled workforce that could operate using its discretion, and in return for so doing the employer would provide employment security, the potential for a satisfying career and good rewards.

As was stated above in connection with the difficulties of achieving coherency in the application of personnel management techniques, the successful integration of HRM strategy with business strategy may also be difficult to achieve for the following reasons: there may be a lack of determination to do so; the required managerial competence at all levels may not be available; the personnel or HRM function may be too traditional in its outlook and operation; entrenched traditional managerial attitudes and behaviour may still prevail; and if traditional business strategy, with its primary emphasis on considerations such as marketing, finance, etc. receives the bulk of attention, human resource issues may be neglected.

However, more recent evidence (Becker and Huselid, 1999; Pfeffer and Veiga, 1999) has shown that there is a strong link between successful adoption of a 'bundle' of best HRM practices and organisational performance. Extensive empirical studies, particularly in the United States, but also in Europe, have substantiated the assertion of the HRM–business success link, and so development of best HRM practice is now seen as a crucial strategic consideration (Becker and Huselid, 1998). An example of this is provided by Vesuvius International (see Case example 1.4).

CASE EXAMPLE 1.4

SHRM IN VESUVIUS INTERNATIONAL

Vesuvius International is the ceramics division of the British-owned Cookson Group, which employs 8,500 people at 74 manufacturing sites in 21 countries (Arkin, 1999). It is located in Scotland and specialises in producing speciality ceramics for use in the steel industry. The Vesuvius plant in Scotland faced the prospect of closure by the parent organisation if it failed to perform to the highest possible standards at the lowest possible costs. In order to deal with this threat a change programme was introduced in 1994 with the aim of creating a culture in which all employees took responsibility for their performance. The HRM strategy had a series of elements:

- ▪ The traditional division of jobs and complicated wage structure were replaced with a single wage structure and flexibility of working, so that there were fewer barriers to job rotation.
- ▪ Self-managing teams were introduced.
- ▪ Training was enhanced so that all team members could carry out all the individual functions required of the team.
- ▪ Two-way communication was promoted through regular team meetings.
- ▪ A positive partnership was fostered with the trade union.
- ▪ The foremen were retrained to take on a new role as facilitators rather than supervisors.

The aim was to increase quality and performance through the management of people and outcomes were impressive. The Investors in People accreditation was awarded, and every employee had an individual development plan linking individual, team and organisational targets. Surveys of employee satisfaction produced an increase in the overall satisfaction score from 70 per cent in 1993 to 89 per cent in 1996. Customer complaints have decreased, and the market share enjoyed by Vesuvius has increased, while prices have been maintained. The introduction of self-managed teams has led to cost savings of £500,000 p.a. and turnover increased from £37 million in 1993 to £55 million in 1998. The company attributed this rise to the competitive edge it had gained through empowering its employees and giving them responsibility for quality.

Source: based on Arkin, 1999

Questions

1. If you were an employee in Vesuvius, what would make you believe that management was really genuine in empowering you?

2. In view of your answer to the previous question, what issues should managers keep in mind when they are seeking to empower employees?

There is further discussion of the interaction of HRM strategy with corporate strategy in Chapter 2 but at this point it is worth considering briefly the role of the HRM specialist with regard to strategic interaction. Pfeffer and Sutton (2006) note that there are regular calls for HRM specialists to become more 'strategic' and act as 'business partners' to the senior management of the company. They argue, however, that there are common misconceptions concerning what it would mean to be a strategic business partner. A stream of research dating back to the 1970s (Mintzberg, 1975) has shown that managerial jobs are typified by pressure, demands for short term-performance and the juggling of many tasks at the same time. Therefore, it is necessary for HRM specialists to be able to operate within business constraints, and to be able to make a contribution to the managerial function. One way of making such a contribution, according to Pfeffer and Sutton (2006), is to promote and exercise 'evidence-based management'. Fundamentally, this is about improving decision making, particularly as it impacts on employees, within the time and resource constraints that are common in most companies.

There are three main steps to evidence-based management. First, ideology and 'gut-feel' should be minimised. Pfeffer and Sutton argue that many managers are unaware of good quality research, which could inform their decisions, because of the time pressure and many distractions that they have to cope with. Hence, for example, managers make false assumptions about what motivates people, and then act on those false assumptions. Therefore, it is incumbent on the HRM specialist to be sufficiently aware of pertinent research and to be able to express its salient findings and facts in a succinct manner so that decision making can be informed but not slowed down. Secondly, there should be a 'commitment to hearing the truth'. This means that the HRM specialist should be able to access opinions of employees and gather perceptions on the decisions that are made – even if those perceptions are negative. Pfeffer and Sutton give the example of the medical services company, DaVita, which puts emphasis on its 'Town Hall Meetings'. At these meetings, groups of employees are invited to give input and comment on decisions. Thirdly, and perhaps most surprisingly, evidence-based management is not about 'getting it right first time'. In many cases it is not possible to make the perfect decision – to do so might take too long or consume too many resources. Rather, the idea is to treat the organisation as an 'unfinished prototype' in which the understanding is that decisions will be as good as possible, but they are not 'finished'. They are experiments aimed at promoting learning. Actions taken should be reviewed and the review information should feed into the next phase of decision making. This approach both reflects the reality of management and plays to the strengths of HRM specialists who will typically have an understanding of learning and feedback processes.

Conclusions

HRM can be seen as a development that originated from traditional personnel management and which has replaced it to some extent. Key managers and some professionals in the personnel function felt the old system was no longer functional and there was a need for a change in the status of personnel practitioners as well as for getting them more involved in business decisions. HRM also reflects changes in philosophies and practices with respect to the management of people in organisations.

In HRM there is a greater emphasis on strategic issues and on the way in which the human resource contributes to the achievement of corporate objectives. Amongst the natural concerns of the organisation are sensitivity to the needs of stakeholders, the development of human resources to meet future challenges, and ensuring that people's energies are sufficiently focused in order to add value to organisational inputs. HRM underlines the importance of flexibility and the ability to react and adapt quickly to changes in the organisation's environment. It is also concerned with quality management, where the requirements of the quality of both the operations of the organisation and the product or service trigger a need for high calibre staff to secure competitive advantage.

Although HRM unashamedly embraces a cost-effective business approach, it values employees for perfectly understandable reasons. Being concerned with the well-being of people is seen as a powerful way to motivate and inspire the workforce. HRM takes a systems approach to the analysis and management of organisations. It likes to see the different parts of the organisation functioning effectively and together moving cooperatively towards meeting the overall goals of the enterprise. This is facilitated through the management of systems such as human resource planning, recruitment and selection, appraisal, training and development, and rewards. These systems must be integrated and 'pull in the same direction'. In this way the HRM function assists the organisation to be more effective and profitable.

The rationale for the structure of the remainder of this book is that we will start with the strategic issues – those that determine the long-term future of the firm. Then three 'macro' issues that draw on a number of HRM practices and approaches will be explored. These are organisational structure, change and culture. Following the macro perspective, we will examine a series of specialist areas within HRM. First, employee resourcing – the processes of planning for and recruiting the workforce; secondly, employee development – focusing on performance, training and reward; thirdly, the topic of employee relations will be examined. We close by discussing how these areas of theory and practice might be integrated, and reflect on some of the theoretical and practical criticisms of HRM.

Review and reflection questions

1. What is the significance of HRM's historical development on the way it is regarded today?

2. What difference in attitude towards employees might be denoted by one professional adopting the title 'Personnel Manager' and another adopting the title 'Human Resource Manager'?

3. HRM has been adopted mainly by large organisations such as Hewlett Packard and Fedex. What issues should managers be aware of in applying HRM concepts and practices to SMEs such as Acme Oyster House?

4. What barriers might be expected to the implementation of HRM? How might managers overcome such barriers?

Activities

If you are in work:

Consider the HRM practices in your organisation.

1. To what extent do they match the models discussed in this chapter?

2. Can you see any differences between your organisation's HRM practices and those of companies such as Hewlett-Packard and Vesuvius?

3. On the basis of your comparison, what lessons might you derive for your organisation?

If you are in full-time study:

Visit the Hewlett-Packard website (www.hp.com/hpinfo).

1. Look at sections that could reveal the company's current approach to HRM, for example, 'corporate objectives', 'diversity and inclusion', 'global citizenship' and 'jobs'.

2. What can you tell about Hewlett-Packard's approach to HRM from the website?

3. Do you think it is a good example for others to follow?

Further Reading and Research

The following article provides a classic explanation of the difference between personnel and HRM and incorporates a critical perspective.

Guest, D. (1989) 'Personnel and HRM: can you tell the difference?' *Personnel Management*, January, 48–51.

A more recent article, also authored by David Guest, provides a review of academic concepts relating to personnel and HRM.

Guest, D. and King, Z. (2004) 'Power, innovation, and problem solving: The personnel manager's three steps to heaven', *Journal of Management Studies*, 41, 401–423.

HRM is an international phenomenon, and this is reflected in the work of the World Federation of Personnel Management Associations. The WFPMA website offers a useful resource to explore the international nature of HRM. The website provides information on a number of ongoing projects and news on what is currently of interest to HRM professionals around the world. The section on 'HR Global Challenges' is produced in several languages and is a helpful overview.

References

Arkin, A. (1999) 'Peak practice', *People Management*, 5, 57–59.

Armstrong, M. (1992) *Human Resource Management: Strategy and action*, London: Kogan Page.

Becker, B. and Gerhart, B. (1996) 'The impact of human resource management on organizational performance: Progress and prospects', *Academy of Management Journal*, 39, 779–801.

Becker, B.E. and Huselid, M.A. (1998) 'High performance work systems and firm performance: a synthesis of research and managerial implications', *Research in Personnel and Human Resources Management*, 16, 53–101.

Becker, B.E. and Huselid, M.A. (1999) 'Overview: strategic human resource management in five leading firms', *Human Resource Management*, 38, 287–301.

Becker, B.E. and Huselid, M.A. (2000) 'Getting an Edge Through People', *Human Resource Management International Digest*, 8, 36–38.

Beer, M. (1997) 'The transformation of the human resource function: resolving the tension between a traditional administrative and a new strategic role', *Human Resource Management*, 36, 49–56.

Beer, M. and Spector, B. (1985) 'Corporate transformations in human resource management', in Walton, R.E. and Lawrence, P.R. (eds), *Human Resource Management Trends and Challenges*, Boston, MA: Harvard Business School Press.

Beer, M., Spector, B., Lawrence, P., Mills, Q. and Walton, R. (1984) *Managing Human Assets*, New York: Free Press.

Bird, A. and Beecher, S. (1995) 'Links between business strategy and human resource management strategy in US-based Japanese subsidiaries: an empirical investigation', *Journal of International Business Studies*, First Quarter, 23–46.

Budhwar, P.S. and Sparrow, P.R. (1997) 'Evaluating levels of strategic integration and development of human resource management in India', *International Journal of Human Resource Management*, 8, 476–494.

Carrington, L. (2007) 'A breath of fresh air', *People Management*, 13, 26–29.

Delery, J.E. and Doty, D.H. (1996) 'Modes of theorising in strategic human resource management: Traits of universalist, contingency, and configurational performance predictions', *Academy of Management Journal*, 39, 802–835.

Dessler, G. (2005) *Human Resource Management*, New Jersey: Pearson.

Du Gay, P. (1997) 'Organizing identity: making up people at work', in du Gay, P. (ed.), *Production of Culture/Culture of Production*, London: Sage.

Dyer, L. and Reeves, T. (1995) 'Human resource strategies and firm's performance: what do we know and where do we need to go?', *International Journal of Human Resource Management*, 6, 656–70.

Fombrun, C., Tichy, N.M. and Devanna, M.A. (1984) *Strategic Human Resource Management*, New York: John Wiley.

Gratton, L., Hope-Hailey, V., Stiles, P. and Truss, C. (1999) 'Linking individual performance to business strategy: the people process model', *Human Resource Management*, 38, 17–31.

Guest, D.E. (1989) 'Human resource management: its implications for industrial relations', in Storey, J. (ed.), *New Perspectives on Human Resource Management*, London: Routledge.

Guest, D.E. (1994) 'Organizational psychology and human resource management: towards a European approach', *European Work and Organizational Psychologist*, 4, 251–70.

Guest, D.E. (1997) 'Human resource management and performance: a review and research agenda', *International Journal of Human Resource Management*, 8, 263–76.

Hendry, C. and Pettigrew, A. (1990) 'Human resource management: an agenda for the 1990s', *International Journal of Human Resource Management*, June, 17–43.

Heneman, H., Metzler, C., Thomas, R., Donohue, T. and Frantzreb, R. (1998) 'Future challenges and opportunities for the HR profession', *HR Magazine*, 43, 68–75.

Hislop, D. (2006) 'Knowledge Management', in Redman, T. and Wilkinson, A. (eds), *Contemporary Human Resource Management*, Harlow, Essex: FT/Prentice Hall.

Huang, T.-C. (2001) 'The effect of linkage between business and human resource management strategies', *Personnel Review*, 30, 123–144.

Hunt, J.W. (1984) 'The drifting focus of the personnel function', *Personnel Management*, February, 14–18.

Kotelnikov, V. (2007) 'Hewlett Packard', www.1000ventures.com

Lawler, E.E. (1986) *High Involvement Management*, San Francisco: Jossey-Bass.

Legge, K. (1978) *Power, Innovation and Problem-solving in Personnel Management*, Maidenhead, Berks: McGraw-Hill.

Legge, K. (1989) 'Human resource management: a critical analysis', in Storey, J. (ed.), *New Perspectives in Human Resource Management*, London: Routledge.

Legge, K. (1995) *Human Resource Management: Rhetorics and Reality*, London: Macmillan.

Miles, R.E. and Snow, C.C. (1984) 'Designing strategic human resource systems', *Organizational Dynamics*, 13, 36–52.

Mintzberg, H. (1975) 'The Manager's Job: Folklore and Fact', *Harvard Business Review*, July–August.

Mohrman, S.A. and Lawler, E.E. (1997) 'Transforming the human resource function', *Human Resource Management*, 36, 157–162.

Needle, D. (2004) *Business in Context: An introduction to business and its environment*, London: Thompson Learning.

Packard, D. (2007) cited in http://uob-community.ballarat.edu.au

Pfeffer, J. and Sutton, R.I. (2006) 'A Matter of Fact', *People Management*, 12, 25–30.

Pfeffer, J. and Veiga, J.F. (1999) 'Putting people first for organizational success', *Academy of Management Executive*, 13, 37–50.

Pickard, J. (2004) 'Riverboat Shuffle', *People Management*, 10, 38–39.

Redman, T. and Wilkinson, A. (2006) 'Human Resource Management: A contemporary perspective', in Redman, T. and Wilkinson, A. (eds), *Contemporary Human Resource Management*, Harlow, Essex: FT/Prentice Hall.

Renwick, D. (2003) 'HR managers, guardians of employee well-being', *Personnel Review*, 32, 341–359.

Roberts, Z. (2006) 'A good courier move', *People Management*, 12, 38–39.

Rousseau, D.M. (2001) 'Schema, promise and mutuality: The building blocks of the psychological contract', *Journal of Occupational Psychology*, 74, 511–541.

Singh, R. (1996) 'Human resource management: a sceptical look', in Towers, B. (ed.), *The Handbook of Human Resource Management*, Oxford: Blackwell.

Sisson, K. (1990) 'Introducing the *Human Resource Management Journal*', *Human Resource Management Journal*, 1, 7–24.

Sparrow, P.R. and Marchington, M. (1998) 'Introduction: is HRM in crisis?', in Sparrow, P.R. and Marchington, M. (eds), *Human Resource Management: The new agenda*, London: FT/Pitman Publishing.

Storey, J. (1992) *Developments in the Management of Human Resources*, Oxford: Blackwell.

Storey, J. (1995) *Human Resource Management: A critical text*, London: Routledge.

Tichy, N.M., Fombrun, C.J. and Devanna, M.A. (1982) 'Strategic human resource management', *Sloan Management Review*, Winter, 47–61.

Ulrich, D. (1998) 'The future calls for change', *Workforce*, 77, 87–91.

Ulrich, D. and Brockbank, W. (2005) *The HR value proposition*, Boston, MA: Harvard Business School Press.

Walton, R.E. (1985) 'Towards a strategy of eliciting employee commitment based on policies of mutuality', in Walton, R.E. and Lawrence, P.R. (eds), *Human Resource Management Trends and Challenges*, Boston, MA: Harvard Business School Press.

Whittington, R., Molloy, E., Mayer, M., Smith, A. and Fenton, E. (2005) 'Look who's talking', *People Management*, 11, 38–40.

Wong, N.C. (2006) 'Churn keeps HP fully staffed', *San Jose Mercury News*, 26 December.

Chapter 2
CORPORATE STRATEGY AND STRATEGIC HRM

Introduction

This chapter examines the nature of corporate strategy and strategic human resource management (SHRM), and the interaction between the two. Different perspectives on strategy are outlined, as are the alternative models of SHRM. The developments in assessing the linkages between HRM and corporate performance are explored, and issues of managing the psychological contract and HRM content and process are highlighted.

Once you have read this chapter, you should:

■ be aware of the different schools of thought on strategy;

■ understand the connections between strategy and HRM, and the implications of these connections for HRM;

■ understand the connections between strategy and specific HRM topics, including involvement, empowerment, flexibility and training;

■ understand the need for an awareness of both content and process in HRM;

■ know the importance of the psychological contract;

■ be able to analyse critically the role and practice of HRM at the strategic level;

■ know the meaning of HRM being a 'business partner';

■ understand the need for organisations to be adaptive to their environments, and recognise the importance of managing ongoing change in organisations.

Corporate strategy

Before entering into a discussion of strategic human resource management (SHRM) the concept of strategic planning in business should be examined. Beardwell *et al.* (2004) maintain that in order to understand the development of SHRM and recognise it as more than traditional HRM with the word 'strategic' tagged on, it is necessary to consider first the nature of strategic management or corporate strategy.

There are a number of generally agreed facets of corporate strategy (Chaffee, 1985). First, strategy affects the overall direction and potential for organisation success; secondly, it is concerned with the fit between the environment and the organisation; thirdly, it deals with the non-routine activities and is seeking innovation and change in the organisation. In its simplest form it amounts to setting organisational objectives, and then deciding on a comprehensive course of action to achieve those objectives. Business strategy is concerned with the efficient use of resources, as well as ensuring that the mobilisation of those resources achieves the maximum impact. In this context a company could, for example, focus on:

■ pursuing markets with high growth potential;

■ improving channels of distribution;

■ reducing its cost structure through the application of modern technology.

According to Johnson *et al.* (2005) strategic decisions are those that are concerned with the long-term direction of the organisation. They are likely to have an impact on a number of facets of the organisation:

■ *the scope of activities* – what the organisation does, whether there is a broad spread of activity or a tight focus;

■ the aim to achieve some *advantage* for the organisation over its competition – for example, by offering better quality services or lower priced products;

■ the *fit between the organisation and its environment* – whether the organisation operates in a mass market or a niche, what the geographical spread of activities is and what technologies are used;

■ how the core *competencies, skills and knowledge* of the organisation will be developed and utilised.

Strategies will also be expressions of the values of the organisation's stakeholders and will be an outcome of the way power operates, for example, through board decisions, but also through the power that employees, customers and competitors have to influence the internal and external business environment.

For Johnson *et al.* (2005) strategic management has three primary aspects: the strategic position; strategic choice; and strategy into action. Strategic position is focused on the external environment and the organisation's abilities to influence its environment. The environment includes the political, legal, economic, technical and social settings of the organisation. These factors can have a strong influence on the sort of strategy adopted. For example, if a new technology is developed that means a product can be produced at lower cost, and competitors take up this technology, then in order to remain in business it is likely that the organisation will have to adopt a similar technology. Strategic choices are the way that strategists react to the external and internal environments. Choices can include allocating resources to some activities and removing them from others, pursuing particular opportunities and not others, and developing the direction and focus of the organisation. Lastly, putting the strategy into action normally entails ensuring that the structure of the organisation is fit for purpose, managing change to gain commitment to the direction, and enabling success through the provision of resources, technology, skills and knowledge.

Each of these elements of strategy affects, and is affected by, the behaviour of people in the organisation. Changing the scope of activities relies on people with the right skills and abilities being available. Gaining competitive advantage typically requires employees to be motivated towards the organisational goals. If people are not driving towards aims such as quality improvement or the development of enhanced service provision, then the success of such aims is likely both to fall short of expectation and be short-lived. Understanding what the organisation's core competencies are, and what its strengths and weaknesses are, requires a good understanding of what staff are currently capable of, and how they might be trained to enhance such capabilities. Therefore, there is a close interaction between HRM and organisational strategies. Neither can operate effectively without understanding the other and organisational success requires an effective fit between the two.

Different conceptualisations of strategy have been developed over time and we will now briefly explore them before discussing the nature of strategic HRM in more depth.

PRESCRIPTIVE SCHOOL

A traditional conceptualisation of strategy has been termed the 'prescriptive school' of strategy (Mintzberg et al., 1998). The three areas emphasised in this school are design, planning and positioning. Design is concerned with the match between internal capabilities and external opportunities (Andrews, 1987), and this is echoed in the early approaches to strategic HRM (Fombrun et al., 1984), which are considered in the next section. The purpose of planning is to predict and prepare for the future, for example, through analysis of strengths, weaknesses, opportunities and threats (SWOT analysis) (Ackoff, 1983). The third area of focus entails deciding on the position the organisation should adopt with regard to its suppliers, competitors and customers.

Walker (1980) encapsulated the essence of design and planning when he identified five steps of strategic planning steps as follows:

1. *Definition of corporate philosophy and the preparation of a mission statement.* In this step, the organisation makes clear its reasons for existence, what it will produce and whom it will serve, and its orientation to business in terms of its values.
2. *Scan environmental conditions.* The organisation systematically investigates the technological, economic, environmental, political and social forces that impact upon it. This scan will give detailed information on the nature of the market the organisation is competing in and will help with the identification of opportunities for developing the business.
3. *Evaluate the organisation's strengths and weaknesses.* In this step the organisation focuses internally to investigate its current resources. Attention is paid to particular abilities that might differentiate the organisation from its competitors and critical limitations in its abilities are identified.
4. *Develop objectives and goals.* Having assessed external conditions (step 2) and internal capabilities (step 3) the next step is to determine specific goals and objectives aimed at fulfilling the mission. Objectives are normally focused on performance and could specify desired achievements such as sales volume, profit levels and return on investment.
5. *Develop strategies.* The last step is to decide what changes are needed to achieve the objectives and goals. Some strategies relate to areas such as finance and technology and are focused, for example, on the nature of investment. Other strategies relate directly to HR policies such as what skills and training are needed to bring the strategy into effect.

With regard to positioning, it has been argued that there are three main positions an organisation can take (Porter, 1980, 1985). First, 'cost leadership' entails the organisation seeking to produce output at low costs to enhance competitiveness, thereby making the market less attractive to competitors. Secondly, the organisation can seek to differentiate itself by producing a product or service that is unique and difficult to copy and offers higher profit margins. The third position would identify the particular customer groups, products or markets (e.g. geographically defined) in which the organisation will specialise. In deciding on which position to adopt, organisations should consider the following (Porter, 1985):

■ the threats of new entrants (how difficult it is for competitors to enter the market);

■ the bargaining power of the firm's suppliers (the extent to which they are substitutable);

■ the bargaining power of the firm's customers (e.g., how easily customers could buy comparable goods or services from other suppliers);

■ the intensity of rivalry amongst competing firms.

While the prescriptive school remains an important force in strategic management, it has been challenged (Mintzberg *et al.*, 1998). The challenge has come in part from theorists such as Lindblom (1969) and Quinn (1980), and also from practice found in successful organisations. For example, in the 1970s, adopting the tenets of the prescriptive school would have led to advising Honda, which at that time was mainly concerned with motorcycle manufacture, not to enter the car market that was already saturated with efficient competitors. Three decades later, however, Honda holds a significant position in the car market. Honda, and other such firms, did not always follow the advice of the prescriptive school, and yet they were still successful. This led to some doubts that the prescriptive school could accurately predict business outcomes in all cases.

From a theoretical perspective, it has been argued that strategic decisions are not fully rational, because managers suffer limitations with respect to the time they can spend on addressing issues, the information they can gather and the processes of decision making they employ (Lindblom, 1969). Typically, rather than carrying out a full analysis, organisations conduct a series of limited comparisons and adopt the most workable position that emerges within the restraints of the analysis. In addition, decision making and implementation are not entirely separate. So, while there might be a decision about the direction in which an organisation should go in attempting to pursue its aims it may come across difficulties or new opportunities that lead it to alter its original decision. Although there may be an initial strategic plan, this is often altered and developed in response to external events and internal pressures as the implementation unfolds (Quinn, 1980); for example, employees may lack the skills that the organisation requires to develop in a particular direction, or customers may demand modifications to the nature of a service supplied. In this sense, strategy may be 'emergent' rather than fully planned in advance of taking any action. The strategy may be adapted to circumstances that arise at the operational stage.

DESCRIPTIVE SCHOOL

An alternative approach known as the 'descriptive school' has been proposed (Mintzberg *et al.*, 1998). This school has at least four important perspectives, namely vision, learning, power and culture.

Vision

The vision of the organisation, as discussed above, provides an image rather than a fully worked-out plan. It is typically concerned with change and providing a general direction (Drucker, 1970; Marzec, 2007), and allows a certain degree of freedom within which employees can decide how to act. This can be particularly important in entrepreneurial organisations and

SMEs (Griener, 1998; Brand and Bax, 2002) and for employees who deal directly with customers or users. Some organisations adopt a top-down approach to vision, with the direction coming from the top team or the entrepreneur. Others have developed visions by involving staff, for example through workshops in which they discuss the purpose of the organisation and their role within it; this has the characteristics of a bottom-up approach. In one example, Northern Foods set up consultation forums in each of its strategic business units in the United Kingdom, Ireland and the Netherlands. Employees were consulted on how the forums should operate, and the communication on strategic issues is becoming upwards as well as top down (Walsh, 2000).

Learning

The focus on learning has been highlighted by Prahalad and Hamel (1990), who argue that it is only through a collective learning process that an organisation will be able to compete effectively with others through speed of modifying standard processes or services in order to meet the demands of customers. Part of a strategic approach to enhancing learning is through deliberate planning, for example, in enabling appropriate training and development in the organisation. However, a view from the other side of the fence indicates that employees must be able to move in a direction dictated by their own learning, rather than being required to adhere strictly to a formal plan. According to Senge (1990), the process is one of changing employees from being simply the implementers of plans to being problem solvers who will move the organisation forward. This implies a degree of bottom-up change and decision making. There is further discussion of the learning organisation in Chapter 10.

Power

The focus on power is justified when we acknowledge that organisations are coalitions of individuals who have different beliefs, interests and information and may have different perceptions of reality (Bolman and Deal, 2003). Groups will naturally seek to influence decisions on organisational direction and resource allocation towards outcomes favourable to themselves. Bourne and Walker (2005) see strategy making as intrinsically linked to organisational politics and the activities of interest groups (or stakeholders), which are manifestations of the use of power. It is argued that in formulating strategy one cannot merely reach rational decisions and expect them to be accepted. Rather, one needs to be aware of the interests and power of the different groups that may be affected by a decision and to take this into account (Pesqueux and Damak-Ayadi, 2005). Sometimes it is possible to do this by incorporating representatives of powerful groups into the decision-making process so that there will be less resistance to the decision. On other occasions it may be necessary to negotiate the implementation of a decision with such groups. On some occasions manipulation or coercive pressure are used.

Culture

Strategy can be seen as a process of social interaction in which decision making is strongly influenced by culture (Johnson, 1992; Li and Putterill, 2007). For example, some cultures are risk averse and others support risk taking: therefore it is easy to conclude that the nature of decision making is dependent upon the prevailing culture. The strategy is likely to reflect the dominant values and taken-for-granted assumptions in the organisation. Culture is discussed in detail in Chapter 5.

The focus on vision, learning, power and culture has implications for SHRM. Of course, it is possible for an organisational culture to be authoritarian, and for the power orientation of leaders to be coercive. In such cases employees would normally be remote from the decision-making arena. However, in the way that the descriptive school is envisaged by Mintzberg, the following would be expected. First, a much greater degree of involvement and upward communication is envisaged. Secondly, attention must be paid to the employees' perceptions of their role in the organisation and the development of their skills and knowledge in order to become problem solvers. Thirdly, it is the incremental process of change that is seen as crucial rather than one-off grand strategic plans. The argument is not that rational analysis is unnecessary, or that top teams do not have responsibility for vision, direction and the welfare of the organisation. Rather the position is that, though all these are necessary, they are not sufficient in today's business environments, which require adaptability, responsiveness to customers and the commitment of employees.

It should be noted that the descriptive school could be subjected to criticism. Clearly, not all organisations and all environments lend themselves to thorough communication and employee involvement; for example, the required speed of decision making may prevent an extensive consultation process. In addition, there are examples of successful organisations that do not extend employee learning beyond the basics of operational training.

Strategic HRM

Over two decades ago a school of thought in HRM, known as the Michigan School (Fombrun *et al.*, 1984), arrived on the scene. This model of HRM placed much emphasis on the importance of the strategic approach, which involves relating corporate strategy to SHRM in areas such as structure (discussed in the next chapter), culture (discussed in Chapter 5), and employee resourcing and development (discussed in Chapters 6–10).

The model of HRM briefly outlined above can be viewed as the traditional model, also known as the matching or best-fit model, discussed below. Alternative models, known as the resource-based model and the processual view of HR strategies, will be discussed later.

MATCHING OR BEST-FIT MODEL

The matching or best-fit model focuses on strategic integration (Beer *et al.*, 1984). Integration in this sense means bringing about a good fit between the HR policy and the company's policy with regard to strategic direction. There are a number of approaches to SHRM that have attempted to come up with a good match or best fit (Beardwell *et al.*, 2004). These include the life cycle approach (e.g. Baird and Meshoulam, 1988), and the competitive advantage approach (e.g. Schuler and Jackson, 2000).

Life cycle approach

To begin with there is the start-up phase in the development of the business and this signals the need for flexibility in order to encourage entrepreneurialism and growth. Once the business reaches the growth stage the emphasis would be towards the development of more formal HRM policies and procedures. The next stage – the maturity stage – is where markets mature and profit margins shrink, and the standing of certain products and the performance of the organisation reach a plateau. At this stage HR strategy is very much concerned with cost control. A challenge for SHRM at the mature stage is to retain organisational viability and sustain competitive advantage, and this demands the cultivation of flexibility and a high capability to respond and adapt to external forces. In the final stage – the decline stage of a product or business – there is a preoccupation with rationalisation whereby HRM is addressing the consequences of downsizing, such as handling redundancies.

Competitive advantage approach

This tends to subscribe to Porter's (1985) ideas on strategic choice (e.g. cost leadership, differentiation through quality and service and niche or focus market) explained earlier on page 28. Schuler and Jackson (2000) use Porter's ideas as a foundation for their model of SHRM, and offer suggestions about the most appropriate HR policies and practices to fit the corporate strategies connected with cost reduction, quality enhancement and innovation. The emphasis is on linking SHRM policy and practices to the strategic direction of the business. Their contention is that the economic performance of the organisation will improve when HR practices are in harmony and complement each other in the service of the chosen strategy for the organisation, which is to foster competitiveness. It is accepted that certain types of behaviour are required of employees if they are to make a successful contribution to the implementation of corporate strategy, and that it is encumbent on HR practices to provide the underpinning and support for the desired employee behaviour. Vertical integration is achieved when these behaviours are effectively directed at the achievement of corporate goals. For example, if the organisation had a primary emphasis on cost reduction, the appropriate HR strategy would be a focus on promoting efficiency through hard HR techniques. On the other hand, quality enhancement and innovation strategies could be supported by softer HR techniques and policies that focus on added value. This latter strategy is evident in the case of Toshiba presented in Case example 2.1.

CASE EXAMPLE 2.1

MATCHING MODEL – TOSHIBA'S STRATEGIC INNOVATION

'In today's ultra-competitive business environment, organisations are increasingly relying on all workers – not just managers – to find new and creative ways to do business. Innovation is the lifeblood of Toshiba, enabling the company to pioneer and drive new high-margin markets ...'

(Susan Stevens, Head of HR for Toshiba Information Systems, quoted in Pollitt, 2006: 5).

Toshiba operate in a highly competitive marketplace and its strategy is to deal with this environment through innovation. In order to execute this strategy, it needed to develop HRM policies that would encourage staff to be innovative. Its process was successful and innovative projects, driven by employees, have yielded £10 million savings in the United Kingdom and £3 billion worldwide (Pollitt, 2006). Projects have included creation of a web-based sales platform, dramatic reduction of telephone bills and a project that enabled Toshiba to become the leading supplier of personal computers to Dixons, a major electronics retailer.

Part of the HRM strategy was concerned with organisational structure. It entailed breaking down traditional functional silos and encouraging what Toshiba termed 'cross-pollination'. One particularly successful example was of a project team formed from members of the information technology and marketing departments. A second aspect of the strategy was to review and reward employees for producing creative ideas. Employees also felt that they were being involved in the company's decision making, and this was found to enhance their commitment to Toshiba. Lastly, innovative processes were carefully managed. Rather than leaving people to find their own ways of developing ideas, Toshiba found it best to provide a framework, not of restrictive rules, but of supportive programmes, such as cross-pollination, which gave employees a structure within which to work. Project teams would have to define their ideas and show how they could be measured, analysed and controlled. However, within these guidelines, employees had discretion to develop innovative ideas.

These aspects of the HRM strategy were chosen to fit with the organisational strategy. They do not cover all aspects of HRM. For example, recruitment and training are not mentioned. Rather, there is a focused approach to creating the right conditions for an innovative workforce.

Question

Toshiba's strategy focused on encouraging employees to be creative. What are the potential benefits and risks of such a strategy?

Criticism of the matching or best fit model

The model has been subjected to criticism in at least four areas:

1. The matching model bears the features of a rational model of decision making. In other words, it assumes that organisational decision makers can plan and act rationally and that those plans will be the ones that are executed in the organisation. But as Mintzberg *et al.* (1998) maintain there are other views of strategy, which are a better representation of the reality of organisational life. Also, the problematic nature of strategic decision making is recognised by Johnson (1992), who raises questions about constraining influences such as political processes in organisations, lack of consistency in management decision making and various manifestations of negotiating and bargaining ploys used by actors in the system. The existence of these constraints makes it very difficult to accept the idea of a rational 'linear' model of organisational decision making.

2. The matching model bears witness to a number of contradictions. It has been argued that in some circumstances there is a certain incongruity between corporate strategy and strategic HRM (Legge, 1995). This could arise when, for example, the corporate plan dictates cost minimisation through a reduction in labour costs following a pruning exercise such as downsizing. Putting such a plan into action could involve making staff redundant, and this could run counter to an HRM perspective that puts the accent on commitment to employees. As a result, the outcome could be lower satisfaction or dissatisfaction and poor organisational performance (Patterson *et al.*, 1997). Even though there may be a certain logic in pursuing the financial strategy stated above in the matching model, the outcome could be less than satisfactory or undesirable in human terms. There lies the contradiction!

3. It has been argued that the act of matching corporate strategy with SHRM in a pronounced way may not be a good idea after all (Boxall, 1996). In seeking to gain competitive advantage through a strategic fit between corporate strategy and HRM strategy, the organisation could end up with structures and processes more inflexible than that of its competitors. The reality of the marketplace today indicates that flexibility is a central requirement for effective organisational performance, and flexibility based on organisational learning (see Chapter 10) is a valuable attribute (Boxall, 1996).

4. The matching model assumes a degree of freedom on the part of organisations, for example to reduce the number of employees as required. However, in reality, the freedom to change terms and conditions of employment are limited by employment law and custom and practice, not to mention the possibilities of industrial action if proposed changes are strongly objected to by the workforce.

Mindful of the criticisms of the matching model, Beardwell *et al.* (2004) advocate a configurational perspective that requires SHRM to develop a HR system that requires both horizontal and vertical integration. In this way the outcome of the horizontal integration of HR policy and techniques (configuration) is linked to the various strands (configuration) of the implementation of corporate strategy.

Torrington *et al.* (2005) can see different levels of vertical integration, as follows:

■ the HR strategy is designed to fit the requirements of the business strategy of the organisation, as is evident in the matching model. This has manifestations of the classical approach to strategy, as business objectives are cascaded down from senior management through departments to individuals and teams.

■ There is only dialogue between those making business strategy decisions and those responsible for making HR decisions. In practice a more correct way of describing the interaction is that those responsible for HR may merely pass on essential information to senior corporate decision makers.

■ There is a high level of interaction between the two camps. Employees are recognised as a key source of competitive advantage, and every effort is made to harness the competency of the human resource (Barney and Wright, 1998).

RESOURCE-BASED MODEL

This model represents a significant shift in SHRM thinking by attracting our attention to the internal resources of the organisation rather than analysing performance in terms of the external context. A noticeable feature of the resource-based model is its primary concern with what is going on within the organisational boundaries in order to be well placed to respond to opportunities in the external environment (Barney, 1991). This approach seeks to understand the distinctive competences of the workforce – which competitors would experience difficulty in imitating – through a process of analysing capabilities, knowledge and skills at the disposal of the organisation. The reason for doing so is to develop a sustainable competitive advantage for the organisation. Kamoche (1996) is of the view that it is important to align the distinctive competences of the organisation with the HR competences if success in the marketplace is to be achieved.

Maintaining alignment of individual competences is particularly an issue where individuals have competences that are no longer relevant to the distinctive abilities of the organisation. In such circumstances there may be a need to retrain the individual, possibly redeploy them, or ultimately make them redundant where there is no other viable alternative.

There may be situations where developments in a market mean that development in organisational competences is required. Under these circumstances it is necessary either to buy in new skills or identify training needs for employees. Maintaining alignment of competences is a dynamic process and has an impact on training and development (which is discussed in greater detail in Chapter 10).

Beardwell *et al.* (2004) point out that to achieve competitive advantage that is sustainable over time, HRM needs to ensure that the organisation's human resources provide value, are rare, are difficult to copy, and that there are appropriate HR systems and practices in place to achieve these demanding objectives.

Value

We have become accustomed to organisations reducing costs through the medium of HRM (e.g. reduction in headcount, introduction of flexible practices to reduce costs), but we should be paying more attention to ways in which HRM can help organisations to create value through enhancing efficiency, customer selection and retention, and meeting customer's needs.

Rarity

Serious consideration should be given to ways and means to nurture rare characteristics of the organisation's human resources to gain competitive advantage. This would necessitate attracting good entrants who are interested in the company's line of business. Once selected every effort should be made to develop such employees and reward them well so that they are motivated to produce distinctive performance.

Inimitability

The aim is to develop characteristics that cannot easily be imitated by the organisation's competitors. It would appear that creating and sustaining a particular culture is crucial in this respect. Barney and Wright (1998) make reference to the culture in South West Airlines, USA in the late 1990s which was supportive of good employee selection, as well as facilitating excellent performance and tolerance of making mistakes – viewed as a learning experience. In that organisation, apart from subscribing to the principle of empowerment, there was a culture of fun, good relationships and trust. These could be viewed as company-specific assets that provide value and are difficult for competitors to copy.

Organisation

There should be a determination that HRM practices are horizontally integrated, or that HRM systems are integrated and complement each other. This requires that the individual subsystems are not contradictory and are well coordinated. This is easier said that done. One could argue that there is limited coordination across the board and in many organisations with a long tradition of adherence to personnel management or HRM it would be possible to find that employee resourcing, employee development, performance management, reward management and employee relations strategies evolved in isolation.

The main message coming across from the resource-based model is that SHRM should be actively framing the future by identifying and developing core competencies for competitive advantage. The experience of Dell (see Case example 2.2) illustrates the importance of subscribing to the enhancement of the organisation's HR base.

KNOWLEDGE-BASED STRATEGIES AT DELL

Dell built on its core strengths to develop a business model that combined both mass customisation and built-to-order specialisation for the customer (Lewin and Massini, 2004). Such a combination was not thought to be possible in traditional views of strategy, but Dell achieved the synergy through its ability to allow customers to book their orders online and sophisticated management of its supply chain. Hence, it was able to pursue a strategy of price reduction which squeezed its competitors who were trying to manage multiple retail channels (traditional and online). The capabilities to develop this strategy were not developed instantaneously. Rather, they were developed over time and emerged after several years of trial and error. Through this process, Dell developed both knowledge and network relations with its supply chain that were very difficult for competitors to imitate. This strategy relied on the establishment of the knowledge resource within the company over time.

Criticisms of the resource-based model

While it may be an attractive theory, it tends to be too introspective, not giving sufficient attention to the external environment and there are relatively few overt examples in practice. In addition, the model does not acknowledge sufficiently the potential for conflicts of interest between employees and their employer – the outcome of which can be that employees may have the necessary competences but they may choose not to employ them fully or effectively in pursuit of the organisation's ends (Bratton and Gold, 1999).

BEST PRACTICE MODEL (HIGH COMMITMENT)

The idea of best practice or high commitment SHRM (universalism) was raised in the early US models of HRM. Contributors circulated the view that the adoption of certain best practices in HRM would be reflected in improved employee attitudes and behaviour, lower levels of absenteeism and turnover, and higher levels of skills leading to enhanced quality and efficiency and improved productivity. The major conclusion is that organisations will be winners if they manage to gain employee commitment to the implementation of a set of HRM best practices. A pertinent question to ask is what constitutes an ideal set of HRM best practices and is it necessary for them to be horizontally integrated into bundles that can be related to issues connected with the implementation of corporate strategy? Marchington and Wilkinson (2002) have identified a number of best practice measures, as follows:

- good selection practices;
- secure employment and opportunities to progress within the organisation;
- a climate of sharing information, with people being extensively involved in various deliberations where they have the freedom to express a firm point of view;
- active fostering of learning and development, aided by well-resourced training;
- reward systems that are firmly related to performance;

■ a reduction of status differentials among employees;

■ Extolling the virtues of teamwork and good use made of self-managed teams.

The central message of the best practice model is that HRM is trying to influence senior management to implement the bundle of best practice techniques. A valid question to ask is, what is the best combination of best practice techniques? Those who advocate the best practice techniques, particularly the universalists, have their critics. One fundamental criticism is that the best practice model, with its strong adherence to high commitment, subscribes to unitarism. But this ignores the inherent pluralist values and tensions present in many organisations.

PROCESSUAL APPROACH

This approach has characteristics in common with the descriptive theories of strategy (Mintzberg *et al.*, 1998) discussed earlier. It conceives of strategy as the outcome of both planned and unplanned activities. In its application to HRM this means that strategy is not simply concerned with setting policy in areas such as organisational structure, recruitment, training and so on. It is also concerned with the impact on the 'realised' strategy (i.e. strategy as it occurs in practice) as a result of the actions of managers and employees. For example, the way managers undertake recruitment at the local level can alter, in real terms, the 'espoused' or formal policy (Watson, 1999). This influence can be positive – for example, when best practice is used as a benchmark for other managers to follow – but it can be negative – for example, where an equal opportunities policy is subverted by personal bias on the part of a manager.

The processual approach often emphasises employee involvement, and in this regard it can have a strategic impact. For example, in recruitment and selection traditional approaches seek to match candidates to a pre-formed 'template' of the ideal employee designed by the organisation, but this approach (Newell and Rice, 1999) envisages selection as a two-way negotiation in which potential employees can have an input to the design of the job! This is carried out through informal and open discussion in which the candidates and the organisation get to know each other, and to understand what the possibilities and limitations of a match are. Subsequently, both sides have a choice in whether or not they take the process further to formalise application and selection. An advantage of this approach is that it increases the information both the individual and the organisation have of each other, but it can impose considerable costs on the organisation as employers will have to spend time with potential candidates, the majority of whom (in normal circumstances) will not end up as employees. Hence it is likely that such an approach cannot be used for all jobs, or in all organisations.

The processual approach can be criticised in a number of ways. Because it operates at the 'doing' level rather than the 'visioning' level it can be seen as 'downstream' of the 'real' strategy (Purcell, 1992) and as reactive rather than proactive (Legge, 1995). If a high degree of freedom is extended to managers then there is the potential for inconsistency and unfairness in the application of policy. For example, variable standards might be used by different managers in making selection decisions, and this would result in unfair treatment of job candidates. Hence there is a need for a framework of policy to ensure sufficient consistency.

HRM and organisational performance

HIGH PERFORMANCE THROUGH PEOPLE

Walton (1985) argued persuasively that the HRM model was composed of policies that promoted mutual goals, influence, respect, rewards and responsibility between employees and the organisation. The theory was that the resultant, reciprocal, positive attitude would lead to enhanced commitment on the part of employees, and that this would in turn lead to increased economic performance of the organisation. The practices Walton endorsed included the following:

- teamworking and undertaking the 'whole task' (rather than fragmentation of task and specialisation of skill);

- agreeing performance objectives that stretch people;

- a flat organisational structure with reduced supervision, coordination and communication through mutual influence, involvement and shared goals;

- group-based reward systems;

- a priority on training; and

- a joint problem-solving approach to employee relations.

He argued that such an approach can be applied in almost all organisational situations, and that it will result in enhanced commitment and performance.

We referred above to the best practice model of HRM and there has been some debate over the detailed contents of the 'bundle' of best HR practice, with a variety of terms being employed, for example, 'high commitment management' (HCM) (e.g. Wood, 1995) and 'high performance work practices' (Huselid, 1995). However, Delaney and Huselid (1996) offer a useful analysis that emphasises the logical flow of, and connection between, the various practices. Their conceptualisation is as follows:

- The *recruitment and selection* of employees can be improved in order to maximise the skills and knowledge that employees bring to the organisation.

- The quality and contribution of current employees can be improved through *training and development*.

- In order to encourage employees to deploy their skills and knowledge with enthusiasm in the direction of organisational objectives it is necessary to have an effective *reward system*. In addition, they argue that motivation also depends on employees believing that they will be treated fairly, that the *performance management* system will acknowledge their efforts, and that they will not be subject to arbitrary treatment by management.

- The way that work is arranged has an impact on effectiveness.

The evidence of research marshalled by Delaney and Huselid (1996) indicates the benefits of organising work so that employees are directly *involved* in determining what the priorities are, and how work is carried out – for example, through *team-based working* and upwards *communication*. Pfeffer (1994, 1998) and Pfeffer and Veiga (1999) summarise the broad agreement amongst researchers on the make-up of the effective bundle of HR practices along the following lines:

- employment security;

- selective hiring;

- teamworking and decentralised decision making;

- comparatively high pay contingent on organisational performance;

- extensive training;

- reduced status distinctions;

- sharing information.

Employment security

Although providing employment security may appear to be an anachronism in competitive conditions where a company may need to reduce costs by reducing the headcount, Pfeffer (1998) argues that it is important for a number of reasons. First, employees are unlikely to agree to increase their flexibility and cooperation in becoming more efficient and productive if there is not some assurance that they will not lose their jobs as a result. Secondly, if the first reaction to financial difficulties is to lay off staff, the effect is to put important strategic assets into the labour market for the organisation's competitors to employ. Thirdly, there are significant costs to reducing headcount, including redundancy payments. Fourthly, providing job security can be an important discipline for managers as it encourages considerable caution and care in recruitment and selection. The chief executive officer (CEO) of Southwest Airlines, quoted by Pfeffer and Veiga (1999), argues that the last approach has helped the company to maintain a smaller and more competitive workforce than its competitors over the long term. Additionally, the competitors have incurred the costs of a fluctuating headcount, both up and down.

Selective hiring

Pfeffer and Veiga (1999) highlight a number of steps in effective recruitment and selection. They advocate generating a large pool of applicants. Some would see dealing with large numbers as an unnecessary expense. However, the most successful companies in the research sample saw it as a necessary step. The selection process should focus on the most critical skills and attributes not only for the job but also for the future of the organisation. These include initiative, judgement, adaptability and the ability to learn, as well as more job-specific skills. Finally, selection, which is discussed in Chapter 7, should focus primarily on attributes that are difficult to change through training. For some organisations this includes finding a good fit between candidates and the organisational culture.

Teamworking and decentralised organisational design

Teamworking is advocated primarily because it replaces hierarchical control with peer-based control of work. This can lead to greater responsibility being taken by people at lower levels in the hierarchy and enables the reduction of supervisory layers of management. While this can result in cost saving it should be noted that there may be a tension between this approach and the approach based on the previous hierarchical model. This tension may be resolved in some companies by having an initial phase of change that reduces layers with a likely reduction in staffing levels or headcount reduction, but thereafter continuous improvement and change is pursued through the existing workforce. Pfeffer and Veiga (1999) cite many examples, but a telling one is that of Vancom Zuid-Limburg, the Dutch transport and bus organisation, which has achieved rapid growth. It is able to win contracts because of its very low overhead costs based on a manager–driver ratio of 1:40 rather than the industry norm of 1:8. The self-managed teams of 20 drivers run their own lines and have budgeting responsibilities, and each driver has responsibilities for high levels of customer care and proactive problem solving.

Comparatively high pay contingent on organisational performance

Part of the argument for comparatively high pay is that it can refocus employees from worrying and complaining about their pay to improving performance. If the pay deal is favourable for employees, organisations have found that they can expect and achieve greater effort, particularly in the area of customer service, from their employees. Pfeffer and Veiga espouse share ownership, where employees hold shares in the company, and as a result they are more likely to act and think like owners. Other forms of reward that seek to achieve this outcome include profit sharing, gain sharing and various forms of team or individual incentives. These issues are discussed in Chapter 9.

Extensive training

Training is essential to the implementation of high-performance work systems, as is argued in Chapter 10, because such systems rely on front-line staff being able to exercise initiative, solve problems, manage quality and initiate changes. Although it would be desirable to be able to evaluate clearly the contribution of training to performance in a cost/benefit analysis, this is difficult, if not impossible, as the isolation and identification of effects specifically due to training are problematic.

Reduced status distinctions

The basic premise of high-performance work systems is that performance is derived from making use of the skills, ideas and efforts of all the people in the organisation. Strong status differentials are likely to obstruct such processes, and successful organisations have often sought to reduce such barriers both symbolically (e.g. through language, dress and physical space) and substantively through a reduction in the number of wage bands and distinctions.

Sharing information

Sharing information is vital to the establishment of trust in the workplace, and it is also crucial if employees are to understand the organisational objectives. In addition, if management is to understand and learn from employees on issues such as problem identification, improvements in systems and other suggestions, the sharing of information needs to be multi-directional rather than top down. Highly successful organisations seek to share information whether it is good or bad. If the organisation only propagates 'good news' employees are likely to think they are only getting part of the story, and will be less able to contribute solutions to real problems.

EVIDENCE OF THE LINK BETWEEN HRM AND PERFORMANCE

Becker and Huselid (1999), surveying research findings, state that high performance HRM systems have now become a source of competitive advantage. In a major study in the United

States covering more than 2,400 firms, Becker and Huselid (1998) found that considerable differences in organisational performance were attributable to the implementation of the bundle of high-performance HRM practices. They devised an index including 24 items of HRM systems, and measured the correlation of this against various indicators of organisational performance. The general finding was that good HRM practice was positively correlated with increased performance. In particular, organisations placed 1 standard deviation higher than the norm on the HRM system index showed differences in performance measures as follows:

market value	+24%
accounting profits	+25%
gross rate of return on assets	+25%
sales per employee	+4.8%
staff turnover	−7.6%

In a study of five-year survival rates of newly quoted companies Wellbourne and Andrews (1996) found a correlation between company survival and HRM practices. When factors such as size, industry and profits were statistically controlled the survival rates varied by 20 per cent with a 1 standard deviation shift in the index of the value the firm placed on HR. The difference in probability of survival between those organisations in line with best practice on employee rewards and those most distant from best practice was 42 per cent.

This research has been supported in the United Kingdom, where Patterson *et al.* (1997) found strong linkages between the acquisition and development of skilled people, job design stressing autonomy, flexible problem solving and positive employee attitudes and performance. They found that HRM practices correlated with 18–19 per cent variation in productivity and profitability, with good HR practice leading to increases, and lack of good HR practice leading to decreases, in performance.

Similarly, a strong link has been found between employee commitment and the business's financial success in the German banking sector (Benkhoff, 1997) and in a study of Taiwanese high-tech firms (Chang and Chen, 2002). They found significant effects on employee productivity from HRM practices such as training and development, teamwork, benefits, HR planning and appraisal. In some research, the successful organisational outcomes are associated with all, or almost all, of the HRM practices (as a bundle). This was the case with Becker and Huselid's (1999) findings, and more recently with studies that have focused on particular organisational outcomes. For example, in Laursen and Floss's (2003) study of innovation in 1,900 Danish firms, innovation is linked to seven out of nine HRM practices. However, other research has discovered strong associations between a more restricted selection of HRM practices and organisational outcomes. For example, Bartel's (2004) study of US banks shows a strong relationship between the 'incentives' dimension of high performance workplace systems (performance evaluation, feedback and recognition) and branch performance.

Notwithstanding the impressive volume of research indicating a strong correlation between HRM and organisational performance, there is a criticism that the research has not fully uncovered the nature of the links. Purcell *et al.* (2003) have argued that there is a 'black box' issue with the research linking HRM and organisational performance. That is, despite research of the type referred to above, we cannot be sure *how* the inputs (HRM practices) lead to particular outcomes. We cannot be sure that in all cases when HRM practices are introduced employees will respond positively and that personal and corporate performance will improve in tandem. Some research has shown mixed results. For example, Guest *et al.* (2003), in a study of 366 UK companies, did not find a clear causal connection between HRM practices and productivity. They did, however, discover links between profit, reduced staff turnover and HRM practices. In a situation where the linkages are not absolute, it may be the case that they are mediated by other factors. It is thought that this is the case as far as HRM and organisational performance is concerned.

The mediating factor is thought to be the way that employees perceive the intention and effect of HRM practices. Garrow (2003) studied employees in four organisations over a year. It was found that the psychological contract of employees was particularly significant. Where there was a positive psychological contract, staff turnover was lower and commitment was higher. Conversely, where the psychological contract was negative, turnover was higher and commitment was lower. The nature of the psychological commitment has been strongly linked to performance and to HRM (Wright *et al.*, 2003; Bartel, 2004) and so it is important that we have a good understanding of the nature of the psychological contract and the influence of HRM upon it.

According to Guest (1998) the 'psychological contract' is crucial in influencing effort and performance. As stated on page 10, the psychological contract concerns the expectations, rights and obligations employees believe to exist between them and the organisation (Rousseau, 2001). Where there is a mutual understanding and perception of fairness then performance is likely to be enhanced. For West and Patterson (1998) such factors are highly significant, because they contribute to the climate of satisfaction in a workplace. Their findings indicate that where there is a good climate the attitudes and behaviour within a peer group foster good relations as workers cooperate. The positive climate also relates to the relationship between employees and their supervisors, and this enables good communication. Conversely, where there are problems, for example the psychological contract is not honoured due to poor communications or lack of involvement, then negatively reinforcing cycles can be expected. In such situations peer groups may expend considerable effort on discussing or worrying about the social situation and on ensuring their own future safety, rather than working together in order to perform.

Recently, there has been some criticism of the concept of the psychological contract. Cullinane and Dundon (2006) see it as a form of managerialism in which the interests of the organisation take precedence over those of the employee. It is argued that managers are in a position of power that enables them to define what good performance means and to alter the terms of engagement. For example, if the organisation is pursuing continuous improvement, behaviour that constituted good performance two or three years ago may not be counted as favourably next year when performance expectations have increased. Hence, it is possible that employees believe that they are performing well and should be recognised, whilst management believes the opposite.

Another potential problem is that focusing on the psychological contract can lead to excessive concentration exchange as the basis of the relationship between employer and employee, to the detriment of other factors such as emotional engagement (Winter and Jackson, 2006). In their study of the psychological contract in Australian credit unions, Winter and Jackson found that managers tended to focus on calculable exchange (such as pay for performance), and were particularly concerned with resource constraints and financial considerations when considering the allocation of reward and recognition. Employees, however, in additional to such forms of exchange, were also concerned with emotional and symbolic matters. For example, where the organisation was perceived as 'uncaring' and management as 'distant', or where managerial actions such as open-door policies were regarded as 'symbolic acts' rather than being genuine, there were negative outcomes for the psychological contract.

Garrow (2003) identifies a similar distinction when she differentiates transactional psychological contracts, which are based on monetary gain and expectations of short-term quid pro quo, from relational psychological contracts, which are based on trust and loyalty. Where there are perceived breaches of the contract, in material, rational, emotional or symbolic terms, the outcome is often a decreased attachment between the employee and the organisation (Restubog *et al.*, 2006). These criticisms do not remove the need to understand and engage with the psychological contract. Rather, they draw attention to the way that it should be managed – as a form of genuine engagement and communication between managers and employees. An illustration of the psychological contract appears in Case example 2.3.

CASE EXAMPLE 2.3

THE PSYCHOLOGICAL CONTRACT IN ACTION AT SAFEWAY

The staff at the supermarket Safeway were accustomed to thinking of it as a very successful business. However, in 2003, Safeway was threatened with a possible takeover, and this led to a lowering of morale and concerns that staff turnover would increase as people sought security elsewhere. 'We introduced financial incentives to encourage people to stay but we also recognized that many staff at Safeway have a relational psychological contract, in that they are long-serving and not motivated purely by money . . . so we knew we had to appeal to them in different ways' (Kellam Greenwood, People Potential Manager, Safeway, quoted in Garrow, 2003: 28). The retention strategy had four main aspects. First, there was an investment in training and development. The aim was to upskill people so that they could be confident about the future, whether or not there was a takeover. Secondly, there was a new approach to leadership in which leaders were trained in new behaviours that were aimed at leading in times of ambiguity and enabling staff to be resilient in the face of change. Thirdly, there was a focus on clear communication. A dedicated part of the intranet was set up to communicate about possible and actual changes; 'meetings for everyone' were held at head office every four weeks, with video-links to distribution centres and regional offices. In addition, colleague councils were set up to enable representatives to meet senior managers for briefings. The briefings were then cascaded through the organisation by the representatives. Finally, motivational payments were made to 25,000 staff. The outcome was successful in that staff turnover did not increase and customer service (measured in the customer service monitoring programme) improved month on month during 2003.

Source: based on Garrow, 2003

Questions

1. Do you think Safeway's approach to improving the psychological contract would work for other types of organisation, such as manufacturing and public sector organisations?

2. What other practices could be added to influence the psychological contracts positively?

While the benefits of high-performance HRM systems have been stressed it is worth considering potential costs as well as benefits. Bratton and Gold (1999) note that there may be increased costs associated with training and investment in employees, and management will also lose some of its decision-making prerogative through devolved systems of management. From an employee's perspective there may be benefits of increased access to information, participation in decision making and sharing in shaping the work processes. However, there will also be the potential for increased stress associated with increased responsibility, and in many cases there is the loss of lifetime employment guarantees.

Another line of critique has questioned the extent to which the linkages have really been proved. Lam and Schaubroeck (1998) found such linkages applied only in a minority of their sample. They found that HRM policies, rather than being rational tools aimed at increasing organisational performance, were actually political tools, aimed at persuading top management to increase expenditure on HRM. Lahteenmaki *et al.* (1998) concluded from their study of Finnish organisations that there was 'hardly any link between the state of HRM and company performance'. They argue further that the linkages may be too complicated to be revealed other than in longitudinal in-depth studies.

Other studies have shown that HRM, exemplified as high-performnance practices in the workplace does have an impact on performance, but not uniquely so. For example, Wood and de Menezes (1998) argue from their analysis of the major UK survey of organisations – the Workplace Industrial Relations Survey – that high-commitment practices do have some performance effects, but that alternative approaches (e.g. control oriented) can also be effective. They found that the high-commitment management (HCM) workplaces had greater growth and financial performance than the two medium categories, but that the results for low-commitment practices were not significantly different from those with high-commitment practices. In other words good results seem to be achievable either through significant adoption of HCM or through a control-oriented approach (at least in the short term).

Wright *et al.* (2003) in a study based on 50 business units of a large food service company in the United States and Canada vouch for a link between HRM practice and organisational commitment; the latter was linked in part to business unit performance. But Purcell *et al.* (2003) echo a word of caution; they state that we cannot be sure *how* the inputs (HRM practices) lead to particular outcomes.

HRM content and process

It is clear when we consider both relational and transactional psychological contracts that merely having good HRM policies is unlikely to be sufficient to motivate employees and derive organisational performance. Hence, there is a need to go beyond HRM *content* and consider HRM *process* (Bowen and Ostroff, 2004). HRM content refers to the people-oriented policies and practices which have the purpose of meeting organisational objectives, for example, the strategic objectives of the organisation might relate to enhancing service provision, quality, profitability or efficiency. There is a debate about which HRM policies best serve each of these particular objectives. However, in general terms, Becker and Huselid (2000) have identified the following factors as being significant in HRM's contribution to the achievement of strategic goals:

■ Seeing HRM as an investment:

  ● HRM professionals are seen as 'business partners' – sharing organisational goals and being part of the management decision-making team;

  ● HRM services are provided to management efficiently and effectively.

- People are seen as a source of competitive advantage:

  - the competencies and knowledge of employees are central to how the company 'adds value' for its customers;

  - managers are focused on leadership and teamworking is often prevalent.

- The role of performance management:

  - behaviours and outcomes are recognised and rewarded;

  - individual and organisational goals are aligned.

- Industry best practice:

  - ideally the company is seen as an 'employer of choice' and hence can both get the best people and get the best out of its people;

  - detailed best practices are similar to those outlined by Marchington and Wilkinson (2002) and Pfeffer and Veiga (1999) above.

However, it is possible for organisations to put best practice in place and yet not achieve their full potential. This is because attention also needs to be paid to the process of HRM (Bowen and Ostroff, 2004). Fundamentally, the policies and practices of HRM can be regarded as a form of communication between management and employees. Even messages sent with the best of intentions can be interpreted and reinterpreted by the 'audience' that receives them. Employees are not merely passive recipients of messages, rather, they actively make sense of them (Weick, 1995) by fitting information into their own cognitive frameworks (or ways of seeing things). Hence, a workforce that feels it has been badly treated and consequently has grown distrustful of management may well reinterpret messages from management in a very negative way. So, for example, an organisation might follow Becker and Huselid's (2000) advice and decentralise decision making with the intention of giving employees greater autonomy. However, the employees might reinterpret this practice as being a way of increasing their responsibility and exposing them to greater potential blame if things go wrong. Bowen and Ostroff (2004) highlight certain aspects of the process which can help to make the most of HRM as follows.

HRM practices need to be:

- highly visible and observable;

- understandable (often there are complicated ideas behind practices such as performance management, but these need to be expressed in simple and memorable terms);

- launched with legitimacy (buy-in from the top is vital if employees are to believe that the practices will have a real impact and be taken seriously by management);

- relevant to day-to-day activities;

- consistent – over time, so that current policies do not appear to needlessly contradict existing ones – and between policies, so that policies reinforce each other.

For Bowen and Ostroff the effectiveness of the HRM process is 'in the eye of the beholder' and hence they place emphasis on perceived fairness. Where employees think the process is fair there is a much greater chance of them positively interpreting the HRM practices.

An illustration of a large company adopting HRM practices is provided in Case example 2.4.

RUSAL – ADOPTING HRM PRACTICES

RUSAL is Russia's largest aluminium producer. It was formed in 2000, incorporating several large Siberian smelteries, and has grown to be the third largest aluminium producer in the world with over 50,000 employees in 12 countries. It is now considered to be an employer of choice and a model for other Russian organisations.

In the Soviet era, according to Victoria Petrova, HR Director, employees were guaranteed lifetime employment, had no contact with the outside world and were never asked their opinion. They worked in poor conditions with outdated equipment, health and safety procedures that were largely ignored and uninspiring facilities. As the first woman on the board and the first advocate for HRM, Petrova faced significant challenges. She needed to convince her colleagues of her own capabilities and of the need to introduce HRM practices. This took a year, but since then the transformation of the company has been dramatic. The HRM practices were aimed squarely at organisational goals and the processes that complemented the practices signalled and reinforced significant change.

A modernisation of HRM practices was undertaken. Previously there had been no performance management system, so an evaluation of job roles and objectives was conducted through one-to-one meetings between employees and their line managers. This formed the basis for a new performance-related pay structure. Training programmes were developed incorporating induction, e-learning and sponsorship for external courses. The 'golden reserve' talent programme invited employees to nominate themselves for management training. Less than 350 applicants were expected, but over 700 applied. Each year 25 per cent of participants have been promoted. A new code of ethics was produced that has helped to wipe out corruption (ranging from minor theft to more significant fraud), which, according to Petrova, had previously been commonplace. In addition, investment was made in facilities so that employees had the tools, equipment and environment within which to perform.

The modernisation of HRM practices was achieved through a set of processes that were designed to shift the relationship between employees and the organisation. Communication and involvement were the central themes. The code of ethics was not changed by top-down edict. Instead, employees were invited to have a say. Some 18,000 made suggestions and 4,000 participated in round-table discussions. The round-table participants elected a committee, which developed and distributed the code. A wide range of communication tools was introduced including an intranet, information days and an encouragement for line managers to talk to their workers. Workers were also encouraged to develop ways of improving productivity by exchanging best practice with colleagues and through visits to other sites.

By the end of 2005 productivity had been doubled and there was a dramatic shift in morale to produce, in the words of the code of conduct, 'a company of which we and our children can be proud'.

Source: adapted from Fuller, 2005

Questions

1. Do you think the nationality of the organisation makes a difference to the way HRM is practised?

2. Whether you answer 'yes' or 'no', what are the reasons for your answer?

In this example the HRM practice developments correlate with the factors identified by Becker and Huselid. There was a clear investment in HR, there was an investment in skills and knowledge and there was a focus on performance and reward. Equally, the process aims highlighted by Bowen and Ostroff were achieved. The high visibility of HRM was constantly maintained. The communication and involvement techniques reinforced a relationship with employees in which there was evidence that their opinions mattered and made a difference in a relevant and understandable way. This helped to encourage employees to interpret the changes in a positive way and, consequently, their performance changes were also positive.

Finally, an example of a bank that has achieved significant strategic shift, incorporating a new HRM strategy, is discussed in Case example 2.5.

CASE EXAMPLE 2.5

HRM AND STRATEGIC CHANGE AT ABBEY

Abbey is the sixth biggest bank and second largest mortgage lender in the UK, having 741 branches and approximately 2,500 ATMs. It employs 20,000 people and specialises in personal financial services such as mortgages, loans, savings, investments, insurance, pensions and life assurance. Abbey's vision is to be 'the best bank on the high street: for customers, employees and investors' (Abbey, 2007). The results for the year end 2006 showed growth in profits (24 per cent higher than 2005), bank account openings up 17 per cent, a doubling of mortgage value lending as compared to 2005 along with a reduction of 5 per cent of costs and a 2,000 headcount reduction.

> 'Abbey made strong progress in 2006. We've accelerated revenue growth and have continued to successfully reduce costs across the business, with cumulative savings of almost £300 million – one year ahead of target. The bank is well on track to meet its three-year plan targets'

(Antonio Horta-Osorio, Chief Executive).

However, this picture of success is markedly different to the situation in 2003. In 2002 Abbey (or Abbey National as it was then) lost close to £1 billion following severe problems with its wholesale banking activity (Edwards, 2004). The new strategy was to focus only on the core business of personal finance services and to divest other parts of the business. Along with this strategic shift was a recognition that there was a need for significant internal change and that the employees would be crucial to any future success. Priscilla Vacassin was recruited as the first board level HR director. She found morale to be low and there was a sense of shock in the organisation that was not used to failure.

Vacassin started a series of HR changes that have contributed to the turnaround of Abbey's fortunes. First, there was a need for effective communication. A pocket-sized booklet – 'Turning banking on its head' – was produced. It explained the organisational purpose – to continuously improve the way people relate to their money; and the vision – to be a first choice provider of personal finance services where customers would want to return. The booklet showed that Abbey recognised the importance of employees as the interface with customers and offered advice on how to go about effective customer interaction. Management made a commitment to understanding the employees better and to aid this extensive staff surveys were launched (Edwards, 2004).

Performance management was a central part of the HR strategy. The aim was to increase individuals' awareness of their impact on the business. Individual objectives were set covering both 'what I'll do' and 'how I'll be'. Bonuses were more closely related to performance, and a forced ranking system was introduced. This allocated people into the top 10 per cent, upper 40 per cent, lower 40 per cent and bottom 10 per cent. Although this form of judgement can appear harsh, Vacassin argued that it pushed managers and employees into having honest discussions, and that people in the bottom 10 per cent generally already knew where they were.

There was a major investment in training with 20,000 training days per month (representing a 50 per cent increase on the previous year).

At the senior management level there were major changes. The top 80 positions were reduced to 60, and about 50 of that 60 were replaced with new staff. There was a new focus on leadership and to team building. In a major exercise, employees were brought together to discuss the gap between what they thought the teams *should* look like and what they were currently like. The outcomes were team action plans and individual plans, the latter contributing to individual performance development plans.

At the same time as investing in training, leadership and organisational development, reductions were being made. Offices were closed and substantial job losses occurred. This was part of the balance for Abbey. In focusing on core business cost reductions were necessary. However, Abbey could not merely reduce costs and continue to operate as before. Therefore, it had to make simultaneous investments in people and the managerial processes that impacted on motivation and performance.

At the end of 2004, Banco Santander Central Hispano aquired Abbey in an agreed takeover. Abbey is now part of one of the 10 leading financial groups in the world, with a presence in 40 countries, 126,000 employees and 63 million customers.

Source: based on information from Abbey, 2007

Question

Select one of the formulations of HRM covered in this chapter and compare it to Abbey's practice. To what extent do you think Abbey is undertaking SHRM?

Thinking performer/business or strategic partner

As can be seen from the foregoing discussion, in modern organisations there is a constant demand for performance, and this drives a need for ongoing change which impacts at the level of the organisation (its strategy and corporate performance) and the individual (realised through the psychological contract). To satisfy these demands HRM must operate at a high level both in terms of its content and in its processes. This has implications for the role and practice of the HRM specialist. Few would regard an old-fashioned administrative role to be sufficient any more and the Chartered Institute of Personnel and Development (CIPD) has led the way in new thinking in this area.

The concept of the thinking performer has taken central stage as a result of the CIPD's recent preoccupation with it so that the new entrants to the HR profession emphasise thinking and reflecting on the one hand and performing and doing on the other (Marchington and Wilkinson, 2005). The thinking performer concept occurs in the CIPD's professional standards devised in 2004, the object of which is to ensure that all CIPD members become 'thinking performers' who continuously update their professional knowledge and 'add value' to the businesses that employ them. The business focus embraces the notion of 'business partner' whereby HR professionals apply a critical, thoughtful approach to their jobs in order to make a contribution to organisational survival, profitability and subscribing to the vision and strategic direction of the organisation (Whittaker and Johns, 2004).

It is interesting to note that the values adopted by the CIPD are similar to those associated with the business partner modelling of HRM developed by Ulrich (1997). In this model there are four key roles, namely strategic partner, administrative expert, employee champion and change agent. Strategic partner is evident where HR professionals enter into partnership with line managers to help them with the challenge of raising standards in connection with both strategy formulation and execution (Ulrich and Brockbank, 2005). Change agents are responsible for bringing about organisational transformation and cultural change. The role of the change agent is discussed in Chapter 4 in connection with managing change. The administrative expert is the type of person who is constantly improving organisational efficiency by re-engineering the HR function and other work processes.

The employee champion puts the spotlight on people as well as a focus on day-to-day operational matters, and is in the tradition of normative models. The role of employee champion has been divided into two roles, that of 'employee advocate' and 'HR developer'. The employee advocate role places the emphasis on the ability of the HR professional to act as a representative of the employees, but at the same time is tuned into the needs of other stakeholders, such as customers and shareholders, and also considers the needs of line managers. It is then that the HR professional communicates with employees specifying what is required of them in order to be successful in creating value. The human resource developer is a more future focused process role. In Chapter 10 there is a discussion of employee development in its many facets.

Reflecting on Urlich's four roles, they seem to have a lot of intuitive appeal and sound plausible, but there is a proviso! Can we realistically expect the HR professional to achieve balance between competing stakeholder interests and values? Is there a danger that the business-oriented performance outcomes as emphasised in the literature overshadow the importance of employee well-being per se (Grant and Shields, 2002), and impact negatively on job satisfaction and the work–life balance? If business oriented performance considerations are ingrained in management practice and culture, is there a likelihood that few HR professionals will consider seriously the role of 'employee champion' even though they recognise it as an important part of the heartland of HRM. In an empirical study (Francis and Keegan, 2006), the researchers found that most of the HR professionals that they had surveyed in the United Kingdom had not heard of the term 'thinking performer' or had a fairly neutral opinion of it. However, several respondents considered it to be a good idea. As to the concept of the 'business or strategic partner' its practical significance seemed to be outside the orbit of the HR practitioner dealing with day-to-day matters.

Conclusions

Organisational environments are turbulent and change is always present. This places a great responsibility on the shoulders of strategic HRM to be proactive in developing the organisation's flexibility and creativity to capitalise on opportunities and to sustain competitive advantage. Interfacing corporate strategy with strategic HRM has significance in highlighting the importance of the human resource in contributing to organisational success. Therefore, having in place sound structures and processes, which allow people to pull together with commitment in a climate of mutual benefit, is a laudable aim. The links between individual and group performance and the achievements of the firm are now one of the central concerns of HRM. Of crucial importance is the psychological contract. Where there is a positive psychological contract individuals feel connected to the organisation and are committed to its goals. Hence, they tend to exert greater effort. If the organisation is following good HRM practice, it will maintain a positive feedback cycle by making sure that there is good communication with the employee and effective recognition and reward.

The contribution of the management of people to the strategic aims of the organisation has been increasingly accepted on the basis of the research evidence published since 1995. There is still increasing evidence that HRM practices can be adapted in beneficial ways both internationally for companies around the world and for small firms. In the case of small companies, the practices might be less formalised than would be the case in large firms, but the central practices ranging from selection, through communication and training to reward are still applicable.

Pursuing best practice in HRM can no longer be seen as a luxury, rather it is a necessity for new firms that want to survive and grow, and for established firms, particularly where high performance is required. The basis of the high-performance HRM models is the engendering of commitment in the workforce. This is achieved through involvement and mutuality, and the fostering of positive psychological contracts. Research in international HRM has shown the transference of HRM best practice to many countries, but it is normally accepted that a degree of adaptation and alteration is necessary in different cultural settings.

The role of managers and HRM specialists as 'thinking performers', in achieving a positive working environment and in establishing trust and open communications that underpin the psychological contract, is central. It is not sufficient to have good HRM policies – it is important to effectively manage both content and process. There will inevitably be difficulties in implementing HRM best practice, and it is those companies that can develop their own solutions to such difficulties that will reap the benefits in achieving competitive advantage.

Review and reflection questions

1. What are the three primary aspects of strategic management according to Johnson *et al.* (2005)?

2. Explain the key differences between the prescriptive and descriptive schools of strategy.

3. Describe the relative strengths and weaknesses of the following models of SHRM:

   (a) Matching or best fit model

   (b) Resource-based model

   (c) Best practice (high-commitment) model.

4. What are the main practices associated with SHRM?

5. Explain the concept of the psychological contract.

6. What is the evidence of the link between SHRM and organisational performance?

7. Describe the role of an HR business partner.

Activities

If you are in work:

1. What is the state of your psychological contract with your organisation?
   - Do you feel attached to the organisation?
   - Do you know what the organisation's goals are?
   - Do your personal goals fit with those of the organisation?
   - Do you feel adequately recognised and rewarded?
   - Do you think that your voice is heard when you want to express an idea or opinion?
   - Is your work adequately challenging?

2. What managerial practices impact (positively or negatively) on your psychological contract?
   - Communication
   - Training
   - Appraisal
   - Rewards
   - Day-to-day interaction and organisational life

3. When you are in a position, either now or in the future, to have an impact on the psychological contracts of other people (e.g. those reporting to you) what are the key lessons you will keep in mind?

If you are in full-time study:

1. Read the case study of Abbey above, and find out more about the company by visiting their website: www.aboutabbey.com.

2. Read the sections above on the 'Evidence of the link between HRM and performance' and 'HRM content and process' and visit the CIPD website regarding SHRM at www.cipd.co.uk/subjects/corpstrtgy.

3. On the basis of your reading and research, what advice would you give Abbey about the SHRM practices it should now undertake? What are the reasons for the advice that you give?

Further reading and research

Having read this chapter, you will be aware that corporate strategy and strategic HRM are vast areas of study and practice. A number of issues arise that are suitable topics for further study. First, there is an on-going question of how HRM is related to organisational performance, and in the following article, Lawler provides some useful insights.

Lawler III, E. E. (2005) 'From human resource management to organizational effectiveness', *Human Resource Management*, 44, 165–170.

Another contemporary issue is the extent to which HRM is a genuinely international phenomenon, and this can be explored further in the following reading:

Budharwar, P. and Mellahi, K. (Guest Editors) (2007) 'Special Issue: Managing human resources in the Middle East', *International Journal of Human Resource Management*, 18 (5).

Thirdly, HRM can be seen as a set of practices that is constantly evolving, both in terms of HRM practices and the nature of the profession. These issues are discussed in the following readings:

Cascio, W.F. (2005) 'From business partner to driving business success. The next step in the evolution of HRM', *Human Resource Management*, 44, 159–164.

Subramony, M. (2006) 'Why organizations adopt some human resource management practices and reject others: An exploration of rationales', *Human Resource Management*, 45, 195 –210.

With a focus on practice, the following readings offer accessible perspectives on key strategic issues for practitioners – the challenge of becoming a business partner and the crucial question of the extent to which HRM activities should be outsourced.

Arkin, A. (2007) 'HR business partners: Street smart', *People Management*, 5 April, 24–28.

People Management (2007) 'The Guide to HR Outsourcing', February, 5–38.

There are many websites that cover HRM. If you want to research the topic further, the following will be helpful.

www.cipd.co.uk/subjects/corpstrtgy This is the CIPD fact sheet that defines strategic HRM; examines the relationships between SHRM, business strategy and human capital management; and explores that impact of SHRM on business performance.

www.hrmguide.co.uk This website provides an overview of a range of SHRM issues such as: people strategies, forming HRM strategies, translation of strategy into action and restructuring. The site also provides links to relevant research articles and news updates.

References

Abbey (2007) www.aboutabbey.com – key facts; www.aboutabbey.com – financial results.

Ackoff, R.L. (1983) 'Beyond prediction and preparation', *Journal of Management Studies*, 20, 59–69.

Andrews, K.R. (1987) *The Concept of Corporate Strategy*, Holmwood, IL: Irwin.

Baird, L. and Meshoulam, I. (1988) 'Managing two fits of strategic human resource management', *Academy of Management Review*, 13, 116–128.

Barney, J.B. (1991) 'Firm resources and sustained competitive advantage', *Journal of Management*, 17, 99–120.

Barney, J. and Wright, P. (1998) 'On becoming a strategic partner: the role of human resources in gaining competitive advantage', *Human Resource Management*, 37, 31–46.

Bartel, A.P. (2004) 'Human Resource Management and Organizational Performance: Evidence from retail banking', *Industrial and Labour relations Review*, 57, 181–203.

Beardwell, I., Holden, L. and Claydon, T. (2004) *Human Resource Management: A contemporary approach*, Harlow: Prentice-Hall/FT.

Becker, B.E. and Huselid, M.A. (1998) 'High performance work systems and firm performance: A synthesis of research and managerial implications', *Research in Personnel and Human Resource Management*, 16, 53–101.

Becker, B.E. and Huselid, M.A. (1999) 'Overview: strategic human resource management in five leading firms', *Human Resource Management*, 38, 287–301.

Becker, B.E. and Huselid, M.A. (2000) 'Getting and Edge Through People', *Human Resource Management International Digest*, 8, 36–38.

Beer, N., Spector, B. and Lawrence, P.R. (1984) *Managing Human Assets*, New York: Free Press.

Benkhoff, B. (1997) 'Ignoring commitment is costly: new approaches establish the missing link between commitment and performance', *Human Relations*, 50, 701–727.

Bolman, L.G. and Deal, T. (2003) *Reframing Organizations: Artistry, choice and leadership,* San Francisco: Jossey-Bass.

Bourne, L. and Walker, D.H.T. (2005) 'Visualising and mapping stakeholder influence', *Management Decision*, 43, 649–660.

Bowen, D.E. and Ostroff, C. (2004) 'Understanding HRM-Firm Performance Linkages: The role of the "strength" of the HRM system', *Academy of Management Review*, 29, 203–221.

Boxall, P.F. (1996) 'The strategic HRM debate and the resource-based view of the firm', *Human Resource Management Journal*, 6, 59–75.

Brand, M.J. and Bax, E.H. (2002) 'Strategic HRM for SMEs: implications for firms and policy', *Education and Training*, 44, 451–463.

Bratton, J. and Gold, J. (1999) *Human Resource Management: Theory and practice*, London: Macmillan.

Chaffee, E.E. (1985) 'Three models of strategy', *Academy of Management Review*, 10, 89–98.

Chang, P.-L. and Chen, W.-L. (2002) 'The Effect of Human Resource Management Practices on Firm Performance: Empirical evidence from high-tech firms in Taiwan', *International Journal of Management*, 19, 622–631.

Cullinane, N. and Dundon, T. (2006) 'The psychological contract: A critical review', *International Journal of Management Reviews*, 8, 113–129.

Delaney, J.T. and Huselid, M.A. (1996) 'The impact of human resource management practices on perceptions of organizational performance', *Academy of Management Journal*, 39, 949–70.

Drucker, P.F. (1970) 'Entrepreneurship in business enterprise', *Journal of Business Policy*, 1, 3–12.

Edwards, C. (2004) 'Called to Account', *People Management*, 10, 33–34.

Fombrun, C., Tichy, N.M. and Devanna, M.A. (1984) *Strategic Human Resource Management*, New York: John Wiley.

Francis, H. and Keegan, A. (2006) 'The changing face of HRM: in search of balance', *Human Resource Management Journal*, 16, 231–249.

Fuller, G. (2005) 'Come the Revolution', *People Management*, 11, 38–40.

Garrow, V. (2003) 'Pact to the Future', *People Management*, 9, 26–30.

Grant, D. and Shields, J. (2002) 'In search of the subject: researching employee reactions to Human Resource Management', *Journal of Industrial Relations*, 44, 335–358.

Griener, L.E. (1998) 'Revolution as organizations grow', *Harvard Business Review*, May–June, 55–68.

Guest, D.E. (1998) 'Beyond HRM: commitment and the contract culture', in Sparrow, P.R. and Marchington, M. (eds), *Human Resource Management: The new agenda*, London: Financial Times/Pitman.

Guest, D.E., Michie, J., Conway, N. and Sheehan, M. (2003) 'Human Resource Management and Corporate Performance in the UK', *British Journal of Industrial Relations*, 41, 291–314.

Huselid, M.A. (1995) 'The impact of human resource management practices on turnover, productivity and corporate financial performance', *Academy of Management Journal*, 38, 635–672.

Johnson, G. (1992) 'Managing strategic change: strategy, culture and action', *Long Range Planning*, 25, 28–36.

Johnson, G., Scholes, K. and Whittington, R. (2005) *Exploring Corporate Strategy*, Harlow: Pearson/Prentice Hall.

Kamoche, K. (1996) 'Strategic human resource management within resource: capability view of the firm', *Journal of Management Studies*, 33, 213–233.

Lahteenmaki, S., Storey, J. and Vanhala, S. (1998) 'HRM and company performance: the use of measurement and the influence of economic cycles', *Human Resource Management Journal*, 8, 51–65.

Lam, S.S.K. and Schaubroeck, J. (1998) 'Integrating HR planning and organisational strategy', *Human Resource Management Journal*, 8, 5–19.

Laursen, K. and Floss, N.J. (2003) 'New human resource management practices, complementarities and the impact on innovation performance', *Cambridge Journal of Economics*, 27, 243–263.

Legge, K. (1995) *Human Resource Management: Rhetorics and realities*, Basingstoke: Macmillan.

Lewin, A.Y. and Massini, S. (2004) 'Knowledge Creation and Organizational Capabilities of Innovating and Imitating Firms', in Tsoukas, H. and Mylonopoulos, N. (eds), *Organizations as Knowledge Systems*, London: Palgrave.

Li, X. and Putterill, M. (2007) 'Strategy implications of business culture differences between Japan and China.', *Business Strategy Series*, 8, 148–154.

Lindblom, C. (1969) 'The science of muddling through', in Etzioni, A. (ed.), *Readings in Modern Organizations*, Englewood Cliffs, NJ: Prentice Hall.

Marchington, M. and Wilkinson, A. (2002) *People Management and Development*, London: CIPD.

Marchington, M. and Wilkinson, A. (2005) *Human Resource Management at Work*, London: CIPD.

Marzec, M. (2007) 'Telling the corporate story: Vision into action', *Journal of Business Strategy*, 28, 26–36.

Mintzberg, H., Ahlstrand, B. and Lampel, J. (1998) *Strategy Safari*, London: Prentice Hall.

Newell, S. and Rice, C. (1999) 'Assessment, selection and evaluation: pitfalls and problems', in Leopold, J., Harris, L. and Watson, T. (eds), *Strategic Human Resourcing: Principles, perspectives and practices*, London: Financial Times/Pitman.

Patterson, M., West, M., Lawthorn, R. and Nickell, S. (1997) *The Impact of People Management Practice on Business Performance*, London: Institute of Personnel and Development.

Pesqueux, Y. and Damak-Ayadi, S. (2005) 'Stakeholder Theory in Perspective', *Corporate Governance*, 5, 2–21.

Pfeffer, J. (1994) *Competitive Advantage Through People*, Boston: Harvard Business School Press.

Pfeffer, J. (1998) *The Human Equation*, Boston: Harvard Business School Press.

Pfeffer, J. and Veiga, J.F. (1999) 'Putting people first for organizational success', *Academy of Management Executive*, 13, 37–50.

Pollitt, D. (2006) 'Toshiba sparks a wave of innovation', *Human Resource Management International Digest*, 14, 5–7.

Porter, M.E. (1980) *Competitive Strategy: Techniques for analysing industries and competitors*, New York: Free Press.

Porter, M.E. (1985) *Competitive Advantage*, New York: Free Press.

Prahalad, C.K. and Hamel, G. (1990) 'The core competence of the corporation', *Harvard Business Review*, 68, 79–91.

Purcell, J. (1992) 'The impact of corporate strategy on human resource management', in Salaman, G. (ed.), *Human Resource Strategies*, London: Sage.

Purcell, J., Hutchinson, S., Kinnie, N., Rayton, B. and Swart, J. (2003) *Understanding the Pay and Performance Link: Unlocking the Black Box*, London: CIPD.

Quinn, J.B. (1980) *Strategies for Change: Logical incrementalism*, Holmwood, IL: Irwin.

Restubog, S.L.D., Bordia, P. and Tang, R.L. (2006) 'Effects of psychological contract breach on performance of IT employees: The mediating role of affective commitment', *Journal of Occupational and Organizational Psychology*, 79, 299–306.

Rousseau, D.M. (2001) 'Schema, promise and mutuality: The building blocks of the psychological contract', *Journal of Occupational Psychology*, 74, 511–541.

Schuler, R.S. and Jackson, S.E. (2000) *Managing Human Resources. A partner perspective*, London: Thomson Learning.

Senge, P. (1990) *The Fifth Discipline: The art and practice of the learning organization*, New York: Random House.

Torrington, D., Hall, L. and Taylor, S. (2005) *Human Resource Management*, Harlow: FT/Prentice Hall.

Ulrich, D. (1997) *HR Champions*, Boston, MA: Harvard Business School Press.

Ulrich, D. and Brockbank, W. (2005) *The HR value proposition*, Boston, MA: Harvard Business School Press.

Walker, J.W. (1980) *Human Resource Planning*, New York: McGraw-Hill.

Walsh, J. (2000) 'Timing of Northern Foods' forum plan is coincidental', *People Management*, 6, 11.

Walton, R.E. (1985) 'From control to commitment in the workplace', *Harvard Business Review*, March/April, 77–84.

Watson, T. (1999) 'Human resourcing strategies: choice, chance and circumstance', in Leopold, J., Harris, L. and Watson, T. (eds), *Strategic Human Resourcing: Principals, perspectives and practices*, London: Financial Times/Pitman.

Weick, K.E. (1995) *Sensemaking in Organizations*, Thousand Oaks, CA: Sage.

Wellbourne, T. and Andrews, A. (1996) 'Predicting performance of initial public offering firms: should HRM be in the equation?', *Academy of Management Journal*, 39, 891–919.

West, M. and Patterson, M. (1998) 'Profitable personnel', *People Management*, January, 28–31.

Whittaker, J. and Johns, T. (2004) 'Standards deliver', *People Management*, 16 June, 24–28.

Winter, R. and Jackson B. (2006) 'State of the Psychological Contract', *Employee Relations*, 28, 421–434.

Wood, S. (1995) 'Can we speak of high commitment management on the shop floor?', *Journal of Management Studies*, 32, 215–47.

Wood, S. and de Menezes, L. (1998) 'High commitment management in the UK: evidence from the Workplace Industrial Relations Survey and Employers' Manpower and Skills Practices Survey', *Human Relations*, 51, 485–516.

Wright, P.M., Gardner, T.M. and Moynihan, L.M. (2003) 'The impact of HR practices on the performance of business units', *Human Resource Management Journal*, 13, 21–36.

Chapter 3

ORGANISATION STRUCTURE

Introduction

Organisation structure is the infrastructure within which strategy is conceived and implemented. Structure can be seen as both the outcome of strategic decisions and a factor that
influences strategy. Since HRM has an overwhelming interest in providing people with space
and opportunity to utilise their abilities and skills to an optimum level, it pays particular
attention to the way organisations and jobs are designed. In this chapter there will be an
examination of theories and perspectives on organisation structure and design.

Once you have read this chapter, you should:

- be aware of alternative organisational structures, from highly regulated bureaucracies
to looser networks;

- be able to reflect on the implementation of such structural designs in reality;

- understand the links between structure and other topics such as power, strategy and
technology;

- be aware of the developments in structure, such as virtual and networked organisations,
and some of the implications of these developments for human resources management.

Classical bureaucracy

A concept of bureaucracy was developed by Weber (1947), a German sociologist. In its ideal
form it was known as the legal–rational framework. This type of organisation is rational
because it is specifically designed to perform certain functions, and it is legal because its operation is based on a set of rules and procedures for every position or job within it. Weber
distinguished the legal–rational model from other models he had in mind, namely charismatic
(leader driven) and traditional (influenced by custom and practice). The features of classical
bureaucracy (legal–rational) are as follows:

- clear definition of duties and responsibilities;

- maximum specialisation;

- vertical pattern of authority;

- obedience to authority;

- post-holders rely on expertise derived from technical knowledge;

- maximum use of rules;

- impersonality in administration;

- remuneration is determined by rank and job responsibility;

- promotion is determined by seniority or achievement as judged by superiors;

- clear separation between ownership of the organisation and its control.

It is now apparent that the bureaucratic organisation in its ideal form is heavily dependent on rules, procedures, well-defined duties, relationships and responsibilities. It is allegedly a rational, impersonal system of organisation, free from the whims and preferences of individuals who occupy roles within it.

Scholars who studied the blueprint of classical bureaucracy felt it had a number of shortcomings. For example, it was felt that the pressure placed on the individual to act methodically and cautiously, with strict adherence to rules and procedures, could create a situation where the preoccupation with the means to the end becomes far more important than the end itself. Also, there could be a ritualistic attachment to rules and procedures, with undue insistence on authority and status rights, which could have the effect of not advancing the interests of the organisation. In such a setting resistance to change could become a real issue. Finally, even if classical bureaucracy could be justified as functional, this is likely to happen only in conditions where tasks are simple and repetitive and are performed consistently over time. But where tasks become more complex and subject to change the conditions likely to be compatible with classical bureaucracy cease to exist.

Classical principles

The classical principles of organisation developed by theorists and practitioners many years ago still have some relevance when the structure of organisation is studied. In this section the classical principles will be acknowledged in their original form, but at the same time interpretations will be forthcoming in order to put them in a present-day context. The following classical principles are examined.

Division of labour

Economic benefits can result from the breaking down of tasks and allowing the employee to specialise in a narrow area. Specialisation makes it possible to apply technology to tasks, with potential for productivity gains, and facilitates ease of training. Although certain segments of the working population may be happy with routine jobs and repetitive tasks that flow from the division of labour and specialisation, others may have a preference for enriched jobs and can be more productive in such conditions. In the final analysis the negative effects of repetitive work have to be offset against the alleged economic benefits.

Unity of command

Subordinates report to only one superior from whom they obtain advice and guidance. Having access to only one official source of direction and assistance might be construed as restrictive, and could be a negative influence when coupled with the division of labour.

Authority and responsibility

Rights vested in the position occupied by the employee are referred to as authority. The obligations placed on employees to perform are referred to as responsibility. Authority and responsibility are co-equal. Authority can be delegated within the organisational 'chain of command', but responsibility probably cannot, though this requires clarification. It is accepted that ultimate responsibility cannot be delegated, but there can be delegation of operational responsibility.

Authority can be referred to as line authority that is the type of authority which each manager possesses, and it flows through the chain of command. This should not be confused with the authority of the staff specialist (e.g. HRM specialist), whose role is to help line managers in executing their responsibilities.

The concept of authority had greater validity in the days when superiors were knowledgeable about all the jobs within their area of influence. Today overreliance on authority could be dysfunctional if subordinates are well trained and superiors are not fully conversant with everything within their section. Also, it would be unwise to place reliance on authority to the exclusion of other factors, such as the persuasive skills and power base of the manager.

What is becoming more apparent in the age of HRM is the strengthening of the role of the line manager with the accent on its 'enabling' aspects in a climate of teamwork, participative management and availability of various specialisms, either internal or external to the organisation. Currently it is customary to refer to authority as part of a larger concept of power.

Span of control

The span of control refers to the number of subordinates reporting to one boss. It was originally suggested that the number should not be more than six. The span of control has an inverse relationship to the number of layers in the hierarchy (e.g. the narrower the span of control, the more layers there are in the hierarchy). When a conscious decision is made to widen the span of control it could be associated with a growth in the number of better qualified and more experienced employees. The flatter organisational structure that is created by the wider span of control is popular today, and this is said to be compatible with growing empowerment, greater flexibility, speedier decision making, and responding to customer needs (Child and McGrath, 2001). In turn this requires knowledgeable and skilled workers.

The following factors are likely to influence the size of the span of control:

- job complexity (the more complex the job the greater the justification for a narrower span of control so that the supervisor has the capacity to assist subordinates);

- physical proximity of subordinates (a wider span of control is more manageable if subordinates are geographically closer to their boss);

- extent of formalisation and standardisation (it is easier to justify a wider span of control when the jobs of subordinates are governed by well-specified rules and procedures) – these will be examined again later;

■ preferred managerial style (some managers feel comfortable and confident supervising a large number of people, and because of the wide span of control they resort to delegation of authority in a pronounced way; such a course of action could cramp the style of other managers who prefer a narrower span of control).

Departmentalisation

In effect this is a form of division of labour, whereby certain cells of specialised activity are created that require overall coordination. This seems to be as far as classical theory goes in addressing the question of departmentalisation. If we take departmentalisation a stage further, the following groupings emerge:

■ Functional – there is a division of the organisation by function, such as finance, manufacturing, HRM and so on.

■ Product or service – there is a division by product (e.g. ICI's Paints Division), with associated functions such as production, marketing, etc., while a division by service is evident when a firm of chartered accountants is organised in accordance with service to clients (e.g. auditing, taxation, insolvency). Birkinshaw (2000), when examining the global product division, states it has a disadvantage in that its standardised approach hinders the ability to respond to country specific differences. Nevertheless, the global product division is emerging as the most common structure among large global companies. British Petroleum, British Telecommunications, Siemens, Ericson, Sara Lee, 3M, and many other global companies use the basic product division.

■ Customer – the nature of the customer base determines the structure used; for example, in a particular company there could be a wholesale division as well as a retail division.

■ Process – in a manufacturing company production processes can be differentiated by section or department; for example, a manager with responsibility for a particular production process would report to the manager of the plant.

■ Geographic – a part of the organisation (e.g. sales/marketing function) is fragmented on a regional or country basis. When analysing territorial groupings by country, Birkinshaw (2000) identifies a disadvantage when he says that coordination across countries suffers, which makes it difficult to achieve economies of scale in development and production. It appears the territorial grouping or area division is on the decline, whilst the global product division or some sort of hybrid between global product and territorial grouping is becoming more popular with large companies.

The types of departmentalisation described can be combined to create a mixed structure. For example, one might find functional departmentalisation having within its boundaries process departmentalisation and a sales function organised by region. Within the region there could be departmentalisation by customer. (An important feature of HRM is giving pride of place to the customer.) The reference to the hybrid structure in the last paragraph is also an example of a mixed structure.

Centralisation and decentralisation

Centralisation is referred to when a small number of people at the top of the organisation exercise significant authority and decision making. By contrast, decentralisation occurs when a lot of autonomy is felt by those working further down the organisation. Both have advantages and disadvantages, but it could be said that centralisation is complementary to a bureaucratic system of organisation, whilst decentralisation is more compatible with an organic system, which will be discussed later.

Matrix organisation

This system of organisation integrates two groupings. For example, a project department is superimposed on the division by function described above. In practice this means that a particular employee belongs to a function (e.g. marketing) but also works on a project. Effectively the employee reports to two supervisors – one is the manager of the project and the other is the boss within the function. A matrix organisation can be a complex system and if it is to be effective it has to be operated with a certain amount of skill.

Among problems to anticipate are role conflict among subordinates because of the dual system of reporting and power struggles about the use of authority in particular situations (Daft, 2004; Larson and Gobeli, 1987). Lorenz (1994a) had this to say about matrices in general:

> the matrix organisation used by multinational companies in the 1960s and 1970s, especially by US companies, was, with a few notable exceptions, plagued by internal conflict, inefficiency, expense and delay, as divisional, geographic management debated and fought with each other. In many cases disputes were only resolved laboriously by powerful coordinators acting as matrix police.

The concept of the team (the project team) seems to be an important feature of matrix organisation. As we shall see later, in the spirit of HRM teams are created to cut across departmental boundaries to promote flexibility and innovation, with the needs of the consumer high on the agenda.

At this stage one might ask, is there a perfect structure? The answer is likely to be that there is no perfect structure. Each structure has its own limitations, and organisational design is influenced by a combination of strategic factors, fashion and the pronouncements of gurus.

Organisational configuration

The configuration or mode of arrangement of the organisation will be examined in the first instance from the angle of the five traditional features listed below. These features indicate the level of complexity within the organisation. Subsequently, there will be a brief acknowledgement of the six types of configuration identified by Mintzberg (1983).

1. *Vertical differentiation.* This is concerned with the number of levels or layers within the hierarchy through which control and coordination are exercised. Because information has to flow through a number of layers the potential for problems connected with the dissemination of information and the monitoring of operations is ever present.
2. *Horizontal differentiation.* This is akin to the division of labour and specialisation, whereby specialist activities are arranged in a lateral form and staffed by employees with specific orientations. For example, employees in the finance function could interpret commercial reality differently from those in the HRM function. This could give rise to communication difficulties that ultimately could affect modes of cooperation.

3. *Spatial differentiation.* If the organisation is fragmented in a geographical sense we refer to spatial differentiation.

4. *Formalisation.* The key characteristics of formalisation are job descriptions and well-defined procedures. When formalisation is rated highly employees have little opportunity to exercise discretion and use initiative in the job. The reverse is the case in conditions where formalisation receives a low rating. The position of a job within the hierarchy can determine the degree of formalisation. For example, we expect employees occupying positions in the higher echelons of the organisation to exercise more discretion in making decisions than employees located further down the organisation. The particular type of function might also be a factor influencing the degree of formalisation. For example, the production function may lend itself to a higher degree of formalisation than the marketing function. Finally, where formalisation is well established the terrain is fertile for standardisation to take root.

5. *Centralisation/decentralisation.* These were briefly mentioned earlier in connection with the principles of organisation; they occupy the opposite positions on a continuum and reflect the location of decision making within the organisation. Factors likely to influence centralisation or decentralisation are as follows:

   (a) The organisation is geographically dispersed (spatial differentiation) and this signals the need for decentralisation. However, if an organisation has sophisticated and comprehensive management information systems aided by information technology it would appear that there is a strong drive to go in the opposite direction and resort to centralisation.

   (b) Where spatial differentiation is not an issue because the organisation is located on one site, decentralisation could be used for reasons connected with stated corporate policy or managerial preferences. A justification to adopt the opposite position and use centralisation could be an attachment to the notion of bureaucratic control or the existence of autocratic tendencies within the organisation.

Mintzberg (1983) identified six types of structure, each appropriate to the dominant needs of the organisation as follows:

1. *Simple structure.* This structure could apply to a recently created organisation where authority is centralised in the hands of the owner-manager or small group. The trappings of a bureaucratic organisation are minimal.

2. *Machine bureaucracy.* This structure has a number of the features of bureaucratic organisation referred to earlier and assumes the characteristics of the mechanistic system of organisation discussed later in the chapter. The organisation is large and long established and operates in a relatively stable environment.

3. *Professional bureaucracy.* This structure allows the exercise of professional expertise where autonomy and the absence of rigid status differentials prevail (e.g. the traditional hospital or college). There is a tendency not to place too much emphasis on bureaucratic practices.

4. *Divisional form.* This structure is appropriate for a large, well-established company with a number of different markets. The company could be organised by, for example, product or service referred to earlier, but there is a tendency to adopt machine bureaucracy.

5. *Adhocracy.* This structure could apply to a total organisation or a division within it. The organisation, which is designed to promote innovation, operates in a complex and dynamic environment. Employees with expertise, who tend to be attached to project groups with a market orientation, exercise a lot of power and influence. The attachment to the project group conjures up images of the matrix organisation examined earlier.

6. *Missionary*. This could be considered to be lacking in features of formal organisation; for example, division of labour and specialisation is not very pronounced. People are bound together by their shared values.

Formal and informal organisations

A distinction can be made between the formal and the informal organisation. Many of the features of organisation discussed earlier (e.g. span of control and hierarchy), coupled with the stated objectives of the organisation and the roles assigned to individuals, reflect the formal organisation. By contrast, the informal organisation is flexible with a fluid structure. In the informal organisation the degree of informality stems from the interaction of role occupants or employees and it can be harnessed to complement the aims of the formal organisation. For example, it could promote a sense of identification with the organisation, a sense of belonging and motivation. However, the informal organisation has the potential to undermine the effectiveness of the formal organisation. The informal oganisation has been found to be particularly important in some functions. For example, in product development, multi-disciplinary teams with fluid structures and the ability to make numerous informal connections within the organisation, are particularly effective at innovation (Morton *et al.*, 2004). However, in other functions, for example where safety is a prime concern, a greater degree of formality may be preferable.

Contingency perspectives

Over the years researchers have studied the form organisations take, and a general conclusion is that structure is determined by circumstances. The topics that will be examined in this section are: technology and structure, size and structure, strategy and structure, and power/control and structure.

TECHNOLOGY AND STRUCTURE

Burns and Stalker (1961) found that mechanistic (bureaucratic) structures had greater relevance when stability prevailed in markets and in the application of technology to operations within organisations. As you would expect, mechanistic structures are characterised by a pronounced vertical and horizontal differentiation, high formalisation, centralisation and limited upward communication.

Where conditions were unstable, that is markets were unpredictable and there was uncertainty with regard to the application of technology, organic structures were considered more appropriate. In the organic structure conditions opposite to those applicable to the mechanistic structure applied, as follows:

- There was a lesser degree of horizontal differentiation, with greater collaboration between staff at different hierarchical levels and across functions.

- There was a lesser degree of formalisation and a greater degree of decentralisation.

- Responsibilities were less clear-cut, with people interpreting and responding to events in the light of circumstances.

- Communication was more likely to take the form of networks in which the giving of information and the exercise of control originated not from the apex of the organisation but from cells of the organisation where the greatest knowledge and expertise resided. Also, lateral communication between employees of different rank, resembling consultation more than command, was considered more important than communication that flowed through formal channels organised on a hierarchical basis.

■ Community of interest – in current parlance 'shared vision and values' – was a more important influence on behaviour than contractual obligations.

■ Teams consisting of different specialists (e.g. design, engineering and production) operate better if they are located near each other, and the best way of managing innovative projects is through multi-functional teams led by the same manager from the idea generation stage through to completion.

The book containing the research evidence of Burns and Stalker was reissued by the publisher 33 years after it was first released, and was praised by a respected journalist in the management field for the quality of its ideas, which he says had a profound impact on contemporary theory and practice (Lorenz, 1994b). The ideas of Burns and Stalker have continued to be applied. For example, Wang and Ahmed (2003) have highlighted the need of knowledge-based organisations to adopt an organic structure. This allows for dynamic interaction of knowledge workers and enables informal contacts which can be a spur to innovative performance.

Another researcher interested in factors that determine organisation structures was Woodward (1965). She studied the influence exerted by technology. The term 'technology' can be broadly defined to embrace the activities associated with the transformation of various inputs into the output of the organisation. In a factory the production system is a technology. In Woodward's research, companies were categorised by the types of production systems used; for example, unit or small batch production, large batch or mass production, and process production.

Certain features of organisation (e.g. hierarchical level or vertical differentiation, span of control, formalisation and standardisation) moved in sympathy with the technology adopted. Successful companies in a particular category of production system tended to have similar organisation characteristics, and generally speaking organic structures were better suited to unit, small batch and process production companies, while mechanistic structures were most effective when aligned with mass production companies.

In later research Woodward and her colleagues studied the ways in which companies used control systems and how these influenced the design of organisations. Control was viewed from the standpoint of personal control (supervision) or impersonal control (administrative monitoring and control systems), and where it was located (i.e. localised or centrally focused).

Another way of looking at the influence of technology was proposed by Thompson (1967). The categories he used to classify all types of organisation are long-linked, mediating and intensive technologies:

■ *Long-linked technology.* Tasks or operations that flow in a particular sequence and are interdependent are referred to as long-linked. This type of production system is found on the assembly line in, for example, a car manufacturing plant, where one operation has to be completed before another starts.

■ *Mediating technology.* This type of technology includes the tasks and operations involved in linking clients using the services of two different functions of the organisation. For example, clients of a bank are treated as depositors in one function and as borrowers in another. The depositors are on the input side of the organisation and the borrowers are on the output side. In this example the success of the bank depends on satisfying the needs of disparate groups, and it performs a mediating function in linking units or groups, which are otherwise independent.

■ *Intensive technology*. When tasks or operations are geared to tackling problems in conditions where the exact response or solution is unpredictable we enter the domain of intensive technologies. For example, a firm of management consultants has a number of specialists on its payroll. The firm is invited by a client to conduct an investigation into problems or difficulties experienced by the client. These could be messy problems requiring in the first instance a judgement on their nature and subsequently a decision on which consultant(s) (e.g. from marketing, HRM or finance) to allocate to the assignment.

There is no direct link between the system of technology used and structural characteristics of organisation in Thompson's research. What he maintains is that the organisation arranges its structural characteristics in such a way as to protect the technology from the uncertainty surrounding it. To confront uncertainty, either in the sources of supply of raw materials or in the distribution network, a manufacturing company may adjust structure in a particular way. In these circumstances the technology used could be instrumental in shaping the structure of the organisation. There is also recognition of a connection between technology and structure when it is stated that mechanistic structures are more likely to be associated with companies using long-linked and mediating technologies, while the intensive technology could fit the organic structure.

A different interpretation of technology was advanced by Perrow (1970). He emphasised technology based on knowledge rather than production technology. The emphasis is on task variability and problem analysis. The interactions of these variables are shown in Table 3.1. Where there are a multitude of ways of performing tasks, i.e. there are many exceptions to the general rule, and the approach to the analysis of problems is ill-defined because of the complexity of the situation, the job is likely to be of a non-routine nature, as shown in Table 3.1 (Cell 4). By contrast, where there are few exceptions to the general rule on job performance, and the approach to problem analysis is well defined, the job is likely to be basic and clear-cut, i.e. routine as shown in Table 3.1 (Cell 1). An example of a routine job is that of a car park attendant who issues tickets in return for a stated sum of money. The job of a management consultant of some stature or a senior social worker who enjoys autonomy and a lot of scope to interpret situations in conducting assignments could be described as non-routine – Table 3.1 (Cell 4). The construction of a unique building uses engineering technology, and although it can be undertaken in a rational and systematic way there could be a large number of exceptions – Table 3.1 (Cell 2). Craft technology could be used by an electrical technician who could face a relatively difficult problem governed by few exceptions – Table 3.1 (Cell 3).

Table 3.1 Dimensions of technology based on knowledge

	Task variability	
Problem analysis	Few exceptions	Many exceptions
Well-defined	Routine 1	2 Engineering
Ill-defined	3 Craft	4 Non-routine

Activities falling into the upper part of the figure lend themselves to systematic analysis, while those in the lower part of the figure call for more discretion and intuition. The former are likely to be more compatible with mechanistic structures, and the latter with organic structures.

NEW TECHNOLOGY

In recent years the impact of new technology on organisations has been analysed. Employees at the lower levels of the organisation have access to a greater quantity of information owing to the availability of information and communication technology (ICT) systems, and the justification for highly centralised structures is difficult to defend. As a result, the cause of decentralisation is advanced. However, one has to acknowledge that the growth of ICT systems could lead to the pendulum swinging in the direction of centralisation. This could arise because senior managers have access to information previously non-existent or difficult to obtain. Because senior managers are better informed about events throughout the organisation there is not the same need as in the past for a number of layers in the hierarchy. As a result, the organisation ends up with a simplified and compressed structure having removed layers of middle management that are no longer required (Huber, 1990; Reed, 1989).

In today's world, new technology has created the intranet which is the fastest form of corporate networking, making it possible for the establishment of the 'virtual organisation'. In this type of organisation key activities are performed by the nerve centre of the organisation (i.e. headquarters), with other functions outsourced to separate companies or individuals connected electronically to the central office. Such an organisational system allows an expansion of operations and reduced costs. There is further discussion of the virtual organisation later in the chapter where emerging organisational trends are addressed.

In the ICT age production technology is also supported by production systems based on 'just in time' (JIT) (Henry, 2004). Japanese car firms were the first to develop JIT and a number of UK companies followed in their footsteps. JIT is a manufacturing and stock system whereby component parts arrive just in time to be used in the manufacturing process, thereby obviating the necessity to hold stock at the levels required under the old system. There are cost advantages arising from reducing buffer stocks in the warehouse, but because of the reduced stock levels employees are expected to be flexible and to solve problems as they arise, otherwise the next stage in the process will be adversely affected (Tailby and Turnbull, 1987). In effect JIT can promote employee flexibility and multi-skilling, but its introduction could necessitate a radical change in the culture of a factory, expressed as a display of serious interest in it by top management and a firm commitment of resources. Finally, there is a view that JIT is more applicable to manufacturing processes of a repetitive nature rather than to processes that are non-repetitive, for example, production geared to the customers' specification (Collins *et al.*, 1997).

It has been argued that virtual workplaces will be the mode in the future. Such arrangements are facilitated by ICT and can include teleworking, dispersed networks of people working from their homes via ICT links to the central organisation, and 'hoteling', which involves employees combining working at home with meetings in convenient hotels. The virtual working trend (see also the discussion of the virtual organisation later) has increased, and in 2000 it was estimated that 40 million people were teleworking on a global basis (Cascio, 2000). By 2007, 6 per cent of the European Union workforce, and 20 per cent of the US workforce were teleworking (Sanchez *et al.*, 2007). Typically, this approach has implications for HRM. For example, many such workers have variable reward packages linked to the achievement of objectives and management styles have to be based on a combination of trust and output measures. There are strong business reasons for such developments. Research has indicated that teleworkers are strongly results oriented (Sanchez *et al.*, 2007) and studies for IBM have shown savings on facilities costs of 40–60 per cent per site where virtual working has been implemented, and this has been combined with productivity gains of between 15 and 40 per cent. Similarly, Hewlett-Packard has doubled revenue per sales person and Andersen Consulting found that its consultants spent 25 per cent more face-to-face time with customers following moves to virtual working (Cascio, 2000). There are costs as well as benefits, for example the cost of setting up and maintaining ICT equipment in the homes of workers, limitations in effective communication and changes in the nature of team working. From an HRM perspective, one of the cost savings has been assumed to be a reduction of the need for supervisory management; however, Cascio argues that in practice managing people remotely actually calls for increased effectiveness of managers. Managers need to shift from a focus on time – overseeing the employees as they operate throughout the working day, to a focus on outputs or results. This requires sophisticated performance management systems in which specific and challenging goals are agreed with workers, measured and reviewed. In addition, the management style needs to be one of facilitating and encouraging performance, rather than trying to control it.

Shell and Manpower formed a consortium to consider the future of work. The impact of ICT was a key issue and their findings are discussed in Case example 3.1 using Stanford University as an example.

CASE EXAMPLE 3.1

STANFORD UNIVERSITY – A NEW ICT-ENABLED WAY OF WORKING

The Shell consortium on the future of work (Smethurst, 2005) identitifed technological changes as the basis for structural and managerial challenges. Traditional ways of working assume that employees are gathered in one place and that their time is controlled. However, these assumptions are becoming less valid over time.

At Stanford University the traditional offices have been replaced by large open spaces. The furniture is mobile and people can take the furniture and equipment they need to an appropriate space in order to work in the team they need for a particular task.

> 'Nothing is fixed anymore. Everyone's doing their emails on their BlackBerry, working at airports, in cars, in Starbucks . . . the whole concept of workplace/office is changing' (Smethurst, 2005: 30).

The result of this is that HR need to enable managers to think and act differently. It can be particularly difficult for middle managers to accept that their workers do not need to be visible, and that workers being away from the immediacy of control may be a good thing. Managers need to switch from measuring inputs (such as hours at work) to outputs. There is also a challenge to traditional structures that were based on the idea that people at certain grades had particular freedoms and responsibilties. In the new ICT-enabled way of working, there is much more flexibility and employees were negotiating packages (including pay, provision of equipment and flexibility of working hours) that were individually-based, rather than adhereing to the traditional rule for a particular grade.

Source: based on Smethurst, 2005

Question

What could be the consequences of the kind of changes that Stanford have introduced for the psychological contract (introduced in Chapter 2) of employees?

SIZE AND STRUCTURE

The outcome of the Aston Studies (Pugh *et al.*, 1968) indicated that it was size rather than technology which bore the strongest relationship to dimensions of organisation structure such as specialisation, formalisation and centralisation, though technology had an impact closest to its area of influence (e.g. the shopfloor). It is easy to appreciate the significance of size. Increasing the number of employees can lead to greater horizontal differentiation (i.e. more specialised activities) and greater vertical differentiation to facilitate the coordination of specialised functions. This sets the scene for greater reliance on rules and regulations (formalisation). With growing complexity owing to the above factors the exercise of personal control by management could become difficult, hence the need to resort to decentralisation. In recent years the opposite to the above trend – i.e. reducing the number of employees in organisations – has been associated with downsizing, and one effect of this approach is the creation of leaner organisations.

STRATEGY AND STRUCTURE

The main emphasis in this relationship is that changes in corporate strategy can lead to changes in the structure of organisation. It has been suggested that decision makers at top management level make choices about the strategic direction of the organisation and that this results in a reshaping of structure (Child, 1972; Child, 1997). A major proposition put forward by Chandler (1962) is that as corporate strategy shifts from a position where it is concerned with a single product to being preoccupied with product diversification, the management of the company will tend to develop more elaborate structures in order to achieve an optimum result. Effectively this means starting with an organic structure and eventually adopting a mechanistic structure.

In the light of recent evidence the strategy/structure proposition is taken a stage further. There is a view that organisations which have embraced an 'innovation' strategy need flexible systems normally associated with organic structures, where prominence is given to a loose structure, a low level of division of labour and specialisation and formalisation, and a pronounced emphasis on decentralisation. In different conditions an alternative arrangement could apply. For example, a mechanistic structure might be considered functional when a company goes through a period of rationalisation and cost reduction. In this case the suggestion is that there is a significant division of labour, with high levels of formalisation and centralisation. Finally, where a strategy of what is called 'imitation strategy' applies (where organisations try to capitalise on the best aspects of both an 'innovation' and 'cost minimisation' strategy), the result is a combination of both mechanistic and organic structures where tight controls apply to current activities and looser controls to new ventures or developments.

Organisations adopting an imitation strategy move into new products or new markets after innovative competitors have proved that a market exists. In essence, they copy the successful ideas of innovators (Robbins, 2004).

POWER/CONTROL AND STRUCTURE

Very briefly, the power/control explanation states that an organisation structure could be determined by the outcome of power struggles among influential competing factions within the organisation who are intent on advancing their personal interests. Power may also be derived from sources external to the organisation. For example, the funding levels of local government can be influenced by their readiness to adopt flexible structures (including a significant amount of contracting-out of work) approved by central government in the United Kingdom.

Power may operate in a number of ways. It may be centralised, in which case decision makers at the top of the organisation exercise a lot of influence. In such circumstances the structure of the organisation may be a tall organisation, with communications and decisions emanating from the apex. Alternatively, in smaller entrepreneurial organisations, the organisation's processes may all have to be ratified by the entrepreneur who is at the centre of a web of relationships with other organisational members. Power may also operate on a functional or expertise basis. Here power springs from being an expert or controlling access to being a technical function. For example, there is a tradition in the United Kingdom for accountants to be influential when making a contribution to discussions on the strategic direction of the enterprise, and accounting terminology has become part of the normal discourse between managers and a formative part of the way ideas can (and cannot) be raised in organisational settings (Coupland, 2006). The outcome is that problems and opportunities are framed in language and concepts, which tend to preserve the status quo in terms of power. The argument is that dominance of one professional language and set of concepts restricts the way problems and decisions are framed, and hence restrict the potential solutions that can be derived.

Finally, power has the capacity to be scattered along a range of stakeholders, including customers, shareholders, subcontractors and other companies with whom the organisation is collaborating (Bovaird, 2005). In this setting management becomes more of a process of negotiation and influence, and the structure may reflect points of contact with stakeholders. For example, an appropriate organisational unit is charged with acquiring and managing subcontractors. In such circumstances the importance of contracts and agreements on the level of service are underlined. This type of development has some of the features of Weber's legal–rational concept of bureaucracy referred to earlier.

Organisations as open systems

Organisations are not closed systems since they relate to an external environment, such as the financial and legal systems, customers or clients, suppliers, the labour market or regulatory bodies. Therefore they are open systems. As such, organisations can face stable or dynamic environments; the latter are more common nowadays and can create environmental uncertainty. In order to reduce or minimise uncertainty emanating from events such as changing customer tastes, serious challenges from new competitors, threats to sources of supply of raw materials and so on, the organisation could modify the way it is structured.

Emery and Trist (1965) examined four types of environment, which they referred to as follows:

1. placid randomised (relatively unchanging);
2. placid clustered (relatively unchanging, but there are clusters of threats of which the organisation ought to be aware);
3. disturbed reactive (more complex environment, with many competitors);
4. turbulent field (a rather dynamic environment with a high degree of uncertainty).

The disturbed reactive and turbulent field environments – a common sight at the present time – are more likely to be compatible with an organic structure, while the placid randomised and the placid clustered environments, which are becoming increasingly rare nowadays, could match a mechanistic structure.

Lawrence and Lorsch (1967) were also interested in the relationship between the environment and organisation structure. They studied companies facing different degrees of environmental uncertainty with reference to two dimensions of structure, namely differentiation (horizontal) and integration.

Differentiation exists when those who control different functional units or departments vary in their outlook and objectives. For example, the head of the manufacturing unit has objectives and an orientation at variance with those of the head of the finance unit and this is understandable because they relate to different external subenvironments. A particular subenvironment for the finance unit or function could be the regulatory agency controlling the disclosure of financial information, while for the manufacturing unit or function it could be externally prescribed technical specifications with regard to product quality or safety. Integration refers to the process of bringing activities together and achieving unity of effort within the organisation, and this function is even more important if there is pronounced differentiation.

Successful companies had structures more suited to the demands of their particular environments. Since an organisation could be relating to a number of subenvironments the key to success was to match particular subenvironments with organisational functions. For example, a certain type of functional activity within the organisation (e.g. product advertising) faces a dynamic subenvironment, and as a consequence adopts an organic structure; whereas a particular accounting activity interfacing with a relatively stable subenvironment operates within the confines of a mechanistic structure. Another finding from the Lawrence and Lorsch study was that the more diverse the environments faced by the company the greater the amount of horizontal differentiation within the organisation; and that successful companies were those which had established a high degree of integration for coordinating the various functions in the achievement of organisational goals.

When focusing on functions or subsystems within organisations we could quite easily turn our attention to the socio-technical systems approach to studying organisations. This approach looks at the organisation as an open system structured in such a way as to integrate two major subsystems, namely the technical (i.e. task) and the social subsystems. The technical subsystem is concerned with transforming inputs into outputs and the social subsystem relates to the interpersonal aspects of life in organisations. The socio-technical systems approach developed from the research of Trist and Bamforth (1951) when they examined the effects of the introduction of new techniques in British coal mining many years ago. The expected productivity gains failed to materialise because of problems with the social subsystem due to the splitting up of well-established work groups. Here we see that improvements to the technical subsystem did not produce the desired result because of the adverse effect this development had on the social subsystem.

The researchers suggested that the technical and social subsystems could be integrated through the medium of autonomous work groups. These groups aim to facilitate cooperation between the two subsystems so that they function for the good of the overall system. Case example 3.2 discusses an example of autonomous work groups. Autonomous work groups are related to task redesign, particularly job enrichment referred to in Chapter 10, and wider issues connected with group interaction, remote supervision and other aspects of organisation design. An important feature of the socio-technical systems approach to organisation design is the belief in the importance of harmony between the social and technical subsystems. Box 3.1 discusses autonomous work groups and their successor concept – self-managing teams.

CASE EXAMPLE 3.2

AUTONOMOUS WORK GROUPS AT SCOTTISH & NEWCASTLE BREWERIES

Fork lift truck crews, responsible for loading and unloading delivery lorries and conveying kegs to and from the production line, were closely supervised and had no discretion on how to perform their work at Scottish & Newcastle Breweries. An experiment in job redesign took place in which each crew was formed into a team and allowed to organise how its work should be carried out. A crew would decide how work should be allocated amongst team members, and were briefed on such matters as the stock position and deliveries. The role of the foreman changed to that of a 'consultant' to the teams when they encountered problems they could not solve for themselves. Features of the new situation were improved communication, regular consultative meetings, better training, a more pleasant physical working environment and the introduction of a revised payment system. The experiment was considered to be very successful.

Source: based on Department of Employment, 1975

Questions

1. Do you think all employees would welcome this degree of autonomy?

2. What skills would managers need to be effective 'consultants' or 'coaches' to autonomous work groups?

Box 3.1: Self-managing teams

Autonomous work groups were conceived as an open form of structure that allowed work groups to be self-determining in their activities, including, for example, stock control, production activities and quality enhancement. After an initial enthusiasm for the concept it became less popular as there were fears that such approaches would not be beneficial for the productivity and profitability of organisations, particularly where employees were not self-motivated to perform consistently at a high level.

The basic concept has subsequently re-emerged as 'self-managing teams'. Such teams are not fully autonomous, but have considerable discretion in the way they work. Job roles are somewhat blurred and team members take on activities as required by the task at hand. According to a recent study, the popularity of self-managing teams has been increasing (De Jong, *et al.*, 2006) particularly in service industries. One example is in US nursing homes (Yeatts *et al.*, 2004) where nurses and other staff operate as relatively independent teams. The result has been improved satisfaction rates amongst patients, families and staff. However, this style of structuring work places certain requirements on the team. They need the emotional resilience to cope with disagreements, resolve conflict and make decisions (Offermann *et al.*, 2004). Similarly, there are additional demands on managers. Although the teams are self-managing, unlike the original practice of 'autonomous groups', managers have a strong role in establishing and supporting constructive team environments (Zárraga and Bonache, 2006), and in giving strong backing to genuine empowerment (Kirkman *et al.*, 2004).

Question

Self-managing teams are 'semi-autonomous' and have less freedom than the original autonomous work groups. What are the advantages and disadvantages of limiting the degree of freedom that teams have?

Postmodern organisation

Clegg (1990) compares the modernist with the postmodernist organisation. The first is the type of organisation with which we are familiar and that has been analysed in the chapter up to this point. It tends to be rigid, caters for mass markets and gives pride of place to technological determinism (as we found in contingency theory). There are also highly differentiated functions and jobs (as in classical theory), and a generous sprinkling of job demarcation and deskilling (Taylorism). There is reference to the work of Taylor, the father of scientific management, in the section on the utilisation of human resources in Chapter 6. Postmodernist organisations are flexible with niche markets, and are the opposite of modernist organisations with respect to differentiation, demarcation and skill, and actors (key employees) exercise choice as far as the use of technology is concerned (absence of technological determinism).

The postmodernist critique of organisations also recognises that there are multiple and competing views of organisation that are legitimate. It appears everything is open to question and there are always alternative explanations in conditions of diversity. Those advocating this approach have not much time for the modernist view of the existence of a universal objective truth that can be discovered by research methods, often referred to as rational and scientific, which the contingency theorists would like to think they use. The postmodernists recognise that we construct reality as we go along after indulging in self-reflection, aided by the use of language. Given the ambiguous and debatable nature of HRM, it is sometimes said that a postmodernist view of the organisational world is compatible with it. The impact of postmodernism on HRM will be examined further in Chapter 12.

Organisational trends

In recent years much has been said about the changes to traditional organisation structures that are considered necessary for companies to meet future challenges more effectively. It has been argued that large established organisations need to maintain the spirit of younger ones. Bryant and Moon (2006) have found, in their study of global organisations in a range of sectors, that it is necessary to challenge inertia and structural barriers to innovation. This can be achieved in part through those at the top of structures deliberately disrupting and challenging the normal way of doing things. Greg Dyke, the former director-general of the BBC, is credited with this type of approach. Rather than merely telling staff to overcome bureaucratic barriers, the traditional bureaucracy was significantly changed and assumptions were challenged. Each time he was told that a particular established approach was the way to proceed, Dyke would find another way, or ask a challenging question. At first, staff found this disruptive, but over several months they found it stimulating and even started to enjoy the discomfort (Bryant and Moon, 2006).

However, it should be acknowledged that this style of disruption would not be welcomed in all settings, and may be dysfunctional in some settings. The findings of Bryant and Moon reflect the views of Kanter (1989) who maintained that future successful organisations would be 'post-entrepreneurial'. By this is meant that organisations need to take entrepreneurship beyond its present position by combining the creative elements of the role of the entrepreneur and the more disciplined corporate approach, which in an HRM sense would entail taking on board a commitment to cooperation and teamwork. There is a need for faster and more creative action within the organisation, and for closer partnerships with stakeholders (e.g. employees, suppliers and customers). Organisations need to be flexible and free from cumbersome bureaucratic structure if they are to cope well with changing markets and technology, and the external environment at large. In Kanter's terminology, 'corporate giants . . . must learn how to dance'.

Acceptance of the model of the post-entrepreneurial organisation would necessitate the adoption of three main strategies, with a consequent change in values, as follows:

1. Restructuring to find synergies

This means that there is an effective rearrangement of the constituent parts of the organisation so that the value added by the cooperative effort of the whole is greater than the sum of the individual parts. Such an eventuality could arise when a company goes through a process of downsizing (cutting numbers) of central corporate staff and the removal of layers at middle management level (see Box 3.2.)

Box 3.2: Downsizing and delayering

Large organisations faced with having to rationalise operations for a variety of reasons have cut back significantly on numbers of employees, generally in the hope of creating leaner but economically healthier entities. Particular targets in this rationalisation exercise have been headquarters or corporate staff, who have become victims of what is called 'organisational downsizing', i.e. reducing the size of corporate staff. Downsizing has also been associated with an across-the-board reduction in the headcount. Some are of the view that downsizing will harm the organisation in certain key functions, whereas others point to positive outcomes in terms of faster decision making due to the existence of fewer management levels through which decisions pass for approval. Downsizing and delayering are complementary in the sense that reducing hierarchical levels is a means to achieve downsizing.

A flatter structure, obtained by a reduction in the number of layers in the management hierarchy, is justified as a means to simplify management structures, reduce bureaucracy, cut paths of communication, speed up decision making, and push responsibility to lower organisational levels (empowerment). Delayering makes an important impact on managers' lives. The flattening of the management hierarchy also reduces opportunities for promotion, and therefore could impose a restriction on career paths. On reflection, its real impact on career advancement for managers need not be negative, because delayering offers managers who remain in the organisation the opportunity to assume greater responsibility at an early point in their careers and also to receive favourable rewards for doing so (Child, 2005).

A distinction is made between reactive downsizing and strategic downsizing. The former refers to situations in which employee reductions are made in response to external events (e.g. severe competition in the marketplace) and short-term needs. This could be indiscriminate across-the-board cuts without regard to a department's strategic value. Strategic downsizing, sometimes called rightsizing, refers to a carefully thought out process and is designed to support the long-term organisational strategy. It could be associated with transforming the organisation with the objective of introducing 'lean production', business process re-engineering, focus on core competencies, or other aspects of organisational reform (Child, 2005).

To make the downsizing process more palatable, managers can consider adopting HR strategies, such as voluntary programmes (based on incentives to leave), keeping people informed, and allowing those whose services are dispensed with to leave the organisation with dignity and a suitable package of benefits, including access to an outplacement service. In order to reduce feelings of anger and grief during the transitional stage, off-the-site therapeutic workshops, training sessions and lectures could be made available (Brockner, 1992). The psychological dimension of downsizing is heavily underlined by Kets De Vries and Balazs (1996) when they focus on the cognitive and emotional effects. They examined the patterns of individual reactions, as opposed to the technical and procedural factors associated with narrowly based downsizing strategies. The critical constituents in their analysis are the victims (those who lost their jobs), the survivors (those staying with the company), and the executioners (those responsible for the implementation of downsizing). They offer practical recommendations on how to facilitate the downsizing process.

Increasingly the spotlight is put on the predicament of the survivors (those who have still got a job). Greenhalgh (2002) has highlighted the following issues attributable to survivors subjected to poorly managed downsizing. A number of studies have shown that survivors of a poorly managed downsizing initiative are likely to feel anxiety and depression. Their work attitudes are also likely to change and their commitment to the company will have largely disappeared. Their productivity will have taken a serious fall (unless their work lends itself to monitoring) and it is unlikely they will put in extra effort to ensure high quality or customer satisfaction. They are likely to resist change and innovation and could demand militancy from their trade unions. If good labour market opportunities exist, they may be inclined to go elsewhere. This could apply particularly to the better employees, who may be difficult to replace.

Greenhalgh also attracts our attention to a good downsizing programme. It gives people some control over their work lives. They are given choices wherever possible, even if the choice is an unattractive one, such as accepting an unwanted transfer or being asked to leave. For a number of years IBM was a model of industry best practice in providing understanding of the process even when market forces forced it into radical downsizing. As a standard operating procedure, IBM managers were briefed on every detail of the downsizing and were entrusted with explaining it to their staff. In addition to direct communication with management through the use of interviews, newsletters were also used to reinforce the message and to address questions asked by employees. In addition, a hotline was set up whereby any employee would have a question answered with 24 hours. Finally, senior managers made themselves available to allow employees to have their concerns addressed directly. This was considered effective in discrediting the rumour mill. All the above processes were influential in tackling job insecurity.

Question

If a function is outsourced and consequently provided by an external supplier the workers performing that function are no longer members of the parent organisation. This can have an impact on factors such as loyalty and 'ownership' of problems. What would be the essence of a HRM argument against outsourcing?

The manifestation of the restructuring could be seen in changes to the tasks previously carried out by the layer of management which has been removed. Authority could be delegated to lower levels of the organisation. This process could be facilitated by giving work groups more autonomy and by enhancing ICT systems to cope with the collection and exchange of information as well as the monitoring of operations.

In order to react more quickly, large corporations have set up small 'business units' within the organisation, and others have contracted out non-core activities (e.g. catering and security), which were previously carried out in-house. The results of these changes can be smaller organisations with flatter and more focused structures concentrating on 'core' business activity. The challenge facing HRM is to ensure that the changes described are introduced without demotivating the employees affected.

2. Opening boundaries to form external strategic alliances

As organisations concentrate on their core activities they can benefit from forming short-term strategic alliances with other organisations. These alliances assume various forms and, for example, may involve two organisations in a particular market collaborating on some aspects of research and development of mutual benefit to both of them, but too costly or difficult to undertake alone. In another situation a management consultancy firm and a hospital form an alliance to market consultancy services to other hospitals. The hospital, as part of the health sector, can establish contact with other health sector organisations more quickly and easily than the consultancy firm that supplies the services.

3. Create new ventures from within the organisation

These are basically ventures based on innovative practices. One way to promote innovation is to commission the formal research and development department (where one exists) to generate new ideas and projects. However, Kanter acknowledges another source from which fertile ideas can spring: essentially the flexibility built into the structure of the organisation and the work-force. For example, to encourage innovation the organisation could establish short-term interdisciplinary teams to undertake particular projects. In this arrangement team leaders would put a lot of emphasis on their advisory role, where they offer support to well-qualified team members, and would prefer empowering people rather than monitoring or controlling their activities in a traditional sense (see Box 3.3). These teams would then disperse on the comple-tion of the projects and subsequently undertake a new set of tasks under a different arrangement.

FLEXIBLE FIRM

Another observer of the organisational scene recognises that companies now operate in a tougher, more competitive and changing environment (Handy, 1989). He sees UK organisations as becoming less labour intensive and moving towards structures where a central core of knowl-edge-based workers controls the technology and operations of slimmed-down companies. Value is added not through the use of muscle power but through an input of knowledge and

Box 3.3: Empowerment

Empowerment is a management practice concerned with giving front-line employees more responsibility, resources and authority. It is something that is far more than delegation: in effect it means harnessing the creativity and brainpower of all employees, not just the chosen few such as managers. Properly empowered employees are well placed to maximise their potential, and in the process enhance the competitive advantage of their organisation. Empowerment is seen as supportive of a no-blame culture, where mistakes are seen as learning opportunities.

Effective empowerment and engagement of staff has been identified as a corner-stone of productivity. Forward-looking chief executives and senior managers are skilled at engaging the enthusiasm of employees by recognising and welcoming their suggestions and input, and by enabling them to take a greater role in decision making at the operational level (Syedain, 2006).

Empowerment is often accompanied by a reduction in the number of layers of management, normally at middle management level. In certain situations there are other changes such as wider spans of control, managers exercising less control coupled with the use of supportive management, and a greater readiness to embrace HRM practices. The aim of empowerment is both to make better use of people's skills and to enhance performance, for example, though customer service or productivity improvements.

Question

Should empowerment be a central part of all HRM policies? Give reasons for your answer.

creativity. According to Handy, the future organisation will have a core of well-informed employees with ready access to relevant ideas and information (i.e. knowledge workers). This is similar to what Drucker (1988) called the information-based organisation. The core workers are referred to by Pollert (1988) as a group with permanent employment contracts and job security who are multi-skilled and able to perform a variety of functions (i.e. functional flexibility) that may cut across traditional occupational boundaries. An example is provided by BP Chemical's approach to its specialist engineers. BP was finding it difficult to recruit engineers with the requisite skills. The solution has been to invest in an intensive training and education programme, 'project Quartz', which developed employees to fill the skills gap. Participants undertook a four-year college course whilst working for BP and many have continued to further part-time study. The result has been a massively reduced need to recruit engineers from the external labour market. In addition, the turnover amongst those on the programme has been low and hence there has been considerable savings in recruitment costs (Simms, 2005).

Surrounding the core of knowledge workers would be outside workers – a contractual fringe – operating on a subcontracting basis and paid a fee rather than a wage. The management of this group (periphery workers) is removed from the organisation that is receiving its services. A further consideration is the use of a part-time and flexible labour force. This group of temporary or casual workers is less costly for the organisation because their services will only be used to meet particular demands, and released when they are no longer required. In essence the organisation is using what Atkinson called 'numerical flexibility' (Pollert, 1988). Recent research on agency workers in the periphery has shown that a common reason for organisations to employ them, rather than permanent employees, is to manage labour costs, particularly in the short term (Forde and Slater, 2006). Whilst organisations might be happy with this arrangement, agency workers themselves often have low levels of satisfaction, feel insecure and regard their skills as being under-utilised (Hall, 2006).

Another form of flexibility is called 'financial flexibility', where the organisation adapts its labour costs to its financial position (Pollert, 1988). Examples of this would be that the size of the pay packet would be determined by the profits made by the company (e.g. profit-related pay), and relating payment to the performance of specific tasks (e.g. the fees paid to a subcontractor for doing a particular job).

How do the different categories of workers respond to the demands of the flexible firm? From the results of a survey, Hunter *et al.* (1993) conclude that full-time employees were considered flexible, highly stable, committed to the organisation and easy to manage. Temporary employees were viewed as less stable and committed depending on the employment contract, and part-time permanent employees were believed to have higher commitment but were more difficult to use continuously because of the hours worked. Generally, it was noted that employers expected women to find part-time work attractive because of their domestic responsibilities (e.g. dependent children). But the opportunities to work part-time are limited in managerial jobs; for example, in the late 1990s only 18 per cent of managers in the United Kingdom worked part-time (Sly *et al.*, 1998). Therefore it could be argued that women are at a disadvantage if they take advantage of 'family friendly' policies in the form of part-time work opportunities and run the risk of damaging their careers.

It is said that employees who choose to go down the part-time work route tend to miss out on factors vital to career advancement in management (such as visibility), have less time to establish relationships, tend to be allocated to marginal roles with a narrow range of duties, and carry the stigma of low commitment (Edwards *et al.*, 1999). It should be noted that there is a distinction between Edwards *et al.*'s (1999) reference to the 'stigma' of low commitment and Hunter *et al.*'s (1993) reference to actual high commitment amongst part-time employees. This may indicate an area where bias derived from unscientific assumptions (such as part-time workers being less committed than others) can have a negative impact on the validity of the recruitment and selection process. In other words recruiters may assume that part-timers will be less committed than full-timers, whereas this is not necessarily the case. This issue may be particularly significant for women as more women than men work part time.

The changes outlined above will have an impact on the management of human resources. The trend towards information-based organisations and the use of computer-aided production reduces the need for unskilled and semi-skilled production workers. There will be a changing pattern of employment and an increase in the proportion of the labour force devoted to short-term contract and part-time employees. As a result of pressure from the European Union part-time workers can now benefit from rights to certain employment conditions, previously the preserve of full-time workers. Case example 3.3 provides examples of flexible working.

CASE EXAMPLE 3.3

WORKING FLEXIBLY

In Japan

In Japan there is an erosion of the social contract which Japanese workers viewed as sacred for half a century. This was exemplified in a job for life in return for dedicated loyalty to the company. Now there is a trend in Japan reflected in a decrease in the number of full-time workers and a substantial increase in the number of part-time and contract workers. Japan has not yet reached the stage where workers can move easily from one job to another. But the labour market has become segmented between relatively highly-paid permanent staff and lowly-paid temporary and contract workers with few prospects of joining the full-time labour force. Interestingly, the growth of the latter has affected the level of consumer expenditure. The stark reality is that the labour force is much more mobile than it was a decade ago.

Source: based on Pilling, 2004

In Germany

Volkswagen (VW), the German carmaker, seems to be adapting to the legislative framework in the European Union and acting flexibly. Not only has the company adapted to Germany's rigid labour market, but it has also introduced new working arrangements held as examples of good practice for others to follow. Redundancies have been avoided by high degrees of flexibility. Rather than dismissing workers, they were put on a four-day working week. Another measure is that extra hours worked earlier in one's employment with the company could be banked and cashed in later, allowing workers to work part-time or take early retirement. VW has maintained its reputation for defending the social consensus on which German post-war economic success was built, and for working with the unions through Workers' Councils on ways to increase productivity. However, investors do not regard VW as benevolently now because its recent financial performance has been lacklustre.

Source: based on Atkins, 2004

In the UK

The findings of an Economic and Social Research Council survey (reported in Timmins, 2002) do not suggest that the UK has the flexible labour market that it urges other European countries to emulate. 'Far from permanent jobs disappearing 92 per cent of the employed workforce held permanent job contracts in 2000, against 88 per cent in 1992. Contrary to popular belief, people are staying in their jobs longer. Temporary and fixed contract working decreased in the 1990s, and portfolio working remains a minority occupation'. The survey also shows a marked divide between skilled and unskilled workers in the use of advanced technology. Among the semi-skilled and unskilled manual workers only 15 per cent use the Internet at work.

Source: based on Timmins, 2002

Questions

1. In what ways could having temporary employees make an organisation more flexible?

2. In what ways could having temporary employees make an organisation less flexible?

The appearance of flatter organisation structures will reduce the opportunities to improve pay through progression within the hierarchy, but such a development offers greater possibilities for the introduction of performance-related pay discussed in Chapter 9. The position of the 'core' workers warrants careful attention because their hours of work and the demands on them (e.g. greater flexibility with regard to working practices) are likely to be on the high side. However, we must not lose sight of the likely disadvantages of being a peripheral worker – lack of job security, which could adversely affect motivation and commitment (Feldman *et al.*, 1994), and perhaps very limited training opportunities.

Reflecting on the flexible firm, Hunter *et al.* (1993) conclude that the core–periphery contrast is too crude to be helpful with analysis. The so-called periphery has different strands (it gives the employer much scope for variation in the pattern of employment), and therefore is not unitary in its composition. This is a view similar to that taken by Barling and Gallagher (1996) when considering part-time employment. Overall, there is a mixed picture with regard to the adoption of flexible working patterns in Europe.

NETWORK ORGANISATION

Finally, the 'network organisation' is likely to pose a different challenge to the management of the traditional organisation. For example, organisations could concentrate on things they do particularly well, outsourcing functions that can be done quicker and more effectively, or at lower cost, by other companies. One company in the network may research and design a product, another may engineer or manufacture it, and a third may handle distribution. This could allow for greater specialisation and encourage innovation; it could require less time and effort to be put into planning and coordination now that a number of functions have been hived off (Snow *et al.*, 1992). There is further comment on outsourcing in Case example 3.4.

It should be stated that network organisations are not free of shortcomings. There may be a problem with control generally because of the existence of a number of subcontractors, and this could extend to the area of quality control. Equally, the subcontractor may take advan-

OUTSOURCING

Companies in Europe and the United States have been under a lot of pressure to reduce costs without compromising quality. Outsourcing opens the way to reduce labour costs significantly. It is a term used interchangeably with off-shoring and sometimes with business process outsourcing. Two types of outsourcing are to be found. One is the outsourcing of value-chain operations, of which outsourcing the supply chain is the most important. The other is the outsourcing of support activities (research and development, human resource activities, etc.), which supports the value chain, rather than being an integral part of it (Child, 2005).

Companies such as Nike and Reebok in the United States have been successful by concentrating their strengths in designing and marketing the product, and contracting virtually all the manufacturing of their footwear to outside manufacturers or suppliers. Computer companies either purchase their hardware ready made or they buy in all the parts and get involved in the final assembly. In the case of Intel, the design of the processor takes place at two sites in the United States and in Asia. Manufacturing is carried out in the United States (Oregon and New Mexico) and Ireland. Assembly and testing is conducted in Costa Rica, Malaysia, and the Philippines. Intel managers who have the responsibility of coordinating projects across continents argue that a strong corporate culture (referred to in Chapter 4) is more important than ever in this type of organisational arrangement (London, 2004).

Sainsbury's, the UK supermarket chain, embarked on a massive overhaul of its technology systems and discovered a number of its systems were dated. They had not been updated for years and this was having an adverse effect on service to the customer and profitability. Accenture, a United Kingdom consultancy firm, took on Sainsbury's 800 IT staff in addition to 200 contractors working on the systems (Voyle, 2003). This must have been a less than satisfactory arrangement because Sainsbury moved its IT team back to its head office in 2005. In recent years British Airways, HSBC, Prudential Insurance and British Telecommunications have switched a number of call centre jobs to India. However, some European countries stand to gain from the outsourcing trend, among them Ireland and countries in Eastern Europe because of the closer cultural and linguistic links with other parts of Europe and the more convenient time zones. The Irish Republic has been a major beneficiary of the off-shoring trend; it attracted an influx of investment from US and other companies over the past decade. East European countries are now trying to follow Ireland's lead.

Unlike the situation in the United States and much of Europe, Japan has not outsourced many of its back-office jobs to organisations in foreign countries. Apart from the language problem, there is the uniqueness of the 'customer language' used in Japan (Pilling, 2004). But hundreds of thousands of jobs (in call centres) have moved to remote parts of Japan. Outsourcing in Japan reflects growing competitive pressures and significant changes in the labour market. As companies cut costs, the traditional job for life culture is gradually giving way to a more contract-based system.

Increasingly higher skilled jobs are outsourced to developing countries, such as India. In May 2003 the mobile 'phone division of Siemens, the German company, designated

Bangalore, India, as its global software Research and Development Centre. Other examples are jobs requiring more complex financial skills, such as equity research and analysis or market research for developing new business. Evalueserve, an outsourcing company located in Delhi, performs research for patent attorneys and consultancy firms in the United States. Novartis, the Swiss pharmaceutical company, employs 40 statisticians in Mumbai, who process data from clinical research (Thottam, 2003). Outsourcing has become a sensitive issue politically in both the developed and developing countries. The transfer of business processes (e.g. accounting, human resources) and manufacturing from advanced countries to developing economies has generated popular resentment, particularly in the United States and France, where some politicians, unions, and lobby groups refer to it as an important cause of unemployment.

Finally, can we expect any reversal of the off-shoring trend? Perhaps we can on a selective basis! A leading Manchester-based manufacturer of control equipment used for measuring water flow, in which it is a world leader, is transferring production jobs from Thailand to the United Kingdom (where the wages are five times the level of Thailand) where it will use an automated production line at the company's home base. The chairman of the company is reported as saying that in spite of the disparity in labour costs it was more effective to do certain kinds of production in the United Kingdom, partly because it could be controlled more easily by senior managers (Marsh, 2004).

There are obvious advantages stemming from outsourcing, such as allowing organisations to concentrate on what they do best, where there were previously operational difficulties with the activity or process earmarked for outsourcing, cost savings, and where access to valuable expertise is obtained. However, certain problems arising from outsourcing should be noted. These are loss of crucial skills or competencies, the unreliability of the new suppliers, the latter exploiting the client's dependence on them, and lack of sufficient flexibility in outsourcing contracts to handle unusual situations (Child, 2005).

Question

If outsourcing to companies or subsidiaries in parts of the world where labour is cheaper continues in the coming years, what will be the implications for HRM in those companies/subsidiaries?

tage of the dependency relationship to increase prices significantly, or prove to be unreliable in a number of ways, or there may be an unacceptable turnover in the number of subcontractors (McKenna, 2006). Miles *et al.* (1997), who previously were preoccupied with the intricacies of the network organisation, have attracted our attention to the cellular organisation, which is founded on the principles of entrepreneurship, self-regulation and member ownership.

VIRTUAL ORGANISATION

The virtual organisation has been defined as a network organisation with a small core of employees that outsources major business functions (Cascio, 2000). Management outsources all the primary functions of business and the organisational core is a small group of executives, assisted by computer network links, whose major function is to supervise and control activities that are carried out in-house and to coordinate relationships with other organisations that manufacture, distribute, and perform any other activities for the organisation. The coordination and control of external relations can be a time-consuming activity.

The features of the virtual organisation identified by Warner and Witzel (2004) are as follows:

■ *Lack of physical space.* There are fewer buildings, and those that exist are geographically dispersed.

■ *Reliance on communications technology.* ICT plays a major enabling role in the virtual organisation and could be considered its lifeblood. There are networks of communication supported by the Internet (which enables many employees to share information simultaneously), intranets (private nets within large companies which are effectively internal communication systems using special software and not available to the public), and extranets (extended intranets accessible only to selected employees and authorised outsiders). There are also inter-organisational networks that facilitate contact between, for example, a company and its supplier.

■ *Mobile work.* It matters less where work is physically located because of the use of communication networks. Therefore people do not have to work close to each other. For example, project teams in large multinational companies can draw on members located in different countries, without establishing physical contact.

■ *Hybrid forms.* Often a feature of the virtual organisation is cooperation and collaboration between individuals or companies within a loose framework in order to achieve a mutual goal. Such hybrids can have a short- or long-term existence.

■ *Flexible and responsive.* A glaring feature of the virtual organisation is flexibility and responsiveness. Success is assured if the constituent elements of the virtual organisation are able to relate in a mutually beneficial way, and employees are able to work flexibly.

■ *Boundaryless and inclusive.* Relationships cut across organisational boundaries. The virtual organisation can comprise of a company working in close relationship with suppliers and distributors.

The potential benefits of the virtual organisation are seen in the way it makes possible the efficient coordination of activities across boundaries of time and space, a reduction in costs, a more flexible combination of activities, and the simplification of management (Child, 2005). But one should be aware of certain limitations. It is often said that a major disadvantage of the virtual organisation is that it reduces management control over important parts of the business. Child (2005) says there are concerns about the limitations of the virtual organisation, especially in terms of its capacity to stimulate learning and innovation, and the vulnerability that may arise from dependence on partners. In connection with the latter, Robbins (2003) makes the following point:

'When you farm out your data processing, manufacturing, and other functions you make your capabilities available to your competitors. So virtualization of work diminishes competitive advantages. It leads to rapidly spreading commoditization of everything. Any function that an organization uses to achieve competitive advantage cannot be outsourced.'

BOUNDARYLESS ORGANISATION

One of the features identified by Warner and Witzel above is the boundaryless organisation. The term 'boundaryless' organisation was actually developed by Jack Welch when he was CEO of GE to describe his vision of how he wanted the company to be. He intended to achieve this by eliminating vertical and horizontal boundaries within GE and also by the breakdown of external barriers between the company and its customers and suppliers (Robbins, 2003). This he hoped would make GE a 'big company/small company hybrid'. The basic ideology behind this boundaryless state is that of trying to eliminate the chain of command, having limitless spans of control, and replacing departments with empowered teams, coupled with a heavy reliance on ICT. Jack Welch found that by removing vertical boundaries, the organisational hierarchy was considerably flattened, which in turn minimised status and rank. This could open the way for greater interaction by employees from different levels of the organisation and promote the practice of participative management and the use of 360-degree performance appraisal.

As for the removal of the horizontal boundaries, this was achieved by a process of replacing functional departments with that of cross-functional teams and to organise activities around processes. The organisation could use cross-functional teams to work on, for example, new product development. In this type of setting budgets could be allocated to processes, not to functions or departments. Another way management could weaken barriers between functions is to promote lateral transfers, which would involve rotating employees into and out of different functional areas. The rationale for taking this line of action is to transform specialists into generalists.

Among the techniques available to weaken external boundaries are strategic alliances. The latter opens up a pathway to another organisation and offers employees from different organisations the opportunity to come together and work on joint projects. Strategic alliances were referred to earlier. Another example is the involvement of customers in key organisational processes, such as the selection of staff. There is reference to this type of activity in the discussion of high-performance systems (customer-focused operating units) later in the chapter.

To achieve the boundaryless organisation is likely to be a Herculean challenge. Robbins (2003) quite rightly says that GE has not achieved the boundaryless state, and probably never will, but it has made significant progress towards the ideal form.

TEAM STRUCTURE

When management uses teams as a central mechanism to coordinate activities, this is referred to as a team structure or horizontal organisation (Forrester and Drexler, 1999). One way in which delayering, referred to above, can be achieved is by the removal of layers in the hierarchy, making it possible to create teams and in doing so to encourage decentralisation of authority and initiative. In the traditional hierarchical structure authority is vested in the manager, and in the team-based structure authority is vested in the team or work unit. An important consideration as far as the team structure is concerned is that teams are composed of members who have the necessary information, expertise and authority to arrive at decisions and execute their responsibilities in an efficient manner.

In the team-based structure there is also a removal or dilution of barriers between departments and functions within the organisation as teams draw their membership from different functions, and this creates a situation whereby more frequent horizontal communication is facilitated. The use of cross-functional teams in an organisational setting can facilitate the coordination of major projects. Finally, a satisfactory outcome would be if the team structure were used to complement bureaucratic structures; that would mean the mechanistic system (formalisation/standardisation) could co-exist with the organic system (flexibility and rapid response), but there could be tension between the two systems.

LEAN PRODUCTION AND HIGH-PERFORMANCE SYSTEMS

Organisational design in manufacturing companies has been influenced by developments such as lean production systems and high-performance systems. In Japan lean production systems became popular and were influenced by the following principles: quality control, continuous improvement, minimum stock buffers, teamwork and customer focus.

The concept of lean production has been applied throughout the world. A substantial part of the success of this approach relies on the effectiveness of the operating system applied. However, the human factors are also significant, and employee practices have been identified as crucial in the success or failure of lean production (Genaidy and Karwowski, 2003). An illustration of the impact of the application of lean production systems in the United Kingdom is provided by Wagstyl (1996). He put the spotlight on changes in management and organisation in certain British companies (e.g. Ford and Nissan UK) in the 1980s and 1990s, and reports on outcomes such as impressive productivity gains, improved work practices and management, a noticeable commitment to good quality standards and continuous improvement, greater cooperation between key constituents (e.g. workers, managers, suppliers), greater effort in detecting faults and taking appropriate remedial action, and an improved relationship with trade unions.

Although lean production systems have been used in the West, as we have seen above, one is more likely to find derivatives of these systems, called high-performance systems, in use in advanced industrial countries such as the United States. The main reasons why they have been introduced are the highly competitive conditions in the marketplace and the demands of shareholders for greater returns on their capital. High performance systems are based on five principles, as follows (Useem, 1997):

1. *Customer-focused operating units*, where there is heightened sensitivity to reactions of customers, relying on market surveys and focus groups. This information would go directly to managers of operating units, and some of it could be used in HRM decision-making processes connected with the performance of employees and the determination of rewards.
2. *Devolved decision making*, where authority is pushed down the hierarchy to an extent that greater power resides in operating units (called strategic business units – SBUs). These consist of broad categories of products in which are placed appropriate functional specialisms (e.g. production, marketing). There is a similarity between this type of structure and the 'product grouping' referred to earlier in the chapter. SBUs are customer oriented, have responsibility for formulating strategy and are accountable for results, and this can provide a useful motivational spur to the management that runs them. The relationship between an SBU and the central controlling cell of the organisation varies; in some companies there are more centralised functions than in others.
3. *Streamlined management control/tighter financial control*, reflected in wider spans of control and flatter structures, arises as a result of downsizing and the removal of layer(s) of management. Although there are likely to be fewer policy directives sent from the nerve centre of the organisation to the operating units, tighter financial targets could be imposed on the latter.
4. *Business process re-engineering* (BPR), which amounts to a fundamental rethink and radical redesign of business processes and practices in order to bring about significant improvements in the quality and speed of the service to the customer as well as a dramatic reduction in costs (Hammer and Champy, 1993). Chapter 5 has further discussion of BPR as a technique that can be used to change culture.
5. *Establishing a connection between organisational actions and decisions and shareholder value*. This amounts to assessing the effectiveness of management at producing wealth for shareholders. In HRM terms the link between management action and shareholder value can be seen in the connection between share option schemes and company performance.

CHANGE

Restructuring is an important feature of the organisational landscape in contemporary times and is likely to continue as an important activity in the future. Unilever, the Anglo-Dutch foods and detergent conglomerate, announced the formation of two global divisions, one for food and the other for home and personal care in 2001. The heads of the two divisions both had executive authority and profit responsibility for Unilever's operations across 88 countries. The company said that the rationale was to accelerate decision making and to strengthen the company's ability to harness innovation, and awaken the entrepreneurial spirit within the company. In addition, the move was designed to put brand management firmly at the centre of Unilever's focus and to speed up its responsiveness to the market (Killgren, 2000; Thornhill, 2000). An observer said that such an arrangement would allow the then co-chairmen – Niall FitzGerald and Antony Burgman – to concentrate more on strategy. It appears that the newly created divisions are closer to the concept of an SBU than the product division, both of which were discussed earlier.

Ruigrok *et al.* (1999) conducted a survey of 450 European companies. The results indicated that over the period 1992–96 companies across Europe reported significant progress with features such as decentralising operational decision making, introducing project-based organisational forms and linking up with external agencies such as suppliers (e.g. outsourcing) and competitors (e.g. strategic alliances). The last point is a theme reinforced by Cravens *et al.* (1996) and Ferlie and Pettigrew (1996) when they state that the organisation's relationship with customers, suppliers and competitors has changed, with an emphasis on building partnerships, alliances and networks inside and outside the organisation. Increasingly initiatives are being taken to combine conventional work practices and settings with non-traditional ones (Apgar, 1998). More attention is being paid to the manner in which work is organised in order to take advantage of the deployment of flexible labour and the introduction of high-performance work practices that can build on employee commitment and lead to a position of competitive advantage (Whitfield and Poole, 1997). Undoubtedly the above changes to organisational structures and work practices will necessitate changes to the nature and style of HRM.

Is there a danger that we have gone too far with diluting the traditional hierarchy of organisation as a result of subscribing to principles behind the emerging forms of organisation referred to above? (See Box 3.4 for a possible answer.)

Box 3.4: In defence of hierarchy: status

According to Adrian Furnham, Professor of Psychology, University of London, in answer to the question posed this could very well be the case. He is reported as saying that:

'there is a backlash against US-style management orthodoxy that has tried to tame the drive for status by flattening hierarchies. The desire for status is a powerful force, and companies should not try to suppress it. Status is all about one-upping the next person. The ego is a very powerful thing and companies must learn to exploit it. People are willing to trade down salary if it means trading up status. It is no coincidence that American companies tend to have dozens of vice-presidents.'

John Hunt, Professor of Organisational Behaviour at the London Business School, makes the point that the contemporary 'egalitarian impulse behind dressing down (informal dress) has been subverted by status conscious workers who outdo their colleagues with designer labels' (Bilefsky, 2000).

Loch *et al.* (2000) argue that the drive for status is primordial and any attempts to tame it are futile. They go on to say that humans are genetically hard-wired to be status conscious, and that the drive for status can act as a catalyst to pursue success. Managers can encourage healthy competition by offering incentives such as a bigger office, invitations to lunch with the chief executive or a chance to work on high-profile projects. Though recognising the validity of what has been said, it must be acknowledged that having a hunger for status can be destructive from the point of view of the organisation. In 1998 the first attempted marriage between Glaxo Wellcome and SmithKline Beecham collapsed because Richard Sykes and Jan Leschly could not decide who would get the top job (Bilefsky, 2000).

Leavitt (2003) recognises that despite some negative features (e.g. encouragement of distrust, authoritarianism and fear), bureaucratic structures have a lot going for them as they provide the means of handling complexity, offer structure and predictability, and fulfil our needs for order and security.

Questions

1. If you had spent your career climbing to become a top manager in a large organisation, would you want to remove or reduce hierarchy?

2. If you were just starting your career, would you like to think that there were steps you could advance up to reach a higher level, rather than having a career of perpetual sideways moves?

 Conclusions

Strategy, discussed in Chapter 2, and structure are interrelated and together are crucial for the success of the organisation. Determining the nature of the organisation's structure can be an important strategic decision where top managerial influence plays a key role. However, the various environments (e.g. technological, market, economic, political) to which the organisation is exposed also play a crucial role in the determination of strategy and structure. Ensuring that the structure does not militate against performance (the accusation levelled at bureaucracy) has led to increases in flexibility of structure.

Such changes present a challenge to HRM that seeks to determine the make-up of the workforce, and ensure that it is managed in such a way as to maximise commitment and performance. Greater flexibility and looser networks in organisational structure may bring advantages such as increasing the speed of response the organisation can make to changes in its environment, but there may be costs such as greater difficulty in achieving a shared vision amongst the workforce and in maintaining effective communication. For example, concepts such as the virtual organisation and boundaryless organisation mean that traditional approaches to careers, training and development and appraisal could be challenged as many of the traditional HRM techniques work on the basis that the employee reports to a manger on the basis of a defined job, whereas flexibility means that this is no longer always the case. The benefits of flexibility can be greater creativity, but managing flexible workers will require flexible thinking from management. This issue and the concept of HR managers as business partners will be discussed further in Chapter 12.

There is no single best way of structuring organisations, and it is important to find an appropriate fit between the structure, the business environment, the size of the organisation, the available technology, the forces for change and the disposition of the employees. In seeking to find such a fit it is worth bearing in mind the development of structure from the classical theories to IT-inspired virtual organisations. Whatever the structure adopted there will still be a need for effective management of performance, communication and the interaction of employees. Some would argue that the need for excellence in these areas of management increases rather than decreases in modern organisational forms.

Review and reflection questions

1. What characteristics of bureaucracies might have led to their successful survival for so long?

2. Do modern forms of organisation, such as the virtual organisation and self-managing teams, imply a break with the classical principles of organisational structure (e.g. the division of labour, authority, responsibility and the span of control) or merely a different enactment of the principles?

3. What are the six types of organisational structure according to Mintzberg?

4. In what ways does technology (old and new) impact on organisation structure and design?

5. What does it mean to think of an organisation as an 'open system'?

6. How can an organisation increase its flexibility?

7. What are the advantages and disadvantages of modern forms such as virtual and networked organisations?

Activities

If you are in work:

Use the typology devised by Mintzberg to analyse your organisation.

1. Which type is it closest to?

2. What are the advantages of this structure?

3. What are the disadvantages?

4. What changes would benefit the organisation?

5. What type of organisation structure would be most suitable for a company that practises progressive HRM ?

If you are in full-time study:

Compare and contrast your experience of being in informal organisations (such as groups of friends) and formal organisations (such as schools and universities).

1. How was authority distributed?

2. How was it decided who would have which role?

3. How successful were the organisations in achieving their aims?

4. What are the strengths and weaknesses of the different styles of organisation?

5. What type of organisation structure would be most suitable for a company that practises progressive HRM?

Further reading and research

Organisational structure and design is a complicated topic of study that has engaged scholars for a considerable time. The following book by John Child has a particular strength in presenting the research and modern perspectives on structure.

Child, J. (2005) *Organizations: Contemporary Principles and Practice*, Oxford: Blackwell.

A current topic of interest is the virtual organisation. Some see this as the future of successful businesses, others argue that it means a loss of 'centrality' of the organisation in employees' lives and can be disorienting. The following references explain the debate and its implications for management practice.

Axtell, C.M., Fleck, S.J. and Turner, N. (2004) 'Virtual Teams: Collaborating across distance', in C.L. Cooper and I.T. Robertson (eds), *International Review of Industrial and Organizational Psychology*, 19, Chapter 7, 205–248, Chichester: Wiley.

Warner, M. and Witzel, M. (2004) *Managing in Virtual Organizations*, London: Thomson.

Outsourcing and offshoring have been introduced in the chapter as recent trends. Often these approaches are aimed at decreasing costs, but efficiency and quality can also be affected, sometimes negatively. The following references provide an insight into these issues.

Cooke, F.L., Shen, J. and McBride, A. (2005) 'Outsourcing HR as a competitive strategy: A literature review and an assessment of implications', *Human Resource Management*, 44, 413–432.

Warren, C. (2007) 'Offshoring: Stars of India', *People Management*, 28 February, 27–30.

The structure of ownership has an impact on the style of organising and on the business targets. The following paper offers a perspective on this issue.

Clark, I. (2007) 'Private Equity and HRM in the British Business System', *Human Resource Management Journal*, 17, 218–226.

A useful general website is The Times 100 (www.thetimes100.co.uk). This covers a range of business topics, but within the People section there are pages covering formal and informal organisation, and developing ideas about the potential clashes between the two aspects of organisation. The associated case study on the Audit Commission (accessible through links from the main site) discusses flexible working patterns and is a good illustrative case.

The link between organisational function and structure is exemplified by the Metropolitan Police on its website (www.met.police.uk). The structure of policing London is explained including organisational structure, ranks, local policing and specialist operations.

References

Apgar, M. (1998) 'The alternative workplace: changing where and how people work', *Harvard Business Review*, 76, 121–136.

Atkins, R. (2004) 'Volkswagen goes down road to flexible working', *Financial Times*, 21 June, 3.

Barling, J. and Gallagher, D.G. (1996) 'Part-time employment', in Cooper, C.L. and Robertson, I.T. (eds), *International Review of Industrial and Organizational Psychology*, Chichester: Wiley.

Bilefsky, D. (2000) 'How to discover your inner chimp', *Financial Times*, 4 August, 14.

Birkinshaw, J. (2000) 'The structures behind global companies', *FT Mastering Management*, Part 10, 4 December, 2–4.

Bovaird, T. (2005) 'Public Governance: balancing stakeholder power in a network society', *International Review of Administrative Sciences*, 71, 217–228.

Brockner, J. (1992) 'Managing the effects of layoffs on survivors', *California Management Review*, Winter., 9–28.

Bryant, B. and Moon, S. (2006) 'Walls come tumbling down', *People Management*, 12, 30–33.

Burns, T. and Stalker, G.M. (1961) *The Management of Innovation*, London: Tavistock.

Cascio, W. (2000) 'Managing a virtual workplace', *Academy of Management Executive*, 14, 81–90.

Chandler, A. (1962) *Strategy and Structure: chapters in The History of the Industrial Enterprise*, Cambridge, MA: MIT Press.

Child, J. (1972) 'Organisation structure, environment, and performance: the role of strategic choice', *Sociology*, 6, 1–22.

Child, J. (1997) 'Strategic choice in the analysis of action, structure, organisations, and environment: retrospect and prospect', *Organisation Studies*, 18, 43–76.

Child, J. (2005) *Organizations: Contemporary principles and practice*, Oxford: Blackwell.

Child, J. and McGrath, R.G. (2001) 'Organizations unfettered: Organizational form in an information intensive economy', *Academy of Management Journal*, December, 1135–1148.

Clegg, S.R. (1990) *Modern Organizations: Organizations in the postmodern world*, London: Sage.

Collins, R., Schmenner, R. and Cordon, C. (1997) 'Rigid flexibility and factory focus', in *Mastering Management: Module 9 Production and Operations Management*, 311–315, London: FT/Pitman Publishing.

Coupland, C. (2006) 'Corporate Social and environmental Responsibility in Web-based Reports: Currency in the Banking Sector', *Critical Perspectives on Accounting*, 17, 865–881.

Cravens, D., Piercy, N. and Shipp, S. (1996) 'New organizational forms for competing in highly dynamic environments', *British Journal of Management*, 7, 203–18.

Daft, R.L. (2004) *Organization theory and design*, International Student Edition, Mason, OH: South Western.

de Jong, A., de Ruyter, K. and Wetzels, M. (2006) 'Linking Employee Confidence to Performance: A Study of Self-Managing Service Teams', *Journal of the Academy of Marketing Science*, 34, 576–587.

Department of Employment (1975) *Making Work More Satisfying*, London: HMSO.

Drucker, P.F. (1988) 'The coming of the new organization', *Harvard Business Review*, January/February, 45–53.

Edwards, C., Robinson, O., Welchman, R. and Woodall, J. (1999) 'Lost opportunities? Organizational restructuring and women managers', *Human Resource Management Journal*, 9, 55–64.

Emery, F.E. and Trist, E.L. (1965) 'The causal textures of organisational environments', *Human Relations*, February, 21–32.

Feldman, D.C., Doerpinghaus, H.I. and Turnley, W.H. (1994) 'Managing temporary workers: a permanent HRM challenge', *Organizational Dynamics*, Autumn, 49–63.

Ferlie, E. and Pettigrew, A. (1996) 'Managing through networks: some issues for the NHS', *British Journal of Management*, 7, 81–99.

Forde, C. and Slater, G. (2006) 'The nature and experience of agency working in Britain', *Personnel Review*, 35(2), 141–157.

Forrester, R. and Drexler, A.B. (1999) 'A model of team-based organization performance', *Academy of Management Executive*, August, 36–49.

Genaidy, A.M. and Karwowski, W. (2003) 'Human performance in lean production environment: Critical assessment and research framework', *Human Factors and Ergonomics in Manufacturing*, 13, 317–330.

Greenhalgh, L. (2002) *FT Mastering Leadership*, Part 5, 29 November, 2–3.

Hall, R. (2006) 'Temporary agency work and HRM in Australia', *Personnel Review*, 35, 158–174.

Hammer, M. and Champy, J. (1993) *Re-engineering the corporation: A manifesto for business revolution*, New York: Harper Business.

Handy, C. (1989) *The Age of Unreason*, London: Business Books.

Henry, A. (2004) 'Analysis of parts requirements variance for a JIT supply chain', *International Journal of Production Research*, 42, 417–430.

Huber, G.P. (1990) 'A theory of the effects of advanced information technologies on organisation design, intelligence, and decision making', *Academy of Management Review*, 15, 47–71.

Hunter, L., McGregor, A., MacInnes, J. and Sproull, A. (1993) 'The flexible firm: strategy and segmentation', *British Journal of Industrial Relations*, 31, 383–407.

Kanter, R.M. (1989) *When Giants Learn to Dance: Mastering the challenges of strategy, management and careers in the 1990s*, London: Unwin.

Kets De Vries, M. and Balazs, K. (1996) 'The human side of downsizing', *European Management Journal*, 14, 111–120.

Killgren, L. (2000) 'Unilever splits operations but denies plans for divorce', *Financial Times*, 5/6 August, 1.

Kirkman, B.L., Rosen, B., Tesluk, P.E. and Gibson, C.B. (2004) 'The impact of team empowerment on virtual team performance: The moderating role of face-to-face interaction', *Academy of Management Journal*, 47, 175–192.

Larson, E.W. and Gobeli, D.H. (1987) 'Matrix management: contradictions and insights', *California Management Review*, Summer, 126–138.

Lawrence, P.R. and Lorsch, J.W. (1967) *Organizations and Environment: Managing differentiation and integration*, Homewood, IL: Irwin.

Leavitt, H.J. (2003) 'Why hierarchies thrive', *Harvard Business Review*, March, 96–102.

Loch, C. *et al.* (2000) 'The fight for alpha position: channelling status competition in organizations', INSEAD.

London, S. (2004) 'Intel's success involves a series of key strokes', Special Report on the Future of Work, *Financial Times*, 27 September, 2.

Lorenz, C. (1994a) 'Ford's global matrix gamble', *Financial Times*, 16 December, 13.

Lorenz, C. (1994b) 'Pioneers and prophets: Tom Burns', *Financial Times*, 5 December.

Marsh, P. (2004) 'Manufacturer switches work from Thailand to Britain to cut costs', *Financial Times*, 5 March, 6.

McKenna, E. (2006) *Business Psychology and Organizational Behaviour*, Hove: Psychology Press.

Mintzberg, H. (1983) *Structure in Fives: Designing effective organizations*, Englewood Cliffs, NJ: Prentice Hall.

Miles, R.E., Snow, C.C., Mathews, J.A., Miles, G. and Coleman, H.J. (1997) 'Organizing in the knowledge age: anticipating the cellular form', *Academy of Management Executive*, 11, 7–20.

Morton, S.C., Brookes, N.J., Smart, P.K., Backhouse, C.J. and Burns, N.D. (2004) 'Managing the informal organization: conceptual model', *International Journal of Productivity and Performance Management*, 53, 214–232.

Offermann, L.R., Bailey, J.R., Vasilopoulos, N.L., Seal, C. and Sass, M. (2004) 'The Relative Contribution of Emotional Competence and Cognitive Ability to Individual and Team Performance', *Human Performance*, 17, 219–243.

Perrow, C.B. (1970) *Organisational Analysis: A sociological view*, London: Tavistock.

Pilling, D. (2004) 'Japan's job spin out of Tokyo', *Financial Times*, 5 July, 8.

Pollert, A. (1988) 'The flexible firm: fixation or fact?', *Work, Employment and Society*, 2, 281–316.

Pugh, D.S., Hickson, D.T., Hinings, C.R. and Turner, C. (1968) 'Dimensions of organisation structure', *Administrative Science Quarterly*, 13, 65–105.

Robbins, S.P. (2004) *Essentials of Organisational Behaviour*, Englewood Cliffs, NJ: Prentice Hall/Pearson Eduction International.

Robbins, S.P. (2003). *Organisational behaviour*, Upper Saddle River, NJ: Prentice-Hall/Pearson Education International.

Reed, M. (1989) *The Sociology of Management*, Hemel Hempstead: Harvester Wheatsheaf.

Ruigrok, W., Pettigrew, A., Peck, S. and Whittington, R. (1999) 'Corporate restructuring and new forms of organising: evidence from Europe', *Management International Review*, 39, 41–64.

Sanchez, A.M., Perez, M.P., de Luis Carnicer, P. and Jimenez, M.J.V. (2007) 'Teleworking and workplace flexibility: a study of impact on firm performance', *Personnel Review*, 36, 42–64.

Simms, J. (2005) 'Chemical Planting', *People Management*, 11, 36–37.

Sly, F., Thair, T. and Risdon, A. (1998) 'Women in the labour market: results from the Spring 1997 Labour Force Survey', *Labour Market Trends*, 106, 97–120, London: Office for National Statistics.

Smethurst, S. (2005) 'The Great Beyond', *People Management*, 11, 28–31.

Snow, C.C., Miles, R.E. and Coleman, H.J. (1992) 'Managing 21st century network organisations', *Organisational Dynamics*, Winter, 5–20.

Syedain, H. (2006) 'Put out of Joint', *People Management*, 12, 28–30.

Tailby, S. and Turnbull, P. (1987) 'Learning to manage just-in-time', *Personnel Management*, January, 16–19.

Thompson, J.D. (1967) *Organizations in Action*, New York: McGraw-Hill.

Thornhill, J. (2000) 'Unilever's rejig takes inspiration from its origins', *Financial Times*, 5/6 August, 12.

Thottam, J (2003) 'Where the good jobs are going', *Time Magazine*, 18 August, 34–36.

Timmins, N. (2002) 'Work myths study shows rise in staff discontent', *Financial Times*, 1 May, 5.

Trist, E.L. and Bamforth, K.W. (1951) 'Some social and psychological consequences of the Longwall method of coal getting', *Human Relations*, 4, 3–38.

Useem, M. (1997) 'The true worth of building high performance systems', in *Mastering Management: Module 8 Managing People in Organizations*, 288–292, London: FT/Pitman Publishing.

Voyle, S (2003) 'Why Sainsbury put its money on a wholesale system change', *Financial Times*, 13 June.

Wagstyl, S. (1996) 'Lifeblood from transplants: a revolution in British manufacturing has been heavily influenced by Japanese groups such as Nissan', *Financial Times*, 29 July, 15.

Wang, C.L. and Ahmed, P.K. (2003) 'Structure and structural dimensions for knowledge-based organizations', *Measuring Business Excellence*, 7, 51–62.

Warner, M. and Witzel, M. (2004) 'Managing in virtual organizations', London: Thomson.

Weber, M. (1947) *The Theory of Social and Economic Organization* (trans A. Henderson and T. Parsons), New York: Oxford University Press.

Whitfield, K. and Poole, M. (1997) 'Organising employment for high performance: theories, evidence, and policy', *Organization Studies*, 18, 745–764.

Woodward, J. (1965) *Industrial Organisations: Theory and practice*, London: Oxford University Press.

Yeatts, D.E., Cready, C., Ray, B., DeWitt, A. and Queen, C. (2004) 'Self-Managed Work Teams in Nursing Homes: Implementing and Empowering Nurse Aide Teams', *The Gerontologist*, 44, 256–261.

Zárraga, C. and Bonache, J. (2005) 'The Impact of Team Atmosphere on Knowledge Outcomes in Self-managed Teams', *Organization Studies*, 26, 661–681.

Chapter 4

ORGANISATIONAL CHANGE AND DEVELOPMENT

Introduction

Change management is a topic that is rich both in theoretical perspectives and application to the practice of management. Important challenges for organisations are to react swiftly and effectively to external forces for change, and to capitalise on the potential for internally driven change and development.

Once you have read this chapter, you should:

■ **understand why employees might resist change;**

■ **be aware of alternative approaches to overcoming resistance;**

■ **be able to discern the psychological stages that people can go through when they experience change;**

■ **understand and be able to judge the applicability of alternative approaches to managing change;**

■ **be aware of ways of executing change at the levels of the organisation, task and individual/group through organisation development techniques;**

■ **be able critically to reflect on the role of change and development in HRM.**

Change is a phenomenon we encounter in life both inside and outside organisations and it is fair to say that the pace of change has accelerated in recent years. We have witnessed changes in the political landscape of the world with the disintegration of the communist system and the collapse of the Eastern bloc. This has generated further changes, such as the creation of independent states within the old Soviet Union and of course the reunification of Germany. The expansion of the European Union has had an impact on trade and the mobility of labour. Change is visible in South Africa, where power sharing between blacks and whites replaced the previous system of rule by the white population. Shifting perspectives in China have had significant impacts on their participation on the world economic stage. Such macro-political changes have an impact on organisations in terms of areas of the world that they can regard as markets, potential sites of production and competition.

At the economic level there will be greater competition as barriers to trade between EU countries have been removed with the creation of the Single Market. This is being accentuated by the rapid development of global markets. The pace of technological developments is reflected in changes across a broad spectrum. For example, there have been impressive advances in the application of new technology to the office and the factory. Technological innovation also finds expression in the development of new products. Change will also affect how people perceive careers. Employee expectations are changing, because now there is recognition of the growing need to have a number of jobs throughout a working life, with much less attachment to the notion of a continuous association with one organisation.

As organisations seek to operate in global markets and to apply products and processes internationally, they may be faced with dealing with increased complexity. On the one hand, globalisation implies a unification to some extent; for example, the same product can become sold more widely, or a particular management technique may be applied across national boundaries. However, it has been argued that internationalisation creates requirements for greater internal diversity of the organisation to deal with the external diversity (Herrmann and Datta, 2005). In some cases differences can be major and clearly identified. In others, differences between people in divergent national cultures (Rondinelli and Black, 2000), with histories of different forms of practice (Mintzberg and Markides, 2000), create subtle but important variation in perceptions of the reasons for, and the rationality of, change.

It is commonplace in today's world for organisations to bring about a variety of changes to their goals, structures and processes in response to both internal and external happenings or in anticipation of these events. At the strategic level corporate goals could be set or adapted (changed) so that the organisation is well placed to derive competitive advantage in its market. At the operational level responses or precipitative action to improve efficiency and effectiveness could be reflected in changes to working practices, contracts of employment, systems and structures. With globalisation, some manufacturing organisations have moved production to countries where labour costs are low. Similarly, some service-provision firms, such as IT services and call centres, have relocated to parts of the world where skilled labour is available cheaply. This puts the onus on achieving innovation and high-quality service for companies that operate with higher labour costs. Given the degree of change at the social, political and economic levels the aim must be to achieve flexibility in response to external change at the operational level. Typically this will require employees to be flexible in their attitude to change and in the application of their skills and knowledge to new tasks. However, managing change is far from straightforward and research has indicated that 40 per cent of reorganisations do not meet their objectives (Kent, 2005).

Reactions to change

Change is not a painless process and it is often resisted by employees when they do not share the employer's view.

RESISTANCE TO CHANGE

The following are some of the reasons why change is resisted. These operate at the individual, group and organisational level and could be based on historical justifications (Tan, 2006; Bedeian and Zammuto, 1991):

■ People perceive that the proposed changes are likely to threaten their expertise, undermine their influence, dilute their power base and reduce the resources currently allocated to their department. If this negative view prevails efforts to introduce the change could be hindered.

■ There is a lack of trust between management and employees. This could have arisen because those likely to be affected by the proposed changes did not receive adequate explanations about what is due to take place, or they recall that past changes did not produce the promised benefits.

■ There are diverse views about the need for change and the anticipated benefits, and this creates some confusion. For example, management holds optimistic views about why the change is necessary and the expected results, whereas the workers are unable to share these views. Of course there could also be differences of opinion within each group. Whatever the reason, the lack of consensus acts as an impediment.

■ People have a low tolerance for change, though it is recognised that there are certain people who thrive on confronting change. Individuals with a low tolerance for change may feel anxious and apprehensive about the uncertainty that accompanies change, and as a result oppose it even though they recognise it is for the benefit of the organisation.

■ As creatures of habit people construe change as uncomfortable because it poses a challenge to established routines to which they have grown accustomed and to relationships developed over time. For example, there is a proposal to overhaul organisational processes and practices by resorting to business processing re-engineering and people feel uncomfortable about the prospect of a major upheaval that is likely to result in discarding established ways of doing things. If the proposed reorganisation leads to the break-up of established groups of colleagues people could feel sad at the disintegration of teams because of the impact this is likely to have on comradeship, mutual support and shared experience. Also, there could be a certain sadness at the prospect of severing contact with people who the organisation feels are superfluous to requirements and as a result are being made redundant.

■ There is a perception that the proposed change challenges cherished values and beliefs; for example, the proposal to remove the system of promotion based on seniority that was considered an attractive HR practice in the past (e.g. as in Japan).

■ People harbour doubts about their ability to cope with the demands of the new situation.

■ People feel that their future job security and income could be adversely affected by the proposed changes, and this is compounded by fear of a future clouded with ambiguity and uncertainty (fear of the unknown).

■ People feel a sense of apathy due to powerlessness and are not well disposed to the proposals for change.

■ Individuals are influenced by group norms – for example, the group is critical of individualised incentive schemes (performance-related pay) – and as a consequence resist the proposed change.

■ Organisational systems are elaborate (e.g. entrenched bureaucratic processes and practices) with an inbuilt resistance to overhauling them even when justified (e.g. in the case of introducing total quality management (TQM) which disperses power); this is because of an attachment to the view that they are functional in maintaining stability. In fact there could be a certain inertia that acts as a counterbalance to change.

OVERCOMING RESISTANCE

A number of measures to overcome resistance to change have been proposed (Fernandez and Rainey, 2006; Eccles, 1994). Some of the measures, which can be viewed as negative, are unlikely to appeal to the HRM specialist. These are 'coercion' in the form of direct threats or force to elicit compliance; or 'manipulation', which amounts to distorting facts and figures so that they look more attractive, or withholding negative data so that the change scenario is more acceptable to the resisters. The following are the positive measures to overcome resistance to change.

Communication

If the source of resistance is poor communication, then action should be taken to communicate with employees specifying clearly the rationale for the change (e.g. change is crucial for the success of the organisation). It is a good idea to keep people fully informed by disseminating all relevant information; as a result, there is less likelihood of rumour or conjecture being a problem. It is also sensible to allow employees time to consider the proposals, and when they respond one should listen carefully to their reaction. When proposals for change are likely to challenge cherished organisational values (e.g. seniority-based pay), solicit the views of influential employees with relevant experience. As a general principle, it is not a bad idea to involve those likely to oppose the change in the decision-making process related to it, in particular those who can make a valid contribution to this form of participation, on the understanding that they are more likely to accept decisions to which they have had an input (i.e. they own the problem). Also, opinion leaders and natural leaders could be targeted to assist with getting the message across to the rank and file. One could also target middle managers who are supporters of change.

Other factors

A bargaining process could be mounted where some position is conceded in return for more compliant behaviour on the part of the resisters. Those who initiate change will benefit from being flexible and adaptable because they need to be receptive to good ideas from those who are reacting to the change proposals. In the final analysis, if people have strong fears and anxieties about the proposed changes some form of counselling and skills development could be beneficial.

Psychological impact

It is understandable that news of profound changes affecting the individual's job or place of work can arouse deep psychological feelings related to self-esteem and achievement, which in turn affect the level of motivation and performance. A 'cycle of coping', which covers five stages and traces the individual's reaction to change, has been proposed (Carnall, 1990). The pronouncements in the cycle of coping that now follow might be viewed as generalisations; however, reflecting on them when considering the management of change could be useful.

Stage 1 is 'denial' as the individual is confronted with the proposal for change. A typical reaction is that change is unnecessary, and there could be an enhancement of the person's self-esteem because of an attachment to the present way of doing things. Where a group is involved the threat posed by the proposal for change could lead to a reinforcement of the ties between members and performance remains stable.

Stage 2 is 'defence' and at this stage the realities of the decision to institute change become apparent as early deliberations lead to the formulation of concrete plans and programmes. Faced with this outcome people become defensive in order to defend both their jobs and the way they have executed their duties and responsibilities. This stage produces an adverse effect, which manifests itself as a lowering of self-esteem, motivation and performance.

Stage 3 is 'discarding' and, unlike the previous stages, which emphasised the past, this stage puts the spotlight on the future. There is a change in perceptions as people realise that change is necessary and inevitable. Although performance is still on the decline, there are signs that self-esteem is improving as people get to grips with the new situation.

Stage 4 is 'adaptation', where people are beginning to come to terms with the new techniques and processes. Naturally it will be necessary to modify and refine the new system and if people are involved in this exercise they are likely to experience an increase in their self-esteem. However, performance still lags behind the growing level of motivation, particularly in situations where it was necessary to have an understanding of new methods and techniques.

Stage 5 is 'internalisation', where people finally make sense of what has happened, and the newly adopted behaviour is now becoming part of people's repertoire of behaviour. One could now expect an improvement in self-esteem and motivation and this coupled with the better use of people's abilities could give rise to raised levels of performance.

Managing change

An organisation must try to anticipate change, not merely respond to it. If so, the planning and management of organisational change must become part of the organisation's strategy. In this section we are going to examine the following schools of thought: (i) force field model, (ii) continuous change process model, (iii) emergent approach, and (iv) Kotter's model

FORCE FIELD MODEL

Before setting out to plan change it is well to recognise the existence of a state of equilibrium between the forces for change and the forces against change. In accordance with Lewin's (1951) force field model this equilibrium must be disturbed in a planned way in order to bring about change. This is done by strengthening the forces for change or weakening the forces against change, or taking both courses of action. However, at the beginning it is likely to be a difficult task to identify the forces for and against change. Lewin postulates a model that could be useful as a means of understanding the process of change from the old to the new situation. It consists of:

$$\text{Unfreezing} \rightarrow \text{Changing} \rightarrow \text{Refreezing}$$

People are not normally receptive to change when they are locked into a state where they are attached to traditional values supportive of the status quo (i.e. they are frozen). It is necessary to unfreeze this state before progress can be made in getting people to adopt new ideas and work methods. The unfreezing stage consists of a number of courses of action, such as highlighting the benefits of moving to the new situation, challenging the status quo and the attitudes that underpin it, using appropriate information and discussion in a supportive atmosphere to remove the psychological defences, and facilitating the movement from the status quo to the new situation by measures such as advice and skills training.

After the unfreezing has taken place we move to the changing stage, where the planned changes in the work situation are implemented. It is hoped that the anticipated benefits have materialised. If so, the final stage – refreezing – has arrived. At this stage the changes to structure (e.g. the development of a more focused and flexible organisation) or processes together with the underlying attitudes and behaviour need to be refrozen so that they can be sustained over time. If this stage is not successfully negotiated there is the danger of reverting to the previous equilibrium state. On the other hand, if the refreezing has gone ahead without a hitch, then the new situation is stabilised as the driving and restraining forces for change are balanced.

CONTINUOUS CHANGE PROCESS MODEL

A model of managing change – called the *continuous change process* model – puts particular emphasis on the role of top management and change agents. Top management specifies the changes that are necessary (e.g. the changes which are crucial in the realisation of corporate objectives), discuss with employees the alternatives available and what the outcome is likely to be (Bhuiyan *et al.*, 2006; Kotter, 1995), and ensure that all parts of the organisation act in unison, supported by HRM strategies (Bredin and Soderlund, 2006; Mabey *et al.*, 1998). Obviously it would beneficial if top management had the right leadership skills, temperament and commitment, and that its proposals were unlikely to be seriously undermined by the prevailing organisational climate and culture (McKenna, 2006).

Change agents, who are either internal or external consultants, have the responsibility for managing the multitude of activities connected with bringing about the desired change. It stands to reason that they should be enthusiastic about the prospect of change and accept the challenges and opportunities it offers, and have the personal qualities and political skills to do a difficult job, which includes relating effectively with managers and others who are involved in the change process. The latter have to be convinced that the proposed changes are necessary and should be given appropriate help and encouragement, including training (Beer, 1980; Buchanan and Badham, 1999; Egan, 1994). Buchanan *et al.* (1999) call for a more effective role for the change agent because of their reservations about the way change management is normally handled.

EMERGENT APPROACH

While acknowledging the important part played by top management in managing change, there is a view that it is functional in dynamic and uncertain business environments to recognise the limited power of managers at the apex of the organisation to prescribe corporate renewal (Beer *et al.*, 1990). This view is encapsulated in the '*emergent approach*' to managing change (Tsoukas and Chia, 2002), where it is conceded that there is scope for initiating and implementing change from the bottom up rather than the top down (Sminia and Van Nistelrooij, 2006). In such circumstances managers further down the organisation can make an important contribution to the change process, and senior managers can learn from those closer to the scene of action. In the emergent approach one has to recognise the existence of power relationships and the strength of interest groups, and acknowledge the need to reconcile the needs of the organisation with the varied interests of its members; also, participants have to recognise the imperfect nature of knowledge and the short attention spans of individuals (Burnes, 1996). In such an approach the role of the manager is likely to be one of facilitation, building-in a variety of views and enabling contributors to develop solutions to problems and new ways of working. This is in contrast to more traditional forms of leadership that typically focus on setting a vision and goals.

KOTTER'S MODEL

Earlier we saw in the continuous change process model that top leaders are influential in articulating the company's vision and setting the agenda for major change. But one must recognise that managers and employees throughout the organisation are involved in the process of change. In Kotter's model of a change process there are eight stages that can be used to successfully implement change (Kotter and Cohen, 2002), and there is a recognition of the validity of the continuous change process and to some extent the emergent approach as well.

The stages, listed below, could be viewed as a change process moving through time, though not necessarily moving in a linear sequence. In reality stages can overlap and change agents need to go back to earlier steps.

- Establish a sense of urgency: Make it clear that change is really necessary for the organisation to survive and prosper. This stage helps with the unfreezing aspect of the Lewin model discussed earlier.

- Establish a coalition: Those who wish to institute change must recognise the need to put together a strong enough team to direct the process, otherwise the change initiative is unlikely to get off the ground. Hence the need to build a coalition of people throughout the organisation who have enough power and influence to lead the change process.

- Create a vision and strategy for change: The guiding coalition should develop a shared realistic vision that provides useful guidance and can easily be communicated to those affected by the change and appeals to their interests.

- Communicate the vision and strategy through a combination of words, deeds and symbols.

- Remove obstacles (such as inappropriate organisation structure, HRM techniques, or values and beliefs) that impede the accomplishment of the new vision, and empower people to move ahead.

- Produce visible signs of progress in the form of short-term victories: Ensure that people involved in making things happen receive recognition for their good work.

- Stick to the change process and refuse to give up when conditions get tough, and don't declare victories or achievements too soon.

- Nurture and shape a new culture to support the improvements and innovations that are taking root: Show that the change has brought about beneficial alterations or modifications to attitudes, behaviour and organisational processes, which in turn have resulted in improved performance. There should be constant reminders of the benefits of the changes introduced until they form part of the accepted culture of the organisation.

Bolman and Deal (2003) have taken Kotter's model and combined it with four ways in which they view organisations (i.e. the structure, symbolic (culture), human resource and political frames) and claim this approach provides a powerful vehicle for successfully managing change.

For example, consider the first stage (developing a sense of urgency) of Kotter's model and apply the Bolman and Deal 'frames' to it. Strategies from the HR, political and symbolic areas all contribute. Symbolically leaders can construct a persuasive story by painting a picture of the current challenge or crisis and why failure to act would be catastrophic. Human resource techniques of participation and open meetings would help to get the story out and gauge audience reaction. Behind the scenes leaders could meet with key players, assess their interests and negotiate or use power as necessary to get people on board.

Another example, Kotter's fifth stage, calls for removing obstacles and empowering people to move forward. Structurally, this is a matter of identifying rules, roles, procedures and patterns blocking progress, and then working to realign them. Symbolically, a few public hangings (e.g. firing, demoting or exiling prominent opponents) could reinforce the message. Meanwhile, the HR frame resorts to counselling and training and provides support and resources to enable people to master new behaviours.

Consider for a moment the emphasis on training in the last sentence. Many change initiatives fail because managers do not spend sufficient time and money developing the necessary new knowledge and skills. But apart from the lack of formal training, there are other contributory factors responsible for the unsuccessful implementation of change. From studies of both successful and unsuccessful change efforts in organisations around the world, Kotter and Cohen (2002) concluded that too many change initiatives fail because they rely too much on data gathering, analysis, report writing, and presentations, instead of a more creative approach aimed at grabbing the feelings that motivate useful action. Therefore, the efforts of change agents are not as effective as they might be because they rely entirely on reason and structure, and neglect human, political and symbolic – culture – elements (Bolman and Deal, 2003). The change conducted at the British Museum (see Case example 4.1) exemplifies a process that incorporates several of Kotter and Cohen's stages of change and Bolman and Deal's frames.

CHANGE AT THE BRITISH MUSEUM

In 2002 the British Museum was regarded as being 'in crisis' (Edwards, 2005). There had been a down-turn in tourism (following the September 11 tragedy) and a considerable reduction in government subsidies. This led to the need to reduce the cost base by £6.5 million. 135 job losses were planned, and as a result the Museum suffered its first strike action in its 250-year history. After initial headcount reductions, the HR strategy was to re-establish the values and skills of staff and to challenge the old structure and industrial relations.

A project was undertaken to establish the core values of the Museum. This had to be achieved as an initial step as it would lay the foundations for establishing a competency framework and skill development. As Martin Moore, Head of HR put it, 'Unless you know precisely what it is you are about, how do you know what training and development you should invest in?' (Edwards, 2005: 32). A Group of 50 people from across the organisation took part in a series of workshops to consider the values. An initial draft had been developed by the directorate and this was opened up for debate. The values of stewardship, openness, providing insights, diversity and excellence were settled on as being meaningful to the staff. Whilst it was felt that the external image of the Museum was well established, the needs of staff were less well catered for.

The response included an innovative approach to training and development. In a programme entitled 'Museum Mission Impossible' security and gallery staff spent time in other museums around the country. They observed the practice in these other organisations, concentrating on staff organisation and customer-related activities. On their return, the staff were thought of as the experts. They made presentations of their conclusions and contributed suggestions for developments. The intention of this programme was not only to gather information, it was also to empower front-line staff.

They subsequently suggested that language training would be beneficial. This enabled them to address visitors in their own language in some cases (e.g. giving directions). These initiatives brought people together from different parts of the organisation and enabled them to acquire skills that were directly relevant to their jobs.

The trade unions had reacted to the initial changes and needs for cuts with understandable opposition. The reaction to this was to seek to build a new style of relationship with the union. The staff body was 90 per cent unionised, and so this was an important issue. Rather than excluding the unions, representatives were brought into decision making to 'represent the interests of staff and what's best for the organisation. That's how you get a partnership' (Moore, quoted in Edwards, 2005: 33). The unions saw this as 'refreshing' and representing a much more open attitude from management. 'It was beneficial for both sides. Because we've had a say in it, it has taken away any problems we've got with it. If you're involved in something from the start and are consulted, it's easier to go forward' (Peter Clennell, trade union site chair, quoted in Edwards, 2005: 33).

The new approach resulted in a restructuring. Rather than the traditional hierarchy a 'family structure' consisting of five professional groups was being developed.

This change process can be examined through the lens of Kotter and Cohen's (2002) theory. There was a clear sense of urgency, and a coalition incorporating front-line staff was established to develop the vision and communicate about the change. Obstacles and forms of resistance were overcome, not through coercion, but through involvement. Bolman and Deal's (2003) frame analysis is also applicable. The downsizing represented one form of structural change and the negative reaction to this was met with a symbolic initiative of the development of new core values. There were some power changes, both through empowerment of the front-line staff in investigating good practice elsewhere and in a partnership relationship with the union. In these instances, the management were letting go of some of their power and transferring it to others. The changing basis of working with the union and the upskilling of the workforce represent HR initiatives. Finally, the structural frame came back into play as the Museum reviewed and refined its traditional bureaucracy.

Questions

1. Which aspects of the change management approach at the British Museum would be likely to enhance trust between management and workers?

2. Why might the issue of trust be particularly important in managing change?

OVERVIEW

When reflecting on models of change we should take particular note of the view expressed by Dawson (2003). In his 'processual/contextual' perspective on change he maintains that there are no universal prescriptions on how best to manage change. Major change is both a complicated and political process that takes time to plan and implement. It is important that change strategies are sensitive to the HR considerations and the context in which they will take root. It must be recognised that change is a phenomenon that is perceived differently by the various actors within the organisation and that communication is an essential ingredient in the change process. Involvement in the change process is a learning experience whether or not it is successful. Training is a natural complement to change, but all too often training is inadequate to underpin change.

Organisational development

Organisational development (OD) is part of the process of planned change and has as its remit the improvement of organisational functioning. It relies on a number of interventionist strategies ranging from modifications to structure and processes to the use of therapeutic techniques and counselling. If it is properly applied, individuals and groups are likely to be better able to solve problems and the organisation ought to be better equipped to respond to the external environment. In the past OD was preoccupied to a significant extent with the improvement of interpersonal relationships, and placed less emphasis on organisational efficiency and effectiveness (Cummings and Worley, 2004). Today it is broader in its perspective and takes its cue from strategic planning. Normally you would expect OD techniques or interventions to apply at three levels: the organisation, the task and the individual/group.

ORGANISATION

Some scholars (e.g. Thompson, 1990) believe that restructuring the organisation (e.g. delayering) is an effective way to bring about change. The result could be that employees are given revised or new duties and responsibilities and as a consequence pressure is put on them to change their attitudes and behaviour. Elsewhere in this text we have seen the application of various techniques and processes (TQM, BPR, new technology – see Chapter 5) to bring about significant changes so as to improve the performance and competitiveness of the organisation. Other complementary methods for transforming organisations (e.g. changing culture and utilising the learning organisation – see Chapter 10) are likely to be a useful means of bringing about change. Typically, such large-scale changes would utilise an 'unfreeze – change – refreeze' approach (Lewin, 1951).

Changes to the whole organisation have the advantage of being all encompassing. They can be used to generate a new mind-set and behaviour-set amongst the employees. Psychological denial of, and resistance to, change on this scale are difficult to sustain. However, disadvantages include the fact that the resources required and the disruption caused are considerable. There is also a danger that repeated restructuring could have a detrimental impact on the attitudes of employees to change as they may start to experience 'change fatigue'. This has been the case for some employees in the British National Health Service, where they feel that they have not yet fully adapted to the last restructuring before the next one comes along (Beech et al., 2004). The result can be a degree of cynicism about how genuine and long lasting the changes will be. This phenomenon may become more general if organisations continue to be subject to increasing change in the social, political and economic arenas.

TASK

It is felt that certain tasks are no longer as relevant as they used to be, and a strategy of job redesign is necessary. In this case job redesign is the intervention strategy. This could result in an enrichment of certain jobs and recognition that some tasks are superfluous to requirements. In Chapter 9 there is an examination of motivational techniques based on job redesign. Tasks are specified in the job description for a post. Traditionally, job descriptions would provide considerable detail, but nowadays they tend to be less specific and more open. The purpose behind this change is to establish an expectation from the outset that the tasks employees have will not remain fixed throughout their term of employment. (These issues are discussed in relation to recruitment and selection in Chapter 7.) Changes in the nature of tasks may lead to training needs as there is a requirement for new skills or knowledge.

INDIVIDUAL/GROUP

There are OD strategies or interventions aimed at changing the attitudes and behaviour of employees, apart from training and development discussed in Chapter 10. Among the well-known, people-focused, change techniques that put the accent on changing attitudes and behaviour are sensitivity training, process consultation, survey feedback, team building and intergroup development.

Sensitivity training

This technique is also referred to as encounter groups, or 'T'- (training) groups. Its objectives are to give people the opportunity to develop awareness of their own behaviour, how others see them, greater sensitivity to the behaviour of others and a better understanding of group processes. The main method used to change behaviour is group interaction in an unstructured setting. For example, a group of 10–15 members interact in an environment characterised by openness and frankness, and they discuss information about themselves and the dynamics of the group. A trainer or adviser is in attendance but refrains from taking a directional stand. Instead he or she creates a setting where people feel able to express their thoughts and feelings. An outcome from a successfully run 'T'-group would be that people are better able to empathise with others, are better able to listen to others, are less inhibited, are more tolerant of others' points of view and are better equipped to confront conflict situations. However, some individuals could find the experience traumatic and the permanency of the benefits is questionable because of the difficulty in transplanting the changed behaviour to the place of work. This could be due to the fact that normal organisational conditions are not conducive to conditions of openness and trust (Makin *et al.*, 1989).

Process consultation

This technique bears some similarity to sensitivity training but is more task oriented, having as its major aim the resolution of interpersonal problems in order to improve organisational effectiveness. In process consultation an outside consultant helps a group (e.g. a management group), who is the client, to solve their own problems (Bedingham and Thomas, 2006; Schein, 1969). The consultant will need to establish whether the project is of interest and one that he or she can handle, and that the client is interested. If so, together they diagnose the problem and explore the most likely solution. The able consultant, adept at devising pertinent questions and listening, uses the interview rather than the questionnaire for gathering information.

Consultants use interventions, such as setting the agenda with the group, provide feedback and offer coaching or counselling. The consultant's role is a sensitive one because all questions asked can be viewed as interventions. The focus is on people-centred problems, helping the client to perceive and understand better key organisational problems, but not suggesting solutions. Also, people are encouraged to come forward with their own solutions to the interpersonal problems they face. Generally, as stated above, the consultant does not offer solutions to technical problems; but there may be exceptional circumstances when technical advice is offered. It needs restating that the consultant's expertise is essentially in the domain of problem diagnosis and developing the most appropriate group dynamics. The consultant can help the group locate a technical expert if it is obvious that this type of help is needed. When questioned about the use of general consultants in change management, many HR professionals expressed a negative view (Kent, 2005). However, it is argued that the reason for this problem is that there is often inadequate management of the consultant by the client. Some organisations hand over too much control to the consultant, rather than identifying key inputs that the consultant can make. This could be an expertise in the process of change (as is the case with process consultation), or specialist skills that the organisation cannot provide itself. Important issues to consider in the relationship between the consultant and the client are the psychological contract between them, the question of trust, and the consultant not being viewed simply as the expert. Finally, a sensitive issue is the disengagement by the consultant and an evaluation of the effectiveness of the process consultation.

Survey feedback

This technique could be used to solicit views on a number of issues (e.g. communication, job satisfaction, supervision) from employees attached to particular sections or departments. At the outset a change agent interviews a cross-section of employees to establish the important issues (e.g. problems) before a questionnaire is prepared. The questionnaire is used to collect information. When the data is analysed a summary of the results are fed back to the participants in the survey (Cummings and Worley, 2004). The summary is used by the employees to help them with the identification and solution of the problem. The change agent organises feedback meetings (i.e. small 'family' groups) to promote interaction and discussion of the issues, and the feedback meetings are run by the managers. In fact the change agent's role is that of an expert and an information resource at the disposal of the group. Before the formal feedback meeting takes place, the change agent helps the manager when together they review the feedback data (e.g. communication, job satisfaction, decision making, leadership), and suggests ways of identifying and solving the various problems. At the formal feedback meeting the group discusses the issues raised by the survey data and, relying on the assistance provided by the change agent, states what they have learnt from the information presented. The next phase is when action plans for improvements are proposed; this stage could require a number of meetings. Finally, there is the implementation of the proposals for solving the problems.

Team building

It is natural to focus on team building as a technique because there are many situations in organisations where members of a team or group frequently work in an interdependent fashion. Interdependency is crucial in teamwork, and so is coordination of the efforts of the group members if a successful outcome is to materialise. The major objective of team building is to create a healthy climate of trust between members and to foster high levels of interaction with the ultimate aim of improving specific aspects of the performance of the team. In team building it will be necessary to make a serious examination of the group's goals and priorities, clarification of each member's role in the group, evaluation of the group's performance, analysis of the problems encountered by the group, and sensitivity to the overall dynamics of the group. During the team-building process different perceptions will surface, and a critical perspective should apply to an appraisal of both the means and the ends in the context of group functioning. A change agent could be employed to facilitate the above activities and help with exploring action plans aimed at bringing about the necessary change. An example of a movement to teamworking appears in Case example 4.2.

CASE EXAMPLE 4.2

TEAMWORKING AT THE INLAND REVENUE

Employees at the Inland Revenue (now renamed Revenue & Customs) worked for many years on an individual basis in their own particular areas and in a unionised environment. When the manager of the main office of the Inland Revenue in Portsmouth was grappling with the idea of introducing team systems of working he was aware of that tradition. He was committed to teamworking because of a belief that this system of working would lead to greater employee involvement, job satisfaction and the realisation of people's potential for the benefit of the business. He knew that teamworking was part of a much wider change programme launched by the Inland Revenue in the early 1990s and recognised that trying to enforce teamworking too quickly would not produce the desired effect.

The manager therefore formed a task group to establish whether teamworking was an appropriate vehicle to process work activities within his domain and, if so, the form it should take. After identifying likely difficulties, the task force felt that it would be desirable to pilot teamworking to a limited extent in the first instance. The services of a change agent were available at the conception and implementation stages of the scheme, and useful information (interpreted for the benefit of management) was provided as a result of his fact-finding exercises. Subsequently, when teamworking was in place it was found that the managers reporting to the overall office manager were operating as self-management teams, making their own decisions on operational matters without having to refer everything upwards, which was previously the case in the traditional hierarchy. These managers now enjoyed autonomy in the way the work was processed, although they had to operate within strict guidelines. The main guideline is that they must involve their subordinates when it comes to reorganising the work.

In this case the emphasis was on teamworking that cut across traditional functional (lateral) and hierarchical (vertical) lines, and it was done gradually in order to elicit support and to bring about a change in culture.

Source: based on Arkin, 1997

Activity

Analyse the Inland Revenue case by comparing the steps taken to Kotter and Cohen's model, which was introduced above.

An interesting example of team building is a model of management team development devised by Dyer (1984). The major objective of the team building session is to remove barriers to the smooth functioning of the team (i.e. to clarify roles, correct misunderstandings, advocate more sharing of information, be more creative). In the first instance data is collected to establish the causes of the problems. The change agent or consultant is committed to open discussion and acts as a catalyst – i.e. an observer/facilitator with a focus similar to the process consultation consultant – and the manager acts as group leader. To start with, the team assembles at a location away from its place of work. Before the team building session starts in earnest the following questions are asked:

- What group practices are worth preserving?

- What behaviour or practices are undermining or interfering with the effectiveness of the team?

- What are the team's proposals for improving the quality of the working relationships within the team and its overall functioning?

At the meeting, answers to these questions are discussed and, using a flip chart, the following points could be emphasised: identification of the barriers to individual and team effectiveness, the tasks people enjoy doing, and the suggestions made for improvements. The next step is for the problems facing the team to be prioritised; this forms the agenda for the remainder of the meeting. The objectives of the session will be re-examined in relation to what has happened. In practice, certain issues will be resolved, others referred to a working party, and yet others remain unresolved. Finally, strategies for action are stipulated, and in this context it is important to secure the commitment of the team leader (the manager) and the change agent (the consultant) to the implementation of the proposals.

The outcome of a serious research project into successful team performance underlined the importance of 'role heterogeneity' – that is, different group members are capable of performing different roles within a team (Belbin, 1993). For example, it would be functional to have members with the following skills: capable of chairing a meeting effectively; full of good ideas; a capacity to ensure that deadlines are met; an ability to put ideas into practice; able to inject useful information into a discussion and negotiate with external agencies; a facility to move the debate forward so that agreement can be reached; able to evaluate individual contributions and analyse complex situations; and able to provide social support to members. A team could consist of individuals each possessing a single but different skill, but it would be more realistic to assume that any one individual has the capacity to exercise more than one skill. If so, this would be a useful resource in a small team consisting of a few members.

At this stage one may very well ask if teamwork penetrates the upper echelons of the organisation. It is sometimes said that senior executives sing the praises of teamwork at lower levels of the organisation, but when it comes to themselves, they often exhibit aloofness and blinkered perspectives (Hambrick, 2000). According to Hambrick, chief executives are resistant to teamwork at the top level, fearing that it amounts to an abdication of their leadership role, or that it runs counter to their organisation culture of unit accountability and initiative. What these executives do not understand is that an effective top management team greatly extends the capabilities of the chief executive; it rarely dilutes them. He goes on to say that a well functioning top management team is an important complement to individual effort directed at driving the business forward. An integrated senior management team is crucial not only to diagnose the company's current predicament, and formulating a plan for large-scale change, but also to engage in implementing change.

Intergroup development

The aim of this technique is to change attitudes and the perceptions that different organisational groups (e.g. finance, marketing) have of each other, so that they are better able to communicate and cooperate. If negative views prevail, this could undermine the quality of interactions and liaisons between teams, and perhaps adversely affect efforts to coordinate activities at the organisational level. If there are problems with intergroup relationships, one could take concrete action to solve them as shown in Box 4.1.

> **Box 4.1:** Solving intergroup relationships
>
> Teams, or their leaders, get together to attempt to solve the problem and in doing so promote better relationships. To start with the groups are located in different rooms and after initial deliberations each group comes forward with its perception of the other group, as well as speculating about what the other group is saying about it. Then the groups meet in a central location to share information, conveying to the other group their perceptions of that group. In this situation the consultant's intervention is confined only to the clarification of meaning. The groups retire to their respective rooms and discuss the insights that apply to themselves and the other group. This forum offers the opportunity to clear the air with respect to differences of opinion and friction between the groups. The groups return to the central location and meet and compare their lists of the issues that divide them. They cooperate in providing lists of outstanding issues (unresolved difficulties) and prioritise them. Action plans to solve the difficulties are created in the expectation that they will be implemented. Finally, it is important to evaluate the implementation of the plans.
>
> Source: Liebowitz and De Meuse, 1982

In contemporary organisations the individual/organisational approach (i.e. people centred approach) to organisational development is not as important as it was in the past. The preferred overall approach nowadays is change management, and its strength is that it draws on a variety of approaches, including the three approaches examined above, to improve organisational performance (Worren *et al.*, 1999).

Finally, note the verdict on OD from Bradford and Burke (2004). Answering the question 'Does OD have a future?', the authors came forward with the following answer:

> 'We believe OD has much to offer in its emphasis on releasing the human potential within the organisation. It has developed many valuable approaches. It has stressed the importance of values at a time when too much behaviour is valueless. It would be a shame to have this lost. But for the field to grow and develop, it must do more in defining what it is and what it is not. It must also be more demanding of what is required to be a competent professional. Doing that will not be easy and we do not offer easy answers.'

Appreciative inquiry

A position opposite to traditional OD is appreciative inquiry. This school of thought takes a position opposite to the traditional people-centred OD approach of identifying a problem and then finding a solution to it. In the appreciative inquiry (AI) approach, instead of being on the look out for problems, the practitioner sets out to identify the unique qualities and special strengths of the organisation. Once this is done effort is directed at improving these features so as to enhance performance and organisational success (Copperrider and Whitney, 2000). At the heart of AI is a strong tendency to place emphasis on learning and understanding of the current system and what works within it. AI at its simplest is:

'a collaborative, participative, system-wide approach that seeks to identify, understand and enhance the life giving forces that exist within all organizations. It seeks to make positive use of the complex networks within the organization and it uses the myths and stories that fill our organizations as both a resource and a tool. Perhaps most importantly it calls upon the desire of all members of the organization to contribute and shape the world of work in which we live' (Passmore and Hain, 2005).

AI takes a Theory Y approach, where people's views are respected, people can be trusted, and there is a recognition that they need to be empowered. The organization becomes a 'possibility to be realised rather than a problem to be solved' (Passmore and Hain, 2005).

In appreciative inquiry the spotlight is on isolating what is good about the organization and making it better, rather than laying blame with the resultant defensiveness for various problems that may have surfaced. Appreciative inquiry can assist in promoting change by building on the organization's strengths. It consists of four steps within the confines of a group with a change agent in attendance and lasts for a few days.

■ Stage 1 (discovery): Group members are given the opportunity to express points of view about the qualities and strengths of the organisation.

■ Stage 2 (dreaming): The information obtained at the discovery stage is used to speculate about a possible future scenario for the organisation. For example, the group could imagine a situation at some point in the future and state in what way it is likely to be different from the situation right now.

■ Stage 3 (design): Group members will give serious consideration to the outcome of stage 2 and try to reach some form of consensus or common ground on the future shape and purpose of the organisation, isolating its unique qualities and strengths.

■ Stage 4 (describe the organisation's destiny): Building on stage 3, the emphasis will be on how the organisation can move forward to the desired or preferred state. At this stage the approach is essentially preparing action plans and implementation strategies.

Role of change and development in HRM

Some have argued (e.g. Thornhill *et al.*, 2000) that managing change is now central to HRM. The HRM specialists are frequently cast as change makers (Torrington *et al.*, 2005) who take on responsibility for leading the implementation of change through initiatives such as OD, structural change, and individual change through training or recruitment. This was the case, for example, in Rolls-Royce, where an initiative was undertaken to professionalise the HR group in the spirit of 'physician heal thyself' (Simms, 2005). The HR professionals underwent upskilling and continuous development so that they could help others do likewise. The result was a significant improvement in the perceptions of internal customers. A number of major challenges act as drivers of change, including the following:

■ Cross-national boundary working requires people to work with different cultures and to be highly adaptive in the way they perform tasks and use management styles.

■ Growth through mergers and acquisitions requires a blend of structures, processes and accepted ways of working.

■ Increasingly, there is a need for organisations to work in partnership with their employees, which can entail significant changes in decision-making processes, communication and industrial relations (Edwards, 2005).

■ There is a need for organisations to enhance performance and achieve competitive advantage through their HRM strategies.

To illustrate the link between HRM and change consider a study of firms in Korea – a country that has been undergoing major change in recent history (Bae and Lawler, 2000). Bae and Lawler examined the relationships between placing value on HRM, high involvement and organisational performance. They found that in Korea, at the initial stages of export growth and economic emergence, firms typically adopted bureaucratic HRM strategies that complemented low-cost production. However, as the country has gone through times of change and economic crisis there was a need to seek alternatives.

While some theorists have argued that in order to be coherent it is necessary for an organisation to have one unified HRM strategy, Lepak and Snell (1999) have argued that it is possible to mix strategies, such as developing staff internally and acquiring staff externally, and Bae and Lawler found a degree of mixed strategy in the Korean firms as they faced globalisation through what they termed the 'new human resource management'. This entailed high-involvement strategies, and typically placing a strong value on HRM. People were now seen as a source of competitive success (realised advantage) and there was much greater effort to empower them. This turned out to be vitally important, because of time-based competitive advantage (Pfeffer, 1994) – i.e. beating the competition by the speed of the work. This required workers who had well-developed intellectual preparation to respond on the spot with speed and sophistication. These skills were fundamental to organisational performance, particularly in times of change. The ability of workers to learn quickly, adopt technologies and translate these into practice (Hobday, 1998) differentiated the high-performance firms from those that struggled in the competitive external environment. Overall, the best performing firms were internally adaptive (i.e. they have an ability to develop new practices and processes in response to new ideas and opportunities internally, as well as responding to forces of change externally). This could be achieved through their developmental HRM strategies, which focused on involvement and creating a workforce that perceived itself to be valued (Bae and Lawler, 2000).

In the modern organisational context change is ever present, and this presents HRM with both a challenge and an opportunity to be involved and add value. The challenge is to the traditional theories of HRM that sought consistency and coherence in a set of policies and practices, which would give employees a sense of stability and meaning over time. In changing market conditions it may be necessary to adopt mixed strategies (Lepak and Snell, 1999), which are contingent upon the strategic environment (e.g. variation in demand for products, changes in the number and type of competitors) but that, nonetheless, engender commitment in the workforce. It has been argued that such an approach could reduce commitment, as employees perceive themselves being treated as a contingent variable (Legge, 1995) – contingent variable in this context means that people perceive themselves to be secondary to the purposes of the organisation. As those purposes change so will people be required to change! For example, by using short-term contracts, people's services can be dispensed with when demand falls. Evidence from the United Kingdom indicates that organisations frequently do not adopt 'complete models', such as high-commitment management; instead they use the mixed approach, which yields performance benefits for the firm (Wood and de Menezes, 1998).

The indications from studies such as those of Bae and Lawler (2000) are that mixed models can work as long as they incorporate involvement and equip the workforce for change through development. However, from the perspective of Pfeffer and Veiga (1999) – discussed in Chapter 2 – a fully integrated approach is preferable. This provides the opportunity for HRM to challenge traditional HRM perspectives and subscribe to individual, team and organisational development (i.e. change management through people). Case example 4.3 shows how a capital investment in a service firm had to be accompanied by distinct HR change in order to be successful.

CASE EXAMPLE 4.3

TRAVELODGE – MATCHING CAPITAL INVESTMENT WITH HR CHANGE

In 2003 the hotel chain Travelodge was experiencing some difficulties. In a survey, whilst nine out of 10 people recognised the brand, they regarded it as 'cold, masculine and stuck in the 1980s' (Hope, 2005: 16). The company was bought by venture capitalist Permira Investment Fund Managers and embarked on significant change. The aim was fast expansion with a new hotel opening every 10 days in 2005 and a doubling of size being the target for 2011. This would involve the creation of 4,500 new jobs.

Significant investment was put into the buildings, both existing and new build. Rooms were redecorated and updated with the aim of producing a warm and inviting experience for customers. However, achieving such a customer experience is also down to the skills and attitudes of staff. 'People want a welcoming smile. Our staff need to be customer-focused, warm, natural people who like to give good service. . . . if we don't get the people aspect right then we don't have a business' (Angus Stewart, HR Director, quoted in Hope, 2005: 16). However, in some locations staff turnover was as high as 80 per cent, so ensuring knowledgeable, high-quality customer service was not an easy task. In addition, at the time of the acquisition, staff were uncertain about the future.

A set of values, based on being simple, fair, friendly and efficient was established. A communication process called 'teamtalk' was initiated. Staff in each hotel were allowed to nominate a spokesperson and a national staff forum was set up. Managers were able to find out directly from staff what their concerns were, and staff representatives were able to have a say in defining issues and identifying ways forward. An incentive scheme offered rewards of up to £1,000 for suggestions.

The recruitment strategy changed both its focus and process. Instead of recruiting on the basis of competencies, the emphasis was placed on attitude. In jobs such as receptionist, people needed a welcoming attitude and the willingness to be trained. In city centre locations, where turnover was often high, a process referred to as 'speed recruitment' was undertaken. This built on the cultural phenomenon of 'speed dating'. Candidates would have a series of short one-to-one conversations to find out what the job entailed and determine their suitability. Selection of managers also emulated popular culture. A 'Management Idol' talent contest was conducted in which potential managers would attend 'auditions' which incorporated role-plays, interviews and assessment workshops that sought to bring out people's personalities. The style of these recruitment initiatives was intended to give a clear message about the culture of Travelodge and to stimulate a more relaxed climate in which person-to-person service was emphasised.

The performance targets were demanding, and wages for some jobs, such as room cleaning, were not high. Therefore, approaches other than payment were needed to retain and motivate people. Term-time only contracts were found to be popular as they allowed parents to look after their children during school holidays. Training also had to be both effective and efficient. Because the business was a 24/7 operation it was difficult to reach all staff with training opportunities. The answer was to establish a bus that toured the United Kingdom delivering training at the hotel sites. This approach had saved the company £100,000 in a year by reducing the need to hire venues and take staff away for overnight training sessions.

In this setting, return on investment was a high priority and many of the jobs were not high status or knowledge-oriented. However, the HR changes were vital to the company's ability to pursue its growth strategy, and Travelodge developed some innovative and popular ways to meet the challenges. Travelodge was sold to Dubai International Captial in 2006. The view was that the brand was strong, and that there were excellent opportunities for growth (Sameer Al Ansari, Chief Executive, Dubai International Capital, 2006). The aim was to be the leading provider of budget accommodation for the 2012 Olympics in the United Kingdom. This strategy of continued growth is supported by innovation. For example, Travelodge has led on internet bookings, with 80 per cent of sales being booked on line by 2006 (Ranger, 2006). Further development was planned with the website operating a membership system, a ratefinder tool and personalised routes through the website to concentrate on what customers prefer in their journey from enquiry to hotel stay.

Question

The change at Travelodge was conducted in order to meet business targets and the business was sold following the changes. To what extent do you think the changes can be regarded as organisation development?

Conclusions

In this chapter we have discussed some of the factors in putting change management through people into practice. It is necessary to understand the potential psychological effects of change, resistance and various means of engaging with and overcoming such resistance. While in some forms of traditional management coercive strategies of change were popular, the more recent research evidence indicates that superior organisational performance is achieved through people-centred approaches to change. Coercion is likely to alienate the workforce and build up resistance. Involvement and development are more likely to equip employees to be flexible and adaptable in the face of the demands of globalisation, the need for rapid reaction to customers, the adoption of new technology and the enactment of emergent strategy (referred to in connection with the descriptive school of strategy in Chapter 2) that are associated with organisational success.

Communication plays a significant role in managing change. Effective communication has been highlighted in the high-performance models of HRM (Becker and Huselid,

1999) and in the context of change it is crucial in ensuring that the various parties retain an open mind and perceive the messages that were really intended by others. Genuinely open communication is only likely to occur where there is a supportive organisational culture and an understanding by management of the implications of change for the workforce. For example, care is needed to match the appropriate management style with the 'stage of coping' or the level of resistance the workforce exhibits. Of course there are circumstances in which ideas for innovation occur not only in the management group but throughout the organisation. Various techniques of organisational development, such as process consultation, team building and intergroup development, can be used to encourage change and development and build on the potential of the whole organisation. Lastly, it is worth noting that change is likely to entail people thinking and acting differently, and so managing change plays a central role in HRM activities.

Review and reflection questions

1. Why might people resist change?

2. What are the psychological stages of coping with change?

3. What are the stages of Kotter and Cohen's model of change?

4. What is organisation development?

5. What activities are employed in OD processes?

6. Why is change considered a central aspect of HRM practice?

7. What are the implications of a HRM philosophy for the way change is managed?

Activities

If you are in work:

Think through a change you have experienced at work.

1. Use Kotter and Cohen's model of change to assess the change

   (a) Did activities take place at each stage of the model?

   (b) Did the order of activities reflect the model?

2. How were the management and leadership of the change received by employees?

If you are in full-time study:

Compare the examples of the British Museum and Travelodge.

1. What was the impetus for change?

2. What processes of change were implemented?

3. To what extent did the examples relate to the theories of Kotter and Cohen and/or Bolman and Deal?

4. How do you think the change programmes were received by employees?

Further reading and research

The following references provide academic insight into the nature of change management, including a pluralistic perspective and an exploration of the links between theory and practice.

Buchanan, D. and Dawson, P. (2007) 'Discourse and audience: Organizational change as a multi-story process', *Journal of Management Studies*, 44, 669–686.

Burnes, B. (2004) 'Kurt Lewin and the planned approach to change. A reappraisal', *Journal of Management Studies*, 41, 977–1002.

Hayes, J. (2002) *The theory and practice of change management*, Basingstoke, Hants: Palgrave.

Change management is a difficult task, and there are many backward steps. The following references provide some insight into the reasons for difficulties in change management.

Baxter, L. and Macleod, A. (2007) 'Change Management: Unhappy endings', *People Management*, 5 April, 39–40.

Sirkin, H.L., Keenan, P. and Jackson, A. (2005) 'The hard side of change management', *Harvard Business Review*, October, 109–118.

Wright, G., van der Heijden, K., Bradfield, R. and Cairns, G. (2004) 'The psychology of why organizations can be slow to adapt and change', *Journal of General Management*, 29, 21–36.

The topics of change and ethics are linked very effectively on the Government Office for the South West's website, www.oursouthwest.com. The pages are concerned with resource efficiency and corporate responsibility and guidance is provided on managing change with the purpose of achieving greater sustainability. Key factors in this process are: pressure for change; clear shared vision; capacity for change; and action. There is a revealing section entitled 'worst practice in managing change'!

The CIPD provides a helpful podcast on the management of change (www.cipd.uk/podcasts, see episode 3). Presenters include Professor Michael West, Professor of Organisational Psychology at Aston University, Vicky Wright in her role as CIPD president and Kevin Green, the People and OD Director of the Royal Mail.

References

Al Ansari, S. (2006) quoted in 'Dubai firm buys Travelodge hotels', BBC news, http://news.bbc.co.uk.

Arkin, A. (1997) 'Tax incentives', *People Management*, 3, 36–38.

Bae, J. and Lawler, J.J. (2000) 'Organizational and HRM Strategies in Korea: impact on firm performance in an emerging economy', *Academy of Management Journal*, 43, 502–517.

Becker, B.E. and Huselid, M.A. (1999) 'Overview: strategic human resource management in five leading firms', *Human Resource Management*, 38, 287–301.

Bedeian, A.G. and Zammuto, R.F. (1991) *Organizations: Theory and Design*, Orlando, FL: Dryden Press.

Bedingham, K. and Thomas, T. (2006) 'Issues in the implementation of strategic change programmes and a potential tool to enhance the process', *International Journal of Strategic Change Management*, 1, 113–126.

Beech, N., Burns, H., de Caestecker, L., MacIntosh, R. and MacLean, D. (2004) 'Paradox as an invitation to act in problematic change situations', *Human Relations*, 57, 1313–1332.

Beer, M. (1980) *Organizational Change and Development: A systems view*, Santa Monica, CA: Goodyear.

Beer, M., Eisenstat, R.A. and Spector, B. (1990) 'Why change programmes don't produce change', *Harvard Business Review*, November/December, 158–166.

Belbin, R.M. (1993) *Team Roles at Work*, Oxford: Butterworth Heinemann.

Bhuiyan, N., Baghel, A. and Wilson, J. (2006) 'A Sustainable Continuous Improvement Methodology at an Aerospace Company', *International Journal of Productivity and Performance Management*, 55, 671–687.

Bolman, L.G. and Deal, T.E. (2003) *Reframing Organizations: artistry, choice, and leadership*, San Francisco, CA: Jossey-Bass.

Bradford, D.L. and Burke, W.W. (2004) 'Is OD in crisis?', *The Journal of Applied Behavioural Science*, 40, 369–373.

Bredin, K. and Soderlund, J. (2006) 'Perspectives on Human Resource Management: an explorative study of the consequences of projectification in four firms', *International Journal of Human Resources Development*, 6, 92–113.

Buchanan, D. and Badham, R. (1999) 'Politics and organizational change: the lived experience', *Human Relations*, 52, 609–630.

Buchanan, D., Clayton, T. and Doyle, M. (1999) 'Organization development and change: the legacy of the nineties', *Human Resource Management Journal*, 9, 20–37.

Burnes, B. (1996) 'No such thing as one best way to manage organizational change', *Management Decision*, 34, 11–18.

Carnall, C. (1990) *Managing Change in Organizations*, Hemel Hemstead: Prentice Hall.

Copperrider, D.L. and Whitney, D. (2000). *Collaborating for change: Appreciative Inquiry*, San Francisco: Berrett-Koehler.

Cummings, T.G. and Worley, C.G. (2004) *Organization Development and Change*, London: Thomson.

Dawson, P. (2003) *Understanding organizational change: The contemporary experience of people at work*, London: Sage.

Dyer, W.G. (1984) *Strategies for Managing Change*, Reading, MA: Addison-Wesley.

Eccles, A. (1994) *Succeeding with Change: Implementing action driven strategies*, Maidenhead: McGraw-Hill.

Edwards, C. (2005) 'Unravelling Change', *People Management*, 11, 30–33.

Egan, G. (1994) *Working the Shadow Side: A guide to positive behind the scene management*, San Francisco, CA: Jossey-Bass.

Fernandez, S. and Rainey, H.G. (2006) 'Managing Successful Organizational Change in the Public Sector', *Public Administration Review*, 66, 168–176.

Hambrick, D.C. (2000) 'Putting the team into top management', Part 2, Mastering Management Series, *Financial Times*, 9 October, 6–7.

Herrmann, P. and Datta, D.K. (2005) 'Relationships between Top Management Team Characteristics and International Diversification: An Empirical Investigation', *British Journal of Management*, 16, 69–78.

Hobday, M. (1998) 'Latecomer catch-up strategies in electronics: Samsung of Korea and ACER of Taiwan', *Asia Pacific Business Review*, 4, 48–83.

Hope, K. (2005) Extreme Makeover. *People Management*, 11, 16–17.

Kent, S. (2005) Outer Limits. *People Management*, 11, 40–42.

Kotter, J.P. (1995) 'Leading change: why transformation efforts fail?', *Harvard Business Review*, 73, 59–67.

Kotter, J.P. and Cohen, D.S. (2002) *The heart of change. Real life stories of how people change their organizations*, Boston: Harvard Business School Press.

Legge, K. (1995) *Human Resource Management: Rhetorics and realities*, Basingstoke: Macmillan.

Lepak, D.P. and Snell, S.A. (1999) 'The human resource architecture: toward a theory of human capital allocation and development', *Academy of Management Review*, 13, 31–48.

Lewin, K. (1951) *Field Theory in Social Science*, New York: Harper & Row.

Liebowitz, S.J. and De Meuse, K.P. (1982) 'The application of teambuilding', *Human Relations*, January, 1–18.

Mabey, C., Salaman, G. and Storey, J. (eds) (1998) *Strategic Human Resource Management: A reader*, London: Sage.

McKenna, E. (2006) *Business Psychology and Organisational Behaviour*, Hove: Psychology Press.

Makin, P., Cooper, C.L. and Cox, C. (1989) *Managing People at Work*, London: Routledge/British Psychological Society.

Mintzberg, H. and Markides, C. (2000) 'Crosstalk', *Academy of Management Executive*, 14, 31–45.

Passmore, J. and Hain, D. (2005) 'Appreciative Inquiry: positive psychology for organizational change', *Selection and Development Review*, 21, 13–16.

Pfeffer, J. (1994) *Competitive Advantage Through People*, Boston, MA: Harvard Business School Press.

Pfeffer, J. and Veiga, J.F. (1999) 'Putting people first for organizational success', *Academy of Management Executive*, 13, 37–50.

Ranger, S. (2006) 'Travelodge does dynamic online booking case study', www.silicon.com/retailand leisure.

Rondinelli, D.A. and Black, S.S. (2000) 'Multinational strategic alliances and acquisitions in central and eastern Europe: partnerships in privatization', *Academy of Management Executive*, 14, 85–98.

Schein, E. (1969) *Process Consultation: Its role in organizational development*, Reading, MA: Addison-Wesley.

Simms, J. (2005) 'High Rollers', *People Management*, 11, 32–35.

Sminia, H. and Van Nistelrooij, A. (2006) 'Strategic Management and Organizational Development: Planned change in a public sector organization', *Journal of Change Management*, 6, 99–113.

Tan, C.C. (2006) 'The Theory and Practice of Change Management', *Asian Business and Management*, 5(1), 153–155.

Thompson, J.D. (1990) 'The structure of complex organization', in Pugh, D.S. (ed.), *Organisation Theory: Selected readings*, London: Penguin.

Thornhill, A., Lewis, P., Millmore, M. and Saunders, M. (2000) *Managing Change: A human resource strategy approach*, Harlow: Pearson.

Torrington, D., Hall, L. and Taylor, S. (2005) *Human Resource Management*, Harlow, England: Prentice Hall.

Tsoukas, H. and Chia, R. (2002) 'On Organizational Becoming: rethinking Organizational Change', *Organization Science*, 13, 567–582.

Wood, S. and de Menezes, L. (1998) 'High commitment management in the UK: evidence from the Workplace Industrial Relations Survey and Employers' Manpower and Skills Practices Survey', *Human Relations*, 51, 485–516.

Worren, N.A.M., Ruddle, K. and Moore, K. (1999) 'From organizational development to change management: the emergence of a new profession', *Journal of Applied Behavioural Science*, 35, 273–286.

Chapter 5

ORGANISATIONAL CULTURE

Introduction

Culture is a central and important topic in HRM. It is concerned with the values, attitudes, beliefs, assumptions, actions and procedures that people adopt in organisational life. It encompasses the range of thought and action as they are reinforced in the corporate setting, and so underlies many of the specific issues of people management. It provides the social framework for the relationship between managers and employees and as such is an influencing factor on the psychological contract, employees' willingness to accept change and the ability of the organisation to be open about, and learn from, its experience.

After reading this chapter, you should:

■ be aware of some of the main theories and models of national and organisational culture;

■ understand the dimensions that are commonly used to analyse culture;

■ be aware of the implications of culture for issues such as leadership style, teamworking and commitment;

■ understand the problems and opportunities associated with managerial attempts to change culture;

■ be able to reflect critically on the interaction between culture and HRM, and on the issues for managers operating within a particular culture.

Societal culture

Goffee (1997) defines culture as guides for living and collective mental programming developed over time. These guides are based on assumptions reflected in the attitudes, values and behaviour of individuals and groups. The assumptions are learnt, they assume a pattern and are passed down through the generations. Culture, which can also be viewed as achievements in art, literature and music in society, has been a subject of investigation in social anthropology where researchers have sought to understand the shared meanings and values held by groups in society that give significance to their actions.

So, to understand actions and behaviour at a religious ceremony in a particular country, it would be most helpful to have an insight into the underlying system of beliefs. Nationality is an important factor to consider in the context of values and behaviour. For example, there is some evidence to indicate that the Americans adhere to values associated with individuality, the Japanese are partial to conformity and cooperation in groups, while Arabs tend to steer clear of conflict and place loyalty ahead of efficiency. In looking at differences between countries considerations other than national culture should be given due weight. For example, the legal system and political institutions can shape the national character.

IMPACT OF NATIONAL CULTURES

Cultural differences between nationalities were found when the views of a large number of employees spread over many countries but employed by the same organisation were solicited (Hofestede, 1980). Hofestede concluded that national cultures could be explained with reference to the following four factors:

1. *Power distance.* This factor measures the extent to which culture prompts a person in a position of authority to exercise power. Managers operating in cultures ranked high in power distance (e.g. Argentina) behaved rather autocratically in conditions of low trust, and there was an expectation on the part of subordinates that superiors would act in a directive way. By contrast, in cultures ranked low in power distance (e.g. Canada) a closer and warmer relationship existed between superiors and subordinates, where the latter would be expected to be involved in decision making.

2. *Uncertainty avoidance.* This factor measured the extent to which culture encouraged risk taking and tolerated ambiguity. People in cultures that encouraged risk taking were inclined to take risks and were ranked low in uncertainty avoidance. Such people (e.g. in Hong Kong) encountered less stress from situations clouded with ambiguity and placed less importance on following the rules. By contrast, people in cultures ranked high in uncertainty avoidance (e.g. Iran) tended to be risk aversive. Features of the behavioural pattern of people displaying risk aversiveness when confronted by situations high in uncertainty avoidance are working hard, displaying intolerance towards those who do not abide by the rules and staying in the same job for a long time, in order to reduce the high levels of anxiety and stress stemming from conditions of uncertainty.

3. *Individualism–collectivism.* This factor gauged the extent to which culture measured an individual as opposed to a group perspective. In a culture with an individualistic bias (e.g. the United States) there would be a pronounced emphasis on the exercise of individual initiative and performance with a tendency to be preoccupied with the self and the immediate family. By contrast, in collectivist cultures (e.g. Singapore) there exists a broader set of loyalties to the extended family and, where appropriate, to the tribe. In return for loyalty the individual gets protection and support.

4. *Masculinity–femininity.* This factor measured the extent to which culture measured what were called 'masculine' as opposed to 'feminine' characteristics and would be reflected in the type of achievements that are valued. Masculine cultures (e.g. Italy) place much emphasis on the acquisition of material possessions and an ambitious disposition, and there is a clear differentiation between male and female roles. By contrast, the emphasis appears to be on concern for the environment, the quality of life and caring in feminine cultures (e.g. the Netherlands).

As a result of more recent work, Hofestede (1994) puts forward a fifth dimension to his scheme. This dimension is called *long-term orientation vs short-term orientation.* A long-term orientation manifested itself as future oriented, with an emphasis on perseverance and thrift, and high levels of adaptability to a changing world. This orientation applied to societies in

South-east Asia (e.g. Japan, Hong Kong, Singapore), where the Confucian philosophy is prevalent. It was also applicable to Brazil.

Trompenaars (1993) also recognises the power of national cultures in the way they influence the behaviour of managers. He identifies seven dimensions as follows, five of which are relevant in this context:

1. *Universalism vs particularism.* Universalism means that, for example, a solid principle can be applied everywhere, while particularism means that particular circumstances are influential in determining whether a principle or line of action should be adopted. Universalism would be more applicable to countries such as the United States and Germany, whereas particularism could apply to Indonesia and Venezuela.

2. *Individualism vs collectivism.* Individualism means that individuals experience personal achievement and assume personal responsibility for their actions, and is attributable to countries such as the United States and the United Kingdom. In societies where collectivism prevails (e.g. Thailand, Singapore and Japan) individuals function through groups and they assume joint responsibility for the collective output. This dimension has already been recognised by Hofestede.

3. *Neutral vs affective.* In societies where a neutral culture prevails expressing anger or happiness in the workplace is not really acceptable. Those with a neutral orientation in societies, such as Japan and the United Kingdom, do not like expressing themselves in an emotional sense in public. But those in societies (e.g. Brazil, Mexico) with an affective disposition openly express their emotions with an expressive face, body gestures and raised voice.

4. *Specific relationship vs diffuse relationship.* In societies with a specific relationship orientation (e.g. the United Kingdom, the United States) there is a preference for people to keep their public and private lives separate, particularly guarding their private lives. The tendency is to display mostly a public face. But in societies with diffuse relationships (e.g. Spain, Chile) it is possible to see more of the inner self of the person. Work and private lives are closely linked.

5. *Achievement vs ascription.* In societies with an achievement orientation (e.g. Switzerland, Germany, the United States) people work hard to improve themselves, they are ambitious and emphasise accomplishment. But in societies where ascription is found (e.g. Indonesia, Chile) there is a tendency to pay respect to those with status in the community (e.g. respected and admired figures), quite independent of their achievement.

Theories of national culture, and particularly those of Hofestede, have inspired a large volume of subsequent research, and much of this has consequences for HRM. For example, Ishida (1986) found that collectivist Japanese managers experienced problems when they were appointed to lead employees from individualist cultures overseas. More recently, Fujimoto *et al.* (2007) have explored the links in multinational firms between HRM, culture and IT. They argue that the design of IT systems is too often the preserve of technical specialists, and that this can result in problems. The organisation of people's work relates to the technology they use (see Chapter 3), but the technology is also a reflection of cultural assumptions. For example, access to the Internet is restricted in Singaporean organisations where there is an adherence to conservative views. In contrast, in Hawaii, online communication is regarded as a way of enhancing diversity by maintaining the language of indigenous groups. In one culture, IT use is restricted, in the other it is encouraged because of cultural factors. In HRM terms, individualistic cultures are substantiated through IT where it is used to monitor individual performance targets and rewards, and to define individual tasks. Conversely, IT systems can be used to foster a collectivist culture, focusing on equality, group-based performance measurement and reward. The danger comes where, in a multinational firm, one approach is imposed on other cultures in a way that will lead to the accentuation of 'value dissimilarity' and negative outcomes such as increased stress and decreased trust. In general, Fujimoto *et al.* (2007) suggest that firms should err on the side of collectivism, but they also suggest that there should be sufficient flexibility in the user-application of IT systems so that they can be adapted to either individualist or collectivist cultures.

Cultural diversity: teams and leadership

Recognising the US roots of HRM, Guest (1994a) draws our attention to a number of factors likely to influence its implementation in Europe. He identified cultural diversity as an important factor. In this section cultural diversity will be viewed from the angle of multi-cultural teams and how managerial leadership is influenced by national culture. In the last decade the development of global markets has created numerous cross-cultural contacts, and the ensuing dialogue has formed the basis for transacting global business (Adler, 2002). This has implications for the development of culturally diverse teams, where people from different cultures relate to each other, aided by the power of new technology when it comes to communication systems. The output of culturally diverse teams can be impressive if diversity is well managed (Bhaskaran and Sukumaran, 2007). It is said that the potential of diverse teams is not fully realised unless one pays particular attention to the way these teams are managed (Kandola, 1995).

To operate successfully across cultures it is important to be able to recognise cultural differences and be adaptable (Marx, 1999), as well as viewing the organisation as international in orientation. To satisfy the latter it would seem necessary to be aware of political currents likely to affect international trade, to have a management and organisation system tuned into the demands of world markets, and management development activities that nurture an appropriate international outlook. Speaking of management development, one may well ask what type of managerial leadership is appropriate in particular cultures. As a broad principle one can acknowledge that culture influences leadership style (Koopman *et al.*, 1999). More specific associations will now be examined.

In some cultures leaders are respected when they take strong decisive action, whereas in other cultures consultative and participative decision-making approaches are more valued. According to Den Hartog *et al.* (1999), in a culture where authoritarian leadership is valued it would be pointless acting in a way more characteristic of a participative or democratic leader. But in a culture that endorses a more nurturing and humanistic leadership style, being sensitive and considerate as a leader could be functional. Using Hofstede's framework, examined above, masculine cultures are probably more tolerant of strong directive leaders than feminine cultures. In the latter case it is more likely that there is a preference for more consultative, considerate leaders. Also, in 'high' power distance cultures, as defined by Hofstede, authoritarian leadership styles may be more acceptable. In this type of setting dominance and overt wielding of power may be considered appropriate. By contrast, in more egalitarian societies and cultures leaders may be more prone to emphasising less social distance between themselves and their followers, thereby striving for equality with others (Den Hartog *et al.*, 1999).

House (1995) reflects on the North American cultural influence on theoretical developments in managerial leadership, and concludes that the following slant is apparent:

- There is an emphasis on individualistic rather than collectivist approaches.

- Rationality takes pride of place over ascetics, spiritual values or superstition.

- Reward systems assume more of an individual rather than group character.

- People are more self-centred than altruistic in their motivation.

- The responsibilities of followers rather than their rights receive emphasis.

- The primacy of work in people's lives and the sanctity of democratic values are conspicuous.

Organisational culture

It is apparent from Hofestede's and Trompenaars' work and the literature generally on cultural diversity that national cultures impinge on practices within the organisation. That provides a cue to direct our attention to a study of organisational cultures. Organisational culture finds expression through the thoughts, intentions, actions and interpretations of members of the organisation (Michailova and Hutchings, 2006). Schein (1990) defined organisational culture as a pattern of basic assumptions that a given group has invented, discovered or developed in learning to cope with its problems of external adaptation and internal integration. This pattern has worked well enough for the group to be considered valid and therefore is to be taught to new members as the correct way to perceive, think and feel in relation to those problems.

Note the concept of 'integration' and 'adaptation' in Schein's definition above. Integration means that members develop a collective identity and are capable of working well together. It is concerned with day-to-day working relationships and determines how people communicate within the organisation, as well as establishing what behaviour is acceptable or not acceptable and how power and status are allocated.

Adaptation is a force that helps the organisation to adapt to its external environment. It facilitates the meeting of organisational goals and dealing with outside influences. This aspect of culture helps guide the daily activities of employees to meet certain goals, and can help the organisation to respond promptly to customers' needs and the actions of competitors.

An alternative definition provided by Moorhead and Griffin (2004) states that organisational culture is a set of values, often taken for granted, that help people in an organisation understand which actions are considered acceptable and which unacceptable. Often these values are communicated through stories and other symbolic means.

Aspects of organisational culture

The culture of the organisation is perceived by Trice and Beyer (1984) as consisting of four major aspects:

1. rites and ceremonies,
2. stories,
3. symbols, and
4. language.

RITES AND CEREMONIES

Rites and ceremonies help employees identify with the organisation and its successes and provide vivid accounts of what a company values. They can be considered special occasions that reinforce special values, that create a bond between people to foster common under-standing, and honour heroes who stand for important beliefs or achievements. The following are examples of the different types of rites.

- Rites of passage (e.g. induction courses) facilitate the entry of employees into new social roles or jobs, and can increase the status of employees.

- Rites of enhancement foster stronger social identities, and increase the status of employees. For example, there could be a ceremonial launching of a new product at which employees are present, or an address by the chief executive at the 'Salesperson of the Year' event. At events of this nature, often held at a large hotel or conference centre, successful sales repre-sentatives receive various gifts for meeting sales targets. Offering public recognition for outstanding performance can have a motivating effect. Other rituals take place when employees take advantage of the opportunity to socialise and relax with each other at informal company social events.

- Rites of renewal (e.g. management training and development) are reflected in various training and development activities.

- Rites of integration are activities that create common bonds and good feelings among employees and can have the effect of increasing commitment to the organisation.

STORIES

This is a form of communication that focuses primarily on vignettes and anecdotes about the dedication and commitment of corporate heroes and managers, or the devotion of ordinary employees. They are told to new employees to inform them about the organisation. There are true stories founded on events showing employees displaying heroism or, for example, adhering to high quality standards. Also, the great achievements of the leadership at the incep-tion of the company could be highlighted, as could accounts of great career achievements, ways of getting round the rules and regulations, what one learnt from past mistakes, how the organisation coped with a major crisis, and how a restructuring of the organisation was carried out (Boye, 1991). Stories like these help with explanation and legitimacy by placing the present in some relevant historical context (Brown, 2006).

However, there could also be myths, lacking foundation in fact, where employees 'recall' past happenings, typically passing them on through word-of-mouth. These could be sup-plemented by legends – accounts of actual events fleshed out with fictional details – as well as by folk tales, which amount to fictional stories with a message. Stories keep alive the primary values of the organisation and provide employees with a shared understanding. To foster rec-ognition there are symbols, slogans, logos or emblems (e.g. the Mercedes symbol), and these represent an important identification sign.

SYMBOLS

A symbol is something that represents something else. For example, rites, ceremonies and slogans are all symbols; they symbolise the deeper values of the organisation. But physical arti-facts are also symbols. They convey something distinctive about the organisation, and range from the physical layout and decor of offices to the nature of office furniture. Open-plan offices with common areas may indicate a certain degree of informality and may convey some-thing about the social and psychological climate of the organisation (e.g. less emphasis on status, flexibility, etc.). Material symbols, such as size of office and quality of its furnishings, access to a company apartment in a prime location, and use of a chauffeur-driven car, convey to employees certain aspects of status and importance, as well as management culture.

LANGUAGE

Organisations develop distinctive terms (specific sayings, slogans, or metaphors) to describe people, buildings and events, and the acronyms and jargon used could be alien to the new entrant. The development of a common language can have a unifying effect within the organisation. A good example of terms used to describe particular groups are those that the Walt Disney organisation uses. It refers to the workforce at its theme parks as the cast, the customers are guests, and when staff work with the public they are on the stage. Likewise, McDonald's refers to its workers as crew members.

CULTURE VS CLIMATE

Is there a difference between culture and climate within the organisation? Some argue that climate is a subset of organisational culture, and that in reality the difference between climate and culture is not pronounced (Furnham, 2005). Others can see a noticeable difference, as follows: climate is concerned with the current atmosphere within the organisation (Denison, 1996), as manifested in communication and reward systems and leadership style, etc. Organisational culture is based on the history and traditions of the organisation with the emphasis on values and norms underpinning the behaviour of employees, and it is more difficult to change in the short term.

TYPES OF CULTURE

Often we refer to organisational culture as strong and weak, as well as a dominant or a subculture. Strong cultures are said to be advantageous in promoting cohesiveness, loyalty and the commitment of employees. This is so because the core values of the organisation are widely shared and eagerly adopted by large numbers of employees. Strong cultures exert powerful behavioural compliance, expressed as high agreement amongst members about what the organisation represents. The result is the creation of an internal atmosphere of high behavioural control, as opposed to bureaucratic control; that is, the stronger the culture of an organisation, the less management need to be concerned with developing formal rules and regulations to guide employee behaviour. In recent years, as organisations have created flatter structures, introduced team systems of working, released bureaucratic control, and empowered employees, some would argue that the shared meaning generated by a strong culture ensures that everyone is moving in the same direction.

From a perspective of 'diversity' a strong culture could be considered a liability because it would not accommodate the diverse behaviours and strengths that people of different backgrounds can bring to the organisation. There could be a bias or insensitivity to people perceived as different on racial, ethnic, gender or other grounds, and this could be reflected in judgements made when recruiting and selecting new employees (Cox, 1993; Brannan and Hawkins, 2007). Even though there might be a view that diversity could have an enriching effect, at the same time there is often a wish to recruit new staff who will experience little difficulty in embracing the organisation's core cultural values.

We should not ignore the potentially dysfunctional aspects of a strong culture. This is evident when strong cultures, which worked well in the past, may have become barriers to change when the old ways are no longer valid. Finally, if there is little agreement among members about the organisation's core values, the culture is said to be weak.

A dominant culture, referred to as the organisation's culture, reflects the core values that are shared by the majority of the employees. This could be referred to as the distinctive personality of the organisation. A subculture, found in departments, divisions and geographical areas, reflects the common problems or experiences of employees in these areas (Tushman and O'Reilly, 1996). But equally a subculture could consist of the core values of the dominant culture as well as the values of the area to which they relate. There could be differences between one subculture and another and between subcultures and the dominant culture (Riad, 2007). The subculture of the dealing room could be different from the subculture of another department of an investment bank (see Box 5.1).

Box 5.1: The culture of the dealing room

Many dealing rooms in merchant banks and stockbroking firms are dominated by one simple system of values: win or be damned. If dealers make large profits for the organisation the rewards – both in a material and psychological sense – are very significant. Not only is personal remuneration substantial, but also the dealers' status in the firm and the market generally is considerably enhanced. However, if the dealers' performance is poor in terms of profits generated or losses sustained the reverse situation applies. They could feel humiliated and isolated and risk losing their jobs with detrimental personal consequences. Always in the background is greed and fear, in particular fear: fear of losing the job and fear of public humiliation. It is fear that prevents dealers from cutting their losses as well as forcing them to get out of profitable positions early.

Dealers live in a unique corporate 'subculture', one that encourages overconfidence and insulates them from the outside world. On the trading floor boldness is looked upon as the most important virtue, and the traders' faith in themselves is boosted by their substantial remuneration package. A moment's hesitation or uncertainty could undermine a transaction. Dealers tend to behave as if they are omnipotent, they brag about the size of their deals, and hero status is bestowed on anyone making large sums of money. Because of the high rewards they are encouraged to take unwise risks.

There is a loss of perspective on outside events, with a tendency for dealers to shield themselves from too much information that could metaphorically lead to paralysis. There is the illusion that the computer screen gives them a window on the outside world, even though it is no more than a series of rapidly changing numbers. Erratic behaviour is condoned if not encouraged, and shouting matches and foot stomping are part of the scene on the trading floor. The dealers display emotional volatility, and this is accepted as long as they are generating good profits. A dangerous cocktail is the mixture of emotional volatility, overconfidence and access to large amounts of capital. In addition to tightening up procedures, Weaving (1995) suggests the following actions to counteract the culture of individualism, competition and insecurity symbolised by Baring Securities, Singapore, in early 1995:

■ Create a culture of teamwork in which dealers help each other and share information. When dealers have bad days colleagues would help them by alerting

> them to the risk management procedures, coaching them through a bad position, and encouraging them to be more rational.
>
> ■ Take steps to build the dealers' self-confidence, which should help them admit when they are wrong. With self-confidence they are less likely to fall into the trap of the 'illusion of invulnerability', which is often associated with arrogance.
>
> ■ Help dealers to recognise their own particular response to stress (e.g. feelings of panic and a deterioration in rational thinking that could undermine good decision making) and train them in how to manage stress.
>
> ■ Institute good management practice exemplified by a competent approach to offering praise, coaching and the provision of feedback. In the appraisal of performance a broad range of behaviour would be considered, and rewards would reflect behaviour somewhat more varied than a single moneymaking criterion.
>
> Source: based on Griffith, 1995; Weaving, 1995
>
> In 2004 in a British court of law the spotlight was on the trading room culture when a senior trader employed in London's financial district was claiming damages because of bullying at work. In this case questions were asked about the extent to which foul language and bullying were part of the dealing room culture.
>
> Source: based on Tait, 2005
>
> ### Question
>
> This dealing room is an expression of a strong culture in which everyone is expected to share the same basic values. What features of the situation are likely to encourage such a unanimous view?

Analysing organisational culture

Culture became an issue in the 1980s with attempts to unravel the secrets of Japanese business. Certain fundamental values in Japanese society, such as social solidarity, respect for elders and a strong work ethic, influenced behaviour in organisations. Generally the Japanese corporate culture is supportive of seniority-based pay, job security, uniformity in dress and facilities (e.g. canteens), importance of duty, careful attention to employee selection and training, and a quality-driven system of organisation and management. However, a direct threat to certain values (e.g. seniority-based pay and job security) has come about as a result of the economic recession in Japan in the 1990s.

In the early 1980s the economic success of Japan was attributed by Ouchi (1981), in his Theory Z, to a mixture of US and Japanese practices as follows:

■ a predominant concern for people;

■ a guarantee of long-term employment;

■ decision making based on shared values and collective responsibility;

■ a 'clan' approach to participation, with strong social pressures to encourage performance;

■ high trust and faith in the managers' ultimate judgement; and

■ non-specialised career pathways.

The end result was mutual commitment, that is employees responded to the commitment made by the employer by a pledge of commitment to the organisation.

The corporate welfare and paternalistic aspects of Japanese organisational cultures can be found in a particular ideology. This is the ideology of loyalty to one lord as derived from the Japanese appropriation of Chinese 'Confucian' principles and the feudal legacy (Wilkinson and Oliver, 1992). As stated earlier, in effect societal values in Japan have permeated the fabric of the organisation. It would appear that the best course of action by management in the West, which would like to import and use Japanese management practices, is to adapt them to their particular circumstances rather than transplant them in their entirety.

The relationship between organisational culture and performance in the United States was emphasised by Peters and Waterman (1982) when they associated certain management practices with success. In essence these were:

■ adopt an action-oriented and decisive management;

■ identify and serve the customers' needs;

■ encourage independence and entrepreneurial flair with assistance provided by small cohesive groups;

■ involve people at all times in the management of the enterprise in conditions where top management are seen to be in touch with employees;

■ confine the organisation's activities to what it knows best and avoid diversification into unknown territory;

■ avoid complex hierarchical arrangements; and

■ combine central direction with autonomy for the work group.

This research captured the spirit of the times (early 1980s) and offered a US solution to the challenge of Japanese competition. Peters and Waterman felt that the curriculum in business schools, with the predominant emphasis on strategy, structure and quantitatively driven systems, was ill-conceived. To them success rested on a number of factors, such as those mentioned above, which gave more weight to the 'soft' characteristics of HRM – namely staff, style, systems, skills and shared values. Acceptance of the 'excellence theories' propounded by Peters and Waterman would entail paying more attention to leadership, corporate culture, quality, management of change and, of course, HRM in general. It is easy to find fault with the research of Peters and Waterman, in particular the methodology, but it should be borne in mind that this work attracted the attention of top management and succeeded in shifting the focus of management thinking so that much more weight was given to policy issues in HRM (Guest, 1994b).

Another framework of analysis was provided by Deal and Kennedy (1982). Their analysis features 'risk' and 'feedback' as important variables. With these variables in mind culture was analysed as follows:

■ *Tough-guy macho culture* (high risk/fast feedback). In this type of organisational setting you are likely to find entrepreneurial types, who are not very interested in teamwork and are prepared to take high risks. This profile was considered to be applicable to a media or consultancy company at the time the research was undertaken.

■ *Work hard, play hard* (low risk/fast feedback). This is an action-oriented environment where work is viewed as a source of fun. Although there are many solo performers they do rely on supportive teams in a climate of low risk and rapid feedback. This profile could apply to a car dealership or estate agency.

■ *Bet your company* (high risk/slow feedback). The influential people in this culture are those who are technically proficient and show respect for authority in organisations faced with cyclical changes in the economy. The key players are risk takers who rely on slow feedback and were found in industries such as oil or mining.

■ *Process culture* (low risk/slow feedback). The people who function in this environment are low risk takers with an eye for detail, and who rely on well-defined procedures. They put a lot of effort into their work, but are not required to exercise much initiative in conditions of slow feedback. The organisations to which they belonged were located in banking, public utilities and governmental agencies.

With reference to the above profiles, ideally job applicants should give serious consideration to the type of organisational culture most suited to their needs. Equally, organisations should strive to obtain the best fit between the individual and the organisation at the selection stage if the optimum outcome is to be achieved.

There have been attempts to relate culture to the design of the organisation. In this context four types of organisational culture have been proposed (Harrison, 1972):

1. *Power culture.* A small number of senior executives exert much power in a directive way. There is a belief in a strong and decisive stance to advance the interests of the organisation.
2. *Role culture.* There is a concern with bureaucratic procedures, such as rules, regulations and clearly specified roles, because it is believed these will stabilise the system.
3. *Support culture.* There is group or community support for people, which cultivates integration and sharing of values.
4. *Achievement culture.* There is an atmosphere that encourages self-expression and a striving for independence, and the accent is on success and achievement.

A modified version of this typology is proposed by Handy (1985), who acknowledges types 1 and 2 above and adds task culture (e.g. utilisation of knowledge and technical competency in project teams) and person culture (e.g. personal needs and preferences are seriously considered in the assignment of tasks). The typologies examined here can be described as ideal types within which organisations can be placed. Individuals may fit better into one type of culture than another, as would management functions and organisational features. A criticism levelled at this work is the lack of empirical evidence to support it (Williams *et al.*, 1989).

A typology devised by Miles and Snow (1978) recognises the potency of managerial ideology and leadership in influencing and shaping the culture of the organisation. The three-part typology consists of the following:

1. *Defender organisations.* The major objective is to secure and maintain a stable position in the market for the product or service. There is an emphasis on formal systems where planning and control are centralised and there is a commitment to efficiency and cost reduction.
2. *Prospector organisations.* The major objective is to develop new products and exploit market opportunities. To this end there is an emphasis on flexibility, ad hoc systems and creativity.
3. *Analyser organisations.* Careful attention is given to research and development and to steady rather than dramatic growth. There is a tendency to follow rather than lead in the product market.

It is more than likely that different attitudes and beliefs are compatible with the different types of organisational cultures. Also, it is important that structure, strategy and culture blend and harmonise to secure a successful outcome. With regard to strategy, it is known that culture can bolster the strategy of the company and provide the impetus for the development of new products, as has been the case with Motorola, the US corporation. Ogbonna and Whipp (1999) consider the Miles and Snow typology useful when looking at the relationship between strategy and HRM in the UK food retailing sector.

In recent years there was an interest in 'reinventing strategy' as a reaction to downsizing, rightsizing and delayering associated with massive cost cutting (Tennant and Wu, 2005; Hamel and Prahalad, 1994). The view is that we should avoid the danger of corporate anorexia and that companies should be energised and stimulated to create new markets.

There are occasions when organisations feel it necessary to reinforce their existing culture and set in motion a series of events or activities to accomplish this objective. Alternatively, there could be a determination to change corporate culture, and this could have significant implications in terms of modification or revision to strategy, structure and processes within the organisation.

Changing culture

In recent years many organisations have felt it necessary to change corporate culture to ensure survival or to gain competitive advantage. Often this was prompted by the realisation that the existing culture did not fit the desired future state for the organisation. In Case example 5.1 there is an account of action taken to address an inappropriate organisational culture.

CASE EXAMPLE 5.1

CITIGROUP – A CORPORATE CULTURE THAT NEEDED CHANGING

Citigroup, the world's largest financial services group, had been hit repeatedly by scandals that cost it billions of dollars in fines and compensation, and in the process damaged its reputation. A major factor responsible for this unsatisfactory situation was the pursuit of short-term profit at the expense of long-term reputation. This was a result of the way the company was formed – a series of mergers and acquisitions during the 1990s that brought together diverse businesses, such as investment banking, credit cards, retail banking and lending to poor people. During this period the emphasis was on cutting the costs of support activities, such as reducing the cost of back office activities, and setting tough profit targets for the operating subsidiaries that enjoyed considerable autonomy. In this cultural setting executives and managers who 'cut corners' to meet quarterly targets could earn large performance bonuses. Therefore it was not surprising that serious irregularities or lapses occurred.

In 2005 the then CEO, Chuck Prince, was unhappy about this state of affairs, and announced plans to change the culture of Citigroup. He was eager to build a corporate culture that struck a good balance between short-term operating profit and the long-term reputation of the company. The measures proposed ranged from basic ones, such as the company's value aspirations and an ethics hotline to report unacceptable practices, to more substantial ones, such as the introduction of a common performance appraisal system for senior managers. This could be described as a primary mechanism, using the terminology used by Schein later, and resulted in replacing 50 performance appraisal systems the company collected from its growth by acquisition. Another primary mechanism – performance-related pay – was to be linked to the profits of the individual businesses as well as to the company's overall performance.

An obstacle in trying to promote a cohesive culture was the difficulty of moving key staff between divisions in order to promote the values now considered important. In this respect it is said that it is difficult for senior executives with no experience of particular businesses to control them. Another difficulty encountered in financial services conglomerates arises in areas where conflict of interests arise, for example, where one arm of the organisation is advising companies on the issue of shares or other securities and another arm is trying to sell those shares or securities to investors. Chuck Prince faced a challenging task in his endeavour to change the culture of Citigroup.

Source: based on editorial comment, *Financial Times* (2005)

Questions

1. Which of the culture types described by Deal and Kennedy above best fits Citigroup?

2. Which type should they aspire to being, and why?

Forces in the organisation's external environment could signal the need for a change in culture. For example, in the late 1980s and early 1990s the UK Conservative government took action to unleash market forces within the National Health Service and this had a significant impact, particularly in the case of the culture of Hospital Trusts. The Labour government that came to power in 1997 also intended on changing culture by means of encouraging the formation of 'joined-up' working and clinically led teams with the spotlight on the patient. Joined-up working can result in a team drawing members from health and social services departments and government agencies to focus on the needs of a service user. So, instead of a service user going from hospital to social housing and then outpatient therapy in turn, their overall care plan would be developed incorporating all the services, so that for the user the provision is 'seamless'. This entails the various providers collaborating over how arrangements should be made and how funding is organised. It is also a challenge to the attitude and power of the professionals involved who are used to holding sway in their own domain.

In Trompenaars' (1993) terms this represents an attempt to move from an individualistic to a collectivist culture. Apart from the external environmental stimulants, the force for cultural change could come from within when senior executives apply new approaches to management, such as total quality management and process re-engineering (approaches discussed later in the chapter). Once it has been established that there is a need for change, a first step would be to analyse the existing organisational culture. Next it would be necessary to envisage the desired end state as far as culture is concerned. Certain commentators see the need for strong leadership to permeate the total organisation, where 'heroes' recognise the need for change and put in place change agents and construct symbols of change in order to create the necessary momentum (Deal and Kennedy, 1982). The major emphasis in cultural change and development is on trying to change the values, attitudes and behaviour of the workforce.

How does one go about changing culture? According to Schein (1985) the organisation can rely on the following 'primary' and 'secondary' mechanisms to change culture. These cultural change mechanisms will now be considered.

PRIMARY MECHANISMS

(a) Matters to which leaders pay most attention

If senior managers place much emphasis on, for example, the control of expenditure or the importance of service to the customer, and this is visible to employees, then a powerful message is transmitted about the significance of this type of activity. Sometimes it may be necessary to mount workshops or discussion groups to get a key message across to all employees, as Co-operative Financial Services did in Case example 5.2 later.

(b) Leader's way of reacting to crises and critical incidents

This could be reflected in the type of situation that is seen as a crisis situation (e.g. a relatively high materials' wastage rate in the manufacturing plant) and the nature of the leader's response to the crisis (e.g. an urgent determination to tackle and solve the problem).

(c) Role modelling, teaching and coaching by leaders

Role modelling occurs when, for example, junior staff copy the behaviour of their seniors and integrate such behaviour into their own pattern of behaviour. This could apply to mannerisms and behaviour, such as ways of managing (see Box 5.2) and interacting with valued clients or customers. With regard to teaching and coaching, working closely with people offering guidance and reassurance in a supportive climate has much to commend it, and has value in promoting commitment. There is reference to coaching in the context of management development in Chapter 10.

> ## Box 5.2: CEO leading by example
>
>
>
> Informality seems to be the hallmark of the management style of Ingvar Kemprad, the Chief Executive of IKEA (the large Scandanavian home furnishing chain). The way he treats his staff and customers reflects his philosophy of life. He is endowed with a genuine warmth and interest in people, which is no doubt one of the most important reasons for his success. Due to his influence the company has a culture in which informality and simplicity is a striking feature. This is also reflected in the neat but casual dress of the employees – jeans and sweaters – and the relaxed office atmosphere where practically everyone sits in an open-plan office (Kreitner *et al.*, 2002).

In (a), (b) and (c) prominence is given to the hierarchical role of the leader exercising the right to lead. Some question this type of cultural leadership and point out that if we want cultural change to be effective then there should be wide agreement and ownership amongst people about the desired change (Torrington and Hall, 1998).

(d) Criteria used for allocating rewards

Recently the visibility of performance in the job as a criterion in the determination of rewards has been apparent. At one time loyalty to the organisation received greater emphasis as a criterion than is the case today. If the relationship between performance and rewards is highly visible there is likely to be an expectation that it is functional to strive for improved performance. There is a discussion of performance-related pay (PRP) in Chapter 9.

(e) Criteria used for employee selection, promotions and termination of employment

The criteria that would apply under this heading relate to what selectors consider important characteristics in hiring staff, the most appropriate work behaviour to secure career advancement, and what to avoid in order to reduce the likelihood of being made redundant.

Redundancy could be used to terminate the employment of employees on a compulsory basis when, for example, performance is unsatisfactory. An alternative way of shedding labour is to offer voluntary redundancy, or early retirement, particularly to those who might have difficulty in fitting into the new culture. It stands to reason that instituting redundancy measures can have a major impact on the lives of those who leave the organisation, but it can also adversely affect those who stay. For example, if there is a lack of fairness or compassion in the implementation of the redundancy scheme, resentment can arise and has a negative effect after the change in culture has taken place. The legacy of this type of managerial behaviour could sour future relations between management and workers.

As regards employee selection, the organisation could take a conscious decision to recruit workers with attitudes deemed appropriate in the light of the company's culture, and such an approach can have a beneficial impact on the psychological contract (Sekiguchi, 2007) discussed in Chapter 2. This approach has been adopted particularly by Japanese companies setting up operations on a 'greenfield' site. Nissan UK used a rigorous and lengthy selection process when selecting its new workforce (Wickens, 1987). This practice was at variance with the much less exacting traditional practices for hiring shopfloor workers. Nissan's intention was to select a group of employees with values and attitudes compatible with the company's culture. It would appear that the type of person likely to be suitable would be one who is basically cooperative, flexible and certainly not the stereotypical rabble-rouser!

The point to bear in mind is that the organisation endeavours to shape behaviour when implementing HRM techniques that utilise the criteria referred to in (d) and (e). An important consideration is the visibility of these criteria in the various decision-making forums.

SECONDARY MECHANISMS

(a) Structures, systems and procedures

There could be a fortification of existing structures, systems and procedures or a significant change in them so that the organisation is repositioned to face the future with greater confidence. For example, the desired change might be to create the post-entrepreneurial organisation (e.g. flexible and free from cumbersome bureaucracy) as suggested by Kanter (1989) and discussed in Chapter 3. Such a transformation, if successful, could bring about a fundamental shift in people's attitudes and behaviour at work.

With regard to changing people's attitudes and behaviour so that they will fit comfortably with the emerging culture, it is suggested in Chapter 10 that training and development have a part to play. For example, in teamwork training people are given the experience of working cooperatively in activities away from the actual work situation. This provides them with an opportunity to encounter the attitudes and processes associated with teamwork, and perceive each other's strengths and weaknesses. There is a view that it would be more productive to concentrate on changing behaviour initially in training sessions in the expectation that attitudes will follow the new or changed behaviour. This approach was adopted in equal opportunities training programmes because early attempts to develop awareness and acceptance of the need for equal opportunities were seen as unsuccessful in challenging entrenched biases. Subsequently the emphasis switched to training programmes that highlighted appropriate behaviour (e.g. unbiased interview techniques in selection and promotions). The hope is that the new experience will pose a challenge to the biased attitudes, leading to the development of more appropriate attitudes.

Another example of a behavioural change was the 'Smile Campaign' mounted by a major supermarket as part of a customer service programme. All front-line employees were expected to put on a smile for customers and could face a reprimand if they did not do so (Ogbonna, 1992). In order to motivate employees to undergo the suggested behavioural change a competition between stores was introduced. Senior managers visited stores before making a judgement on which store offered the best level of customer service. Apart from being profiled in the company's magazine, the winner received a financial reward. This example illustrates the importance of providing feedback on performance and the allocation of extrinsic rewards (referred to in 'Primary mechanisms' (d), above) as part of a strategy to bring about changes in attitudes and behaviour within an organisation.

(b) Artefacts, façades and physical spaces

These are aspects of the physical environment that convey images, which make an impact. For example, a certain impression is created when a person attending a job interview walks into the reception area of the company and perceives an expensively furnished setting. Another manifestation of the physical environment likely to capture the attention of the person and convey a message is the number of open spaces, the layout of the offices and the nature and distribution of office equipment. When organisations change situations identified in (a) as part of a cultural facelift they could also change certain aspects of the physical environment so that they blend with the changes made. They may also change their logo (the symbol of corporate identity) if the old one is out of keeping with the changed circumstances.

(c) Stories and legends about important events and people

There could be stories and legends containing a mixture of fact and fiction about heroic deeds in the past that may have contributed in a significant way to the company's success or saved the company from disaster. Earlier in the chapter there was also reference to stories. The message is that present employees must not lose sight of dedication to duty and the need to continue with unselfish commitment to the success of the organisation. Where accounts of management incompetence or greed circulate perhaps the expectation is that these are things we should learn from and avoid now and in the future.

(d) Formal statements of philosophy and policy

These could include mission statements, which are explicit articulations of the direction in which the organisation is going and the values to which it will adhere. These statements should reflect reality and ideally should be reinforced with reference to their practical significance in a discussion forum.

Culture change initiatives

Three initiatives or interventions worthy of note are quality circles (QCs), total quality management (TQM) and business process re-engineering (BPR). Before examining these initiatives our attention could profitably be diverted to events at Co-operative Financial Services and RWE in connection with cultural change. These are described in the Case examples 5.2 and 5.3.

CASE EXAMPLE 5.2

CULTURAL CHANGE AT CO-OPERATIVE FINANCIAL SERVICES

Co-operative Financial Services is part of the Co-operative Group which incorporates food retail, specialist retail, banking and insurance. The group prides itself on an ethical approach to business and this is made overt in its objective which is to 'optimise profit where our co-operative values give us a positive marketing advantage, to serve our members and to deliver our social goals ... [whilst] making a reasonable financial return' (www.co-op.co.uk). Co-operative Financial Services (CFS) was formed in 2002 by bringing together The Co-operative Bank, Smile (the internet bank) and the Co-operative Insurance Society (CIS). CFS has 7 million customers and employs 12,000 staff. There has been a comprehensive modernisation programme which has entailed reducing costs and 2,500 job losses with the aim of achieving a tighter market focus. Some staff were redeployed elsewhere in the business. Alongside these structural changes, there has been a significant effort to change culture. This example focuses on the CIS part of the business.

In 2002 CIS was a technically-oriented organisation which was run by actuaries. As professionals, the actuaries were promoted from within and length of services was a consideration in promotion. As a result the culture was hierarchical, traditional, status-dominated and male-oriented (Simms, 2005). Helen Sweeney, HR Director at Co-operative Financial Services recalls her initial impressions:

> 'Men had to wear their jackets when they moved between floors and sometimes had to ask permission to remove them in meetings. I was told I couldn't wear high heels in the boardroom as they might damage the carpet. And instead of using first names, everyone referred to each other as "Mr" – or, very occasionally, "Mrs"' (quoted in Simms, 2005: 35).

The status differentials were also apparent, with senior managers being a distinct group. People's status was indicated by access to executive dining facilities, styles of chair, different coloured furniture and the number of windows in an office.

A survey in which CIS was compared to a database of 1,000 other companies indicated that, whilst there were strengths, there were significant perceived weaknesses in clarity, change orientation and recognition. Focus groups indicated that there was a dominating, even bullying, management style.

In order to change this traditional, hierarchical and change-averse culture a number of steps were taken. First, significant effort was put into changing the leadership. A programme for the top 70 directors was introduced and this was extended to 700 middle and senior managers. The next phase of roll-out was to incorporate 6,000 team leaders in the training. Prior to this, people who were promoted for their technical ability and long service in the company were given little or no management training. The old style was typified as a 'telling' management style. Following the retraining, a much greater emphasis was put on listening and involvement. Senior managers were present in the general office and were approachable. One of the top managers made a point of walking round the office four times every day. Much greater freedom was given to employees to make suggestions and decisions, and managers were encouraged not to simply 'wade in and give the solution' when there was a problem. By allowing employees to develop solutions, some innovative outcomes occurred that had a positive impact on individual and group performance.

The second significant target was to enable people to be more accepting of change. 'Change agent' workshops were organised for 1,000 middle managers. These helped people to understand their own preferences in managing change and to explore ways of achieving a common language and better understanding. The workshops equipped the managers with tools to apply in their own work settings.

The third focal area was to make change happen. 'Direction setting' workshops were introduced. In these workshops employees helped to clarify their objectives and identify ways of translating the objectives into meaningful actions. These were then linked to daily activities and targets. Individuals have action plans which are discussed with line managers. They report finding this motivational, particularly as they are clear where they need to expend their efforts.

The organisation now has a different look and feel. It is much more informal. Jackets are no longer required, people address each other by first names and the executives are visible and present alongside other employees. The satisfaction ratings in the 2005 survey had increased significantly with a 25 per cent increase in employees rating their managers as having good people skills (Simms, 2005). This cultural shift of greater informality, problem solving and individual action has also had a beneficial impact on the performance of the business. The Co-operative group has performed well during these changes. Group operating profit for 2006 was up 12.5 per cent from 2005 to £181.5 million. CIS was identified as a significant part of this performance. Although revenues from insurance fell by 13.2 per cent from 2005 to 2006, operating profit increased by 84.8 per cent to £17 million (www.co-op.co.uk).

Questions

1. What were the main symbols of the culture before and after the change?

2. What might make the culture difficult to change?

3. What would you consider doing differently to the way that the management approached the change process?

CHANGING CULTURE AT RWE

RWE, the Essen-based power and water corporation (utility), is
adapting to the forces of globalisation. Less than a decade ago the
100-year-old former Rheinisch-Westfalische Elektrizitatswerk was
a stuffy industrial organisation of considerable size with interests as diverse as printing
press manufacturing and telecommunications, and with a shareholder base dominated by
Rhineland municipalities with multiple voting rights.

In 1998, after much discussion and negotiations, RWE abolished the municipalities'
multiple voting rights and over the next few years became a global player, growing by
expensive international acquisitions at a fast pace. Among the companies acquired were
Thames Water in the United Kingdom and American Water Works. In a short space of time
50 per cent of income was generated abroad and 50 per cent of employees were working
outside Germany. RWE became Europe's third biggest listed utility, after German rival Eon
and Italy's Enel. But the company grew too fast and debts soared. What was the company's
response to this serious situation? In 2002 the late Friedel Neuber, former Head of the
state-owned West LB Bank and then Chairman of RWE's Supervisory Board, appointed a
Dutchman, Harry Roels, as CEO. It was a rare example of a foreigner taking a top job at a
big German group. Roels, aged 56, a chemistry graduate, had spent 30 years working for
Royal Dutch Shell.

Roels stated that 'culture change' was one of his priorities at RWE, and he expected it
would be going on for five years. He also said that to be 'a truly international company you
need a culture and leaders that are as international as its assets, and that is what we are
working on'. The following are some of the changes introduced, as well as Roel's views on
critical issues:

■ A programme of disposals was undertaken, particularly non-core businesses (e.g. the
printing machinery manufacturer), leaving RWE focused on gas, electricity and water. A
key consideration when Roels became CEO was to reduce the company's debt, which
was in excess of €23 billion. Debt has now fallen to below €15 billion. The current
policy for the company is to engage in organic growth, instead of growing by major
acquisitions. However, Roels does not rule out smaller or medium-sized acquisitions
to round off the product portfolio, particularly in the gas and electricity industries
rather in the water industry where links between water companies and municipalities
make consolidation unlikely.

■ Roels created a 'group business committee' consisting of 12 executives from across the
group (RWE), as opposed to the five strong, legally required Vorstand (management
board). He found that the Vorstand had weaknesses in taking a balanced view of
business issues across the group. By contrast, the group business committee became
much more effective as a forum in which individual executives had to raise issues and
defend their ideas. Something similar to the group business committee was set up by
Josef Ackermann (the Swiss born chief executive) at Deutsche Bank.

The creation of the group business committee has significance beyond mere
organisational change. Previously RWE operated like a classic German conglomerate,
whereby different parts of the group acted independently or competed with each other.

It was said that Roels has driven another nail in the coffin of the traditional German conglomerate. He was very keen to emphasise the importance of the group, and that means 'not putting the division first, but putting the group first'.

- Non-German ways of working have been introduced. Certain formalities in addressing people (e.g. Herr Doctor) have been discouraged. All members of the board of directors have agreed to call each other by their first names. Harry Roels is always addressed as Harry by his subordinates.

- There are other little symbolic things one should note. Roels feels that senior executives should eat with other employees in the canteen. He has abolished the practice of somebody standing by the door and opening it for him the moment he arrives at the company's headquarters by car.

- Roels speaks English fluently. He says, we have international groups of people meeting together and communication is part in German and part in English, leaving people to use the language with which they feel most comfortable.

- Roels sees limits to culture change, something he shares with a number of German chief executives, including Jurgen Schrempp (CEO of DaimlerChrysler), in that he is not in favour of reforming Germany's Mitbestimmung or co-determination laws, by which half the supervisory board is made up of employee representatives. He says, RWE has had a long and basically positive experience with Mitbestimmung, and he values the involvement of employees. He goes on to say, 'at the end of the day change can best be executed in a climate of trust and cooperation or consensus than in a conflict-ridden environment'. Incidentally, Germany's main employer organisations think Mitbestimmung is an anachronistic system that makes German companies uncompetitive.

Source: based on Atkins and Milne, 2004

Questions

1. What were the main symbols of the culture before and after the change?

2. What might make the culture difficult to change?

3. What would you consider doing differently to the way that management approached the change process?

In the case of Co-operative Insurance Society a clear need to change culture was established. The old culture had been what Harrison (1972) would refer to as a 'role culture'. The emphasis was on conforming to the role of the professional actuary and gradually working your way up the functional hierarchy. Training was focused on qualifying as a professional and maintaining professional expertise. Such cultures can be effective, particularly in relatively stable business environments. However, this was no longer the case in the financial services sector. Customers were becoming more demanding and discriminating and the market was fluctuating more frequently. The aim was to constrain costs and increase innovation and performance simultaneously. In Schein's (1985) terms, both primary and secondary mechanisms were used to implement the change. Primary mechanisms included a shift in leadership. Leaders now paid more attention to communication and particularly to encouraging employees to contribute ideas. Leaders role modelled a new form of behaviour. Instead of telling people what to do and 'providing solutions', they acted in a more facilitating manner to draw out solutions from employees. They then made sure that innovative ideas and solutions developed by employees were recognised. Secondary mechanisms employed included changes to the physical space and artefacts which had previously reinforced a strong division between senior managers and others. Structures were also reviewed with roles being redefined so that they focused on customers. In Harrison's terms the culture achieved was more akin to a support or achievement culture.

In CIS the imperative for change came from a need to be more customer- and market-oriented, and the resultant need to be more flexible. In the case of RWE the stimulus for change was another common pressure – that of globalisation. It was felt necessary to change culture in order for the organisation to become more competitive in the light of its programme of acquisitions internationally. This necessitatated modification of processes and practices internally. The leadership was altered, bringing in a wider range of perspectives and seeking to represent the international flavour of the organisation at the highest level. The approach was changed from fast growth by acquisition to organic and considered development. In addition, there was an effort to form a more integrated culture in which divisions thought of the group first, rather than being focused on their own 'silos'. There was also symbolic change, for example, in the way that people were addressed more informally and a removal of the status differentials in dining arrangements. These changes combine Schein's primary and secondary mechanisms. It is worth noting that along with the changes, certain facets of the old culture were conserved. In particular, the inclusion of employee representatives on the supervisory board. This arrangement would be in keeping with the new culture which stressed integration and accessible leadership.

Returning to the theme raised in the opening of this section, the three initiatives or interventions – QCs, TQM and BPR – will be discussed shortly. But first something should be said about quality. The control of quality was an original US idea enthusiastically taken on board by Japanese business and subsequently adopted by both US and UK organisations. The central idea is that quality becomes the concern of all employees and should be totally immersed in the management process. The latter is characterised by delegated authority and empowerment in all activities connected with quality. The needs and expectations of customers are an overriding preoccupation for those charged with responsibility for quality. It is suggested that one reason for the greater uptake of the idea of quality in Japan was due to the greater scarcity of resources and the resultant need to eliminate waste and maximise getting things right first time (Oliver and Wilkinson, 1992).

QUALITY CIRCLES (QCs)

The QC is a group joined by shopfloor workers to solve problems related to barriers to quality improvement, cost reduction, working conditions, health and safety, etc. The group, normally led by a team leader, consists of 5–10 volunteer employees who meet regularly (weekly or fortnightly) to identify and solve problems of the type described above. In order to equip the QC members to sharpen and develop their problem-solving skills, they are offered training programmes covering topics such as problem definition, statistical analysis and teamwork and communication skills. In Japan the QC was viewed favourably as a factor in its industrial success, and was imported to the West in the late 1970s.

It is claimed by some commentators that QCs have a beneficial effect on a number of fronts (e.g. communication, participation, job satisfaction and personal growth), which leads to increased quality and efficiency. For instance, Dale *et al.* (1998) believe that QCs represent an advanced form of employee participation which is associated with favourable employee attitudes and productivity. It is suggested that social needs are satisfied in QCs because an outlet is provided for the expression of grievances and irritations, and instant recognition is provided for the accomplishments of members. All this could have a beneficial effect in terms of a sense of dignity, morale and group cohesiveness. However, there is evidence to challenge these claims. It is suggested that the significance of the QC in Japan has been overrated because the difficulties addressed were relatively trivial; in fact a rather small percentage of 'quality' problems were confronted (Schonberger, 1982). The alleged benefits of the QCs have also been challenged in the United Kingdom. There were low levels of participation – not more than 25 per cent of eligible employees joined QCs – and widespread indifference and often active opposition on the part of employees (Hill, 1991).

TOTAL QUALITY MANAGEMENT (TQM)

TQM is a major management philosophy that embodies the important aim of satisfying customers' requirements as efficiently and profitably as possible, to improve performance continually as situations allow, and to ensure that all work activities achieve the corporate objectives and are completed right first time. Quality is seen as the key to the organisation's success, and the success of any policy on quality lays firmly on the shoulders of every employee. To underpin this approach to management would probably require a mixture of soft (e.g. customer care, participation, training, teamwork and performance) and hard factors (e.g. production standards and techniques, and quantitative analysis in the assessment of quality). The proponents of TQM would see it as a total system that fundamentally affects the culture of the organisation rather than as a 'bolt-on' technique, which was often attributable to QCs. In the case of QCs the training and cultural change techniques necessary to embed the circles in the values and attitudes of employees were rarely instituted. But TQM is strategically driven by top management and almost prescribes involvement of all employees in matters connected with quality in their jobs. Since TQM emphasises commitment, trust and self-control within a unitarist perspective it is consistent with HRM. Also, the introduction of TQM gives HRM the opportunity to play a more strategic role in the organisation, such as the creation and maintenance of a supportive culture. Whilst much of the early research on TQM focused on the technical design of systems and solutions (Wilkinson and Marchington, 1994), there is now a body of research which relates TQM and HRM issues (Ooi *et al.*, 2007). Ooi *et al.* conducted research in Malaysian semiconductor production companies and found strong positive links between TQM and employee satisfaction, particularly where there was a culture of teamwork. Guest (1992) sees quality improvement as inextricably linked to HRM in the following ways:

- Training and development is the normal technique for communicating the importance of quality.

- Because the quality and commitment of the employees is crucial in improving the quality of the product or service there is a need for systematic recruitment, selection and training.

- Top management commitment to TQM is a function of the quality and development of management.

- Adherence to quality takes root in a process of employee involvement and a flexible mode of operation, and this is likely to be more compatible with an organic type of organisation imbued with high trust.

TQM has also been linked to national culture. TQM seeks to empower employees and hence has been associated with low power distance, low uncertainty avoidance cultures in which people are willing to take on decision making (Chin and Pun, 2002). However, it can also apply in other cultures. For example, Kumar and Sankaran (2007) have argued that India's collectivist culture can be productive when TQM is implemented. Although there is a hierarchical element to the Indian culture the nurturing nature of relationships (the 'guru–shishya' or teacher–student relationship) and a collectivist approach compensate for the hierarchical orientation.

The experience of an organisation that adopted TQM as a key feature of a corporate culture the company wished to establish is reported in Case example 5.4. Although TQM has its supporters as an effective intervention in changing and developing culture it has been the subject of criticism. It is argued that it is questionable whether employee empowerment or greater autonomy is a reality. On the basis of a case study of an electronics manufacturing company where TQM was adopted it was clear that problem-solving teams worked on problems identified by management, and the implementation of the solutions and any deviations from the standard format for the execution of a task led to the exercise of management control (Sewell and Wilkinson, 1992). Putting TQM into practice is no easy matter. It has been suggested that there is a high failure rate in the application of TQM in Europe (Zairi *et al.*, 1994). In the United States the results of a study showed that there was a lack of managerial skill in handling it, a resistance to change on the part of those involved, and a recognition that it took longer than expected to produce results (Lorenz, 1993). However, improvements in implementation have been observed more recently (Chapman and Al-Khawaladeh, 2002; Yang *et al.*, 2003).

CASE EXAMPLE 5.4

TQM AT BOSCH

Bosch, a supplier of car components and electronic products to many of Europe's leading car manufacturers, introduced TQM when it opened its first manufacturing plant in the United Kingdom on a greenfield site in Wales in 1990. Many of the company's customers had specific quality demands so it was necessary to have a corporate culture in which quality was firmly ingrained. The values forming part of the culture included a quality product to secure global competitive advantage, continuous improvement of the employees' skills, improved quality of operations and productivity, and ensuring that the company met its responsibilities to customers, employees, suppliers and the local community.

High on the list of priorities was the continuous improvement of employee skills, production methods and productivity, and relations with customers. There was an emphasis on teamworking and team development. This was understandable because the company believed in synergy as applied to the efforts of people – that is, the effect of the group working in concert is greater that the sum of the individual contributions. Teams would be used to tackle problems, to enhance commitment and to further the cause of quality improvement.

The customer–supplier (employee) relationship was emphasised across the board. The supplier would endeavour to deliver to the external customer the appropriate product or service and then ensure that it was delivered 'right first time, on time, every time'. An internal customer is an employee who is a recipient of the company's internal output or service and is entitled to quality customer care. He or she is not the recipient of the finished product or service of the company, but is, for example, the next person on the production line.

The company considered it important that constant feedback flowed from both customers and management to employees to enable them to maintain and improve their standards of performance. The staff newspaper was also used as a vehicle to provide general feedback and reinforcement.

Source: based on Fowler *et al.*, 1992

Questions

1. To what extent do you think the success of TQM is reliant on having a supportive culture?

2. What aspects of an organisational culture would be supportive of TQM?

BUSINESS PROCESS RE-ENGINEERING

BPR has been defined as 'a radical scrutiny, questioning, re-definition, and re-design of business processes with the aim of eliminating all activities not central to the process goals' (Thomas, 1994). As a process of change that questions the way activities are carried out in the organisation, BPR focuses on core business (i.e. activities that add value), leaving non-core activities to be contracted out. A special characteristic of BPR from an organisational design perspective is that it advocates a departure from the rigid compartmentalisation of processes in hierarchical organisation arranged on a functional basis, which can lead to unacceptable delays in processing tasks (e.g. executing orders from customers), to acceptance of the cross-functional project team approach, which is similar in some respects to matrix organisation and project management. It poses a direct challenge to the division of labour and the need for hierarchical control.

The proponents of BPR point to advantages in terms of speed of response, quality, delayering and the scope to apply information technology to handle the complex interdependent and cross-functional processes. In the early 1990s IBM introduced a new management structure after the arrival of its new chairman and chief executive. Shortly afterwards the focus was on business processes, i.e. the way the company carried out the multitude of tasks related to forming and maintaining customer relationships. The main justification for the company's adoption of BPR was to satisfy the needs of customers more effectively (Kehoe, 1994). An application of BPR to a US insurance company appears in Case example 5.5.

In this case job enlargement and job enrichment (explained in Chapters 9 and 10) were experienced by those who participated in the new system. This would suggest that some form of empowerment took place, but this is not always the case. For example, a high street outlet in the United Kingdom, Argos, instituted change processes, which resulted in the simplification and deskilling of tasks. In a survey of UK-based companies that had adopted BPR, Tennant and Wu (2005) found that the key barriers to success were short-term, 'solution-driven' approaches that took inadequate consideration of the people issues. Success was more likely where people did not believe that the change was really a front for downsizing, and where there was a genuine coordination between people and technology.

BPR AT MUTUAL BENEFIT LIFE

Before BPR was introduced the company dealt with new applications for insurance by using a complex administrative process in which applications went through 30 steps, five departments, and were handled by 20 people who performed simple repetitive tasks. The total process could take anything from 5 to 10 days to complete.

After the implementation of BPR the situation changed radically. All new applications were dealt with individually by case managers, with the exception of the most complicated cases. The case manager had at his or her disposal an information technology workstation utilising a database and an expert system, which was invaluable as an aid to decision making. The end result was that the time taken to process each application was reduced by 3 to 5 days and the administrative capacity to handle applications nearly doubled. A reduction in staff amounting to 100 posts led to considerable savings.

Source: based on Hammer, 1990

Questions

1. To what extent do you think the success of BPR is reliant on having a supportive culture?

2. What aspects of an organisational culture would be supportive of BPR?

There are some parallels between BPR and TQM, since both interventions include major organisational and cultural changes. Both require vision and commitment from top management as well as gaining the commitment of employees. Some recent applications of BPR have taken root in greenfield sites. This has inbuilt advantages, as we saw in the Bosch case earlier, because the company can select a workforce compatible with the culture it wishes to adopt and avoid the problems connected with changing the outlook of an existing workforce. First Direct, an autonomous offshoot of Midland Bank (now HSBC), set out to establish a new system of banking involving processes different from traditional banking, and considered it more appropriate to recruit a new workforce with terms and conditions of employment and industrial relations practices different from those in the parent company, but more functional from its own point of view.

It would appear that BPR does not draw on a particular mix of HRM practices. The prevailing circumstances within an organisation are likely to determine the most appropriate mix. However, the following HRM practices are likely to occupy a prominent position: recruitment and selection, job redesign and rewards, training, team building, transformational leadership, and counselling. Opponents of BPR are quick to point out that its claims to success are wildly exaggerated and they would no doubt get some satisfaction from the fact that the Mutual Benefit Life, referred to by Hammer earlier in Case example 5.5, collapsed shortly after the appearance of his article in 1990. They would also point out that there is very little in BPR that has not been incorporated in other management and organisational approaches, such as the matrix organisation and TQM.

Some argue that BPR is a cost-cutting and restructuring technique at a time when the prevailing management emphasis is switching to growth. In other words its focus is on corporate mechanics, not on vision or strategy, and left to its own devices it will drive out all strategies except cost minimisation (Lloyd, 1994). A scathing attack on BPR comes from Case (1999), who in observing that its popularity amongst management is on the decline goes on to say that it has an exploitative dimension to it.

OTHER TECHNIQUES

A technique that originated within General Electric (Bolman and Deal, 2003) and which has become popular is known as 'WorkOut'. An application and explanation of this technique is given in Case example 5.6.

CASE EXAMPLE 5.6

USING 'WORKOUT' TO CHANGE CULTURE AT EAGLE STAR

When Patrick O'Sullivan joined Eagle Star as chief executive in 1997 he confronted a high degree of inefficiency and complacency within the company. The system of creating reserves was inadequate, the pricing in the marketplace left much to be desired, the marketing function was unduly influencing risk assessment decisions, information technology was completely disconnected from the business and was consuming large amounts of resources and going nowhere, the actuaries and underwriters were not talking to each other, the finance function was not well integrated into the business (it was a reporting function that did senior management's bidding), and the chain of accountability was deficient. The new chief executive was alarmed to find that only his predecessor and a few of his senior staff were aware of the seriousness of the company's plight. Generally the employees – who were getting more and more rewards (e.g. flexitime, benefits and bonuses) – thought the company was wonderful to work for.

In his first three months the new chief executive visited 40 sites and addressed more than 90 per cent of employees, telling them about the seriousness of the situation affecting the company and the changes that were being contemplated. He experienced subtle resistance from a layer of senior and middle managers, and the rest of the staff were rather cynical. O'Sullivan was convinced that the technique 'WorkOut' could be used to bring about change. He knew that General Electric, USA used WorkOut successfully when in the past he worked for one of its subsidiaries in Europe.

It is claimed that WorkOut can shorten the decision-making process as well as improving it, and enhances responsiveness to customers' needs by using the collective intelligence of the entire company, not just the management elite. The employees are encouraged to come forward with well-prepared and properly costed proposals, and these are presented to 'town meetings' where senior managers are present and are expected to listen to the proposals for change. A WorkOut could consist of groups of 50–100 employees from a cross-section of business units, and three days can be allocated to solving problems. There is likely to be heated debate in these forums and the key decision makers (i.e. the senior managers) are required to give a 'yes' or 'no' answer there and then. If they give a 'yes' answer then implementation will take place over a 2–3 month period, but if the answer is 'no' then senior managers have to offer credible reasons why the proposal(s) cannot be adopted.

The WorkOuts in the company started in 1998 with the Eagle Star Direct Group, who were considered to be an innovative team, and they responded positively to this technique. Members came together for three-day WorkOuts and worked long hours without receiving any overtime pay, even though they would normally expect to receive such payments in their jobs. The problems they confronted were response times, and concrete proposals were put forward to increase productivity. Although O'Sullivan acknowledged that much work had to be done in perfecting the technique, he considered WorkOut had been a key factor in turning round Eagle Star. Following a merger in 1998 the company, which was part of BAT Financial Services, was now in the same stable as Zurich Financial Services. O'Sullivan used WorkOut to bring together Eagle Star and Zurich, two companies with different corporate cultures.

Source: based on Bolger, 2000

Question

Do you think that the WorkOut technique could work in isolation, or does it need to be implemented in line with other culture change processes? Give reasons for your answer.

Some contemporary issues

When giving further thought to the most appropriate culture to develop within an organisation, it would be wise to pay attention to the issues raised here. The link between culture and contemporary issues, such as ethics, customer responsiveness, spirituality, and the learning organisation, will now be briefly examined.

ETHICS

Ethics, which is the code of moral principles and values that govern the behaviour of people with respect to what is right and wrong, can go beyond behaviour governed by the legal system. (There is a discussion of ethical issues in Chapter 11.) In recent years serious corporate accounting scandals, charges of insider trading and company executives making personal use of company funds have helped to focus on issues related to corporate ethics. Organisations should be active in promoting an ethical culture. The following measures might be considered relevant (Robbins, 2003; Smith *et al.*, 2001):

■ Management, particularly top management, should lead by example and act as a responsible role model on ethical issues.

■ Strive for the minimisation of ethical ambiguities by producing and circulating an organisational code of ethics. This document should state the organisation's primary values and ethical rules that employees are expected to follow.

■ Be visible when it comes to rewarding ethical acts and disapprove and punish unethical ones.

■ Put in place procedures to enable employees to discuss ethical dilemmas and report unethical behaviour without fear of reprimand. An individual, such as an ethical counsellor, could oversee this process.

Steare (2006) argues that an ethical culture should be developed not only to avoid risk of prosecution, but also because it can lead to enhanced performance. In his view companies should 'do the right thing because it is the right thing to do'. By this he means that being ethically good also encourages businesses to make effective decisions and manage people well. Research has indicated that employees' perceptions of their company's level of corporate social responsibility (CSR) has a significant influence on their commitment to the firm (Brammer *et al.*, 2006). In order to capitalise on this, Steare (2006) suggests that the crucial step is to distil values into behaviours. Employees should not only be aware of ethical dilemmas, but should also be aware of the choices of action open to them. This should be reinforced by an effective performance management system which overtly checks ethical behaviour. One might question whether adopting an ethical culture mainly in the pursuit of self-interest is genuinely ethical, but this can be a way of gaining commitment to such a change.

CUSTOMER RESPONSIVENESS

In recent years there has been an emphasis on customer-responsive cultures. In this type of culture one could expect to find a number of measures to promote the interests of the customer, such as the following (Bettencourt *et al.*, 2001; Robbins, 2003):

- Recruit and select people who possess personality attributes and attitudes, in line with a high service orientation. These could include an outgoing and friendly disposition coupled with a desire to provide high standards of service.

- Key managers within the organisation should show their commitment to customer care by words and deeds.

- Employees who engage in a good level of service to customers should be well rewarded – in effect the organisation makes pay and promotion dependent upon impressive service to the customer.

- Inject flexibility and autonomy into the jobs of those charged with meeting customers' requirements. This would be consistent with the concept of empowerment.

SPIRITUALITY

Spirituality in the workplace is not concerned with organised religious practices. However, it is concerned with the inner life of the person, and looks at ways in which that inner life can enrich and be enriched by meaningful work in an organisational setting. Those who subscribe to spirituality in this sense would like to see the development of an organisational culture which recognises that people have a spiritual side to their makeup, are eager to seek meaning, purpose and fulfilment in the work they do, as well as striving for satisfaction from connecting with other people and feeling they are part of a community (Ashmos and Duchon, 2000; McCormick, 1994). A number of reasons are given for the preoccupation with workplace spirituality. These include a desire to obtain something of significance from life in a world where increasingly organised religion has less meaning for many people, where existing work may lack meaning, where there is a need to counter-balance occupational and life's pressures, and where there is a desire to bring personal values and beliefs more into line with work-based values.

If one were to profile the culture of the spiritual organisation it is likely that the following features would be heavily underlined (Robbins, 2003). There would be a climate of openness where people felt free to air their feelings and emotions without the realisation that they would be disadvantaged; where mutual trust and honesty exist; where people are highly valued and their growth and development is a key issue; and where empowerment is a striking feature of the organisational landscape. Some would not condone this type of emphasis when it comes to shaping the culture of the organisation and are likely to point out that spirituality and profitability are not natural bedfellows. However, there is evidence to indicate that there is a positive relationship between the two.

LEARNING ORGANISATION

In Chapter 10 the concept of the learning organisation is examined, and it is stated that the learning organisation could help with the development of the company's capacity to respond well to changes in its environment by facilitating the learning of all its employees, and by being alert to the need for continuous transformation. In essence the aim is to create a culture of continuous learning for all employees.

Following a review of the relevant literature, Daft (2004) maintains that one of the potent characteristics of the learning organisation is a strong organisational culture that incorporates the following values: employees are aware of the whole system and how the constituent parts fit together; the emphasis on the whole minimises the significance of boundaries, and despite the existence of subcultures there is a strong commitment to the dominant culture. Also, equality and trust are primary values and it is apparent that the culture of the learning organisation creates a pronounced sense of community and caring for one another. The emphasis on treating everyone with care and respect generates an atmosphere of trust where people feel secure. This allows experimentation in a climate where people do not feel too inhibited about making mistakes and learning is an ongoing process. Finally, the culture within the learning organisation encourages risk taking and a commitment to change and the improvements of systems and processes. A basic value of the learning organisation is to question the status quo. For those who are innovative with respect to products and processes there is due recognition for their contributions with the dispensing of appropriate rewards.

This approach changes the nature of training so that it becomes learning-focused (Sloman, 2006). Rather than a training approach in which skills are 'passed on' from instructors, a learning culture entails trainers becoming 'people developers'. In this role they seek to support and accelerate learning in which the learner is highly active in deciding on priorities and engaging purposively. Such an approach has been significant in service-sector and knowledge-based firms where it is not easy to codify skills and knowledge. However, the idea is spreading. The pharmaceutical giant, Pfizer, has gone down this path in dealing with cultural differences in its research and development wing. It employs 14,000 people in the United States, the United Kingdom and Japan. Considerable effort has gone into developing understanding across the cultural differences, ranging from practicalities such as how to run meetings to broader cultural issues such as how hierarchy is regarded. As a result, communication and learning between the different centres has become much more open (Sloman, 2006). Some might view the values of the learning organisation outlined here as rather idealistic, but as a set of principles they are worth considering.

Culture and HRM

A link between HRM and culture is emphasised when it is suggested that an important role of HRM within high performance work organisations is the development of 'core' organisational values to inform the strategic direction of the business (Drummond and Stone, 2007; Huselid, 1995).

HRM adopts a unitarist position, which espouses the view that it is in the interests of organisational members to work together towards the achievement of common goals without the intrusive influence of conflict. It takes the view that it is to the benefit of employees, in terms of rewards and job security, for the organisation to achieve its goals successfully. In taking this stand HRM is supporting a particular view of organisational culture, which could be seen as management driven, where conflict does not exist and common interests prevail.

This could pose a dilemma because HRM also espouses a flexible approach to job design. Adopting this approach, which has the ingredients of a pluralist perspective, could mean employees experiencing greater control over their work, including greater responsibility for the outcome of their effort, as well as greater group autonomy through, for example, quality circles and autonomous work groups. Apart from specific initiatives in job design HRM is partial to the removal of layers within the organisation, which has the effect of pushing decision making further down the organisation. This results in reducing managerial control over employees. In addition, HRM expects effective and dedicated performance from members of the organisation when it stresses the need for employees to be creative and innovative in pursuit of higher performance standards, and to commit themselves to hours at work over and above their contractual hours.

Therefore the challenge for HRM is to reconcile the unitarist perspective with the pluralist perspective of greater individual and group autonomy. The reconciliation of these two positions is unlikely to be an easy task, and begs the following question: can we create an organisational culture in pluralist conditions where there can be reasonable harmony between the interests of the organisation and the interests of employees to pursue objectives based on self-interest, which may not be in congruence with company objectives?

There have been a number of criticisms of the role of culture in HRM. Above it is acknowledged that, in the pluralist perspective, managerial control is removed to a certain extent, and subordinates are empowered, thereby creating conditions for a greater diversity of views. In such a climate is it realistic to assume that a uniform culture with strongly held shared values and beliefs can coexist with 'deviant' values held by individuals? According to Willmott (1993) the conditions for the expression of heretical views, or the adherence to competing values by individuals or groups, could be severely limited if the uniform culture is strong. Referring to strong cultures to which organisational members subscribe, alluded to earlier, it is suggested that a disadvantage could be reduced flexibility and adaptation to changing environmental conditions because people subscribe to cultural norms more suited to the previous conditions than to the changed conditions (Legge, 1989). However, one should not be left with the impression that, generally speaking, weak culture is synonymous with flexibility. It may be that the metaphor of relative strength is not the best way to conceive cultures.

In a development of Legge's critical appraisal Watson (2004) argues that a conceptualisation that posits too great an autonomy on the part of managers to decide on a high or a low commitment culture is as problematic as one which presumes that the context determines the culture with no input from management. The argument here differs from that of Willmott (above) in that managers are seen to have a role of interactively interpreting the context and making use of this to develop a position between pure high and pure low commitment cultures. However, managers are not totally free from the constraints of their business environment and hence a balanced approach is called for.

Other critics draw our attention to the distinction between the 'practitioner' literature and the 'academic' literature in the way organisational culture is dealt with in HRM (Mabey and Salaman, 1995). Those espousing the practitioner view are seen as simplifying the complex nature of culture and adopting initiatives to control the environment within which people work in order to enhance performance. By contrast the academic perspective appeals to social anthropology to capture the complexity of culture by focusing on the rituals, behaviour, beliefs and language of participants. The views expressed in the academic literature are not sympathetic to the views found in the practitioner literature. In a similar vein, some approaches to HRM and culture management are regarded as overly 'managerialist'. In such cases, too much emphasis is placed on the interests of the organisation and not enough on those of the employees. Some research has indicated that overly managerialist approaches may be self-defeating as organisational strategies that incorporate employee involvement and the possibility of genuine challenge are likely to be more successful (Diefenbach, 2007).

We would call for a reconciliation of the opposing 'academic' and 'practitioner' views and for the goodness of both approaches to be preserved. This may require practitioner-oriented literature to acknowledge a degree of complexity and tension between competing options rather than espousing the best way of doing things. Conversely, in the academic literature, the needs of practitioners to decide on a course of action should be given due weight, on par with critical comment on policies and practices.

COMMITMENT

A commentary on HRM and culture would not be complete without a serious comment on organisational commitment, which is a key concept in HRM. It is one of the four 'Cs' in the Harvard Model (discussed in Chapter 1) and amounts to a certain degree of identification with the stated aims, objectives and values of the organisation as well as involvement on the part of employees. In attitudinal and behavioural terms this could be reflected in their desire to stay with the organisation, and putting more than adequate effort into the achievement of business objectives. Employees are more likely to be committed to their employing organisation if they feel confidence in their employer's commitment to them. It should be said that real commitment is unlikely without mutual trust.

At one time western companies expressed a strong interest in developing the type of commitment shown by Japanese workers. Values at the heart of the Japanese workers' commitment, apart from its reciprocal nature, are as follows:

■ work ethic – seen to work hard, and long hours spent at work;

■ conformity – a high need to belong, and not to be isolated from one's community;

■ avoidance of shame – failure to discharge duties in accordance with normal social rules can bring shame, loss of face and could result in isolation.

It would be difficult to transplant these values in their pure form to a western context. In any case commitment is likely to receive a battering in the age of the leaner, fitter and delayered organisation, where opportunities for advancement and security of employment are not what they used to be.

Conclusions

It should now be clear that the organisational culture and attempts to change and manage it are legitimate concerns of HRM. Culture is closely linked to strategy and structure and influences activities such as recruitment, selection, appraisal, training and rewards, which are covered in subsequent chapters. Changing culture is a prolonged and costly process. For example IBM, having failed to read correctly developments in the microcomputer market at one stage, subsequently embarked on major cultural change through a different type of leadership, questioning many of the old values, a process that continues to the present day. Likewise, the former Rover Motor Car Company spent 15 years trying to gain acceptance for its changed philosophy of management. In HRM terms the latter is based on mutual commitment, which has the potential to increase cooperation and performance and lead to competitive advantage.

Theories of culture have been criticised on a number of grounds. For example, it can be asked if all individuals in an organisation (or nation) really share the same culture. Equally questionable is the view that an organisation can really change the deeply held values of employees. Nonetheless the policies adopted by the organisation, and management action, reflect organisational culture. The combined effect of policy and management action, coupled with the way employees are treated on a daily basis within the organisation, can lead to employees making judgements about the organisation's culture and their place in it. Culture is not just the rituals and ceremonies – it is also reflected in the basic processes of organisational life. Therefore it is crucially important for managers to bear these issues in mind when performing their normal activities. The way managers use power, express emotion, make decisions, involve and reward others will create the setting for the formation of attitudes and commitment of the employees.

Review and reflection questions

1. What are the dimensions used in Hofestede's model of culture?

2. What does the term 'organisation culture' mean?

3. What are the four major aspects of an organisation culture?

4. What are the types of culture according to Deal and Kennedy?

5. When changing culture, what, according to Schein, should managers pay attention to?

6. What is the relationship between initiatives such as TQM and BPR and organisation culture?

7. How can a culture encourage ethical (or unethical) behaviour?

8. What is the significance of culture to the successful practice of HRM?

Activities

If you are in work:

1. Choose one of the descriptive models (e.g. Harrison or Deal and Kennedy) and use it to analyse the culture of your organisation.

2. What are the main strengths and weaknesses of your organisational culture?

3. What changes would you see as desirable?

If you are in full-time study:

1. Choose a well-known organisation (e.g. a retail company or a business with a high media profile) and collect as much information as you can about it:

   (a) artifacts such as products

   (b) communications such as adverts, press releases, websites

   (c) stories of the organisation, for example, in case studies or the media.

2. Analyse the information in order to make a judgement about the type of culture the organisation has.

Further reading and research

We started the chapter by examining national culture and more on this topic can be found in:
Smith P.B. (2004) 'Nations, cultures, and individuals', *Journal of Cross Cultural Psychology*, 35, 6–12.

The links between culture, HRM and improving performance are central to the line of reasoning advocated in HRM. The following reference throws more light on this topic:
Detert, J.R., Schroeder, R.G. and Mauriel J.J. (2000) 'A framework for linking culture and improvement initiatives in organizations', *Academy of Management Review*, 25, 850–863.

In the course of the chapter, we raised the issue of ethics and its connection to culture. The following article provides a view of how to develop an ethical culture:
Clarke, E. (2007) 'Stop thief: develop a culture of ethics to beat employee fraud', *People Management*, 8 February, 34–36.

There are many websites relating to organisational culture and culture change. Two that are worth a visit are:
■ www.mindtools.com, which provides an outline and example of Gerry Johnson's Culture Web technique of analysis. More information on the culture web is available in Johnson, G., Scholes, K. and Whittington, R. (2005) *Exploring Corporate Strategy*, Harlow: Pearson.
■ http://humanresources.about.com: this human resources website has a number of short articles on understanding and changing organisational culture.

References

Adler, N. (2002) *International dimensions of organisational behaviour*, Cincinnati, OH: South Western College Publishing.

Ashmos, D.P. and Duchon, D. (2000) 'Spirituality at work. A conceptualization and measure', *Journal of Management Inquiry*, June, 139.

Atkins, R. and Milne, R. (2004) 'How a Rhineland behemoth changed course', *Financial Times*, 22 November, 8.

Bettencourt, L.A., Gwinner, K.P. and Meuter, M.L. (2001) 'A comparison of attitude, personality, and knowledge predictions of service oriented organizational citizenship behaviours', *Journal of Applied Psychology*, February, 29–41.

Bhaskaran, S. and Sukumaran, N. (2007) 'National culture, business culture and management practices: Consequential relationships?', *Cross Cultural Management: An International Journal*, 14, 54–67.

Bolger, A. (2000) 'How Eagle Star was saved by a high flier', *Financial Times*, 30 June, 16.

Bolman, L.G. and Deal, T.E. (2003) *Reframing Organisations: Artistry, choice and leadership*, San Francisco, CA: Jossey-Bass.

Boye, D.M. (1991) 'The storytelling organization: A study of story performance in an office-supply firm', *Administrative Science Quarterly*, March, 106–126.

Brammer, S., Millington, A. and Rayton, B. (2006) 'Do CSR policies affect employees' commitment to their organizations?', *People Management*, February, 52.

Brannan, M.J. and Hawkins, B. (2007) 'London Calling: selection as pre-emptive strategy for cultural control', *Employee Relations*, 29, 178–191.

Brown, A.D. (2006) 'A narrative approach to collective identities', *Journal of Management Studies*, 43, 731–753.

Case, P. (1999) 'Remember re-engineering? The rhetorical appeal of a managerial salvation device', *Journal of Management Studies*, 36, 420–441.

Chapman, R. and Al-Khawaldeh, K. (2002) 'Quality Management Worldwide: TQM and labour productivity in Jordanian industrial companies', *The TQM Magazine*, 14, 248–262.

Chin, S.C. and Pun, K.F. (2002) 'A proposed framework for implementing TQM in Chinese Organizations', *The International Journal of Quality and Reliability Management*, 19, 272-294.

Cox Jr., T. (1993) *Cultural diversity in organizations: Theory, research, and practice*, San Francisco: Berrett-Koehler.

Daft, R.L. (2004) *Organization theory and design*, International Student Edition, Mason, OH: South Western.

Dale, B.D., Cooper, C.L. and Wilkinson, A. (1998) *Managing Quality and Human Resources: A guide to continuous improvement*, Oxford: Blackwell.

Deal, T. and Kennedy, A. (1982) *Corporate Cultures*, London: Penguin.

Den Hartog, D.N., House, R.J., Hanges, P.J., Ruiz-Quintanilla and Dorfman, P.W. (1999) 'Culture specific and cross-culturally generalizable implicit leadership theories: are attributes of charismatic/transformational leadership universally endorsed?', *Leadership Quarterly*, 10, 219–256.

Denison, D.R. (1996) 'What is the difference between organizational culture and organizational climate? A native's point of view on a decade of paradigm wars', *Academy of Management Review*, 21, 619–654.

Diefenbach, T. (2007) 'The Managerialistic Ideology of Organisational Change Management', *Journal of Organizational Change Management*, 20, 126–144.

Drummond, I. and Stone, I. (2007) 'Exploring the potential of high performance work systems in SMEs', *Employee Relations*, 29, 192–207.

Financial Times (2005) 'Editorial comment: Ethics and business: changing Citigroup's corporate culture will not be easy', 18 February, 16.

Fowler, A., Sheard, M. and Wibberley, M. (1992) 'Two routes to quality', *Personnel Management*, November, 30–34.

Fujimoto, Y., Bahfen, N., Fermelis, J. and Hartel, C.E.J. (2007) 'The global village: Online cross-cultural communication and HRM', *Cross Cultural Management: An International Journal*, 14, 7–22.

Furnham, A. (2005) *The psychology of behaviour at work*, Hove, UK: Psychology Press.

Goffee, R. (1997) 'Cultural diversity', in *Mastering Management: Module 6 Organisational Behaviour*, 240–246, FT/Pitman Publishing.

Griffith, V. (1995) 'Hero one day, villain the next', *Financial Times*, 3 March, 13.

Guest, D.E. (1992) 'Human resource management in the UK', in Towers, B. (ed.), *The Handbook of Human Resource Management*, Oxford: Blackwell.

Guest, D.E. (1994a) 'Organizational psychology and human resource management: towards a European approach', *European Work and Organizational Psychologist*, 4, 251–270.

Guest, D.E. (1994b) 'Human resource management: opportunity or threat?', in Indoe, D. and Spencer, C. (eds), *Survival and Quality, Annual Course Proceedings 1994, Educational and Child Psychology*, 11, 5–10.

Hamel, G. and Prahalad, C.K. (1994) *Competing for the Future*, Boston, MA: Harvard Business School Press.

Hammer, M. (1990) 'Re-engineering work: don't automate, obliterate', *Harvard Business Review*, July/August, 104–112.

Handy, C. (1985) *Understanding Organisations*, London: Penguin.

Harrison, R. (1972) 'Understanding your organization's character', *Harvard Business Review*, May/June, 119–128.

Hill, S. (1991) 'Why quality circles failed but total quality management might succeed', *British Journal of Industrial Relations*, 29, 541–568.

Hofestede, G.H. (1980) *Culture's Consequences*, Beverly Hills, CA: Sage.

Hofestede, G.H. (1994) *Cultures and Organizations: Intercultural cooperation and its importance for survival*, Maidenhead: McGraw-Hill.

House, R.J. (1995) 'Leadership in the 21st century: a speculative inquiry', in Howard, A. (ed.), *The Changing Nature of Work*, San Francisco, CA: Jossey-Bass.

Huselid, M.A. (1995) 'The impact of human resource management practices on turnover, productivity, and corporate financial performance', *Academy of Management Journal*, 38, 635–670.

Ishida, H. (1986) 'Transferability of Japanese human resource management abroad', *Human Resource Management*, 25, 103–121.

Kandola, R. (1995) 'Managing diversity: new broom or old hat?', in Cooper, C.L. and Robertson, I.T. (eds), *International Review of Industrial and Organizational Psychology*, 10, Chichester: Wiley.

Kanter, R. (1989) *When Giants Learn to Dance: Mastering the challenge of strategy, management, and careers in the 1990s*, London: Unwin.

Kehoe, L. (1994) 'Down in the dirt to clean up IBM', *Financial Times*, 5 December, 8.

Koopman, P.L., Den Hartog, D.N. and Konrad, E. (and others too numerous to mention) (1999) 'National culture and leadership profiles in Europe: some results from the GLOBE study', *European Journal of Work and Organizational Psychology*, 8, 503–520.

Kreitner, R., Kinicki, A. and Buelens, M. (2002) *Organizational Behaviour*, Maidenhead: McGraw-Hill.

Kumar, M.R. and Sankaran, S. (2007) 'Indian Culture and the Culture for TQM: a comparison', *The TQM Magazine*, 19, 176–188.

Legge, K. (1989) 'Human resource management: a critical analysis', in Storey, J. (ed.), *New Perspectives in Human Resource Management*, London: Routledge.

Lloyd, T. (1994) 'Giant with feet of clay', *Financial Times*, 5 December, 8.

Lorenz, C. (1993) 'TQM: alive and kicking in the US', *Financial Times*, 23 July, 15.

Mabey, C. and Salaman, G. (1995) *Strategic Human Resource Management*, Oxford: Blackwell.

Marx, E. (1999) *Breaking through Culture Shock*, London: Nicholas Brealey.

McCormick, D.W. (1994) 'Spirituality and Management', *Journal of Managerial Psychology*, 9, 5.

Michailova, S. and Hutchings, K. (2006) 'National Cultural Influences on Knowledge Sharing: A comparison of China and Russia', *Journal of Management Studies*, 43, 383–405.

Miles, R.E. and Snow, C.C. (1978) *Organisational Strategy, Structure, and Process*, New York: McGraw-Hill.

Moorhead, G. and Griffin, R.W. (2004) *Organisational behaviour: Managing people and organisations*, Boston: Houghton Mifflin.

Ogbonna, E. (1992) 'Organisation culture and human resource management: dilemmas and contradictions', in Blyton, P. and Turnbull, P. (eds), *Reassessing Human Resource Management*, London: Sage.

Ogbonna, E. and Whipp, R. (1999) 'Strategy, culture, and HRM: evidence from the UK retailing sector', *Human Resource Management Journal*, 9, 75–90.

Oliver, N. and Wilkinson, B. (1992) *The Japanization of British Industry: New developments in the 1990s*, Oxford: Blackwell.

Ooi, K.B., Bakar, N.A., Arumugam, V., Vellepan, L. and Loke, A.K.Y. (2007) 'Does TQM influence employees' job satisfaction? An empirical case analysis', *International Journal of Quality and Reliability Management*, 24, 62–77.

Ouchi, W.G. (1981) *Theory Z: How American business can meet the Japanese challenge*, Reading, MA: Addison-Wesley.

Peters, T. and Waterman, R. (1982) *In Search of Excellence*, New York: Harper & Row.

Riad, S. (2007) 'Of mergers and cultures: What happened to shared values and joint assumptions?', *Journal of Organisational Change Management*, 20, 26–43.

Robbins, S.P. (2003) *Organisational behaviour*, Upper Saddle River, NJ: Prentice-Hall/Pearson Education International.

Schein, E.H. (1985) *Organisational Culture and Leadership*, San Francisco, CA: Jossey-Bass.

Schein, E.H. (1990) 'Organisational culture', *American Psychologist*, 45, 109–119.

Schonberger, R. (1982) *Japanese Manufacturing Techniques*, New York: Free Press.

Sekiguchi, T. (2007) 'A contingency perspective on the importance of PJ fit and PO fit in employee selection', *Journal of Managerial Psychology*, 22, 118–131.

Sewell, G. and Wilkinson, B. (1992) 'Empowerment or emasculation? Shopfloor surveillance in a total quality organisation', in Blyton, P. and Turnbull, P. (eds), *Reassessing Human Resource Management*, London: Sage.

Simms, J. (2005) 'Spirit of Co-operation', *People Management*, August, 34–37.

Sloman, M. (2006) 'Just your Cup of Tea?', *People Management*, December, 34–36.

Smith, D.B., Grojean, M.W. and Ehrhart, M. (2001) 'An organizational climate regarding ethics: The outcome of leader values and practices that reflect them', *Leadership Quarterly*, Summer, 197–217.

Steare, R. (2006) 'How to create an ethical culture', *People Management*, February, 46–47.

Tait, N. (2005) 'Cantor close to settlement with bullied trader', *Financial Times*, 22 March, 2.

Tennant, C. and Wu, Y.-C. (2005) 'The application of business process reengineering in the UK', *The TQM Magazine*, 17, 537–545.

Thomas, M. (1994) 'What do you need to know about business process re-engineering?', *Personnel Management*, 26, 28–31.

Torrington, D. and Hall, L. (1998) *Human Resource Management*, Hemel Hempstead: Prentice Hall.

Trice, H.M. and Beyer, J.M. (1984) 'Studying organisational cultures through rites and rituals', *Academy of Management Review*, 9, 653–669.

Trompenaars, A. (1993) *Riding the Wave of Culture. Understanding cultural diversity in business*, London: Nicholas Brealey.

Tushman, M. and O'Reilly, C.A. (1996) *Staying on Top: Managing strategic innovation and change for long-term success*, Boston, MA: Harvard Business Press.

Watson, T. (2004) 'HRM and Critical Social Science Analysis', *Journal of Management Studies*, 41, 447–468.

Weaving, K. (1995) 'Sweeping fear from the floor', *Financial Times*, 3 March, 13.

Wickens, P. (1987) *The Road to Nissan*, London: Macmillan.

Wilkinson, A. and Marchington, M. (1994) 'TQM: instant pudding for the personnel function?', *Human Resource Management Journal*, 5, 33–49.

Wilkinson, B. and Oliver, N. (1992) 'HRM in Japanese manufacturing companies in the UK and USA', in Towers, B. (ed.), *The Handbook of Human Resource Management*. Oxford: Blackwell.

Williams, A., Dobson, P. and Walters, M. (1989) *Changing Culture*, London: Institute of Personnel Management.

Willmott, H. (1993) 'Ignorance is strength, freedom is slavery: managing culture in modern organizations', *Journal of Management Studies*, 30, 515–555.

Yang, T., Chen, M.C. and Su, C.T. (2003) 'Quality management practice in semiconductor manufacturing industries – empirical studies in Taiwan', *Integrated Manufacturing Systems*, 14, 153–159.

Zairi, M., Letza, S. and Oakland, J. (1994) 'Does TQM impact on bottom line results?', *TQM Magazine*, 6, 38–43.

Chapter 6

EMPLOYEE RESOURCING: HUMAN RESOURCE PLANNING

Introduction

Human resource planning (HRP) is an activity that directly links HRM to organisational strategy. It is concerned with setting out the size, quality and nature of the workforce in order to meet corporate objectives. Increasingly there is a need for flexibility in planning, and resource-based strategies (discussed in Chapter 2) to put people centre stage in the strategic planning process. There is a need to be able to meet the demands of the business environment and also to be able to motivate and develop employees. These twin demands mean that HRP has to focus both internally and externally – making the most of external opportunities and enabling current employees to progress and develop their skills. Hence there is a strong link between HRP and recruitment and selection and training and development.

Having read this chapter, you should:

- understand the role of HRP in an integrated approach to HRM;

- be aware of the issues in achieving a balance between the demand for, supply and utilisation of labour;

- be aware of some of the analytical techniques of HRP;

- understand the effects that changes in external factors, such as legislation and demographics, can have on HRP;

- know what the different types of flexibility are, and have an appreciation of how they can be applied;

- have an understanding of some of the current critical issues and developments in HRP.

Employee resourcing, the process of acquiring and utilising human resources in the organisation, consists of a number of specialist activities that need to act in harmony to ensure that human resources of the right quantity and quality are available to meet the overall objectives of the company. The specialist activities referred to are human resource planning (HRP), which is dealt with in this chapter, and recruitment and selection, which are examined in Chapter 7. These activities are operationalised in the context of strategic human resource management (SHRM), a topic discussed in Chapter 2. As was stated there, strategic human resource planning is an approach that links the management of human resources to the organisation's overall strategies for achieving its goals and objectives.

A starting point for HRP is to assess the future needs of the organisation for employees, noting the blend of skills required. As stated earlier, HRP is part of the framework set by the interaction of SHRM and corporate strategy. By contrast, traditional manpower planning was concerned principally with making sure that the organisation had the right number of employees in the right place at the right time. Human resource planning has not rejected this perspective but it has changed our understanding of it. In traditional manpower planning a strong quantitative bias was evident, with an orientation towards dealing with 'hard' problems and their solutions. But in HRM, with its strong emphasis on people as a key resource, there is the recognition that the 'hard' problem approach has to be supplemented by the 'soft' problem approach. In the latter case qualitative issues connected with employee creativity, innovative practices, flexibility, messy problems and so on are taken very seriously.

The anchor of HRM comprises three facets, as follows:

1. demand for human resources, which can be gleaned from the strategic human resource plan;
2. utilisation of human resources in a cost-effective and efficient manner;
3. supply of human resources manifested in the current number of employees (internal supply) and the potential pool of suitable applicants external to the organisation (external supply).

There is a dynamic interplay between the three facets mentioned, and the overall process is mediated by happenings within the organisation (internal environment) and forces external to the organisation (external environment). Both environments generate turbulence where change is omnipresent and has to be managed.

Demand for human resources

Demand for human resources can be defined as the number of staff required to meet the organisation's future needs as well as the composition of the workforce in terms of the necessary skills. For example, an expansion of the organisation's activities could result in recruiting extra staff with the appropriate skills. On the other hand an organisation may be planning to reduce staffing levels because of an anticipated fall in the demand for its product(s). Of course rationalisation of staffing levels could also be prompted by other considerations, such as scope to cut costs or improve working practices, which offers the opportunity to maintain the existing output, or in some cases to increase output, with fewer employees. As was mentioned earlier, competitive forces emanating from the external environment can have a material bearing on the magnitude of the demand for human resources. This could be reflected in a reduction of staffing levels as well as changing the character and skills associated with the jobs that remain

A telling example of such changes is the UK banking sector in the 1990s. During this time, the banks faced increased competition from building societies, coupled with customer expectations of low charges and quality of services. The result was a need not only to reduce costs but also to maintain levels of service. A method to achieve this was greater use of new technology which removed many of the old paper-handling jobs of the early 1990s and before. As a consequence there was a reduction in staffing levels in order to avoid overstaffing. This resulted in a significant reduction in demand for human resources, and led to a preoccupation with the quality of the human resources. For example, it was felt that the staff needed new information technology skills, and to develop their abilities in customer relations, sales and knowledge of the products and services offered by the bank.

The traditional approach to calculating the demand for human resources is to make use of ratios, for example the simple ratio of 4:1 used in a research and development department within a company. In this particular situation that means four scientific officers to one technician. The company decided that an extra four scientific officers would be appointed, in which case it must set aside funds for a new technician as well.

A first step when using ratios in the example given is to decide on the number of new scientific officers that the company requires. To assist with this task data are collected and projected into the future, and this can be presented diagrammatically using trend analysis (see Figure 6.1).

Projection A in Figure 6.1 shows a constant ratio. This means that in every situation the work of four scientific officers will require the work of one technician. Projection B indicates that in certain circumstances the ratio may be variable. In this case there are 'economies of scale', which means that although the first four scientific officers need a full-time technician, in a larger department of 20 scientific officers, three rather than five technicians are needed. This could occur because of efficiency gains from the technicians working as a team, or from them specialising and becoming expert in particular tasks. Projection C indicates achieving a different ratio because of implementing a change, for example, the introduction of new technology, which results in each technician being able to service six scientific officers.

This type of analysis can also be used to plot the number of employees needed against projected demand for production. For example, there could be a ratio of four scientific officers to 1 million units of production per annum. Therefore, if production were to be raised from 4 million units to 6 million units, the complement of scientific officers would need to rise from 16 to 24 (where a constant ratio was applied). Current thinking in some areas of hospital-based health care is that as changes in technology enhance the care that can be provided to patients, the ratio of technical to clinical staff is likely to increase. Innovations require an increased technical component to medicine and, as a result, current ratios are being revised in order to prepare for future demand.

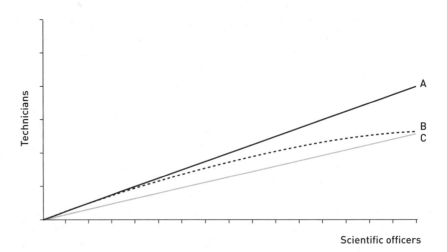

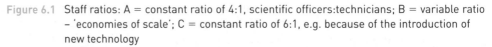

Figure 6.1 Staff ratios: A = constant ratio of 4:1, scientific officers:technicians; B = variable ratio – 'economies of scale'; C = constant ratio of 6:1, e.g. because of the introduction of new technology

The use of ratios in calculating the demand for human resources was more prevalent when the influence of trade unions was pronounced. They were used in union–management negotiations on staffing levels. However, as competitive conditions have increased a more flexible approach has been called for (Sanchez *et al.*, 2007). This meant assessing particular requests on the basis of merit. A more flexible approach may involve achieving the same level of output with a reduced number of staff through gains in productivity, the introduction of new technology, or it may involve changes to job design such as job enlargement.

In the heyday of manpower planning statistical forecasting techniques were based on assumptions of stability and absence of radical change when predicting future demand for labour. Such an approach would now be unrealistic given the likely future turbulence and uncertainty in markets. When considering the demand for human resources in an HRM framework a preoccupation with customers and quality in conditions of change is very much in evidence (Bramham, 1989; Torrington *et al.*, 2005). Formal HRP techniques are still used, typically by large organisations. However, in fluctuating and speedily changing business environments, predictions of future needs based on extrapolation from the past are regarded as lacking reliability and hence there is a focus on pragmatism and flexibility that allows the organisation to meet unexpected needs (Torrington *et al.*, 2005). Nowadays planning needs to possess the characteristics of speed and response if it is to be successful. Managerial judgement seems to be asserting itself in the process of establishing demand for human resources where a balance has to be achieved between the use of systematic data drawn from formal planning and the views of those managing the day-to-day reality of the organisation concerning the range of skills required (Arnold and Pulich, 2007).

One approach that caters for this is scenario planning (Van der Heijden *et al.*, 2002). Scenarios are not traditional forecasts, rather they are possible 'stories of the future' that are derived from managerial judgement about key variables that will affect the company. For any variable, such as changes in technology, demand, competition or legislation, some things are known (and hence should be planned for using traditional techniques) and others are uncertain. Scenario planning takes the uncertain things seriously and asks a series of 'what if . . .?' questions on the chosen variables. For example, what would the business environment be like if a new technology changed our potential mode of production and global markets contracted because of increased conflict in ten years' time? What would the environment be like if the same technological changes were accompanied by global peace? By switching the variables that are focused on, a number of scenarios can be constructed (sometimes framed as very positive, mixed and very negative outcomes). The scenarios can then be used to consider what the demand for staff would be under these circumstances. As time moves on, the scenarios can be used as 'early warning' systems. For example, if global conflicts start increasing then certain scenarios become closer to operational reality, and hence become more informative of decision making. At present the relevant questions appear to be 'What are the business needs?' and 'What is the ideal complexion and size of the HR factor to meet those needs?'

Utilisation of human resources

Establishing the demand for human resources cannot be achieved without considering the way employees' skills and talents will be used. Utilisation of human resources impacts directly on the demand for staff. For example, a company improves its systems of work as part of a programme to make better use of its employees. As a consequence there are now more staff than are needed to process the workloads. The end result could be a need for fewer staff, and could lead to voluntary or involuntary redundancies. However, if opportunities exist elsewhere within the company there could be a redeployment of all or some of the staff who are super-fluous to requirements. An increasing trend has been the use of computer-aided design and production in manufacturing. This trend has reduced the number of human resources needed to carry out processes, which used to be labour intensive. It has also had an effect on the quality of employees required, since people with particular skills are needed to create and maintain the systems.

Another trend has been the use of teamworking arrangements (Sanchez *et al.*, 2007). Small groups of employees take responsibility for the total production of goods or services where individuals had previously specialised in small sections of the production process. This has an implication for the skill levels of the employees, as in a team they need to be able to carry out a wider range of tasks to complete the process. This type of utilisation of human resources is linked to quality approaches and the devolvement of responsibility from supervisors and middle managers to the teams that actually carry out the work.

There has been a long tradition of trying to foster efficiency and effectiveness of the oper-ations of an organisation through work study and related management services techniques. The basic approach is to subject to detailed analysis the way tasks are undertaken and then to make recommendations for the improvement of systems and the better utilisation of staff. The forerunner of present-day work study was the research undertaken by Taylor (1947), the father of scientific management. He examined the tasks undertaken by employees in order to estab-lish how wasted time could be eliminated and how human effort and work techniques could be better used. His approach was to observe employees engaged in the performance of tasks and to document and analyse their movements. On the basis of his analysis he postulated action strategies for improving techniques, making better use of time, and introduced training and incentives, with a view to increasing productivity. Taylor's intentions were felt to be more partial to the interests of management and detrimental to the interests of workers according to commentators such as Braverman (1974). Modern day approaches which share a central concern for efficiency, such as business process re-engineering (BPR) and lean production were explained in Chapter 3. Such methods seek to measure objectively the work that is being done and to streamline the work methods such that either more can be produced by the same number of employees, or savings can be made by reducing the number of staff employed (Wickramasinghe, 2007). Dangers of such approaches are that they can have a negative impact on the motivation of employees and can neglect the significance of performance management as a route to increased commitment and productivity. These issues are considered in Chapters 8 and 9. An alternative to observing workers, as Taylor and his followers prescribe, is to engage them in the analysis process. Torrington *et al.* (2005) say that focus groups are increasingly popular where, for example, a chief executive meets representatives of employees to discuss their views of the organisation's strengths and weaknesses, as well as the action necessary to improve matters.

Prominence was given earlier to the role of work study as a technique to quantify the util-isation of human resources. But a question to ask is: does this technique live up to the expectations of its adherents? Some people would harbour certain reservations. Workers can disguise their capacity to produce when they are being observed and assessed. Naturally they are very conversant with the various facets of the job, and when they are assessed by the work study practitioners in order to set standards of work and output it could be in their interest to underperform. By so doing they create a situation whereby softer or less difficult targets or standards are allocated to them.

In contemporary reflections on the scientific management approach, of which work study is a part, there has been a challenge to the 'carrot and stick' approach where control by man-agement features strongly. An approach more acceptable to a HRM perspective would be to concentrate on worker motivation, where the emphasis would be on creating enriched jobs and greater self-control so as to provide employees with more scope for self-fulfilment. It is in this climate that appraisal systems that focus on personal/self-assessment have emerged which seek to encourage people to realise their potential. Performance management is discussed in Chapter 8. Finally, making a judgement about HR utilisation currently involves a greater recognition of the importance of the qualitative approach (i.e. obtaining soft data from managers and workers about the reasons behind what is done and future intentions), though the quantitative approach is still relevant.

Human resource supply

The next stage of HRP is to evaluate the supply of labour. This is done by reference to the amount of labour needed as a result of having calculated the demand for labour (examined earlier in this chapter). The approach to HR supply has two parts: internal and external supply.

INTERNAL SUPPLY

When reference is made to the number of employees already employed by the organisation we speak of the internal supply. The first step is to report on key characteristics of the internal supply as follows:

1. age,

2. grade,

3. qualifications,

4. experience,

5. skills.

Before conducting exercises, such as the above method of profiling, policy decisions taken by the organisation with respect to expansion or contraction should be kept firmly in focus. For example, if contraction is contemplated (e.g. downsizing referred to in Chapter 3) it may be decided that employees aged 50 and over could be considered for voluntary early retirement, but given the legislation on age and employment in the UK, great caution is needed in such exercises and employees cannot be discriminated against on the basis of age. Therefore it is felt necessary to profile staff by age and grade. However, when this exercise is completed and the analysis shows that a substantial number of senior and middle managers are over the age of 50, it would appear necessary to reconsider the policy on early retirement, because releasing a large number of managerial staff over the age of 50 could strip the organisation of most of its experienced managers.

Succession planning

If conditions suggest that an increase in the supply of managers from within the organisation is needed then the organisation has to pay attention to 'succession planning'. This calls for an assessment of the actual performance of the person in his or her position, with that person's potential for promotion firmly in mind. It normally entails a formal plan to broaden the person's knowledge and experience of many aspects of work in a particular area, and/or training in skills at the technical and human relations levels.

Beardwell *et al.* (2004) suggest we should recognise two approaches to succession planning. One is the traditional approach (above), which relies on identifying a few key individuals capable of taking on senior roles at some future date. For this system to take root a stable environment and long-term career plans are required. The other approach is more contemporary and takes as its starting point the existence of a rapidly changing environment with an uncertain future, and then the focus moves away from identifying an individual to fill a specific job towards developing talent for groups of jobs as well as planning for jobs that do not yet exist. In addition, the contemporary approach stresses the need to balance the needs of the organisation with the aspirations of employees and broaden the competencies of the senior management group. Succession can be managed on an individual basis, with particular people being picked out for the future. Alternatively, a cohort, or group-based approach can be adopted in order to foster a new generation of leaders. The latter approach has been adopted in Cartus, and is illustrated in Case example 6.1.

CASE EXAMPLE 6.1

FOSTERING LEADERS AT CARTUS

Cartus is a subsidiary of Realogy, the global relocation services company. In 2000 it identified a problem with filling its leadership (upper management) ranks. In part this was because of a desire for cultural change that meant that service provision through people was central to the strategy.

Potential leaders were identified through application of a new set of leadership standards and were invited to join a regular leadership forum (Maxwell, 2006). By 2006 the forum was functioning as a 'hot house' in which future leaders were developed. Members met on a regular basis and exchanged information and understandings of their hands-on activities. More experienced leaders were able to discuss their experience in an open way with junior colleagues. Reading and reflection was encouraged through the provision of cutting-edge articles that would then be discussed in the forum. There was an emphasis on bringing outside knowledge into the organisation and developing skill-development opportunities. As a result of these activities, a new cadre of leaders developed who had an open approach, were able to measure themselves against best practice internally and externally, and as a result the succession problem was overcome.

Question

Ethical questions can be raised where 'hot housing' selected people is based on favouritism. What steps might Cartus take to ensure that the nurturing of future leaders is not achieved at the expense of equal opportunities?

Talent Management

Recently, the practice of talent management has become popular in HRM. According to Barner (2006) a distinguishing characteristic of successful organisations is their ability to win the 'war for talent'. He reports on surveys that indicate that many companies (particularly in the United States) believe that they do not have sufficient talent for future leadership, and that attracting and retaining talent is difficult because of the high mobility of talented people.

Managing talent entails careful observation to identify high performers and sensitive management of internal politics to maximise retention and progression of talented individuals whilst minimising alienation of staff more generally (Barner, 2006).

Cunningham (2007) proposes two possible approaches to talent management which are resonant of Beardwell *et al.*'s (2004) approaches to succession planning above. The two approaches are aligning people with roles (APR) and aligning roles with people (ARP). In the case of APR, the roles are fixed and talent management is about fitting people to them. Four factors are identified as important in achieving this. First, recruitment and selection are used to get the right people and to promote them. Secondly, learning and development focused on developing skills for the business needs of particular positions are supported. Thirdly, succession 'development' (rather than 'planning') is used to generate a pool of people from whom the organisation can select a successor for vacated positions. This approach does not line an individual up with a future job, but creates a group of people who can compete with each other for future vacancies. Lastly, career guidance needs to be provided so that people are aware of the choices that are open to them. ARP (aligning roles with people) takes a different approach. This is based on the understanding that if an organisation design does not accommodate the aspirations of talented people, they may not want to stay. In this approach, roles are viewed more flexibly such that they can grow and change with the individual. Rewards may be flexible and customised for individuals rather than people receiving the set reward package for the grade they are on. Attention is paid to the working environment, and particularly the opportunities for on-the-job learning. Lastly, working methods should allow talented people to see through a range of work processes rather than being restricted to a fragment of the whole task (Cunningham, 2007). One has to guard against the misuse of succession planning and talent management where they are seen to disadvantage certain groups.

Where the decision about which individuals gain access to this form of development is a matter of managerial judgement it is important to ensure that there is parity between the judgements of different managers. Conscious or unconscious bias on the part of the manager could result in criteria being used that unfairly discriminate against particular groups. For example, if a manager regards an aggressive or 'macho' style of management as preferable this may give unwarranted advantage to men over women in terms of who is seen as having the potential to make a good manager.

Rosabeth Moss Kanter has criticised what she regards as an obsession with talent management (Pickard, 2005). Her concern is that focusing all efforts on attracting a few stars can make everyone else in the organisation feel less valued. What makes an organisation successful is not, in her view, a preoccupation with talented individuals, but the creation of an environment that makes everyone perform well.

Traditionally, upward movement was a feature of career progression (the linear approach). As organisations move to flatter structures (see Chapter 3), with fewer layers of management, the potential for gradual movement upwards is reduced, and lateral moves (e.g. moves to different positions in a work group at the same level) are entertained. Obviously this can create greater employee versatility as new skills are learnt and familiarity with new roles within the group or team grows. Metaphorically, career ladders give way to career climbing frames (Inkson, 2006), where sideways and sometimes downward moves become increasingly a feature of employee development within organisations.

Reducing staff numbers

An organisation could be contemplating a reduction in the internal supply of labour because of a reduced demand for the services of all those currently employed. It is felt that labour is superfluous to requirements in one or more sections. A variety of conditions could have contributed to this state of affairs, including the advent of new technology, that has reduced the labour intensiveness of operations. A programme of redundancy is mounted because reliance on natural wastage would not be good enough to get rid of the surplus. It is also important for management to control the outward flow of skills, experience and knowledge from the organisation rather than leaving this solely to the choice of individual employees, as the outcome may be the loss of important skills and the retention of employees who are not as valuable to the organisation.

The law on redundancy must be considered by the organisation because there are legal provisions which state that the company must make every reasonable attempt to find a comparable position for an employee whose job ceases to exist. Therefore, if a situation arose where the organisation is reducing staffing levels in one section, and expanding numbers in another, those whose positions are redundant should receive first consideration for the newly created vacancies over those external to the organisation.

In some situations it is inevitable that the staffing of an organisation will have to be 'downsized' or redundancies made. This is a difficult process, not only for the individuals directly involved but also for others who may have had friendships with those made redundant, and who may fear for their own future security. From an HRM perspective the organisation should seek to minimise the negative impact of staffing reductions by managing the process professionally. It is easy for the organisation to be perceived as having breached the psychological contract, not only by those who have to leave, but also by staff who stay, when downsizing occurs (Tzafrir *et al.*, 2006). 'Outplacement' – a process through which the organisation will help employees facing redundancy to find other jobs – can have a positive impact on the psychological contract. The following activities may be included in managing outplacement (Graham and Bennett, 1998; Tzafrir *et al.*, 2006):

- communicating the reality of the situation and its consequences as soon as they are known;
- counselling for the individuals facing redundancy;
- helping employees to discover their aptitude for alternative types of work (e.g. through the use of psychometric testing);
- offering training in new and relevant skills;
- using corporate networks (e.g. with supplier organisations) to identify vacancies;
- support for job search (e.g. through helping employees to compose a CV and providing stationery and postage);
- allowing employees to take time off from work to seek other employment and attend interviews.

Although such services may be regarded as a cost it should be borne in mind that there is some moral responsibility for employees, and from a public relations perspective such an approach can cast the organisation in a favourable light with the employees who remain.

Internal labour supply analysis

Inevitably during the process of collecting and analysing data on the internal supply of labour we encounter the staff turnover rate, which could indicate that the organisation has problems. The formula used to compile this rate was given in Chapter 1. The rate in itself is relatively uninformative, but what is useful is the comparison of rates across sections or departments.

For example, if in a department of 50 staff 10 left in the previous year, that is a rate of 20 per cent. This may signal grounds for concern if most other departments in the organisation have a rate of 5 per cent or less. In certain industries a high staff turnover is normal. For example, catering staff and kitchen workers have a tradition of staying in a job for a relatively short period of time. In their study of a major UK food retailer, Booth and Hamer (2007) found that it was useful to break down the overall turnover figure by geographical region. They found that turnover in Wales was over 4 per cent lower than in the North of England, whilst stores in the South had a more than 6 per cent higher turnover than the North. Consequently, different approaches to staff retention were required in the different regions. It appeared that these differences were related to the existence of alternative employment in the local environment.

It is always a good idea to establish the reasons why the turnover rate is on the high side (or exceptionally low). Reasons for high turnover can include a local competitor offering better conditions and benefits or general dissatisfaction in a department due to, for example, job insecurity or very poor management. Similarly, it is a good idea to learn more about a group of employees who entered the organisation together. An example of such a group is a cohort of graduates recruited as trainee managers. The progress of the group could be analysed at regular intervals to see how many complete the training, how many achieve certain levels of performance and grades, and how many leave the company. Cohort analysis using statistical techniques can be used to explore the extent of wastage or loss due to turnover. One such technique is Bowey's (1974) stability index, which takes account of the length of service:

$$\frac{\text{Sum of months served (over 'N' period) by staff currently employed}}{\text{Sum of possible months service (over 'N' period) by a full complement of staff}} \times 100 = \% \text{ stability}$$

This formula measures the experience of current staff as a proportion of the maximum experience that could have been gained over the period ('N') being examined if all the staff had been in constant employment for the whole period.

The following example may serve to clarify the use of this index. A group of 20 management trainees is recruited by an organisation, and after two years Bowey's stability index is to be calculated. The sum of the possible service/experience in months is:

$$20 \text{ (people)} \times 24 \text{ (months)} = 480 \text{ person months}$$

This supplies the figure for the bottom of the equation (the denominator).

The current management trainees have the following profile: 5 have served 24 months, 5 have served 12 months and 10 have served 6 months. This indicates that some members of the cohort have left and been replaced during the 2 years. The 15 members of staff who have less than 24 months' experience are replacements. The total number of months served by the current employees is 240. If these figures are inserted into the equation (240/480 × 100) the stability is 50 per cent. This would indicate that the group is not very experienced – it has amassed only half the possible experience it could have gained in the time period. This level of staff stability would be likely to be seen as relatively low.

Further analysis may be undertaken to establish the pattern of leaving. A wastage or stability rate may be distorted by a disproportionately high (or low) number of people passing through one particular position or a specific job type. If this were found to be the case it would indicate that there might be a problem with the particular job or position, which is not general to the whole department. It would be important to discover the reasons behind this phenomenon.

Quantitative techniques, such as Bowey's stability index, are a vital part of the planning of the internal supply of labour. However, they should not be viewed as the ultimate explanation but as a starting point for further explanation. As mentioned earlier when focusing on the application of quantitative techniques we need to go behind the statistics and try to establish the reasons for a particular result or trend. With regard to cohort analysis, what contributed to a high rate of turnover in a particular situation? It could be that employees are leaving to take up better posts elsewhere, or to broaden their experience, or to escape from an unpleasant atmosphere within the organisation.

This type of qualitative information can be obtained from 'exit interviews' with those leaving the organisation (Clarke, 2007). Exit interviews are probably best conducted by a HR specialist who is likely to be seen as less threatening and as someone to whom one can divulge frank views. A departing employee is often able to voice criticisms about many facets of the organisation and its management, views one would not expect to hear from a person who plans to remain in the organisation. The latter may be reticent about voicing criticism because of a belief that such action would be damaging for their career and future remuneration. Of course a departing colleague could also express complimentary views. Therefore the exit interview provides useful information not readily available from other sources.

EXTERNAL SUPPLY

If the organisation cannot draw on an internal supply of labour when extra staff are needed it will need to recruit from the external labour market. The external supply of labour will be discussed with reference to the following:

- tightness of supply;
- demographic and gender factors;
- social/geographic aspects;
- the type of employee required.

Tightness of supply

A tight supply of labour arises where there are relatively few external candidates with the requisite abilities to do the job. By contrast, a loose supply indicates a large number of able candidates are available. Given the current relatively low level of unemployment in the United Kingdom one might conclude that the external supply of labour is low (tight). Though it is useful to think of external labour supply in quantitative terms, such as low or high, the picture is more complex when viewed qualitatively. For example, the particular skills and abilities required by the organisation are not necessarily found among the unemployed. For example, historically there have been times when demand has far outstripped supply for IT professionals. Where the organisation experiences difficulty in attracting people with the necessary skills it may resort to the use of subcontractors or consultants to overcome the shortage. This could be a one-off arrangement or alternatively a continuing relationship. 'Skilled contingent workers' (SCWs) have increasingly been used to provide a flexible component of staffing, with 78 per cent of US organisations using some form of alternative employment relations (such as agency and subcontract workers) (David, 2005). However, according to David (2005), the use of SCWs can have a negative influence on the productivity and turnover of permanent staff, as a demotivational effect can occur where full-timers believe that SCWs are better rewarded than they are.

An alternative to recruiting people with the necessary skills is to recruit people with potential and train them to the required standard. This involves the cost of training and carries the risk that their potential will not be realised. It can be time consuming to train people and, particularly for small organisations that do not have training systems already established, this course of action could be prohibitively expensive and difficult. However there are advantages to training people internally. It can lead to an increased sense of commitment on the part of the employees, the training could be directly related to the organisation's needs, and it is a form of investing in people and treating them as assets. There is more detailed discussion of training in Chapter 10. Apart from the strategies mentioned, labour shortages could be met by attracting certain groups back to work (e.g. married women with children) and then providing appropriate conditions (e.g. hours that coincide with the school day). The increase in flexible employment practices, such as the latter, has been one of the reasons for an increase in the proportion of women in the workforce. Another potential source of staff in tight supply situations is migrant labour. An example is provided in Case example 6.2. In this case, there was an insufficient supply of labour in the locality and so workers were employed from overseas. This has worked out very well for the organisation, which has experienced a degree of culture change and greatly increased productivity. In order to gain these benefits, however, the HR approach also had to change.

CASE EXAMPLE 6.2

MIGRANT WORKERS AT STRATHMORE FOODS

Strathmore Foods is a producer of quality Scottish foods, such as scotch pies, both under its own brands and supplied to supermarkets under their brand names. Strathmore Foods is located in the East of Scotland in an area where about 3000 people are employed in the food industry. Strathmore Foods employs 150 staff in its production factory. The supply of labour has become tight in the recent years due to economic growth in the United Kingdom that has provided a range of alternative employment and the ageing population, according to Liz Jackson, former Director of HRM. This has meant that it was difficult to recruit sufficient staff to meet demand for produce. The answer for Strathmore Foods has been to employ migrant labour and one third of the workforce now come from other European countries that have recently joined the EU or 'accession states' that are on the route to joining the EU. The result for Strathmore Foods has not just been to replace one source of labour with another but has also had a significant positive impact on the way the factory operates. However, in order to accrue this benefit Strathmore Foods has had to employ a holistic and innovative HRM approach.

The experience of employing the migrant workers has been very positive according to Jackson. The migrant workers have a strong work ethic, their attendance levels are very good and their productivity is exemplary. The migrant workers approached management to ask if they could work 10-hour shifts rather than the normal eight hours, hence further lifting production levels. This had an impact on the indigenous workers. Initially they were fearful that they would be replaced and so they sought to match the production levels of the migrant workers within their eight-hour shift.

When viewed purely from a business perspective, this situation looks highly desirable for the organisation. However, there was clearly a potential for conflict and resentment as although workers had voluntarily increased production, their motivation had been fear and internal competition.

When management realised that this was the case, it made a concerted effort to communicate with all workers that there was no threat to them or their jobs. Once this was clear, productivity levels stayed high and the atmosphere became much more positive.

In order to establish the migrant workers in the factory, a new approach to HRM has developed. There has been a need to provide extra training for management and supervisors so that they can manage in the new situation. In addition, an in-house translator has been provided, and policy documents and induction packs have been tailored and translated for migrant workers. Beyond this, Strathmore Foods has taken care of its workers outside work. This has included help in finding suitable accommodation (Strathmore Foods now rent flats which are sublet to the workers), help with personal administration (such as setting up bank accounts) and establishing a partnership with a local college to provide English language training for employees.

The culture in Strathmore Foods has developed to the point where 'it is as if it has always been like this' as Liz Jackson put it. Some migrant workers are now in a position to be promoted when positions arise, and some indigenous workers have gone on holiday with the migrant workers to their home countries.

Question

The experience at Strathmore Foods is a positive one, but there are potential pitfalls with this type of employment strategy. What issues should organisations employing migrant workers focus on in order to achieve a positive outcome?

Demographic and gender factors

Demographic changes (e.g. the number of young people entering the labour force) affect the external supply of labour. In the United Kingdom, the proportions of the population analysed by age are changing. The relative numbers of young to old are decreasing. According to the Office of National Statistics, in 1971 people under 16 made up 25 per cent of the population, whereas by 2005 they accounted for 19 per cent. In a converse trend, those over 65 increased from 13 per cent to 16 per cent of the population. These trends are a result of reductions in the birth rate and recent declines in mortality rates. The result is that the proportion of the population that is within the traditional working age will continue to fall over the coming years (see Figure 6.2).

Figure 6.3 shows the shape of the UK population at 2005. As the thick middle moves up the graph over time, and presuming that mortality rates continue to improve, instead of there being a large group in the working-age population, the large group will be older people with smaller groups following through.

This change will affect the supply of labour to organisations that have traditionally recruited young people and trained and developed them by using a training process and exposure to the organisation's ethos or culture. The stated demographic change will alter the age composition of the workforce and will force employers to review their recruitment policies. The outcome of such a review could be to give more consideration to employing older workers who will constitute a higher proportion of the workforce than hitherto.

Research on employing the older worker conducted in Canada can offer some insights into how organisations might go about this. Armstrong-Stassen (2006) combined a survey of 1,500 Canadians aged over 50 (with a response rate of 45 per cent) and a case study of Home Depot

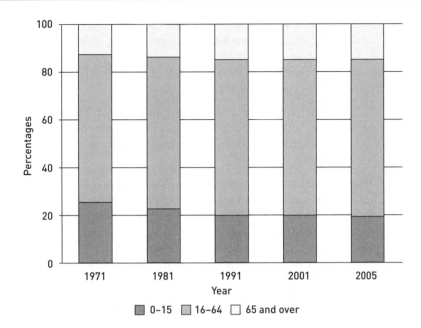

Figure 6.2 UK population, by age

Source: National Statistics, www.statistics.gov.uk

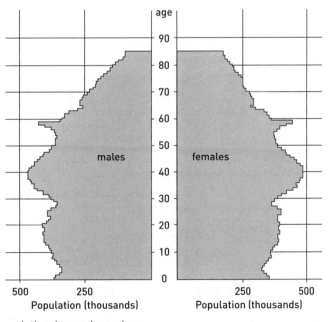

Figure 6.3 UK population, by gender and age

Source: National Statistics. www.statistics.gov.uk

Canada, which was winner of the first 'Best Employer for 50-Plus Canadians' award. Five factors were identified as most strongly influencing retirees' decisions to return to work:

1. ensuring that the organisational culture recognises and rewards the contributions of older workers;
2. adopting flexible work schedules and policies;
3. promoting continued development and training for older workers;
4. designing jobs to be both challenging and meaningful;
5. developing innovative incentives incorporating not only finance, but additional time off/holidays.

Home Depot had deliberately targeted older workers and retirees. The organisation found that these employees brought knowledge to the job and particularly good customer service skills. The older workers had responded well to offers of training and had shown that they were fully capable of taking on new skills. This research reflects similar findings in previous research in the UK (Jetter, 1993) in which older workers were not only found to be trainable in the same time as other employees, but their absence and turnover rates were also found to be lower.

The composition of the workforce has changed in its gender composition. Over the past 20 years there have been significant changes as women have moved from 45 per cent to 49 per cent of the workforce (see Table 6.1). This trend of an increasing proportion of women in employment will put pressure on organisations to become more 'family friendly'. Progressive organisations are likely to employ more women and older workers than was traditionally the case. This will entail the application of appropriate strategies of recruitment, retention and training.

In the United Kingdom, employment legislation has given more rights to people who want to work part-time and it has also had an impact on temporary employment. Part-time work has increased in the past decade (from 25 per cent to 30 per cent of jobs). However, the proportion of part-time workers who report not wanting a full-time job has fallen over the same period from 85 per cent to 71 per cent (see Tables 6.2 and 6.3).

Table 6.1 UK employment by gender

	Total employment	Women	Men
1987	21,307,000	9,679,000 (45%)	11,628,000 (55%)
2007	24,957,000	12,170,000 (49%)	12,787,000 (51%)

Source: National Statistics, www.statistics.gov.uk

Table 6.2 UK part-time employment by gender

	Total part-time employment	Women	Men
1997	5,392,000 (25% of all jobs)	4,617,000 (86% of part-time jobs)	775,000 (14% of part-time jobs)
2007	7,440,000 (30% of all jobs)	5,726,000 (77% of part-time jobs)	1,714,000 (23% of part-time jobs)

Source: National Statistics, www.statistics.gov.uk

Table 6.3 UK part-time employees who did not want a full-time job

	Total	Women	Men
1997	4,609,000 (85% of part-time jobs)	4,160,000 (91%)	449,000 (9%)
2007	5,295,000 (71% of part-time jobs)	4,490,000 (85%)	805,000 (15%)

Source: National Statistics, www.statistics.gov.uk

Another factor to note is EU legislation, which has increased the potential mobility of labour within the European Union. Under this legislation workers are free to undertake employment in other member states. On the demographic front it should be noted that the proportion of young people in the population will decline even more sharply in Germany and Italy. It could be that this will result in a net movement of skilled workers out of the United Kingdom to take up positions in Europe (Hendry, 1994; Mayrhofer and Larsen, 2006). However this predicted outcome is subject to varying influences, for example, linguistic skills, culture and economic growth.

Social/geographic aspects

The external supply of labour is influenced by socio-geographic factors. In certain parts of the United Kingdom (e.g. north of England, Scotland, Wales), where rapid decline of the older industries has taken place, there have been large pools of labour with skills available following periods of industrial decline. This has prompted industrialists to consider moving their operations to these areas. Amongst the other factors influencing a company's decision to move to an area where an adequate supply of suitable labour exists are the quality of transport systems and access to the market for its output.

Many Japanese companies that have invested in the United Kingdom have done so in greenfield sites where there is high unemployment (Wilkinson and Oliver, 1992). For example, Komatsu, which manufactures earth-moving vehicles, set up its operation in the north-east of England. In the case of many of the Japanese consumer electronics companies, the company was not attracted by skills, which already existed in an area, but was more concerned to recruit inexperienced labour. The selection process has been principally concerned with testing candidates' teamworking ability and their attitudes to cooperative modes of working, as well as numeracy and dexterity skills.

Type of worker

The category of worker is another variable to consider when discussing the external supply of labour. Traditionally, graduates and professional staff have been more prepared to move location for a job than blue-collar skilled and semi-skilled workers. As was stated earlier, freedom of movement of labour within the EU is now enshrined in legislation, but in practice mobility tends to occur either where professionals and managers can gain rewards and build their careers, or where the income that skilled and semi-skilled workers can achieve in a host country significantly outweighs their earning potential at home. Initiatives have been taken by the European Union to increase mobility in the labour market (Mayrhofer and Larsen, 2006).

These initiatives include promoting common vocational standards, transferability of qualifications and student exchanges.

Internal vs external supply

Using the internal supply of resources as a source of labour has certain advantages over the external supply. Those already employed in an organisation are well placed to understand the way things are done and how the different parts of the organisation fit together, and to appreciate the nature of the culture. The people responsible for selecting internal candidates for vacant positions have access to more comprehensive information relating to their abilities, track record and potential achievement than they would have if they were selecting people originating from the external labour market. Drawing on an internal supply of labour to fill vacancies, whereby the internal candidate receives a promotion, sends a powerful signal to employees that the organisation is committed to their advancement and development.

However, one must be aware of certain disadvantages associated with drawing on an internal supply of resources. Although there may be more information about internal candidates at the disposal of selectors, it is not always free of bias. Also, there is greater likelihood of more negative information about internal candidates being available, while external candidates are better placed to conceal information about their past failures and difficulties. Finally, internal candidates could be steeped in the culture of the organisation: if this culture is risk aversive and conservative, it could act as a constraint when innovative practices and initiatives are required of the successful candidate. An external candidate could feel less inhibited where the introduction of fresh ideas to working practices and job performance is highly desirable. However, for this to happen it may be necessary to change the corporate culture.

One way in which companies bring about a change in culture is by tapping the external supply of labour (Reger, 2007). This could be reflected in an attempt to create a workforce with values and attitudes compatible with the desired corporate culture. For example, Toshiba aimed to increase cooperation and flexibility on their shopfloor. This was done by carefully wording its recruitment literature, which referred to 'assembly operators' rather than to specific jobs, and through the use of a video shown to candidates offering themselves for employment so that they could engage in self-selection if they felt comfortable with the projected organisational environment on screen. Therefore candidates with a flexible attitude, who were prepared to take on a variety of tasks, were selected rather than people who wanted to assume only one specific and fixed role.

Labour markets

In recent years pressure has been mounting from the European Union and international bodies, such as the OECD, to take on board flexibility in labour markets and working practices. As a result of high levels of unemployment, high social costs (such as generous benefits and pensions) and long working hours in some parts of the EU, member states have been encouraged to embrace work sharing initiatives, part-time working, and to reconsider the balance between work and non-work, and the division of labour by gender within households. It is apparent that much of the ensuing restructuring has been driven by a desire to cut costs, and in the words of Legge (1998), by the urge to extend the scope of managerial regulation of the employment relationship. As Japan coped with its economic problems there were some indications that labour markets were becoming more flexible (Tett, 2000). However, in the

United States, where flexible employment took off in a big way in the past, there is evidence in an authoritative report by the Economic Policy Institute (a Washington think tank) to suggest that the proportion of workers in temporary or part-time jobs has declined due to the progressive return of full-time employment over the past five years (Taylor, 2000). The numbers employed in temporary work has also declined in the United Kingdom, and a minority of temporary workers reported not wanting a permanent job (see Tables 6.4 and 6.5).

In this section flexibility is dealt with specifically, a topic also considered in connection with developments in restructuring in Chapter 3. In addition, there will be comment on the changing composition of the EU labour force. Flexibility can be construed as consisting of at least five components, as follows:

1. *Numerical flexibility* – use of part-time and temporary workers whose numbers and hours can be varied relatively easily and cheaply to meet organisational needs.
2. *Distancing flexibility* – the use of contract staff or self-employed freelancers who are provided with a contract for service but are not employees of the organisation.
3. *Functional flexibility* – employees possessing skills that cut across functional areas within an organisation; it implies a certain degree of versatility with an emphasis on both the acquisition and updating of appropriate skills through on-the-job training. However, Reilly (2001) maintains that there is a likelihood of resistance on the part of employees and an increased likelihood of errors when functional flexibility is introduced.
4. *Temporal or working time flexibility* – relates to the more intensive use of labour, or the closer matching of organisational requirements with staffing levels (e.g. moves to seven-day working, shift working and overtime).
5. *Financial flexibility* – linking rewards more closely with individual or organisational performance, and including incentives such as performance-related pay, share options and share ownership schemes (Murton, 2000).

Table 6.4 UK temporary employees by gender

	Total	Women	Men
1997	1,711,000 (8% of total jobs)	943,000	768,000
2007	1,496,000 (6% of total jobs)	801,000	695,000

Source: National Statistics. www.statistics.gov.uk

Table 6.5 UK temporary employees who did not want a permanent job

	Total	Women	Men
1997	503,000 (29% of temporary jobs)	184,000	319,000
2007	444,000 (29% of temporary jobs)	187,000	257,000

Source: National Statistics. www.statistics.gov.uk

Although there are advantages attached to restructuring based on flexibility, some argue that greater flexibility has meant job insecurity, lack of status and reduced bargaining power for workers (Legge, 1998). Others point out the partial nature of flexibility schemes. For example, Ford UK achieved some flexibility in its assembly line operations by getting rid of demarcation lines and redefining jobs in such a way as to reduce 500 differently defined assembly jobs to a mere 50. However, Ford UK failed in the early 1990s to obtain union agreement to accept both quality circles and a formalised system of employee involvement at a time when employee involvement achieved some success in Ford USA (McKinlay and Starkey, 1992). The reader is asked to refer to Chapter 3 for further observations on the concept of flexibility.

Atkinson and Rick (1996) reported that temporary work can be used as a stepping stone to permanent employment, with at least 20 per cent of employers using it in this way. The advantage of this approach is that it gives the organisation the chance to judge the individual on the basis of his or her performance in reality, rather than as hypothecated through recruitment and selection techniques such as interviews and in-tray tests. It also gives employees a chance to judge whether or not they will fit into the organisation. The downside, however, is that if the match between employee and organisation does not work out, for the employee the job ends.

Clearly, flexibility can have both advantages and disadvantages. Emmott and Hutchinson (1998) summarise survey evidence on employee attitudes to flexible working as follows:

Advantages:

- the ability to combine work with outside interests (e.g. caring responsibilities or hobbies);

- greater job satisfaction;

- improved motivation;

- less tiredness.

Disadvantages:

- unequal treatment in terms of pay and benefits;

- reduced career development opportunities;

- limited training opportunities;

- the 'psychological contract' is threatened;

- increased job insecurity;

- increased stress.

According to Emmott and Hutchinson the majority of part-time employees work part-time because they do not want a full-time job.

Although much has been written about the flexibility of home working, in the United Kingdom there was no increase in the number of home workers (i.e. those who mainly work in their own homes) between 1996 and 2000, with the figure constant at 0.7 million (Office for National Statistics, 2001). By 2007, however, 6 per cent of companies across the European Union, and 20 per cent of companies in the United States had adopted teleworking (Sanchez *et al.*, 2007). A survey of 2,500 employers and 7,500 employees by the Institute of Employment Research and IFF Research (Skills and Enterprise Executive, 2001) found that many employees wanted flexible working arrangements, and 62 per cent of organisations allowed some level of flexible hours. Men were found more likely than women to want flexitime, compressed hours and annualised hours. Women were found more likely to want term-time working or reduced hours.

The individual and the organisation: change and careers

The concepts of stable identity and form, both of organisations and individuals, are one of the fundamental assumptions of traditional HRP. While it has long been acknowledged that organisations will change and people will develop, the assumption was that it was possible to plan for the future through analysis of the past and present. As organisations changed the changes could be accounted for by changes in demand for employees, and development of individuals would be accounted for through career management. However, in the social and economic environment of the twenty-first century change has been such that predictions based on an assumption of stability have been challenged in a radical way.

CHANGES IN ORGANISATIONS

The drive for productivity, particularly in competitive organisational environments, has had a significant impact on HRP (O'Doherty, 1997). Traditionally, if a department lost people through turnover, promotion or retirement, it would be reasonable to assume that they would be replaced in the HR plan. Nowadays it may be more realistic to assume that there will be a question mark over vacancies because of the need to control costs and increase productivity (and hence shareholder value) (Ramlall, 2006). Similarly, efforts to increase employee performance, for example, through quality initiatives and high commitment management, have often been associated with reduced supervision, which leads to cost savings. So in HRP terms the focus is on utilisation rather than supply of labour.

In addition the nature of utilisation has also been changing. Traditionally the focus would be on developing the way that currently employed staff worked. However, with structural changes that have resulted in 'permeable boundaries' between organisations (creating alliances, close relationships with suppliers, such as just-in-time procedures and outsourcing), the workforce on a particular task may be drawn from different organisations. Such arrangements rely on contracting between organisations, and so the planning for labour supply becomes part of the overall contracting arrangements of a contingency nature undertaken by the organisation.

One example is taken from the film and television industry (Bilton, 2007), where in an organisation such as the BBC the planning of a major project such as a drama series does not necessarily use in-house design, production, editing, technical and facilities staff. The planning of such a project will involve a temporary network of many staff drawn together for a particular purpose and specific time period. The choice of people is often made through reputation and personal contact. The nature of contracts, working requirements and conditions will relate to the individuals' ability to negotiate, and there is a lack of standardisation of plans and arrangements.

CAREER MANAGEMENT

In a unitarist definition of HRM (see Chapter 11), career management, which is also discussed in Chapter 10, has been seen as the 'organizational processes which enable the careers of individuals to be planned and managed in a way that optimizes both the needs of the organization and the preferences and capabilities of the individual' (Mayo, 1991). While career management has traditionally been available to managerial and professional employees there have been attempts to incorporate a broader range of employees in 'people-centred' approaches, which seek to define jobs around the individual rather than exclusively the converse (Crawshaw, 2006). In such models counselling sessions, typically between the manager and the employee, will seek to find matches between the organisation's needs for human resources emerging from the business strategy and the individual's aspirations and competences (Whiston and Rahardja, 2005). Clearly this requires managerial competency in career counselling, and achieving a balance in which it is likely that some of the employee's aspirations will not be achievable within the existing opportunities provided by the organisation. In addition it requires the organisation to be flexible enough to meet some of the aspirations of the employee if the scheme is to retain credibility and enhance the motivation of staff. Traditional career counselling models (e.g. Verlander, 1985) tended to focus on manager-led interactions. More recently the focus has swung towards individuals driving their own progress, with an emphasis on personal development plans, learning centres and career workshops (Rowold, 2007). In research in Taiwan, Chen *et al.* (2004) found a positive relationship between professional career development within companies and productivity levels. They relate this to a high degree of satisfaction that is expressed by workers. However, in organisations where delayering has greatly reduced the chances for upward progression the experience of many is, of necessity, that the career is not available to be managed in the mode envisaged by Mayo (1991).

Overview

Armstrong (2003) suggests an alternative to traditional HRP which he refers to as the contemporary approach. The latter puts greater emphasis on the soft side of HRP (e.g. employee attitudes, behaviour and commitment), though elements of the hard approach are retained such as the balance between demand and supply forecasting. The contemporary approach also underlines the importance of the internal labour supply. The key ingredients of the contemporary approach are as follows (Armstrong, 2003):

- attract and retain the staff with the appropriate skills, expertise and competences required to staff operations;

- develop a capacity to anticipate problems that arise as a result of surpluses or deficits in human resources;

- develop a well-trained and flexible workforce to enhance the organisation's capability to adapt to dynamic and turbulent environments;

- place less reliance on external recruitment when skilled workers are in short supply – instead put effort into retaining and developing staff;

- make better use of the human resources at the disposal of the organisation by identifying and using more flexible systems of work.

Another perspective that is mentioned in discourse connected with HRP is scenario planning. This can be used to supplement or replace the more traditional demand and supply forecasting (Beardwell *et al.*, 2004), but it may be difficult to determine the required number of scenarios. However, scenarios could be useful to sketch alternative options for the future state of the organisation and how HRM techniques and processes might respond to these. Instead of prescribing detailed plans, building of scenarios allows us to assess the impact of different courses of action on resources and costs.

Human resource plans could be developed to coalesce with the strategic goals of the organisation, or they can contribute to the development of business strategy. Either way they can be perceived as a major facilitator of competitive advantage (Marchington and Wilkinson, 2005). Human resource planning can also contribute help build flexibility into the organisation, either through the use of more flexible forms of work or by identifying qualities and skills that one would like to see in employees.

There are influential voices that have fundamental reservations about planning as far as human resources are concerned. However, some point out that the planning process is of critical importance in the complex organisational environments we encounter today. Those with reservations simply state that it is difficult to forecast in conditions resembling a turbulent environment. In particular, Sisson and Storey (2000) seem to be inclined to the view that the planning process is based on two highly questionable assumptions: (i) that the organisation has the necessary personnel information to purposely engage in meaningful HRP or for that matter succession planning, and (ii) that the planner will have at his or her disposal the perfect plan that the prescriptive literature advocates. Taylor (2002), reflecting on HRP in today's organisation, feels that it might still be appropriate when used by organisations operating in relatively stable product and labour markets, but it could be impracticable in conditions where decentralisation is pronounced and HR issues are devolved to managers operating at the business unit level. Other reasons (e.g. flexible job descriptions, new organisational forms, flexible employment contracts) make objective forecasting difficult and therefore long-term planning may feature in a lowly position in the organisation's list of priorities.

Finally, HRP has often been denigrated with the result that it has received relatively little attention in the literature and has become less widely used in organisations (Taylor, 2002).

 ## Conclusions

Human resource or manpower planning has always been an area of interest in personnel and HRM. Emphasis has been placed on different parts (hard and soft) of the planning process at different times in its history. The approach taken has largely reflected the business environment and the state of development of the subject. It is important to strike a balance so that no area of the planning process is neglected.

The current focus is on the need for flexibility in planning so that organisations are able to adapt to situations steeped in change. The impact of information and communication technology (ICT) on organisations has been pronounced. It has enabled arrangements such as teleworking, and increased the substitutability of some employees (those whose jobs can be replaced or changed significantly by ICT), while at the same time increasing the value and scarcity of others (typically the ICT professionals). Where there is power on both sides of the employment contract, accommodating the needs of employees and employers in a flexible way is becoming the vogue.

Increasingly the focus is not just on planning but also on managing the nature of contractual arrangements through flexible accommodation, subcontracting and outsourcing. Through such arrangements the organisation can spread the risk of failing to find future business, which it formerly absorbed when taking on permanent employees. Whether the focus for a particular organisation is on cost control and outsourcing, or developing staff through career management, there is a need for proactive HRM. At both ends of the scale there is a need for effective selection decision making – whom to subcontract to, or whose career to support. Although there has been a swing towards 'managerial judgement' and away from more traditional quantitative approaches, it is important to optimise the decision-making process, and this does not imply simply moving to the exclusive use of intuitive judgement, it means contracting the space reserved for intuitive judgement.

HRP is concerned with proactively analysing the external environment and making the best possible use of employees. In these ways HRP can provide an input to the organisational strategy by outlining the possibilities and costs of current and potential workforce configurations. It maps out the implications of strategic decisions for subsequent HRM activities such as recruitment and development. HRP can therefore be seen as an important linking factor between strategy and operation.

Review and reflection questions

1. What are the three key facets of HRP?

2. What can organisations do to improve employee utilisation?

3. When is it a good idea to use the internal supply of labour?

4. When is it a good idea to use the external supply of labour?

5. What are the main aims of talent management?

6. When staffing is being reduced, what can organisations do to minimise the pain and discomfort?

7. What are the implications of the demographics in the United Kingdom for the future supply of labour?

8. What are the different types of flexibility, and what are their advantages and disadvantages?

Activities

If you are in work:

Think about your career and where you want to get to. Consider how this can best be achieved with your current employer. Using the websites on career management at the end of this chapter will help with this process.

If you are in full-time study:

Consider the demographic information provided above and the career websites provided at the end of this chapter. On the basis of this information, and on that of your personal goals, think about what area of the labour market you would most like to enter on leaving full-time study.

Further reading and research

As has been seen above a range of topic areas fall within the remit of HRP. The following suggestions for further reading are either chapters that give a good overview of the subject or are books dedicated to the area which go into more depth.

Iles, P. (2001) 'Employee Resourcing', in J. Storey (ed.), *Human Resource Management: A critical text*, London: Routledge.

Liff, S. (2000) 'Manpower or human resource planning: what is in a name?', in S. Bach and K. Sisson (eds), *Personnel Management: A comprehensive guide to theory and practice*, Oxford: Blackwell.

Taylor, S. (2002) *People Resourcing*, London: CIPD.

Turner, P. (2002) *Strategic Human Resource Forecasting*, London: CIPD.

Talent management is a topic of current interest. The CIPD has a helpful report: 'Talent management: understanding the dimensions'. This is available at www.cipd.co.uk/subjects/recruitment.

A paper that draws on empirical research to report 13 factors of talent management is as follows:

Lubitsh, G. and Smith, I. (2007) 'Talent Management: A strategic imperative', *The Ashridge Journal*, Spring, 6–11. This is available at www.ashridge.org.uk.

Talent management tends to take an organisational perspective. The alternative perspective is that of the individual and from this perspective there has been an increasing focus on career management. The CIPD has a number of useful resources on careers. There is practical advice in fact sheets/tools on: 'Succession Planning', 'Career Outplacement Consultants' and 'Career Discussions at Work'. These are available at www.cipd.co.uk/subjects/career.

There are many agencies offering help and practical tools for individuals seeking to manage their careers. One that has a range of accessible tools is Agency Central that covers activities such as career analysis, CV writing, psychometric testing and agencies. The website is www.agencycentral.co.uk.

References

Armstrong, M. (2003) *A Handbook of Human Resource Management Practice*, London: Kogan Page.

Armstrong-Stassen, M. (2006) 'Encouraging Retirees to Return to the Workforce', *Human Resource Planning*, 29, 38–44.

Arnold, E. and Pulich, M. (2007) 'The Department Manager and Effective Human Resource Planning: An overview', *The Health Care Manager,* 26, 43–52.

Atkinson, J. and Rick, J. (1996) 'Temporary work and the labour market', Institute of Employment Studies, Report 311.

Barner, R. (2006) *Bench Strength*, New York: American Management Association.

Beardwell, I., Holden, L. and Claydon, T. (2004) *Human Resource Management: A Contemporary Approach*, Harlow, Essex: Pearson Education.

Bilton, C. (2007) *Management and Creativity*. Oxford: Blackwell.

Booth, S. and Hamer, K. (2007) 'Labour Turnover in the retail industry', *International Journal of Retail and Distribution Management,* 35, 289–307.

Bowey, A. (1974) *A Guide to Manpower Planning*, London: Macmillan.

Bramham, J. (1989) *Human Resource Planning*, London: IPM.

Braverman, H. (1974) *Labour and Monopoly Capitalism*, New York: Monthly Review Press.

Chen, T.-Y., Chang, P.-L. and Yeh, C.-W. (2004) 'An investigation of career development programs, job satisfaction, professional development and productivity: The case of Taiwan', *Human Resource Development International,* 7, 441–463.

Clarke, M. (2007) 'Choices and Constraints: Individual perceptions of the voluntary redundancy experience', *Human Resource Management Journal,* 17, 76–93.

Crawshaw, J.R. (2006) 'Justice Source and Justice Content: Evaluating the fairness of organizational career management practices', *Human Resource Management Journal,* 16, 98–120.

Cunningham, I. (2007) 'Talent Management: Making it real', *Development and Learning in Organizations,* 21, 4–8.

David, J. (2005) 'The unexpected employee and organizational costs of skilled contingent workers', *Human Resource Planning,* 28, 1–23.

Emmott, M. and Hutchinson, S. (1998) 'Employment flexibility: threat or promise?', in Sparrow, P. and Marchington, M. (eds), *Human Resource Management: The new agenda*, London: Financial Times/Pitman.

Graham, H.T. and Bennett, R. (1998) *Human Resources Management*, London: Financial Times/Pitman.

Hendry, C. (1994) 'The Single European Market and the HRM Response', in Kirkbride, P.S. (ed.), *Human Resource Management in Europe*, London: Routledge.

Inkson, K. (2006) *Understanding Careers: A metaphor-based approach*, London: Sage.

Jetter, M. (1993) 'The wisdom factor: B&Q's employment of older people', in McIntosh, M. (ed.), *Good Business*, Bristol: School for Advanced Urban Studies.

Legge, K. (1998) 'The gift wrapping of employment degradation', in Sparrow, P. and Marchington, M. (eds), *Human Resource Management: The new agenda*, London: Financial Times/Pitman.

Marchington, M. and Wilkinson, A. (2005) *Human Resource Management at Work: People Management and Development*, London: Chartered Institute of Personnel and Development.

Mayo, A. (1991) *Managing Careers*, London: IPM.

Mayrhofer, W. and Larsen, H.H. (eds) (2006) *Managing Human Resources in Europe: A thematic approach*, London: Routledge.

Maxwell, W.J. (2006) 'Leaders Developing Leaders: leadership and succession planning', *Human Resource Planning,* 5, 40–47.

McKinlay, A. and Starkey, K. (1992) 'Strategy and human resource management', *International Journal of Human Resource Management,* 3, 435–450.

Murton, A. (2000) 'Labour markets and flexibility: current debates and the European dimension', in Barry, J., Chandler, J., Clark, H., Johnston, R. and Needle, D. (eds), *Organization and Management: A critical text*, London: Business Press (Thompson Learning).

O'Doherty, D. (1997) 'Human resource planning: control to seduction?', in Beardwell, I. and Holden, L. (eds), *Human Resource Management: A contemporary perspective*, London: Pitman.

Office for National Statistics (2001) 'Labour force survey', *Social Trends*, 31.

Pickard, J. (2005) 'Stars in their eyes', *People Management*, 11, 17.

Ramlall, S.J. (2006) 'Strategic Human Resource Management Creates Value at Target', *Journal of Organizational Excellence*, 25, 57–62.

Reger, S.J.M. (2007) 'IBM's "tangible culture" approach can smooth the way to successful transformation', *Human Resource Management International Digest*, 15, 24–26.

Reilly, P. (2001) *Flexibility at Work*, Aldershot: Gower.

Rowold, J. (2007) 'The effect of career exploration on subsequent training performance', *Human Resource Development*, 10, 43–58.

Sanchez, A.M., Perez, M.P., Carnicer, P.L. and Jimenez, M.J..V. (2007) 'Teamworking and Workplace Flexibility: A study of impact on firm performance', *Personnel Review*, 36, 42–64.

Sisson, K. and Storey, J. (2000) *The Realities of Human Resource Management*, Buckingham: Open University Press.

Skills and Enterprise Executive (2001) *Get a Life, Get a Work Life Balance*, Issue 1.

Taylor, F.W. (1947) *Scientific Management*, New York: Harper & Row.

Taylor, R. (2000) 'Labour market: dramatic shift from flexible employment towards regular work – job security back in booming US', *Financial Times*, 4 September, 10.

Taylor, S. (2002) *People Resourcing*. London: Chartered Institute of Personnel and Development.

Tett, G. (2000) 'Time to rectify a period of disappointment', *Japan – Financial Times Survey*, 19 September, 1.

Torrington, D., Hall, L. and Taylor, S. (2005) *Human Resource Management*, Harlow, Essex: Pearson Education.

Tzafrir, S.S., Mano-Negrin, R., Harel, G.H. and Rom-Nagy, D. (2006) 'Downsizing and the impact of job counseling on effective employee responses', *Career Development International*, 11: 125–144.

Van der Heijden, K., Bradfield, R., Burt, G., Cairns, G. and Wright, G. (2002) *The Sixth Sense: Accelerating Organizational Learning with Scenarios*. Chichester, John Wiley & Sons.

Verlander, E.G. (1985) 'The System's the thing', *Training and Development*, April, 20–23.

Whiston, S.C. and Rahardja, D. (2005) 'Qualitative Career Assessment: An overview and analysis', *Journal of Career Assessment*, 13, 371–380.

Wickramasinghe, V. (2007) 'Staffing Practices in the Private Sector in Sri Lanka', *Career Development International*, 12, 108–128.

Wilkinson, B. and Oliver, N. (1992) 'Human resource management in Japanese manufacturing companies in the UK and USA', in Towers, B. (ed.), *The Handbook of Human Resource Management*, Oxford: Blackwell.

Chapter 7

EMPLOYEE RESOURCING: RECRUITMENT AND SELECTION

Introduction

Recruitment and selection are crucial decision-making points in the establishment of the working relationship. The psychological contract is established in part by the expectations that the organisation and employee have of each other from early impressions, so it is important that the best possible information flows in both directions. Success in selection has been highlighted as integral to high-performance models of HRM, and the cost of poor decisions, both for the organisation and the individual, can be extensive.

Having read this chapter, you should:

■ **understand the role of recruitment and selection in an overall system of HRM;**

■ **be aware of the nature of job analysis;**

■ **know the purpose and make-up of job descriptions and specifications;**

■ **be able to make judgements about the appropriateness of the various sources of recruitment;**

■ **understand the alternative tools of selection – their strengths and weaknesses.**

The process of recruitment and selection is the planned way in which the organisation interfaces with the external supply of labour. Recruitment is the process of attracting a pool of candidates for a vacant position, and selection is the technique of choosing a new member of the organisation from the available candidates. These processes incur significant costs, so it is natural for organisations to pay attention to these activities from a cost-effective viewpoint. Placing advertisements and using the services of managers in selection interviewing can be costly, as it can be if the person selected to fill a particular vacancy does not perform satisfactorily in the job. Substandard performance on a production line can lead to having to correct a mistake, and a lack of skill in interacting with a customer could lead to loss of business. Within a work group a poor performer can affect the rhythm and output of the team.

Certain advantages are said to accrue from external recruitment. It offers the organisation the opportunity to inject new ideas into its operations by utilising the skills of external candidates. When internal promotions have taken place, external recruitment could be used to attract candidates to fill positions, that have been vacated by insiders. Also, external recruitment is a form of communication, whereby the organisation projects its image to potential employees, customers and others outside the organisation.

Prerequisites to recruitment

Recruitment and selection need to be underpinned by solid preparatory work in the form of job analysis and preparing a job description and job specification.

JOB ANALYSIS

Job analysis procedures are designed to produce systematic information about jobs, including the nature of the work performed, the equipment used, the working conditions and the position of the job within the organisation (Arnold, 2005).

To start off this process one could interview the previous job-holder as well as their supervisor and other staff connected with them in the natural course of events. This approach has value in describing the tasks that constitute the vacant post, and highlights the reporting relationship (to the job-holder's superior) and other forms of liaison (e.g. with colleagues). There is also a tradition in job analysis whereby the job holder may be asked to keep a work diary to record how time is actually spent.

Smith and Robertson (1993) have put forward the following six-step approach to job analysis, which covers some of the points mentioned above:

1. Utilise appropriate existing documents, such as job descriptions and training manuals.
2. Ask questions of the line manager in whose department the job is located about the main purposes of the job, the tasks involved and how the job relates to other jobs.
3. Ask questions of the person doing the job about the main purposes of the job, the tasks involved and how the job relates to other jobs. In addition, the job-holder could be asked to provide supplementary information in the form of a record (e.g. work diary) of the activity in the job over a set period (e.g. two weeks).
4. If practicable, an observer could be assigned the task of noting what the job-holder does, normally over a period of more than one day and at different times.
5. The job analyst could go through the motions of performing the job in order to obtain the necessary insight, but it should be noted that this approach may not be possible if the job analyst has not got the necessary training or is unable to use the machinery, where appropriate, because of lack of familiarity with its use.
6. The final step is to produce a description of the job.

Other methods are the work profiling system, consisting of a computerised questionnaire produced by Saville and Holdsworth (Smith *et al.*, 1989), designed to provide a detailed job description and a profile of the ideal candidate, and the 'critical incidents technique'. The latter is applied in situations when job-holders are asked to describe a number of specific real-time events that have contributed to successful job performance.

Job analysis is not an unbiased source of information (Price, 2004). Subordinates are capable of exaggerating in the sense that they convey that their jobs are more demanding or complex than they really are; they can also be guilty of omission when they remember the interesting tasks but somehow forget the boring ones. Information provided by supervisors could err on the side of understatement – jobs are portrayed as being easier and less complex than they are in reality. Misunderstanding could also arise, as frequently supervisors do not have a detailed view of the subordinates' jobs.

When conducting a job analysis exercise one should keep firmly in mind the justification for the job in the light of current and future organisational needs. Corporate strategic considerations should therefore be a guiding force.

Job analysis will normally take place when a position becomes vacant, but as organisations become more flexible it can be an ongoing process of updating so as to enhance the adaptability of the organisation. Job analysis provides the fundamental information, which will subsequently be used in formulating the job description and job or person specification, i.e. information about the tasks that are carried out and the skills and attributes needed to achieve successful performance.

Finally, some work psychologists have expressed reservations about the relevance of job analysis in the contemporary world and speak of the demise of traditional job analysis (Doyle, 2003; Furnham, 2001). If jobs have a short life span, job analysis is somewhat impractical. Also, bear in mind that technology affects and changes jobs frequently, so it is becoming exceedingly difficult to predict the type of person the organisation will need in the future. However, that does not rule out the need to base HR decisions on good information that also takes into account the needs of business.

JOB DESCRIPTION

Having defined the job after analysing it, the next step is the preparation of a job description. This should contain an outline of the job, the tasks involved, the responsibilities and the conditions. A job description is a foundation stone for a number of HR practices, ranging from selection to the determination of pay and training. But the traditional job description is now being challenged with the advent of the 'flexible' job description. This has become popular for some organisations, particularly those influenced by Japanese management practices in the 1990s. The flexible job description will normally outline the nature of the tasks, and mention 'competencies' and skills required for the job-holders; but it will not specify which team or group they belong to, nor will it state the precise nature of their responsibilities. The reason for the open-ended nature of the job responsibilities is to provide flexibility in the event of changes in the emphasis or direction taken by the organisation.

Note the reference to competencies above. The move towards underlining the importance of competencies shifts the emphasis away from closely specifying tasks to be carried out towards stating the abilities and skills required of the job occupants. Michelin, the tyre production company, has defined a set of core managerial competencies as follows: decision making; managing a team; people development and coaching; and openness to others (relationships). These competencies are used at the point of selection and are also broken down into more detail to form part of the performance management and development systems. As a result there is an integrated approach to employee resourcing, and this can aid the effective establishment and maintenance of a positive psychological contract (Sutton and Griffin, 2004). By adopting the competency approach it is hoped that the individual and the organisation will utilise the flexibility to adapt to new job requirements and situations. Also, the rigidity imposed by specifying a closed set of duties and responsibilities is removed.

JOB (PERSON) SPECIFICATION

Job or person specification describes a process whereby the information contained in the job description is used to assist in profiling the type of person capable of successfully executing the tasks associated with the job. It lists the essential criteria that must be satisfied. However, it should be pointed out that the leap from job description to person specification is never entirely objective – it requires inference or intuition and it offers employers the opportunity to exercise discrimination by ruling out particular types or groups (Ross and Schneider, 1992).

A traditional approach to help with this exercise of matching job applicants and jobs is Rodger's (1952) seven-point plan:

1. physique (health, appearance);
2. attainments (education, qualifications, experience);
3. general intelligence (intellectual capability);
4. special aptitudes (facility with hands, numbers or communication skills);
5. interests (cultural, sport, etc.);
6. disposition (likeable, reliable, persuasive);
7. special circumstances (prepared to work shifts, excessive travel, etc.).

To make the seven-point plan operational would mean specifying essential and desirable characteristics under each of the above headings. More modern interpretations are likely to place emphasis on skills, work attitudes and interests apart from the above factors. In particular, restrictive personality requirements and criteria such as having a 'likeable' disposition could introduce an element of bias into the process, and so tend to be treated very carefully.

An alternative person specification is the five-fold grading system proposed by Munro Fraser (1958):

1. impact on others (through physique, appearance, mode of expression);
2. acquired qualifications (education, training, experience);
3. innate attitudes (quick to grasp things, appetite for learning);
4. motivation (sets goals and is determined to achieve them);
5. adjustment (stable with high threshold for stress, relates well to others).

Current practice tends to pick items from the traditional models outlined above and adapt them to the job and setting at hand. McGrath (2006) provides an example of a person specification for a lobbyist. Lobbyists operate in and around politics, advocating for particular policies or clients. They are often regarded with suspicion and distrust by the general public and there are many misapprehensions about the job and the sort of people who do it. On the basis of 60 interviews with lobbyists in Washington, London and Brussels, McGrath complied a composite set of personal characteristics that are desirable in successful lobbyists:

■ listening ability,

■ observation skills,

■ relationship building,

■ courtesy,

■ honesty and integrity,

■ credibility,

■ ability to deal with issues surrounding gender and sexuality.

Whilst this specification does not strictly adhere to the Munro Fraser formulation, there are clear parallels. For example, impact on others, attitudes and adjustment are highlighted, whilst qualifications are less pronounced.

The central fact to note is that the preparation of a job or person specification is critical as a step in the process prior to recruitment because it tells us about the type of person needed to fill the vacant post. It provides a benchmark of the desirable qualities and important qualifications below which the organisation must not go. In many cases current practices are modifications of one or more of the above systems.

Key result areas

It is now customary to pay attention to making explicit 'key result areas' for the job around the time the job or person specification is prepared. In this approach getting results is heavily underlined, and so the emphasis is on outputs, not inputs. Outputs could be expressed in the form of quality, quantity, time and cost. A feature of 'key result areas' is that objectives are set for the new recruit, in accordance with stated criteria (e.g. quality/quantity of output), and this can provide the basis for subsequent performance appraisal.

Increasingly the language used in job or person specifications tends to reflect recent cultural shifts in HRM (e.g. creative management of change, performance oriented), so words such as initiate, achieve, stimulate, etc., seem to have wide currency. It is now commonplace to highlight critical competencies likely to be associated with successful job performance when specifying the format and content of the job or person specification. A competency has been referred to above in connection with the job description and relates to an underlying individual characteristic such as ability to communicate, solve problems, delegate effectively and act as a good team player. There has been some criticism of competencies. For example, Griffiths (2005) has argued that the way that statements of competency are worded can favour men over women where they focus on individualism and competitiveness. There is a debate on the findings of this research, but it is important to note that one should be careful in the phraseology that is used to make sure that it does not play into unconscious biases that might exist in the minds of those making selection decisions. An elaboration of what we really mean by competencies appears in Box 7.1. There is further discussion of competencies in a training and development context in Chapter 10.

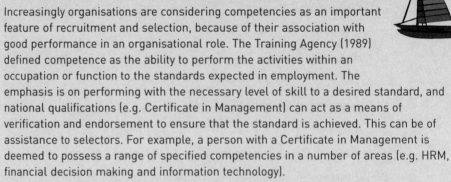

Box 7.1: Competencies

Increasingly organisations are considering competencies as an important feature of recruitment and selection, because of their association with good performance in an organisational role. The Training Agency (1989) defined competence as the ability to perform the activities within an occupation or function to the standards expected in employment. The emphasis is on performing with the necessary level of skill to a desired standard, and national qualifications (e.g. Certificate in Management) can act as a means of verification and endorsement to ensure that the standard is achieved. This can be of assistance to selectors. For example, a person with a Certificate in Management is deemed to possess a range of specified competencies in a number of areas (e.g. HRM, financial decision making and information technology).

Of course there will be certain elements of competence not assessed by national awards, and organisations are expected to compensate for this omission when they analyse jobs. For example, London Transport carried out a competency-based analysis of the position of supervisor, and now bases recruitment and selection around such criteria as written and oral communication, planning and organising, customer awareness, quality consciousness and attention to detail. Within these general headings more specific criteria are identified. For instance, a person competent in oral communication is able to convey information and instructions that can be easily understood, and a person competent in planning and organising has the ability to prioritise work and plan or schedule it. The above competencies must be kept firmly in mind when assessment of skills is made during the formal selection process.

Tesco make use of competency-based selection when taking on staff in their Contact Centre. The competencies used include: achievement of task; people skills; thinking style; personal style and serving our customers. Each of these main competencies is broken down into more detail. For example, 'people skills' is made up of communication, teamworking and interpersonal skills. These competencies are used throughout the recruitment and selection process. The initial stage is a telephone interview during which particular competencies are tested. For example, as part of the communication competencie, evidence of the candidate's ability on the following items is sought:

- voice: tone, pitch and pace, clarity;
- language: vocabulary, enunciation;
- motivation: enthusiastic, positive;
- confidence: positive self-image.

These competencies are directly related to performance on the job and to the business needs.

Activity

Apply the competencies approach to the person specification of a lobbyist provided above.

Before leaving the discussion of job or person specification it should be mentioned that the process so far should be considered within a framework of equal opportunity. This means keeping in mind that all job applicants should be given the chance to demonstrate their abilities irrespective of their sex, ethnic origin, disability or age where these factors are considered irrelevant to job performance.

Recruitment

In this section the spotlight will be on how to attract applicants, the sources of recruitment and the shortlisting of candidates, which takes place before the formal selection techniques are activated.

ATTRACTING APPLICANTS

Now that the organisation has a good idea of the profile of the candidate suited to the vacant position, the next step is to attract the attention of suitable applicants. The job or person specification will be used as a basis to create a shortened profile of the ideal candidate and likewise the job description will be used to extract information on the duties and responsibilities of the job-holder. This information is then used to advertise the position and to send an 'information pack' to applicants. This is an important stage in the process because the primary aim of the organisation is to attract a sufficient number of good candidates. It should be noted that it is disadvantageous to attract too many candidates, because sorting out large numbers of applications is time consuming and costly. It is also disadvantageous to attract too few applicants because the organisation is faced with insufficient numbers, which limits choice.

SOURCES OF RECRUITMENT

How does the organisation go about finding suitable applicants? A number of options are open to it. Before exercising these options a decision will be made on whether to handle the process internally or externally. In certain situations the personnel department or HR function has the resources and competency to mount a recruitment campaign. One might expect this to happen where the job is fairly routine and applicants are in plentiful supply, but it could apply to other situations as well. Where the internal function does not have the expertise and confidence to provide the service reliance could be placed on an external provider. External recruitment could run concurrently with activity to advertise vacancies internally, thereby encouraging internal candidates to apply.

The following are examples of situations where the organisation uses external recruitment.

Job centres

A job centre is a free external service, which the organisation could find to be of great assistance. It will advertise the job and help with shortlisting suitable candidates. This can be most helpful where there is a large pool of available candidates.

Recruitment agencies

These agencies are likely to have a list of suitable applicants on their files, and charge a certain percentage of the salary attached to the job for making these available to the organisation. They will be responsible for advertising the vacant position and shortlisting candidates. The obvious advantage to the organisation using the services of recruitment agencies is the saving of time; and the small organisation without an adequate personnel or HR function has the advantage of having specialist advice and assistance. The disadvantages are the costs involved and the fact that control of such an important process is outside the organisation. Another drawback might be that some agencies do not adhere to the organisation's equal opportunities policy and its implementation in a way the organisation would do when dealing internally with job applicants.

Executive search agencies

When the organisation wishes to fill a very senior position, or a highly specialist position where applicants are in short supply, it may resort to the use of executive search agencies. These agencies charge very high fees, but organisations using them believe that the benefits outweigh the cost. To derive benefits will certainly necessitate providing the search consultant or headhunter with a thorough job specification relating to the vacancy.

Casual callers

These are respondents who read vacancy notices at, say, a factory gate, and could be attracted by the image of the company as an employer. They may show a reluctance to register with a job centre or agency, or to respond to a newspaper advertisement.

Friends or relatives of existing employees

The advantage of introductions through friends or relatives already employed in the organisation is that the prospective employee gets an insight into the nature of the job and conditions within the company. However, it is important to bear equality of opportunity in mind because if certain groups (such as ethnic minorities or women) are under-represented in the current workforce they may also be under-represented in the friends and relations of the current workforce.

It is claimed that employers are rewarding employees who spot talent on their behalf. According to the CIPD almost 50 per cent of employers offer an incentive to employees to encourage friends and associates to make job applications. Another form of talent spotting on the increase is alumni programmes that encourage former employees to feed back recruitment leads to the company and to consider rejoining the company at a future date. In a sense all this amounts to using the power of word of mouth, prompted by internet social networking facilities such as MySpace and Friends Reunited. Others would argue that these developments are influenced by a desire to cut recruitment costs. Whatever the motivation, social networking appears to be an increasingly significant recruitment source, and it is discussed further in Case example 7.1.

CASE EXAMPLE 7.1

EMPLOYEES' NETWORKS AS A RECRUITMENT SOURCE

Xansu

Xansu, a UK-based outsourcing and technology business, rewards employees for introductions that result in permanent appointments. Payments reflect the seniority of recruits and range from £100 for clerical staff up to £7,000 for directors. According to the HR director of the company, in the UK employee referrals bring in 20 per cent of recruits, but in India it is close to 75 per cent. As to the advantages of this type of recruitment, the person referred is more likely to share the cultural attributes of the company, but equally there are reservations that it could be restrictive to the flow of new ideas into the organisation and exacerbates workplace biases because existing staff are likely to recommend people in their own image. But if the organisation is already socially diverse and staffed by open-minded people, this may be less of a problem. Another reservation relates to how reliable the average employee is as a judge of who is the right employee for a particular organisation. For example, friendships could influence employees' views of their friends' capabilities.

BUPA, UK

Safeguards ought to be built into the social networking process. According to the HR director of BUPA, UK, referred candidates should be assessed on the same basis and by the same methods as external applicants. Another safeguard is to conceal, where possible, the referral source. Finally, only pay the introduction bonus after the referred candidate has completed the probation period.

Astra Zeneca

Astra Zeneca, the pharmaceutical company, does things differently with respect to social networking in recruitment. It invites staff, particularly those in areas of skill shortages, to enrol as 'talent scouts'. They then receive an online magazine that highlights recruitment priorities and offers tips on how to network. About 15 per cent of the company's employees are talent scouts, and they are on the look out for talented people among those they meet through their work or know by reputation. Also, the company does not subscribe to the view that a bonus is only paid after a referred candidate successfully completes the probation period. The job of the scout should only be concerned with populating the pool of suitable candidates.

Source: based on Clegg, 2007

Question

What are the potential dangers of recruiting friends and acquaintances of current employees?

Schools, colleges, universities

Organisations that have traditionally taken on young people directly from the education system have operated a number of processes to recruit from this source. These include the 'milk round', where employers visit universities publicising their vacancies and interviewing final-year students. Some employers have built up links with schools, encouraging visits and supporting education. Other employers, such as the Royal Navy and some large electronics companies, have funded the education of students on the understanding that the graduates will work for the organisation following completion of their courses.

Internships, in which students, typically prior to their final year of study, spend the summer working for an organisation, are becoming increasingly popular with companies (Beckett, 2006). Internships have historically had a bad name as some organisations treated them as a way of getting cheap labour on a temporary basis. Forward looking companies, such as Deloitte, however, put the students onto a structured programme of work, which develops them and delivers for the company. The company pays a decent rate for the job and as a result has a high degree of competition for places (Beckett, 2006). The process gives the company a good opportunity to get to know the students and vice versa, and this exchange of knowledge can be very helpful in subsequent selection decisions.

Advertisements

A popular source of recruitment is an advertisement in national, provincial or local newspapers, or specialist magazines or journals. The organisation could liaise directly with the media or use the services of advertising agencies. The latter, which receive their commission from the media, can offer advice on advertising copy and choice of media, and may be better placed than the typical organisation to book advertising space at short notice.

It is important to give serious consideration to the contents of the advertisement. There should be an emphasis on the necessary qualifications and experience, duties and responsibilities, the organisation where the job is located, salary (unless negotiable), method of application, and closing date for applications. Any special requirements such as non-standard hours or travel arrangements might be included to facilitate a prospective applicant's decision. The advertisement is effectively projecting the image of the company, and as such it is a selling document – it is selling the company and the job in order to elicit a good response. The language used in the advertisement and the style of presentation should have intrinsic appeal. In the final analysis it should be uppermost in the recruiter's mind that the potential applicant has the choice to apply or not to apply. Therefore what appears in the advertisement should assist rather than hinder applicants in deciding whether or not they are interested in joining the organisation.

One should recognise cultural differences in the approach to recruitment advertising. On this theme Price (2004) draws a distinction between the French and the British scene, as follows:

> British recruitment marketing normally features salaries and benefits but French equivalents are vague in this respect, reflecting different approaches to rewards (Barsoux and Lawrence, 1990). UK companies base pay on job requirements; in France it depends on the candidate's qualifications. French advertisements define educational requirements in detail, sometimes indicating the number of years of study after the Baccalaureate as the main heading. Attendance at specific Grandes Ecoles may be requested. Management in France is regarded as an intellectual rather than interpersonal matter. Hence recruitment is geared towards cleverness (Barsoux and Lawrence, 1990). Instead of the managerial buzzwords, such as dynamic, energetic, and high calibre, found in British advertisements, French equivalents seek out les éléments les plus brilliants. The nuance is telling.

Telephone hotlines

In most cases the first major contact between a candidate and the organisation after receiving the appropriate information will be a written submission in the form of either a completed application form or a curriculum vitae (CV). An alternative first contact is a telephone 'hotline'. This may be publicised through an advertisement, and candidates will be encouraged to contact the organisation to discuss the vacancies, conditions of work and so on. This has the advantage of facilitating a speedy response and can encourage a larger pool of recruits, which may be important if there is a tight external supply of labour.

Open days

Some organisations use open days to encourage recruitment. Potential candidates are invited to come into the organisation to meet managers or team leaders, and to see what working for the organisation involves. This allows people to decide whether or not they are attracted to the vacant positions and to the organisation, and it can encourage them to enter the next phase of recruitment. As with telephone hotlines, open days can be useful where there are a number of similar vacancies and a relatively tight supply of labour.

Internet

The use of the Internet as a mechanism of recruitment has been increasing, and most major UK employers now use it as a significant part of their recruitment strategy citing the following most common reasons (Smethurst, 2004):

■ reducing the cost per hire;

- increasing the speed to hire;

- strengthening the employer brand;

- greater flexibility and ease for the candidates;

- broaden the applicant pool.

Woolworths had reduced the cost per hire by 70 per cent and administration time by 40 per cent, and B&Q have cut hiring costs by 30 per cent (Smethurst, 2004). It is not necessarily the case that all companies would make similar savings, but these examples make the concept attractive to others.

Applicants can gain information about the organisation, its vacancies and processes of application via the Internet. In some organisations this has been taken further. One example is Dell, which has used the Internet to enable applicants for some jobs to 'shadow' current employees via desktop web cameras. This gives the applicants an understanding of what it is like to work for Dell. A problem encountered by Dell, and other popular computer-based companies, is oversubscription for their vacancies. The company attempts to limit this by providing online self-screening so that candidates can determine whether or not they are fundamentally suitable for the position. On the Dell website (www.euro.dell.com) potential candidates can access information on careers with Dell in different countries by category, such as student, graduate or experienced staff. They can then see information on 'working at Dell', rewards and benefits, learning and development and career paths. It is possible to click on the type of job that is of interest, and this yields a job description and specification of the knowledge, skills, abilities, competencies, education and experience necessary for the post. If suitably qualified, enquirers can submit their CVs. This access allows a large number of interested people to get a better understanding of Dell and the job they are specifically interested in without taking up any significant time from Dell's point of view.

Another example is Cisco Systems, which recruits exclusively through the Internet. For some jobs it is possible to interact with current employees via email, and informal conversations enable candidates to assess the nature of the organisation and whether or not they would fit in (Welch, 1999). More generally, on the website (www.cisco.com) it is possible to view a video introduction to Cisco and to access information about jobs and internships. Information of the culture and approach of the Cisco 'family' is provided and there is the ability to search by location and job and to submit a CV. Job descriptions for vacancies, incorporating main duties, knowledge and skills, and personal qualities (such as teamworking and problem solving) are downloadable.

Although the Internet is a very popular source of recruitment it does have shortcomings. For example, 11 per cent in a survey of 534 students admitted cheating in online tests, often by consulting friends or family for help (Phillips, 2006). Hence, it is important to treat information cautiously and to corroborate the apparent performance of candidates with other methods (which are discussed in the following section on selection). Issues regarding the implementation of online recruitment are discussed in Case example 7.2.

Evaluation of sources

Recruitment is an expensive and time-consuming process, so its effectiveness needs to be monitored. A basic approach is to establish whether vacancies are filled at acceptable cost, with people possessing at least the minimum qualifications, or whether a sufficient number of

ONLINE RECRUITING

British Airways

British Airways has a high level of technology use, and employees are expected to use the Web as a basic tool of the job. It follows that the Web should be a central recruitment mechanism for the organisation. While there used to be a number of separate micro sites advertising different types of post, including jobs for graduate trainee pilots, IT staff and engineers, there is now a discrete site encompassing all occupations. This is the result of a recruitment strategy that deliberately focuses on online processes and which seeks to represent the BA brand in a coherent way. The focus is on BA as an employer of choice and candidates should expect to compete with each other to join the organisation.

There is an emphasis on providing information as follows:

- advertisements of the BA vacancies;
- details of the required skills;
- profiles of current BA employees;
- explanations from current employees of what it is like to work at BA;
- electronic application forms;
- simulations and games.

The aims are to present BA clearly, so that candidates can judge whether or not they would fit in with the style of the organisation, and to attract the best candidates. The graduate management training programme 'Leaders for Business' now recruits exclusively through electronic media. BA was warned that this would reduce the number of applications, and the number fell from the usual 12,000 to 5,000, but the view of the organisation was that the quality of applicants was very high, and that there was no difficulty in filling places. Similarly, an advertisement on the Web for 147 customer-service agents was successfully filled through online recruitment alone.

The Web is not only functioning as a source of recruitment but also as a means of filtering out potential candidates. BA is not uncomfortable with this on the grounds that in areas such as graduate recruitment and IT professionals one would expect candidates to be web literate. For many jobs traditional media, such as newspaper advertisements, are still used in conjunction with the Internet. The expenditure on newspaper advertisements has been reduced, however, with a typical advertisement appearing in one outlet rather than four as was often the case in the past. The result of this is that the development of the Internet for recruitment has been cost neutral.

The BA jobs site includes a flight simulator. Although the feature is regarded simply as a game by BA the simulator is being used by about 30,000 people per day, and so is obviously popular with the public. This fun factor is part of the drive to make the site 'sticky' for potential candidates.

It is not expected that online application will totally replace traditional methods, but for BA the jobs' website combines communicating corporate image with up-to-date recruitment and information provision to candidates.

Source: based on Merrick, 2001

KPMG

Recruitment experts are predicting that the lengthy process of applying for a graduate appointment by filling in a complicated form will be consigned to the dustbin. Instead most employers are expected to adopt online application systems, though at present only a small number of companies (e.g. KPMG, Deutsche Bank, Merrill Lynch) are going down this road.

KPMG, the professional services firm, gets more than 8,000 applications a year for the 650 places on its graduate-appointment programme, and it is now asking universities to inform students that it is going online, pointing out that there are benefits to both the recruiter and the candidate from adopting this approach. The national director of graduate recruitment at KPMG is reported as saying that 'the entire graduate application process has been redesigned to take advantage of the speed, accuracy, and flexibility of the Internet. Also the cost per hit will be much lower.' He expects the online system to halve the paperwork and quadruple the speed of the process.

Online recruitment offers employers an abundance of information at their fingertips – how many people applied, their profiles, their progress, which universities they attended – and this information can be circulated widely within an international firm such as KPMG. The national director of graduate recruitment at KPMG goes on to say that this 'means we can identify good applicants and get them to the offer of employment stage quickly. After all the sooner we can focus on outstanding candidates the more likely we are to get them.'

Job applicants will also save a lot of time because an online application will take much less time to complete than a paper application. But it should be noted that the onscreen form incorporates some kind of test or assessment, so it is important that candidates are prepared and read the instructions carefully. It is claimed that the online recruitment process is much fairer because it is more objective: 'Whatever a candidate's name, racial origin or accent, the computer will score him or her impartially.' Another advantage, according to the spokesperson from KPMG, is that 'online recruitment systems are so efficient that instead of a rejected candidate getting the standard type of reject letter, they can be told why they failed'. KPMG developed its approach with consultants in online recruitment systems and occupational psychology.

Source: based on Eglin, 2000

Question

Do you think that web-based recruitment and selection will eventually supplant other methods? To what extent would this be a good thing?

applicants were attracted by the organisation's efforts to gain their attention (Dessler, 2005). Wright and Storey (1994) suggest that the following data could be collected:

- the number of applicants who completed application forms;
- the number of candidates whose applications are processed at different stages in the recruitment process, including those who get on the shortlist;
- the number of candidates recruited by the organisation;
- the number of successful candidates who are still in the organisation after six months.

As a general principle, it would be desirable to obtain evaluative data or information from those involved in the recruitment process, including staff who dealt with initial inquiries in response to the advertisement, as well as from both successful and unsuccessful candidates. Obviously it is unlikely that the unsuccessful candidates would be forthcoming in this type of exercise; however, they could be asked to comment if they contacted the organisation requesting information on the reasons why they were not selected.

SHORTLISTING

The outcome of the recruitment process is to produce a shortlist of candidates whose background and potential are in accordance with the profile contained in the job or person specification. If there are large numbers of applicants this can be a time-consuming process. Those engaged in the shortlisting exercise will hopefully be making good use of the information provided by candidates on a well-designed application form, although in some situations candidates are asked to submit a CV instead of completing a pre-printed form.

An advantage of the CV is that it allows candidates to state their qualifications, experience, etc., in a way that reflects their written communication skills. However, one should be aware that some candidates may receive professional help with the preparation of a CV. A problem with a CV as opposed to a standard application form is that the candidate specifies the information to include or exclude, whereas with the application form it is the organisation that controls events and requires information specific and relevant to organisational needs. The application form could be considered more reliable, because all applicants are forced to divulge information under set headings.

With regard to what is expected of job applicants, practice varies between countries. For example, as a general principle, there could be a request in advertisements in France for a handwritten letter of application to accompany a CV and photograph. The emphasis on handwriting could be due to the use of graphology in the selection process (see page 204). It is said that French CVs are shorter and more factual than the Anglo-Celtic type, and contain little or no personal information such as hobbies and leisure pursuits. In Japan an official family registry record, a physical examination report, and letters of recommendation, as well as a CV and photograph, are expected (Price, 2004).

Whatever approach is adopted the organisation will be looking for information on the person's education, qualifications, training, experience, present salary, special qualities, state of health and reasons for leaving the present job; and the candidate is normally given the opportunity to provide any additional relevant information. Some employers provide less elaborate application forms for applicants seeking manual work. Although the application form is designed with selection firmly in mind, the completed form also serves another purpose. It can be used as an input to the personnel records of the successful candidates who join the organisation. At this stage additional information, such as the national insurance number, may be required. In the not too distant future the traditional application form could become obsolete (see Case example 7.1 above.)

Selection

Selection is referred to as the final stage of the recruitment process when a decision is going to be made on who the successful candidate will be. As you can imagine, this is an important decision and should be made in an impartial and objective way, drawing on some or all of a number of selection techniques as follows:

- interviews,

- psychological tests,

- work-based tests,

- assessment centres,

- biodata,

- references,

- graphology,

- polygraphy,

- telephone screening,

- the Internet.

INTERVIEWS

Interviewing, either on a one-to-one basis or by interview panel, could be considered the most popular selection technique. Interviews offer the opportunity for a genuine two-way exchange of information that can be useful in judging whether or not the interviewee will relate well to colleagues and fit into the culture of the organisation. With reference to the last point, interviewers could be looking for attributes that go beyond the specific job-related skills of the applicant. For example, there could be a focus on 'the applicant-organisation fit', in the sense that selectors are looking at the personality characteristics of the candidates, their personal values and attitudes, and their flexibility and commitment, to see if they will fit into the organisation's culture. The applicant–organisation fit approach could be very relevant when conditions within organisations are in a state of flux, and significant change affecting jobs is on the horizon (Torrington *et al.*, 2005). Cisco Systems developed culturally consistent selection criteria that targeted candidates 'who were frugal, enthusiastic about the future of the Internet, smart and not concerned with status. . . . Also, the company targeted "passive applicants" – people who were satisfied in their current jobs, and not job hunting, but who might be lured to Cisco; and it developed a fast easy-to-use website for them to learn about Cisco' (Chatman and Cha, 2002).

According Newell (2006), the interview is the most common selection tool across many countries. Some of the basics of conducting interviews are highlighted in Box 7.2.

> ### Box 7.2: Interviewing
>
> 1. *Be clear on the objectives of the interview.* The main objective is to foster an effective two-way exchange of information between the interviewer and interviewee. The process can be thought of as 'a conversation with a purpose'.
>
> 2. *Decide who should conduct the interview.* The advantage of one-to-one interviews is the possibility of building up a good rapport between interviewer and interviewee.

The disadvantage is the possibility of unchecked bias on the part of the interviewer. Panel interviews mean that more than one interviewer hears the information supplied by the interviewee, and so the process may be less biased, but if panels are too large it can be intimidating for the interviewee.

3. *Conduct careful advance preparation.* Questions should be well planned, and if it is to be a panel interview an appropriate division of labour between panel members should be agreed. The physical layout of the room should be welcoming, and all distractions such as telephone calls should be banished.

4. *Structuring the interview.* The interview should have a clear structure, with major topics being clearly identified and dealt with in a coherent way. This makes more sense to a candidate than a random selection of questions ranging over diverse topics. The interviewers need to decide how much structure they are going to impose, and what degree of freedom will be given to the candidates to lead the conversation.

5. *Framing the questions.* The key areas identified in the job description will need to be covered, but in addition interviewers will want to get beyond the 'stock' responses of candidates. This requires open questions to establish a topic, for example, 'Could you tell us about your experience of leading teams?' and following the response with 'probing' questions, for example, 'could you give us more detail on what you actually did to motivate the team members?'

6. *Managing the climate of the interview.* A good interviewer is able to monitor the reactions of the candidate, and to put them at their ease. This enables them to speak more openly, and a better exchange of information to take place.

7. *Gathering and exchanging information.* Good questioning and active listening are necessary to bring out the information required. It is wise to keep a record of the key points of answers the candidate gives as the interview progresses. It is important to maintain attention throughout the interview, otherwise crucial points may be missed, and bias can creep into the decision-making process.

8. *Controlling the interview.* Some candidates will talk too much, others too little. The interviewer must make sure that questions are directly answered (repeating them if necessary) and that the time spent on the various topic areas is suitably controlled.

9. *Closing the interview.* The candidate should be invited to give any information they have not so far offered, and the interviewer should check that they are clear on what happens next (e.g. further selection testing, or a letter from the HR department).

Some forms of interview are said to have low validity but they continue to remain popular often because managers would not want to contemplate employing a candidate without meeting them (Klehe, 2004). (The issue of validity will be examined later in this chapter.) The crux of the matter with conducting interviews is not the irrelevance of interviewing as a selection device; it is the widely held view that the process itself is carried out in a flawed way. So what are the dysfunctional aspects of selection interviews?

- Subjective, unsound judgements are made by untrained interviewers.

- There is a tendency for interviewers to arrive at a judgement early on in the interview, and this could be perceived as unjust by the interviewee who picks up this impression from the nature of the questioning and body language.

- Where interviewers have prior unfavourable biases about interviewees, there is the danger of highlighting negative data about the candidates so that it fits the biases. The 'halo' effect is where the interviewers are positively disposed towards interviewees because they like or are attracted to them. The result is that the interviewers look more benignly on the answers of the candidates instead of judging the raw content of what they say. The 'horn' effect is the reverse of this, where interviewers are predisposed to 'hear the worst' in what the candidates are saying. If a number of interviewers are involved (e.g. a panel interview), it is hoped that such individual biases will be reduced.

- There are many times when a consensus view does not emerge from a panel of interviewers, simply because interviewers see different things in the same interviewee.

What can be done to mitigate the worst effects of the selection interview and improve its overall standing?

- Set in motion a training programme for those who conduct interviews, be they managers, supervisors or 'personnel' specialists, using closed-circuit television. In such a setting the trainees would receive coaching in good practice.

- Ensure that the appropriate documentation (i.e. job specification, job description, completed application form or CV) is circulated to the interviewer or interview panel members well in advance, and carefully studied before the start of the interview.

- The venue should be suitable for conducting interviews, and the furniture in the interview room should be appropriately arranged.

- A reasonable amount of time should be allocated for the interviews, and generally each interviewee should receive the same time allocation.

- Where appropriate, open-ended, job-related questions, which require more than a yes/no response, should be asked of interviewees. The information received can be summarised and relayed to the interviewee to check that a correct understanding has been gained.

- Normally towards the end of the formal questioning the interviewee should be given the opportunity to ask his or her own questions, and be free to make observations.

- Complement the information gleaned from the interviewee with the outcome of psychological tests (where used), and references (preferably written). (There is a discussion of tests and references later in the chapter.)

- Using panel rather than one-to-one interviews can reduce the amount of individual interviewer bias (such as the halo and horn effects), and can yield more information than where one interviewer is trying to take in all the information being disseminated. However, interview panels should not be so large that they become intimidating for the interviewees. Between three and five interviewers would be seen as normal.

The selection interview is a process that is evolving on a continuous basis. The discussion above concentrated on the structured as opposed to the unstructured interview.

Structured vs. unstructured interview

In recent years the superiority of the structured interview over the unstructured interview has been endorsed; there are advantages in standardising questions, recording information and rating applicants. But it is said that the selection interview is frequently conducted in an unstructured way (Van der Zee *et al.*, 2002). The interview is unstructured when the interviewee has been given a degree of control to ask questions and raise issues, rather than the interviewer leading the process through a series of pre-planned questions. This can be a useful approach to encourage a genuinely two-way exchange of information. The unstructured interview, however, has its shortcomings, among them being their casual nature, random questions and short duration (Campion *et al.*, 1997).

One particular approach to interviewing is called the situational interview (Latham *et al.*, 1980; Huffcutt *et al.*, 2004). Here critical on-the-job incidents are identified and recorded following a job analysis exercise. Questions are then prepared to elicit the views of the interviewees on these events. For example, an interviewee is asked, 'What would you do in a particular situation?' The answers are entered on a form and rated on a five-point scale. Research has shown the situational interview, which is akin to the structured job-related interview, to be more valid and reliable than unstructured interviews (Sue-Chan and Latham, 2004). The superiority of the structured interview over the unstructured interview has been advocated. Boyle (1997) speaks highly of the structured interview as a selection method when it is used by trained interviewers using systematic assessment procedures to target key skills and attributes identified by job analysis. However, some interviewers who are more attached to a discursive style complain that the structured interview is too constraining.

Another development in the selection interview that is worthy of note is the patterned behaviour description interview (Newell, 2006). The interviewer probes major life change events in order to ascertain the interviewee's reasons for taking the reported career direction. The aim is to create a 'picture over time' to help with predicting the candidate's likely reactions to future career challenges and changes. Patterns of behaviour could relate to educational choices, ways of approaching particular problems and opportunities at work, and decisions about career development. A pattern may emerge in which candidates are either more proactive or reactive to situations, or information may be gained on whether they deal with problems aggressively, assertively or passively. The emerging pattern is compared with the pre-established desirable pattern of behaviour. Like situational interviews, pattern behaviour description interviews have also been shown to have relatively high validity when executed properly (Klehe and Latham, 2005).

Another development is 'competency-based interviewing' (Johnstone, 1995; Newell, 2006). Instead of looking at what the candidates have achieved, the focus is on how they achieved the results they claim. With competency-based interviewing the interviewer is looking for specific traits reflected in past achievements. To identify those traits interviewers are instructed to look for STARs – an acronym that stands for situations, tasks, actions and results. This is likely to unfold as follows: first, examine the job specification to establish what the job requires. For example, a managerial job could require the exercise of leadership skills, or the ability to make a presentation at a senior level, or skills in promoting interaction in teams. Secondly, having identified the relevant roles, the candidates are asked whether they played such roles or found themselves in such 'situations' in the past or previous job. Once interviewers have found an appropriate situation in the candidates' past the next step is to identify the 'tasks' they were responsible for, followed by identifying the 'actions' they took if a problem arose, and finally what effect or 'result' the actions had.

As a final comment on interviewing, one should note evidence that is supportive of the suitability of the interview in assessing a job applicant's intelligence, level of conscientiousness, level of motivation, and interpersonal skills (Cascio and Aguinis, 2005; Huffcutt *et al.*, 2001). It is suggested that these attributes are related to performance in management positions. Therefore, it is not surprising that applicants for senior management positions attend numerous interviews with headhunters, board members and other executives before a final selection decision is made. Likewise, interviews are used frequently when deciding on the composition of teams.

PSYCHOLOGICAL TESTS

Two of the more important psychological tests (often referred to as psychometric tests) used for selection purposes are intelligence tests and personality tests. The justification for considering both intelligence and personality tests in the field of selection is the belief that scores on those tests have some validity in predicting future job performance.

Intelligence testing

If an organisation gave intelligence tests to recruits, which took the form of tests of numerical and verbal ability, and found from experience that good test scores were associated with good subsequent performance in the job, then we could conclude that there is a high correlation between a particular test of intelligence and job performance. Tests of verbal and numerical ability, with questions on vocabulary, similarities, opposites, arithmetical calculations, etc., are often referred to as general intelligence tests. When people score highly on these tests they are said to have a good capacity to absorb new information, pass examinations and pick up things quickly and perform well at work. But it should be noted that a particular test might only be valid for a particular type of job or activity.

Apart from general intelligence tests, there are aptitude tests and attainment tests. Aptitude tests can measure specific abilities or aptitudes (e.g. spatial ability, manual dexterity, numerical ability, verbal ability) and are used to gauge the person's potential. It should be noted that individuals differ markedly in their ability to do certain things – for example, the ability to learn to do tasks requiring eye–muscle coordination. Attainment tests, which are sometimes called achievement tests, measure abilities or skills already developed by the person. For example, a word-processor operator could be tested for speed and accuracy on a typing test prior to the interview for a secretarial post.

The concept of emotional intelligence has been recognised as an important concept capable of practical use (Goleman, 1998; Woodruffe, 2005). It is concerned with the person's emotional and social skills, and consists of emotional attunement or self-awareness (being in touch with one's feelings and able to empathise with others); emotional management (being in control of one's emotions – e.g. anger – so that one is not overwhelmed by them); self-motivation (able to delay gratification of a need, such as waiting a while for a reward rather than taking it immediately); and self-management skills (well able to handle situations). Those scoring high on the factors described above could be considered good at handling personal relationships and diffusing difficult or explosive situations. There are measuring instruments on the market to gauge emotional intelligence (Watkin, 1999), such as the Emotional Intelligence Inventory (Hay McBer) and the Emotional Intelligence Questionnaire (NFER-Nelson).

Personality tests

There is a recognition that personality has a bearing on the competence of the individual to perform effectively at work, and that personality defects can nullify the beneficial aspects stemming from having the appropriate aptitude or ability. It goes without saying that a highly motivated, psychologically well-adjusted employee is of greater value to a company than an employee who is emotionally unstable and demotivated.

As a broad statement we could refer to personality as that part of us that is distinctive and concerned more with our emotional side and how it is reflected in our behaviour. In a major theory called the 'Big Five' factor theory (see Table 7.1), five basic dimensions of personality are introduced. This theory can be used to illustrate personality characteristics.

By contrast, intelligence is concerned with the cognitive or thinking side of us, though, of course, there are some areas of overlap. For example, in Cattell's (1963) 16 personality factors (16PF) inventory or test, one factor refers to intelligence, and the same applies to intelligence in the model in Table 7.1.

After the administration of a test such as Cattell's 16PF, a profile of the job applicant is produced. There are a number of personality inventories on the market with the same basic aim as Cattell's 16PF, such as Saville and Holdsworth's occupational personality questionnaire. When personality is assessed using one of the published tests, the next step would be to compare the resulting profile with some standard profile believed to be appropriate or relevant to the job for which the candidate is being considered. Obviously a good fit would be advantageous, but one must be aware of the extreme difficulty of creating the standard or ideal profile of a job occupant.

When a person is completing a standard personality questionnaire the organisation would like to think that honest responses are given, and that the respondent avoids giving socially acceptable answers. In practice there could be problems meeting these conditions, as there could be difficulties in establishing clear links between certain personality traits and job outcomes (good performance). Personality questionnaires or measures should be used with great caution in selection (Doyle, 2003). They can provide useful additional information, but their use requires very careful interpretation of individual scores and sensitive feedback. Doyle goes on to say that the conclusion drawn from the results of personality inventories must always be regarded as tentative and that the real value of personality inventories may be more in career guidance/management and personal development, than in selection. They can also be very useful in teambuilding.

The characteristics of a good psychological test should be noted:

■ The measuring device is able to discriminate between individuals.

■ The test is reliable and valid (this will be explained later).

Table 7.1 The 'Big Five' personality dimensions and representative traits

Dimensions	Traits	
	Desirable	Undesirable+
Extraversion (1)	Outgoing, sociable, assertive	Introverted, reserved, passive
Agreeableness (2)	Kind, trusting, warm	Hostile, selfish, cold
Conscientiousness (3)	Organised, thorough, tidy	Careless, unreliable, sloppy
Emotional stability (4)	Calm, even tempered, Imperturbable	Moody, temperamental, nervous
Intellect or openness (5)	Imaginative, creative, intelligent	Shallow, unsophisticated, Imperceptive

Source: based on Hampson, 1999

■ The test is properly standardised, whereby it has been used on a significant sample of the population to which it is related, allowing individual scores to be compared with norms derived from that population when interpreting the results.

Certain assumptions underlie the administration of psychological tests: there is the belief that there are significant differences in the extent to which individuals possess certain characteristics (e.g. emotional stability, intelligence, motivation and finger dexterity); there is a direct and important relationship between the possession of one or more of these characteristics and the ability of the person to do certain jobs; selected characteristics can be measured in a practical sense; and finally an evaluation can be made of the relationship between test results and job performance.

Those who argue that psychological tests have advantages are likely to cite the following:

■ Tests provide quantitative data on the person's temperament and ability that makes it possible to compare individuals on the same criteria (e.g. emotional stability, intelligence).

■ Tests are based on comprehensive theoretical foundations that underpin various behavioural patterns; they are reliable and valid and allow us to draw distinctions between people.

■ Tests are fair because they prevent corruption and favouritism in the selection and promotion of people.

■ Test data can be referred to again at a later stage to see how good the test was in predicting actual success in the job (Furnham, 2005a).

Critics would be keen to cite the following disadvantages:

■ Those tested may lack the ability to give responses that reflect their true feelings, so their responses are meaningless.

■ Questions in the test booklet could be misinterpreted due to a lack of understanding on the part of some subjects, and this affects the accuracy of the response.

■ The performance of an individual tested is not what one might expect because the person is feeling unwell.

■ There could be some individuals who try to confuse the situation by giving irrelevant and stupid responses.

■ There could be others, particularly in personality tests, who are intent on creating a false impression; this amounts to faking in order to project a good image (certain action can be taken to reduce faking!).

■ Tests fail to measure certain important personal characteristics (e.g. trustworthiness).

■ Tests are unfair because they disadvantage members of particular racial and gender groups.

■ Tests are invalid because they do not measure what they are supposed to measure, and test scores are not good at predicting the testee's work performance over time.

■ There are certain weaknesses in the way testers administer tests, such as lack of skill in interpreting the results, and using inappropriate 'norms' (the figures to which the raw scores are related).

■ Given the widespread use of tests nowadays, subjects could be motivated to get hold of copies of them to obtain practice at tackling the questions. If so, performance in the real tests may reflect prior preparation more than the candidates' true ability (Furnham, 2005a).

Whatever the shortcomings of psychological tests, there has been a growth in their use in the field of selection and this has been most pronounced in managerial positions and larger organisations.

Other issues

To conclude the section on psychological tests, other issues – tests and job performance, impact of culture, and integrity and ethics – will be briefly examined.

Tests and job performance: The value of selection test scores to predict future job perform-ance has been the subject of much debate with challenges to the validity of such exercises (Blinkhorn and Johnson, 1990). Later Blinkhorn (1997) continued to express profound reser-vations about the usefulness of psychometric tests, as did Barrett (1998) who has also closely studied this subject. However, it has been argued that part of the early reported low validity of tests occurred because there was no agreement amongst the experts on the nature of tests. Since the emergence of the 'Big Five', and with advances in testing, validity scores have increased, particularly where a specific item (such as conscientiousness) is associated with par-ticular aspects of the job (Newell, 2006). Some people might object to the narrow focus, when personality test scores only are used, because of the failure to consider other relevant factors that influence behaviour, for example, demands of the immediate environment. Others point out, again in the context of personality, that there can be a danger of recruiting the same or similar personality types and producing a situation where there is a lack of variety in the per-sonality composition of work teams.

There is now evidence of developments aimed at putting forward alternatives to conven-tional psychometric tests. Robert McHenry of OPP and Steve Blinkhorn of Psychometric Research and Development felt it necessary to develop tests that measure people's ability to apply knowledge. The new range of tests are called Aptitude for Business Learning Exercises (ABLE), and it is their hope that these tests will be superior to conventional tests when it comes to predicting the performance of those tested and reducing the disadvantages alleged to be suffered by ethnic minorities who have taken tests. ABLE rests on the notion that people are given concepts to learn and are then tested on their ability to apply the concepts (Rogers, 1998).

Impact of culture: There are variations across national boundaries with regard to interest in and acceptance of testing. Italy does not permit the use of tests in selection. In Sweden and Holland applicants have the right to see the test results before the employer sees them, and can destroy the results in the event of a withdrawal of the application (Arnold *et al.*, 1998). The results of a study by Feltham *et al.* (1998) indicated that personality tests made little allowances for cultural differences between countries. On the basis of this revelation Feltham and his colleagues embarked on a project to get rid of cultural incompatibility in a test used. In practice, however, although some improvements are reported, there are still reservations (Cronshaw *et al.*, 2006). Finally, those interested in the selection of expatriates, a topic dis-cussed later in this chapter, should note that the effectiveness of personality tests used in selection may be questionable when it comes to predicting candidates' capability to adjust to different cultures (Dowling and Welch, 2004).

Integrity and ethics: The issue of ethics is becoming increasingly important in organis-ations, and as a consequence there are now tests to measure integrity (Baldry and Fletcher, 1997; Furnham, 2005b). Integrity in this context could cover a variety of issues including theft, fraud, malingering, absenteeism, inadequate effort, drug and alcohol problems, cases of bullying and violence, and so on. When integrity tests were first introduced in questionnaire form in the selection process they were generally considered an alternative to the polygraph (the lie detector). The application of integrity tests is fraught with difficulty, and if used should be carried out with extreme caution. In the final analysis a decision to reject an applicant because he or she poses a high risk to engage in dishonest or deviant behaviour is a decision difficult to justify on the basis of a score on a single integrity test.

The ethics of the use of tests in selection has become in important issue (Alder and Gilbert, 2006). Porteous (1997) raises the following issues:

■ Tests should be filed securely and only administered by qualified users.

■ Conditions for the administration of the tests should be suitable, and candidates ought to be put in the picture as to what is in store for them – it would be beneficial if they had the chance to try sample questions before the actual test.

■ The tests should be up to date by reflecting changes in jobs and the calibre of applicants presenting themselves, and the tests should be relevant to the job under review.

■ There should be a connection between the test result and at least some aspects of the person's performance in the job.

■ Candidates should receive sensitive feedback on their performance in tests (particularly intelligence tests) when they are unsuccessful, because of the association with failure.

■ The test results of unsuccessful candidates should be destroyed, or the anonymity of the candidates should be protected if the results are retained.

WORK-BASED TESTS

When an organisation needs to assess the level of candidates' competence in particular areas behavioural tests can be used. These are sometimes referred to as 'in-tray' tests because the candidates are presented with a representative sample of the work they would be doing if appointed – i.e. a sample of what they might find in their 'in-tray' – and they are required to undertake the typical tasks associated with the job. The quality of their work is then assessed. Normally the test will have a time limit. Candidates will have to prioritise the work they are presented with and carry out as many tasks as they can. For a secretarial position, this may include typing sample correspondence, dealing with enquiries (presented verbally or in writing) and so on. As an extension of this approach applicants could be presented with a series of hypothetical situations, and then asked how they would respond. This is similar to situational interviewing. Another example of work-based tests is evident in the selection of social workers, where candidates join in the examination of hypothetical cases to decide on the appropriate programme of action or care. A further variant of the work-based test arises in situations where an assessment is made of the individual's performance in a group setting. In this case two or more applicants meet to discuss a particular topic. Subsequently, their performance in the discussion is assessed.

Work-based tests are valuable in that they provide evidence of the candidate's competence in actually carrying out specific tasks, and hence their use has become popular (Newell, 2005). However, as the situation of the test is simulated, rather than real, certain factors may affect the performance of candidates. Candidates may perform poorly if they are nervous or lack the background information and experience they would have if they were actually in the job. There is a further question to raise and that is what is being assessed? Work-based tests concentrate on the current competencies of candidates. However, where the organisation is concerned with flexibility and the future potential of candidates – a stand that would be compatible with an HRM perspective – it would be necessary to use other selection techniques as well.

ASSESSMENT CENTRES

Assessment centres, which are events rather than places, use a variety of selection methods in order to increase the likelihood of making a good decision. The methods used include the interview, psychometric tests, and individual and group exercises such as role playing and task simulations, including in-tray exercises referred to earlier.

A feature of the assessment centre is that a competency or skill is assessed from at least two angles. For example, the ability to exercise leadership could be assessed by the use of a group exercise, arranged as a meeting, and by the use of a personality test. Similarly, the candidates' numerical strengths could be assessed using a test of numerical reasoning and by a work statistics exercise (McKenna, 2006).

Before assessment commences the organisation should ensure that the relevant job or person specification and competencies are spelled out and are available. The assessment takes on an individual form when psychometric tests are administered and the candidates are interviewed individually. But an important part of the assessment centre is the evaluation of the candidates' interactive and interpersonal skills in a group exercise. This is done by a number of trained assessors, many of whom are line managers within the organisation. One reason for having a number of assessors is to minimise bias in the assessment process. Also, a number of assessors are needed to observe closely the behaviour and interactions of the various candidates. Because a number of methods are used, and it is an intensive process, it stands to reason that the overall exercise is time consuming (say two or three days) and costly.

Normally one finds that assessment centres (or development centres when applied to management development) are used by large organisations to select key staff, and this could include graduate entrants. The cost of mounting an assessment centre for selection purposes is justified if it is effective in channelling a flow of able employees into the organisation. A spin-off of the assessment centre could be the provision of feedback to candidates who have gone through the process that helps them to build on their strengths and tackle their weaknesses. It should be noted that assessment centres have high validity as a selection device.

Over the years there has been an impressive increase in the use of assessment centres. It is reported that 65 per cent of larger companies (employing over 1,000 people) in the UK use assessment centres (Newell, 2006). Increasingly they are being used with occupational groups other than managers in the area of both selection and career development.

Finally, it is acknowledged that assessment centres are good at predicting the potential of people (Cook, 2003).

BIODATA

This method is used to relate the characteristics of job applicants to the characteristics of successful job-holders, and is most likely to be used by organisations faced with a large number of vacancies for which they receive a very large number of applications (McKenna, 2006). When candidates apply for a job in an organisation they normally complete a standard application form or submit a CV. In these documents one would expect to find certain 'biographical' information related to age, education, personal history, and current and past employment. When one uses biographical information or biodata in a systematic way as a selection tool a questionnaire is used to collect information on a large number of successful performers in the job, and the data are then correlated with the data from candidates. From this exercise could materialise an awareness of biodata (e.g. a certain type of qualification) that is associated with career success. Particular features of a person's biographical profile could receive a higher score than others because of such features' prime importance in influencing good performance. The basic assumption of this approach is that if we know enough about people's life histories we can improve selection by being better able to predict the likely future performance of candidates.

To operationalise the biodata approach the specially designed questionnaire, with weighted items, is used for each candidate. A score is given for responses under each item, and individual item scores are then summed. This technique can be used at the shortlisting phase or later at the time of a structured interview. The discriminating factor in either case is the score given.

There are certain advantages stemming from the use of the biodata approach. It is a useful technique when it is necessary to screen a very large number of applications in response to an advertisement. It is relatively objective and underlines the importance of using a systematic approach to compiling biographical information as a means to improving selection decisions. An obvious disadvantage is the large amount of time needed to ascertain the key biographical items in the first instance, as well as the cost of such an exercise.

There are certain potential dangers in the use of biodata. The features of personal background, which are accorded the status of highly rated desirable features, might be biased against certain minority groups. For example, bias could occur where the sample of employees from whom the biodata profile is drawn – which forms the standard used to judge the candidates – is an unrepresentative group, or has distinctive features that could unfairly exclude others. For instance, if all the successful performers coincidentally had a particular type of family background, to use this as a discriminating factor would introduce bias.

A study found that 20 per cent of organisations used biodata as a selection device for some vacancies, but only 4 per cent used it for all their vacancies (Shackleton and Newell, 1991), and more recent studies have indicated that the use of structured biodata has remained unpopular in comparison to other techniques (Newell, 2005). There is evidence to support the usefulness of biodata in selection (Harvey-Jones and Taffler, 2000). However, one should be vigilant at all times about the strength of the relationship between particular biodata items and outcomes, such as good performance on the job, and be prepared to make adjustments to the questionnaire items when circumstances make it necessary. Finally, Torrington *et al.* (2005) point out that a drawback of the biodata approach is the time involved in its use and the size of the sample needed.

REFERENCES

A candidate for a job is normally asked to nominate more than one referee. One function of a reference is to provide confirmation that the information provided by the candidate is true, another is to provide a character reference. Today employers have to be aware that employees may challenge and possibly resort to litigation if they were to receive an unsatisfactory reference, even if it amounted to an honest assessment (see Box 7.3).

Normally a reference is taken up when the applicant appears on a shortlist and is seriously considered for the particular job, though there are times when a 'long' shortlist is prepared

Box 7.3: Legal implications of providing references

Comments in a reference that prove to be ill judged or inaccurate can result in legal action. An employer should not defame the employee who is hoping to leave the organisation. There are exclusions in the UK Data Protection Act that may prevent employees seeing what they believe are erroneous references; however, these exclusions will not prevent the references being disclosed in general litigation.

Avoid making any comment that could be discriminatory. Recent UK case law has extended both the Race Relations Act and the Sex Discrimination Act to cover the issue of references. Statements such as, 'A left our employment and subsequently brought a claim against us for sex and racial discrimination' will create liability for the employer because such statements could be seen as victimising the employee for taking action. Prospective employers should be cautious on acting on information received from former employers. A prospective employer who decides not to appoint someone, knowing that he or she has claimed against a previous employer, is also guilty of discrimination. This situation is similar to where an employee has a disability and this is mentioned in a reference, or where there is reference to a poor attendance record, without adequate explanation.

An employer should not forget obligations to other employers. If an employer writes a misleading reference where the qualities or skills of the employee are overstated, and the new employer suffers loss, the provider of the reference may be liable to the new employer. For example, an employee, suspected of dishonesty but whose guilt is not proven, enters into an arrangement with the employer to leave the company on grounds of redundancy and receives a good reference containing a statement indicating that he or she was a trustworthy employee. The employee obtains a job with a new employer and subsequently is caught stealing in the new job. Then the new employer reviews the reference and seeks the assistance of a lawyer.

Generally, employers are under no obligation to provide a reference, and would be better off not providing one if the reference cannot be balanced and fair. Increasingly employers are adopting strict policies on giving references. Some issue references with a minimum amount of information such as name, rank and serial number, which are sometimes a little bit more informative when it is stated that further information may be given over the telephone. At least in the latter case it is more difficult to prove what is said. Perhaps in future references will only be provided where a good employee has decided to leave for reasons unconnected with the employer's behaviour or business.

Source: based on Bradley, 2004

and a reference has a part to play in the production of the final shortlist. Some candidates are not too keen for a potential employer to approach their current employer with a request for a reference unless a job offer is on the table. They may not want their present employer to know that they wish to move on. Others might positively welcome their current employer being approached, even though they have not received a job offer, because they feel that being considered seriously for another job of some significance is something they would like their current employers to hear about.

References are considered to be an important input to the selection process where honesty and moral rectitude are crucial considerations. But there are cases where the information contained in references is of doubtful value, particularly when referees provide little beyond confirmation of the dates of employment. Obviously references have greater value when informative data on the candidate's track record are provided and the contents of the application form are verified. A reliable form of reference is one that has been prepared specifically in response to a list of relevant questions posed by the potential employers.

A drawback of references as a selection device is that the applicant nominates the referee(s), and he or she is unlikely to choose a person who will provide a negative assessment. In practice referees are often hesitant to express negative views about a person in writing; although some would feel less inhibited if asked to provide a reference over the telephone. However, giving references over the telephone gives employers less time to marshal their thoughts and use words carefully, unless of course they had advance notice and adequate time to consider the views to be expressed.

Generally the validity and reliability of references are rather poor (Hunter and Hunter, 1984; Reilly and Chao, 1982), but they are still popular and a survey of 700 HR managers in the United States indicated that 87 per cent always take up references as part of the selection procedure (Dessler, 2005).

Finally, Doyle (2003) makes an interesting point with regard to the substance of references. She asks, is it realistic to assume that insight into the past behaviour of a candidate, found in a reference, is useful in predicting future behaviour, particularly if the job applied for and its setting is so different from the present or previous job?

GRAPHOLOGY

Graphology is a technique that makes predictions about future performance on the basis of handwriting analysis. The basic premise is that applicants reveal their personality characteristics through their handwriting. Employers using this method would ask candidates to submit handwriting samples for analysis. Generally, handwriting analysis would not be used alone as a method of assessment; where it is used it is more likely to be one of a number of techniques selected to provide a total profile of the candidate (McGookin, 1993).

Although not very popular in the United Kingdom or the United States (Dessler, 2005), graphology has greater acceptance in France and Germany (Shackleton and Newell, 1991) (see Box 7.4). Drawing inferences about the personal qualities of people from an analysis of their handwriting has been challenged as a reliable form of assessment. A report by the British Psychological Society expressed serious reservations about its effectiveness as a selection device (McLeod, 1994). The CIPD, having assessed the data relating to graphology, concluded that the evidence in its favour is inconclusive, anecdotal and therefore prone to bias and misinterpretation (CIPD, 2001).

POLYGRAPHY

Advocates of the lie detector test or polygraph might consider it suitable for selecting people for certain jobs (e.g. the handling of large quantities of cash) or to detect fraudulent claims (see Box 7.5). The polygraph is used to measure emotional stress shown by variations in blood

Box 7.4: Graphology in selection

Exponents of handwriting analysis believe that graphology can show the potential and ability of a person not apparent from the normal scrutiny of a CV or completed application form. The British Institute of Graphologists claims that analyses from trained graphologists are generally described by clients as extremely accurate and compare favourably with other methods of personality assessment, such as psychometric testing.

A graphologist will require a candidate to submit at least a page of spontaneous writing in fountain or ball-point pen, preferably on unlined paper. The content of the submission is unimportant, but the writer is told not to copy a piece of text as this impedes the flow of writing. Precise rules are followed to measure the writing size, slant, page layout and width of letters and pressure on the paper. These measurements are interpreted to reveal the emotions and talents of the writer. Apparently the degree of pressure on the page conveys the writer's level of energy. Nowadays, more than 75 per cent of French companies use graphology as a standard selection procedure, and its use by Swiss companies is even higher. Companies in countries such as Germany, Austria, Belgium, Holland and Italy also use graphology regularly. Job advertisements in Continental European newspapers frequently ask for handwritten letters, and applicants expect their handwriting to be analysed.

Source: based on Altman, 1995

The Fike Corporation, a producer of valves and industrial products in the United States employs 325 workers. It uses graphology as a screening mechanism for its employees. However, the process is used to design an interview in which the analysis can be followed up with the candidates, rather than a secret analysis which candidates do not know about and cannot respond to.

Source: based on Dessler, 2005

pressure, pulse rate, perspiration, sweating of the palm and respiration, whilst applicants answer questions. In recent years brain activity has also been measured, and the bodily and brain activity can be displayed via ink writing pens on to charts or via a computer screen (BPS, 2004). More recently, the voice is also considered. The reasoning behind the polygraph is that telling a lie is stressful, and the stress will be reflected in physiological reactions. But it should be kept firmly in mind that the polygraph measures emotional stress and is not a measure of lying. Many causes of emotional stress not related to lying may cause a person to fail a lie detector test. Also, many people can lie without being detected by a polygraph.

At one time the polygraph was widely used in an employment context in the United States of America, but in 1988 the US Employee Polygraph Protection Act was passed. This legislation prevented the use of the polygraph for pre-employment screening except by some government agencies and certain strategic industries, such as nuclear power. A Working Party consisting of prominent psychologists was set up by the British Psychological Society (BPS) and reported that the use of the polygraph in employment and security screening is not justified by the available research evidence, and that the use of the polygraph in attempts to detect deception raises issues concerning human rights and professional codes of practice (BPS, 2004).

Box 7.5: Lie-detector test to identify those making fraudulent claims

It is estimated that £650 million in housing benefits is overpaid annually in the United Kingdom through fraud or error. Birmingham Council, the largest local authority in the United Kingdom, is concerned that more than £1 million a year in social benefit payments is being claimed fraudently. As a result, it is to use a telephone lie-detection system in an effort to identify benefit cheats and will rely on expert assistance provided by Capita, the outsourcing business. In the pilot scheme a telephone-based assessment will replace the interview.

Capita, acting for Birmingham Council, is engaged in mounting a pilot scheme using software that will scan claimants' speech patterns, looking for irregularities consistent with lying, such as changes in speed or tone. The pitch of the human voice tends to rise when a person is lying, and a tremour may become apparent. It is said that the measurement of callers' voices would be carefully calibrated so that nervousness or shyness is not a trigger to arouse suspicion.

It is often asserted that techniques used to identify fraud are not infallible. A spokesperson for the Trades Union Congress has criticised the pilot scheme, maintaining that the problem with this type of technology is that a lot of the time it does not work. Also, it could discourage genuine claims and accomplished liars would be able to outwit the technology. It remains unclear whether those claimants using the telephone system will be warned that they are taking a lie-detector test. Apparently it will still be possible to request an interview assessment.

Source: based on Guthrie, 2007

Question

Under what, if any, circumstances do you think it would be appropriate for an employer to make use of such technology?

TELEPHONE SCREENING

This method, which could be part of a wider selection process, could be used instead of an application form and has the advantage of a prompt response. It is important that this method is used in such a way that standardised information is asked of each candidate. What is not straightforward is deciding on the spot the person's suitability in the light of the set standards. B&Q, the UK DIY retailer, has used telephone screening (Overell, 2002). To begin with a human being at a call centre will note personal details and preferred hours the applicant hopes to work, but the interview is conducted by machine. The aim of the automated system is to assess applicant's values, outlook, conscientiousness, aspirations, integrity and cleanliness. By pressing numbers on the telephone, candidates respond to questions designed to assess their personalities to establish whether they fit the culture the company wants to create in its stores.

After conducting the interview, the system generates a score and creates a letter that informs candidates whether they are suitable for work at B&Q. Those who make the grade are put on to a database and managers at one of the numerous stores can choose from the shortlist. Names, dates of birth, and other indicators of ethnicity, gender, etc., are removed to try to eliminate discrimination. It is only at this stage that previous skills and experience are scrutinised. The final selection is done by the traditional face-to-face interview.

INTERNET

This has a lot of potential as a recruitment and selection device, and has grown in importance in recent years. It could consist of the employer's own website, and jobs could be advertised alongside the organisation's products and services. Alternatively, the job could be advertised by an employment agency on the Internet, and when the responses are processed the agency sends off a shortlist of suitable CVs to the employer. Although it is cost effective, a shortcoming is the enormous amount of applications that could be generated. A number of issues have been raised (Torrington *et al.*, 2005). Sometimes a candidate is asked to apply online by completing an application form or taking a psychometric test, but there is no guarantee that the candidate has in fact completed the test, or that it has been completed within a standard, pre-determined time limit. Some candidates might be harbouring fears about confidentiality and security when inputting their personal details online. Sometimes there are concerns about the tactics of agencies (e.g. copying CVs from competitors' sites) in building up a stock of good CVs in order to impress client organisations.

Selection of expatriate employees

In recent years concern has been expressed about the management of repatriation of employees who work for large companies on overseas assignments (Tayeb, 2005). Given the importance of this topic to multinational companies, it would be wise to raise certain issues impinging on the selection of expatriate employees (Briscoe and Schuler, 2004). It is claimed that UK expatriates have had to face harsh conditions on their return by having to cope with downward mobility and even redundancy; also, it seems that UK companies have adopted a 'sink or swim' policy to returners and their families. A prominent theme in the international recruitment and selection literature is that of expatriate failure. This could be defined as the premature return of an expatriate manager to the home country before the period of assignment is completed. One can conclude that an expatriate failure represents a selection error, compounded in some cases by poor expatriate management (Dowling and Welch, 2004).

In an interesting review of the relevant literature a number of issues connected with expatriate success and failure were examined, and these are issues that selectors should seriously consider (Dowling and Welch, 2004). Amongst the traits and characteristics identified as predictors of expatriate success are: technical ability, managerial ability, cultural empathy and ability to function in a foreign environment, language ability, diplomacy, adaptability (self and family), positive attitude and maturity, and financial stability. The major factors contributing to failure are said to be: lack of adjustment, inability of spouse to adjust, and personal or emotional problems. With regard to failure to adjust to and cope with a foreign environment, one should always consider national differences.

In addition societal trends, such as dual career families, must always be given serious consideration because they can impede the organisation's efforts to attract the best candidates for an overseas assignment. For example, a first-rate manager, with a spouse who has an interesting and stable position, is reluctant to take a foreign posting because of the disruption that is likely to ensue if he or she accepted the position. The issue of gender in the selection of expatriates is said to be an important variable. There is evidence to indicate that women are less likely to be considered suitable for international assignments, and are less willing to relocate in order to advance their careers (Brewster and Scullion, 1997; Harris, 1995).

Validity and reliability

Validity measures how successful a selection technique is in predicting the future performance of the job occupant. Before we can measure validity, criteria have to be established as to what constitutes successful performance in the job, and also what constitutes successful performance during, for example, the interview process or test. Measuring performance on a psychometric test, for example, is not too difficult, but measuring performance when another selection device is used (e.g. the interview) is much harder. Statistical methods are used to relate measures of performance during the selection process to measures of subsequent job performance (such as the quantity and quality of the employee's contribution).

A valid selection process could be expressed as follows: those who score highly on a selection test perform better on the job than those registering lower test scores. A statistical relationship showing the correlation between test scores and indicators of performance could amount to +1 (a perfect positive correlation) or the opposite −1 (a perfect negative correlation), and 0, where there is no evidence of correlation and no predictive value (i.e. the selection method is no better at predicting performance than reliance on pure chance). In practice, a very good figure for correlation would be 0.5–0.6, and a range between 0.3 and 0.4 would be acceptable. Finally, one should realise that ascertaining the validity of a selection method is by no means an easy task, and psychologists use different types of validity.

The reliability of a test is the extent to which it measures consistently whatever it does measure. For example, all candidates for a job are subjected to the same tests and are questioned by the same interview panel, and if the procedures remain the same the selection methods are said to be reliable. If a test is highly reliable, it is possible to put greater reliance on the scores individuals receive than if the test is not very reliable.

An example of an unreliable test is as follows: a person is examined on two separate occasions, using a finger dexterity test. He or she scored highly on the test on the first occasion, and was placed near the top of the group. However, without any material change in factors affecting the individual that person scores badly on the test on the second occasion and is placed near the bottom of the group.

Reliability of tests is something one might consider in the context of the implementation of an equal opportunities policy. It is important that all candidates have an equal chance to express themselves and show their competencies.

Fairness

If standards of fairness were universally accepted in the selection process it would be commonplace for all applicants to be provided with equal opportunity to gain employment. Such an ideal is difficult to attain, as practice bears witness to a number of situations where people are discriminated against in the selection process on the grounds of, for example, race, colour, sex or disability. In the case of people with a severe sensory disability (poor eyesight), Reid (1997) concluded that there were an inadequate number of tests for assessing the intellectual functioning of visually impaired adults. There is a view that some racial and ethnic minorities do not do as well as other applicants in many tests of intelligence and aptitude, and as a result are not selected at the same rate. The difference in the selection rate is usually referred to as 'adverse impact' (Kellett *et al.*, 1994). On this theme one should recognise that a good test is not unfair simply because members of different societal groups obtain different scores. However, it has to be acknowledged that despite relevant legislation (e.g. race relations) and guidelines, unfair discrimination still exists.

Cost effectiveness

It is important that the selection techniques used are cost effective. As was mentioned earlier, the cost of a selection decision mistake can be very high and this has to be balanced against the cost of extensive procedures to minimise mistakes. Consequently, many organisations will use assessment centres (which are costly) for managerial jobs and other positions considered important, but would not incur the same cost for lower level positions in the organisation. Similarly, biodata and psychological tests can be expensive to set up and use because the services of specialist professionals will generally be required. As a result they tend to be used for more senior positions.

Debate in recruitment and selection

The traditional approach to recruitment and selection discussed in this chapter is referred to as the 'systems approach' (Graham and Bennett, 1998). In this approach it is a matter of defining the ideal candidate who most closely fits the ideal profile for the job. A number of problems have been identified with this approach. First, it assumes there is 'one best way' of doing the job, and this assumption is often based on what happened in the past rather than what is likely to happen in the future. It is argued that the systems approach underestimates the degree of change affecting jobs in today's organisations (Sekiguchi, 2007). Secondly, it presents a fairly static view of the individual, whereas it has been argued that people change and develop over time, and when they take up a new job there is evidence that they can change quite dramatically as a result of the new experience (Iles and Robertson, 1997; Watson, 2005).

In line with these criticisms, Scholarios and Lockyer (1996) identified two key challenges to recruitment and selection practice. First, there is a question over how far fixed or constant criteria associated with successful job performance can be identified. Fixed criteria would be based upon a firm understanding of the contents of the job and the ability to predict the stable elements of the position. However, HRM lays emphasis on processes, such as empowerment, delayering and functional flexibility, that are likely to lead to change, some of it unpredictable, and so there may be problems in establishing such criteria. In the future job-holders may be required to undertake activities that are not currently envisaged, and so which remain outside established criteria. Secondly, it is argued that a suitable alternative to the systems model of recruitment and selection (which has a tendency towards fixed criteria) has yet to be found (Scholarios and Lockyer, 1996).

In response to problems such as these the processual approach has been proposed (Newell and Rice, 1999) taking a more 'emergent' view both of the strategy of a company and of the work and performance of employees (Watson, 2005). Under this approach neither the job nor the individual are regarded as fixed entities. Negotiation between the individual and the organisation are envisaged over the nature and content of work, and the adaptability of the organisation to individuals' needs. However, it should be noted that companies that have actively pursued such approaches, for example Cisco Systems and Dell (referred to earlier in this chapter), are highly profitable organisations and are dealing with sections of the labour market where demand exceeds supply.

The processual approach to recruitment and selection has as its starting assumptions the view that both the job and the individual can (and are likely to) change over time. Hence the approach should not be one of ensuring the most accurate fit between the job and the individual, but rather there should be a process of exchange and negotiation (Watson, 2005) in which both parties get around to understanding their current and future needs and values. Newell and Rice (1999) argue that the analysis used in the processual approach should not be restricted to one level, but should examine the person–job fit, the person–team fit, the person–organisation fit and the person–environment fit (Sekiguchi, 2007), and should do so flexibly through keeping the nature and design of the job as open as possible for as long as possible in the recruitment and selection process.

The procedure for implementing the processual approach would be a series of 'episodes' in which increasing amounts of information are exchanged between the individual and the organisation, and through which both adapt to the expectations of the other, in such a way that a psychological contract of mutual understanding is arrived at. This could be operationalised, for example, through informal contacts between existing employees and potential candidates over time, as in the case of Dell and Cisco Systems mentioned earlier. These contacts could then be more formalised in the selection procedure drawing on traditional methods such as interviews and work-based tests.

Although this approach may sound attractive there can be drawbacks. First, if the organisation remains flexible to the extent specified above, appointments will not necessarily complement its strategic direction and business needs. Secondly, the process can become very convoluted, involving a number of ongoing conversations with rival candidates through which criteria that would act as 'common denominators' to judge between candidates would not necessarily be clearly identified. Thirdly, allowing this degree of openness with a fair number of potential candidates is likely to increase greatly the costs (in terms of employee time) compared to more traditional approaches to recruitment and selection.

As increases in the flexible use of the workforce occur, recruitment and selection need to adapt to changing circumstances. This can entail speedier approaches to attracting temporary workers and the use of specialist agencies. It is important that these changes do not reduce the quality and fairness of the procedures.

Conclusions

The processes of recruitment and selection interact with other systems. In particular they are part of the way HR plans are implemented and they provide input to the training and development functions of the organisation. As recruitment involves advertising, publicity and corresponding with members of the public it needs to be implemented in a way that supports the image of the organisation.

Employee selection has attracted considerable research and scholarly attention. As a result there has been extensive critical debate about the effectiveness of selection methods. There is now a wide range of techniques available, and the HR manager should be aware of each technique's strengths and weaknesses so that the best method for the job and the organisation can be chosen. Scholarios and Lockyer (1996) concluded that evidence from surveys over the past 20 years indicates that the use of sophisticated multi-method selection is confined to larger companies, in the main because of the prohibitive costs of more sophisticated methods for smaller companies. They argue that the 'classic trio' of application form, references and interview remain the most popular methods of selection for most vacancies. However, the practice involved in interviewing and the design of application forms has developed (Newell, 2006) such that best practice now offers a more valid set of techniques than it did 20 years ago.

Traditionally HR managers have felt that their expertise in this area is an important part of their professionalism. Increasingly, however, organisations are devolving aspects of recruitment and selection work to line and functional managers. This means that there is a change in focus from providing a high-quality, inclusive service to providing support so that other managers can carry out the process legally, effectively and efficiently.

The use of the Internet in recruitment and selection has been increasing, although for many organisations it is mainly a tool for recruitment and a supplement to advertising rather than a fully fledged selection device. It can offer effective access to information, but ultimately the human decisions of who will best fit the job and work environment have to be made, and most people feel that face-to-face interaction is an important part of making that judgement.

Review and reflection questions

1. Why is job analysis important?

2. What is the distinction between a job description and a person specification?

3. What is a competence? What is meant by the competency-based approach to recruitment and selection?

4. What is the recruitment phase?

5. Name at least three recruitment methods.

6. What is the selection phase?

7. Name at least three selection methods.

8. What are the strengths and weaknesses of the following methods:

   (a) interviews

   (b) psychometric tests

   (c) work-based tests.

9. What is meant by the 'processual' approach?

Activities

If you are in work:

Choose a job that has recently been advertised in your organisation and gather as much material on it as possible. Review:

■ job description,
■ further particulars,
■ person specification,
■ selection methods used.

On the basis of your review, what changes or developments would you make to the process used?

If you are in full-time study:

Choose a job of the type that you would like to apply for on completion of your studies. Gather as much material on it as possible. Review:

■ job description,
■ further particulars (e.g. structure, mission, department details),
■ person specification,
■ selection methods used.

On the basis of your review, what changes or developments would you make to the process used?

Further reading and research

The following two references explore trends in the use of selection methods and some of the reasons for employer's choices.

Borman, W.C., Hedge, J.W., Ferst, K.L., Kaufman, J.D., Farmer, W.L. and Bearden, R.M. (2003) 'Current directions and issues in personnel selection and classification', in J.J. Martocchio and G.R. Ferris (eds), *Research in Personnel and Human Resources Management*, 22, 287–356, Oxford: Elsevier.

Wilk, S. and Cappelli, P. (2003) 'Understanding the determinants of employer use of selection methods', *Personnel Psychology*, 56, 103–124.

Assessment centres are valid approaches to selection, but can be costly. The following book provides insights into when to use assessment centres and how to organise them.

Woodruffe, C. (2000) *Development and assessment centres. Identifying and assessing competence*, London: CIPD.

There are some international differences in approaches to recruitment and selection and the following reference is helpful in understanding the impact of the national context.
Roe, R.A. and vanden Berg, P.T. (2003) 'Selection in Europe: Context, developments, and
    research agenda', *European Journal of Work and Organizational Psychology*, 12, 257–287.

The ACAS website provides a guide to recruitment and selection that stresses ethical issues and fairness in decision making. It also includes practical tips. www.acas.org.uk.

There are numerous websites relating to psychometrics. A useful one can be found at: www.personalityresearch.org/bigfive. This has information about the 'Big Five' personality typologies and links to relevant articles. There is also a link to a version of the questionnaire that you can fill in online.

References

Alder, G.S. and Gilbert, J. (2006) 'Achieving Ethics and Fairness in Hiring: Going beyond the law',
    Journal of Business Ethics, 68, 449–464.
Altman, W. (1995) 'The write way to a job', Business Recruitment Feature, *London Evening Standard*, 24
    January, 34.
Arnold, J. (2005) *Work psychology: Understanding human behaviour in the workplace*, Harlow, Essex:
    FT/Prentice-Hall.
Arnold, J., Cooper, C.L. and Robertson, I.T. (1998) *Work Psychology: Understanding human behaviour in
    the workplace*, London: Pitman.
Baldry, C. and Fletcher, C. (1997) 'The integrity of integrity testing', *Selection and Development Review*,
    13, 3–6.
Barrett, P. (1998) 'Science, fundamental measurement, and psychometric testing', *Selection and
    Development Review*, 1, 3–10.
Barsoux, J.L. and Lawrence, P. (1990) *Management in France*, London: Cassell.
Beckett, H. (2006) 'All Good Practice', *People Management*, 12, 38–40.
Blinkhorn, S.F. (1997) 'Past imperfect, future conditional: fifty years of test theory', *British Journal of
    Mathematical and Statistical Psychology*, 50, 175–185.
Blinkhorn, S. and Johnson, C. (1990) 'The insignificance of personality testing', *Nature*, 348, 671–672.
Boyle, S. (1997) 'Researching the selection interview', *Selection and Development Review*, 13, 15–17.
Bradley, D. (2004) 'References: No comment, no legal action', *Financial Times*, 25 September.
Brewster, C. and Scullion, H. (1997) 'A review and agenda for expatriate human resource
    management', *Human Resource Management Journal*, 7, 32–41.
British Psychological Society (BPS) (2004) Final report of a working party: A review of the current
    scientific status and fields of application of the Polygraphic Deception Detection, Leicester: BPS.
Briscoe, D.R. and Schuler, R.S. (2004) *International Human Resource Management*, New York:
    Routledge.
Campion, M.A., Palmer, D.K. and Campion, J.E. (1997) 'A review of structure in the selection
    interview', *Personnel Psychology*, Autumn, 655–702.
Cascio, W.F. and Aguinis, H. (2005) *Applied psychology in human resource management*, Englewood
    Cliffs, NJ: Prentice Hall.
Cattell, R.B. (1963) *The 16PF Questionnaire*, Champagne, IL: Institute for Personality and Ability
    Training.
Chartered Institute of Personnel Management (CIPD) (2001) *Graphology: Quick Facts*, London: CIPD

Chatman, J.A. and Cha, S.E. (2002) 'Culture of growth', *FT Mastering Leadership Series*, Part 4, 22 November, 2–3.

Clegg, A. (2007) 'Social networking hits the workplace', *Financial Times*, 16 April, 9.

Cook, M. (2003) *Personnel selection. Adding value through people*, Chichester: Wiley.

Cronshaw, S.F., Hamilton, L.K., Onyura, B.R. and Winston, A.S. (2006) 'Case for non-biased intelligence testing against Black Africans has not been made', *International Journal of Selection and Assessment*, 14, 278–287.

Dessler, G. (2005) *Human Resource Management*, New Jersey: Pearson Education.

Dowling, P.J and Welch, D.E. (2004) *International Human Resource Management*, London: Thomson Learning.

Doyle, C.E. (2003) *Work and organizational psychology: An introduction with attitude*, Hove, East Sussex: Psychology Press.

Eglin, R. (2000) 'Online recruiting is just a click away', *The Sunday Times*, Appointments Section, 5 November, B14.

Feltham, R., Lewis, C., Anderson, P. and Hughes, D. (1998) 'Psychometrics: cultural impediments to global recruitment and people development', *Selection and Development Review*, August, 16–21.

Furnham, A. (2001) 'Keys to unlock path of career fulfillment', *The Sunday Telegraph* (Appointments Section), A1.

Furnham, A. (2005a) *The Psychology of Behaviour at Work*, Hove, East Sussex: Psychology Press.

Furnham, A. (2005b) 'Keeping crooks out of your business', *The Sunday Times* (Appointments Section), 6 February, 7.

Goleman, D. (1998) *Working with Emotional Intelligence*, London: Bloomsbury.

Graham, H.T. and Bennett, R. (1998) *Human Resources Management*, London: Financial Times/Pitman.

Griffiths, J. (2005) 'Masculine Wiles', *People Management*, 11, 20–21.

Guthrie, J. (2007) 'Council to subject benefit claimants to lie-detector test', *Financial Times*, 7 September, 4.

Hampson, S. (1999) 'State of the art: personality', *The Psychologist*, June, 284–288.

Harris, R. (1995) 'Organizational influences on women's career opportunities in international management', *Women in Management Review*, 10, 26–33.

Harvey-Jones, J.E. and Taffler, R. (2000) 'Biodata in professional entry-level selection: statistical scoring of common format applications', *Journal of Occupational and Organizational Psychology*, 73, 103–118.

Huffcutt, A.I., Conway, J.M., Roth, P.L. and Stone, N.J. (2001) 'Identification and meta-analytic assessment of psychological constructs measured in employment interviews', *Journal of Applied Psychology*, October, 910.

Huffcutt, A.I., Conway, J.M., Roth, P.L. and Ute-Christine, K. (2004) 'The Impact of Job Complexity and Study Design on Situational and Behavior Description Interview Validity', *International Journal of Selection and Assessment*, 12, 262–273.

Hunter, J.E. and Hunter, R.F. (1984) 'Validity and utility of alternative predictors of performance', *Psychological Bulletin*, 96, 72–98.

Iles, P. and Robertson, I. (1997) 'The impact of personnel selection procedures on candidates', in Anderson, N. and Herriot, P. (eds), *International Handbook of Selection and Assessment*, Chichester: Wiley.

Johnstone, H. (1995) 'Beat the interview blues' (Business Recruitment Feature), *London Evening Standard*, 8 March, 46.

Kellett, D., Fletcher, S., Callen, A. and Geary, B. (1994) 'Fair testing: the case of British Rail', *The Psychologist*, January, 26–29.

Klehe, U.-C. (2004) 'Choosing How to Choose: Institutional Pressures Affecting the Adoption of Personnel Selection Procedures', *International Journal of Selection and Assessment*, 12, 327–342.

Klehe, U.-C. and Latham, G.P. (2005) 'The Predictive and Incremental Validity of the Situational and Patterned Behavior Description Interviews for Teamplaying Behavior', *International Journal of Selection and Assessment*, 13, 108–115.

Latham, G.P., Saari, L.M., Pursell, E.D. and Campion, M.A. (1980) 'The situational interview', *Journal of Applied Psychology*, 65, 659–673.

McGookin, S. (1993) 'Graphology: a waste of money', *Financial Times*, 19 November, 12.

McGrath, C. (2006) 'The Ideal Lobbyist: Personal Characteristics of Effective Lobbyists', *Journal of Communication Management*, 10, 67–79.

McKenna, E. (2006) *Business Psychology and Organisational Behaviour*, Hove, East Sussex: Psychology Press.

McLeod, D. (1994) *Graphology and Personnel Assessment*, Leicester: The British Psychological Society.

Merrick, N. (2001) 'Wel.com aboard', *People Management*, 7, 26–32.

Munro Fraser, J. (1958) *A Handbook of Employment Interviewing'*, London: Macdonald and Evans.

Newell, S. (2005) 'Assessment, selection and evaluation', in Leoplod, J., Harris, L. and Watson, T. (eds), *The Strategic Managing of Human Resources*, Harlow, England: Pearson.

Newell, S. (2006) 'Selection and Assessment', in Redman, T. and Wilkinson, A. (eds), *Contemporary Human Resource Management*, Harlow, England: Prentice Hall/Financial Times.

Newell, S. and Rice, C. (1999) 'Assessment, selection and evaluation: pitfalls and problems', in Leopold, J., Harris, L. and Watson, T. (eds), *Strategic Human Resourcing: Principles, perspectives and practices*, London: Financial Times/Pitman.

Overell, S. (2002) 'The right personalities in store', *Financial Times*, 5 December, 12.

Phillips, L. (2006) 'Be on your guard for online test cheats', *People Management*, 12, 15.

Porteous, M. (1997) *Occupational Psychology*, Hemel Hempstead: Prentice Hall.

Price, A. (2004) *Human Resource Management in a Business Context*, London: Thomson Learning.

Reid, J.M.V. (1997) 'Standardised ability testing for vocational rehabilitation in visually impaired adults. A literature review', *Journal of Visual Impairment and Blindness*, 91, 546–554.

Reilly, R. and Chao, G. (1982) 'Validity and fairness of some employment selection procedures', *Personnel Psychology*, 35, 1–62.

Rodger, A. (1952) *The Seven-point Plan*, London: National Institute of Industrial Psychology.

Rogers, A. (1998) 'Psychometric tests go on trial', *The Sunday Times*, 9 August, 7.7.

Ross, R. and Schneider, R. (1992) *From Equality to Diversity: A business case for equal opportunities*, London: Pitman.

Scholarios, D. and Lockyer, C. (1996) 'Human resource management and selection: better solutions or new dilemmas?', in Towers, B. (ed.), *The Handbook of Human Resource Management*, Oxford: Blackwell.

Sekiguchi, T. (2007) 'A contingency perspective of the importance of PJ fit and PO fit in employee selection', *Journal of Managerial Psychology*, 22, 118–131.

Shackleton, V. and Newell, S. (1991) 'Managerial selection: a comparative study of methods used in top British and French companies', *Journal of Occupational Psychology*, 64, 23–36.

Smethurst, S. (2004) 'The Allure of Online', *People Management*, 10, 38–40.

Smith, M. and Robertson, I.T. (1993) *The Theory and Practice of Systematic Personnel Selection*, Basingstoke: Macmillan.

Smith, M., Gregg, M. and Andrews, R. (1989) *Selection and Assessment: A new appraisal*, London: Pitman.

Sue-Chan, C. and Latham, G.P. (2004) 'The Situational Interview as a Predictor of Academic and Team Performance: A Study of the Mediating Effects of Cognitive Ability and Emotional Intelligence', *International Journal of Selection and Assessment*, 12, 312–320.

Sutton, G. and Griffin, M. (2004) 'Integrating expectations, experiences, and psychological contract violations. A longitudinal study of new professionals', *Journal of Occupational and Organizational Psychology*, 77, 493–514.

Tayeb, M.H. (2005) *International HRM: A multinational company perspective*. Oxford: Oxford University Press.

Torrington, D., Hall, L. and Taylor, S. (2005) *Human Resource Management*, Harlow, Essex: Pearson Education.

Training Agency (1989) *Training in Britain: A study of funding, activity, and attitudes*, London: HMSO.

Van der Zee, K.I., Bakker, A.B. and Bakker, P. (2002) 'Why are structured interviews so rarely used in personnel selection?', *Journal of Applied Psychology*, February, 176–184.

Watkin, C. (1999) 'Emotional Competency Inventory (ECI)', *Selection and Development Review*, October, 13–16.

Watson, T. (2005) 'Organisations, strategies and human resourcing', in Leopold, J., Harris, L. and Watson, T. (eds), *The Strategic Managing of Human Resources*, Harlow, England: Prentice Hall/Financial Times.

Welch, J. (1999) 'British firms lag behind surfing USA', *People Management*, 5, 13.

Woodruffe, C. (2005) 'Emotional Factors as Selection Criteria', in Evers, A., Anderson, N. and Smit-Voskuijl (eds), *Handbook of Personnel Selection*, Oxford: Blackwell.

Wright, M. and Storey, J. (1994) 'Recruitment', in Beardwell, I. and Holden, L. (eds), *Human Resource Management*, London: Pitman.

Chapter 8

EMPLOYEE DEVELOPMENT: PERFORMANCE MANAGEMENT

Introduction

Performance management incorporates the review of past performance and the setting of objectives for the future. It should be regarded as a fundamental managerial activity that to some extent formalises the everyday processes of feedback between manager and employee. Various approaches to appraisal can be adopted and the choice of system will reflect the style and culture of the organisation. Some will be top down and judgemental, others will be more open and developmental. In either case it is important that a sound basis is established for other associated elements of HRM practice – training and development and reward management.

Having read this chapter, you should:

■ be aware of the purpose of performance management and appraisal;

■ understand the different techniques that can be applied in performance management;

■ know the alternative perspectives and the implications of these for implementation of a system;

■ have an awareness of some of the key skills of appraisal;

■ be able to compare and contrast different examples of good practice;

■ understand some of the considerations of performance management in an international context;

■ be able to critically reflect on the purpose, nature and outcomes of performance management.

Frequently judgements are made, both formally and informally, about the performance of employees at work. In an informal system we are aware that superiors are continually making judgements about their subordinates' performance on a subjective basis. By contrast, superiors could resort to using formalised appraisal techniques when assessing the performance of subordinates, and these judgements are considered to be more objective. The supervisor could note the extent to which the subordinate has met the objectives set for him or her for the period under review, with or without the involvement of the appraisee in the setting of the objectives. It is important that the appraiser is sensitive to issues affecting performance, which lie outside the control of the appraisee.

In formalised systems the terms 'performance appraisal' and 'performance management' are used. Both refer to a process whereby managers and their subordinates share understanding about what has to be accomplished, and the manager will naturally be concerned about how best to bring about those accomplishments by adept management and development of people in the short and long term. Also, the subordinate's performance could be appraised against each task specified in the job description or key accountability. Performance could also be appraised against job competences using some of the techniques discussed in this chapter, and it would subsequently be related to targets or plans. In this way the subordinate receives feedback on his or her progress. In the final analysis an overall competency profile could be identified for a particular job and this could be used in performance appraisal. Performance management systems have been identified as being particularly important for organisations that experience competitive markets (de Waal, 2006), and success in enhancing productivity in such circumstances has been related to the formal and frequent linking of organisational goals to individual goals through effective managerial communication (de Waal, 2007).

A distinguishing feature of performance management is its integrating strength in aligning various processes with corporate objectives: for example, the introduction of performance-related pay (PRP) systems and the mobilisation of training and development resources to achieve corporate objectives (Bevan and Thompson, 1991). Alignment and integration are regarded as important for the effective functioning of performance management. For example, the global company Astra Zeneca used four principles to govern the systems and behaviours of performance management as follows (Torrington *et al.*, 2005):

1. Aligned objectives: a cascade of objectives from business level via department/function and team to the individual.
2. Joint responsibility: both managers and individual workers being accountable for giving their best performance and contributing to a challenging environment.
3. Constructive conversations: an open and honest dialogue between managers, project leaders and individuals.
4. Reviewing and rewarding performance: having a clear link between performance and reward and recognition.

The purpose of these principles is to link individuals closely into their teams and the organisation more generally, and to support these links via processes that emphasise integration, such as dialogue and shared accountability. For a more detailed explanation of performance management see Box 8.1.

Box 8.1: Performance management

In performance management there is an emphasis on mutual objective setting and ongoing performance support and review in a sympathetic organisational culture setting, but according to Torrington *et al.* (2005) the term performance management remains beyond precise definition. Performance management needs to be line manager driven rather than HR driven, and for this to happen appropriate action has to be taken. Putting line managers side by side with HR managers in a working party to develop the system is important because the influence of the line manager is crucial.

According to Doyle (2003), performance management is best thought of as a philosophy (like that of a learning organisation), rather than a particular set of policies and practices. Williams (1998) feels performance management is essentially concerned with creating conditions whereby employees share the organisation's goals, and then helping people to understand their contribution to these goals. In this way the performance of people and organisations is managed. The building blocks of performance management are the creation of a mission statement and business plan, which is clearly communicated throughout the organisation, with ample opportunities for everyone to contribute to its formation. Then one has to clarify how the individual's performance is going to fit into the whole, subsequently defining, measuring and rewarding individual performance (Doyle, 2003).

Questions

1. In your organisation, or one you know of, is performance management a 'philosophy' in the way that Doyle suggests it should be?

2. What is the impact of the present (or absence) of such a philosophy on day-to-day activities?

When defining performance management in a British context, Williams (1998) stated that it was a logical progression in the history of the development of appraisal systems and can be seen as a set of interventions with the aim of harnessing the contribution of the employee's performance to organisational performance. This trend has continued, and in recent years there has been a focus on ensuring that individuals can see the correlation between their own efforts and the performance of their team/department (Mendibil and MacBryde, 2006).

Following a survey by the Institute of Personnel Management (IPM; now the Chartered Institute of Personnel and Development) in the early 1990s, a list of characteristics, which distinguished organisations with formal performance management from those having other policies for managing employee performance, was produced. This appears in Table 8.1. It should be noted that a relatively small number of the organisations surveyed had performance management policies which would match the list of characteristics (Williams, 1998), however, more recently a CIPD survey in the UK has indicated that 87 per cent of respondents had formal performance management systems (Baron and Armstrong, 2004), and the figure is over 90 per cent in the US (Redman, 2006).

The current perspective of the CIPD (Cannell, 2007) draws upon the definition by Armstrong and Baron (2004) that performance management is a strategic process that is fundamentally aimed at establishing a shared understanding in the organisation of what is important and where effort should be deployed. The concept is that performance management is about:

■ establishing a culture in which everyone takes responsibility for continuous improvement;

■ sharing expectations between managers and individuals;

■ improving the quality of interrelationships and communication;

> **Table 8.1** Distinguishing characteristics of organisations with formal performance management
>
> Performance management organisations were more likely to:
> - have mission statements that are communicated to all employees;
> - regularly communicate information on business plans and progress towards achieving these plans;
> - implement policies such as total quality management and performance-related pay;
> - focus on senior managers' performance rather than manual and white-collar workers';
> - express performance targets in terms of measurable outputs, accountabilities and training/learning targets;
> - use formal appraisal processes and presentations by the chief executive as ways of communicating performance requirements;
> - set performance requirements on a regular basis;
> - link performance requirements to pay, particularly for senior managers.

Source: based on Williams, 1998

- a joint planning process to define objectives;

- enabling measurement of performance of all employees and teams;

- having a continuous and holistic process, which pervades all aspects of running the organisation (Cannell, 2007).

The main changes over the past ten years have been the roll out of performance management to affect all employees, the focus on continuous joint processes of communication and the view that performance management is part of efforts to manage the culture of the organisation. The following elements of performance appraisal are identified (CIPD, 2006):

- Measurement – assessing performance against agreed targets.

- Feedback – providing information to the individual on their performance and progress.

- Positive reinforcement – emphasising what has been done and giving constructive criticism about what can be improved.

- Exchange of views – about what has happened, how improvements can be made and what support is needed.

- Agreement – coming to a joint understanding of what needs to be done.

Aims of appraisal

The following aims might be considered when examining a performance appraisal system:

- Set targets, which are acceptable to those whose performance is going to be appraised and do so in a climate characterised by open communication between superior and subordinate, striving for partnership in action.

- Use reliable, fair and objective measures of performance, compare actual with planned performance, and provide feedback to the appraisee.

- Where performance is suboptimal, after going through the previous step, signal the need to specify and agree with the appraisee a personal improvement plan that could be based on an assessment of the person's training and development needs.

- Provide an input to succession planning.

- Make provision for the allocation of both extrinsic rewards (e.g. performance-related pay) and intrinsic rewards (e.g. opportunity to enhance one's skills) following the assessment process.

- Place emphasis on the use of good interpersonal skills in the appraisal process, so that frank exchanges are encouraged, and recognise that the appraiser and the appraisee have the opportunity to influence each other.

- Validate the effectiveness of the selection process and previous training.

- Obtain information on the quality of management and organisational systems from the appraisee.

- Subscribe to desirable outcomes in the form of employee fulfilment, full utilisation of the individual's capacity, change of corporate culture (where appropriate), and the achievement of organisational objectives in conditions where there is harmonisation of individual and organisational objectives.

- Recognise that performance management is at the heart of the general management process.

Appraisal techniques

Certain techniques are available to evaluate the performance of the employee. This section briefly reviews the major techniques used.

WRITTEN REPORT

The appraiser writes a narrative about the strengths, weaknesses, previous performance and potential of the appraisee, with suggestions for improvement. It is important that the appraiser is perceptive with reasonable writing skill.

CRITICAL INCIDENTS

The appraiser highlights incidents or key events that show the appraisee's behaviour as exceptionally good or bad in relation to particular outcomes at work. This exercise would depict desirable behaviours as well as behaviour that signal a need for improvement.

GRAPHIC RATING SCALES

This is a popular appraisal technique and, unlike the written report and critical incidents techniques, it lends itself to quantitative analysis and comparison of data. A set of performance factors is identified, including such characteristics as quality of work, technical knowledge, cooperative spirit, integrity, punctuality and initiative. The appraiser would go through the set of factors rating them, for example, on a scale 1 to 5 where the highest number would denote the best rating. This technique is economical in the time devoted to its development and use, but it does not provide the depth of information provided by the other techniques described above.

A variation of the graphic rating scales is the 'behaviourally anchored rating scales', where descriptions of the type of behaviour associated with each point on the rating scale is clearly stated. Behaviourally anchored rating scales specify job-related behaviour associated with each performance factor along a continuum. The appraiser then selects the appropriate point on the continuum for each performance factor. For example, an appraisee, who is a middle manager, is rated as 4 under the performance factor referred to as 'leadership'. The statement of behaviour associated with this point on the continuum or scale is 'exceptional skill in directing others to great effort'. By contrast, a rating of 1 on the same continuum could be described as 'often weak in command situations; at times unable to exert control'.

MULTI-PERSON COMPARISON

This technique, which is a relative rather than an absolute measure, is used to assess one person's performance against one or more other individuals. It comprises three well-established approaches, as follows:

1. *Individual ranking*. This approach orders appraisees from the best to the worst performer with no provision for ties.
2. *Group ranking*. This approach requires the appraiser to place appraisees in particular categories that reflect their performance. For example, a person who performed exceptionally well would be placed in the top 10 per cent, while a person who performed very poorly would be placed in the bottom 10 per cent.
3. *Paired comparison*. This approach allows for the comparison of each appraisee with every other appraisee. Appraisees are paired and each person is rated as either the stronger or the weaker individual. When the exercise of paired comparisons is completed, after all appraisees have been paired with each other, each appraisee is given an overall ranking score, which reflects the stronger points. Although this approach permits everybody to be compared with everybody else in a particular organisational setting, it can be difficult to handle when large numbers are involved.

Multi-person comparisons can be used in conjunction with one of the other techniques in order to mix the best features of the relative and absolute measures. For example, a graphic rating scale could be used alongside an individual ranking approach.

MULTI-RATER COMPARATIVE EVALUATION

One example of this technique is an assessment centre, which was examined in Chapter 7 in connection with selection. One can adopt a comparative evaluation approach in an assessment centre, using multiple raters. When used in the context of management development it is often referred to as a 'development centre', where the appraisal of managerial abilities and skills with a view to establishing the suitability of subjects for promotion can take place over a few days. The total appraisal process consists of interviews, psychometric testing, simulations of relevant work activities, peer appraisals and appraisals by trained assessors.

Another example of the multi-rater technique is the 360-degree feedback system. This technique uses ratings from several people (e.g. superiors and their counterparts from other departments, customers or clients, and consultants) and is potentially useful because of the wide range of performance-related feedback it offers, more so than the traditional evaluation techniques. It considers qualitative issues in performance (e.g. leadership qualities) apart from quantitative issues, such as increases in output. Eventually a feedback report is produced and this is discussed with the appraisee at a feedback session (see Table 8.2 on issues to consider in the feedback interview). According to Goffin and Anderson (2007) multi-source and 360-degree appraisals have become increasingly used, although the CIPD survey of UK employers indicated that only 14 per cent used 360-degree feedback (Baron and Armstrong, 2004).

It goes without saying that the confidential nature of the 360-degree process must be accepted by the raters, and it is important that they feel confident about being open and honest in their judgement. On a different note, Fletcher (1998) expressed reservations about some of the questions that appear in the 360-degree appraisal systems when he points out, on the basis of his research, that they did not measure the behaviour they were designed to assess. He admonishes companies to be vigilant and evaluate the worth of these systems before using them. In a survey conducted by Watson Wyatt's Human Capital doubts have been cast on the effectiveness of 360-degree appraisals (Donkin, 2002).

For the 360-degree feedback process to be effective the corporate culture must be supportive of this type of appraisal (Warr and Ainsworth, 1999). It should be noted that given the range of appraisal data available from this technique the potential for appraisers to make remarks perceived as threatening is high (Clifford and Bennett, 1997). If this is the case, the operation of the 360-degree appraisal system could be impaired. Research by Goffin and Anderson, (2007) has indicated that the experience can be more positive where honest disagreement is possible between appraisee and appraiser in such settings. Finally, it has been suggested that 360-degree feedback can help create an ethical culture (Steare, 2006). Gaining information on how well values have been enacted and giving feedback to an employee from internal and external 360-degree processes is said to motivate people towards the values.

The use of input from customers or service users in appraisals has become more widespread. According to Redman (2006) this is achieved in three main ways:

1. Customer views can be gathered through surveys conducted by telephone, post, interview or the Internet.
2. Surveillance techniques can be used by managers to monitor samples of the service encounter. For example, in contact centres, phone calls can be monitored.
3. 'Mystery' or 'phantom' shopping can be conducted in which staff employed by a specialist agency pose as customers and report back on how they were treated. This technique is commonly used in banks, insurance sales, retail and parts of the public sector.

Table 8.2 Feedback interview

- Be thorough in preparation for the event.
- At the outset state the primary purpose of the interview.
- It is advantageous if the appraiser is seen as a person who has credibility and authority.
- A positive emotional disposition on the part of both the appraiser and the appraisee is desirable.
- The focus should be on issues rather than personality.
- The appraiser ought to praise good performance early on in the session, as this could create a less defensive appraisee.
- The appraiser should be helpful to the appraisee.
- If criticism is voiced by the appraiser, it should be done without hostility in words and gestures.
- The appraisee should be given the opportunity to comment on his or her performance.
- The appraiser ought to articulate what is required of the appraisee in the future at the end the interview.

Whilst such approaches can garner useful information, there are dangers. These approaches do not necessarily reinforce a trusting relationship between management and workers and staff can feel 'spied on' and demotivated. These problems are exacerbated where the 'customer' feedback is used in a negative way. However, where the feedback is used to give positive messages and spread good practice a positive impact can result (Redman, 2006), although it is fair to say that such techniques should only be used with great caution and consideration of the rights of the employees.

MANAGEMENT BY OBJECTIVES

Back in the 1970s management by objectives (MBO) became fashionable. MBO stressed the link between individual performance and departmental performance and in doing so advanced the notion that subordinates should play an active role in the appraisal process in order to achieve a degree of commitment to the achievement of targets. The necessity for this approach had been pointed out many years before by Peter Drucker in his classic book *The Practice of Management* (Lundy and Cowling, 1996), and this gave credence to appraisal being a two-way process rather than top down. In MBO objectives are formulated and agreed at the beginning of the period under review, and the appraisee is given the necessary assistance and training to facilitate the achievement of those objectives. At the end of the period there will be an appraisal of performance and new objectives are set. Dessler (2005) sets out 'six steps' of MBO which emphasise integration as follows:

1. Set the organisation's goals (on the basis of the strategic plan).

2. Set departmental goals (jointly between departmental leaders and executives).

3. Discuss departmental goals (between departmental heads and staff, in some cases at a departmental meeting).

4. Define expected results (set individual goals including short-term targets).

5. Review performance (comparing actual and targeted performance).

6. Provide feedback (evaluate and discuss progress made).

Price (2004) adds that it can be desirable to go beyond setting individual goals and develop action plans for implementation jointly between manager and individual workers.

Dessler points out that problems can occur where targets are misunderstood or where there is a 'tug-of-war' in agreeing aims. However, in a survey of US companies, 32 per cent said that they used MBO (Dessler, 2005) and most incorporated an element of objective setting into their procedures. The figure in the UK is that 62 per cent of companies surveyed by the CIPD report using objective setting as part of their appraisal systems (Baron and Armstrong, 2004).

SELF-APPRAISAL

As a rider to the discussion of the major appraisal techniques, which are frequently used by superiors in evaluating the performance of subordinates, consider for a moment the practice of self-appraisal in the context of employee development. Michelin, the tyre manufacturer, introduced on a pilot basis a self-appraisal scheme as a means of empowering workers, enhancing teamwork and raising awareness of quality. The pilot scheme covered 30 workers who were asked to complete appraisal forms on which they evaluated themselves against criteria such as attendance, productivity, quality, safety, teamwork and commitment. The completed appraisal forms were then used as a basis for a discussion with the managers of the participating workers. Freeing the managers from form filling meant they had more time for communication with their subordinates. It was concluded that the workers who participated in the self-appraisal scheme were not backward in coming forward with criticisms of themselves, more so than if the managers conducted the appraisals. It is the company's intention to expand the scheme (Huddart, 1994).

Finally, Fletcher (1993) suggests that one of the best ways for individuals to assess themselves is to rate different aspects of their performance to other aspects of their performance, rather than relative to the performance of colleagues or others. In that way individuals can be more discriminating. The advice of the CIPD is that self-assessment works best where individuals have clear targets against which to assess themselves, and the organisation has a culture of trust such that appraisees believe that appraisers will not take unfair advantage of an open self-assessment (CIPD, 2006). However, this method has been regarded as problematic. Dessler (2005) reports a study in which 40 per cent of employees rated themselves in the top 10 per cent and virtually all the remaining employees rated themselves in the top 25 per cent ('well above average') or the top 50 per cent ('above average'). Only 2 per cent placed themselves in the 'below average' category. Hence, systems that ask employees to rate themselves against others are not recommended. However, self-rating against particular criteria as part of a system that involves other methods of assessment in addition can be very effective as it provides a basis for a dialogue between the appraisee and appraiser.

TEAM APPRAISAL

An important point to note is that, given the growing popularity of team systems of working, acknowledged earlier in the book, serious attention will have to be given to evaluating teams rather than individuals. The difficulty likely to be encountered with the assessment of teams is finding appropriate performance measures and relating team performance to goal achievement. Robbins (2003) suggests a number of actions along the following lines: relate the team results to the organisation's goals; assess the effectiveness of the team in meeting customers' requirements, with the accent on delivery and quality; consider the part played by individual team members in supporting team processes and accomplishments; ensure that both individuals and the team define their objectives, as this helps clarify individual roles and promotes team cohesiveness. Uptake of team appraisal is still relatively low with a figure of 6 per cent reported in the CIPD survey (Baron and Armstrong, 2004).

BALANCED SCORECARD

There is a preoccupation with demonstrating the contribution of SHRM to organisational performance. One method for doing this is the balanced scorecard (Kaplan and Norton, 1996). A stakeholder's perspective, focused on performance management issues, is adopted, operating on the assumption that for an organisation to be successful it must satisfy the requirements of key stakeholders, namely investors, customers and employees. Investors are interested in financial performance (economic added value); and customers are interested in availing themselves of products or services that are measured by customer value added. But for the employees (the human resources) the organisation can use attitude surveys, skill audits, and performance appraisal data to measure factors, such as the quality of the place of work, opportunities for professional development and growth. These data throw light on what people do, what they know, and the role played by HRM and other systems in helping to identify targets and measure performance in relation to those targets (see Case example 8.1). When the spotlight is on the HR aspect of the balanced scorecard there is a natural preoccupation with the impact of key HR activities, for example, employee growth and development and its effect on the performance of the company broadly conceived (Beardwell *et al.*, 2004; Kaplan and Norton, 2001).

BALANCED SCORECARD IN THE NHS

The NHS was set a number of performance targets by the government. This incorporated the interests of different stakeholders (Chang, 2007). At the organisational level improvements were sought in terms of inputs (including efficient use of resource), service delivery (including service users' satisfaction), clinical effectiveness and long-term health (including public health targets). Six high-level performance indicators were produced:

1. health improvement (e.g. measures of death from particular causes);

2. fair access (e.g. waiting lists, number of GPs, surgery rates);

3. effective delivery of appropriate health care (e.g. childhood immunisation, acute care, cost of effective prescribing, returning home after treatment);

4. efficiency (e.g. day case rate, length of stay, costs);

5. patient/carer experience of the NHS (e.g. cancelled operations, delayed discharge, outpatient services);

6. health outcomes of NHS health care (e.g. conceptions below age 18, dental health, cancer survival rates, hospital readmissions).

These indicators incorporate long- and short-term targets and items that can be directly controlled along with outcomes that can only be indirectly influenced. At the local level, these indicators were converted into applicable indicators. For example, in the Merseyside Health Authority a balanced scorecard was produced for coronary heart disease. It included measures such as:

1. Effectiveness

   (a) Percentage life threatening calls reached within 8 minutes

   (b) Percentage patients with chest pain, door to needle <1 hour

2. Patient expectations

   (a) Percentage patients waiting >12 months for revascularisation

   (b) Standardised mortality rate for various categories of patient

3. Efficiency

   (a) Percentage of patients readmitted

   (b) Number of evascularisations

   (c) Number of catheters

(CASE EXAMPLE 8.1)

4. Organisational development

   (a)   Percentage practices with pro-active secondary prevention programme

   (b)   Number of patients reviewed by CVD nurses

The targets have an impact on what employees focus on and on how they can review their own performance, as well as receiving feedback from their managers. Feedback from within the system indicated that whilst the process did achieve a focus, there was a perception that the situation was over-politicised.

Source: Based on Chang, 2007

Question

If you were a senior manager in the NHS what difficulties might you expect to find in implementing this balanced scorecard approach?

UPWARD APPRAISAL

This is a bottom-up approach to appraisal, whereby subordinates rate superiors, which has been used by organisations such as British Petroleum (BP), British Airways and Cathay Pacific. Upwards appraisal is more common in the United States than the United Kingdom and other countries (Redman, 2006), but it is spreading, particularly where US parent companies have operations elsewhere in the world. It is felt that subordinates are well placed to gain a solid view of the strengths and weaknesses of their bosses. Typically, views of subordinates are gathered via anonymous questionnaires and managers can gain feedback that helps them see how they are perceived by others. A representative view could materialise from the combined ratings of a number of subordinates. For this system of performance management to work well requires it to be efficient and equitable in an appropriate cultural setting. For example, a prerequisite is that the organisation feels it can trust employees to be honest, fair and constructive. Also, there should be a firm belief in the value of two-way communication within the organisation.

Upward appraisal is not without its problems. One has to recognise that some subordinates could feel somewhat inhibited when asked to offer a frank and fair view of their superiors for fear of reprisal. Others might show an aversion to rating at either the upper or lower ends of the rating scale, instead they settle for the unadventurous middle point of the range. Sometimes the suggestion is made that subordinates should come forward with anonymous ratings, and therefore might feel less inhibited. However, there could be a downside to such an approach when subordinates avail themselves of the opportunity to be vindictive towards a superior who has been putting pressure on them to reach exacting performance standards.

Finally, subordinates would need training on how to conduct appraisals, and from the organisation's point of view it is desirable that subordinates' ratings are acted upon. The latter could necessitate a significant change of corporate culture (Furnham, 1993).

Different perspectives

There are two main perspectives on the performance appraisal process; one is evaluative and the other is developmental (Anderson, 1992; Harris *et al.*, 1995; Houldsworth, 2007). An evaluative appraisal amounts to making a judgement about the appraisee and this follows a historical analysis of the latter's performance over the period under review. The judgement is made after comparing the appraisee's performance against previously established objectives or targets, or against all operational items on the job description. This type of appraisal could be linked to the allocation of extrinsic rewards, such as pay.

A development appraisal sets out to identify and develop the potential of the appraisee with the spotlight on future performance, and could be linked to career planning and management succession. A major aim is to establish what type of knowledge and skill the individual should develop. After identifying the appraisee's development needs, appropriate development objectives can be established. Because it is necessary for the appraisee to be open and frank about his or her perceived personal limitations and difficulties encountered in performance, it is necessary for this type of appraisal to be imbued with a high level of openness and mutual respect between the appraiser and the appraisee; restrictive bureaucratic control should also be avoided.

The two performance appraisal perspectives stress the need for feedback on both good and bad performances and underline the importance of indicating future personal development. By doing so they acknowledge the part played by motivation in feedback sessions; for example, being recognised for good performance or being told where there is scope for improvement has real motivational significance. Further discussion of the evaluative and developmental perspectives follows.

EVALUATIVE APPRAISAL

Performance factors were briefly referred to earlier when examining appraisal techniques. Here we will have something more to say about them. When engaged in performance-related behaviour the employee is concerned with the behavioural, social and technical aspects of the job. The appraiser, normally the immediate supervisor or manager, with perhaps assistance from a HR specialist, has to establish what aspects of employee performance should be examined, and what combination of objective and subjective appraisal techniques should be used.

In research undertaken by Income Data Services, London (an independent research body) (IDS, 1989) it was concluded that the performance factors most usually appraised were as follows:

- knowledge, ability and skill on the job;

- attitude to work, expressed as enthusiasm, commitment and motivation;

- quality of work on a consistent basis with attention to detail;

- volume of productive output;

- interaction, as exemplified in communication skills and ability to relate to others in teams.

Other performance factors that were less commonly used consisted of the following items: flexible mode of operation, ingenuity in tackling problems, capability to act with little supervision, skill at managing others, conversant with job requirements, track record at meeting performance targets, attendance record and punctuality, ability to plan and set priorities, and awareness of health and safety regulations. Obviously there is an overlap between some of these factors and the key factors listed above (e.g. job knowledge, ability and skill).

Cannell (2007) states that the list of factors currently popular is as follows:

- achievement of objectives;

- levels of competency;

■ standards of performance;

■ work outputs.

However, he points out that the emphasis varies with the category of staff being appraised. Whilst senior managers are commonly measured on the meeting of corporate objectives, production workers, for example, are normally assessed on achieving outputs.

Those involved in the appraisal of performance will pay a lot of attention to the choice of both performance factors and techniques. They will be interested in the outcome of the appraisee's performance. This could be something tangible, such as a quantitative record of the employee's output (see Case example 8.2), or more qualitative, such as the display of appropriate behaviour. What should be avoided is the recording of personality traits, which are not related to actual behaviour on the job.

A feature of the evaluative appraisal is the link between the outcome of the appraisal process and pay or financial benefits (Cannell, 2007). Proponents of this association are likely to point out that it is equitable and has real motivational effect. Employees are likely to consider the appraisal process as being significant because good performance is recognised and rewarded, but poor performance is not rewarded. Also, a performance-oriented culture is fostered (Anderson, 1992). By contrast, opponents of the process of linking pay to appraisal feel that the purpose of the performance review is blurred, that it is almost tantamount to a pay review, and that performance appraisal should be separated from a review of pay. According to Anderson (1992):

■ pay assumes a position of overriding importance when it is linked to performance;

■ appraisees try to extract from their boss performance targets that are easily attainable;

■ the appraisee's behaviour is too narrowly focused on those targets to the detriment of a broader view of performance in order to receive good ratings;

■ appraisees show an inclination to conceal negative information about their performance; and

■ those charged with performance appraisal give appraisees a higher ranking when they know a lower ranking would disadvantage them in financial terms.

When looking at the relationship between pay and performance appraisal it is wise to consider the influence of culture. In an organisational culture supportive of individualism and achievement there could be firm expectations on the part of employees that the appraisal process should coincide with the review of pay. An example of such a culture would be the dealing arm of a stock broking firm (see Box 5.1, p. 122). The dealers are likely to welcome a situation of loose organisational control with a minimum amount of guidance from above. The outcome of the appraisal process would form an input to the activity connected with the determination of rewards. It is unlikely that the organisational culture would be supportive of conditions where performance appraisal and the review of pay take place at different times.

There are circumstances where, at the target-setting stage, the performance appraisal process is used to transmit organisational values or culture. The latter could then be reinforced at the evaluation of performance stage when acceptable behaviour in which the organisational values are enshrined is recognised and rewarded. A company subscribing to this viewpoint could be concerned with encouraging appropriate behaviour (e.g. reliability, cooperativeness, able team player, good attendance record, enthusiastic, efficiency conscious and being a good example to others in improving methods and practice) with less emphasis on actual output. This was the approach adopted by Polaroid in its appraisal process when determining who should be promoted (Townley, 1989).

It appears that compliance is exacted from the subordinate in return for some advantage or reward when the evaluative appraisal is used, and the process has ingrained in it images of a power relationship between the superior and subordinate. Such an arrangement could run counter to a system of industrial relations where collective bargaining has taken root. In such circumstances there could be trade union resistance. Now we seem to have moved into territory where the performance appraisal system is seen as a medium of management control and manipulation. However, not everybody would take that view because there is a body of opinion that believes the appraisal process could create a performance culture that gives due recognition to the individual's actual and potential performance and development needs.

CASE EXAMPLE 8.2

A FOCUS ON MEASUREMENT AT NCCI

NCCI is the US-based National Council on Compensation Insurance. It had the aim of improving customer service by getting employees who engaged with customers to focus on particular goals. The goals were set within the context of corporate objectives such as providing clients with more service and selling more software products. Each employee met with his or her supervisor to agree goals that would contribute to the corporate objectives. Each month, employees would receive a report including statistics on how much time they had spent with clients, how many new products had been sold and how many problems had been solved for clients. The statistics would be aggregated for the department, the division and the company so that each employee could see how they fitted into the performance of the company.

Source: based on Dessler, 2005

Questions

1. Why is it important to have measurable elements in a performance management system?

2. Why might it be important to have elements that are not straightforwardly measurable?

DEVELOPMENT APPRAISAL

In this type of appraisal the interview features prominently, with the emphasis on the future development of the appraisee. The provision of open and constructive feedback is used to create the right motivational disposition (Walsh and Fisher, 2005). In practice the appraisee could gain sight of the appraisal forms and say what he or she thinks of the performance of the person carrying out the appraisal (the appraiser). We now appear to be moving towards emphasising a partnership between the manager and the subordinate in the appraisal process. The importance of personal objectives, which flow from corporate objectives, being agreed by both the appraiser and appraisee as realistic and challenging is strongly advocated, with the rider that appraisal techniques should be appropriate measuring devices of actual performance and kept under review (Williams, 1991).

One should also note the reinforcing qualities of solid feedback in an appraisal session when good behaviour is praised and deficiencies identified, though this is something that should happen on a periodic basis and not just once a year. Where deficiencies have been found steps should be taken to prepare a performance improvement plan to help the appraisee rectify the deficiencies and build on his or her strengths; self-development should be encouraged in these circumstances (see Case example 8.3).

There is no doubt about the status of the development appraisal: it is an integral part of the management process. It is suggested that counselling should be coupled with the normal deliberations associated with running the appraisal process. This occurred at IBM in a climate supportive of employee development, with the added dimension of determining merit pay (Sapsed, 1991). Introducing pay determination into the development appraisal is unlikely to be the normal practice in organisations that subscribe to the basic tenets of assessment aimed at development. Apart from counselling and developing a relationship of mutual trust and respect, the manager might give serious consideration to empowering subordinates so that they have the opportunity to stretch their capabilities in a problem-solving context.

Given the developments in HRM, whereby ownership of the appraisal process has moved from the personnel function to the appropriate manager, it is imperative that the latter is trained in operating the techniques of appraisal. When using the appraisal data to diagnose development needs the manager will be expected to use counselling and communication skills, including effective listening, and perhaps, in appropriate circumstances, inviting the appraisee to practise upward appraisal. If the manager is found wanting in the utilisation of these skills, this could signal the need for a skill-based management development experience for the manager. Where a number of different but complementary appraisal techniques are used, as found in a development centre (discussed earlier), managers could find themselves rubbing shoulders with a number of other suitable assessors.

CASE EXAMPLE 8.3

DEVELOPING COMPETENCIES IN A BRAZILIAN RESEARCH CENTRE

The organisation concerned is a unit of a federal public research body in Brazil. Over 8,000 employees are based at 37 research centres. The approach to appraisal was to develop performance by focusing on the inputs to research, and in particular the competencies of the staff. There are links between the organisation's competence-based approach and developmental appraisal. The three main aspects of the appraisal are people's development, effort and behaviour (Ubeda and Santos, 2007). The purpose of the appraisal is to help develop staff abilities and to stimulate the direction of their application to further organisational goals.

The organisational competencies for the unit were defined as research skills in agriculture and breeding to support agribusiness with sustainability and supplying research that would encourage the population's health and improve nutrition. These organisational competencies were translated into individual competencies including abilities to run and monitor research projects, abilities to produce and transfer technology to practical uses, and the ability to work with others to produce research outcomes and publications.

Individual appraisals focused on the appraisee's competencies and defined routes for development. The ethos of appraisal was to stimulate creativity. The research centre operated on the basis of temporary teams put together to work on particular research projects and a key mode of development was to agree with researchers which teams and projects they should be allocated to next so that they were being exposed to new knowledge. In addition, there was considerable investment in courses for researchers and on enabling them to visit and work with researchers at other leading-edge research institutions.

This developmental process highlighted the need for some modification of the strategic positioning of the centre, and as researchers brought in new knowledge and spread it to others through team activities, the focus and performance of the centre became more clearly defined. Hence, organisational development was spun off the back of personal development, and this, in turn, had been driven by an open attitude towards creativity and new competencies.

Source: based on Ubeda and Santos, 2007

Question

Do you think that the approach adopted in this case would be as successful in other settings where there is less integration, for example, in a networked organisation (see Chapter 3)?

Before we conclude our analysis of the development appraisal, Box 8.2 provides the views of an occupational psychologist with experience of the developmental appraisal.

Box 8.2: Reflections on development appraisal

Doyle (2003) believes, 'if a development appraisal is done well and it is linked to personal development plans that are aligned to business objectives, the interview based on it can offer a great deal'. She states that: 'development reviews can raise difficult issues in a constructive context, can clear the air of misunderstandings, resentments and frustrations, can raise the performance of weaker staff and encourage the best, improve superior–staff relationships, motivate the demoralized, and help everyone to work towards common goals ... Development reviews can give people the chance to discuss what they really want to do in the future to further their goals/aspirations.'

It is considered good practice not to combine the judgemental and development aspects of appraisal. Should they be combined in one session, people may not be frank and truthful about their strengths and weaknesses if they felt this could be detrimental to their career advancement or level of pay. Equally an appraiser cannot easily play a counselling role, normally associated with a developmental appraisal, if adopting a critical stance whilst operating in an evaluative or judgemental mode.

Question

Do you agree with Doyle that the judgemental and developmental aspects of appraisal should not be combined?

Before looking at the problems associated with appraisal, we shall turn our attention to two cases dealing with the use of performance management. In Case example 8.4 two different cases of good practice are presented. In both the purpose is to pursue the organisation's strategy through developing employees' understanding of their roles in corporate performance, and their places in the organisation's culture. However, the organisations take different routes to this goal. For Barclays Bank the answer is a formal but frequently implemented system with quarterly reviews, objective setting and feedback on attributes or competences. By contrast Humberside Training and Enterprise Council, with its focus on development, took a highly flexible and informal approach to 360-degree feedback in order to reinforce a culture of empowerment and responsibility taking by employees. It is clear that there is not a single best way of conducting performance management, and the onus is on the organisation to establish the right approach in its own circumstances. Considerations in making the decision on what type of approach to adopt will include an understanding of the employees, the culture, the nature of the business and the purposes of the performance management system.

CASE EXAMPLE 8.4

GOOD PRACTICE IN PERFORMANCE MANAGEMENT

Barclays Bank

The mortgages section of Barclays Bank employs about 800 people in the north of England. It operates in a very competitive market in which aligning the commitment of employees to organisational objectives is seen as crucial. All employees are on the same system, which focuses 50 per cent on objectives ('what you do') and 50 per cent on attributes ('the way you do it').

Business objectives were developed on the basis of the corporate strategy, and were translated into departmental objectives. In order to achieve buy-in from employees, they are facilitated by team leaders to develop their own key responsibility areas, objectives and measures that reflect the departmental objectives. The aim is to set expectations, and to include measurable outcomes in the objectives. Where possible, the nature of exceptional performance is specified. One of the dangers with setting objectives is that they can be filed away and neglected. In order to make the objectives a 'living document', a quarterly review is conducted in which the individual's 'achievement log' is updated. The frequency of reviews enables changes in business priorities to be reflected in the individual's aims.

'Attributes' are the behaviour and qualities that are expected from employees who are performing effectively. An 'attribute library' of 18 attributes, such as 'delivering results' and 'attention to detail', is subdivided into dimensions reflecting jobs at different levels in the organisation, and performance bands. Eight attributes are selected as core to a particular role, and these are assessed in the quarterly review. The review consists of a self-assessment and a reviewer assessment. Feedback is delivered in writing and the attributes library specifications and objectives are used as benchmarks to judge the employees' performance. Ratings on the scale 'exceed', 'meet', 'fall short' and 'fail' are communicated. In addition the individual is required to gain feedback from six other people during the course of a year. Where there are deficiencies in performance development plans are drawn up.

Source: based on Bratton and Gold, 1999

Humberside Training and Enterprise Council

Humberside Training and Enterprise Council (now part of the Learning and Skills Council: www.lsc.gov.uk/regions/YorkshireHumber) is a public sector body concerned with the stimulation of business and provision of training in an area in the north of England. It employs 200 people. A fundamental part of the strategy is to stimulate and facilitate business activities by others, and the style and approach of its employees is fundamental to its success. The performance management system seeks to reinforce an organisational culture that will inspire employees to be effective facilitators who take responsibility for their own actions. An unstated but clear objective is to avoid the pitfalls of traditional bureaucracies.

Feedback from employees about a previous performance management scheme indicated that the most valuable part of the process was the face-to-face feedback, and the least valuable part was the form filling. Taking this message to heart, the new scheme is paperless. There are no strict rules about the running of appraisals, and people are trusted to develop suitable approaches, although the clear intention is that feedback should be sought from a 360-degree system and that each individual should have at least one appraisal per year. The purpose of appraisal is to improve performance and help people learn and grow.

Typically feedback is given in groups. It was found that group sizes above seven were less effective as the feedback became mainly generalities, but in suitable sized groups clear feedback and behavioural examples could be given. Any written material produced belongs to the appraisee, and there are no files or records. The outcome is that the process is one of dialogue rather than recording.

Employees say that the system is effective, noting that the feedback they receive may not be that different to the feedback they had formerly received from managers in a top-down approach, but they add that hearing six other people say the same thing has a much stronger effect. Employees are also expected to take responsibility for their development plans emerging from the feedback meetings. Initially employees tended to select a 'safe' group of friends to give them feedback. But as confidence has grown in the system people have started to select more challenging groups to give feedback, knowing that this can provide an effective stimulus for changing behaviour and learning. Employees report that this is reinforcing the culture of empowerment, and that communications have greatly improved.

The managing director of Humberside TEC argued that everyone involved in the 'three-dimensional perspective' on performance takes something out of the process. Further, it has the advantage of being very flexible, so that it can change as individuals develop and the business changes. The process has enabled individuals to reflect on their practice and be involved in planning their training and development. It has also thrown up a number of discoveries for the organisation as a whole as it seeks to become a learning organisation.

Source: based on Storr, 2000

Question

Compare the relative strengths and weaknesses of the approaches of Barclays and Humberside.

In interviewing senior HR managers, Baron and Armstrong (2004) found that although they were aware of the distinction between development-led and evaluative and pay-led appraisal, most wanted to achieve the 'best of both worlds'. Rather than make the distinction, the HR managers stressed performance management as an integral part of running the organisation, incorporating both measurement and development. In a similar finding, Houldsworth (2007) in a survey of 400 line managers, found that top-performing organisations were seeking to combine the positive features of both types. One example was the supermarket chain Metro AG. Metro AG used both 'hard measures' and 'people measures', the latter being assessed via the Gallup Group's 12-question engagement inventory. Houldsworth believed that achieving the fine balance between development and evaluation would be the key challenge for the performance management agenda of the future.

Problems with appraisal

Appraisal has many strong points when it is well conceived and executed as a process for providing systematic judgements to support pay reviews, promotions, transfers and the provision of feedback on actual performance, with pointers to performance improvement through changes in attitudes, behaviour and skills. Also, as mentioned earlier, it provides an opportunity for counselling and can sow the seeds for personal development. However, one has to acknowledge a number of potential problems associated with performance appraisal as follows:

1. Poorly designed appraisal forms are compounded by some irrelevant items.
2. Insufficient time is devoted to preparing for the event, completing the appraisal forms and ensuring the necessary training is undertaken.
3. Inadequate interview and counselling skills are used by the appraiser.
4. Feedback given to subordinates is deficient in a number of respects.
5. Action strategies (e.g. training) that stem from the appraisal are not seriously entertained.
6. There is unreliable judgement because of subjectivity on the part of the appraiser, despite efforts to minimise it. One way to minimise subjectivity and promote objectivity is to make sure that there are explicit, previously agreed performance criteria against which judgements are made. Also, a senior manager could take responsibility for overseeing a number of appraisals to check that differences between the ratings that individuals receive are not due to appraiser bias.
7. Related to point 6 is the appearance of other imperfections. These include invalidity and unreliability (the measure is not measuring what it is supposed to be measuring or it is unreliable), ratings are either too lenient or too severe, and the evaluation is distorted by personal likes and dislikes.
8. Target setting and use of techniques leave much to be desired.
9. Where the appraiser acts as both judge and counsellor, this could give rise to confusion as well as leading to certain difficulties for the appraisee. For example, the appraisee is subjected to an evaluative appraisal at which past performance is assessed and rewards determined, and then there is a switch to a development appraisal; in such circumstances there could well be a reluctance on the part of the appraisee to be open and frank about past mistakes and problems. Randell *et al.* (1984) argue that the solution to this problem would be to arrange different meetings for the different types of appraisal, with a different appraiser for each meeting. The development appraisal might be conducted by a manager from another department or by a HR specialist in training and development.

10. In connection with ownership and rewards, Lundy and Cowling (1996) cite an IPM-sponsored study (Fletcher and Williams, 1992) in which the following weaknesses in performance management practice in the United Kingdom were identified:

'There was frequently little indication of a real sense of ownership of performance management among line managers, and therefore no depth in commitment. Too many managers perceived it as a top-down process with no feedback loop operating, there was a widespread perception that performance management was 'owned' by the HR department, and there was a lack of thought and imagination when tackling the issue of rewards.'

However, as performance management and appraisal become more widely practised and embedded in organisational systems, there is evidence that perceptions are changing. In a more recent CIPD survey, 61 per cent of line managers believed that performance management was very or mostly effective (Baron and Armstrong, 2004). This is reinforced by Houldsworth's (2007) survey of 400 line managers. She concludes: 'the survey results suggest that the persistent myth of the unpopularity of performance management processes within organizations should finally be put to rest. The majority of respondents are largely convinced of the usefulness of performance management, with 68 per cent indicating that the process used in their own company was either "effective" or "very effective" ' (2007: 35).

There are further observations in Box 8.3 on why the appraisal system can fail to live up to expectations.

Box 8.3: Failures in appraisal

Longenecker (1997) conducted a survey and found that the most common reasons for the failure of an appraisal system for managerial staff were (a) unclear performance criteria or an ineffective rating instrument, (b) poor working relationship with the boss, and (c) the appraiser lacking sufficient information on the appraisee's actual performance. Other reasons given were lack of ongoing feedback and lack of focus on the improvement of performance through management development schemes. Lesser concerns that were expressed were inadequate skills of appraisal and the performance review process lacking adequate structure or content.

A particular concern voiced by Torrington et al. (2005) is the importance of the ownership of the appraisal scheme. If it is designed and imposed by the HR department that would leave little ownership of the system by line managers. Also, if the paperwork has to be returned to the HR department, the system may be viewed as a form filling exercise for somebody else's benefit with no practical value as far as performance on the job is concerned.

Doyle (2003) also recognises unskilled behaviour on the part of the interviewer conducting the appraisal, and goes on to point out that often there are difficulties experienced by appraisers (managers) when relaying negative feedback to the appraisees. Also, many employees will react with defensiveness, anxiety, and depression when negative feedback is poorly given.

Shaun Tyson, Professor of HRM at the Cranfield School of Management, UK is quoted as saying that 'appraisal requires interview and counselling skills of a high order, which many managers don't possess. They don't prepare, don't have time, don't have skills to conduct interviews and, where the relationship with the person being appraised is not good, might make it even worse. People go into the appraisal highly motivated and come out highly demotivated.' This comment by Tyson has been endorsed by Overell (2003) who cites evidence that a lot of managers don't have the interpersonal skills to give negative comments in a constructive way – there is a very British fear of criticism.

The Director of Organisation Development at Amersham Pharmacia and Biotech, UK, who used a 360-degree feedback system for three years, says that 'generally appraisal causes confusion because it tries to do too many things. It tries to set objectives and set performance against them, give personal development planning and obtain information for salary planning. The part that loses out the most is development ... We use the 360-degree feedback as an optional extra to help our leaders and managers increase their self-awareness and improve their performance. But it must be done with care. They are given help to understand the feedback and translate it into development plans.'

The Head of HR at Coutts Banking (part of the Royal Bank of Scotland), UK, says that '360-degree feedback, which is being used increasingly, is valuable but not enough ... It is naive to rely on appraisals for staff development. The problem we encounter is that people fill in forms that are then filed and then forgotten. Most organisations would recognise that fact.'

Source: based on Coles, 1999; Overell, 2003

Question

Do you think having some parts of the appraisal process (such as 360-degree feedback at Amersham Pharmacia and Biotech) is a good idea?

International considerations

In this section some important issues are considered when taking a snapshot of performance appraisal in an international context. Technical competence is a necessary but not sufficient condition for successful performance in international management positions. Amongst the matters to consider are cross-cultural interpersonal skills, sensitivity to foreign norms and values, understanding of differences in labour practices or customer relations, and ease of adaptation to unfamiliar environments. It follows that cultural sensitivity has to be considered in the practice of performance appraisal. In Japan, for example, it is important to avoid confrontation to 'save face', and this custom affects the way in which performance appraisal is conducted. It is said that a Japanese manager cannot draw attention in a direct sense to a mistake or error attributable to the subordinate. Instead the emphasis right at the beginning is to focus on the strengths of the subordinate followed by a general discussion of the work, and then explain the consequences of the type of error or mistake made by the subordinate without identifying the actual mistake or the person making it. From this discourse the subordinate is supposed to recognise the mistake and put forward suggestions to improve his or her work (Dowling *et al.*, 1994). Amongst the matters to consider are cross-cultural interpersonal skills, sensitivity to foreign norms and values, understanding of differences in labour practices or customer relations, and ease of adaptation to unfamiliar environments (Briscoe and Schuler, 2004).

Pepsi Cola International, with operations in over 150 countries, used 'instant feedback' as one of five aspects of its common appraisal system, which allows for modification to suit cultural differences and local circumstances. In utilising the process of instant feedback the following national differences were noted (Schuler *et al.*, 1991):

- Americans use it because it fits a fast-paced way of doing business.

- In most Asian cultures feedback is never given in public, and in some Asian cultures head nodding during an instant feedback session does not signify agreement, it merely denotes that the message has been heard.

- Some Latins will argue strongly if they do not agree with the feedback.

- Some Indian nationals will ask for a great deal of specific information.

It is no easy task to devise a performance appraisal system for multinational companies that caters adequately for employees consisting of expatriates, host country nationals and third country nationals. Producing documentation and ways of operationalising the system, so that it will not disadvantage a particular group, could prove to be a Herculean task, but it has to be seriously addressed if effectiveness and equity are to be achieved.

These issues are being tackled by Alliance UniChem, a merged organisation that needed to bring together people from different cultures. Its approach was to implement a package that combined 360-degree feedback with the ability to communicate simultaneously in different languages (see Case example 8.5).

CASE EXAMPLE 8.5

360-DEGREE FEEDBACK IN AN INTERNATIONAL SETTING

In 1999 UniChem, the UK pharmaceuticals company, merged with Alliance Santé of France to form Alliance UniChem. The company then employed 17,000 people in several European countries, becoming the second-largest pharmaceuticals business in Europe. Pre-merger, neither organisation had well-developed corporate HR functions, but HR was chosen as the first area to tackle following the merger as it was seen as being essential to thriving in a market characterised by low profit margins. A central HR department was established in Paris and its top priority was to encourage people to cooperate effectively across cultural boundaries. A main thrust of their approach to achieve this end was the introduction of a new 360-degree performance appraisal package.

The proposal to set up 360-degree appraisal was not met with general acceptance. The method was virtually unheard of in three of the countries (Italy, Spain and Portugal) and in France it was viewed with suspicion as an 'American tool'. However, the board was convinced that the process was important because it recognised the need to develop multi-cultural management in the group and it wanted to be able to move managers between countries so that they would get a more holistic and integrated understanding of the business. Integration was important because the previous style had been for entrepreneurial managers to lead their own business units, whereas now there was a need to bring them together to drive an organisation on a completely different scale.

The system was based on four key values that came out of the merger: excellence, service, innovation and partnership. Competencies were drawn up in each area as the basis for feedback. Because the system allows for translation, it is possible for an individual to receive feedback from someone in a different country on the same system, even if they do not have any shared language. The system was developed to operate in five languages; it includes targets and records of individual progress. Development activities on each competency are devised through suggestions from the employee, the system and the manager. Alliance UniChem sees this development of a set of common behaviours as fundamental to getting employees to focus not just at the national level, but on the needs and goals of the organisation as a whole.

Source: based on Johnson, 2001

Questions

1. If you were a middle manager in Italy, Spain, Portugal or France how do you think you would react to the introduction of 360-degree appraisal?

2. If you were the board member with responsibility for implementing the system in Europe, how would you persuade middle managers that 360-degree feedback was a good idea?

Notwithstanding the difficulties, the uptake of performance management has been increasing across the world. It is almost ubiquitous in the United States with over 94 per cent of companies reporting having appraisal systems (Redman, 2006). An international survey which received 3,500 responses reported that 35 per cent of respondents said they had never received an evaluation from their employer. Figures were poor for Brazilian (53 per cent) and Spanish (49 per cent) respondents reporting no evaluations, however it is reported as being increasingly common in China, Hong Kong, Japan, Africa and India (Redman, 2006). One source of influence is the pervasive performance management of expatriates in multinational enterprises, where it is common for expatriates to be included in the system adopted by the home headquarters (Shih *et al.*, 2005).

Some critical issues

Reflect for a moment on the meaning of performance management. Though the term performance management is open to a number of interpretations, in the United Kingdom it has come to take on a particular meaning. It denotes a system where the level of intervention is that of the individual employee, and the overall intent is to align individual performance with organisational performance. But this is a unitarist view, and it fails to recognise the plurality of interests (i.e. varied interests that are part of organisational reality – see Chapter 11). We should not expect it to be an easy task to align individual performance with goals that are possibly conflicting and contradictory.

It appears that traditional performance appraisal, with appraisal pay bolted on, is alive and kicking in many organisations. This reflects an outmoded theory X view of motivation

(McGregor, 1960), but it has appeal, in terms of control, to a number of practitioners operating in a climate where expenditure is continually pruned. An alternative view – Theory Y (McGregor, 1960) – would be preferable as it is more expansive in accommodating diverse needs and interests, and would embrace the following progressive activities: good communication, job enrichment and empowerment, participation in goal-setting, frequent feedback, a broad view of performance to include behaviours/competencies, a broad view of reward, and the promotion of employee well-being. However, to implement such a scheme has traditionally been regarded as costly (Williams, 1998). Nowadays, the question is whether a good return can be expected for such an investment (Cannell, 2007).

Conclusions

Performance management has an evaluative and developmental dimension to its make-up, and is crucial in both linking rewards to performance and providing a platform for the development of employees. Over-concentration on the assessment of performance can work to the detriment of effort aimed at establishing the development needs of the individual in an open and honest way. The manager, as an appraiser, may encounter difficulties in reconciling the roles of 'judge' and 'mentor'. Managers need to develop the skills of coping with such tensions in their roles. In some organisations this problem is solved by having different managers carry out performance and development appraisals.

Appraisal provides the context in which managers can seek to ensure that there is acceptable congruency between the objectives of the individual and those of the organisation. Although one recognises the part played by performance management in the determination of rewards, we believe that, if treated as a way of providing feedback on progress and of jointly agreeing the next set of aims, the appraisal can have a positive effect on individual motivation. This view is substantiated by the research linking HRM practices to corporate performance (see Chapter 2).

For many organisations it is important to ensure that employees are fully aware of the corporate objectives and the part they can play in fulfilling these objectives. This can be achieved with relative formality, as in the case of Barclays Bank, or more informally, as in Humberside TEC (see Case example 8.4). Either approach can be highly effective, but it is necessary for the approach to fit with the style and culture of the organisation and its members. Performance management is a chance for the organisation to learn about what employees are really doing, and to understand what will motivate them in the future. Innovations such as 360-degree feedback, and in some cases the use of computerised systems, can help facilitate this learning process. The issue of enhancing mutual understanding through such learning is particularly important in international settings where there is a possibility of misunderstandings across cultures, and in some cases having a system that can cope with translation between languages (as in the case of Alliance UniChem, see Case example 8.5) is a positive advantage.

Review and reflection questions

1. What are the four principles of Astra Zeneca's performance management system?

2. What is the 'philosophy' of performance management?

3. What are the aims of appraisal?

4. Name four appraisal methods.

5. Compare the strengths and weaknesses of the following

    (a) management by objectives

    (b) graphic rating scales

    (c) 360-degree feedback.

6. What is the balanced scorecard method?

7. Compare and contrast evaluative and developmental appraisal.

8. What problems can occur with appraisal?

Activities

If you are in work:

For your own position, devise a 360-degree feedback process:
- Who would be consulted?
- What methods would be used (e.g. graphic rating scales, free narrative, etc.)?
- Would the approach be evaluative or developmental?
- Who would conduct the feedback interview?

If you are in full-time study:

For the job you gathered information on in the activity for Chapter 7:
- Review the requirements of the job and translate these into:
    (a) objectives
    (b) competencies.
- Think how information could be gathered on the performance of competences and/or completion of objectives.

Further reading and research

In the following article the compatibility of developmental and evaluative approaches is discussed:

Houldsworth, E. (2007) 'In the same boat. Can soft and hard approaches to managing performance co-exist?', *People Management*, 25 January, 35–36.

An international evaluation of 360-degree feedback is provided in the following:

Brutus, S., Derayeh, M., Fletcher, C., Bailey, C., Velazquez, P., Shi, K., Simon, C. and Labath, V. (2006) 'Internationalization of multi-source feedback: a six country exploratory analysis of 360-degree feedback', *International Journal of Human Resource Management*, 17, 1888–1906.

The following chapter explores the relevance of the practice of current thinking in psychology on appraisal:

Latham, G.P. and Mann, S. (2006) 'Advances in the science of performance appraisal: implications for practice', in G.P. Hodgkinson and J.K. Ford (eds), *International Review of Industrial and Organizational Psychology*, Vol 21, Chapter 7, 295–338, Chichester: John Wiley.

The following articles have a practical flavour:

People Management (2007) 'Trouble shooter: An appraisal problem and a way to solve it', (discussants: S. Jones, T. Russel and S Stevens), 19 April, 58–59.

Arkin, A. (2007) 'Performance management. Forced ranking: force for good', *People Management*, 8 February, 26–29.

The CIPD provides a very helpful insight into performance management in its fact sheet 'Performance Management: an overview'. This can be found at www.cipd.co.uk/subjects/perfmangmt.

Examples of appraisal forms and guidance on assessment centres can be found at the following site: www.businessballs.com/performanceappraisals.

References

Anderson, G. (1992) 'Performance appraisal', in Towers, B. (ed.), *The Handbook of Human Resource Management*, Oxford: Blackwell.

Armstrong, M. and Baron, A. (2004) *Managing Performance: performance management in action*, London: CIPD.

Baron, A. and Armstrong, M. (2004) 'Get into Line', *People Management*, 10, 44– 46.

Beardwell, I., Holden, L. and Claydon, T. (2004) *Human Resource Management. A contemporary approach*, Harlow, Essex: Pearson Education.

Bevan, S. and Thompson, M. (1991) 'Performance management at the crossroads', *Personnel Management*, November, 36–39.

Bratton, J. and Gold, J. (1999) *Human Resource Management: Theory and practice*, Basingstoke: Macmillan.

Briscoe, D.R. and Schuler, R.S. (2004) *International Human Resource Management*, New York: Routledge.

Cannell, M. (2007) *Performance Management: an overview*, CIPD factsheet, www.cipd.co.uk

Chang, L.-C. (2007) 'The NHS performance assessment framework as a balanced scorecard approach', *International Journal of Public Sector Management*, 20, 101–117.

CIPD (2006) *Performance Appraisal Factsheet*, www.cipd.co.uk

Clifford, L. and Bennett, H. (1997) 'Best practice in 360-degree feedback', *Selection and Development Review*, 13, 6–9.

Coles, M. (1999) 'Reappraise the way you develop staff', *Sunday Times*, 14 February, 7–22.

de Waal, A.A. (2006) 'Managing performance for improved productivity: The importance of performance management analysis', *Strategic Direction*, 22, 23–25.

de Waal, A.A. (2007) 'The characteristics of a high performance organization', *Business Strategy Series*, 8, 179–185.

Dessler, G. (2005) *Human Resource Management*, New Jersey: Pearson.

Donkin, R. (2002) 'Challenge to human "capital" assumptions', Appointments (Recruitment) section, *Financial Times*, October 3, X.

Dowling, P.J., Schuler, R.S. and Welch, D.E. (1994) *International Dimensions of Human Resource Management*, Belmont, CA: Wadsworth Publishing.

Doyle, C.E. (2003) *Work and organizational psychology: An introduction with attitude*, Hove, East Sussex: Psychology Press.

Fletcher, C. (1993) *Appraisal: Routes to improved performance*, London: IPM.

Fletcher, C. (1998) 'Assessing the effectiveness of some 360 degree appraisal systems', Paper presented at the BPS Occupational Psychology conference, Birmingham, UK.

Fletcher, C. and Williams, R. (1992) 'The route to performance management', *Personnel Management*, October, 42–47.

Furnham, A. (1993) 'When employees rate their supervisors', *Financial Times*, 1 March.

Goffin, R.D. and Anderson, D.W. (2007) 'The self-rater's personality and self–other disagreement in multi-score performance ratings', *Journal of Managerial Psychology*, 22, 271–289.

Harris, M.M., Smith, D.E. and Champagne, D. (1995) 'A field study of performance appraisal purpose: research vs administrative-based ratings', *Personnel Psychology*, Spring, 151–160.

Houldsworth, E. (2007) 'In the Same Boat', *People Management*, 13, 34–36.

Huddart, G. (1994) 'Firm runs self-appraisal', *Personnel Today*, 17 May, 1.

IDS (1989) *Common to All*, IDS Study no. 442, December.

Johnson, R. (2001) 'Double entente', *People Management*, 7, 38–39.

Kaplan, R. and Norton, D. (1996) *The Balanced Scorecard: Translating strategy into action*, Boston, MA: Harvard Business School Press.

Kaplan, R. and Norton, D. (2001) *The strategy focused organization*, Boston, MA: Harvard Business School Press.

Longenecker, C. (1997) 'Why managerial performance appraisals are ineffective. Causes and lessons', *Career Development International*, 2.

Lundy, O. and Cowling, A. (1996) *Strategic Human Resource Management*, London: Routledge.

McGregor, D. (1960) *The Human Side of Enterprise*, New York: McGraw-Hill.

Mendibil, K. and MacBryde, J. (2006) 'Factors that affect the design and implementation of team-based performance measurement systems', *International Journal of Productivity and Performance Management*, 55, 118–142.

Overell, S. (2003) 'Employee appraisals: Let's have a little chat about work, shall we?', *Financial Times*, 3 March, 13.

Price A. (2004) *Human Resource Management in a Business context*, London: Thomson.

Randell, G., Packard, P. and Slater, J. (1984) *Staff Appraisal: A first step to effective leadership*, London: Institute of Personnel Management.

Redman, T. (2006) 'Performance Appraisal', in Redman, T. and Wilkinson, A. (eds), *Contemporary*

Human Resource Management, Harlow: FT/Prentice Hall.

Robbins, S.P. (2003) *Organisational behaviour*, Upper Saddle River, NJ: Prentice-Hall/Pearson Education International.

Sapsed, G. (1991) 'Appraisal the IBM way', *Involvement and Participation*, February, 8–14.

Schuler, R.S., Fulkerson, J.R. and Dowling, P.J. (1991) 'Strategic performance measurement and management in multinational corporations', *Human Resource Management*, 30, 365–392.

Shih, H.-A., Chiang, Y.-H., Chuan, M. and Kim, I.-S. (2005) 'Expatriate performance management form MNEs of different national origins', *International Journal of Manpower*, 26, 157–176.

Steare, R. (2006) 'How to create an ethical culture', *People Management*, 12, 46–47.

Storr, F. (2000) 'This is not a circular', *People Management*, 38, 38–40.

Torrington, D., Hall, L. and Taylor, S. (2005) *Human Resource Management*, Harlow, Essex: Pearson Education.

Townley, B. (1989) 'Selection and appraisal: reconstituting social relations', in Storey, J. (ed.), *New Developments in Human Resource Management*, London: Routledge.

Ubeda, C.L. and Santos, F.C.A. (2007) 'Staff development and performance appraisal in a Brazilian research centre', *European Journal of Innovation Management,* 10, 109–125.

Walsh, K. and Fisher, D. (2005) 'Action inquiry and performance appraisals', *The Learning Organization*, 12, 26–41.

Warr, P. and Ainsworth, E. (1999) '360-degree feedback: some recent research', *Selection and Development Review*, 15, 3–6.

Williams, R. (1991) 'Strategy and objectives', in Neale, F. (ed.), *The Handbook of Performance Management*, London: Institute of Personnel Management.

Williams, R. (1998) *Performance Management* (Essential Business Psychology Series), London: Thompson Business Press.

Chapter 9

EMPLOYEE DEVELOPMENT: REWARD MANAGEMENT

Introduction

Fostering a motivated workforce lies at the heart of HRM. If people are motivated towards appropriate goals then the likelihood of organisational success is enhanced. Motivation theory has developed over time, and a good understanding of motivation is necessary if we are to manage rewards effectively. There are several different systems of payment and reward, some of which can be used in combination, and others provide alternative choices. Ultimately, what gets rewarded will be a focus of attention for employees, so it is important that their focus is directed on to behaviours that will be advantageous for the organisation and its members.

Having read this chapter, you should:

- know about the methods for determining the nature and level of rewards;

- understand the various types of reward system – their applications, advantages and disadvantages;

- gain a perspective on the issues for reward management in the international environment of multinational companies;

- understand the pertinence and application of motivation theories to reward management;

- be aware of current issues of debate in reward management.

The purpose of managing the system of rewards within the organisation is to attract and retain the human resources the organisation needs to achieve its objectives. To retain the services of employees and maintain a high level of performance it is necessary to increase their motivation, commitment and flexibility by a variety of means, including appropriate management style, competitive compensation package and supportive culture (Armstrong and Murlis, 1998; Armstrong and Brown, 2006). In effect the organisation is aiming to bring about an alignment of organisational and individual objectives when the spotlight is on reward management. To achieve that aim requires a flexible reward strategy – a product of the corporate plan and the human resource plan – that is capable of responding to internal influences (e.g. demand for skilled employees, resources available to meet the costs of labour) and external influences (e.g. government policy on the minimum wage), and the rewards offered by competitors (Boyd and Salamin, 2001).

In an HRM context reward management is not restricted to rewards and incentives, such as wages or salaries, bonuses, commission and profit sharing, which relate to extrinsic motivation. It is also concerned with non-financial rewards that satisfy the employee's psychological needs for job variety and challenge, achievement, recognition, responsibility, opportunities to acquire skills and career development, and the exercise of more influence in the decision-making process. The non-financial rewards can be equated with intrinsic motivation. Later in the chapter there will be a brief examination of motivation theories.

An important issue to consider when reflecting on reward management in a contemporary setting is equal opportunities, in particular parity in a gender context. Research commissioned by the Equal Opportunities Commission (EOC) in the United Kingdom showed that a woman graduate aged 22–24 is likely to earn 15 per cent less than a man with the same degree in the same subject (Eaglesham *et al.*, 2004). The inequality of pay between men and women is compounded by motherhood, particularly for women in lower-skilled jobs. According to the EOC, more than one third of the pay gap stems from the problems women face juggling childcare and paid work. The EOC also mentions other causes for the pay gap between men and women as (i) discrimination, (ii) occupational segregation (e.g. meaning that more women are employed as low-paid care assistants than as higher earning plumbers), and (iii) the unequal impact of responsibility for other people (e.g. elderly relatives) (Briscoe, 2004).

The older the age group studied, the wider the gender pay gap becomes. This is partly because older women are more likely to have spent time out of the labour market caring for children or elderly dependants. There is also a generational factor. While the gender pay gap with respect to educational qualifications has closed in recent years, the difference is still significant between men and women over 40 years old. The then British Prime Minister, Tony Blair, was reported as being committed to equal pay for men and women, as part of 'a fair deal for all at work'. Measures taken in an attempt to honour this commitment are in the policy pipeline. For example, a Commission on Women and Work was set up and given the brief to consider measures to tackle the pay gap between the sexes, including a statutory requirement for employers to carry out regular pay audits (Eaglesham *et al.*, 2004).

A valid question to ask at this stage is how does the organisation determine the level or magnitude of reward?

Determination of rewards

Traditionally, many reward systems have been determined by collective bargaining whereby management and employee representatives (usually trade union officials) negotiate wage rates for large groups of employees. In certain UK organisations, such as hospitals in the National Health Service and local authorities, pay grades were established for groups of employees on a national basis. For example, a nurse assuming a particular set of responsibilities in the south of England would be on the same grade as a nurse shouldering identical responsibilities in the north of the country despite differences in the cost of living between the two regions. However, it should be noted that there is a special cost-of-living allowance for those working in London.

Underlining this approach to wage determination is the use of a technique called job evaluation. Job evaluation could be described as a process used at the level of a company or industry to determine the relationship between jobs and to establish a systematic structure of wage rates for those jobs. It is concerned with 'internal relativities'; that is, that individuals doing the same type of work receive equal rewards. Job evaluation is only concerned with the assessment of the job, not the performance of the job occupant, and it goes without saying that the preparation of reliable job descriptions is a prelude to embarking on administering job evaluation schemes. Job evaluation measures differences between jobs, and places them in appropriate groups and in rank order. Schemes of job evaluation can be classified as either the quantitative or the non-quantitative approach, as follows:

- *Quantitative*   – factor comparison;

   – points rating.

- *Non-quantitative*   – ranking;

   – job classification.

FACTOR COMPARISON

Different jobs are ranked against agreed factors such as minimum level of education, level of skill, task difficulty, supervisory responsibility, level of training and decision-making responsibility. These are referred to as criteria, each with a scale 1 to 5, against which jobs are placed in rank order. A factor comparison system is more applicable to the evaluation of clerical and administrative positions than to more senior positions with pronounced problem-solving characteristics.

POINTS RATING

Job evaluation systems based on points rating require an analysis of factors common to all jobs and at one time were widely used. The factors commonly used include skill, responsibility, complexity and decision making. Each factor is given a range of points to allow the award of a maximum number of points. The relative importance of a factor is the weighting it receives, which is determined by the number of points allocated to it, and is related to the level at which the factor is present in the job. For example, the well-known Hay-MSL system identified nine factors common to all jobs at different levels, as shown in Table 9.1.

Levels 1, 2 and 5 are key indicators for senior jobs, and 3, 4 and 5 are key indicators for all other jobs. In the evaluation of jobs using the Hay-MSL system three characteristics are considered, namely 'know-how', 'problem solving' and 'accountability'. When jobs are matched

Table 9.1 The Hay-MSL system

Level	Factor
1	Purpose
2	Accountability
3	Activities
4	Decision making
	Context
	Relationships
5	Knowledge
	Skills
	Experience

against these criteria a numerical exercise is undertaken and points are awarded. Generally, the more important the job the greater the number of points.

To make schemes, such as the above, operational requires a lot of preparation and effort. Although these schemes help in the design of graded salary structures, whereby the scores obtained by a particular job under each factor are aggregated, and have the appearance of objectivity, they can be highly subjective. Among the disadvantages of the points rating system are the following:

- The evaluation of all jobs, or even just 'benchmark' jobs, can be a complex, time-consuming and costly exercise. Benchmark jobs are a small number of jobs covering the range of jobs subjected to evaluation and considered by the evaluators to represent a good example of the right relationship between pay and job content.

- The assessment is static and not dynamic because the analysis refers to a moment in time.

RANKING

This procedure involves comparing jobs on the basis of, for example, knowledge/skill, discretionary features of decision making and task complexity, and then arranging the jobs in order of importance, difficulty or value to the organisation, with the appropriate levels of pay. To begin with the most and least important jobs are identified, followed by ranking all jobs within this framework. In this hierarchical arrangement 'benchmark' jobs are established at key points and the remaining jobs are put in position around them. Establishing the position of the most and least important jobs is relatively easy but deciding on the position of the middle range jobs can be difficult. In a ranking exercise it is important to be aware of the potential for the introduction of bias or prejudice on the part of evaluators, and to avoid the pitfall of assessing the performance of the job occupant rather than evaluating the job itself.

JOB CLASSIFICATION

Jobs are placed into a number of grades in which differences in skill and responsibility are accommodated. These differences embrace areas within a job such as required knowledge, training and type of decision making. A definition of a job grade should be sufficiently comprehensive so as to permit a comparison of a real job description with the corresponding grade definition. The job classification approach with a predetermined number of grades and a pay structure to match is relatively straightforward and inexpensive. However, using the job classification approach with a large number of grades can take a long time and it cannot cope with complex jobs, often found at the more senior levels, which do not fit comfortably within one grade.

ADVANTAGES AND DISADVANTAGES OF JOB EVALUATION

The advantages and disadvantages of job evaluation should be acknowledged. As to the advantages, it is said to be an objective, fair (free from managerial influence) and logical approach in the determination of a pay structure. Murlis and Fitt (1991) view job evaluation as a good way to improve objectivity in the management of vertical and lateral job relativities with respect to pay, though they are prepared to admit that it is not a totally scientific process. With regard to objectivity, the point should be made that this could be undermined if job descriptions were prepared subjectively. It is worth noting that job evaluation is often viewed favourably by industrial tribunals as a foundation for a reward system that is visible and amenable to adjustment when correction is necessary.

As to the disadvantages, there could be a problem where the objectivity of the evaluators is questioned; it could also be costly to install and maintain. In connection with maintenance, it should be noted that upgradings following the evaluation could mean extra expenditure but savings on downgradings may not follow where protected grade status exists for current employees. The validity and reliability of job evaluation is called into question. One particular bone of contention is that the initial choice and weighting of 'benchmark' jobs is arbitrary (Armstrong, 2003). The rigidity of job evaluation systems and of the attitudes that underpin them has been criticised (Wickens, 1987). He feels they result in a level of bureaucracy that runs counter to the notion of flexibility and adaptability ingrained in HRM thinking. Job evaluation operates on the assumption that there is a collection of tasks performed by a job occupant working in a stable reporting relationship in a traditional bureaucratic organisation. But as new organisational forms emerge, epitomised by delayering and flattening of structures, employees will be required to be more flexible and versatile in the work domain. This rules out a job demarcation mentality and introduces a recognition of the need for flexible job descriptions and acceptance of frequent changes to job boundaries. In such circumstances the level of stability required by job evaluation no longer prevails. In such an environment the traditional job evaluation system may lack significance (Stredwick, 2005). This could herald the advent of simplified job evaluation systems, for example Nissan's 15 job titles.

Another matter to consider in connection with traditional job evaluation systems is that while it may seem equitable to offer the same reward to different individuals doing the same job on a particular grade, one has to recognise the possibility of variations in their performance. Therefore, one can challenge the fairness of a system that dispenses a uniform rate to workers irrespective of their level of performance. Apparently, a criticism more valid in the past than at the present time is that job evaluation reinforced discrimination, particularly sexual discrimination, amongst employees (Cowling and James, 1994). This arose when greater weightings were given to factors supportive of men (e.g. physical strength or having completed an apprenticeship), while aspects of women's work, such as dexterity or caring, received a lower weighting.

OTHER SYSTEMS

In recent times there is a view that instead of abandoning job evaluation it should be made more flexible to reflect the internal and external worth of jobs (CIPD, 2004). Armstrong and Brown (2001) maintain that the demise of job evaluation has been overstated, and refer to new perspectives such as competency-based job evaluation, associated with broad banding; the latter is considered a way of retaining the positive features of traditional pay scales while reducing some of the less desirable effects. Broad banding entails compressing a hierarchy of pay grades or salary ranges into a number of wider bands with the aim of rewarding people who adapt to new challenges and expand their roles (CIPD, 2004). Broadband structures could be viewed 'as increasing the extent to which managers have discretion over the setting of internal differentials, introduce more flexibility and permit organisations to reward performance or skills acquisition as well as job size. Their attraction is that they achieve this while retaining a skeleton grading system which gives order to the structure and helps justify differentials' (Torrington *et al.*, 2005).

As a single factor approach, competence and skill analysis amounts to an analysis of the competence or skill requirements of a job using an appropriate technique. The relevance of the individual's competence to the needs of the organisation is emphasised simply because there is no point in rewarding employees for knowledge and skills that have no operational significance for the organisation. This approach has particular value in situations where the deployment of skills has a material bearing on outcomes, as in the case of the jobs of scientific and professional staff, and could be suited to modern conditions of flatter organisational structures where there is an emphasis on flexibility, multi-skilling and teamwork.

This system, as a non-analytical approach to job evaluation, would be difficult to use in equal value claims and is likely to be unsuitable when used in organisations with firm bureaucratic structures. (An equal value claim arises when an employee asserts that his or her job, though different, is equal in nature to a job that has been given a higher rating. The first legal case in the United Kingdom governed by the Equal Pay Act 1970 (amended 1984) was *Haywood v Cammell Laird Shipbuilders*, where a cook's work was found to be equal to that of a printer, carpenter and thermal insulation engineer.)

Over the years implementation of the Act has become highly complicated, with cases typically involving expert witnesses on both sides. *Pickstone v Freemans plc* (1988 IRLR 357; HL), for example, took nine years to reach a decision and was won in the end because the tribunal agreed with Pickstone's expert witnesses rather than those of Freemans. Other complicating factors include access to rewards beyond the immediate payment, for example to pensions, and questions over extending the time limits on entitlement to back pay (currently two years) where an employee wins a case (Newman, 2001). Ways of streamlining the system, for example through appointing assessors to help tribunals come to decisions without referring cases to higher courts, are under consideration, but any new system could not be in contravention of the right to a fair trial established under the Human Rights Act 1998.

EXTERNAL INFLUENCES

The 'internal relativities' emphasis outlined in the previous section when examining job evaluation is no longer the overriding consideration when it comes to the determination of rewards. It appears that external market and environmental conditions are now of greater importance. Over the past decade the political environment has had an impact on the determination of rewards. Since 1979 employment legislation in the United Kingdom has weakened the power of the trade unions. The system of the 'closed shop', where everyone doing a particular job governed by a trade union agreement is required to join the same union, is illegal. A large number of employers have taken steps to move away from collective bargaining systems to more individualised reward systems. Performance-related pay, which will be discussed later in this chapter, is a good example of this trend. It is a payment system that takes into account the quality of performance on the job instead of being specifically related to a wage or salary grade.

External competitiveness, rather than internal equity that is associated with job evaluation schemes, is now a live issue in the determination of rewards. This is evident when organisations set out to adopt market-driven reward systems where the rate for the job reflects the rate required to attract recruits rather than being based on a payment system that is underpinned by an internal grading structure.

There are a number of 'sources of information' on the levels of pay and employment conditions amongst organisations employing (and hence competing for) employees of particular types, such as specific professions in the labour market. These would include official national statistics on incomes and economic data, data services relating to income from private agencies, company surveys whereby HRM specialists solicit relevant information on remuneration from their counterparts in other organisations, groups of organisations that are committed to the exchange of information on remuneration on a frequent basis, and data collected from external job advertisements and external job applicants.

It is important to compare like with like, and to do so necessitates the preparation of a job description, and not reliance on a job title alone. Of the sources of information listed above, it would appear that well-conceived exchanges of information on pay between companies are highly effective if they are based on reliable job descriptions. Apart from the competitiveness of the remuneration package on offer, one should endeavour to ensure that it is fair. Finally, the role of performance appraisal, which has been discussed in Chapter 8, should be considered in the context of the determination of rewards.

Types of reward system

There are a variety of schemes on offer, such as the following:

■ time rates

■ payment by results;

■ individual/group performance-related pay (including profit-related pay);

■ skill/competency-based pay;

■ cafeteria or flexible benefit systems.

TIME RATES

When a reward system is related to the number of hours worked it is referred to as a payment system based on time rates; this is common in collective bargaining. Time rates can be classified as an hourly rate, a weekly wage or a monthly salary. Time rates became an issue with the establishment of the national minimum wage in the United Kingdom (see Box 9.1).

Box 9.1: The minimum wage

In 1999 the minimum wage was set at £3.60 an hour for employees over 21, and £3 for those aged 18 to 21. In October 2005 the rate was increased to £5.05 an hour, and as at November 2007 was £5.52. It applies to most workers in the United Kingdom, including home workers, commission workers, part-time workers, casual workers and pieceworkers. Extra money paid to workers who work overtime or do shift work is not included. The National Insurance Contributions Office, part of HM Revenue & Customs, is charged with ensuring the minimum wage is paid, but there is no separate agency to police the system. The Low Pay Commission monitors how the system operates in practice. Refusing to pay the national minimum wage is a criminal offence, which can result in a fine of up to £5,000. Dismissing a worker because he or she becomes eligible for the national minimum wage will count as unfair dismissal.

The trade unions are worried about the effectiveness of the system to force compliance with the minimum wage. There is a view that it could lead to job losses, but equally certain categories of workers (e.g. women in part-time employment) could benefit. With regard to job losses, shortly before the minimum wage was implemented on 1 April 1999, a poll of more than 2,200 small businesses carried out by Peninsula

Business Services, a Manchester law consultancy, revealed that 65 per cent of respondents expect that the introduction of the minimum wage will lead to job cuts or a reduction in recruitment and 67 per cent expect the minimum wage to have a negative financial impact on their business. The results of a survey (Taylor, 2000) of companies by Income Data Services would challenge the expectation with regard to job losses. There was no evidence of job losses in low paying sectors of the economy because of the minimum wage. Where job losses do occur in low paying areas, such as the textiles and clothing industry, the main reason for the contraction in numbers employed was said to be overseas competition.

In the above survey it was also suggested that a growing number of companies are paying a minimum wage higher than legally required, because of the competitive conditions in a tightening labour market. It is interesting to note that more companies are paying the adult minimum rate to workers from the age of 18, and some even from 16, instead of 21.

Source: based on Department of Trade and Industry, 1999; Oldfield, 1999; Taylor, 1999, 2000

Question

Do you think it is a good idea to have a legally enforceable minimum wage?

According to Income Data Services (IDS), increasing numbers of employers in business are setting pay rates for the lower paid above the official minimum wage in order to maintain a competitive advantage in hiring staff. Established UK retailers, such as Tesco, Marks & Spencer's, and Dolland and Atichison, pay rates well above the national minimum wage (Turner, 2004). The body representing employers in the United Kingdom – the Confederation of British Industry (CBI) often suggests that restraint should be exercised in raising the minimum wage, the reason given is to preserve levels of employment. The CBI's position is in sharp contrast to that of the Trades Union Congress (TUC), who advocates a higher percentage increase (Moules, 2004). However, according to a CIPD survey of employers whilst 40 per cent employers benchmark reward packages against inflation and 35 per cent benchmark against competitors, only 10 per cent took the minimum wage into consideration, hence reinforcing the impression given by the retailers referred to above (Fuller, 2006).

Traditionally, factory workers received a weekly wage and it is common for office workers to receive a monthly salary. By contrast, part-time employees receive an hourly rate. As stated earlier, jobs have grades attached to them following job evaluation, and each grade has a particular level of pay associated with it. Within a grade it is common to have an incremental scale in which employees move along on the basis of one point each year until the maximum of the scale is reached. This system rewards experience rather than performance; in effect the employee receives an incremental award normally on an annual basis for serving time in the job. Time rates place the main emphasis on the value of the task (the work system process) as influenced by job evaluation, and not explicitly on the value of the skills and abilities the employee brings to the job, or on the quality or quantity of performance.

A stated advantage of the time rates system is that it is open to inspection and is equitable in the sense that employees doing the same job will be on the same grade, though there could be differences in income owing to staff being on different positions on the incremental scale. Other advantages are the following:

■ The system encourages the retention of human resources by creating stability, staff knowing that there are gradual increases in rewards within given grades. The rationale is that employee retention and the stability of the labour force offer staff the chance to enhance their skills and efficiency over time with obvious cost advantages.

■ The system is relatively easy to administer and allows labour costs to be predicted.

■ The system does not emphasise quantity of output to the detriment of quality.

A criticism levelled at the time rates system is that while theoretically costs of output decrease as the competence of employees grows, employees have no motivation to become more productive. For example, a worker receiving a wage of £300 a week increases output dramatically from 200 to 300 units per week. This clearly is to the advantage of the organisation but not to the employee in monetary terms. The reward received by the employee in the example is the same whether the output figure is 200 or 300. This raises the issue of why an individual should want to be a good performer if good and bad performers on a particular grade receive the same pay. Another matter to consider is that the traditional form of progression up the hierarchy from one grade to the next by way of promotion or career development has to be revised in the light of delayering and flatter organisational structures.

PAYMENT BY RESULTS

One way to address the criticisms levelled at the time rates system is to introduce a payment by results (PBR) scheme. PBR links pay to the quantity of the individual's output. A forerunner of PBR is the piecework system where pay is linked to the number of units of work produced. This was common in manufacturing industry; for example, if the piece-rate is £2 per unit and a worker produces 200 units of output, the income received is £400. Any figure above or below 200 units would lead to more or less than £400. Another example is the commission received by sales representatives, and this depends on sales volume. The rationale usually put forward to support the PBR scheme consists of the following:

■ The employee is motivated to put in extra effort because by doing so they will receive additional income.

■ Although there is an absence of overall equity in the sense that not everybody doing the same job will receive the same level of income, there is fairness in that the level of reward is related to the level of production.

■ There are likely to be cost advantages since wages are directly linked to production and less supervision is required.

Prior to the introduction of a PBR scheme method study techniques are used to establish the best procedures to do the job. Then rates of pay are fixed after calculating the time taken to complete the tasks by the employee working at the appropriate or correct speed. As a general principle, in accordance with the British Standards Institution 100 Scale, one could expect that an employee on a PBR scheme working at the correct speed should be able to earn a third more than a colleague on a time rates system (Cowling and James, 1994).

When considering the measurement of output it has to be acknowledged that in certain jobs output cannot be easily measured. Managerial jobs and many jobs in the service sector do not have easily quantifiable output. For example, a swimming pool attendant's pay could not be based on the number of lives saved. In this example the output is not controlled by the worker (the attendant). Obviously the expenditure of effort and the exercise of skill are critical variables when it comes to life saving, but factors such as the number of swimmers in the pool and their levels of expertise are outside the control of the swimming pool attendant.

It is likely that PBR schemes geared to the individual will stimulate the quantity of output, but management must be on its guard in case increased output is at the expense of quality. An example of an adverse impact on quality is a dramatic increase in the scrap rate following an increase in a PBR worker's output in a factory. Therefore, if there is a PBR scheme in operation, there are obvious advantages in having quality control mechanisms firmly in place.

Apart from the question of quality, the following reservations should be noted:

- As was stated above, it could be difficult to measure output in certain jobs.

- In the drive to increase production safety standards may be compromised.

- Passions could be aroused between workers and management if the workers view the PBR scheme as a device to obtain greater effort from them without commensurate reward, and where they have to haggle over money. If workers feel that they have been short-changed there is the inclination to withhold critical information about job performance.

- In a climate of suspicion and distrust between trade unions and management the trade union representatives may use the PBR scheme, particularly in relation to pay, as a means to put pressure on management and create conflict.

Taking a positive view, it is suggested that PBR schemes can be effective where they are well conceived, where work measurement and output measurement are possible, where good prior communication and consultation with employees have taken place, and where there is a healthy rapport between management and workers (Cannell and Long, 1991). As a final comment one might pose the question if PBR schemes are still valid? According to Torrington *et al.* (2005), there is evidence to show that they are in decline, but then they go on to say that 'the results of the New Earning surveys, however, show that PBR is still widely used in some shape or form by employers of manual workers'.

PERFORMANCE-RELATED PAY (PRP)

Unlike payment by results examined in the previous section, performance-related pay considers not only results or output but also actual behaviour in the job. The individual's performance is measured against previously set objectives, or compared with the various tasks listed in the job description, using performance appraisal techniques discussed in Chapter 8. Following this assessment, normally conducted by the manager, with or without professional assistance, there is an allocation of rewards. Rewards linked to performance could consist of a lump sum, or a bonus as a percentage of basic salary, with quality of performance determining the magnitude of the percentage increase; or alternatively accelerated movement up a pay scale.

In connection with the last observation, excellent performance might, for example, justify a movement upwards of two points on the scale, while poor performance could result in staying at the current level. Some incremental pay scales have a bar at a particular point, beyond which there is entitlement to discretionary points. To go beyond the bar and benefit from the discretionary points it would be necessary for the individual to receive a favourable performance evaluation. It should be noted that management reserves the right to award discretionary points.

Designing appropriate schemes, which provide satisfactory incentives for employees, is not straightforward, but Fisher (2001) offers the following steps as a guideline:

■ Take account of the corporate environment through a research phase – that is, analyse business performance over the past five years and classify the contribution of employee groupings (such as departments or teams) to the performance.

■ Combine goals with emotions – be aware that people's reactions to incentives will not only be rational but will also depend on how they feel about the situation; for example, employers who use only money as the reward may be perceived as cynical and uncaring.

■ Ensure congruency between organisational goals and personal goals.

■ Focus on communication – agree a statement of morale, motivation and performance with departmental heads and make sure that the process is properly explained. Use success stories to spur people on. Crucially, it is important to avoid the 'launch it and leave it' attitude amongst managers.

■ Provide adequate skills training for employees.

■ Respond effectively to feedback from employees.

Certain conditions are said to be necessary for a PRP scheme to be effective (Applebaum and Shappiro, 1991):

■ In order to make the measurement of performance a meaningful activity it is essential that there should be sufficient differences between individuals on the basis of performance.

■ The pay range must be of sufficient width to accommodate significant differences in the basic pay of employees.

■ The measurement of performance must be a valid and reliable exercise, and it must be possible to relate the outcome of the measurement process to pay.

■ Appraisers are skilful in setting performance standards and in conducting appraisals.

■ The culture of the organisation is supportive.

■ The remuneration package offered is competitive and fair, and the organisation is adept at relating pay to performance.

■ Mutual trust exists between managers and their subordinates, and managers are prepared to manage with an eagerness to communicate performance criteria and face making difficult decisions.

While the above conditions are supportive of PRP schemes it is possible to encounter conditions, such as the following, which produce a negative impact (Applebaum and Shappiro, 1991; Goss, 1994):

■ No attempt is made to relate individual performance to organisational objectives.

■ Appraisals are not conducted fairly, because either output is difficult to measure or the appraiser is incompetent.

■ Openness, trust, joint problem solving and commitment to organisational objectives are adversely affected by the introduction of PRP schemes.

■ The introduction of PRP schemes produces adversarial conditions when it creates supporters and opponents of such schemes.

Having examined the conditions necessary for the introduction of PRP schemes, and being aware of conditions likely to produce a negative impact, it is legitimate to ask: what are the advantages and disadvantages of such schemes? First we shall note the following advantages of individually based PRP schemes (Goss, 1994):

- Incentives are linked to meeting targets or objectives, as well as to the quality of perform- ance as perceived by superiors. Linking pay to performance that lends itself to measurement is considered fairer than awarding across-the-board cost-of-living increases, which do not discriminate between high and low performers.

- Where employee performance can be measured and the amount of money available to reward performance is sufficient to motivate effort, it saves money if the organisation targets rewards on those who perform.

- High performers are attracted to PRP cultures in the knowledge that pay is linked to pro- ductive effort, and that poor achievement is discouraged.

- Employees receive useful feedback on their performance.

- There is an emphasis on a results-oriented culture, with the accent on effort directed at activities that the organisation values.

The following could be considered disadvantages of individually based PRP schemes:

- Behaviour is rewarded, which one would expect to occur anyway in accordance with the employment contract. The argument goes that good performance is expected and pro- vision is made for it, and where there is poor performance it is the job of management to sort it out.

- Open communication between managers and subordinates could be discouraged, because subordinates are less likely to divulge information on personal shortcomings just in case such disclosures act to their disadvantage.

- The rewarding of self-centred individualism can undermine cooperation and teamwork, which are necessary for coping with climates characterised by complexity and interdepend- ency (Pearce, 1991).

- The growth of managerial control over subordinates is promoted, with the effect of iso- lating the individual; this could affect teamwork.

- Poor performers are punished; this is unfortunate because it is in the organisation's interest to motivate this group in order to improve their performance.

- The existence of trade union opposition could sour relationships between management and the representatives of the workers. Sometimes trade unions object to the individual- istic nature of rewards that run counter to the spirit of collective bargaining, and there is currently a view that too great a part is played by subjective managerial judgement in the determination of rewards. With respect to the latter, there is the fear that equitable criteria are not applied objectively to all employees.

A number of practitioners have endorsed PRP schemes particularly in the West: however, they are being adopted globally, albeit with some adaptation for local culture (see Case example 9.1).

CASE EXAMPLE 9.1

PERFORMANCE-BASED PAY AT SINOELECTRONICS

Sinoelectronics is a large manufacturer, with over 7,000 employees, producing consumer electronic goods in China. It has achieved a high rate of growth since the mid-1990s and is principally targeting the domestic and developing economy markets. The success and growth of the company are related to its low cost base, but equally, quality assurance and sufficient innovation are requirements of the market. The culture in China has tended to be fairly egalitarian, and hence individually-based PRP has had to be introduced carefully in order to gain acceptance. It is combined with other forms of reward. A typical example for an engineer is as follows: monthly base pay (46 per cent of total reward), monthly production bonus (23 per cent), annual profit-related bonus (23 per cent), annual bonus (8 per cent). The annual bonus is paid at the time of the Annual Spring Festival which is an expensive time for most Chinese (similar to Christmas in the West).

This combination of traditional monthly pay and various forms of variable pay, including individual performance, has enabled Sinoelectronics to move its employees gradually towards adopting a more entrepreuneurial perspective. Whilst this has been embraced by the younger generations, some older workers have been less enthusiastic but in the main have accepted the new ways.

Source: based on Lewis, 2006

Question

To what extent do you think worker reactions to reward strategies relate to national and organisational culture?

In a survey of European employers it was found that 14 per cent of UK employees receive PRP, which compares to a European average of 21 per cent (Fuller, 2006). Significant differences were found between different sectors. In financial services 28 per cent of employees received PRP whilst in education the figure was just 5 per cent. Other figures are provided in Table 9.2.

The motivational significance of PRP schemes has been challenged (Kohn, 1993; Thompson, 1993). The results of a survey of managers at British Telecom indicated that the PRP scheme was unfairly administered and there was scepticism of its effect on performance; in fact the payments made had an adverse effect on performance (IRS, 1991). British Telecom suspended its PRP scheme for managers following a pay comparison study in which it was established that the company was paying its managers between 11 and 14 per cent above remuneration levels for managers in similar jobs in outside organisations (Taylor, 1994). This line of action was driven by the need to keep costs in check and to retain competitiveness. The importance of external comparability in the determination of rewards is evident in this situation.

The difficulties encountered with individually based schemes were also highlighted in a research study carried out amongst Inland Revenue employees. A major finding was that performance-related schemes generated much resentment as employees faced conflict as a result of the quantity of work demands putting pressure on quality. Also, 60 per cent of respondents

Table 9.2 Proportions of employees receiving PRP in Europe

Occupational area	Percentage of employees receiving PRP
Financial services	28%
Transport/distribution	23%
Retail	21%
Travel/leisure	20%
Engineering	18%
Business sevices	16%
IT	13%
Science/pharmaceutical	11%
Manufacturing	8%
Education	5%

Source: based on Fuller, 2006

were not too happy at having individual performance targets imposed rather than being the outcome of discussion. The researcher concluded that group-based schemes might have the edge over individually-based schemes (Halligan, 1997).

An IRS survey (2007) of 87 PRP schemes reported mixed results. Some 80 per cent thought that the scheme had led to improved individual performance, approximately 75 per cent thought that it provided a better system for rewarding performance, only 50 per cent thought that it had actually motivated staff. Some 67 per cent thought the process was very time consuming and 60 per cent thought that the sums involved were too small to motivate employees.

Even though one has to admit there are problems with PRP schemes, as reported above, nevertheless Torrington *et al.* (2005) maintain that there is case study evidence to indicate that it is possible to implement PRP successfully in appropriate circumstances. Supportive circumstances or conditions have been identified earlier in this chapter.

Group PRP schemes

These schemes, which link rewards to outcomes such as meeting budget targets or organisational profitability, are said to avoid the threat to cooperative modes of working associated with individually based PRP schemes by de-emphasising the individualistic nature of rewards. According to Murlis (1994), team-based pay seeks to eliminate the divisive nature of individually-based PRP schemes. Reilly *et al.* (2005) found that a trial of team-based pay in the UK health service had been successful. However, while team-based pay improved service and staff attitudes, it was recognised that certain contextual factors were needed to make the reward system work. Significantly, the task (in this case a public health project) had to be directly attributable to the team, and the team members had to be relatively equal in their functions (and hence in their basic pay). Difficulties could have arisen if the team was made up of staff from significantly different professional groups with different pay structures and levels.

The CIPD (2007a) states that team- and group-based pay is most effective where the team has standalone targets, autonomy, and is composed of people who work interdependently in a stable way over time. It is vital that communication is good so that everyone understands and accepts the targets, process and reward outcomes. The effective schemes can encourage team-oriented behaviour including a sharing of skills and knowledge.

The group PRP schemes include the exercise of share options (see Box 9.2) and profit sharing. A group scheme related to profit is called profit-related pay.

Box 9.2: Options for senior executives

The use of share options by senior executives of large companies in the United Kingdom is a contentious issue and much criticism has been levelled at share option schemes. Though the cost of such schemes is not a charge to the company's profit and loss account under current accounting conventions, it is a potential claim on the company's future profits and so reduces the payouts available to the other shareholders. These rewards are inadequately related to management performance and send a poor signal to employees who are not included in the scheme. In many cases executives receive big rewards if their companies achieve no more than the average growth of the economy. A finding from a survey by the National Institute of Economic and Social Research in the United Kingdom (*Financial Times*, 1999) suggests that there is little obvious link between the rewards generated by such schemes and company profitability or total shareholder returns.

Share option schemes are attractive to the recipients. If the company's shares increase in value then the directors stand to gain, but if they decrease they merely lose a potential profit opportunity. By contrast, shareholders incur genuine losses in the latter situation. Share options fail the key test of a good incentive scheme, which is that the interests of shareholders and managers should be as closely aligned as possible.

There is a growing feeling that share incentive schemes should be reserved for exceptional performance, and not for meeting the requirements of a normal job. Also, it would appear that not enough is done to share the benefits of success throughout the workforce. However, there is an indication of some movement in this direction. For example, Safeway – the supermarket chain – provides a share option scheme for all its permanent employees.

Following the publication of the Greenbury Report in 1995, L Tips (long-term incentives) were considered appropriate. They have been viewed as an alternative to share option schemes for senior executives who can profit from the sale of these shares three years later if targets (earnings per share measured against a comparator group of companies) are met. In 1997 Niall FitzGerald, the then Chairman of Unilever, expressed reservations about the usefulness of L Tips if the stock market became bearish. In the scheme designed by Unilever the company's performance will be based on the real growth of the business and the value it creates above inflation, instead of relying on performance relative to other companies forming the comparator group. (*Financial Times*, 1995; FitzGerald, 1997).The results of a 2004 survey on executive directors' pay, undertaken by Deloitte and Touche in the United Kingdom, indicated that a number of companies are cutting back on share option schemes as changes in accounting rules, pressure from shareholders, and weak equity markets have combined to make this system of remuneration less attractive. The survey also showed that only 20 per cent of pay schemes introduced in the past year were share option

▶

plans, compared with 60 per cent in the same survey three years earlier. Overall, 83 per cent of FTSE 100 companies had share option plans in place, down 10 per cent from a year earlier.

Companies tend to be moving towards other forms of incentive pay, including deferred bonuses or performance share plans where stocks are awarded to directors or senior executives only if certain benchmarks are met, rather than granting share options whose worth is entirely dependent on the movement in the share price. The new international accounting standard on share options, as from January 2005, will force companies to account for the giving of share options in the profit and loss account. This is a stimulus for a lot of companies to look at their share option schemes with a view to establishing whether they are getting value for money. The rethink of share option schemes has also been influenced by the reaction of shareholders, who view them as an expensive and inefficient way to reward executive performance that may not be related in a significant way to share price movement. Also the weakness of the market for equities in the past few years has reduced the value of previously granted share options, and this could also be another justification for dispensing with their use.

Source: based on Beattie, 2004

If you have to fail, it is best to fail as the boss of a big US corporation. When Bob Vardelli left Home Depot the shares held by shareholders were worth somewhat less than they were when he arrived six years ago, but he walked away with a severance package worth $210 million. One recognises that it is not easy to find the right mix of incentives for executives. A miserly pay package will attract weak candidates. A package that does not reward success will invite bureaucratic box ticking, and poorly designed executive compensation can also encourage excessive risk taking, short-sightedness, or even fraud.

If American business leaders were appropriately remunerated one would not see, for example, stock options revalued as the share price falls, a reward for failure if ever there was one. Nor would we see backdated options, which are simply an illegal attempt to hide legal but embarrassing generous handouts. Perhaps this reflects certain inadequacies in the way Compensation Committees operate generally in corporations.

High executive salaries and bonuses are now political dynamite, with a high risk of populace backlash. More regulation does not seem to be the answer. It would be preferable if CEOs themselves showed restraint and stopped giving capitalism a bad name. Such action might be in their own interests. Jeff Immelt, who succeeded Jack Welch at General Electric, has not delivered substantially better returns than Bob Nardelli at Home Depot, but with a modest pay package he has more friends and more respect.

Source: based on *Financial Times*, 2007

Question

Does the reward level of top managers have an impact on the motivation of workers?

PROFIT-RELATED PAY

The original idea of profit-related pay was that by linking pay to profits companies could make their wage costs variable. Employees would be given an incentive to work harder, and in good times would reap the rewards, while in bad times they would share the pain, though it is possible to design schemes so that the employees are safeguarded when profits fall. Companies can use profit-related pay as a bonus paid in addition to existing salary, or by getting employees to swap part of their salary for profit-related pay. A major reason why many companies that use profit-related pay, such as Boots, do so is because it is a more tax-efficient means of paying bonuses.

The tendency now is for schemes to cover all or most employees as opposed to senior grades as in the past. According to the recruitment manager at Boots, 'the scheme gives our workforce a greater stake in the business. It means they switch off the lights at night and don't keep the machinery running, and may have lessened pay claims' (Kellaway, 1993). Profit-related pay may not be suitable for all companies however. The companies that have little to gain from such schemes are those with very low paid workers – who pay little tax – or where profits are so volatile that they are impossible to predict. Some companies steer clear of profit-related pay because they prefer incentive schemes based on individual rather than group performance. But other companies, such as Boots (now Alliance Boots) and the Halifax Building Society (now a bank and amalgamated with the Bank of Scotland), view profit-related pay as an addition rather than an alternative to individual incentives (Kellaway, 1993).

Amongst the alleged benefits of group profit-related pay schemes are the following:

■ Employees identify more closely with the success of the organisation, and this has obvious advantages in terms of commitment and improved organisational performance.

■ There is a breaking down or removal of the 'them' and 'us' barrier.

■ Cooperation and working together for mutual benefit is encouraged.

■ There is an awareness of the link between performance and organisational profitability, leading to a greater awareness of costs and their impact on performance. This realisation is beneficial to the organisation when wage claims are submitted.

■ When adverse trading conditions, such as a recession, hit the organisation the element of profit devoted to pay can fall. Such an eventuality is a preferable alternative to laying off employees.

■ Group pressure could raise the performance levels of poor performers.

Research evidence (Freeman, 2001) has indicated that profit sharing and share option schemes may have a positive impact on performance. A study of 299 UK companies between 1995 and 1998 indicated that companies with such schemes involving non-managerial employees tended to strike the right note with employees, giving them information about business performance. Subsequently, company-wide productivity was seen to increase following the introduction of the schemes. Those adopting profit sharing showed increases of 17 per cent value added per worker, and those choosing share option plans recorded 12 per cent value added per worker. But when attention is focused on chief executives they seem to benefit unjustifiably from bonuses based on profit. It was concluded from a study conducted by the Economic and Social Research Council (ESRC) in the UK that annual bonuses paid to chief executives lacked disclosure and are poorly linked to company performance (Tucker, 2004). An example of company-wide profit sharing is provided in Case example 9.2.

STAFF ENGAGEMENT AND REWARD AT THE JOHN LEWIS PARTNERSHIP

The John Lewis partnership is a well-known retailer in the United Kingdom. Staff are partners in the organisation which does not have external shareholders. 'There's a danger when we talk about partners that people think it's all about brotherhood and apple pie, but we're a commercial business' (Tracey Killen, Personnel Director, cited in Faragher, 2007). The partnership approach means that there is extensive consultation with partners. According to Killen this is an advantage when compared to traditional company ownership structures because, although it can take a little time to consider the views of partners, the company is not driven by the short-termism that typifies many shareholder structures. 'It's always going to be 100 per cent important to be regarded as a good employer by those who work here, so we should be most focused on how we're perceived internally. Our most important audience is our internal one' (Tracey Killen, cited in Faragher, 2007).

When it comes to reward, a similar philosophy underlies the approach. Because of the co-ownership structure, all staff share in its success. Every March, partners share any profit the Partnership has made. Reward is distributed in the form of a 'partnership bonus'. According to Killen, this has a strong impact on people's commitment to the organisation: 'People's commitment still impresses me. I'm amazed by their ability to put their personal concerns aside to secure the best outcome for the business. This business is stuffed full of seriously good and committed people.'

This commitment has translated into notable success. In 2007 pre-tax profits rose by 27 per cent and John Lewis and Waitrose, the partnership's main two brands, were rated first and second place as the United Kingdom's favourites by the Verdict poll of 60,000 shoppers. As a result, partners received a share of a record 'bonus pot' of £155 million (up by 29 per cent on the previous year). The typical partner received a bonus worth 18 per cent of their annual salary. This is a good example of the reward system supporting the HRM ideal of mutuality – shared and mutual benefit between the employee and the organisation.

It is worth noting that in addition to profit-related bonuses, John Lewis offers a reward package that incorporates other aspects. For example, there is a bonus saving scheme through which partners can save all or part of their bonus tax-free, flexible working arrangements are available to all, regardless of family circumstances, and a final salary pension is provided. Somewhat unusually, there are also other schemes that add to commitment. The Golden Jubilee Trust is the Partnership's charity that funds about 50 people each year to spend up to six months working for a UK charity whilst still receiving full pay. 'Once in a Lifetime' is another scheme that enables groups of partners to apply for funding to take a 'once in a lifetime' trip.

Source: based on Faragher, 2007

Question

Which aspects of the approach at John Lewis might be exported to companies with different business models?

A disadvantage of group-based schemes, where rewards are linked to company profitability, is that the employee may see the rewards as too distant from individual effort, more so because of having to rely on others as well as the influence of external factors (e.g. competitors and markets).

Cases where management rewarded employees for working as members of teams or groups appear in Case example 9.3.

GROUP-BASED REWARDS

Pearl Assurance

Pearl Assurance was unable to pass on the cost of significant salary increases to its customers because of the prevalence of acute market competition and economic conditions of low inflation. Therefore it had to give serious consideration to the most appropriate remuneration system in these circumstances. Previously a PRP system was in operation, but when salary settlements were below 3 per cent of payroll cost managers under this system had little scope to use their discretion and reward staff on the basis of merit.

Team-based pay was introduced and it was the job of the heads of the sections or teams to meet and rank the performance of each section, and to determine the pay increase each section was to receive. Then each head was expected to evaluate the performance of individuals as team players and exercise discretion in the award of individual salary increases.

Source: based on Trevor, 1993

The Automobile Association

At the Automobile Association team-based incentives were introduced following the creation of a flatter organisation structure. The aims of teams of 30 were to provide high-quality service and maintain a quick response rate, but it was proving difficult to create team spirit because teams spent much of their time on the road with a high level of individual autonomy.

Targets were set for teams covering such criteria as the number of jobs completed at the roadside, the average time taken to complete the job, and the average time taken to respond to a Relay call when the motorist's car had to be transported to the home or to a garage. The performance of teams was measured against the above criteria, and teams competed in leagues. The winners received tangible prizes, such as outings and vouchers to use in stores, coupled with the intrinsic reward of the status stemming from being the winning team. The winners were announced quarterly and annually.

Source: based on Pickard, 1993

Replacing PRP at Citizen's Advice

Citizen's Advice is a UK nationwide voluntary sector organisation that provides advice to people on issues such as finance and legal rights. They have 400 employees who support a large volunteer workforce. In 2001 they had introduced an individual PRP scheme along with a 'toil' scheme through which employees could build up hours to take as holiday through working overtime. The reward process had become dysfunctional because it fostered individualism that clashed with the organisation's collectivity-oriented culture. In addition, staff retention was difficult and there were many unfilled vacancies. As a result, many employees had to cover extra work and so built up large amounts of 'toil'. Managers ended up with very little discretion to manage the workforce, which was constantly overworked, and alternately having to do overtime and taking time off earned through toil.

Citizen's Advice reviewed its reward scheme and introduced signficant changes. Instead of having the individualism of PRP a simpler structure of three salary tiers (administrators, professionals and executive management) were designated. The pay rates were set using internal job evaluation and external benchmarking against similar voluntary sector organisations. The basic pay is supplemented by annual bonuses that are paid to teams. This approach has been found to fit much better with the culture and as David Harker, CEO put it: 'we have taken the opportunity to remove this potential for conflict (the PRP scheme) as well as improving our reward package for our many committed staff' (cited in Fuller, 2005). However, Citizen's Advice has retained the ability to give individuals a bonus where it is warranted.

Following the changes to a more egalitarian reward system vacanies have dropped from over 20 per cent to 8–12 per cent (depending on the department) in 12 months and 17 per cent productivty improvements have been made in active working time.

Source: based on Fuller, 2005

Questions

1. The intention of team- and group-based rewards is to increase in-group ties and mutual motivation. Are there circumstances under which group-based reward could be devisive?

2. What might managers do to avoid such outcomes?

SKILL-BASED PAY

The schemes examined above have concentrated on the 'outputs' of work activity, such as volume and quality of production or profit. By comparison skill-based pay, which is established in the United States and growing in its appeal to employers in the United Kingdom, places the emphasis on 'inputs' that consist of knowledge, skills and competencies injected into the job by employees (Donkin, 1998; IRS, 2003). In the distant past the craftsman received differentiated rewards at different stages of his career. As he moved from apprentice to master the development of skill was reflected in increased reward. In the not too distant past the growth of mass production systems accompanied by advances in technology gave rise to the simplification of work and to a significant amount of deskilling, which had the effect of maintaining a steady demand for unskilled workers.

In the current climate the march of new technology has meant that there is a contraction in the number of unskilled jobs and a growth in the demand for multi-skilled workers. This has been brought about by a team-based approach towards work and the need for flexibility in staffing arrangements. To foster a multi-skill capability in the labour force calls for the acquisition and use of more skills than required hitherto. In order to provide an incentive to employees to broaden their skill base some employers are linking rewards to skills' acquisition and deployment.

According to IDS (1992), before introducing a skill-based system there should be good planning, a fair amount of consultation and employee participation, as well as training directed at the acquisition of new technical skills and teamworking skills. Subsequently, rewards would be linked to both skills' acquisition and use, and perhaps also to the level of performance directly associated with the deployment of those skills, if such an exercise is possible. If it is not possible then an organisation can only hope that skills will be utilised in a manner compatible with high levels of performance.

A point to note in connection with skill-based pay is that management is well placed to use rewards to encourage and support changes in behaviour, i.e. acquisition of a broader range of skills, which are necessary to implement contemporary changes in organisational design and functioning. Also, the operation of a skill-based pay system requires attention to the skills to be rewarded, setting the right rate of pay, providing the appropriate level of training, putting in place the necessary procedures, and ensuring that sufficient time is invested wisely in the process. It said that skill-based pay schemes are beneficial in terms of job satisfaction and performance (Lawler *et al.*, 1993). However, Torrington *et al.* (2005) alert us to what they see as a major disadvantage associated with skill-based pay: that is skills obsolescence, which could arise in conditions of rapidly changing technology. In such an environment there is a danger that a skills-based pay system does not keep abreast of developments and the organisation pays enhanced rewards for skills that are no longer significant or are not required at all.

The cases shown in Case example 9.4 stress the importance of skill-based pay. In the UNISYS case the main emphasis is on the input of skill, but there is also an aspect of performance assessment. In the IBM case the interaction between organisational design and rewards is highlighted.

SKILL-BASED PAY

UNISYS

UNISYS moved away from a PRP scheme to a skill (competence)-based pay scheme. Behaviour was assessed using criteria such as teamwork, customer orientation, innovative practices, accountability and motivation. Employees assessed using these criteria were placed in four categories, with different levels of reward associated with each category.

Source: based on Huddart, 1994

IBM

IBM introduced changes to its pay structure involving a move towards skill or competence-based rewards and sensitivity to job market pay rates. The rates attached to particular jobs are linked to market pay rates within a system of general job categories. The number of levels of jobs in the management and professional area was reduced from 12 to four. The newly created levels represent broad bands containing a range of jobs within which individual employees move from one area to another within the organisation. Moving in this way means there is no change to the cost of the remuneration package because the employee remains within a broad pay band.

The new approach to pay has been influenced by IBM's changed philosophy linked to work design and career structures. The 'job for life' culture and automatic annual pay rises have been challenged. The intention is to create a 'human growth' culture where individual competence is recognised and rewarded. This will put pressure on employees to be concerned with their development and employability so as to secure their future with the company.

Source: based on North, 1993, 1994

Questions

1. What is the rationale for skill- or competence-based pay?

2. Is this approach likely to ensure high performance?

CAFETERIA OR FLEXIBLE BENEFIT SYSTEMS

The flexible benefit system is a departure from the traditional model of a single system of remuneration for everybody (Meyer, 2000). These systems are a way of managing rewards that are gaining in popularity in the United Kingdom, and are established in the United States where they are referred to as 'flexible benefits'. In Australia they are called 'packaged compensation', and in the United Kingdom they are known as the 'cafeteria' system. Since they are substitutes for pay they must be calculated within an overall remuneration or compensation package. Their popularity in the United States has no doubt been prompted by tax advantages, unlike the position in the United Kingdom, and mainly comprises life and accident insurance, medical and dental care, and care for children. In addition the growing costs of health care for companies in the United States motivated them to take flexible remuneration seriously. Companies give employees pre-tax 'flex credits' that they could use to meet the cost of health benefits.

In the United Kingdom flexible benefits have captured the imagination of HR practitioners as a means of providing employees with a degree of choice over the form that their remuneration takes, and as a useful measure in the recruitment and retention of human resources. According to Debbie Harrison, Human Resources Director, Financial Services Authority in the UK, the beauty of flexible benefits is that you can change your selection each year to suit your lifestyle (Harrison, 2001). A cafeteria system in the United Kingdom could be made up of such benefits as the company car, additional holiday entitlement, private health insurance, membership of social clubs, modification to working hours, special pension arrangements, mortgage loan subsidies and other benefits. Employees exercise choice when selecting a range of benefits from a menu that they consider important and to which they are entitled. Although a number of schemes apply to executive and managerial staff there is evidence to indicate that these schemes are becoming progressively available to other employees (Trapp, 2004). This trend is illustrated in Case example 9.5.

A CIPD survey (Richards, 2007) found that just over 10 per cent of respondents had adopted flexible pay schemes. Many organisations that had introduced schemes had done so as part of a move towards greater flexibility in organisation and working generally. The advantages, according to Richards (2007) are as follows:

■ Employees choose benefits to meet their needs and value those benefits more highly.

■ During periods of change (such as a merger) flexible benefits can be used to harmonise rewards.

■ Employers provide benefits at a known cost, regardless of the choices employees make.

■ Employees can have an idea of the full worth of the benefits they receive.

■ Employees are given a sense of control and involvement.

■ Employers are seen as more responsive to employees' needs.

■ The awarding of benefits such as company cars becomes less divisive than when this is done as a top-down decision.

■ Employers' requests for flexible working practices are seen as being more justifiable.

The disadvantages are:

■ The schemes can be complex to operate

■ Choices can cause problems (e.g., there could be difficulties if all employees decide to maximise their holidays).

CASE EXAMPLE 9.5

CAFETERIA SYSTEMS

Poplar Herca

Trapp (2004) reports a significant increase in companies implementing flexible reward packages. Some examples are as follows. Poplar Herca, a London-based housing association, was finding it difficult to recruit and retain employees in a tight labour market. It wanted to differentiate itself from other public sector employers and so introduced a cafeteria reward scheme. Its 240 employees can now choose from a range of benefits including private medical and dental insurance, annual health checks, subsidised home-computers and the option to 'buy' or 'sell' holiday entitlement. Poplar Herca has put considerable effort into communicating the scheme and has found it helpful in changing company culture and the perceptions of employees.

UBS

UBS, the investment bank, employs 6,500 people in the UK. It has used flexible benefits since 1996, but has now extended these to all employees. It has taken a consultative approach to developing the new scheme by using focus groups to understand what employees are really interested in.

Royal Bank of Scotland

Similarly, the Royal Bank of Scotland has also made extensive efforts to consult its workforce in this area. As a result it now has the option to take retail vouchers when profit share and bonuses are being awarded.

Source: based on Trapp, 2004

Question

Later in this chapter equity theory of motivation is discussed. Use equity theory to evaluate the potential motivational effects of a cafeteria reward system.

The following are issues to consider when adopting cafeteria or flexible benefit systems in the United Kingdom (IDS, 1991):

- Flexibility in the way remuneration systems are determined is necessary because of demographic changes (e.g. using the services of more women and older workers). However, it should be noted that the economic recession of the early 1990s and the continuing high levels of unemployment largely nullified the effects of demographic change. The economic situation improved as we moved into the latter part of the 1990s and this called for flexibility. For example, Price Waterhouse (now PricewaterhouseCoopers), an international firm of accountants/consultants, introduced a flexible benefits system in the United Kingdom in 1997 because it was losing too many female employees. But the scheme was designed in such a way as to appeal to all staff (Maitland, 1998).

- If flexible benefit systems are too individually based there is a danger that teamwork will be undermined.

- Every effort should be made to communicate the total benefits portfolio.

- Those who participate in the scheme have the advantage of choosing benefits considered relevant to their needs from a menu that is publicly available. This could have a beneficial effect on commitment.

- The position of spouses/partners with careers should be considered in order to avoid duplication of certain benefits (e.g. health insurance).

- When flexible benefits are costed there is greater awareness of the costs of employing people.

- Full advantage should be taken of the potential of information technology in the administration of schemes in order to keep the costs of operation within reasonable levels.

- The costs of schemes should be kept under review; in particular the administration of schemes when employees choose benefits that happen to be in great demand as an alternative to underutilised benefits.

- The tax implications of schemes should be considered. Some of the benefits are not taxed in the United Kingdom; for example, holidays, home computer purchase, life assurance (up to a maximum of four times salary), long-term disability and pension contributions. But other benefits are subjected to tax (Harrison, 2001).

■ The schemes may be more appropriate to situations where non-unionised labour exists. There is a belief that trade unions may consider such schemes a potential threat to standard remuneration packages. In appropriate circumstances it would appear sensible to involve the trade unions in the various deliberations. In the Price Waterhouse scheme referred to above there was widespread consultation with employees, because it was recognised that these schemes are complex and take time to become integrated into the firm's culture (Maitland, 1998). Therefore involvement of employees in this delicate process is necessary.

■ A feature of the schemes in the United Kingdom is their flexibility and individual bias, but in the United States the major attraction seems to be the tax implications and medical insurance cover.

Other matters to consider are that flexible remuneration arrangements are useful for multinational companies looking for ways to manage expatriate costs; that companies get rid of the perks-driven mentality of employees who expect certain entitlements as a right; and that employees who take part of their total income by way of flexible benefits experience a cost advantage (Donkin, 1994). In connection with the latter, it would be more economical to acquire, say, private medical cover through a company's group plan than on an individual basis out of personal disposable income.

PENSIONS

A pension can be viewed as a form of deferred pay and is a costly and widely used fringe benefit, but the reward management literature shows little interest in this topic (Marchington and Wilkinson, 2005). The occupational pension, as well as paid leave and sickness benefit, developed as part of a personnel policy with a paternalistic bias in the past. Initially the pension was seen as a way of managing retirement and later as a means of attracting and retaining a workforce. The tax relief aspect made pensions particularly attractive and that contributed to their growth. Recent developments in the form of a trend towards discontinuing final salary schemes and instead offering money-purchase alternatives, because of financial pressures, could have important HR implications (e.g. damaging the psychological contract as well as adverse motivational and recruitment consequences).

As stated, two main forms of pension are final salary and money purchase schemes. Final salary pensions provide benefits as a fraction of the final pay. They do not depend on investment returns and the employer contributes costs in excess of employee contributions and takes the financial risk. These schemes work particularly well for long-serving employees who have progressive increases in pay during their career. Money purchase pensions are provided by an accumulation of the contributions invested and so the level of benefit depends on investment returns and the cost of annuities at the point of retirement. The costs are fixed for the employer and the employee takes the financial risk. These schemes can work best for portfolio workers who move on regularly from one job to another. In recent years there has been a trend towards money purchase schemes because of the cost involved for the employer in final salary schemes.

In the United Kingdom all organisations employing more than five staff have to offer access to a stakeholder pension scheme. Stakeholder pension schemes are effectively low-cost personal pensions that are subject to government regulation. The schemes are run by recognised pension companies and employees can make contributions directly from their pay on a tax-free basis.

The CIPD (2007b) argues that choices in the provision of an occupational pension are a significant strategic issue for organisations. The cost is high but, apart from action at the points of recruitment and retirement, it is argued that employers do not put sufficient effort into communicating with employees the nature, benefits and costs of pension provision. The CIPD also notes that the choice of scheme relates to organisational culture. For example, some pensions encourage the view that employees are part of the organisation and are closely bound to it. Others promote the idea of employees as independent individuals who must take care of their own financial responsibilities.

International compensation

Companies operating internationally face a demanding challenge when devising and operating reward systems compatible with the achievement of their strategic long-term objectives. According to Dowling and Welch (2004):

> 'the successful management of international compensation and benefits requires knowledge of the laws, customs, environment, and employment practices of many foreign countries, familiarity with currency fluctuations, and the effect of inflation on compensation. Also, it is necessary to have an understanding of why and when special allowances must be supplied, and which allowances are necessary in the different countries – all within the context of shifting political, economic and social conditions.'

Since compensation programmes should be used to improve the international competitive standing of the global corporation, it is no surprise to find that flexibility and cost consciousness feature prominently in their delivery.

The following are considered likely objectives of international compensation (Dowling and Welch, 2004):

■ The policy should be consistent with the overall strategy, structure and business needs of the multinational enterprise.

■ The policy must be able to attract and retain staff in the areas where the multinational has the greatest needs and opportunities.

■ The policy should facilitate the transfer of international employees in the most cost effective manner for multinational enterprises.

■ The policy should be consistent and fair in its treatment of all categories of international employees.

Achieving the above objectives is likely to be a complex activity, primarily because of the different categories of employees that have to be catered for – expatriates, third country nationals and host country nationals (local employees). The company will be faced with a decision whether to have an overall compensation policy for all employees, or to deal separately with the different categories of employees. In this respect Hollinshead and Leat (1995) argue that multinational organisations can take one of three broad approaches:

1. The *ethnocentric* company seeks to export established practice from its country of origin to the other countries it operates in. In such cases the remuneration system is established at the centre, but may have some local variation as market rates are taken into account. The base salary for expatriates and third country nationals would be linked to the salary structure of the relevant home country.
2. The *polycentric* company prefers decentralisation because the assumption is that local managers are best placed to formulate reward policies, which will reflect local needs. In

this approach there is variability of reward across the company and an emphasis on salary determination at the domestic level. So, for example, the host country salary level could be offered, with significant international supplements (e.g. cost-of-living adjustments, housing and school allowances). This approach could create problems when the person returns home and reverts to the home country salary levels. Friction or feelings of inequity could arise between third country nationals and expatriates because the former feel that their total packages are not up to the level enjoyed by the latter.

3. The *geocentric* company is seen as a more developed form than the previous two types. At this stage of development the aim is to combine strengths from both the ethnocentric and polycentric approaches. Managers should be able to respond locally while holding corporate values and objectives in mind. This introduces potential conflicts in seeking to balance fair internal relativities with responsiveness to international market rates. Although such a balancing act may be difficult to maintain Hollinshead and Leat (1995) argue that it is likely to be the most effective approach in the long term for multinational companies.

The Price Waterhouse/Cranfield Survey (Fillela and Hegewisch, 1994) has indicated a number of trends in reward strategies internationally. First, there is a connection between pay determination and approaches to collective bargaining. In Finland, France and Sweden company-level negotiations tend to complement national- or industry-level negotiations. By contrast, in Portugal, Spain, Turkey and the United Kingdom company-level negotiations have tended to displace higher (national or industry) levels of bargaining. The tendency for companies from the latter countries may, therefore, be towards polycentricism. Secondly, in general there is a trend towards flexibility and away from centralised and collective determination of pay. Thirdly, the operationalisation of this flexibility is increasingly determined at lower levels in the corporation, particularly in the United Kingdom and France, although multi-employer bargaining has persisted longer in the Nordic countries, Ireland and the Netherlands. Fourthly, there is a general trend towards increased variability in pay. In Germany and France this trend has often found expression through profit sharing, while in Italy, Switzerland and the United Kingdom merit- and performance-related pay has been generally preferred (Fillela and Hegewisch, 1994). The greatest flexibility and uptake of cafeteria systems has been in the United States (Hollinshead and Leat, 1995). Company size could also be an important factor in shaping the uptake of new forms of reward system. For example, a study of the uptake of profit-related pay in Italy (Amisano and Del Boca, 2004) has shown that large companies are significantly more likely to adopt this reward strategy. It should be noted that although it is possible to identify some general trends, variations may affect their implementation and local culture may be expected to influence the styles of reward that are perceived to be attractive.

In a survey of 360 companies in 19 European countries a degree of uncertainty has been revealed (Berry, 2005). Only 30 per cent of responding organisations believed that their reward structure was very effective in attracting and retaining talented employees, and only 20 per cent believed that their rewards were effective in influencing employees towards desired behaviours. Some 57 per cent had strong links between their reward strategy and their business strategy, but the conclusions were that there was still a notable proportion of European companies in which links were lacking between reward and strategy, and further, that there were widespread concerns that the burden of current reward levels could prove to be unsustainable.

It is no easy task to come forward with well-conceived international packages to motivate employees. This area of reward management could be a hornet's nest. Because of its complexity, ranging from the determination of salary and incentives to considerations concerned with taxation liability, currency fluctuations, pension rights and various allowances, it presents the HR specialists with a stiff challenge (Briscoe and Schuler, 2004).

Relevance of motivation theories

Those with responsibility for designing reward systems will benefit from an understanding of motivation theories. Work motivation theories delve into psychological explanations about what motivates people in formal organisations. Therefore motivation and rewards are connected because rewards are given on the understanding that employees are motivated to commit themselves to perform to satisfactory levels at the workplace.

Pay, as an important component of a system of rewards, has been singled out by Thierry (1992) as having psychological and social significance, because it sends a number of messages to employees, quite apart from its status as a desired material reward. Pay says something about the appropriateness of the employee's work behaviour, it is a symbol of recognition and it conveys what the organisation thinks of the person's behaviour. In addition, pay performs the following roles (Thierry, 1992):

- It satisfies personal needs (e.g. provides an escape from insecurity, creates a feeling of competence and opens up opportunities for self-fulfilment).

- It provides feedback on how well a person is doing on a variety of fronts and it acts as an indicator of that person's relative position in the organisation.

- It is a reward for success in controlling others where the individual has a supervisory or managerial position.

- It conveys a capacity to spend in the sense that pay reflects purchasing power in the consumer market.

In the above situational interpretation of pay it is clear that a reward could mean different things to different people. For example, one person desires a certain level of income to satisfy their security needs, to another person money serves as a means to portray relative success at work, and to a third it is a means to provide spending power compatible with expectations of status. For the greater part of this century researchers in work motivation have stressed the importance of different factors in the motivation of workers, though in some cases there was a convergence of view.

'ECONOMIC MAN'

Money as a major motivating factor was endorsed by Taylor (1947), the founder of scientific management, in the early part of the last century. People were seen to be motivated by self-interest and were keen to accept the challenge to maximise their income. From the organisation's point of view, the opportunity to maximise production rested on creating reward systems (e.g. piece-rates, payment by results) where financial returns (extrinsic rewards) vary with levels of output. The greater the level of output, the greater the level of individual reward.

HUMAN RELATIONS

The 'economic man' school of thought gave way to the human relations perspective expounded by Mayo (1949). Following a series of experiments on the social and environmental conditions at work, the importance of recognition and good social relationships at work as motivational factors contributing to morale and productivity was heavily underlined.

NEED THEORIES

Next to appear on the scene were the need (content) theories, principally represented by Maslow (1954) and Herzberg (1966). Maslow arranged human needs in the form of a hierarchy with basic needs (e.g. hunger, security and safety) at the lower end, self-actualisation needs at the top, and ego and social needs in the middle. The individual moves up the hierarchy as lower needs are satisfied, and it should be noted that a pressing need is a powerful motivator of behaviour until it is satisfied.

Basic pay, sick pay and pension entitlement could satisfy security needs, and a work environment where hazards are well controlled could satisfy safety needs. The provision of sports and social clubs, which facilitate interaction at work, and works outings, could satisfy social needs. Position in the organisation and symbols of success, such as a valuable company car, have relevance in the context of satisfying status and recognition needs. An experience whereby the individual acquires key knowledge and skills, and successfully completes an exacting and challenging assignment, could contribute to the satisfaction of self-actualisation needs. Finally, adequate pay has significance at the lower end of the hierarchy, although one should take note of the broader interpretation of the psychological implications of pay attributed to Thierry (1992) earlier in this section.

Using concepts similar to Maslow, Herzberg (1966) concluded from his studies that satisfied feelings at work stemmed from a challenging job, extra responsibility, personal accomplishments, recognition from superiors and progress in one's career. These were referred to as real 'motivators'. On the other hand, negative feelings and dissatisfaction could arise from poor relationships with colleagues and superiors, less than satisfactory company policy and administration, poor pay and adverse working conditions. These were referred to as 'hygiene' factors, and if improved could lower the level of 'dissatisfaction' and negativity. Improving the hygiene factors and then building motivators into a job was considered the best way to motivate people. Note the status of pay in the Herzberg model – a hygiene factor – a position challenged later in the expectancy model of motivation.

There is a strong similarity between Maslow's higher level human needs and Herzberg's motivators. Both would be considered when designing or redesigning jobs by way of job enrichment (see Box 9.3).

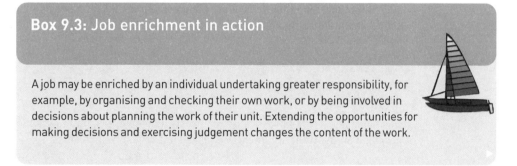

Box 9.3: Job enrichment in action

A job may be enriched by an individual undertaking greater responsibility, for example, by organising and checking their own work, or by being involved in decisions about planning the work of their unit. Extending the opportunities for making decisions and exercising judgement changes the content of the work.

Job enrichment programmes attempt to build in, over time, scope for the development of an individual's skills to provide a sense of personal achievement. This approach frequently affects the nature of other jobs and therefore careful consideration needs to be given to the whole process of reallocating responsibilities, redefining roles and providing the necessary retraining. Over the years there have been a number of instances where job enrichment led to increased job satisfaction and favourably influenced performance.

Source: based on Department of Employment, 1975

ICI – experimenting with job enrichment

In the 1960s ICI was one of a handful of companies in the United Kingdom that experimented seriously with job enrichment. One job enrichment study within ICI examined the role of sales representatives who appeared to be satisfied with their job but were given very little discretion over the way they operated. The following changes were instituted as part of the job enrichment programme. Sales representatives no longer had to write a report on every customer call. Instead they passed on, or requested, information at their own discretion. They were also given total responsibility for determining the frequency of calls to customers, deciding how to deal with faulty or unwanted stock, requesting service from the technical services department and making immediate settlements up to a certain sum in case of customer complaint, if they felt this would prejudice further liability of the company. In addition, they were given discretion to adjust prices on a range up to 10 per cent on the price of most of the products sold, the lower limit often being below any price previously quoted by the sales office. Following the implementation of the job enrichment scheme both job satisfaction and performance increased.

Source: based on Paul and Robertson, 1970

Dejobbing at Cheseborough-Ponds USA

A modern iteration of job enrichment has been termed 'dejobbing' (Dessler, 2005). In many organisations a number of factors have stimulated dejobbing. These factors include: the demands of regular innovation and change of products and services; flatter structures in which there are fewer middle managers to make the decisions; and a move towards 'boundaryless' organisation in which cross-functional teams form and reform as the task changes. In these circumstances it is inappropriate for workers to have one fixed job description that they do not vary from – hence the need for dejobbing.

Cheseborough-Ponds USA (a subsidiary of Unilever) has embraced this style of job enrichment. The organisation has flattened and many people now work in multi-functional self-managing teams. Shopfloor employees make decisions about scheduling, assigning tasks, managing production times and changeovers, cost control and quality control. Employees' jobs change on almost a daily basis and there is a deliberate intention that employees should not think of themselves as 'one trick ponies'.

Source: based on Dessler, 2005

Question

Dejobbing is likely to introduce training costs as employees are required to develop new skill areas. What arguments could you use to justify such costs?

The notion of job enrichment – attempting to make tasks more intrinsically interesting, involving and rewarding – is updated in the Hackman and Oldham job characteristics model (Hackman, 1977).

This model incorporates the following five core dimensions, which are key factors when designing or redesigning jobs:

1. *skill variety* (scope for the exercise of different skills and abilities);
2. *task identity* (extent to which the job requires the completion of an identifiable segment of work);
3. *task significance* (extent to which the job has an impact on the life of others);
4. *autonomy* (extent to which the job offers freedom and the use of discretion in performing tasks);
5. *feedback* (extent to which the job-holder receives information on his or her performance).

The five core dimensions are linked with motivation and performance through critical psychological states (i.e. experienced meaningfulness of the work, experienced responsibility for work outcomes, and knowledge of the consequences of work activities). The model recognises that people differ in their levels of 'growth need'. For example, people with a high need for personal growth are more likely to react favourably in a psychological sense when the five core factors are improved.

OVERVIEW

The motivational factors discussed above can be classified as intrinsic (e.g. job challenge, skill-based pay) or extrinsic (e.g. pay, PRP, working conditions). Skill-based pay is classified as an intrinsic factor because it refers to the reward an individual receives for the baggage (input) of knowledge and skill the employee takes to the job. The outcome could be the enhancement of competences and personal development. By contrast, basic pay in the form of 'time rates' can be related to the need theories, since they call for fairness and relative security, which in turn can generate social satisfaction at work.

EXPECTANCY THEORY

Another theory of motivation is expectancy theory (Porter and Lawler, 1968; Vroom, 1964), which could be considered very relevant to reward management (Lundy and Cowling, 1996). People bring to work various expectations about the likely consequences of various forms of behaviour reflected in work performance. For example, if people expect that the expenditure of effort will lead to good work performance and generate a satisfactory outcome in terms of intrinsic and extrinsic rewards, which are valued, and such expectations are realised in practice, then productive effort is likely to be forthcoming in the future. If this scenario was altered, so that the relationship between effort and reward did not stand, it is possible that the motivational disposition of the employee would change and future effort may be adjusted downwards or discontinued.

In more specific terms Lundy and Cowling (1996), drawing on expectancy theory, state that high performance by individuals or teams will only come about if they are clear about their tasks, to which they have a positive attitude, and that they possess the necessary aptitudes, abilities and competencies. Effort will then be expended resulting in a high level of performance when people perceive that their energy and effort results in high performance, that high performance will lead to rewards, and that the rewards available are those that they desire. The critical final stage is the receipt of positive feedback, when they obtain the desirable intrinsic and extrinsic rewards.

In practice it may be difficult to implement expectancy theory. For example, profit-related pay attempts to bring about convergence between individual and organisational goals, in the sense that the individual is motivated to achieve organisational goals, for by so doing the employee is achieving personal goals, particularly with reference to extrinsic rewards. However, with profit-related pay employees may not be sure that specific rewards will be the consequence of particular actions because of the involvement of others. But in the quoted example, social needs could be satisfied in the process because the organisation is trying to link the interests of employees with those of its own. Social needs could also be considered relevant in the context of group- or team-based pay.

GOAL SETTING

The setting of goals is said to have an impact on the motivation of the individuals, provided the goals set are clear, realistic and challenging, but not too difficult, and that the person subjected to them is able to participate in their setting. Other considerations are feedback on performance, goal acceptance and commitment to the goal (Locke and Latham, 1990). Management by objectives, which was mentioned as a performance appraisal technique in Chapter 8, is an example of a process in which there is an emphasis on participation in the setting of goals. An alternative approach to goal setting as described would be for goals to be set and assigned to the individual, but this approach might not have the motivational impact outlined above. Goal setting, when combined with job enrichment to give greater autonomy, has been found to have motivational value (Garg and Rastogi, 2005).

A reward system anchored in extrinsic rewards (e.g. PRP), utilises the concepts of expectancy and goal setting when judgements are made about the extent to which performance meets objectives, and the adequacy of rewards.

EQUITY THEORY

This theory is concerned with the equitable nature of reward and has significance when the employee perceives the relationship between effort and reward, as would occur in the application of expectancy theory. In an employment situation one considers two important variables: inputs and outputs. Education, skill, experience and effort would be considered inputs, and salary, fringe benefits and career advancement would be viewed as outputs. People compare each other's inputs and outputs and, if they perceive unfairness, feelings of inequity can arise (Adams, 1963). The latter could have an adverse effect on production and possibly lead to absenteeism and resignation. Apparently, if after engaging in the comparative exercise some employees consider themselves overcompensated, there could be a feeling of unease.

We shall give the final say to Robertson *et al.* (1992) on the issue of the ideal interaction between the organisational environment and levels of motivation, as follows:

- Expectations in terms of performance are translated into specific and hard goals that are attainable.

- Employees are allowed to participate in the setting of these goals, and they have a realistic appreciation of the link between effort and performance aimed at goal attainment.

- Employees are endowed with the necessary competence and confidence to ensure that effort made results in appropriate performance.

- Jobs are designed in such a way as to offer employees variety, autonomy, and frequent and clear feedback on their performance.

■ Control systems that regulate people's work are only used as and when necessary.

■ Rewards received by employees for successful performance are geared to their individual requirements and preferences, and are perceived as equitable.

From the discussion of the motivation theories it is clear that motivation theory has evolved from a simple assumption based on notions of a rational economic perspective of employees, who are considered to be primarily motivated by money, to a more sophisticated psychological perspective that takes note of the numerous and divergent employee needs. This more complex but realistic assessment of what motivates employees requires managers to develop strategies that enable employees to develop an ever-greater sense of personal achievement and satisfaction in return for their contribution to the organisation (Beardwell *et al.*, 2004).

HRM and rewards

Systems of pay, such as time rates and payment by results, tend to be associated with the more traditional styles of management, while reward systems, such as PRP and skill-based pay, reflect the spirit of HRM and appear to be growing in popularity. In a PRP culture the aim is to make employees more like entrepreneurs, i.e. people who earn a direct return on the value they create (Kanter, 1987). This approach to reward would fit into the category of hard HRM referred to in Chapter 2, as it assumes that people are motivated by economic self-interest. However, PRP is subtler than this; it can also include 'goal setting', referred to in the previous section. As the goals set can be qualitative as well as quantitative, the issue of quality is addressed (Guest, 1989).

Lawler (1991) maintains that traditional reward systems (e.g. time rates) tend to motivate a large number of people to climb the organisational hierarchy. This arises when rewards are given as a result of progressing within salary grades and scales. But given the advent of flatter organisational structures and flexible work designs – developments that receive the HRM seal of approval – skill-based pay would appear to be more appropriate than traditional reward systems. Skill-based pay is a reward system that credits individuals in a way that benefits the organisation in terms of goal attainment. It is congruent with the aim of HRM to invest in human assets, and it tries to promote flexibility by ensuring that employees are equipped to carry out a variety of tasks. There is also an element of trust involved: given the acquisition of the right blend of skills there is the expectation that employees will motivate themselves to perform to a high standard, though this may have to be complemented by good management. Overall, it is compatible with soft HRM.

The CIPD (2007c) has reported on a survey of 466 organisations across all industrial sectors, employing in all about a million people in the United Kingdom. It was found that the main priorities of reward strategies were to support business goals and, as part of this aim, to support high performers. Base pay was normally set by benchmarking against market rates, internal job evaluation, or a combination of both. Some 54 per cent of employers were giving an annual pay increase, typically as a 'cost-of-living uplift'. Cash-based bonuses were the common variable incentive and most were individually-based. Bonuses based on business performance (such as profit sharing) were next most common. Given the legal requirement, almost all organisations were providing pensions. The most common types were final salary schemes and personal/stakeholder pensions. However, in the private sector most final salary schemes had closed to new members. Table 9.3 summarises key findings from the CIPD survey.

A final key finding of the survey was that 41 per cent of respondents reported having a 'total rewards' approach and a further 32 per cent were planning to take up this approach. This

Table 9.3 Key findings from the CIPD survey

	Reward approaches	Percentage of respondents using the approach
Reward strategy goals	Support business goals	67
	Reward high performers	62
	Recruit and retain high performers	58
	Achieve/maintain market competitiveness	79
Pay structures	Individual pay rates	44
	Broad salary bands	40
	Job families	31
	Narrow graded pay structures	22
	Pay spines (harmonising a range of jobs)	16
Types of bonus and incentive	Individual-based	64
	Based on business results	53
	Combination of the above	47
	Team-based	27
	Project-based or ad hoc	21
	Gainsharing	2

Source: CIPD, 2007c, www.cipd.co.uk

popularity is confirmed internationally by studies in countries such as Finland and China (Chiang and Birtch, 2006) where it is seen to have led to benefits for both organisations and employees. According to Brown (2006) total reward has become increasingly important as it is recognised that: reward is a very significant part of the way that organisations communicate with their employees; it is important to put employee commitment and needs back at the centre of reward; and companies need to fit their reward strategies to the internal and external contexts within which they operate.

Armstrong and Brown (2006) define total reward as bringing together traditional pay and benefits with additional components such as learning and development and aspects of the work environment. Typically, it is regarded as part of building and maintaining the company culture and is concerned with issues such as giving employees a voice. The aim is to encourage a higher degree of employee engagement.

Total reward incorporates financial and non-financial elements. Financial elements include aspects such as base pay, variable pay, share ownership and other benefits. Non-financial rewards incorporate recognition, opportunities to develop skills, career opportunities and the quality of working life. The benefits of total reward schemes are thought to be (Thompson, 2002):

■ easier recruitment of better quality staff;

■ reduced labour turnover;

■ better business performance;

■ an enhanced reputation as an employer of choice.

The style of holistic reward implied by total reward strategies has been shown to have a positive impact. The combination of financial and non-financial rewards has produced a 30 per cent performance improvement in US service firms, which is almost twice the impact of using either financial or non-financial rewards alone (Dessler, 2005).

Conclusions

There is evidence to indicate that UK companies are continually preoccupied with pay systems, with change in reward systems being very common (Goodhart, 1994). A number of large companies have been using a third version of PRP since the early 1980s, with bonus schemes and share options for senior executives in a constant state of overhaul and revision. Now there is a more sober and realistic view of what a reward system can achieve than was the case in the 1980s. The view that a company's success rests principally on adopting state-of-the-art pay systems is now considered too simplistic (Armstrong and Brown, 2006). This is not surprising, because motivation is a complex phenomenon and designing and managing pay systems is a difficult task.

There appears to be a tendency to address a number of operational issues, such as the tension between individual performance and group commitment in PRP. The delicate connection between performance appraisal and PRP has given rise to experimentation with appraisal techniques, such as assessment by colleagues. Apparently some companies justify their attachment to PRP in order to prevent them giving increases in pay to inadequate or poor performers. Progress is being made in developing skill-based pay and gain sharing. The latter are incentive schemes that give employees who are responsible for initiating specific improvements a return for their contributions. A number of institutional investors would like to see advances in the determination of executive pay, in particular more realistic share option schemes.

The system of 'national rates' for employees is being challenged, and there is a movement away from pay systems that reward managers for loyalty expressed as commitment in terms of length of service, towards rewarding managers on the basis of individual performance and company performance in order to cultivate loyalty. Linking rewards to the success of the enterprise was considered a sensible way to proceed, as it was likely to promote commitment. There is a danger that the commitment of a number of employees could be undermined because of significant income inequality within the company. The weakened state of national bargaining pay systems has resulted in the centralisation of greater power in the hands of top management in matters connected with pay determination. Regrettably, it appears that members of top management have been overgenerous in awarding themselves pay increases at a time when pay restraint is advocated for most employees.

As organisations increasingly operate on an international scale there is a need for consideration of how best to manage rewards internationally. Alternative approaches can be adopted that are focused either on the systems of the country of origin or on localised variation in the approach to rewards. There is some pressure towards localisation, particularly in view of the differences in trends that are discernible in international comparative studies. In addition, we might expect differences in motivation in divergent cultures. In particular, the effects of expectancy theory will relate to what is valued by the employees, and what is regarded as being of value will vary with culture.

Finally, an unexpected verdict from Professor John Purcell in a 'Rewards Debate' should be noted. He stated that reward management interventions do more harm than good in building trust, commitment and motivation (Purcell and Brown, 2000). The reasons behind this statement are that linking pay to business objectives and cascading this down through the organisation may sound like an attractive option for increasing commitment amongst employees, but it contains a contradiction. Not only does it perpetrate the illusion that companies are rational, top-down, directed organisations (rather than being involved in fast and messy change), it also assumes that people need incentives to work in an acceptable way; in other words, they cannot be trusted to work effectively without such a control mechanism. This is a contradiction because as we have seen mutual trust is at the heart of high commitment management (see Chapters 1 and 2). The movement towards total reward systems (Brown, 2006) goes some way to addressing this issue. Crucially, simplistic views that it is possible to pay for trust and commitment are not longer generally accepted. Current foci on involving employees in flexible systems and in understanding their connections to the organisation as incorporating development, career opportunities and variety of tasks, has shifted the emphasis in reward management thinking from merely an exchange to part of a psychological contract which will only work if there is mutuality.

Review and reflection questions

1. Name three approaches to job evaluation.

2. What are the advantages and disadvantages of job evaluation?

3. What are the strengths and weaknesses of the following types of reward system:

    (a) time rates

    (b) individual PRP

    (c) flexible/cafeteria systems?

4. How can reward systems be used to 'engage' staff?

5. According to Hollinshead and Leat, what are the three approaches to international compensation?

6. Explain the expectancy theory of motivation.

7. Explain the equity theory of motivation.

8. According to the CIPD survey, what are:

    (a) the main purposes of reward systems

    (b) the most common pay structures

    (c) the most prevalent types of incentive pay?

Activities

If you are in work:

Read the sections on expectancy, equity and goal setting theories of motivation.

1. Which theory, or combination of theories, is most helpful in explaining your reaction to the rewards your organisation provides?

2. On the basis of your analysis, what changes to the reward system might be justified?

If you are in full-time study:

Consider the assumptions about motivation that are embedded in the ideas of individual PRP and job enrichment.

1. What theories are implicit in these reward systems?

2. Where might the different approaches be most appropriate in terms of fit with

   (a) industry norms

   (b) organisational culture

   (c) national culture?

Further reading and research

A comprehensive introduction to the topic of reward management is provided in the following book:
Wright, A. (2004) *Reward Management in context*, London: CIPD.

The following chapter develops an understanding of underlying theories and principles:
Child, J. (2005) 'Questions of Reward' (Chapter 6) in *Organizations: Contemporary Principles and Practice*, Oxford: Blackwell.

Practical applications of reward management are covered in:
Arkin, A. and Downard, B. (2005) 'Reward: Eyes on the prize. The process of developing the best packages to attract and retain staff is becoming more complex', *People Management*, 10 February, 29–35.
People Management (2007) 'The Guide to Reward', 5 April, 47–61.

The CIPD provides comprehensive information on pay and rewards. The PRP trends report includes information on team-based pay and profit related pay. There are also sections on incentive-based pay and employee benefits (see www.cipd.co.uk/subjects/pay).

Another website that is less research based, but which does carry news, features on rewards and web links is www.ereward.co.uk.

References

Adams, J.S. (1963) 'Towards an understanding of inequity', *Journal of Abnormal and Social Psychology*, 67, 422–436.

Amisano, G. and Del Boca, A. (2004) 'Profit Related Pay in Italy', *International Journal of Manpower*, 25, 463–478.

Applebaum, S. and Shappiro, B. (1991) 'Pay for performance: implementation of individual and group plans', *Journal of Management Development*, 10, 30–40.

Armstrong, M. (2003) *A Handbook of Human Resource Management Practice*, London: Kogan Page.

Armstrong, M. and Brown, D. (2001) *New Dimensions in Pay Management*, London: Kogan Page.

Armstrong, M. and Brown, D. (2006) *Strategic reward: Making it happen.* London: Kogan Page.

Armstrong, M. and Murlis, H. (1998) *Reward Management*, London: Kogan Page.

Beardwell, I., Holden, L. and Claydon, T. (2004) *Human Resource Management*, Harlow, Essex: Pearson Education.

Beattie, A. (2004) 'New accounting rules push share option deals further out of favour', *Financial Times*, 25 October, 3.

Berry, M. (2005) 'Doubts surface over value of reward programmes', *Personnel Today*, 28 October.

Boyd, B. and Salamin, A. (2001) 'Strategic reward systems. A contingency model of pay system design', *Strategic Management Journal*, 22, 777–792.

Brisco, S. (2004) 'Missing data mean causes of lower wages are hard to establish', *Financial Times*, 30/31 October, 11.

Briscoe, D.R. and Schuler, R.S. (2004) *International Human Resource Management,* New York: Routledge.

Brown, D. (2006) 'Home Grown', *People Management*, 17, 38–40.

Cannell, M. and Long, P. (1991) 'What's changed about incentive pay?', *Personnel Management*, October, 58–63.

Chiang, F.F.T. and Birtch, T.A. (2006) 'An empirical examination of reward preferences within and across national settings', *Management International Review*, 46, 573–596.

CIPD (2004) *Reward Management: A survey of policy and practice*, London: CIPD.

CIPD (2007a) *Team Reward factsheet*, www.cipd.co.uk

CIPD (2007b) *Occupational Pensions: Strategic Issues*, www.cipd.co.uk

CIPD (2007c) *Reward Management: Annual survey report*, www.cipd.co.uk

Cowling, A. and James, P. (1994) *The Essence of Personnel Management and Industrial Relations*, Hemel Hempstead: Prentice Hall.

Department of Employment (1975) (Report), 'Making work more satisfying', London: HMSO.

Department of Trade and Industry (1999) 'A detailed guide to the national minimum wage', London: DTI.

Dessler, G. (2005) *Human Resource Management*, New Jersey: Pearson.

Donkin, R. (1994) 'An option on perks (flexible remuneration systems)', *Financial Times*, 6 April, 16.

Donkin, R. (1998) 'Reward for know-how', *Financial Times* (Recruitment Section), 24 July, 1.

Dowling, P.J and Welch, D.E. (2004) *International Human Resource Management*, London: Thomson Learning.

Eaglesham, J., Turner, D., and Guthrie, J. (2004) 'Mind the gap: Labour puts equal pay for women in its election agenda', *Financial Times*, 30/31 October, 11.

Faragher, J. (2007) 'John Lewis Partnership: Working in Partnership', *Personnel Today Magazine*, 17 April.

Fillela, J. and Hegewisch, A. (1994) 'European experiments with pay and benefits', in Brewster, C. and Hegewisch, A. (eds), *Policy and Practice in European Human Resource Management: The Price Waterhouse/Cranfield Survey*, London: Routledge.

Financial Times (1995) Editorial comment, 13 February, 17.

Financial Times (1999) Editorial comment, 21 August.

Financial Times (2007) Editorial comment: Shareholders of the world unite – time for performance pay to live up to its name, *Financial Times*, 6 January, 8.

Fisher, J. (2001) 'How to design incentive schemes', *People Management*, 7(1), 38–39.

FitzGerald, N. (1997) 'Incentive plans under fire', *The Sunday Times* (Business Section), 25 May, 31.

Freeman, R. (2001) 'Upping the stakes', *People Management*, 7(3), 25–29.

Fuller, G. (2005) 'Advice Squad', *People Management*, 11, 36–39.

Fuller, G. (2006) 'Performance related pay fails to grip nation', *Personnel Today Magazine*, 28 March.

Garg, P. and Rastogi, R. (2005) 'New model of job design: motivating employees' performance', *Journal of Management Development*, 25, 572–587.

Goodhart, D. (1994) 'In search of wages that work', *Financial Times*, 27 June, 16.

Goss, D. (1994) *Principles of Human Resource Management*, London: Routledge.

Guest, D. (1989) 'Personnel and HRM: can you tell the difference?', *Personnel Management*, January, 48–51.

Hackman, J.R. (1977) 'Work design', in Hackman, J.R. and Suttle, J.L. (eds), *Improving Life at Work*, Santa Monica, CA: Scott Foresman.

Halligan, L. (1997) 'Performance-related pay attacked', *Financial Times*, 10 June, 8.

Harrison, D. (2001) 'Flexible pay deals: Pick-and-mix benefits keep staff sweet', *Financial Times*, 28 March, 18.

Herzberg, F. (1966) *Work and the Nature of Man*, London: Staples Press.

Hollinshead, G. and Leat, M. (1995) *Human Resource Management: An international and comparative perspective*, London: Pitman.

Huddart, G. (1994) 'UNISYS links rises to personal skills', *Personnel Today*, 17 May, 1.

IDS (1991) *DIY Benefits for the 1990s*, IDS Study no. 481, May, London: Income Data Services.

IDS (1992) *Skilling Up*. IDS Study no. 500, February, London: Income Data Services.

IRS (1991) 'BT managers hostile to PRP', *Employment Trends 495*, September.

IRS (2003) 'Looking ahead: the 2004 pay round', *IRS Employment Review*, 787, November.

IRS (2007) *Performance Related Pay*, www.IRSemploymentreview.com

Kanter, R.M. (1987) 'The attack on pay', *Harvard Business Review*, March–April 111–117.

Kellaway, L. (1993) 'Nice little earner (profit-related pay)', *Financial Times*, 23 April, 14.

Kohn, A. (1993) 'Why incentive plans cannot work', *Harvard Business Review*, September/ October, 54–63.

Lawler, E. (1991) 'Paying the person: a better approach to management', *Human Resource Management Review*, 1, 145–154.

Lawler, E.E., Ledford, G.E. and Chang, L. (1993) 'Who uses skill-based pay and why?', *Compensation and Benefits Review*, March/April, 22.

Lewis, P. (2006) 'Reward Management', in Redman, T. and Wilkinson, A. (eds), *Contemporary Human Resource Management*, Harlow, Essex: Pearson.

Locke, E.A. and Latham, G.P. (1990) *A Theory of Goal Setting and Task Performance*, London: Prentice Hall.

Lundy, O. and Cowling, A. (1996) *Strategic Human Resource Management*, London: Routledge.

Maitland, A. (1998) 'Benefits all round, thanks to flexible work options', *Financial Times*, 21 April, 22.

Marchington, M. and Wilkinson, A. (2005) *Human Resource Management at Work*, London Chartered Institute of Personnel and Development.

Maslow, A. (1954) *Motivation and Personality*, New York: Harper & Row.

Mayo, E. (1949) *The Social Problems of an Industrial Civilization*, London: Routledge & Kegan Paul.

Meyer, J.J. (2000) 'The future of flexible benefit plans', *Employee Benefits Journal*, 3–7 June.

Moules, J. (2004) 'CBI urges freezing of minimum wage', *Financial Times*, 17 November, 2.

Murlis, H. (1994) 'The challenge of rewarding teamwork', *Personnel Management*, February, 8.

Murlis, H. and Fitt, D. (1991) 'Job evaluation in a changing world', *Personnel Management*, May, 39–44.

Newman, C. (2001) 'Imbalance of Payments', *People Management*, 7, 18–19.

North, S.J. (1993) 'IBM trims pay grades in salary shake-up', *Personnel Today*, 9 November, 1.

North, S.J. (1994) 'IBM hives off its payroll services', *Personnel Today*, 31 May, 2.

Oldfield, C. (1999) 'Minimum wage to force job cuts', *The Sunday Times*, 21 March.

Paul, W.J. and Robertson, K.B. (1970) *Job Enrichment and Employee Motivation*, Epping: Gower Press.

Pearce, J. (1991) 'Why merit pay doesn't work', in Steer, R. and Porter, L. (eds), *Motivation and Work Behaviour*, New York: McGraw-Hill.

Pickard, J. (1993) 'How incentives can drive teamworking', *Personnel Management*, September, 26–32.

Porter, L.W. and Lawler, E.E. (1968) *Managerial Attitudes and Performance*, Homewood, IL: R.D. Irwin.

Purcell, J. and Brown, D. (2000) 'Pay per view: reward debate', *People Management*, 6, 41–43.

Reilly, P., Philipson, J. and Smith, P. (2005) 'Team-based pay in the United Kingdom', *Compensation and Benefits Review*, 37, 54–60.

Richards, J. (2007) *Flexible Benefits*, London: CIPD (www.cipd.co.uk).

Robertson, J., Smith, M. and Cooper, D. (1992) *Motivation: Strategies, theory and practice*, Hemel Hempstead: Prentice Hall.

Stredwick, J. (2005) *An Introduction to Human Resource Management*, Oxford: Elsevier Butterworth–Heinemann.

Taylor, F.W. (1947) *Scientific Management*, New York: Harper & Row.

Taylor, R. (1994) 'Must try harder', *Financial Times*, 2 February, 9.

Taylor, R. (1999) 'Both sides of industry anxious on minimum wage', *Financial Times*, 29 March.

Taylor, R. (2000) 'Minimum wage is being exceeded', *Financial Times*, 27 November, 4.

Thierry, H. (1992) 'Pay and payment systems', in Hartley, J. and Stephenson, G. (eds), *Employee Relations*, Oxford: Blackwell.

Thompson, M. (1993) 'Pay and performance 2: the employee's experience', *Personnel Management Plus*, November, 2.

Thompson, P. (2002) *Total Reward: executive briefing*. London: CIPD.

Torrington, D., Hall, L. and Taylor, S. (2005) *Human Resource Management*, Harlow: Pearson Education.

Trapp, R. (2004) 'Keeping your options open', *People Management*, 10, 42–43.

Trevor, G. (1993) 'Pearl Assurance', *Personnel Management Plus*, November, 13.

Tucker, S. (2004) 'Executive bonuses poorly linked to success', *Financial Times*, 2 August, 1.

Turner, D. (2004) 'Pay rates reflect action on national minimum wage', *Financial Times*, 6 October, 4.

Vroom, V. (1964) *Work and Motivation*, New York: John Wiley.

Wickens, P. (1987) *The Road to Nissan: Flexibility, quality, teamwork*, Basingstoke: Macmillan.

Chapter 10

EMPLOYEE DEVELOPMENT: TRAINING AND DEVELOPMENT

Introduction

If employees are to behave flexibly and effectively they need to acquire and develop knowledge and skills. If employees are to believe that they are valued by the organisation they need to see visible signs that the company has taken their training needs seriously. Training and development are the processes of investing in people so that they are equipped to perform; these processes are part of an overall HRM approach that hopefully will result in people being motivated to perform.

Having read this chapter, you should:

■ understand the importance of training and development from a strategic perspective;

■ have knowledge of the national training and development scene in the United Kingdom;

■ be able to identify the key features of management development and career management;

■ be able to distinguish the various approaches to training and development, and know the advantages and disadvantages of the alternative options;

■ understand the methods of evaluating training and development;

■ be aware of the key issues when training employees for international assignments;

■ be aware of some of the international comparisons in training and development.

The training and development of employees has become a topic of increased focus for a number of reasons. First, distinctive knowledge has been recognised as a key competence in many organisations, and some see becoming a 'learning organisation' as a process that will enable them to achieve competitive advantage over their rivals. Secondly, change is endemic in many industries, and this may require employees to exercise new skills and to have a positive attitude to change. Thirdly, it is thought that companies whose employees are able to problem solve, understand and react effectively to customers will be able to enhance the perceived quality of their services. Effective training and development underlie achievements in each of these areas.

Training and development are terms that are sometimes used interchangeably. Traditionally development was seen as an activity normally associated with managers with the future firmly in mind. By contrast, training has a more immediate concern and has been associated with improving the knowledge and skill of non-managerial employees in their present jobs. Such a distinction could be considered too simplistic in an era characterised by developments in HRM, because nowadays development of all employees is considered crucial. Such development would be reflected in a commitment to multi-skilling and a flexible mode of operation. There is also the recognition that the human resources are valuable and must be developed if the organisation is to hold on to staff and retain their commitment while they are at work. One should bear in mind that even managers need to be trained in the here and now, because they need current operational skills or competencies quite apart from the qualities (e.g. creativity, synthesis, abstract reasoning, personal development) associated with management development.

From what has been said it would be sensible to regard training and development as interactive, each complementing the other. Finally, the logical step is for the organisation to produce a plan for HR development (i.e. training and development) which will dovetail into the employee resourcing plan (i.e. selection) and the organisation's overall strategic plan. Training and development of employees is not an option, it is an intrinsic part of the practice of HRM and an investment in people (Keep, 1992; Grugulis, 2006).

Systematic training

In the 1960s training received a fillip with the establishment of the Industry Training Boards in the United Kingdom. The emphasis was on the acquisition of behavioural skills and what a training programme could achieve. This is referred to as systematic training and it put emphasis on off-the-job training as opposed to the then popular method of 'sitting next to Nellie'. Quite simply a systematic approach would start with a definition of the training needs of employees, that is the attitude, knowledge, skills and behaviour required by the employee in order to do the job adequately. Next the required training necessary to satisfy these needs is put in motion using suitable trainers, and finally there is an evaluation of the training undertaken in order to ensure it is effective.

A more comprehensive description of the training process, according to Armstrong (1992), is the concept of planned training. Planned training is a deliberate intervention designed to bring about the necessary learning to improve performance on the job (Kenney and Reid, 1988), and it includes the following points. Apart from the issues raised above with respect to systematic training, there is reference to the importance of setting training objectives (i.e. what the trainee should be capable of doing after the training course has been completed) and the planning of the training programme, using the right combination of training techniques and locations, in order to achieve the training objectives.

Above, the importance of assessing training needs was briefly stated. This could be executed on at least three levels, namely organisational analysis, task analysis and person analysis. At the organisational level there is an emphasis on the identification of deficiencies (e.g. poor financial control within the company) that could be remedied by training. Also, at this level the importance of mobilising training so it is congruent with the achievement of corporate objectives is considered important. Here the needs of the organisation are paramount, though the needs of the individual employee could be satisfied indirectly. It would be functional to stress the importance of training in contemporary organisations in order to create a more flexible, committed and loyal labour force, as well as equipping employees with skills so that they can secure another job if their services are no longer required.

Case example 10.1 shows how a small engineering firm responded to a major threat to its continued existence by adopting a developmental approach. It subsequently reaped the benefits, and not only survived but moved from a loss-making position in to one of profit, with a 150 per cent increase in turnover.

In Case example 10.2 we can see that the reasons for undertaking training and development are not always as dramatic as was the case in Hindle Power, but business needs constantly arise which require new skills. For example, changes in technology, geopolitical factors and ethical failures can all provide strong imperatives to develop the workforce.

DEVELOPMENT AT HINDLE POWER

Hindle Power was a family-owned engineering firm, employing 32 people. Most of its business (75 per cent) came from its contract with Perkins Engines to sell, customise and service their engines in machinery ranging from forklift trucks to crop-sprayers. In 1996 Perkins gave warning that Hindle Power, along with other distributors, would have to meet tougher customer service targets or face having the contract terminated. This provided the impetus for a culture change in which training was featured prominently.

Staff were given considerable scope to determine their own training needs through a new appraisal system, which was designed to help people clarify their career goals. Every employee was able to take up to 26 days training per year, and some made radical moves in their careers as a result. A service manager, for example, having studied for a qualification in business management became a parts manager, in charge of stock control, and his performance is enhanced by his understanding of other parts of the business. In another case a sales manager is currently studying for a science degree. Most people, however, volunteered for training that was directly relevant to their work roles. There was an emphasis on the following areas: business management, customer care, IT skills and induction. Some of the training was formal and involved attendance on courses that offered qualifications. Other approaches were less formal, for example suppliers were invited to run product awareness programmes for staff. As a direct result of training and development 10 of the staff have either been promoted or moved to new posts.

Hindle Power also opened its doors to student interns, and as a result of playing host to marketing undergraduates it developed a database of all its customers and potential users. A survey showed that while 90 per cent of the potential customers had heard of Hindle Power only 40 per cent had purchased any services. Customer care training improved employee's ability to provide written quotations, and reminders were sent out to add antifreeze to engines. Subsequent to these profile-raising activities, 60 per cent of the potential market became customers.

The employees are now better placed to expand the customer base, and to ensure that existing customers are happy with the level of service. As one put it: 'processes such as problem solving have a real use – I certainly work with more confidence now'. Performance briefings and monthly financial reports have become a normal part of the operation of the business, and the company has gained IiP (Investors in People) accreditation.

By 2000 the workforce had expanded to 49 people, turnover had grown from £6 million in 1996 to £15 million, and a situation of making losses and being in danger of going out of business had been turned into one of greater security, growth and profit. Business has expanded and a new franchise to sell engine control products for the company has been set up. Additionally, Hindle Power became Perkins' first UK distributor to sell parts in China. Such developments require a workforce that is adaptable and people who are problem solvers.

Rarely has the link between training and the bottom line been so clear.

Source: based on Littlefield, 2000

Question

How could Hindle Power's experience be used as an example to argue for other companies to invest in systematic training?

CASE EXAMPLE 10.2

TRAINING INITIATIVES

British Telecom

British Telecommunications (BT) has accepted the importance of training to support the achievement of business objectives. One of the biggest business units within BT is supplying services to corporate customers with multiple sites, and this has become a £1billion enterprise, employing 20,000 people. But BT is eager to extract more milk from this cash cow, and is working hard to win more contracts and squeeze more revenue out of existing deals. BT felt it was losing out on the opportunity to develop further business from its existing clients. In partnership with a sales training and development consultancy, BT has launched a 'business managers' academy', a series of workshops and programmes designed to develop the skills of its executives in building relationships with customers. The company wanted something more sophisticated than selling equipment out of a box. The introduction of new technologies, such as broadband, wideband and mobile, enabled salespeople to offer more complex solutions, and this could lead to the client outsourcing all its telecommunications to BT. The BT Academy offers a range of opportunities for managers to develop their skills, with a focus on customers.

Source: based on Eglin 2005

Keeping up to date

A number of training areas have been identified as important (Witzel, 2004). With war and terrorism affecting a number of regions of the world, security training must remain a priority. Another area of importance must be corporate governance. This is supported by much legislation getting on the statute book in 2005: for example, the full implementation of the Sarbanes–Oxley Act (USA) and the European Information and Consultation Directive. This means that relevant employees need to be aware of the consequences. Therefore, training programmes have been developed to provide the knowledge needed to ensure compliance with the legislation and directives. There will be other training programmes to explore ethical dilemmas and learn how better to make ethical judgements.

Citigroup

Following a number of scandals that damaged the reputation of Citigroup, the world's largest financial services company, thousands of employees throughout the globe attended presentations and watched a film on the history of Citigroup. The film emphasises that the group's reputation rests on the integrity of past employees and that it is up to current employees to enhance not damage that reputation. This training initiative, related to culture change, is supported by a number of other actions such as changes to the PRP system, the strengthening of internal controls, and the establishment of an 'ethics hotline' for staff to give anonymous feedback on managers.

Source: based on Wighton, 2005

Question

What are the different reasons that companies might have for initiating training?

At the level of task analysis a first step is to establish that jobs are necessary in the light of corporate objectives. Having established this the next step is to identify the necessary patterns of behaviour that are critical for effective performance in the job. The pattern of behaviour would normally include the expression of knowledge, ability, attitudes and competences that are required to do the job successfully. Finally, the third level – person analysis – puts the spotlight on employees needing training. This information could be gleaned from, for example, the records relating to the outcome of the selection and performance appraisal processes and leads to specifying the most appropriate form of training. With respect to personal analysis, Furnham (2001) makes a valid assertion; that is, because of the spread of change in technology all jobs appear to be in a state of flux. Therefore, personal analysis will have to focus on potential, rather than current, knowledge and skill, as well as motivation.

Competition and change

Competitive conditions facing an organisation can lead to changes in working practices, habits, cultures and the redesign of work. To prepare employees for such an eventuality, we can resort to training with the emphasis on development to maintain or enhance the quality of the operations and output. Nowadays words such as flexibility and teamwork enter the organisational vocabulary when talking about change, as we saw in Chapter 4. To promote the cause of teamworking requires training of the team and developing multi-skills so that members can do different tasks within the team. Also, the team leader should be trained in leadership skills.

A move to team-based processes had an impact on the training needs in many manufacturing companies. For example, the Nissan car factory in the United Kingdom delegated decision-making authority to teams who were required to carry out a range of production tasks. The competencies for each team role were identified and employees were trained in each area, and ultimately were able to pass on their knowledge to others. This style of 'up-skilled' working also spread through the supply chain and organisations (e.g. Lucas) that supplied the car manufacturers with component parts also adopted multi-disciplinary teams with enhanced skills (Storey, 1992).

By way of comparison, in the manufacture of biscuits in both Germany and the United Kingdom differences in performance have been attributed to the training of multi-functional teams in broad skill sets. In the United Kingdom there is a demand for simple biscuits that are either plain or have a single coating such as chocolate. By contrast, Germans have a preference for complicated biscuits that combine decoration and multiple textures (e.g. soft biscuits with a jam filling in chocolate cases) (Grugulis, 2006). On basic performance measures, UK factories operate 25 per cent above German ones. However, when adjustments are made for the complexity of the product, the UK workers are 40 per cent less productive than the Germans. In the German factories, 90 per cent of the workers were craft-trained bakers who could work in any of the main operations areas (mixing, forming and oven control) in a flexible way. As a result, three-person teams could manage at least two oven lines at a time. In the United Kingdom, training was more narrow and so each line required its own dedicated team of three people to cover the line as each employee was restricted to their skill area (Grugulis, 2006).

In recent years there have been a number of internal and external initiatives in training following developments aimed at improving the competitive advantage of organisations. The major ones that will be examined in this section are training to underpin management processes, such as total quality management, and national schemes to set standards of competences for all industries.

QUALITY MANAGEMENT

Quality management, and particularly approaches such as total quality management (TQM), already considered in Chapter 5 in connection with changing culture, emphasise the importance of improvements in business operations and output. The final judge of its effectiveness will be the customer in the market. Those responsible for quality improvements and TQM will try to ensure that quality pervades all organisational activities. It is the task of every function and every employee to contribute to activities connected with improvements, and quality systems and a quality culture are essential prerequisites (Hill, 1991; Ooi *et al.*, 2007). Training serves quality improvement programmes by developing employee skills to cope with change, as well as imparting an understanding of quality monitoring techniques.

At Michelin a training programme was mounted to support a quality improvement initiative and this was aimed at improving existing knowledge and skills, and teaching new skills, as well as knowledge of the inspection process. The company tested the trainees on what they absorbed during the training programme and the outcome of this exercise showed that quality improvements had taken place. As a result, skill-based pay was introduced to reflect the new responsibilities (IRS, 1992). In Chapter 8 skill-based pay was discussed as a reward for the acquisition of skills; in effect pay is linked to some extent to the successful completion of authorised training. This is an attempt to underline the importance of training as an aspect of corporate strategy.

NATIONAL SCHEMES

Historically, there have been criticisms of Britain's poor record in education and training. The education system is criticised for not appealing to large numbers of 18-year-olds, who finish their education earlier than many students from some neighbouring countries, and for not providing an educational experience compatible with the needs of industry. Employers have also been criticised for the lack of investment in training. At the national level these criticisms have been taken on board.

The government felt that previous training initiatives (e.g. the Industry Training Boards referred to earlier) failed because they were both too bureaucratic and too centralised. A preferred alternative in the 1990s was to decentralise responsibility for training, making sure that industry and commerce participated in the scheme. Training and Enterprise Councils (TECs) and their Scottish equivalent were set up as the hub of local initiatives. TECs were allocated government funds, which they controlled, but they were allowed to raise private funds as well. The majority of the membership of a TEC was from commerce and industry; the rest came from the field of education and training, trade unions and voluntary organisations. TECs made assessments of their local labour markets and then developed training solutions. In some cases, TECs encouraged local employers with similar needs to cooperate in training support and provision. TECs were replaced with a national Learning and Skills Council (LSC), which gives local skills and learning councils the job of coordinating and funding all work-related further education and training.

The LSC has the stated aim of improving the skills of young people and adults to ensure that the country has a world-class workforce and hence can be more competitive on the global stage (LSC, 2007). It has an annual budget of £10.4 billion and its major tasks are to:

■ raise participation and achievement by young people;

■ increase adult demand for learning;

■ raise skill levels for national competitiveness;

■ improve the quality of education and training delivery;

■ improve the effectiveness and efficiency of the sector.

The LSC was set a range of targets and it has been successful in achieving these. The target for further education colleges was that by 2007 they should achieve a rate of 76 per cent of students achieving a qualification. This target was achieved (at 77 per cent) two years early in 2005. The success rate of young people completing apprenticeships has increased from 40 per cent to 53 per cent and work-based learning rates of successful completion of qualifications is now about 59 per cent, so the targets for employees in work are also being hit (LSC, 2007). The LSC is discussed further in Box 10.1.

Some time ago the government took a particular initiative in the field of training by setting up a national framework – National Vocational Qualifications (NVQs) – that linked the provision of training in a direct way to skills used in jobs. NVQs were designed to set occupationally based standards, to recognise competence in the workplace and to provide a ladder of achievement. The standards are usually defined by national training organisations (NTOs), whose membership is drawn from the relevant industrial sector. On offer are competency-based qualifications applicable to jobs at all levels within organisations across all industries. The qualifications can be acquired by employees while they are engaged in normal job activities at their place of work. Each NVQ is typically divided into units around functional roles. The actual training would be monitored by an accredited tester, normally a manager or supervisor, who is qualified to act in this way. The employee should be able to demonstrate performance that can be assessed. If the employee has met the standard required at a particular level in the NVQ hierarchy a pass grade is given. If the employee does not meet the standards required this signifies a fail and indicates a training need. The NVQs give employees scope to go on developing their skills and experience and hopefully the overall experience will advance the mobility of labour between employers.

The Department of Innovation, Universities and Skills developed plans to invest £500 million per year from 2008 to provide over seven million training places (BBC, 2007). These include 120,000 new apprenticeships, 30,000 places for older workers and basic skills training in literacy and numeracy. The purpose is to enhance the performance of the economy by expanding the participation of skilled labour. John Denham, the Universities and Skills Minister said: 'The primary reason we are expanding skills and training places is to make sure the British economy is prosperous and competitive in the future and to make sure everyone can share in that prosperity' (cited in Siddique, 2007).

Already reference has been made to 'competency'. This is a term used in preference to knowledge and skills on the understanding that competence, unlike knowledge and skills, has a better relationship with improved performance. The jury is still out on this one! The Training Agency defined competence as 'the ability to perform the activities within an occupation or function to the standards expected in employment'. This definition would include the ability to transfer knowledge and skills to new situations within employment, and takes on board activities such as organising and planning, creative and innovative pursuits, tolerance for handling non-programmed situations, and interpersonal skills used in liaising with fellow workers and clients. Case example 10.3 illustrates the use of the 'competency' approach in a training and development context.

CASE EXAMPLE 10.3

A COMPETENCY APPROACH IN NORTH CAROLINA COUNTY

In North Carolina, County land agents were being recruited but it became clear that both new recruits and existing agents had learning needs when it came to an understanding of the technicalities of horticulture. A competency-based approach was adopted by the County. A planning team was drawn from volunteer agents and horticultural specialists to identify the training needs and define the competency types and levels. The agents had a range of experience and knowledge and so it was helpful to standardise the 'output' in terms of when agents would be deemed competent in horticulture and to have a degree of flexibility in terms of input that could cope with the diverse extant skill levels. This pattern fitted the competency approach well. Five tiers of competence were established and these were encompassed within a personal approach called personal and organizational development (POD). The five tiers were:

- technical orientation,
- basic horticultural topics,
- intermediate topics,
- advanced topics,
- graduate level courses.

The graduate level courses were taught flexibly to accommodate agents' diaries. The programme was piloted and has now been rolled out. It is regarded as being highly successful by agents, trainers and managers and the competence level of agents in horticulture has risen to the required levels.

Source: based on Monks *et al.*, 2004

Question

What are the advantages of a competecy-based approach such as that at North Carolina County?

In Case example 10.3, the competency approach is used at different stages – at the assessment of training needs, the setting of learning objectives and the evaluation of training – but the focus is always on the output of the training.

Reservations have been expressed about the competency approach in the sense that it is considered too restrictive. Doubts have also been expressed about whether increasing individual competencies enhances organisational performance, that the focus is on discrete areas of a job and not generalised ability in relation to a whole job, and that too little attention is given to the complexity of the process of skill acquisition and the transfer of skills for the benefit of the organisation (Holmes, 1990). There is also the view that the competency approach does not consider management style, bureaucratic structure, corporate culture, the environment, career patterns and personal learning abilities. These factors were identified as being necessary to operate a sound training programme (Training Agency, 1989). The above criticisms are likely to be too harsh when the advanced stages of the NVQ are considered where management training takes place; the earlier stages would focus on operative training and perhaps the criticisms are more valid at this level. More recent research on the use of competency training at leadership and management levels has found the approach to be quicker and cheaper to develop and equally as effective as traditional systematic training (Naquin and Holton, 2006).

In recent years there appeared to be some unease about the lack of attention to the general skills of numeracy and literacy. There is no requirement for general literacy and numeracy skills to be developed to gain an NVQ award (Steedman, 1998). Therefore, it would be beneficial to have incorporated within the NVQ framework the literacy and numeracy skills currently outside it; this could have the effect of motivating a number of adults low in literacy and numeracy to improve these essential skills (see Box 10.1).

Box 10.1: Learning and Skills Council

The new Learning and Skills Council (LSC) in the United Kingdom, with a strong business representation, replaced the TECs and the Further Education Funding Council and is set to carry out a major reform of post-16 skills and education. The LSC will consist of 47 local councils or subsidiaries, which will enjoy considerable freedom to reflect local needs; the national council – which will assume real strategic power – will oversee the work of further education and sixth form colleges, and work-based training and education.

The LSC has an ambitious plan to spend more than £2.5 billion on training and teaching adults, especially those with poor basic skills needed by industry and those coming from disadvantaged areas. A priority is to tackle Britain's chronic record in adult illiteracy and innumeracy. Those with poor reading, numeracy and writing skills would be introduced to learning via Internet access points in the workplace, libraries and other public areas. It is hoped that the LSC will act as a regulator for industrial spending on training, helping to direct and increase the £20 billion spent privately by companies and other employers, and provide quality assurance so that companies could choose effective training schemes. Under the new system multinational companies will not have to negotiate with numerous local councils or subsidiaries; instead they can go directly to the national council. This arrangement is likely to be an improvement on the old system. Another important activity to be undertaken by LSC would be to gather high-quality intelligence data in the marketplace to enable it to track skills gaps in industry (Kelly, 2000).

The debate continues; in recent years the government outlined proposals for more and better vocational and occupational courses and arrangements with employers to improve skills levels, with a promise of selective support for them.

Source: based on Bream, 2003

Question

Do you think it is the proper role of government to fund training, or should investment in employees' skills be the responsibility of the employer?

A national UK initiative is the Investors in People (IiP) scheme. This attempts to relate training and development to business strategy and provides guidance to companies on how to develop their training programmes to nationally recognised standards. The key issue is the adequacy and relevancy of the company's training requirements in the light of business strategy. The IiP is not too interested in detailed prescriptions on the contents of training programmes, and it is not essential to link training to the NVQ scheme. IiP uses a range of criteria to judge organisations' eligibility to be accredited, but it recognises that companies of different sizes and types will need to meet the criteria in their own way. The IiP standard is based on three principles as follows (IiP, 2007):

- **plan** – developing strategies to improve the performance of the organisation;
- **do** – taking action to improve the performance of the organisation;
- **review** – evaluating the impact on the performance of the organisation.

In order to be recognised by IiP an organisation is required to engage in systematic planning, to audit its training operations to establish if things are going according to plan and, where necessary, to take appropriate corrective action. Trained IiP assessors will visit the company to evaluate the progress made and report on whether or not to offer recognition. By 2007 over 30,000 UK organisations had achieved the standard.

It appears that IiP's interpretation of training and development closely coincides with an HRM perspective in this area. There is no distinction between training and development and there is a recognition that all employees have development potential. Also, training is something that permeates the thinking and behaviour of managers at all levels, it is not something that belongs to the training function in the organisation, and it is relevant to the efficient operation of the company. Such a view, if upheld, could be protective of training in adverse economic situations.

There have been criticisms of IiP by the Confederation of British Industry (CBI) to the effect that the procedures used are overly bureaucratic and the costs of assessment are too high

(Hilton, 1992). But more recently the IiP has reviewed its procedures to make them more flexible and less bureaucratic. The intention is that they should be equally applicable to smaller organisations and there have been more favourable comments from employers. In a report based on a three-year government-funded study and produced by the Institute for Employment Studies at the University of Sussex it was stated that IiP was having a positive effect in the workplace (Bolger, 1996). In the report employers were attributing a number of benefits to their involvement with IiP, such as a more systematic and focused approach to training based on business needs, improved employee communications, a better understanding of business amongst employees and higher levels of motivation and skill among the workforce. Two examples, one relating to a small company and the other a large manufacturer, of successful IiP initiatives are provided in Case example 10.4.

CASE EXAMPLE 10.4

SUCCESSFUL IiP INITIATIVES

Purbeck Ice Cream

Purbeck Ice Cream is a small company employing eight people. It was set up by dairy farmers to make good use of excess milk and is famous for its chilli and cocktail-flavoured ice creams, supplying the major supermarkets.

Purbeck pursued IiP accreditation because it wanted to be highly team focused and saw its people as 'the most important ingredient in the ice cream'. Purbeck put regular appraisals in place and reviewed its documents and procedures. As a result staff had a much better understanding of what was going on and where they fitted in.

The company has achieved all its market and financial targets and now has an ethos of mutual reliance. Recently, when new machinery was introduced, staff were somewhat intimidated by its complexity. However, staff approached the necessary learning as a team and not only achieved productivity gains, but also further strengthened group bonds and loyalty.

Komatsu UK

In contrast to Purbeck Ice Cream, Komatsu UK is a large manufacturer, employing 700 people and producing about 3,000 medium-sized hydraulic excavators per annum, most of which are exported throughout Europe. Komatsu has been recognised by the IiP since the early 1990s and is well established as a leading example of training provision, having been reaccredited recently.

There is a strong focus on quality and the company has many quality circles concerned with improving the quality of the products and processes, and this has implications for employees' skills. About 50 staff are involved in quality circles at any one time. Not only do they develop new skills along with new operational processes, but they also develop problem-solving and decision-making skills through their involvement.

Komatsu puts a lot of emphasis on communications and there are regular briefings and presentations. Everyone is aware of the performance measures and feedback is a significant part of the culture. Staff are encouraged to be strongly involved in making suggestions and discussing innovations.

Komatsu is convinced that this approach has led to its quality and innovation, which has resulted in its strong export position.

Source: based on IiP, 2007

Questions

1. Is the need for training equally likely in small and large organisations?

2. What might be distinctive about how small and medium companies can approach the provision of training?

Management development

Management development is an activity that sets out to ensure that the organisation has the required managerial talent to face the present and future with confidence. It is concerned with improving the performance of existing managers, giving them the scope for personal growth and development, and makes appropriate provision for the future replacement of managers (i.e. management succession). Over the past two decades there has been a substantial increase in management training and development (Storey *et al.*, 1997; Stewart, 2005). Amongst the objectives for a management development scheme are the following:

- Identify managers with potential and ensure they receive the right experience, training and development.

- Set achievable objectives for the improvement of performance that are amenable to measurement, clearly specifying responsibilities.

- Create a climate where serious thought is given to instituting a management succession scheme, which would be kept under regular review.

Sisson and Storey (1988) suggested that the following key organisational issues should be considered before creating a management development strategy to increase managerial effectiveness:

- *Job definition*: strive for exactitude in defining what is expected of managers.

- *Selection*: be thorough in screening new entrants to the organisation with managerial potential to ensure the acquisition of the appropriate 'raw material'.

- *Identification of development needs*: adopt an enlightened appraisal process in order to assess the precise nature of managerial needs.

- *Training or development*: try to achieve a complementary balance between off-the-job training (e.g. management education) and on-the-job development to meet identified needs.

- *Reward systems*: recognise the significance of compensation packages linked to performance, as opposed to the traditional promotion system.

For some companies management development is a very considerable undertaking. This is the case for BP, which has a workforce of 100,000 spread across the globe. BP realised that development would only have a limited impact if it was restricted to top executives and so they set about developing the first-line managers (roughly 10,000 people) in an approach combining systematic analysis, off-the-job courses and on-the-job informal support. More details of BP's approach are given in Case example 10.5.

Some approaches have stressed the structure of needs analysis and targeted training for management, whilst others have proposed a more flexible and personalised approach (Stewart, 2005). The various options are discussed later in the section on approaches to training and development.

CASE EXAMPLE 10.5

FIRST-LINE MANAGEMENT DEVELOPMENT AT BP

BP operates in the competitive and challenging environment of global energy provision. In this environment, the company has to be constantly renewing itself and changing. It has to achieve this development across widely dispersed geographical sites and functions, and hence relies strongly on local managers not only to control their 'patch' but to enable the 70–80 per cent of employees that report to them to provide top quality service.

The management development initiative had strong backing from the Chief Executive and started with a phase of analysis. This included telephone interviews with first-line managers and 250 were chosen to participate directly in the design of the development programme. Until this point their training had mainly been ad hoc and delivered locally with little or no follow-up. Subgroups of the 250 were brought together in a series of workshops to identify learning needs, opportunities and priorities. The workshops were attended by top-level managers so that a dialogue was possible. It had been assumed that local managers would want local provision, but in fact they wanted a global development programme with strong backing from the centre.

A group of learning and development professionals was brought together to consider the potential designs of the programme and in this set of workshops the focus was on what the business needed from the front-line management positions both in terms of current skills and future strategic needs.

The management development programme included the following elements:

■ supervisory essentials – delivered through face-to-face, web-based materials and CDs;
■ context and connections – a two-day session covering the BP strategy, links to local operations and the need for change;
■ the leadership event – a four-day session using action learning, briefings from top executives and role-plays to improve communication and leadership skills;
■ peer partnerships – new first-level managers are paired with experienced colleagues for coaching to enable ongoing learning on-the-job.

So far 8,000 managers have attended some or all of the programme, and those who have attended are consistently ranked above those who have yet to attend both by their subordinates and superiors.

Source: based on Priestland and Hanig, 2006

Question

How will BP be able to judge whether or not the management development programme has been successful?

CAREER MANAGEMENT

This activity is complementary to management development and is concerned with planning and shaping the path that people take in their career progression within the organisation. It normally applies to managerial staff, but not necessarily so, and follows an assessment of the needs of the organisation for managers and the preferences of employees for development. Assessment centres, discussed in connection with selection in Chapter 7, could be used to identify managerial talent or confirm its existence.

The underlying assumption of career management is that, in the context of management succession, the organisation should be alert to providing able people with the training, guidance and encouragement to enable them to fulfil their potential. This view is not shared by all organisations, which would take in 'fresh blood' as and when needed and do not subscribe to elaborate internal promotion policies. Another view is to promote competent people who have proved themselves in their current jobs to higher positions when the opportunity arises. But progressive companies are likely to take a considered, long-term view when they set in motion sophisticated reviews of employee performance and potential and plan job moves on the basis of the outcome of these processes. In this sense a preoccupation with current performance and effectiveness can go hand in hand with considerations regarding future career moves.

It should be noted that the upward and onward view of a career is not always compatible with organisational settings characterised by leaner and fitter companies with fewer promotion opportunities. These issues were discussed in Chapter 6 on HR planning. With a decreasing number of rungs on the career ladder the reality of the career plateau will face many people earlier than was the case in the past. On the basis of research conducted in the UK finance sector, Herriot and Pemberton (1995) describe the following career development alternatives to promotion, as perceived by managers, which are not mutually exclusive:

- *Career flexers*: These tend to be young ambitious managers who move about and are likely to accept a variety of interesting jobs.

- *Ambitious careerists*: These managers tend to be confident about their capacity to evolve to higher positions, and are optimistic about the future in this respect. This disposition seems to be more pronounced when they are younger and have spent little time in their existing or previous jobs.

- *Career disengagers*: These managers are more likely to be older employees who are no longer ambitious or find their work interesting, possibly expecting to be made redundant or being able to avail themselves of an early retirement scheme, though they could be found in younger age groups. They would like to cease working full time either abruptly or gradually.

- *Career lifers*: These managers tend to be older and recognise that advancement is a thing of the past, but are overjoyed when told that they can stay on until retirement. They would welcome a loyalty bonus.

Organisations should recognise the variety of career aspirations of managers, including those listed above, and accept the challenge of recasting the traditional career structure and removing the stigma attached to the plateau. Finally, even though the notion of a career for life in an organisation is becoming more remote, this does not absolve employers from commitment to providing career paths for able employees (Herriot, 1992). Herriot maintains that only those organisations that negotiate careers will retain the people they need to face the future with confidence.

Finally, it should be said that the careers experienced by numerous people are less predictable than they once were, and therefore a sense of injustice and broken promises are quite common among employees in organisations. In this context the concept of equity is crucial and this raises the question of the status of the psychological contract that exists between the employer and employee (McKenna, 2006).

Approaches to training and development

A large number of methods are available to the organisation when it is considering the training and development of both managerial and non-managerial staff. To start with we shall examine job-related experiences, such as demonstration, coaching, mentoring and job rotation/enlargement/enrichment. Later the emphasis is on formal training methods, self-development (e.g. action learning) and outdoor courses.

SITTING BY NELLIE (DEMONSTRATION)

In this traditional method, the trainee is shown how to do the job by an experienced member of staff and is then allowed to get on with it. The advantage of this method is that learning is directly related to the job. The disadvantages are that the experienced member of staff (who may not be a training expert) may have difficulty explaining things and empathising with the trainee, and mistakes made by the trainee could be costly. Also, this method does not provide for the creation of structure in the learning process, neither does it provide appropriate feedback, which is required to improve effective performance.

COACHING

Coaching, which could be considered an improved version of demonstration and has the advantage of interaction between the trainer and trainee, is typically a short-term phenomenon that starts with a learning goal and is concerned primarily with performance and the development of definable skills (Clutterbuck, 2001), and it is on the increase. It has key ingredients not associated with demonstration, such as structure, feedback and motivation. The immediate supervisor or close colleagues normally provide advice and feedback about aspects of the performance of employees. Coaching is predominantly about showing people how to apply knowledge they already possess, and it can be particularly useful in generating ideas and getting people involved in the management of change. Coaches set challenging tasks, carry out appraisals, monitor progress and counsel and prepare people for promotion (Conway, 1994). When coaching is used with senior staff it could be geared to the development of soft skills (e.g. self-awareness, greater understanding of interpersonal processes, flexibility and conceptual thinking) so as to complement the more technical skills developed through other forms of training (O'Reilly, 1998). For an example of the uptake of this method see Case example 10.6.

MENTORING

Mentoring, a method of on-the-job training, particularly for aspiring senior managers, appears to be growing in importance and is usually a longer-term phenomenon, more concerned with helping the employee or executive to determine what goals to pursue and why. It seeks to build wisdom – the ability to apply knowledge, skills and experience in new situations and to new problems (Clutterbuck, 2001). The practice of mentoring could be viewed as a

COACHING AT THE BBC

During the past decade coaching has become embedded in the BBC. It started in the late 1990s when it was confined to senior executives who had external coaches. However, it was felt that staff more generally could benefit from coaching. The cost of hiring external coaches would have been too great, so the BBC developed a team of internal coaches who have achieved success in the corporation and are willing to give some of their time to enabling others. There are now 65 coaches delivering coaching to over 200 people from across the organisation.

Initially, the approach was informal, but now training courses have been set up for the coaches to ensure that they are equipped with the right skills to develop others. Coaches are selected through an assessment centre and given continuous support via a supervisor. Coaching is divided into three 'routes' that are designed to meet the needs of executives in their first 100 days, senior managers and middle managers. Demand is growing and the BBC believes that coaching plays an important role in building the internal community.

Source: based on Syedain, 2007

Question

Coaching can be very effective as a form of individual development. What should companies do to ensure that the learning that occurs is helpful for the group and organisation as a whole?

relationship between two people, one is senior and acts as an adviser to a younger executive preferably in a different section. The role of mentor has at least three functions: to give advice on career options; to provide social support; and to help mentorees be more effective in their current roles (Hunt, 2001). The trainee (mentoree or protégé) observes the skills displayed by the mentor, usually a senior manager who is not their boss, and copies and adopts the senior manager's behaviour. The mentor provides support and help in the various assignments undertaken by the protégé and can provide an invaluable insight into the politics and culture of the organisation. The protégé can benefit from the continuous dialogue with the mentor who, if influential within the organisation, can exert much influence in securing interesting tasks for the protégé as well as opening windows of opportunities. As a result the mentor contributes to confidence building and the career development of the protégé and provides him or her with a useful informal network within the organisation.

Mentoring is said to provide a channel through which core organisational values and meanings are conveyed and fortified by mentors of the status of senior managers at the twilight of their careers, and absorbed by those who will eventually succeed them (Collin, 1992). The characteristics one would expect to find in a mentor are summarised in Table 10.1. Mentoring is a growing activity, with perhaps 50 per cent of medium to large organisations either operating organised schemes or actively encouraging the creation of informal mentor–protégé pairings (Arnold, 2005).

Reflecting on mentoring Arnold (2005) makes the following observation:

Table 10.1: Characteristics of a mentor

■ The relationship between the mentor and the protégé tends to be open ended with less immediate concern for attaining goals than you would expect to find in situations where a boss sets targets for a subordinate. It is a protected relationship in which learning, experimentation and risk taking can occur and potential skills are developed with outcomes expressed as competencies.

■ The mentor is knowledgeable, has high status, a strong power base in the organisation, and has the ability to place issues in a broader context. He or she also has a capacity for conceptual modelling (i.e. has a broad portfolio of models to help the executive analyse and understand interactions, as well as being able to evolve new models as part of the dialogue).

■ The mentor is a good listener, is well able to empathise with the protégé, is able to relate well to people and establish rapport with the protégé (which is often based on shared interests) and is willing to use his or her power to influence events. The mentor should avoid encouraging an over-dependent relationship and recognise the boundaries of his or her capacity to help.

■ The mentor is involved and willing to share his or her expertise with the protégé and promote the latter's self-development, and does not feel threatened by the protégé's potential for equalling or surpassing him or her in status.

■ The mentor has a commitment to developing others, having a genuine interest and pleasure in the protégé's achievements.

Source: based on Clutterbuck, 2001; McKenna, 2006

'It is likely that some mentoring schemes work better than others. It is probably important that mentors and protégés want the relationship, and they may well need training and orientation in order to make the most of it. The goals of the mentoring scheme should be clear and specific. The mentor's work performance should be assessed and rewarded partly on the basis of how effectively he or she is carrying out the mentoring role. The culture of the organization should be one that values personal and professional development. Even then there is a danger that mentors will hand on outdated knowledge and skills to protégés, especially in times of rapid change.'

Those who have received good mentoring early in their careers are likely to experience certain advantages, such as accelerated promotions, improved income and satisfaction with their careers. However, we must be mindful of its negative aspects, which could be listed as follows (Bell, 1998; Goss, 1994):

■ There may be charges of elitism from those who were denied protégé status.

■ There may be a certain incompatibility between the mentor and the protégé.

■ The protégé may be over-dependent on the mentor.

■ The mentor may show an inability to manage the relationship effectively: for example, he or she lacks the appropriate interpersonal skills, is too patronising, is too interventionist, and is inclined to lavish too much praise.

■ Generally, line managers are suspicious of the process and display resistance and lack of cooperation because of its disruptive effect on reporting relationships already established.

The role of the mentor is changing (Bell, 1998). Its hierarchical nature is changing in the sense that it is no longer necessary for the ideal mentor to be a senior executive. Mentoring could also be conducted long-distance where there is a significant geographical space between the parties, and it can last for a short time as opposed to continuing over a long period.

MENTORING VS COACHING

There is some overlap between mentoring and coaching. The most effective coaches share with mentors the capability to help the learner develop the skills of listening to and observing themselves, which leads to much faster acquisition of skills and modification of behaviour. Coaches also share with mentors the role of 'critical friend' – confronting executives with truths no one else feels able to face them with. Whereas the coach is more likely to approach these issues using direct feedback, the mentor will tend to approach them through questioning processes that force the executive to recognise problems for themselves (Clutterbuck, 2001). A related technique is counselling, which is directed at helping the individual overcome specific psychological barriers to performance or helping them deal with dysfunctional behaviour.

Coaching and mentoring are approaches that could be usefully applied in management development, but there are some signs that coaching as a preferred way of developing people is superseding mentoring. It may well be that the terms coaching and mentoring are interchangeable, but it may also suggest a shift to a more performance-focused approach where the emphasis is more on improving quality of work now (the coaching emphasis) than on long-term career or general psychological well-being, as in mentoring (Arnold, 2005).

JOB ROTATION

This involves moving people around on a systematic basis in order to broaden their experience. The advantages of this method are that links between departments are fostered, and employees develop flexibility because of the range of activities undertaken. However, a disadvantage is that it does not offer people the opportunity to practise the complete range of skills because of the limited time spent on any one job. Also, a problem could arise when errors materialise because of the inexperience of the transferred employee, and when managers nominate poor performers for the job rotation scheme.

OTHER JOB-RELATED EXPERIENCES

Apart from job rotation, job enlargement could be used to broaden the job experience of the employee. Job enlargement expands a job on a horizontal basis, as opposed to a vertical basis found in job enrichment, which was discussed in the previous chapter. Diversity is promoted by increasing the number of tasks an employee performs. For example, a word processor operator's job could be enlarged to include tasks such as acting as a receptionist periodically and doing some filing. Job enlargement, along with participating in the work of a project team or task group, could be a useful developmental exercise.

FORMAL TRAINING METHODS

Amongst the methods used are lectures and discussions, together with case studies, role-playing and simulation, and programmed learning. Case studies make use of predetermined situations to provide opportunities for the analysis of data and the presentation of solutions without the risks of failure associated with real-world situations. Role-playing and simulation offers the trainee the opportunity to perform in situations as if they were real, as in, for example, the training of airline pilots. Programmed learning with the aid of the computer can be used to test knowledge and ability at a basic level to begin with, progressing to more difficult tasks later.

Formal training can take place off the job. There could be long college courses that cater for the overall development of the employee, but are not specifically targeted to the job. This gives the employee the opportunity to think afresh and to meet people with different experiences outside the job. Nowadays open learning courses have become popular. The learner proceeds at their own pace with the help of a pack of course material, but unless certain measures are taken (e.g. provision of tutorial support) the learner can feel somewhat isolated.

There are also short courses. Although certain of these are general in nature, others are specifically targeted to satisfy an organisational need. Formal courses can be expensive, and there is no guarantee that learning is transferred to the work situation. Supporters of on-the-job training would argue that learning on the job is more likely to find its way into work practices.

SELF-DEVELOPMENT

In self-development control and direction are primarily in the hands of the individual, with a focus on learning from experience. This approach does not have to be unstructured experience tantamount to a process of trial and error, with an intention to steer clear of past mistakes. It can be structured with an agreement between interested parties at the workplace on the best way to make it operational; this could include guided reading and specified work activities.

An influential theorist in the field of self-development is Kolb (1985). The learning cycle he postulated is as follows:

1. The individual has a concrete experience, either planned or unplanned.
2. Next there is reflective observation, and this amounts to thinking about what was responsible for the experience and the implications, etc.
3. Abstract conceptualisation and generalisation follow where general principles can be drawn from the experience or incident.
4. The final step is experimentation in new situations, and this forms the basis for the development of new experiences.

The application of the learning cycle would necessitate managers diagnosing the work situations they encounter, evaluating the avenues open to them and finally formulating a strategy to attain their objectives. Ideally a programme of self-development will bear some relationship to career development for managerial staff and both could be linked to organisational needs as gleaned from corporate plans. It would appear that any good system of management development based on self-development must prepare managers to exercise control of events and to take responsibility for outcomes within their domain, and particularly control over their own actions and learning (Pedlar *et al.*, 1988).

ACTION LEARNING

The basic ingredients of self-development are ingrained in action learning, but in addition it has a social dimension. Basically, the trainee relies heavily on experience of what happens at work and adopts questioning and exploration in a group setting as a mode of operation (Revans, 1971). In action learning the spotlight is on real problems, where the learner or trainee questions the causes of these problems. This is followed by generating solutions that are capable of implementation.

A small group (called a set) is created and members cooperate in a process that amounts to questioning and testing each other until there is a certain amount of clarity about the nature of the problem and the best way to tackle it. Set members are very supportive as they go about the review of individual projects, and they are keen to provide feedback. A climate of mutual support and mutual constructive criticism can be found in a set that works well. Once the deliberations are completed the set disbands, and trainees are expected to be committed to their chosen action strategies following the various questioning and exploration episodes that took place in the set.

A feature of action learning is the challenge to and the criticism levelled at the status quo and traditional practices. In certain organisational cultures such an approach would not be welcome, but it could certainly take root and produce results in organisational conditions where there is a commitment to action learning. It would appear that action learning as part of a management development programme is a useful approach when the organisation is interested in increasing the effectiveness of its managers in a behavioural sense (Lawrence, 1986), but it is not necessarily the best approach to develop technical competence or to assimilate new knowledge about managing people.

An action learning approach has been adopted by the North Western Health Board in Ireland. The organisation was undergoing significant change, and the aim was to develop a training programme for 500 people. With that number a cost-efficient approach was necessary. Self-managed action learning sets have been established, and so far 160 people are taking part. At the meetings the set focuses on the concerns of each person in turn, and the sets have been likened to 'personal think tanks'. Projects are undertaken, and report-backs occur at the start of the next meeting.

In order to develop skills in managing the sets, facilitators were brought in for the first two meetings of each set, but thereafter they became self-facilitating. A number of projects have been launched, including developing support frameworks for GPs, measuring user satisfaction in the mental health service and schemes for the reduction of waiting lists. In one example, the consultant clinical coordinator at Sligo General Hospital joined a set including a social worker, a nursing sister, two physiotherapists and an occupational therapist. Just working with the group itself proved to be an insightful process, and his project has resulted in the introduction of a hospital-wide clinical audit system (O'Hara *et al.*, 2001).

A prominent feature of action learning is learning to learn. This amounts to developing a greater understanding of the learning process, and of the trainee's preferred approaches to learning. Earlier we noted that Kolb (1985) recognised that people learn in different ways. Honey and Mumford (1992) in the United Kingdom developed a model based on the work of Kolb. For example, a person may prefer to learn in one of the following ways:

- through new experiences: the *pragmatist* – they are more effective learners when they see a connection between new information and the problems they encounter;

- by observation and reflection: the *reflector* – they are more effective learners when they evaluate and reflect on their own experiences;

- by conceptualisation: the *theorist* – they are more effective learners when they relate information that they receive to concepts or theories;

- by experimentation: the *activist* – they are more effective learners when they are actively involved in tangible or concrete tasks.

The Global Leadership Programme offered by the University of Michigan in the United States, which was designed to provide individuals with a global perspective, was based on the principles of action learning. Over a period of five weeks teams of American, Japanese and European executives would learn global business skills through action learning (Dowling and Welch, 2004). To build cross-cultural teams the programme made use of seminars and lectures, adventure-based exercises, and field trips to investigate business opportunities in developing countries (e.g. India, China and Brazil).

OUTDOOR AND INDOOR COURSES

Outdoor training sessions could be on the use of initiative, problem solving and cooperation, and could be used by organisations interested in the development of team building and leadership skills. Invariably there is a sharing of experience by members of the group in the face of adverse physical conditions, such as a challenging mountain climb, and this can contribute to the development of cooperative modes of operation and psychological closeness.

These training sessions can produce good results if attention is given to a number of issues connected with the planning and operation of the course, and relating the course to conditions in the home organisational environment. For example, does the course have clear objectives? Is the course a natural part of the organisation's total training provision? Are the course organisers familiar with the culture and practices in the organisation from which the participants are drawn? Have the course organisers taken the necessary action with respect to safety? In addition, the instructor/trainee ratio should be low and where possible what takes place during the training sessions should be related to the participant's workplace.

One should be aware of potential problems. If some or all of the members of the training course originate from the same organisation but are of different statuses, superiors might feel uneasy about their image in the eyes of subordinates when they have not performed as well as expected. On the other hand, subordinates might act in a predictable organisational way by adopting a typical behavioural pattern (e.g. submissiveness or compliance) where they perceived superiors to be acting officiously. There might be difficulties in transferring the benefits derived from the training session to the work situation because of constraints with respect to implementation. Certain key people in the organisation might feel uncomfortable if those returning were equipped with behavioural skills that enabled them to challenge cherished practices (Lowe, 1991).

There has been a dip in the demand for outdoor courses according to an Industrial Society survey (Hegarty and Dickson, 1995). Some trainers in the late 1990s were keen to get rid of the macho image of training in the great outdoors, and turned their attention to developing minds and building teams rather than testing endurance. The new approach relies on communication workshops, using body language only, and the live arts rather than freezing mud to provide a new source of inspiration to extract the best from employees (Ashworth, 1999). In the case of the live arts, course participants stage their own shows with the help of stage performers and technical staff drawn from the opera, theatre, circus and film. Those who support this approach believe that the arts have a role to play in the release of creativity. In recent years a Management College offered a one-day management development course on the art of leadership in the form of a workshop based on Shakespeare's *The Tempest* led by Olivier Mythodrama. The 'Tempest' play is said to be steeped in magical mystery, revealing the vital ingredients of the successful change initiative, and can be viewed as a unique form of experiential learning combining theatre practice, psychology, mythology, and organisational development to develop authentic leaders (Roffey Park's Newsletter, 2004). It is claimed that by 'acting out' their desired leadership behaviours, and the leadership role they find most challenging, the participants can overcome their leadership 'blind spots' and enhance their expertise. This process creates an embodied memory of their learning, which they then apply in their everyday challenges in the workplace (Roffey Park's Newsletter, 2005). It remains to be seen if this form of management development is successful in the long run.

There appears to be constant experimentation on the best way to achieve teambuilding, creativity, and other goals of outdoor training events. Strategic planning, exchanges of best practices between different departments, and creative thinking, can be generated through carefully structured 'away days'. Away days are gaining popularity in the public sector (White,

2002). One technique in exercises of this nature is to 'road test' proposed changes by having participants play the part of people with typical organisational problems and then ask them to examine how new processes or structures might address those problems.

E-LEARNING

E-learning refers to information and knowledge delivered via information and communication technology (ICT), and is typically associated with the Internet. Learners can operate online to carry out programmed exercises, read material and gain information pertinent to the performance of their job. Technology-based learning is said to have a number of advantages. First, it means that learners can access knowledge at any time convenient to them. Secondly, information can be transmitted to employees at high speed, and regular updates to material are possible. Thirdly, organisations whose workforce is geographically dispersed can enable all employees (or particular groups) to have the same information (Masie, 1999).

Glenmorangie, the Scotch whiskey distiller, used e-learning packages on a range of courses over the company's intranet to reach those in its far-flung outposts. This is a tremendous advantage for the distillery employees, who would otherwise face a three-hour drive to get to the training room at the company's headquarters. Those working in the Isle of Islay would need to catch a flight. Glenmorangie has halved its training budget since adopting the technology two years ago (Moules, 2004). The need to deliver cost-effective training to geographically dispersed employees has also driven the e-learning philosophy at Hilton International hotels, and this case is discussed in Case example 10.7.

However, one should be aware that e-learning may not be suitable for all learning styles and tasks. Particularly, hands-on learning may be necessary for practical topics, and for many learners a social aspect to learning is important. This does not just mean the socialising that is associated with training courses, but the elements of peer feedback and discussion that can provide an important stimulus in learning. In most e-learning packages these aspects are missing. Lloyds TSB (a high street bank) has made an attempt to tackle some of these potential problems. It has made ICT-based training available at 450 centres throughout the United Kingdom, and staff attend planned sessions in which there are pre- and post-course discussions, although the basis of the training input remains technology based (Hills and Francis, 1999).

Similarly, an approach to leadership training has been developed by General Motors, which makes extensive use of technology. After a course had taken place, participants were supported using a database that removed the need for them to remember everything. Information was available as and when they needed it, and they were supported in 'learning by doing'. They had access to other participants who had similar experiences and were able to share their learning and receive feedback. Through enabling such interactions the database built up live examples that participants could use in deciding how to respond to their own situation (Ulrich and Hinkson, 2001).

In a radical move, Pearl Assurance has acknowledged that use of ICT is an area where 'upward learning' can be fostered in the organisation. Pearl Assurance was then part of the Australian Mutual Provident Society. Its managers on a visit to the parent company in Sydney found an answer to problems they were experiencing in integrating the use of the web: 'e-possums'. The e-possums were a group of ICT literate staff who acted as enthusiastic guides to senior managers, enabling them to get to grips with the technology in a way which focused on solutions to problems that were live for the managers. In a sense this is a form of coaching but, in this case, the normal hierarchical arrangement is reversed (McLeod, 2001).

A survey by the CIPD (CIPD, 2007) collected the views of HR professionals on which methods of training are most effective in terms of participants' learning. The advice appears

E-LEARNING AT HILTON INTERNATIONAL

In 2001 Hilton International had ambitious plans to launch a major training initative. However, following the downturn in trade after 11 September, the budget was cut and the plans had to become more modest. The reaction of the HRM team was to develop a significant e-learning resource which is seen as highly successful and has grown significantly since its initiation in 2002.

The group operates hotels in 70 countries and so running residential training for staff from the over 400 hotels at a central location is difficult, costly and inconvenient for a business that relies on having its staff at the 'customer interface' around the clock.

Initially, the e-learning resource had 60 business courses and was not accessible at all venues as some were in parts of the world where there was restricted access to the Internet. Although there was uptake of the courses, it was a little sporadic. The answer was to make the process more systematic. After a review, staff had to apply for a password to enter the 'Development Zone' and they were encouraged to take and complete particular courses that were related to their training needs, rather than browsing courses that they thought they would like.

The content of the courses is partly internally generated and partly provided by external partners such as business schools. Most hotels now have a physical area where staff can access the e-learning resource, which had grown to offer 600 courses. There are three achievement levels – foundation, intermediate and advanced – and seven 'faculties' – executive foundation, management, operations, finance, business development, HR and research.

Having evaluated the provision, Hilton believes that not only are new skills and knowledge generated but the provision is also helpful in retaining staff. It has also seen a correlating improvement in customer satisfaction. However, Hilton does not think e-learning will replace other methods. As Andrea Kluit, Director of International Learning, put it: 'certain areas can be learnt only up to a point with e-learning'.

Source: based on Smethurst, 2006

Question

If you were designing the overall training and development strategy for Hilton, in what areas would you seek to supplement e-learning, and what approaches to training in these areas would you advocate?

to remain that a sensible mix of methods is best, along with a focus on job-centred learning. A summary of the CIPD's findings is provided in Table 10.2.

Continuous professional development

It is almost commonplace nowadays to hear the view that training should be a continuing process with the accent on self-development, as mentioned earlier. This is prompted by the

Table 10.2 Views about the most effective way for people to learn

Method	Percentage
On the job	41
Formal courses	21
The experience of work	15
Coaching/mentoring	10
Informal help from colleagues	7
Other	4
E-learning	2
Self-study in own time	1

Source: based on CIPD, 2007

suggestion that employees cannot, in a rapidly changing world, rely on the knowledge and skills acquired in gaining their initial qualifications. In 1987 the Institute of Personnel Management (now the CIPD) produced a code of practice with respect to personal development and the demands posed by jobs. A starting point is the assessment of the organisation's present and future training needs; this is done by extracting from the corporate plan the pool of employee knowledge and skills required to implement that plan. Predictably the importance of learning from confronting and solving problems at work is underlined. The current CIPD view, whilst retaining the strategic perspective of business-driven training also puts emphasis on individually-driven approaches:

> 'In our rapidly changing and increasingly knowledge-based economy, competitive advantage is built where individuals actively seek to acquire the knowledge and skills that promote the organisation's objectives. Organisations are learning environments, and employment in them is (or should be) a continuous learning experience.' (CIPD, 2007)

According to the CIPD learning is taking place all the time through experience, but not all such learning is necessarily positive. Therefore it is sensible to structure the learning sufficiently to enhance the mutual benefits for both employee and organisation.

The role of top management in cultivating a climate of continuous professional development (CPD) is given special mention. Top management is admonished to place high on the corporate agenda the frequent formal review of training activities aimed at the development of employee competencies. In the final analysis it should be recognised that it is wise to promote the view that one should make learning a habit and to accept the idea that work problems offer opportunities for learning. Ideally it is hoped that well-conceived continuous development aimed at helping the individual also helps the organisation to achieve its objectives.

Continuous professional development has become compulsory in most core accountancy disciplines. Also, lawyers (solicitors and barristers) need to show evidence of the minimum number of hours devoted to CPD in order to retain their practising certificates (Plimmer, 2004). The British Psychological Society (BPS) has made CPD mandatory and it applies to all chartered psychologists who hold a practising certificate (BPS, 2004). It requires individuals to be able to show that they are engaging in the CPD process. The CPD records should be submitted to the BPS in the form of a summary log, which includes details of the CPD process undertaken in the previous year, as follows:

- the professional development needs identified for that year;

- the professional activities undertaken;

- an overview of the individual psychologist's review and reflection of the learning outcomes, and how this relates to their own professional practice;

- any further development needs identified as a result of the review and reflection.

It is apparent that professional bodies are paying more attention to CPD. These bodies are naturally concerned with maintaining professional standards, staving off government interference, and retaining their grip on self-regulation of the profession. However, much of the burden has fallen on the shoulders of the members who have been forced to foot the bill for training and development themselves.

The UK Financial Services Authority takes a tough line, presumably influenced by the mis-selling of financial products in the past. It now requires employers to be responsible for keeping their staff's competencies up-to-date, with companies who fail to do so being liable to severe fines (Plimmer, 2004).

Learning organisation

The arrival on the scene of the learning organisation is associated with the need to provide for the internal renewal of the organisation in the face of a competitive environment. A learning organisation has been defined as one that facilitates the learning of all its members and continually transforms itself (Pedlar *et al.*, 1988). It is said that a learning organisation has the capacity to respond well to changes in its environment and creates space and formal mechanisms for people to think, to ask questions, to reflect and to learn, as well as encouraging them to challenge the status quo and to suggest improvement (Handy, 1989).

The climate within the learning organisation should permeate all collective activities (e.g. meetings, conferences) where there is an acute sensitivity to what is going on in the organisation and a willingness to experiment in the light of opportunities or threats. The learning organisation is keen to assist people in the identification of their learning needs; such needs would be reviewed regularly along with the provision of feedback on performance to date. Also, there would be a commitment to providing new experiences from which people can learn and a willingness to mobilise training resources. Learning from others could be extended to 'benchmarking', which is an ongoing investigation and learning experience that aims to identify, analyse, adopt and implement the best practices in the company's industry (Garvin, 1993).

In summary, the learning organisation puts the accent on a number of important issues, such as the following:

- self-development and continuous development that creates able performers;

- sharing knowledge leads to shared visions of the organisation's future, which could be facilitated by managerial leadership;

- promoting team learning when organisational members get together and share ideas and opinions with each other so as to improve decision making and achieve objectives;

- double loop learning where organisational members use feedback to test the validity of current values and practices, and a desire to keep the total organisational picture in mind with sensitivity to the external environment (Beard, 1993; Senge, 1990).

Finally, some are sceptical about the concept of the learning organisation because there could very well be a clash between the insights and benefits derived from it and those obtained from normal training activities (Price, 2004). Also, Doyle (2003) maintains:

> 'the greatest obstacle to implementing the principles of the learning organization concerns the transmission and management of knowledge. Much organizational knowledge is tacit or implicit. It is based on unvoiced assumptions, is often rooted in action and is often learned unconsciously through the process of socialization into the organization and through imitation. It is very hard to communicate and transfer to others. As anyone who has been involved in developing an expert system knows, getting human experts to make all their knowledge explicit can be difficult because much of their knowledge does not lend itself to being represented verbally.'

While it would not necessarily be claimed that Fox's Biscuits in Case example 10.8 has achieved 'learning organisation' status, it has nonetheless been able to link training and development to strategy, culture change and employee involvement. The outcome has been significant cost cutting and the enhancement of performance.

CASE EXAMPLE 10.8

TRAINING AND DEVELOPMENT AT FOX'S BISCUITS

Fox's Biscuits is part of the Northern Foods Group. It produces biscuits at the rate of 12,000 per minute for supermarkets. Up to 1995 millions of pounds had been invested in new technology, but there had been almost nothing spent on training employees to use it. The workforce had a low skills base, and in some cases poor literacy. There were communication problems and although people worked in teams these tended to be insular with little interaction between teams. The result was that there were grey areas surrounding who was responsible for what stage of the process, and so the process could, and did, collapse quickly and frequently. There was a traditional autocratic culture with eight layers of management and little trust between managers and workers.

The training initiative started with basic levels of training for an NVQ in food and drink. The programme allowed individuals a lot of flexibility, and employees were encouraged to work together. This was helpful because, with all the employees working towards the same study goals, they were able to support each other to improve. Employees reported that they were not afraid to admit that there was something they did not know, whereas in the previous culture no one would have made such an admission. People have gained confidence, and many have gone on to further training and education. The teams are now multi-skilled and can cover for each other's jobs, although each person has a 'principal job'. The shift system has been simplified and the layers of management reduced. Five core action teams were established and they receive suggestions from the workforce. Once the suggestions are assessed, voluntary action teams work to develop them. There is now a culture of people wanting to be involved, and 60 per cent of staff have joined in the projects.

Over the period, £300,000 has been invested in training. As a result 181 employees have achieved NVQ level 1, 128 have achieved level 2 and 25 have achieved level 3. Absence rates have fallen significantly and staff turnover has fallen from 11 per cent to 9 per cent. Suggestions for the year 2000 alone saved the site more than £350,000, thus more than paying back the investment in training in a single year. In 1995, the factory was seen as a poor performer by Northern Foods, but it is now seen as a success and the general manager sums it up by saying: 'Improving capability through developing and involving our people has been the catalyst for our success.'

Source: based on Poole, 2001

Questions

In what ways could associating training with certificated awards:

(a) be motivational

(b) be demotivational?

Evaluation

Eventually the organisation will need to know if its training and development activities are achieving the anticipated results. To put it technically, we are trying to establish the reliability (consistency) and validity (effectiveness in meeting objectives) of training programmes. This will be easier to establish in some areas than in others. For example, outcomes are more tangible and measurable where there is a change in the way a psychomotor skill is performed (e.g. driving a fork lift truck) than when a shift in values or attitudes has taken place. The central point is to establish a relationship between the training methods used and some measure of performance, and this can only be achieved by assessing the trainees' capability after the training has taken place.

We refer to *internal validity* when it is found that the training objectives are met after the trainees are assessed at the end of the training programme. On the other hand, *external validity* is achieved if, after completing the training programme, the trainees' performance is in line with the laid-down standard (Goldstein, 1978).

One would consider a number of issues other than validation in a restrictive sense when evaluating a training programme. The following are indicative of the approaches adopted. At the end of a training session trainees are asked to complete a questionnaire stating which parts of the training were most useful, relevant and interesting. The results of this exercise could be useful to the trainer, and could lead to an improvement next time round. However, the following weaknesses are associated with this method:

■ Positive responses are made because trainees were happy with the training encounter, possibly having been entertained by the instructor. Such responses would not give any insight into the effectiveness of the training session.

■ The trainees feel that the training session was useful and relevant to their occupational sphere, but unfortunately this judgement may be based on a lack of sufficient awareness of their training needs.

■ Because of the close proximity of the evaluation exercise to the end of the training session, there is no information on the transfer of learning to the workplace.

As a means to remedy the last weakness, follow-up questionnaires could be sent to respondents some time after the training took place (e.g. three months). Questions are asked about the extent to which the learning was used in practice in terms of using knowledge, skills and attitudes acquired during the training session. In the responses there could be an indication of impediments or blocks to the transfer of learning. Of course this may not be the fault of the trainee: it could be due to a lack of suitable equipment or software, or where there is resistance from other employees to the material learnt on the course.

Tests of varying kinds, such as examinations and grading of coursework and projects, can be used to evaluate learning, particularly on longer courses. These tests are likely to affect the processes and culture of the group engaged in learning as competitive and secretive tendencies develop following a realisation that a trainee can be given either a pass or fail mark or grade. A less formal version of tests is that of exercises where trainees engage in role-playing, or tackle a case study or in-tray exercise. Then they are given the opportunity to evaluate their own performance, subsequently receiving feedback from colleagues and the trainer. It is hoped that the feedback expressed as criticism is constructive. Although tests and exercises play a useful part in informing us about what learning has taken place we are none the wiser about the transfer of learning to the workplace.

Kirkpatrick (1967) provided what has become a widely-quoted framework for collecting information for the purposes of evaluating training. It consists of four levels, as follows:

1. *Reaction* (e.g. responses on the difficulty, depth, and length of the training).
2. *Learning* (e.g. knowledge acquired as a result of the training, following the use of an appropriate method of assessment soon after the end of the training session, or alternatively much later). The learning stage could entail providing tests on a pre- and post-training basis to establish the extent to which the trainee has achieved the learning outcomes of the training session.
3. *Behaviour* (e.g. if skills are developed following training, the extent to which the trainee uses those skills to an appropriate standard). The behavioural stage is connected with the transfer of learning, discussed in Chapter 7, and deals with the extent to which trainees demonstrate the skills acquired during training when they return to the workplace. One should be realistic about the time factor, because new skills may be competing with the old ones and take some time to be fully operational. The evidence collected at this stage is the unbiased views of the trainee's manager on the improvements detected, aided by indicators of performance, such as number of customer complaints, number of mistakes, etc.
4. *Results* (e.g. the extent to which the training has produced the requisite results in the workplace). The extent to which the training produced an impact on organisational effectiveness can be difficult to establish, as is mentioned below. It is said that a relatively small percentage of companies evaluate post-training behaviour (Patrick, 1992). Perhaps if there is a reluctance to measure its impact, there is an implicit belief in the effectiveness of training, particularly if adequate resources are devoted to it and it is recommended by authoritative personnel in the organisation.

The normal expectation is that the above framework would unfold in the manner indicated. However, this has been challenged. For example, it does not automatically follow that 'learning' would definitely lead to 'results', simply because a situation could arise where the trainee learns the appropriate knowledge but subsequently is not able to use it in the job as a result of lack of encouragement and support from superiors or colleagues (Alliger *et al.*, 1997).

Another approach is evaluation at the 'job behavioural level' (Hamblin, 1974). Here the transfer of learning could be evaluated by the manager or training specialist to establish whether or not behaviour has changed as a result of the training. The following include some of the techniques used for this purpose:

■ *Activity sampling and observer diaries*: the trainees are observed to see to what extent they are putting into practice the knowledge, attitudes and skills acquired through training.

■ *Critical incidents*: key incidents at work are analysed to establish to what extent 'new patterns of behaviour' are present.

■ *Self-recording*: the trainees record how they perform certain activities.

Eventually, the organisation will be looking for evidence of how the changed job behaviour influences other employees and the way the company functions. This would mean measuring changes in overall organisational functioning with respect to productivity, output and costs, but such an exercise would be difficult to undertake. In a recent development, an approach to evaluating training in terms of return on investment has been developed, and this is considered in Box 10.2.

Finally, at the evaluation stage it is worth considering why the training was undertaken in the first place. There could be a number of reasons, such as to rectify a skills deficiency, to project an image as a responsible employer, to convey to employees that the organisation is committed to their development, and as a reward to able performers.

Box 10.2: Return on investment approach to training evaluation

Phillips (2005), in response to the regular calls for a way of measuring the contribution of training, has developed an approach which, he argues, provides good evidence of the pay-back for the expenditure of the training budget.

First, there is a requirement for effective evaluation planning. This entails setting clear objectives at five levels:

1. reaction and satisfaction objectives

2. learning objectives

3. application objectives

4. impact objectives

5. ROI objectives.

There is then a need to collect data that are pertinent to each of the objectives. Hard data include output quality, volume, cost and time. Soft data include job and customer satisfaction. Data are collected via questionnaires, tests, on-the-job observations and performance monitoring as appropriate.

A common problem is to isolate the impact of the training. Several options are available, but two which are particularly useful are control groups and trend analysis. Control groups are groups of similar employees who have not received the training. The data for the control group can be compared to that for a group that has received the training, and if the training is the only significant difference between the groups, then difference in performance could be attributed to it. Where it is not appropriate to have a control group, for example, where it is necessary for all employees to go

▶

through the training, levels of performance post-training can be compared to extrapolations of expected performance using pre-training data. For example, performance could be compared to the figures for the same month in the previous years.

In order to be able to assert a return on investment, it is necessary to convert the analysis into monetary values. This can be done by establishing the value of the difference in performance using standard values, cost statements or expert estimation. The return on investment is a ratio based on the monetary benefits in relation to the costs of the training. The net benefits (i.e. the benefits after deducing the costs) are divided by the costs and multiplied by 100, hence giving a percentage figure.

Although this approach puts great emphasis on monetary calculation, it is also acknowledged that intangible benefits, such as improved teamwork and increased job and customer satisfaction, also occur. Where it is difficult or inappropriate to measure these intangibles, they are listed along with an explanation of the change.

Source: based on Phillips, 2005

Question

1. Do you think organisations should adopt a return on investment approach?

2. What additions or alterations might be considered to this method?

Training for international assignments

In order to compete successfully in global markets, multinational companies recognise that it is vital to train and develop expatriates, host country nationals and third country nationals so that high-calibre staff are available when required to achieve the corporate objectives. In this section attention will be devoted to issues related to the training and development of expatriates, but later the importance of training and developing other employees of multinational companies will also be considered.

It would appear that an effective approach to expatriate training and development includes:

■ development of expatriates before, during and after foreign assignments;

■ development and training of expatriate families before, during and after foreign assignments;

■ development of the headquarters staff responsible for the planning, organisation and control of overseas operations.

According to Dowling and Welch (2004), studies indicate that there are three areas that contribute to a smooth transition to a foreign post: cultural training, language instruction and assistance with practical day-to-day matters.

CULTURAL TRAINING

A major objective of cultural training is to help people cope with unexpected events in a new culture. Cross-cultural training, in addition to the task-specific knowledge necessary for the position, enables individuals to adjust quickly to the new culture (Black and Mendenhall, 1990). Without training of this sort, most people will not be successful in learning how to adapt to their new cultures (Briscoe and Schuler, 2004).

With regard to expatriates, cultural training seeks to develop an appreciation of the host country so that individuals can behave accordingly. For example, in the culture of the Middle East emphasis is placed on personal relationships, trust and respect in business dealings. In addition there is much emphasis on religion that influences almost every aspect of life. Take the case of a highly-paid expatriate who took two miniature bottles of brandy with him into Qatar (a Muslim country in the Middle East). The alcohol was found by Customs, and the expatriate was promptly deported and ordered never to return. It stands to reason that it is important to accept the host country's culture in order to avoid getting into difficulties on an international assignment.

One developmental technique considered useful for putting international employees in the right mind-set is to send them on a preliminary trip to the host country. A suitably arranged visit overseas for the candidate and spouse (where appropriate) can give them the opportunity to establish whether they are interested in the assignment and assess their suitability to embark on it. For example, the Ford Motor Company offered a one-week visit to the foreign location for both the employee and spouse, during which time the employee visited the Ford subsidiary company to meet colleagues, consider future challenges and discuss job requirements. The couple were favourably placed to do some viewing of houses, visit schools and get a 'gut' feeling for the new location and its cultural environment. As a result, they derived first-hand experience of some of the cultural differences so that they were better equipped to make more informed decisions about the overseas assignment. There is no doubt that effective and comprehensive cultural training can make it easier to negotiate the transition from the home to the foreign environment and assist with the development of productive expatriates. Such training could prevent mistakes, such as the case of the expatriate who took alcohol to Qatar, referred to above.

LANGUAGE TRAINING

Though English is the language of international business it would be unwise to rely exclusively on it. Clearly the ability of an expatriate to speak a foreign language can improve his or her effectiveness and negotiating ability in a non-English speaking country. As Baliga and Baker (1985) point out, the ability to speak a foreign language can improve the manager's access to information regarding the host country's economy, government and market; in addition, expatriates can fit in socially more easily, whether or not English is spoken by foreign nationals. One would expect to find orientation and local language programmes provided by the company's personnel or HR function in the host country.

PRACTICAL TRAINING

It seems logical to assume that some form of training is needed to assist the expatriate's family to acquaint themselves with the normal practical aspects of life in the host country (e.g. transport, shopping, use of banks, etc.), including help with establishing a new support network. A useful method of adaptation involves interaction between the expatriate's family and other established expatriate families. Such a process facilitates the exchange of information and adaptation, and contributes to building a suitable network of relationships for the expatriate family. If fluency in the host country language is essential for adaptation, further language training for expatriates and their families should be provided after arrival in the host country.

In Table 10.3 the different approaches to preparing managers for international postings are listed in ranked order. 'It is now widely accepted by both academic researchers and HR practitioners that pre-move training and cross-cultural briefings can help expatriate staff, and their families, adapt to living and working in new environments' (Forster, 2000). Evidence presented by Forster shows that pre-move training and briefings for a large group of UK employees and their dependants, who embarked on international assignments in the mid-1990s, had beneficial effects for most of them. However, the dependants rated the cross-cultural briefings rather negatively.

Contingency approaches

Black and Mendenhall (1989) cite Tung's research in the 1980s into a contingency framework for deciding the nature and level of rigour of training. Tung argued that the two determining factors in her contingency model were: (i) the degree of the 'interaction' required of the expatriate in the host culture, and (ii) the similarity between the expatriate's native culture and the new culture. If the expected interaction between the individual and members of the host culture is low and the degree of similarity between the expatriate's native culture and the host culture is high, then the training initiatives should be geared to job-related issues, rather than culture-related issues, and the level of rigour necessary for effective training should be relatively low. If the reverse situation were applicable, then one would expect greater attention to be paid to the new culture and cross-cultural skills, as well as to the task, with a moderate to high level of rigour of training.

TRAINING HOST COUNTRY AND THIRD COUNTRY NATIONALS

The discussion above has laid emphasis on the training of expatriates. However, it is also important to emphasise the importance of training for host country and third country nationals (Dowling and Welch, 2004). For example Fiat, the Italian vehicle manufacturer, used staff transfers as part of its training programme, with host country nationals spending time at corporate headquarters in Italy. Pepsi Cola International brings non-US citizens to its Management Institute in the United States for training in the systems the company uses. While there trainees are developing managerial skills but also being exposed to the corporate culture. It is recognised from the perspective of the parent company that interacting with the foreign employees can broaden the outlook of corporate staff. It should be noted that the training of host country and third country executives and managers in the way outlined above can be

Table 10.3 Preparing managers for international postings

(Percentage of respondents ranking an activity as amongst the five most important methods in their organisations.)	
Arranging for managers to visit host country	79
Language training for managers	73
Briefing by host country managers	67
In-house general management course	44
Cross-cultural training for managers	42
Cross-cultural training for family	38
General management course at business school	29
Language training for family	23
Training in negotiating within business norms of host country	17

Source: adapted from Barham and Devine (1990), cited in Dowling et al. (1994)

instrumental in developing global management teams. Finally, Matsushita arranged for the company's overseas managers to spend time in Japan working alongside their Japanese counterparts, though this initiative was not without its difficulties.

International comparisons in training and development

It is important to note that any cross-cultural and international comparisons should be read with a 'health warning' in mind: that is they entail generalisations which are likely to subsume many differences within overall classifications. Having said that, there have been some studies that survey the international scene on training and management development, and it is worth acknowledging them.

The indication is that there is considerable variation in training and development between different countries. The question is why this should be so. According to Collin and Holden (1997) this can be traced to national culture. In France, where the majority of companies spend more than 2 per cent of salaries on training, there is a directed culture with regard to training in that the law requires employers to spend 1.2 per cent of total gross salaries on training. Vocational training is incorporated into the school curriculum, there is a mathematical/engineering orientation, and competition to get into the best schools is strong because the establishment attended can have a significant impact on a person's career. Similarly, in Sweden, where there is also a high proportion of companies investing in training, there is a directed culture of training. Vocational content is emphasised in schools, there is considerable free adult education and companies are strongly encouraged to train their workers. In Germany, there is a dual system of practical in-company training and theoretical learning with a vocational bent in schools, with the culture broadly directed. The focus is functional and engineering/industry oriented.

In the United Kingdom the training culture is voluntarist (voluntary participation) and the amount spent on training tends to be less than in France, Germany or Sweden. Investors in People awards have encouraged investment, and management development is growing (Storey *et al.*, 1997; IiP, 2007). However, apprenticeships are declining and there are only about 13,000 apprenticeship places per annum, compared to France and Germany, both of which have over 300,000. The class divide between theoretical and vocational approaches to learning is long established and is still influential, with 'traditional' universities perceived as distinct from 'new' universities that offer more vocational education.

In Japan, the training culture combines directed and voluntarist tendencies. Central and local government set and reinforce training standards. There is a meritocratic/elitist system in which top companies recruit from top universities. There is considerable in-company continuous learning, which is associated with lifetime employment, and there is an emphasis on self-development.

In the United States, the training culture is voluntarist. There is a focus on individual effort and payment, and wide variation between areas and organisations. There is excellent training by top companies, but this is not universal (Collin and Holden, 1997).

Doyle (1997) conducts what he terms a 'Cook's Tour' of management development in a number of geographical areas. The essence of his findings are as follows:

■ *United States/United Kingdom*: A rational–functional philosophy dominates and the justification for management development is that it corrects individual 'weaknesses' and contributes to business strategy and performance. There is a focus on developing the generalist manager.

- *Europe* (apart from the United Kingdom): Here there is a weaker conception of management. Rather than being seen as a discrete set of skills and knowledge it is a 'state of being' (especially in France), which is added on to a functional specialism. Development in a functional specialism is primary and generalist training is less important, particularly in Germany.

- *Japan*: As opposed to the Anglo-Saxon approach, management development consists of short bursts of intensive activity. In Japan there is a longer-term and more collectivist approach in which the significant factor is the relationship between the boss and the individual. The aim is to nurture growth.

- *Central Europe*: In countries such as Russia, Poland, Hungary and Romania there has been a rush to adopt 'western' practices of management, but in a number of cases western models have failed to translate well into the central European situation, and a clear 'road map' has yet to emerge in these areas.

- *Hong Kong and China*: Similarly, in this large area there has been an importation of 'western' techniques of management. But discursive and group-work methods of western management development do not necessarily translate easily to a culture in which there is a strong emphasis on conformity, social status, the need to 'preserve face' and the unchallenged position of the 'expert'.

- *Developing countries*: Although it is difficult to generalise at this level, there is a question over the extent to which individualistic modes of management development from the West are applicable and transferable to developing countries. For example, in Africa there is an emphasis on group solidarity rather than self-development.

Of course, such generalisations are open to criticism. But they do raise certain questions. First, should it be assumed that the direction of learning should be in one direction – the West outwards? It may be that in an era of internationalisation learning requires to be more challenging and that some of the taken-for-granted aspects of the western approach would benefit from critical analysis. Secondly, if change and uncertainty continue to be the dominant features of global economy, how should organisations develop in order to cope with the pressures of change? The answer is unlikely to be a singular one best way, but finding a developmental path that fits with the local culture is more likely to yield results. Thirdly, the emphasis of HRM is about training for the purpose of organisational performance, and doing so on an individualised basis. There are a number of tensions contained within this conceptualisation, and the question is how these tensions should be resolved. There is a tension between learning directed at self-development and learning to promote organisational performance. Another tension concerns the causal connection between training and development and corporate performance.

While it is assumed that individuals who are developed will perform better, and consequently the organisation will also perform better, each of the links in this chain of reasoning can be questioned. It could be that people are developed and yet, because of circumstances in the economic environment, the organisation fails, for example, because of substitution by technology or because the potential customers cannot afford the product. As a final comment, one should heed the advice of Briscoe and Schuler (2004) when they state that there comes a time in the growth of global enterprises when the development of managers from an international perspective has to be recognised. Probably the most formidable task in the HR area facing many global firms today is the development of a cadre of managers and executives who have a deep understanding of the global marketplace and possess the capability to transfer this knowledge into resolute global action, while at the same providing them with adequate rewards and opportunities for personal growth and career development.

Benefits of training

Training, as a vehicle for HR development, is concerned with improving the skills of employees and enhancing their capacity to cope with the ever-changing demands of the work situation. It could also make a positive contribution to the empowerment of employees. Specific benefits have been identified by Armstrong (1992), Beardwell *et al.* (2004) and Kenney *et al.* (1990) as follows:

- Training facilitates getting to grips with the requirements of a job quickly, and by improving the knowledge and skill of the worker it allows him or her to better the quantity and quality of output with fewer mistakes and a reduction in waste. The enhancement of the skill base of the employee allows more challenge to be built into the job (job enrichment) with benefits to both the individual and the organisation.

- When the outcome of training leads to greater competency in the execution of tasks by subordinates the manager is relieved from tasks related to remedial or corrective effort.

- Training is an invaluable process when the organisation wishes to introduce flexible working methods and wants to create appropriate attitudes to equip employees to cope with change. Training could be used as a confidence builder in a management of change programme when employees are given help in understanding why change is necessary, how they might benefit from it, and when they are given the skills to participate in the implementation of change.

- Training has significance in a public relations sense in that it has value in projecting the right image to prospective workers of good calibre.

- Where training incorporates safety training as an integral part of the programme the outcome could be favourable in terms of health and safety at work.

- Training could have a favourable impact on the level of staff turnover, and the costs of redundancy schemes and recruitment of staff could be reduced when displaced staff are retrained.

- The motivational impact of training is manifest when staff feel a sense of recognition when they are sent on a training course, and after been trained they are motivated to acquire new skills, particularly when rewards follow the acquisition and use of these skills.

- The value of training in a communication context is evident when core values, such as those relating to product quality and customer service, are disseminated to employees, with the hope that they will be adopted and generate commitment.

- Identification with the organisation could be fostered when a better understanding of mission statements and corporate objectives is achieved through a training programme.

- Training aimed at operationalising certain management techniques (e.g. quality circles) could generate certain desirable side effects, such as analytical, problem-solving and presentational skills.

As a means of complementing the above list of beneficial points associated with training one should note the following issues related to the success of training programmes reported by the CBI, the employers' organisation in the United Kingdom (CBI, 1989):

- Training fosters a common vision throughout the organisation.

- Training enjoys high status when it is seen to satisfy the needs of the organisation and produces results.

- It is important that there is in place an organisational structure that facilitates the acquisition and nurturing of skills where employee development is geared to the meeting of corporate objectives. Likewise, business systems should be flexible enough to cater for the investment in people, with agreed budgets and clear targets against which performance is assessed on a regular basis. It is apparent that in this climate training is an integral part of corporate strategy. It is certainly not viewed as a peripheral organisational activity with a narrow remedial brief but is seen as a mechanism for fostering employee motivation with implications for the recruitment and retention of staff.

The success scenario outlined above might, in the eyes of some commentators, err on the side of optimism. But one must recognise the formidable constraints affecting a successful outcome. Factors contributing to the failure of training programmes are as follows (CBI, 1989):

- Management fails to consider seriously the existing and future skills needed by the organisation. (Often one finds that training budgets are all too easily trimmed when the organisation is looking for savings; the belief is that training does not pay off in the short term, and that an investment in training is lost when people leave the organisation.)

- Management relies too heavily on local or national labour markets to satisfy the needs of the organisation for relevant skills at all levels.

- Too often a natural response to skill shortages is to poach key employees from other employers even if such action leads to wage inflation.

Conclusions

If HRM is to fulfil its aim of valuing human 'assets' it is necessary to invest in them. This implies a positive attitude towards training and development. In organisations where there is a core of knowledge-based workers, development is vital to maintain their ability to add value to the enterprise. This is equally true where multi-skilled workers are required to participate in teamwork. Even in workforces that are relatively low skilled, training and development can have a significant impact. On the issue of flexibility it will be necessary to ask the question: how much investment should be made in temporary workers?

Training and development cannot be seen as a panacea for all organisational ills. However it is clearly important to equip employees with skills and knowledge and to motivate them to utilise their abilities. This is particularly so when it comes to training staff to operate internationally. There is an increased demand for employees to be flexible in their location of work and to be able to operate globally, but it should be recognised that even where there is the willingness to work in this way additional skills, language, knowledge and orientation training will be needed. It is also important for the organisation to be aware of the issues associated with the return of employees to their home country when they have spent considerable time abroad.

The CIPD reports annually on trends in learning and development in the United Kingdom (CIPD, 2007). Some 40 per cent of managers who responded admitted that they were not very effective in supporting the learning and development activities of employees because either they themselves were not given sufficient training or they were too busy to help workers improve their skills or further their careers. The Learning and Development Adviser at the CIPD is reported as saying that training and development activities are vital in order to ensure the workforce is kept up-to-date with the demands of organisations for skills that are subject to rapid change.

Even though the HR managers tended to be self-critical, the CIPD survey revealed that a considerable amount of training was being conduced. Some of the current highlights from the survey include a growth over time of coaching (63 per cent of organisations reported coaching activity). Most coaching is carried out by internal coaches, but questions remain over the support for coaches as only 17 per cent of organisations train a majority of their managers who act as coaches. There is some development of the recognition of learning and development as strategic issues. Some 32 per cent of respondents said that learning and development were considered 'very important' when the business strategy was being formed and 49 per cent said it was 'quite important'. However, this still leaves some way to go and 19 per cent said that learning and development were not regarded as important during strategy formation.

The use of competency frameworks is increasing and 60 per cent of organisations had one in place, with just under half of those who did not have one expecting to introduce competencies within two years. There was a 50/50 split between organisations that had one framework for all and those that had different competency frameworks for particular groups of staff.

Different countries have adopted alternative approaches to encouraging companies to invest in training. Some (such as France) have formalised requirements, while others (such as the United States) have taken a more voluntarist approach. In the United Kingdom there had been a decline in training in the 1980s under a voluntarist approach. In the 1990s, however, this trend was reversed (Storey et al., 1997). Traditionally, when companies experienced financial difficulties the training budget would be the first to be cut. Nowadays some forward-looking companies, when faced with difficulties, actually increase training.

The integration of training and development policies with other areas of HRM strategy is seen as important. In the view of Myers and Kirk (2005) it is now possible to identify strategic human resource development (SHRD). This reflects the popularity of SHRM referred to in Chapters 1 and 2. SHRD is conducted in partnership with line management and is differentiated from traditional training and development by taking a more proactive stance, for example, seeking to shape rather than reflect business strategy, organisational culture and future leadership. If the organisation is planning change, and particularly when that change can have an impact on tasks, skills and organisational culture, the training employees receive will be a determining factor in the success or failure of the change programme. If there is an aim to form closer and more adaptive relationships with customers and suppliers, which is often the case in current forms of organisational restructuring, then employees need to have sufficient training to enable them to understand and solve problems for customers. When an organisation is seeking to pursue a policy of employee involvement then the success of the implementation of the policy will depend on employees having the relevant skills and appropriate attitudes. Clearly there are links between training and development and recruitment and selection. The basic question is whether an organisation should buy in skilled people from the external labour supply or develop its own people internally. Nowadays it is thought that whichever approach is taken it will be necessary to have an ongoing training policy if employees are to keep up to date and if they are to believe that the organisation is committed to them.

Review and reflection questions

1. What is meant by systematic training?

2. What are the initial reasons that organisations have for introducing training and development?

3. How can national schemes be supportive of training in organisations?

4. What does a competency-based approach to training and development entail?

5. How does IiP encourage a strategic approach to people development?

6. Compare and contrast mentoring and coaching.

7. What are the principles of action learning?

8. What personal development is e-learning good at providing?

9. How can training be evaluated?

10. What are the potential benefits of training:

    (a) for individuals

    (b) for organisations?

Activities

If you are in work:

1. Think of an event or process from which you have learnt a lot:

   (a) What motivated you to learn?

   (b) What process of learning was involved?

   (c) How did you know that the learning had been effective?

2. Review your answers to these questions and compare them to examples of 'normal' training in your organisation (e.g. induction, technical training).

3. Are the normal training events likely to be as effective as the first event/process you thought of?

4. What might be done to improve the success of training and development in your organisation?

If you are in full-time study:

1. Which processes of learning/development have you experienced?

2. What were the most effective processes for you?

3. How will you seek to influence your own processes of learning in the future?

Further reading and research

Learning is important in all sectors of the economy, but is particularly highlighted in knowledge-intensive areas:
Stewart, J. and Tansley, C. (2002) *Training in the knowledge economy*, London: CIPD.

As organisations change, approaches to training also need to adapt. The following article examines the needs of virtual teams and organisations:
Rosen, B., Furst, S. and Blackburn, R. (2006) 'Training for virtual teams: An investigation of current practices and future needs', *Human Resource Management*, 45, 229–248.

As has been explained above, there are many alternative processes of training and development. One innovative approach is discussed from a practical angle in the following article:
Syedain, H. (2007) 'Positive action: Appreciative Inquiry at the Hammersmith Hospitals NHS Trust', *People Management*, 22 March, 31–33.

Management development is crucial to the success of HRM strategies but, as the next article suggests, there are potential pitfalls:
Mabey, C. and Terry, R. (2007) 'The manager in the mirror. Management development yields organisational results when it mirrors business strategy. But can the reflections become distorted?', *People Management*, 12 July, 38–40.

The next article raises the question of how we can best achieve the strategic fit of training:
Reynolds, J. and Slowman, M. (2004) 'In the Driving Seat. Traditional training has its place, but is teaching people what the organization wants them to know the best way to unlock their potential', *People Management*, 12 February, 40–42.

The IiP website offers business improvement tools including a profile self-check, access to case studies and news items at www.investorsinpeople.co.uk.

The *International Journal of Training and Development* provides a range of academic articles on all aspects of training and management development. It can be found at www.blackwellpublishing.com/journals.

References

Alliger, G.M., Tannenbaum, S.I., Bennett, W. (Jr), Traver, H. and Shotland, A. (1997) 'A meta-analysis of the relations between training criteria', *Personnel Psychology*, 50, 341–358.

Armstrong, M. (1992) *Human Resource Management: Strategy and action,* London: Kogan Page.

Arnold, J. (2005) *Work psychology: Understanding human behaviour in the workplace*, Harlow, Essex: FT/Prentice-Hall.

Ashworth, J. (1999) 'Management training is changing: dramatic change to the art of team building', *The Times,* 5 February, 26.

Baliga, G. and Baker, J.C. (1985) 'Multi-national corporate policies for expatriate managers: selection, training, and evaluation', *Advanced Management Journal,* Autumn, 31–38.

Barham, K. and Devine, M. (1990) 'The quest for the international manager: a survey of global human resource strategies', *Special Report No. 2098,* London: Economist Intelligence Unit.

BBC (2007) BBC News http://news.bbc.co.uk – BBC News 16/11/07.

Beard, D. (1993) 'Learning to change organisations', *Personnel Management,* January, 32–35.

Beardwell, I., Holden, L. and Claydon, T. (2004) *Human Resource Management: a contemporary approach*, Harlow, Essex: Pearson Education.

Bell, C. (1998) *Managers as Mentors,* Maidenhead: McGraw-Hill.

Black, J.S. and Mendenhall, M. (1989) 'A practical but theory-based framework for selecting cross-cultural training methods', *Human Resource Management,* 28, 511–539.

Black, J.S. and Mendenhall, M. (1990) 'Cross-cultural training effectiveness: a review and a theoretical framework for future research', *Academy of Management Review,* 15, 113–136.

Bolger, A. (1996) 'Investors in People: both sides reap the benefits', *Financial Times,* 22 November, 13.

Bream, R (2003) 'Tackling the skills shortage', *Financial Times*, 27 March, 16.

Briscoe, D.R. and Schuler, R.S. (2004) *International Human Resource Management*, New York: Routledge.

British Psychological Society (BPS) (2004) *Requirements for continuing professional development*, Leicester, UK.

CBI (1989) *Managing The Skills Gap,* London: Confederation of British Industry.

CIPD (2007) www.cipd.co.uk

Clutterbuck, D. (2001) 'Human Resources: Mentoring and coaching at the top', Part 13, *Mastering Management Series, Financial Times,* 8 January, 14–15.

Collin, A. (1992) 'The role of the mentor in transforming the organisation', Paper presented at the Annual Conference, Employment Research Unit, Business School, University of Cardiff, September.

Collin, A. and Holden, L. (1997) 'The national framework for vocational education and training', in Beardwell, I. and Holden, L. (eds), *Human Resource Management: A contemporary perspective,* London: Pitman.

Conway, C. (1994) 'Mentoring managers in organisations: a report of a study of mentoring and its application to organizations with case studies', Ashridge Management College, Berkhamsted.

Dowling, P.J. and Welch, D.E. (2004) *International Human Resource Management*, London: Thomson Learning.

Dowling, P.J., Schuler, R.S. and Welch, D.E. (1994) *International Dimensions of Human Resource Management*, Belmont, CA: Wadsworth Publishing Company.

Doyle, C.E. (2003) *Work and organizational psychology: An introduction with attitude*, Hove: East Sussex: Psychology Press.

Doyle, M. (1997) 'Management development', in Beardwell, I. and Holden, L. (eds), *Human Resource Management: A contemporary perspective,* London: Pitman.

Eglin, R. (2005) 'BT aims to go on the right track', *The Sunday Times*, 23 January (Appointments Section), 9.

Forster, N. (2000) 'Expatriates and the impact of cross-cultural training', *Human Resource Management Journal,* 10, 63–78.

Furnham, A (2001) 'Keys to unlock path of career fulfillment', *The Sunday Telegraph* (Appointments Section), A1.

Garvin, D. (1993) 'Building a learning organization', *Harvard Business Review,* July–August, 78–91.

Goldstein, I.L. (1978) 'The pursuit of validity in the evaluation of training programmes', *Human Factors,* 20, 131–144.

Goss, D. (1994) *Principles of Human Resource Management,* London: Routledge.

Grugulis, I. (2006) 'Training and Development' in Redman, T. and Wilkinson, A. (eds), *Contemporary Human Resource Management,* Harlow, England: FT/Prentice Hall.

Hamblin, A.C. (1974) *Evaluation and Control of Training,* Maidenhead: McGraw-Hill.

Handy, C. (1989) *The Age of Unreason,* London: Business Books.

Hegarty, S. and Dickson, T. (1995) 'Rise and fall of corporate thrills', *Financial Times,* 9 January, 7.

Herriot, P. (1992) *The Career Management Challenge: Balancing individual and organisational needs,* London: Sage.

Herriot, P. and Pemberton, C. (1995) *New deals: The revolution in managerial careers,* Chichester: Wiley.

Hill, S. (1991) 'Why quality circles failed but total quality management might succeed', *British Journal of Industrial Relations,* 29, 541–568.

Hills, H. and Francis, P. (1999) 'Interaction Learning', *People Management* 5, 48–49.

Hilton, P. (1992) 'Shepherd defends training policy', *Personnel Management,* December, 11.

Holmes, L. (1990) 'Trainer competences: turning back the clock', *Training and Development,* April, 17–20.

Honey, P. and Mumford, A. (1992) *Manual of Learning Styles,* London: P. Honey.

Hunt, J.W. (2001) 'Mentoring: Wise friends in high places', *Financial Times,* 31 August, 10.

IiP (2007) www.investorsinpeople.co.uk

IRS (1992) 'Skill-based pay: the new training initiative', *Employee Development Bulletin,* 31, July, *Industrial Relations Review and Report,* No. 516, 2–7.

Keep, E. (1992) 'Corporate training strategies', in Salaman, G. (ed.), *Human Resource Strategies,* London: Sage.

Kelly, J. (2000) 'Skills Council targets adult illiteracy', *Financial Times,* 11 December, 6.

Kenney, J. and Reid, M. (1988) *Training Initiatives,* London: Institute of Personnel Management.

Kenney, J., Reid, M. and Donnelly, E. (1990) *Manpower Training and Development,* London: Institute of Personnel Management.

Kirkpatrick, D.L. (1967) 'Evaluation of training', in Craig, R.L. and Bittel, L.R. (eds), *Training and Development Handbook,* NY: McGraw-Hill.

Kolb, D. (1985) *Experiential Learning: Experiences as the source of learning and development,* Englewood Cliffs, NJ: Prentice Hall.

Lawrence, J. (1986) 'Action learning: a questioning approach', in Mumford, A. (ed.), *Handbook of Management Development,* Aldershot: Gower.

Learning and Skills Council (LSC) (2007) www.lsc.gov.uk

Littlefield, D. (2000) 'Four-stroke of genius', *People Management,* 6, 52–53.

Lowe, J. (1991) 'Teambuilding via outdoor training: experiences from a UK automotive plant', *Human Resource Management Journal,* 2, 42–59.

McKenna, E. (2006) *Business Psychology and Organisational Behaviour,* Hove: Psychology Press.

McLeod, M. (2001) 'Surfers' paradigm', *People Management,* 7, 44–45.

Masie, E. (1999) 'Joined-up thinking', *People Management,* 5, 32–36.

Monks, D.W., Bilderback, T.E., Sanders, D.C. and Boyette, M.D. (2004) 'Competency based training program in horticulture', *Acta Horticulturae,* 641, 131–134.

Moules, J. (2004) 'More opting for outside helping hand', Professional Development (Special Report), *Financial Times,* 11 October, 2.

Myers, J. and Kirk, S. (2005) 'Managing processes of human resource development', in Leopold, J., Harris, L. and Watson, T. (eds), *The Strategic Managing of Human Resources.* Harlow, England: FT/Prentice Hall.

Naquin, S.S. and Holton, E.F. (2006) 'Leadership and Managerial Competency Models: A Simplified Process and Resulting Model', *Advances in Developing Human Resources*, 8, 144–165.

O'Hara, S., Webber, T. and Murphy, W. (2001) 'The joy of sets', *People Management*, 7, 30–34.

Ooi, K.B., Bakar, N.A., Arunugam, V., Vellapan, L. and Loke, A.K.Y. (2007) 'Does TQM influence employees' job satisfaction? An empirical case analysis', *International Journal of Quality and Reliability Management*, 24, 62–77.

O'Reilly, S. (1998) 'Smart money goes on coaching', *The Sunday Times*, 12 July, 7.14.

Patrick, J. (1992) *Training: research and practice*, London: Academic Press.

Pedlar, M., Boydell, R. and Burgoyne, J. (1988) *Learning Company Project*, London: Manpower Services Commission.

Phillips, J. (2005) 'Measuring Up', *People Management*, 11, 42–43.

Plimmer, G. (2004) 'Emphasis should be on more skills investment', Professional Development (Special Report), *Financial Times*, 11 October, 1–2.

Poole, C. (2001) 'Smart cookies', *People Management*, 7, 46–47.

Price, A. (2004) *Human Resource Management in a Business Context*, London: Thomson Learning.

Priestland, A. and Hanig, R. (2006) 'Fuelling the Fire', *People Management*, 12, 40–42.

Revans, R. (1971) *Developing Effective Managers*, London: Longman.

Roffey Park's Newsletter (for managers and developers) (2004), Autumn, 6.

Roffey Park's Newsletter (for managers and developers) (2005) 'Introducing a dramatic change in leadership', Spring, 2005, 1.

Senge, P. (1990) *The Fifth Discipline: The art and practice of the learning organization*, New York: Random House.

Siddique, H. (2007) 'Government Pledge to Train 7.5 M Workers', Guardian Unlimited, 16 November 2007. http://politics.guardian.co.uk.

Sisson, K. and Storey, J. (1988) 'Developing effective managers: a review of the issues and an agenda for research', *Personnel Review*, 17, 3–8.

Smethurst, S. (2006) 'Staying Power', *People Management*, 12, 34–36.

Steedman, H. (1998) 'Basics are essential: vocational training must include literacy and numeracy', *Financial Times*, 26 August, 9.

Stewart, J. (2005) 'Developing Managers and Managerial Capacities', in Leopold, J., Harris, L. and Watson, T. (eds), *The Strategic Managing of Human Resources*, Harlow, England: FT/Prentice Hall.

Storey, J. (1992) *Developments in the Management of Human Resources*, Oxford: Blackwell.

Storey, J., Mabey, C. and Thomson, A. (1997) 'What a difference a decade makes', *People Management*, June, 28–30.

Syedain, H. (2007) 'Inside Broadcast', *People Management*, 13, 42–43.

Training Agency (1989) *Training in Britain: Employees' perspectives, Research Report*, London: HMSO.

Ulrich, D. and Hinkson, P. (2001) 'Net heads', *People Management*, 7, 32–36.

White, D. (2002) 'Away-days. How to build boats and boost morale', *Financial Times*, 1 April, 8.

Wighton, D. (2005) 'Citigroup in global drive to boost standards', *Financial Times*, 2 March, 29.

Witzel, M. (2004) 'Memo to the CEO (Part 4): Why businesses must stay in training', *Financial Times*, 12 December, 7.

Chapter 11

EMPLOYEE RELATIONS

Introduction

Employee relations, having emerged from industrial relations, is one of the main subjects of research related to HRM. It is concerned with the theory and practice of the relationship between management and workers in an organisational context. Important influences on this area of study include Marxist, structural and critical theories in which workers and organisations are seen as being arranged in opposition, and power is a focus of attention. Although there has been a tradition of adversarial relations between managers and workers in the United Kingdom, HRM espouses a unitarist approach in which their mutually shared interests are emphasised.

Having read this chapter, you should:

- be aware of the main theories and frameworks for understanding employee relations;

- understand models of communication and alternative practical approaches to communicating;

- be able to assess and criticise employee involvement and participation schemes at the macro and micro levels;

- be aware of changes in the relations with trade unions and collective bargaining;

- be aware of trends in international employee relations;

- understand how conflict arises in organisations, and know some of the alternatives for dealing with it;

- recognise the nature of ethics and diversity and their relevance to HRM;

- understand the importance of health and safety in the workplace, and know what the key issues are.

Employee relations ranges widely as an area of study, so it is necessary to be selective in the choice of issues to cover. The following topics will be discussed in this chapter:

- industrial relations vs employee relations;

- communication;

- participation;

- trade union representation;

- national and international trends and perspectives in employee relations;

- conflict;

- health and safety.

Industrial relations vs employee relations

Prior to the advent of HRM, employee relations was often called industrial relations and was concerned with the interactions between the employer (represented by management) and the workforce (typically represented by trade unions). It involved the processes of collective bargaining, negotiation and consultation, and occurred at two levels – the organisation and the industry. Industrial relations tends to be associated in a negative sense with conflict between trade unions and employers and in creating images of bitter strikes and walk outs (Blyton and Turnbull, 2004).

Employee relations, with its milder tone, differs from industrial relations insofar as there is an emphasis on direct communication with the workforce and liaison with employees at the level of the individual; this creates a scenario where there is reduced interaction with trade unions (Bright, 1993). However, Purcell (1994) makes the valid point that the adoption of HRM does not in every case result in a radical individualisation of the practice of workplace relationships. While traditional collective bargaining concentrated on pay settlements and conditions of work, HRM approaches based on employee relations have sought to broaden the involvement of employees and take a more participative approach to management through increased communication, thereby impinging on power relationships within the organisation. On the face of it employee relations may be seen as a positive development, but there is always the danger that the rhetoric of HRM may be used to disguise a policy of anti-unionism.

TYPOLOGIES

A classic way of conceptualising traditional industrial relations was put forward by Fox (1974). He constructed two ideal types: the unitary and pluralist perspectives. There has been reference to this terminology when examining HRM elsewhere in this book. The unitary view has the following features:

- management is the only source of authority and power;

- there is a view of everyone pulling in the same direction, united by common goals;

- conflict and opposition are abnormal and dysfunctional (conflict may be caused either by poor communications, so that workers misunderstand the direction of the organisation, or by the presence of dissidents in the workforce);

- trade unions are viewed negatively, and are discouraged.

By contrast, the pluralist perspective has the following features:

- organisations are expected to contain groups that have divergent interests and perspectives;

- each group (the trade unions and the management separately) have power bases from which they can operate;

■ conflict occurs naturally where there is a clash of interests;

■ management does not have sole authority, but must compete with other sources of leadership (such as trade union representatives).

Purcell and Sisson (1983) further developed the work of Fox and an extended typology of the relations between organisations and workers can be represented as follows:

■ *Traditional approach*: Workers are viewed as a factor of production, they are excluded from decision-making processes, power is concentrated in the hands of management, and trade unions are excluded or opposed.

■ *Sophisticated human relations or paternalists*: Workers are well treated, and sophisticated approaches to recruitment, selection and training, and generous reward packages are believed to remove any need (or justification) for opposition by workers. Trade unions are unlikely to be recognised by the organisation.

■ *Sophisticated moderns*: Workers, normally via the trade union, are seen as legitimately involved in specified areas of decision making. Some (the *constitutionalists*) who adopt this view take a legalistic approach to collective bargaining, clearly set out areas where management exercises power and areas where management and workers engage in joint decision making. Others (the *consultatives*) take a less formal approach, and will bargain with trade unions over a range of issues, which may change and develop over time.

■ *Standard moderns, opportunists*: This approach can be seen to swing between unitarism and pluralism as the situation demands. A firefighting approach is taken to industrial relations. When union power is low management may take control of most of the decisions, but when union power is high a negotiating or consulting approach may be adopted. In large organisations there may be a lack of standardisation across different workplaces, with union recognition and collective bargaining being applied in some but not others.

In terms of the Purcell and Sisson model, HRM approaches would tend towards the sophisticated modern or sophisticated human relations approaches. Some would argue, however, that in reality it is possible for organisations to adopt the language of these types while continuing with traditional and modern organisational practices.

INFLUENCE OF CULTURE

Poole (1986) argued that the style of industrial relations adopted could be related to culture. He examined three distinctive national cultures: Japan, the United States and Nigeria. Japanese industrial relations were typified as 'benevolent paternalism'. This style was thought to derive from a modified Confucian view in which original virtue rather than original sin was assumed. This led to an emphasis on morality as well as economic success, and the desire of business people to be seen as good moral citizens, hence the tendency to treat employees well.

In the United States the wider culture exhibited an embedded individualism. In organisations this was expressed through unitarism, and through an anti-union approach, which went along with developed communications and information sharing. In the Nigerian case Poole found evidence of a style that combined authoritarianism and arbitrariness with a people-centred paternalism. This led to unions often being ignored or dealt with informally, and strikes occurring in response. (It should be noted, however, that not all researchers in the field of culture would accept that such generalisations at the national level are valid.)

Communication

Communication is a process at the disposal of the organisation to keep management and employees informed about a variety of relevant matters. For example, it is important for managers to let people know about the mission statement, if there is one, and the objectives of the company. Also, people are informed of what is expected of them in terms of performance, and how changes in the strategic direction of the company are likely to affect their jobs. It is also important to give employees the opportunity to communicate with management so that their reaction to proposals put to them is heard, as well as having the chance to put forward counter proposals. Good communication, as the lifeblood of the organisation, helps to promote the involvement of employees in the decision-making processes, and in so doing can enhance the individual's identification with the organisation, which in turn can lead to improved performance.

According to Welch and Jackson (2007) it is important to know who is being communicated to, about what and through what processes. Their review reveals that communications between senior managers and line managers are predominantly two-way and concern employee roles and impact. Such communication is often conducted through appraisal discussions and team briefings. Communication within teams between peers tends to be two-way and is concerned with team information and task discussions. Similarly, communications within project groups tends to be two-way and focused on project information. Communication from senior managers to employees in general, however, tends to be one-way and is concerned with conveying corporate goals, developments and activities.

Effective communication involves the sending and receiving of clearly understood messages between management and subordinates in a two-way process. In this respect one should keep in mind the following steps:

1. Have a clear idea of the message to be put across.
2. Ideas should be put across in a suitable form using, where possible, the language of the recipient.
3. Choose the most appropriate communication medium (e.g. telephone/fax, e-mail, meeting, memo or report). Consider building 'redundancy' (i.e. same information in more than one form) into the process when circumstances justify it.
4. Ensure the message gets to the receiver, but it must be recognised that in the final analysis it is the responsibility of the receiver to tune in to the contents of the message.
5. Ensure that the intended meaning of the transmitted message gets across. This is more likely to be established where two-way communication exists.
6. Monitor the reaction of the recipient if a response is required.
7. Elicit feedback from the recipient not obtained in step 5.

Feedback is a two-way process and for it to be open and constructive requires the establishment of the right climate by management. Managing this climate is seen as a vital activity for success, because if employees do not feel they are being dealt with openly and honestly resentment and conflict may arise.

The potential for barriers to effective communication to exist within organisations is great, and sensitivity to these impediments is advocated. These barriers consist of the following:

■ The message is distorted because of the use of unsuitable language.

■ The message does not get through because of interruptions due to physical noise (e.g. a noisy place of work) or psychological noise (e.g. biases and prejudices harboured by the recipient of the message).

- The message is interpreted selectively by the recipient (e.g. the person hears what they want to hear rather than what is said).

- The recipient of the message arrives at a conclusion prematurely, or becomes defensive as a result of being insulted by what has been said.

- Difficulties arise owing to an overload of information in the message.

- The sender of the message is in the dark as to the views of the recipient because the sender misinterprets the feedback or gets no feedback from the recipient.

The size of the organisation will influence the style (e.g. formal or informal) of communications. The following internal approaches to communication can be used in different circumstances, but equally they can complement each other.

NOTICE BOARDS AND MEMORANDA

Written information (e.g. details of vacancies, forthcoming events) is disseminated in a formal sense to employees generally. In the case of the notice board, obsolete information should be removed and overcrowding the board with pieces of paper should be avoided; also, censorship, either unintentional or deliberate, whereby only certain types of information gets on the board, should be guarded against. A drawback of this medium of communication, which could also apply to magazines and newsletters (examined below), is that it does not provide an immediate reaction where the sender of the message can check that the intended message has been properly received and understood and the recipient can express a point of view. In cases where full attention is not paid to memoranda and notice boards the message fails to get through.

MAGAZINES AND NEWSLETTERS

This medium should strive for a balance in its coverage of human-interest stories and organisational issues. It is customary for magazines to be produced by management, whereas the newsletter may be subject to more employee control.

INTRANETS

Many organisations have intranets that allow them to provide information to employees in a timely and up-to-date manner. Intranets operate in a number of ways. Some are relatively passive and store information, such as policies, press releases and general information that employees can look up when they need to. A more active version entails alerting employees to new information, typically by e-mail, so that they are prompted to refer to news items or new policy documents. Lastly, there are highly active forms. These can be used to gather employee perceptions (e.g., via electronic questionnaires) and enable consultation on management decisions. In some cases, room bookings for meetings, operations scheduling and personal diaries are managed online so that there is a high degree of transparency.

CONSULTATIVE COMMITTEES

These committees consist of both management and employees and are formally constituted with an agreed procedure. Minutes of the meetings are prepared and could be displayed on a notice board. Such committees could be used if there is a tradition of industrial relations within a company.

PRESENTATIONS

These could be used by top management on a regular basis. In particular a chief executive interested in human relations could periodically visit the various company sites and address the rank and file on such matters as the financial health of the company, present problems and future challenges. This approach was adopted successfully by a past managing director (Trevor Owen) of Remploy Ltd. Presentations give the chief executive the chance to meet all employees over time and, provided people do not feel inhibited in such a setting, they can be a useful mode of communication. The former chief executive of the Body Shop – the late Anita Roddick – regularly made presentations to people in the various retail outlets of the company using a video recording.

TEAM BRIEFINGS

This is a technique originally conceived and promoted by the Industrial Society in the United Kingdom and has been adopted by organisations seeking to extend face-to-face communications. Briefing sessions take place at various levels within the organisation, and observations on important issues discussed further up the organisation can cascade downwards. Team leaders address a group, varying from 4 to 14 in size, on a regular basis (monthly or bi-monthly). Information is disseminated on company policy and decisions, and the reasons for them, can be explained. At any particular level within the organisation the greater part of the briefing could be devoted to local issues, but circumstances will dictate the amount of time devoted to important issues originating further up the organisation (e.g. the implications of a takeover bid for the company).

Team briefings offer the opportunity for employees to interact in the process of clarifying and understanding decisions and policies and are an example of a more direct form of communication. It is important that part of the session consists of two-way communication so that the organisation is aware of the concerns, ideas and suggestions of the workforce. In such circumstances it would be necessary to have an upward reporting system following the briefing session. Amongst the problems surrounding the operation of team briefings are not having enough to report on a given occasion, the numbers in the team being either too small or too great, and the system not being uniformly applied in the sense that certain parts of the organisation are not taking them seriously. Team briefings can have a favourable impact in improving the status of the supervisor as a provider of information and can create a positive participative climate for resolving problems.

However, in conditions where good industrial relations are absent, team briefing could be viewed by trade unions as a technique used to undermine their influence (Marchington, 1987). Additionally, although managers often claim benefits for team briefings, employees have a more mixed view. In some cases they reported briefings being rushed or irregular, and in research conducted in 25 companies 77 per cent of employees said that team briefings left their commitment unchanged, and 4 per cent reported that their commitment was actually reduced (Marchington *et al.*, 1989). Finally, it is important that the 'briefer' receives appropriate training (Beardwell *et al.*, 2004).

ATTITUDE SURVEYS

The organisation is keen to feel the morale pulse of its employees and mounts attitude surveys to gauge their attitudes and opinions on a variety of issues. This could highlight areas of concern as perceived by employees. If exercises of this nature are to be taken seriously it is important that management acts on the results, otherwise employees could consider participating a waste of time.

SUGGESTION SCHEMES

This is a form of upward communication whereby employees are encouraged to put forward ideas and proposals for the improvement of work practices, which in its own right is a worthwhile pursuit. Schemes of this nature normally have a short life.

Communicating with employees is obviously an important process. The results of a survey suggest that 90 per cent of organisations sampled used one or more of the methods outlined above (Millward *et al.*, 1992). While reflecting on a number of the above communication methods, Ramsay (1996) reviewed a survey of 400 companies and noted that management rate notice boards and memos as relatively poor methods of communication, but nonetheless use them more than any other method. Team briefings, employee opinion surveys and management accessibility (e.g. through 'open-door' policies or management by walking around) are more highly rated. However, such oral and face-to-face approaches are also more time consuming, which is perhaps the reason for their lower level of implementation. Even where they are practised they cannot guarantee effective two-way communication because, as Ramsay argues, such attempts to engender trust may result in a 'catch-22' situation in which the existence of a climate of trust is a prerequisite for employees to speak out.

Ramsay (1996) identified a number of typical problems with communications that hold implications for managerial practice. They are as follows:

■ managerial failure to specify the objectives of a communication scheme;

■ the loss of momentum after initial enthusiasm;

■ the wrong amount of information – too little or too much;

■ too much 'tell and sell' in management style, provoking mistrust amongst employees;

■ attempts to undermine trade unions, which can backfire;

■ failure to specify those responsible for communicating at each level in the organisation;

■ lack of training (e.g. in presentation and communication skills) for both presenters and recipients of information;

■ overformality.

Being aware of the complexity of communication, and the issues raised above, is a useful starting point to bring about improvements in this important process.

Participation

The level of employee participation has a major impact on the way an organisation works, and is generally related to two key areas, i.e. management style and employee representation or involvement, such as the worker-director of old. The issue of employee involvement is addressed in Box 11.1.

Dundon and Wilkinson (2006) report research on employee involvement and participation based on a nationwide survey. A summary of the key findings is given in Table 11.1.

Box 11.1: Employee involvement

Employee involvement (EI) schemes fall into four categories, as follows: downward communication, upward problem solving, financial participation, and representative participation. Differences between EI schemes can be reflected in the degree of involvement (the extent to which employees have influence over a decision), the level of involvement (e.g. at job, departmental or organisational level) and the form it takes (direct, indirect or financial). These distinctions are discussed below.

Downward communication can involve methods discussed in the previous section, such as newsletters, presentations and videos in which management send messages to employees. Downward communication would be seen as fairly low in degree of involvement because it affords little influence to employees. However, such schemes have the potential to be extensive in terms of the levels, range and direct form of involvement.

Upward problem-solving schemes are those that seek to tap into the knowledge and understandings that employees have developed through doing the job. Schemes can involve small groups in solving specific problems, or can be more general and seek opinion on a broader level, for example, through the use of employee attitude surveys. The upward problem-solving schemes can produce a greater degree of involvement than downwards communication, and have the potential to address a range of matters.

Financial participation schemes represent attempts to create clear connections between the performance of the organisation (or unit) and the rewards the individual employee receives. Schemes in which participation occurs can include profit sharing, employee share ownership and bonus payments determined on the basis of corporate or business unit performance. These types of reward system are discussed in Chapter 9 on reward management.

Representative participation schemes tend to be those that give the greatest degree of involvement, typically by enabling employees to be part of decision-making bodies. Examples include joint consultative committees, advisory councils and works councils. Such approaches can provide an extensive range of involvement, and send a serious message to the workforce that its views are taken seriously. They also derive from the assumption within management that many heads are better than one, and that better decisions can be made through opening up to more people the traditional boundaries of the managerial prerogative to decide.

One can draw a number of practical suggestions from a serious consideration of EI schemes, as follows:

■ Management commitment to the scheme should be firm, and should acknowledge that schemes can be demanding of managerial time and effort.

■ Support for the scheme must be secured throughout the management structure, that is not just from the top, but also from the middle and supervisory levels whose actions (or lack of them) will strongly impact on the success (or otherwise) of the scheme.

■ The objectives of the scheme need to be well thought through in advance.

■ Training in the necessary skills must be provided for all involved.

■ Impartial monitoring of the scheme should be carried out in order to record where objectives are met and make changes where they are not.

■ Excessive expectations of the scheme should be tempered – EI can make a significant contribution but it is not a panacea.

■ Be aware of existing relationships, particularly with trade unions, as a scheme that is thought to undermine their position is likely to meet opposition.

Source: based on Holden, 2001; Marchington *et al.*, 1992; Ramsay, 1996

Table 11. 1 Involvement/participation practice

Involvement/participation practice	Percentage of workplaces
Team briefings for groups of employees	65
Staff attitude surveys	45
Problem-solving groups (e.g. quality circles)	42
Regular meetings of the entire workforce	37
Profit-sharing scheme for non-managerial employees	30
Workplace level join consultative committee	28
Employee share ownership scheme	15

Source: Dundon and Wilkinson, 2006: 386

An example of a non-union organisation that adopts a multi-process approach to communication and participation is given in Case example 11.1.

CASE EXAMPLE 11.1

COMPUCOM'S COMMUNICATION AND PARTICIPATION APPROACH

Compucom is a medium-sized company employing 220 people specialising in the design and manufacture of personal computers. The business started in 1982 and has since grown to have a turnover in excess of £30 million. It employs 90 people in technical and design work at its UK headquarters, 100 people in its manufacturing plant in Malta, and 30 people in distribution and sales offices in the United States, Europe, Asia and Australia.

Direct communications are carried out via monthly team briefings and informal day-to-day communications between managers and workers. The matrix structure incorporates cross-functional teamworking on specific projects (such as a new product design) and the communications are seen as a way of enabling team members to have a suitable degree of professional freedom.

In addition, indirect communication and participation is via a works council. This meets every second month in the United Kingdom. There are 10 elected worker representatives and the council is chaired by the personnel manager. The council considers both work and non-work related matters including health and safety, staffing levels and welfare. It does not discuss pay and conditions.

The belief in Compucom is that this process is good for business, helping to improve innovation and quality of performance, and that trust has improved as a result of the processes. The employees have led a number of initiatives such as a flexi-time arrangement which has led to a decrease in absence levels.

Source: based on Dundon *et al.*, 2006

Questions

1. What advantages might SMEs have over large organisations in communicating with employees?

2. What disadvantages might they have?

MACRO PARTICIPATION

At the macro level, participation with employees as a collective is governed by procedures related to consultation and negotiation with trade unions and workers' representatives. These issues are also addressed later in this chapter in the section on trade union representation.

A present-day manifestation of macro participation is the type of works council increasingly used by companies. Works councils are committees usually made up of representatives from workers and management, and can be found in a number of European countries. They operate at the organisational level and meet to discuss issues such as employee relations and business matters and to engage in joint decision making (Holden, 2001). For example, in Germany regulations governing recruitment and selection, regradings and dismissals require the agreement of Works Councils (Sparrow and Hiltrop, 1994). Works councils and the impact of European legislation on employee consultation will be discussed below in the national and international trends section.

MICRO PARTICIPATION

At a micro level, the degree of individual participation will depend on the management styles adopted. Forms of participation in HRM tend to be broadly conceived. The Harvard model of HRM (Beer *et al.*, 1984) holds that the various stakeholders in an organisation should be taken into account when making decisions. The stakeholders include shareholders, customers, employees and unions. It is thought that if employees and unions are involved in the decision-making processes they will feel a greater sense of 'ownership' of the decisions made and will be more committed to their implementation. Workers will be more motivated to perform tasks where they have had some input into the determination of work goals and to the way they will be met. Participation can be seen as an important aspect of the way HRM can seek to enhance employee commitment.

Employee participation can be viewed as consultative or delegative. Consultative participation encourages and enables staff to contribute their views, but management retains the right to make the final decision. Delegative participation goes further and allows workers to take on decisions that had traditionally fallen within the managerial prerogative (Geary, 1994). However, one should acknowledge certain reservations about participative leadership. Stace and Dunphy (2001) argue that the participative style may be inappropriate in specified circumstances. They feel that if conflicting views were likely to surface in a discussion forum that were difficult to reconcile, then it is highly likely that a participative style would not be suitable because it consumes too much time. Equally, where a strategic change in direction is called for in order to ensure organisational survival, it is likely that a participative style would be inappropriate whereas a more directive style would be functional. For example, the restructuring of the police force in New South Wales, Australia was spearheaded by a newly appointed Police Commissioner charged with stamping out corruption and modernising the force. A firm directive style was considered functional in this context, at least in the initial stages (Stace and Dunphy, 2001). This finding endorses the view that a contingency theory of leadership is of prime importance.

In previous chapters various types of participative practices (e.g. autonomous work groups and quality circles) have been examined. An analysis of non-unionised organisations on 'greenfield' sites (Guest and Hoque, 1994) found that nearly half had high involvement/high commitment practices and HRM strategies. Less than a quarter had authoritarian and non-participative management styles. As to the functionality of the various leadership or management styles, cross-cultural issues should be considered (see Case example 11.2).

CASE EXAMPLE 11.2

CULTURAL INFLUENCES ON LEADERSHIP

A few years ago the results of a survey of 200 chief executives, chairmen and directors of companies in the United Kingdom, Germany, and France, conducted by MORI for DDI (an international HR consultancy), showed that there were differences in national attitudes to responsibility, status, and decision making.

- The French senior executive enjoys autonomy in the job expressed as freedom to make decisions with the minimum of interference. On this dimension the Germans and the British are less concerned.
- The British senior executive feels that the best thing about the job is the development of talent in the company. The Germans are closer to the British than to the French on this issue.
- The French captains of industry relish being in a position of power as one of the three attractive features of the job, the Germans are less likely to share that view, whilst the British occupy an in-between position.
- Public recognition is said to be more important in France, reflecting the kudos attached to senior business positions.
- The German leaders stand out in their social conscience and the way they view the responsibility that goes with power.

Question

What impact is leadership style likely to have on communication and employee participation?

A particular perspective on managerial leadership, i.e. transformational leadership (Bass, 1990), seems to be compatible with an HRM outlook on organisational life. This type of leadership is executed in a way that empowers and respects people. Leaders are expected to be innovative, creative, charismatic and visionary risk takers who subscribe to exacting targets and are able to influence their followers to share their inspiring visions of future accomplishments. In the process leaders will be supportive and keen to encourage those subjected to their influence to be entrepreneurial in outlook and bold in seizing opportunities to exploit their talent and make innovative contributions (McKenna, 2006).

Although traditional approaches have focused on the hierarchical relationship between leader and subordinates, another view is that in order to be effective in modern organisations leadership also needs to be 'lateral' and even 'upward'. These issues are discussed in Box 11.2.

Box 11.2: Vision, strategy and other leadership capabilities

A powerful vision is a precondition for leading a company or a country at any time. It is a persuasive picture of where you want to go, how you want to get there, and why anybody should follow. Herb Kelleher formed Southwest Airlines USA in 1971 to make flying affordable and the company profitable. That vision has guided the company ever since. The airline has some of the lowest ticket rates in the industry. A strong vision in a vacuum is not good enough; it must be considered in a strategic context influenced by intensifying competition and not enough time to achieve corporate goals.

Professional investors and analysts in the City and Wall Street expect top management to produce good performances. Although vision and strategy are essential, they are joined by new critical abilities, namely leading out, leading up and moving fast.

With regard to leading out (lateral leadership), companies require managers who can lead out (not just down to subordinates) as they increasingly outsource services, use joint ventures and construct strategic alliances. In other words, the skill of delegating to subordinates is being supplemented by a talent for arranging work (e.g. outsourcing contracts for information services) with partners outside the company. Such lateral leadership is essential for obtaining results when you have no formal organisational authority to guarantee the desired outcome. Lateral leadership could entail, in this case, the identification of the service to contract out, dealing with the right outside partners to provide the service, and convincing sceptical internal managers that the arrangement would deliver what they wanted. Lateral leadership requires the following:

■ strategic thinking to understand when and how to collaborate in order to gain competitive advantage;

■ deal-making skills to secure the appropriate arrangements with outside companies and to ensure that they provide a quality service;

■ monitoring the progress of the partnership by overseeing and developing the collaborative contract; and

■ change management to spearhead new ways of doing business despite internal resistance.

As to leading up, in conditions of decentralised authority companies place a premium on a manager's capacity to mobilise support from superiors as well as subordinates. Effectively one expects managers to lead their own bosses. Where the manager's manager lacks data the subordinate manager should provide the superior with what is needed. Upward leadership depends upon followers who are ready to speak out, solve problems and compensate for weaknesses at the boss's level, but if it is not done in a subtle way it could be disadvantageous to the person exercising it. When handled delicately, it can be beneficial in career terms to those using upward leadership because it gives them the opportunity to be noticed.

With regard to moving fast, the widespread use of the web has increased the availability of information to buyers and sellers and reduced the costs of transactions between them. Acting decisively and quickly with the help of new technology in changing markets, and modifying strategy in response to changes in the company's competitive position is essential. When competitors of eBay – the world's largest online auction site – began competing in the auction market, the chief executive adopted some of their features on eBay's website, as well as adding new features.

Source: based on Useem, 2000

Question

If you were a senior trade union representative in an organisation where traditional leadership was the norm, how might you react to the idea of decentralisation and 'lateral leadership'?

Cynics might suggest that the rhetoric of progressive management practices belies the reality in today's world characterised by delayering and downsizing or rightsizing, in which job insecurity, occupational stress and poor morale are not difficult to find. Therefore it is not surprising that at times managers are prone to outbursts that one would not normally associate with a more humane management style.

Processes such as employee involvement, upward leadership and a team orientation have an impact on and reflect the nature and distribution of power in the organisation. Hardy and Leiba-O'Sullivan (1998) developed a typology of power, based on a review of the research, that can be informative in analysing such processes. They argue that there are four dimensions of power:

1. overt power in the decision-making arena;
2. power over non-decision making;

3. unobtrusive controls;
4. power as a network of relations and discourses.

Overt power may be derived from control of resources, position in the structure and the control of rewards and sanctions. The location of power is observable, and it can be exercised when there is conflict in order to achieve compliance with the dominant order.

However, the decision-making arenas are not open to all who have an interest in the outcomes. Power can also be exercised in deciding who should be involved and who excluded, what items appear on the agenda, and in forming alliances in order to control the outcome of meetings. In other words, not all power is exercised overtly in making decisions, but much occurs behind the scenes.

A third level of sophistication in analysis reveals unobtrusive controls – those that are not simply observable in the way rewards are controlled, or alliances formed. Unobtrusive controls operate through cultural norms, generally held assumptions and structures that legitimise the demands and interests of some but not others. So, for example, the operation of power occurs in conditions of political inactivity. One should not assume that silence indicates agreement – it may be that those with little power are unable to voice their desires and needs as these would not be regarded as legitimate. Power in this sense operates in unseen ways, and attention should be paid not only to actions and words but to silence and inaction.

Lastly, power can be discerned in the network of relationships and discourses. At this level of analysis power is not regarded as an object that can be owned, or a force that an individual can marshal to achieve his or her ends in a straightforward way. Rather, the concept is that we are all subject to the influence of a web of power relations that resides in every individual perception, action and interaction. Discourses determine what is seen as important and what is ignored, and they determine how people are perceived and the way they are interacted with. Hence certain expectations will be held of leaders, and if they do not live up to these expectations they will be regarded as poor leaders, and will suffer the consequences. Similarly, depending on the social context, the same people could be 'constructed' quite differently. For example, in one setting X would be a conservative, and Y a radical, whereas in another setting X would be regarded as being concerned with quality and Y with the generation of new revenue. The way these individuals are assessed will be based on deeply embedded, and often unconscious, sets of concepts and relationships that cannot be controlled by any single individual – even those who are apparently powerful.

Hardy and Leiba-O'Sullivan (1998) analyse a case of empowerment, a topic of relevance to team leadership and motivation, using the four dimensions of power discussed above. In empowerment there is some transfer of overt power in decision making from managers to employees; however, there may be limitations to what an empowered team can decide – for example, their overall budget may be fixed, and hence they have only limited power over the 'non-decision-making arena' that sets their own arena of power. Unobtrusive controls may operate through peer pressure on attendance, perception and performance within the team. For example, those who oppose empowerment might be seen as 'dinosaurs' and 'neanderthals'.

Lastly, when power is regarded as a network of relations and discourses, attention is drawn to the complexity and ambiguity of empowerment as experienced by individuals. The same event can be seen as empowerment, exploitation, or even as not constituting change. At this level of analysis it is not that one could check the objective facts to see which version is true. Rather, the different people are operating in different 'realities' that are real to them. So for some empowerment is experienced as a subtle form of control in which management is extracting greater effort from the workers, for others it is the chance to exercise greater self-determination. In a sense both are right and both are wrong simultaneously. Greater effort and performance are required and yet there is greater self-determination. But there are still strong limitations to individual freedom as the organisation will measure output and the manager and peer group will have expectations that, if flouted, will at least lead to social sanctions such as exclusion from the group. However, the immediate control of supervisory management is removed. The challenge for managers in such situations is to recognise these different levels of reality and enable employees to cope with the ambiguities they entail (Beech and Cairns, 2001).

Trade union representation

Workers are often represented by trade unions in negotiations with management about pay and conditions, in which case both parties enter into collective bargaining. The latter takes place when employees are members of trade unions that undertake to negotiate on their behalf in matters such as pay grades and systems, working conditions, holidays and other benefits, the content of work and its allocation, and when employers recognise trade unions and their officials as legitimate bargaining agents (Price, 2004). Collective bargaining came into existence because unions felt it was a better system than individual bargaining to increase employees' bargaining power and to challenge attempts by employers to create competition between workers. In return for the best possible deal, the unions required solidarity between their members.

A demonstration of a move towards collective bargaining is given in Case example 11.3. This was presented as a partnership approach, and it is clear that the union felt they had gained through the deal.

CASE EXAMPLE 11.3

CARLSBERG-TETLEY AND THE TRANSPORT AND GENERAL WORKERS' UNION

Carlsberg-Tetley, the beer producers, reached a deal with the Transport and General Workers' Union (T&G), which they saw as being a partnership approach. Collective bargaining replaced the traditional local negotiations for transport workers. This was seen as an indication of the maturity of the relationship between the employers and the union, as previously there was great hesitancy on the part of the employers to enter into collective bargaining on the grounds that, if it were to go wrong, beer transportation would be halted right across the country.

The partnership agreement has led to major changes in working practices, terms and conditions. The traditional overtime pay, bonuses and supplements have been replaced by a standard salary. Workers are now expected to stay until the job is completed. The structure has been simplified with 25 job titles reduced to four: driver, driver's mate, team leader and warehouse operative. The result was, according to the director of HR, 'substantial and essential cost savings'. These savings were regarded as necessary given the competitive situation the company found itself in. An implication of the agreement was that the company would not be seeking to outsource its transport; but this was not an explicit statement.

It is worth briefly considering the context of this development in employee relations. Other brewers had recently outsourced their transport functions and, given the company's need to cut costs, the T&G feared that the same approach could be taken by Carlsberg-Tetley. It was believed that if transport were outsourced the terms and conditions of employees would deteriorate radically over time.

Although this agreement was presented as a partnership, Carlsberg-Tetley did not have equally good relationships with all unions. They had derecognised the Manufacturing, Services and Finance union (MSF), which represented 400 middle managers, saying that they were in the minority, and that no one had complained. The HR director denied that the company was 'into union bashing'.

Source: based on Thatcher, 1998

Questions

1. What are the advantages of a 'partnership' approach from the perspective of trade union members?

2. What are the advantages for management?

In the above case it can be seen that Carlsberg-Tetley also gained considerably in flexibility and cost savings. The impact of contextual factors, such as the industry norm for local bargaining, and the highly competitive situation, had an impact on the agreement. The trade union accepted and was influenced by the need for a change in employee performance. The approach may be represented as the 'sophisticated modern' approach (Purcell and Sisson, 1983), examined earlier, in that the organisation was extending the way in which it worked with the union but, in view of the way it treated other unions, it would be possible to raise the question of whether the company also displayed 'standard modern' tendencies in the way it displayed opportunism.

Should one consider *national cultures* when viewing the dynamics of collective bargaining? According to Dowling and Welch (2004) cross-national differences ought to be considered when examining the objectives of the collective bargaining process and the enforceability of collective agreements. They go on to say: 'many European unions view the collective bargaining process as an ongoing class struggle between labour and capital, whereas in the United States union leaders tend toward a pragmatic economic view of collective bargaining rather than an ideological view'. Such a pronounced distinction between the two continents is less likely to be the case in the future.

Relations between employers and trade unions can be characterised as either consultation or negotiation, as shown in Table 11.2.

In the case of consultation, the union may be involved in joint consultative committees, whereas negotiation may be conducted through collective bargaining, which, as we have seen, can only take place where the union has been recognised by management as a legitimate representative of the company's employees. Negotiation can take place in a single organisation, or on a wider scale, when, for example, a union can represent workers doing similar jobs in different organisations in the public sector.

HRM has been associated with an opposite trend – a move towards local level bargaining. This is partly because centralised bargaining (e.g. where pay rates and conditions are centrally determined without reference to local conditions) was seen as time consuming, but it also

Table 11.2 Relations between the parties

Consultation	Negotiation
The views of the trade union are invited by management	Both sides have a right to make an input to the decision
The decision remains within the managerial prerogative	An agreed outcome has to be reached
The decision may or may not take on board the trade union view	The decision is a bargain between the two positions

reflects the changing relations between management and unions. Throughout the 1980s a number of changes occurred in the United Kingdom, which affected the nature of the interaction between management and unions, and as a result we have witnessed the emergence of the new industrial relations. A series of factors has contributed to these changes. For example, there was a decline in manufacturing industry, economic recession, high unemployment, a move to flexible job descriptions, the disappearance of job demarcations in the face of flexible working practices, and an increase in the number of part-time workers with the advent of the flexible firm.

Changes such as these brought in their wake more non-union organisations where contact between employers and individual employees (individualised systems) is prevalent, which could be seen as contributing to the weakening of employee power and growth of employer power within the organisation due to the waning influence of collectivism (Hendry, 1995). In the United Kingdom, the Workplace Employment Relations Survey, the WERS (2004) (www.data-archive.ac.uk; www.wers2004.info) is a large-scale periodic review of the state of employee relations. It has been running since 1980 and has shown a decline in union recognition and membership. The proportion of workplaces employing more than 10 people which recognised unions for negotiating pay and conditions fell from 33 per cent in 1998 to 27 per cent in 2004. In 2004, 34 per cent of employees belonged to a union, compared to 37 per cent in 1998. The decline is more obvious when we consider that slightly over 55 per cent of employees were union members in 1979 (Marsh and Cox, 1992).

It has been mooted by some that the decline in union membership could be because non-union forms of employee representation have taken over (Bewley, 2006). However, there is little evidence to suggest that this is the case. There had been a decline in consultative committees in smaller companies between 1998 and 2004, whilst in larger companies the numbers had remained fairly stable. Equally, there was evidence in the 2004 WERS that consultation and information provision on matters such as organisational change, company financial positions and internal investment plans had either remained stable or declined slightly.

Various pieces of legislation in the United Kingdom have been enacted that have worked against traditional union activity. A secret ballot is required before industrial action can take place, and secondary action (in support of other workers not employed by the same employer) is no longer allowed. 'Closed shops', where all employees are required to join a particular union, are no longer enforceable, and the way of handling those who take industrial action has changed. Prior to the new legislation strikers could be dismissed (as they were considered to have broken the contract to supply their labour in return for remuneration), but everyone striking would have to be dismissed. Individuals could not be singled out; and if one or more strikers were re-employed the others could lodge a complaint with an industrial tribunal. Under the new legislation it is now permissible to dismiss strikers and to re-employ them selectively after a break of three months. These changes have limited the power of the unions and changed the nature of industrial relations.

In the new industrial relations scene management has greater power to impose its will without negotiation or the need to enter into joint consultation. Trade unions, which in the past were opposed to management initiatives, such as increased flexibility and reductions in demarcation lines between jobs, have become less confrontational. The UK Trades Union Congress (TUC) formed the view that properly practised 'soft' HRM is not incompatible with unionism (Monks, 1994). Increasing employee involvement, good communications and treating employees as valued assets rather than factors of production are developments supported by the TUC. Wood (1996) argued that there is some evidence to suggest that unionism can coexist with contemporary strategies for bringing about HRM-based changes that are compatible with the demands of the external environment, but adds that a condition for this coexistence is a continual emphasis on negotiation and collective bargaining. More recently, Willman (reported in Motzko and Perkins, 2007) has argued that we should no longer think in terms of union versus non-union models. In Willman's view it is more appropriate to focus on 'alternative voice regimes'. In this perspective, strategic decision making can be categorised under three labels:

1. 'making', in which there is no union voice;
2. 'hedging', in which there is 'dual voice' incorporating employees but not necessarily via a union; and
3. 'buying', in which employee voice in decision making is enabled via the union.

Some companies, such as Dell, favour the 'making' approach. Dell adopted a 'direct business' model in which communications with the workforce were often related to performance and were made direct to employees without mediation by a union. From Dell's perspective, the direct contact with employees enabled them to enhance trust, feedback and team solidarity (Motzko and Perkins, 2007). However, Bewley (2006) has pointed out that trade union representatives tend to be far better trained than non-union employee representatives, and so there may be less protection for employees and less effective negotiation in business models such as that of Dell.

HRM can view unions as a positive factor, assisting in the process of communicating with and involving employees. In some cases this attitude has resulted in single union deals. Single union agreements are those where sole negotiating rights are granted to one union. They are particularly prevalent in companies that set up operations on greenfield sites and in Japanese-owned organisations. In these situations consultation may be carried out through 'company councils', where the employees' representatives are elected by the workforce rather than appointed by the trade union, although there may be some degree of compromise on this arrangement.

Another feature of the new industrial relations are 'no strike agreements'. Normally these have an automatic referral to an independent arbitrator built into the negotiation procedures where there is failure to reach an internal agreement. The arbitration is often of the 'pendulum' form, which means that rather than the arbitrator making a compromise decision a choice is made between the last offer of the employer and the last claim of the union. Because of the normal obligation of the union not to take industrial action while the procedures are in progress, this means that in effect there is an agreement not to strike. However, unconstitutional industrial action may still occur. Single union and no strike agreements represent a more cooperative approach from unions, and in some cases this is reciprocated by positive HRM practices. For example, in Lucas Flight Control Systems (United Kingdom), the union (the Amalgamated Engineering and Electrical Union) agreed with management an extensive programme of reorganisation, including increases in teamworking and skill flexibility, on the understanding that employment conditions for blue- and white-collar workers will be harmonised, and that the working week will be shorter, with no loss of pay.

However, with the change in the power relations between management and the trade unions, some organisations have sought to impose the managerial prerogative, which has produced a negative effect for workers. For example, in the printing industry there has been a decline in collective bargaining, a derecognition of unions and the imposition of 'individual' contracts.

Finally, according to Roche (2000):

'we may be witnessing the end of new Industrial Relations as a working model for unionised enterprises and sectors in advanced economies and as a major explanatory paradigm for comprehending the dynamics of industrial relations systems. A new perspective is emerging in which the growing influence on industrial relations regimes of contingencies of various kinds actually constitutes the trend in advanced economies.'

In other words, the tradition of employee representation through trade unions and collective bargaining as the focus of engagement between management and unions is being replaced by new relationships in the workplace, but the replacement is not of a single type. Rather, it is made up of a number of different (sometimes contradictory) trends. In some cases the traditional model is retained, in others there is increased individualisation, and in yet other cases a 'partnership' approach is adopted in which unions take on some of the concerns of the organisation, and work with management in order to maintain the profitability and longevity of the firm.

National and international trends

In the United Kingdom there has been a steady decline in union membership. According to the figures from the National Office of Statistics (Granger, 2006), union membership has fallen over the past decade from 33 per cent to around 27 per cent, although the figure rose slightly in 2005 due to an increased proportion of women joining a union. The pattern is different in public and private sectors, with 58 per cent of public sector employees being unionised in 2005 (down from 61 per cent in 1995), whilst less than 20 per cent are unionised in the private sector. By 2005, 6.39 million employees were in a trade union and, as Emmott (2007) points out, this is roughly half the number of members in the 1970s. However, the proportion of employees covered by collective agreements has remained fairly steady since 1997, with nearly 37 per cent of employees being covered in 2005.

The European Industrial Relations Observatory (www.eurofound.europa.eu) collects data on union membership in the EU member states and candidate countries. For the period 1993–2003 records are available for 19 of these countries. These data are presented in Table 11.3 There is a mixed picture in which some countries have seen increases and others decreases in overall numbers. However, it should be noted that the data are mainly drawn from self-reporting by trade unions and that the figures are relative to changes in the working population. That said, there are some trends that are worth noting. The biggest falls were in Eastern Europe and may be related to political and macro economic changes. The largest falls in absolute numbers were in larger economies such as Germany and the United Kingdom. Several countries recorded modest increases, but Luxembourg and France are recorded as having significant growth, although in France the figures available related to one major union and the indication is that others showed much smaller growth of about 4 per cent. Overall, the pattern for Europe was a fall of about 17 per cent because the size of the decreasing union populations outweighed those that were increasing.

Hollinshead and Leat (1995) offer an analysis of the trends in other countries. They argue that the high level of membership in Sweden can be explained by the 'corporate social partnership', which has been established over many years. This has been reinforced by a partnership between trade unions and what was, until the early 1990s, the dominant political party. Consequently, trade unions have enjoyed favourable legislation and governmental support.

Beyond the issue of trade union membership, different styles of employee relations can be seen in Europe. Significant countries in continental Europe have adopted a more regulated approach than the voluntarist style that has been dominant in Britain. Hence, there has often been a tension between Brussels and London concerning the agreement and implementation of labour legislation (Leopold, 2005). Continental Europe has traditionally adopted a more consultative style of employee relations, for example having worker representatives on boards and works councils that enable an employee 'voice' at the top table. These influences have had an impact on legislation such as the Transfer of Undertakings Regulations (TUPE 1981) which apply when one business is acquired by another, or when a public sector service is taken over by another organisation. The TUPE regulations require the acquiring organisation to consult with trade unions or worker representatives and impose duties on the acquiring organisation that prevent it dismissing large sections of the existing workforce in order to achieve economies of scale. Similarly, other legislation (the Trade Union and Labour Relations Act 1992) requires that employers consult with trade unions when 20 or more redundancies are proposed.

Table 11.3 Union membership in Europe

Country	1993	2003	Percentage change
Austria	1,616,000	1,407,000	−12.9%
Belgium	2,865,000	3,061,000	+6.8%
Bulgaria	2,192,000	515,000	−76.5%
Cyprus	159,000	175,000	+10.1%
Denmark	2,116,000	2,151,000	+1.7%
Finland	2,069,000	2,122,000	+2.6%
France	617,000	889,000	+44.0%
Germany	11,680,000	8,894,000	−23.9%
Greece	721,000	639,000	−11.4%
Ireland	432,000	515,000	+19.2%
Italy	10,594,000	11,266,000	+6.3%
Luxembourg	97,000	139,000	+43.3%
Malta	74,000	87,000	+17.6%
Netherlands	1,810,000	1,941,000	+7.2%
Norway	1,325,000	1,498,000	+13.1%
Poland	6,500,000	1,900,000	−70.8%
Portugal	1,150,000	1,165,000	+1.3%
Sweden	3,712,000	3,446,000	−7.2%
UK	8,804,000	7,751,000	−12.0%

Source: based on European Industrial Relations Observatory (2007), www.eurofound.europa.eu

The Transnational Information and Consultation of Employees Regulations (1999) incorporated the influence of the Social Chapter of the 1997 Amsterdam Treaty on European Union into British regulation. These regulations required companies employing more than 1,000 people to extend their information giving and consultation procedures. Subsequent developments in regulations have also required smaller organisations to consult with, and inform, their workforces. The approach of many British companies (such as BT and United Biscuits) had been to form voluntary agreements prior to the regulations coming into force. This allowed them to maintain some aspects of the voluntarist style, for example, in deciding whether representation would be employee- or union-based. In addition, it has been argued that consultations were used as a way of getting employees to 'buy in' to strategic plans, rather than being genuinely open processes by which employees could influence decisions (Leopold, 2005). However, the requirements to communicate responsibly with employees fits well with the HRM approach and so, as long as systems do not become overly bureaucratic, there are benefits to be gained from a positive approach to involvement and consultation.

By contrast, the United States has been typified as a 'business movement' rather than a social partnership. It is argued that the lack of a traditional class base and the high degree of opposition to trade unions from employers and government in the United States have led to the situation of low membership and collective bargaining. Where unions have been active they have tended to focus at the workplace rather than industry level. Additionally, they have tended to adopt a conflictual approach, and so HRM in the United States has tended towards a non-union stance in line with the national trend. In the United States about 35 per cent of employees belonged to a union in the 1960s. This figure had dropped to about 13 per cent by 2002. It has been argued that this is due to a number of factors including societal norms, a shift towards service sector from manufacturing (now about 15 per cent of employees are in manufacturing, whereas the figure was about 25 per cent in the mid-1980s), and the influence of foreign-owned companies such as Toyota and Nissan that have largely taken a non-union approach (Dessler, 2005). There are some exceptions, for example in health care there is a higher proportion of nurses and doctors who are in unions.

In Japan enterprise has been in a dominant position as far as the unions are concerned since the 1950s, and trade unions have generally operated in a cooperative mode rather than the conflictual approach typified by US unions. In France there is the interesting apparent tension between low and decreasing membership and as yet the increasing numbers of employees covered by collective bargaining. According to Hollinshead and Leat (1995) this can again be explained by the political characteristics of the country. In France the trade union movement is politically and religiously fragmented, but it has gone beyond focusing on workplace terms and conditions, and has held broader political aims. In pursuing these aims it has sought to achieve collective bargaining at industry level and to exert pressure on the government, and has had a degree of success in doing so.

Conflict

Conflict in organisations can occur at the collective level (i.e. organised) or the individual level (i.e. unorganised). Collective conflict can lead to industrial action including strikes, go-slows and overtime bans. Individual conflict may manifest itself in absenteeism, a high turnover rate or even sabotage. Any of these actions or outcomes is potentially damaging for the organisation, so it is necessary to use methods for resolving conflict at the earliest opportunity.

Collective conflict may occur when there has been a breakdown in collective bargaining, as, for example, in a dispute about pay levels. Disputes can also arise when there is opposition to changes in working patterns and jobs. At one time the trade unions in the United Kingdom were accused of creating the 'British disease', a high level of strike action. However, in recent years the number of days lost due to industrial stoppages in the United Kingdom is not worse than those of its main competitors. In fact the figures fell gradually throughout the 1980s with one or two exceptions (such as the miners' strike in the mid-1980s).

The Organization for Economic Cooperation and Development (OECD) has carried out a thorough review of strike activity (OECD, 2007). A longitudinal comparison was made of 25 OECD countries for the aggregated periods of 1980–84 and 2000–04. The overall trends are quite clear. Strike rates have roughly halved each decade since the 1980s and the number of workers in each strike has fallen in general. Canada, Iceland, Italy and Spain had the largest number of days lost per employee through conflict and countries with the lowest number lost were Japan, Germany, the Netherlands and Switzerland. Britain was tenth (with first being the lowest number of lost days) of the 25 countries in the study.

There was no simple correlation between strikes and trade union membership or the presence of collective agreements. Strike rates were low both in low trade union membership countries, such as the United States, and in high trade union membership countries, such as Denmark. Similarly, strike rates were low in countries where workers were covered by collective agreements (e.g. Finland and Sweden) and where few workers were part of a collective agreement (e.g. Japan). The analysis of the OECD was that changes in the structure of employment, with increasing proportions of the workforce being employed in the service sector, which tends to have lower strike activity than manufacturing, and a general decline in industrial conflict were behind the strike-rate reductions. However, it may be that workers are hesitant to take industrial action for reasons connected with the economic situation and the fear of losing their jobs.

RESOLVING CONFLICT

To continue with the theme of collective conflict, where it is not possible for management and the representatives of the workers to resolve their conflict, a third party could be invited to intervene. A third party could perform any one of three roles, i.e. conciliator, mediator or arbitrator. A conciliator acts as a facilitator when the main parties are trying to resolve the conflict. A mediator also acts as a facilitator, but in addition puts forward recommendations. An arbitrator actually makes decisions to resolve the conflict.

In cases of individual conflict, as opposed to collective conflict, an employee can be subject to disciplinary procedures or can make a grievance claim where there is a feeling that he or she has been treated unfairly or in an unacceptable manner. In the United Kingdom, statutory dispute procedures came into force in 2004. These set out minimum three-stage processes for dismissal and grievance as follows:

Disciplinary and dismissal procedure:

1. The employer must explain in writing the grounds of the disciplinary issue and invite the employee to a meeting to discuss the issue.
2. The employer must hold a meeting with the employee and notify them of the decision and their right to appeal.
3. Where requested, the employer must invite the employee to attend a further meeting to allow an appeal against the decision.

Grievance procedure:

1. The employee must explain their grievance in writing to the employer.

2. The employer must invite the employee to a meeting to discuss the issue, and then inform them of the decision and their right to appeal.

3. If the employee wishes to appeal they must inform the employer, who must then arrange a meeting.

A CIPD survey (2007a) concluded that the new procedures have led to an increase in formalisation of the way that conflict is managed, but that there has not been a clear impact (positive or negative) on the frequency and nature of tribunal cases. The West Midlands Police Force used the legal changes to update their procedures. It carried out extensive consultation with the Police Federation and other relevant trade unions. As a result it developed a simpler system with a different focus. The new system was entitled 'The Resolution Procedure' in order to highlight the purpose of achieving resolution rather than imposing discipline or establishing blame. Employees can now raise submissions and identify their desired outcome from the process (CIPD, 2007a).

There are occasions where an employer has to dismiss an employee. According to Walsh and Bott (2005) dismissal falls into two broad categories: resulting from employee deficiency, or resulting from a managerial decision with regard to the business that means redundancy for the employee. In both types dismissal can occur through 'exclusion', where blame is attributed, or through 'release' where no blame is attributed. In the case of employee deficiency, exclusion dismissal typically occurs through the disciplinary process. This can be because of gross misconduct or because of persistent problems that were not resolved. To manage this process in line with an HRM approach a 'corrective' style is often adopted. In this style of discipline the aim is to rectify capacity and conduct so that the employee can remain in the organisation. However, it is acknowledged that unless improvement occurs, dismissal will follow. The 'release' version of employee deficiency occurs, for example, where the employee has become unable to perform their job through long-term sickness. In these circumstances, the HRM aim is often to enable the employee to leave in the best way possible in terms of financial settlement and possibly support in finding future employment. In the case where a business decision has led to a significant change in the organisation (such as shutting down a loss-making operation) redundancy is the outcome. Redundancy means that the job has disappeared. Exclusion redundancy can occur where some, but not all, employees, are selected to be made redundant. The selection can be made, for example, on the basis of job performance. The 'release' version of redundancy is where the flexible organisation can come into play. For example, people employed on short-term contracts, who did not have expectations of a full career with the organisation, could be selected as the first to be made redundant. Another common practice is to offer voluntary redundancies to those whose stage of life and personal circumstances mean that this is a reasonable outcome for them.

When dismissal is occurring it is important that it is regarded as being fair as, apart from the obvious ethical implications, former employees can take out a legal complaint against their former employer for 'unfair dismissal'. Many employers want to avoid such proceedings not only because of the cost, but because of the bad publicity and bad feeling of employees that remain that can occur. This does not mean that companies should avoid dismissal where it is justified, but that they should ensure they are acting fairly. A dismissal is deemed to be fair where it is on one (or more) of the following grounds:

■ lack of capability or qualification to do the job;

■ unacceptable conduct of the employee;

■ redundancy (the job has disappeared);

■ legal restraint (e.g. an employee works as a truck driver but is disqualified from driving);

■ another substantial reason (e.g. the employee sets up a rival company).

In addition, employers must be seen to have acted 'reasonably'. This means that they followed the appropriate set of procedures. The Advisory, Conciliation and Arbitration Service (ACAS) has a model disciplinary procedure, which is adopted by many organisations. The purpose of the procedure is to provide a breathing space for the employee whose performance or behaviour has fallen short of acceptable standards so that the necessary improvement can be made.

Certain principles underlie the procedure. These include that the employee will be given full information, and that careful investigation will take place before any disciplinary action is taken. Before the formal procedure is invoked, particularly where the fault is a minor one, the option of dealing with the problem informally should be explored. This might take the form of a counselling session. However, where it is necessary to use the formal procedure, the employee (accompanied by a friend or representative where appropriate) should be given the opportunity to put his or her side of the case at a forum, which sits at a time to be arranged between each of the stages listed below. The stages of the ACAS procedure are as follows:

1. *Oral warning.* A note of this is kept on the employee's file.
2. *Written warning.* This is activated where there is repetition of the offence following an oral warning, or where the offence is more serious.
3. *Final written warning or disciplinary suspension.* For repeated misconduct where previous warnings have not been effective. (A serious alternative may be suspension without pay.)
4. *Dismissal.* Where the employee has failed to comply with the requirements of the final written warning.

For gross misconduct, where the offence is very serious (e.g. theft, fraud, fighting, serious negligence), following an investigation the employee may be dismissed without going through stages 1–3. The employee will normally have the right to appeal against the decision at each stage of the procedure.

Apart from unfair dismissal there is wrongful dismissal. An employee can exercise a 'common law' right to sue the employer for damages if dismissed wrongly. A case of wrongful dismissal arises when, for example, the employer has not given proper notice, or the behaviour of the employee did not justify such treatment. A case of unfair dismissal would be heard before an employment tribunal. However, a case of wrongful dismissal would be referred to an ordinary court where the damages awarded could be higher than the maximum stipulated by the employment tribunals. Always remember that dismissal has to take place before a tribunal or court can act.

When we reflect on the role of grievance procedures and the use of discipline our concern should be to solve a problem and make matters better, and not to be totally preoccupied with the administering of punishment. For example, there is a problem where an employee is persistently late for work. Our aim should be to discover the causes of this behaviour (e.g. lack of motivation, difficult domestic circumstances, travel difficulties, a personal problem), and then to help the employee confront and hopefully remove the underlying cause(s), rather than just dealing with the symptom.

Handling conflict in an organisation is facilitated by the rules and procedures in place. However, we cannot overlook the part played by management style and organisational culture. An aim of HRM is to create a culture in which employees are committed to the goals of the organisation. Where this prevails and is reflected in, for example, increased employee participation, a situation can emerge where employees become more involved in their own 'discipline' (Edwards, 1994). If employees are working in a team, they are not only carrying out the tasks allocated to them but are also interacting with others. In the course of interaction, approved behaviour is likely to be supported, while deviant behaviour could be subjected to sanctions (group discipline). If the team is committed to a goal of achieving high-quality work, it is likely to reward team members whose performance meets the requisite standards.

Ethics, HRM and managing diversity

Increasingly, ethical issues are being raised as matters of concern in organisations. Issues may range from the micro, such as harassment and bullying (discussed in Case example 11.7) to unfair discrimination in selection decision making (e.g. in relation to the use of tests, as discussed in Chapter 7) through to macro issues such as protection of the environment. While people have a personal view of what is right and wrong there is a cultural dimension, for example, the practice of bribery is acceptable in some cultures but not others (McKenna, 2006; Montagnon, 1998). It has been argued by some (e.g. Eccles *et al.*, 2001; Hartley, 1993) that it is necessary to formulate ethical codes of conduct and to reinforce them through measurement in order to persuade organisations to behave ethically. However, this in itself may be insufficient to have a genuine impact and it has been argued that the HRM function should be proactive in raising awareness of ethical issues and the need for consistency between the values and behaviour, particularly in the age of the 'green consumer' and the 'ethical investor' (Pocock, 1989).

An example is provided by the Co-operative Bank. In 1992 it produced a 12-point code that specified it would not lend money to companies involved in cruelty to animals, the arms trade or environmental destruction. By 1998 the Bank's market share had increased by about 3 per cent and it is thought that this is at least partially attributable to its overt focus on ethical issues. In addition, the Bank has enjoyed considerable loyalty from its workforce, with over 60 per cent of employees having in excess of 20 years' service. Commitment is regarded as a two-way thing, and the Bank has made no-redundancy agreements with staff and placed an emphasis on providing training, annual pay increases and an examination of the balance between work and family life (McKenna, 2006). One can ask how far such policies are genuinely ethical if they also bring economic benefits. This has been a matter of debate in HRM, and Legge (1998) offers an analytical framework that is applicable in such matters of judgement.

The framework includes three alternative perspectives on ethics as follows:

1. *Deontological theory* – derived from the philosophy of Immanuel Kant – is based on a belief in moral laws that describe what is ultimately right and wrong. Ethical behaviour is a matter of doing what is right, for example, treating others as we would want to be treated ourselves and operating in a fair and just way.
2. *Utilitarianism* – based on the philosophy of John Stuart Mill – does not accept that there are ultimately right and wrong actions, rather rightness is contingent. Choosing the right action is a matter of calculating what the consequences of alternative actions will be and selecting the one that will lead to the greatest good (or least harm) for the greatest number of people in the circumstances.
3. *Stakeholder theory of justice* – based on the philosophy of John Rawls – argues that justice is neither an ultimate truth nor straightforwardly a matter of calculation of consequences. An alternative is proposed based on a 'mind experiment' as follows: imagine that people existed, but are not yet in the world – they are able to choose the ethical structure and 'rules of engagement' for society, but do not know in advance their own position, strengths

and weaknesses. Rawls believes that people in such a position would choose a system of distribution in which no one would lose out completely, and in which care would be given to all people, no matter how weak. This choice would be made because no individual would know in advance how strong or weak they would be. In application to the organisational world, such thinking emerges as a concern with the needs and desires of divergent stakeholder groups, while maintaining the long-term survival of the organisation.

The different perspectives provide a framework through which the ethical value of HRM policies and actions can be judged. In the case of the Co-operative Bank described above their policy would be ethical in terms of stakeholder justice, but would not necessarily be seen as fully ethical from the deontological perspective as it appears that the 'ethical' policies may have been a means to the end of business success. Ultimately ethical decisions would be the ones taken because they were right no matter what the business outcomes (good or bad). An example of the operationalisation of the ethical framework is provided in Case example 11.4.

CASE EXAMPLE 11.4

ETHICS AND THE PRODUCTION OF JEANS

The different perspectives on ethics lead to different ways of assessing a situation. For example, an ethical question for HRM can be drawn from Abrams and Astill's (2001) investigation of the production of denim jeans. They found that mid-priced jeans being sold in Europe were composed of materials from 13 countries around the world, and while some suppliers were operating a reasonable approach to employment others (in the view of Abrams and Astill) were not. For example, the copper for rivets and buttons was being mined by people working for low wages in poor conditions, and at the cost of environmental contamination in Africa. Similarly, the final product was being assembled and stitched by people working for very low wages under circumstances that would be seen as well below the acceptable standards of health and safety in the United Kingdom.

If we were to think of this situation from the deontological frame it could be argued that this policy of sourcing production at low cost is unethical because it treats people in a way that is always unacceptable. From a utilitarian perspective there would be a number of questions. Although there are bad consequences for some, overall are the interests of the majority served? If so, does the benefit, in human terms, outweigh the costs? If the answers to these questions were yes, then the policy would be seen as ethical. Similarly, from a stakeholder perspective there would be further issues of balance to explore. In particular there is the question of whether some level of employment is better than none. In the mining situation the benefits for the local population may outweigh the costs, notwithstanding the long-term environmental effects. Similarly, although the pay of the production workers is very low by European standards, in their own economic setting it does allow them to live, and the alternative of unemployment would be worse. For the deontological theory perspective it is possible to make an assessment of clear right and wrong. For the other two ethical theories this judgement is contingent on outcomes and degree of balance of the stakeholders.

Question

Should HR managers adopt an approach to ethics in which there are absolute rights and wrongs, or is it ethically acceptable to take a contingent perspective that could, for example, justify low wages in certain situations?

In recent years, corporate social responsibility (CSR) has been firmly on the agenda. Taking a responsible approach to employment incorporates a range of factors including the nature of governance, responsibility towards all stakeholder groups and a concern for sustainability. One aspect of CSR that can have a significant impact is the way that company pension investments are made. Box 11.3 discusses this issue.

A question arises – how ethical is HRM? The answer for Legge (1998) depends on what is meant by HRM and which ethical perspective is adopted. The elements of HRM that are concerned with cost cutting and ensuring that workers are flexible on the terms of the organisation are unlikely to be seen as ethical unless they lead to the greatest good for the greatest number. For example, it could be argued that making some people redundant maintains the viability of the firm, without which everyone would ultimately lose their jobs. It is more likely that the developmental side of HRM – encouraging mutuality, investing in people and rewarding them appropriately – would be regarded as ethical from all three perspectives.

Box 11.3: Socially responsible investing in business

The London Pensions Fund Authority (LPFA), whose Chief Executive is Mike Taylor, appointed in 2006, was established in 1989 to take over the running of the Greater London Council pension fund and subsequently of the Inner London Education Authority, when both were abolished. It has £3.6 billion in assets under management and 73,000 members. The chief executive is now answerable to a board appointed by Ken Livingstone, the Mayor of London. Mr Taylor believes in investing responsibly, taking account of environmental, social and governance issues (ESG), a view held by the Mayor.

In advancing the responsible investment agenda Mr Taylor will try to codify the beliefs of the board. The LPFA board believes that it wants the pension fund to be a long-term responsible investor, though an important consideration is to ensure that there is enough money to pay pensions. To demonstrate the LPFA's credentials of being long term, the quarterly meetings with fund managers have moved away from a performance focus to understanding how they are positioned for the longer term. Fund managers who were not taking a long-term view would be challenged. The most recently appointed fund manager, ING Real Estate, was selected partly on the basis of its ESG credentials. The LPFA has used Trucost, the environmental research organisation, to conduct a carbon assessment of its equity portfolios, so that there is a better understanding of the nature of portfolios in relation to the benchmark. Mr Taylor is prepared to take the findings of this research to some of the influential fund managers asking to discuss them. This could be seen as a first step in a process to change fund managers' thinking on matters connected with investing responsibly.

Source: based on Skypala, 2007

Sue Round, Manager of Allchurches Investment Management Services' Amity fund (£66.9 million assets under management), says that the fund seeks to invest in companies that make positive contributions to communities and the environment. The fund was established to meet the needs of the clergy, enabling them to invest in a way that matches their ideals, and the company provides insurance for churches. Since its inception in 1988 the fund has avoided companies that are involved in alcohol, gambling, arms and tobacco. Ms Round acknowledges that although this policy has harmed the performance of the fund in some instances, it has helped it in others. She points out that making ethical investment decisions is not a black and white exercise and it requires careful examination. For example, there are some large companies operating in countries with oppressive regimes. A natural first reaction might be to avoid investing in those companies. But what if those companies did good things such as providing education, medical care, and housing to workers, then a pragmatic view is called for?

Source: based on *Financial Times*, 2007

Question

Do you believe that companies should use an ethical investment policy in investing their pension funds, or is financial performance alone the most important issue?

MANAGING DIVERSITY

The issue of managing diversity is one that has been raised as a particular ethical issue for HRM. The term diversity emerged from the focus on equal opportunities which was concerned with eliminating unfair bias and using only criteria for selection decision making that were strictly relevant to the job. This would normally exclude criteria based on gender or race.

Managing diversity has broader aims and is concerned with 'creating a working culture that seeks, respects, values and harnesses difference' (Schneider, 2001: 27). Diversity is not a policy of assimilation in which minorities are absorbed into the culture of the majority. Rather it is a deliberate attempt to bring into one organisational setting people who differ in nationality, ethnic origin, gender, religion, sexual orientation, background and so on. The argument for this is based on business logic, and in particular the need to operate in a globalised environment. For organisations operating across national boundaries there are questions of how they are going to be most effective with different groups of employees and different groups of customers. This means having people who can speak the local language and who understand local culture – in Unilever's term being a 'multilocal multinational' (Schneider, 2001). It can also be the case that diverse teams can be highly productive and creative. One example is Intel's development of the Pentium chip, which was undertaken by a 'global product development team'. Following this success such teams have become the norm for Intel.

In order to implement diversity policies Schneider proposes a systematic approach. This starts by gathering three types of measures in a diagnostic phase: employee statistics (such as the make-up of the workforce by gender, ethnicity and disability), internal perceptions (e.g. running focus groups to gather the perceptions of minority groups and employee surveys incorporating diversity questions) and external perceptions (e.g. gathering information from customers on how they regard the organisation). Following the diagnostic phase the targets for progress should be set in a meaningful way. For example, terms such as 'diversity' may have little meaning for the workforce, and structuring policies in terms of 'respect' and 'fairness' may be more effective. In addition to policies it is important to identify the behaviours that will support the vision of diversity. For companies such as Barclays Bank, which has been following this process, it has encompassed a culture change, and thus cannot be regarded as a stand-alone activity. Rather there is a need to link policies and behaviours to the recruitment and selection practices and the performance management system. In Case example 11.5 regarding BAE Systems there is a link between managing diversity and quality improvement that incorporates an integrated approach to change.

CASE EXAMPLE 11.5

BAE SYSTEMS' DIVERSITY POLICY

BAE Systems employs 120,000 people in four continents. In the United Kingdom it employs 70,000 of whom 12 per cent are women, 5 per cent are from ethnic minorities and 1 per cent are disabled. There are two female managing directors and one female non-executive board member. Traditionally the industry has been white-male centric, but BAE fears that unless it can broaden its appeal it will be difficult to recruit the 2,000 engineers (including ICT specialists) it needs every 12 months. Its aim is to create an inclusive culture that does not demand that minority staff should 'fit in'. The reasoning behind this is that job-holder value (i.e. the value of the job and company to the employee) should be regarded as highly significant alongside shareholder value. BAE believes that if this can be achieved then staff will feel valued by the company and will contribute to its success. In addition, it will make the company attractive to graduates and others who will become sources of recruitment.

The approach has been to integrate the diversity policy with an agenda for change that incorporates the European Foundation for Quality Management (EFQM) business excellence model. A SWOT analysis of the current situation was conducted, and best practices identified. In order to foster behavioural change local implementation teams took responsibility to help move their business units from being 'learners' to 'world class' by progressing through bronze, silver and gold measured standards under the EFQM model. Audits are conducted and achieved outcomes are rewarded.

There is some evidence of improvement on the business profile measures that are important to BAE. In the *Sunday Times* survey of 'employers of choice' they rose from 74th to 25th between 1999 and 2001. At the same time benchmarking against industry norms has shown improvement. In the Opportunity Now Survey of 1999 BAE was 6 per cent below the manufacturing sector's norm, but by 2001 it was 11 per cent above the norm. For BAE the link of diversity to business needs is crucial.

Source: based on Benwell, 2001

Question

Should companies adopt diversity policies because they are 'the right thing to do' or because they can be used to enhance the company's reputation or performance?

The Employment Act of 2002 introduced a range of family friendly rights such as maternity and paternity leave, adoption leave and the right for employees with young children to have requests for flexible working arrangements considered seriously by their employers.

The CIPD (CIPD 2007b) conducted a survey of 285 organisations across all sectors on their diversity practices. A scale of 'diversity sophistication' was developed. This incorporated 146 variables of good practice as far as diversity was concerned. The average score was 52 out of 146, with the highest score being 122 and the lowest being 0. The conclusion was that almost all companies could make considerable improvements in their practice. The survey also sought data on the drivers for developing diversity policies and practices. Legislative pressures were the biggest reasons for companies to act, followed by the need to recruit talent, corporate social responsibility and to be an employer of choice. Table 11.4 is adapted from the CIPD research (2007b: 7) based on the percentage of respondents ranking the reason as either 'most important' or 'very important'.

Health and safety at work

Devoting a short section to health and safety is in no way meant to condone its relatively low position in the pecking order of HRM topics. It is recognised that the health, safety and welfare function within the organisation has been very much the 'Cinderella' of HRM despite the enormous human and economic benefits that can flow from a well-conceived and properly implemented health and safety policy within a company. Under the UK Health and Safety at Work etc. Act (1974) employers have a duty to ensure (so far as is reasonably practicable) that they provide a safe and healthy environment both for their direct employees and for other people (including contractors) who may be affected by the work activities. This means that employers are responsible for the following:

- providing safe equipment for the job and ensuring that it is used in accordance with correct procedures;

- making sure that employees do not undertake dangerous activities;

Table 11.4 Reasons for adopting diversity practices

Drivers	Percentage ranking as most/very important	Rank order
Legal pressures	45	1
Because it makes business sense	31	2
To recruit and retain best talent	30	3=
Corporate social responsibility	30	3=
To be an employer of choice	30	3=
Because it is morally right	24	6
Belief in social justice	20	7
To address recruitment problems	19	8=
To improve products and services	19	8=

Source: adapted from CIPD, 2007b

■ checking that all the procedures involved in jobs are safe;

■ providing a safe and healthy environment in which to work (including adequate light, heat and ventilation).

Employees are required to comply with the employer's reasonable instructions with regard to health and safety. So, for example, if instructed to wear safety goggles, or to ensure that a guard is fitted when operating a machine, they are expected to comply. The Management of Health and Safety at Work Regulations (1992) were enacted to implement the European Commission Directive on health and safety. Employers are required to perform the following tasks:

■ carry out assessment of hazards and risks and surveillance;

■ plan and monitor preventive measures;

■ make sure that employees have adequate information;

■ provide necessary training.

Directives have also been implemented on limiting the manual handling of loads, use of computer (display screen) equipment and the provision of personal protective equipment. A legitimate concern of health and safety practitioners, in association with appropriate HRM specialists, could be the provision of counselling and other services to those who succumb to stressful conditions at work often brought about by a climate of profound change. Such action could lead to people being able to cope better with the demands made on them and could have a beneficial effect on absenteeism and staff turnover.

Traditionally managers have confined their attention to health and safety issues within the workplace, reacting to problems as they arise. Nowadays a number of employers have decided to adopt a more proactive stance in health care. This often takes the form of fitness and health screening schemes designed to change the lifestyle of employees inside and outside the organisation (see Case example 11.6). Another manifestation of preventive health management programmes is the employee assistance programme (EAP) highlighted below (Glendon *et al.*, 2006).

CASE EXAMPLE 11.6

HEALTH CARE AT UNIPART

Unipart in the United Kingdom spent £1 million on preventive health care for its 2,500 employees, and opened a £500,000 extension to its on-site sports facilities, which include squash courts, an aerobics studio and a centre for alternative health therapies. The facilities, known as the Lean Machine, compare very favourably with the best of the private health clubs.

Unipart's approach to revolutionising occupational health is seen as a way to combat stress while staying ahead of the competition. According to Unipart's chief executive, the rapid pace of change means that employees are facing more and more stress, which can have damaging consequences. In the 'Lean Machine' employees have the opportunity to get fit so that they can cope with stress. Also, they receive treatment to deal with some of the problems created by stress, and learn to avoid problems and manage stress through the medium of exercise and therapies.

Source: adapted from Wolfe, 1995

Question

To what extent do you think companies should take care of 'the whole person' rather than focusing only on employees' welfare to the extent that this is necessary because of legislation?

EAPs – in which employees are counselled on problems ranging from alcohol and drug abuse to financial, marital and legal difficulties – have only taken root in the United Kingdom in recent years, but are well established in the United States. The main purpose of EAPs is to enhance the quality of the employee's personal life (Berridge and Cooper, 1993), but offering these programmes could be viewed by some companies as a way of projecting a caring image. A main reason why employees use this service is that it gives them the opportunity to address issues connected with relationships, family problems and financial worries. This may not be a surprising development because in many cases traditional support services (e.g. family, church and GP) are not readily available.

Although it is changes in the workplace – for example, widespread downsizing and restructuring often resulting in greater pressure and more work for those left behind – that often persuade companies to introduce EAPs, many of the problems dealt with by the programmes are frequently unrelated to work (Hall, 1995). Normally the types of problem presented vary according to whether they are discussed face to face or over the telephone. According to Michael Reddy of ICAS (an EAP provider), about half the people calling telephone helplines seek financial or legal help, with less than a third of calls related to work. People may want to talk about drink driving, or social security benefits, or eviction threats by a landlord, or separation, or behavioural problems in children experienced by single mothers, or one partner reluctant to move following the relocation of a job.

GlaxoSmithKline, the pharmaceutical company, introduced an EAP programme and found that many of the problems presented were not work-related (e.g. Child Support Agency assessments or meeting the needs of an elderly parent living far away). The company found that those who participated in the programme were subsequently happier, more punctual and productive. At the Post Office stress counselling was said to be beneficial in terms of a decline in anxiety levels and depression, improved self-esteem, and a reduction in absenteeism.

The question sometimes asked is whether the provider of the service should be from within the organisation or from an external source? Some organisations, such as British Telecommunications and HM Revenue & Customs, prefer an in-house service. However, the use of an outside provider can help reassure staff that their problems remain confidential (Hall, 1995).

Workplace counselling is usually offered as part of an EAP. This is a process aimed at helping people to explore a problem and find alternative ways of dealing with it so that some resolution is achieved. The overriding goal is to help clients to help themselves and to take responsibility for their own lives. It is based on the belief that within individuals there is a capacity to grow in maturity and to take on responsibility if the conditions are right. Counsellors are expected to be sympathetic, genuine, nonjudgmental and able to create an atmosphere of trust and acceptance in the quest to understand in a empathetic way the client's behaviour and the reasons for it. Other counselling skills include active listening, clarifying issues, reflecting what comes across in disclosures, summarising the position put forward by the client, and offering guidance. Evidence suggests that organisations benefit as they receive a good return from their investment in well conceived counselling services and EAPs (Glendon *et al.*, 2006).

A psychological issue with pronounced occupational health implications that has captured attention in recent years is that of bullying and harassment. This is highlighted in Case example 11.7.

BULLYING AND HARASSMENT

Bullying is often referred to in the context of the plight of some workers in the financial district of London, but can be found in a wide range of employment sectors and occupations. Workplace bullying has been described as the silent epidemic (McAvoy and Murtagh , 2003). Although managers are the most common perpetrators of bullying, individuals can also be bullied by their colleagues, subordinates and clients. It is said that younger workers who know little about their workplace rights, and members of ethnic minorities, are particularly vulnerable.

Bullying not only makes people ill so that victims have to use sleeping tablets and sedatives, but it also leads to a deteriorating performance, job dissatisfaction, and obsessive-compulsive behaviour, such as constantly checking one's work.

The following illustrates how bullying can be experienced (Cartwright and Cooper, 2007) :

■ having your opinions or views ignored;
■ being exposed to unimaginable workload;
■ someone withholding information that affects your performance;
■ being given tasks with unreasonable or impossible targets or deadlines;
■ being ordered to do work beyond one's competence;
■ being ignored or facing hostility (i.e. being frozen out);
■ having gossip spread about you;
■ excessive monitoring;
■ having insulting or offensive remarks made about your person (i.e. habits and background), your attitudes or your personal life;
■ having key areas of responsibility removed or replaced with more trivial or unpleasant tasks;
■ being disciplined or put down in public.

Organisational culture or conditions that can promote bullying are: where there is a high level of competition; heavy work loads; radical change is present; there is a climate of insecurity (e.g. redundancies are contemplated); there is a macho style of management, and hierarchical organisation is pronounced; there are low levels of participation or consultation; and a lack of procedures to tackle bullying and harassment.

Organisations are advised to increase awareness of workplace bullying and clearly specify the kinds of behaviour that are deemed unacceptable, indicating the procedures that should be followed in the event of a complaint.

One employee's experience

Helen Green, who worked in the secretarial section of Deutsche Bank in London, claimed she suffered psychiatric injury because she was subjected to offensive, intimidating, denigrating, bullying, humiliating, patronising, infantile and insulting words and behaviour. She alleged some colleagues ignored and excluded her, undermined her authority and increased her workload from time to time to wholly unreasonable levels. The bank challenged the various allegations. However, the court ruled in her favour and awarded her £800,000 for damages in respect of the psychiatric injury she had received as a result of being bullied.

Source: based on Cartwright and Cooper, 2007

Question

What HRM practices could be mobilised to reduce bullying?

The Director of Human Resources at Chelsea and Westminster Healthcare NHS Trust is quoted as saying in the June 2001 issue of *Trust News* (an internal newsletter) that the Trust is committed to the physical and psychological health, safety and welfare of its employees:

'The trust believes that all individuals have the right to be treated with dignity and respect at work and affirms that harassment, discrimination, or bullying at work, in any form, is unacceptable ... We are firmly committed to promoting a working environment free from all forms of hostility, so that staff are enabled to achieve their full potential, contribute more effectively to organizational success, and achieve higher levels of job satisfaction.'

The Trust introduced a Dignity at Work Policy, which specifies the different forms harassment can take. In this document there is advice on both formal and informal ways in which staff can tackle the problem. In particular it is said that any employee who believes that he or she is being bullied or harassed should avail themselves of the opportunity to discuss the situation confidentially with someone who is impartial, empathetic and trained in issues of equality.

The Trust has a team of harassment advisers: 'The Harassment Adviser will be part of a team. The aim is to provide a professional, yet informal and friendly service, which staff can use with confidence, and which is independent of line management systems' (*Trust News*, 2001). Staff who are interested in taking on this role are asked to come forward, and receive special training on a course lasting three and a half days. When trained they offer confidential advice, guidance and support to any member of staff who feels they are being harassed.

The field of health and safety at work is well provided with regulations and directives with the noble intention to create greater safety awareness and to protect people from hazards in the workplace. Nevertheless, accidents do happen and frequently the cause is human error. Where this is the case the human element in the man–machine system at work is found to be wanting. Mindful of the prominence given to accidents and mental health in the UK government's White Paper 'Health of the Nation' in 1992, Glendon *et al.* (2006) have attempted to mobilise applied psychology within an HRM framework to shed light on the human factors in safety and risk management. Organisations benefit from investing in well-conceived counselling services and EAPs.

Conclusions

Enhanced communications are central to HRM. Without effective multi-directional communication it is unlikely that there will be mutuality and commitment between employer and employees. A range of media are available for communication in the modern organisation, but the essence of effective communication remains encoding, transmitting and decoding messages with the minimum of interference. Media such as suggestion schemes and attitude surveys are important for maximising the number of staff who can make an input, but face-to-face modes of communication, such as team briefings, remain vital as they offer a greater opportunity for clearing up misunderstandings and for generating direct feedback.

Participation is another central feature of HRM systems. At the macro level this can include consultative committees and works councils. At the micro level decision making on certain issues can be placed in the hands of the workforce. The extent to which there is such delegation is related to the management style adopted. There are calls for forms of management and leadership that increase the focus on involving employees, such as transformational, lateral and upward leadership. These approaches include a shift in the location and nature of power. Traditionally, power was in the hands of those at the top of organisations. In flatter and more empowered organisations power may be more dispersed throughout the structure, and it may be exercised through networks and expertise rather than in the setting of organisational rules and procedures.

The emergence of the new industrial relations and HRM is reflected in an increase in the amount of direct communication and an elevation of the status of individualism as seen in the importance given to individually based performance-related pay, which tends to replace collectively negotiated pay settlements in the United Kingdom. These changes, and falling membership, have meant that a response was needed from the trade unions. One type of response that is likely to be on the increase is the merger of unions to form 'super unions', for example, the creation of Unison in the public sector. The new industrial relations has also seen a more cooperative stance on the part of the trade unions.

The influence of the European Union is likely to increase pressure for consultative forums with employees (Gollan, 2006), involving elected members of the workforce rather than trade union-appointed representatives. However, the tradition of management–union relations is not being eradicated. It has been found that although organisations are increasing the amount of direct communication with employees and offering them greater opportunity to engage in participative processes, these developments are taking place within a framework called 'dual arrangements', i.e. alongside existing trade union institutions and procedures (Tailby *et al.*, 2007). Currently, there is no single view on what constitutes best practice in establishing employee voice. In the United Kingdom, research indicates that a mixture of processes for involving and communicating with employees is adopted by firms, not necessarily in a thoroughly integrated way (Gollan, 2006), and it looks as though practice will continue to develop

along the lines of both union and non-union processes. New flexible and delayered structures, coupled with environments of constant change, call for care and sensitivity in the
way conflict is managed, and signal the need to create participative forums to elicit
mutual benefits for the workforce and the organisation.

There are different trends in trade union membership and collective bargaining on the
international stage, and these can be understood in terms of the model originally proposed by Fox (1974) and subsequently developed by others (Purcell and Sisson, 1983).
Certainly, the rhetoric of many UK organisations has moved towards that of the 'sophisticated moderns', who seek to expand employee involvement and who are not averse to
the idea of trade unions playing a role. However, internationally, for example in the
United States, it could be argued that a 'sophisticated human relations' or paternalistic
approach is in vogue. Having said that, critics may argue, with some justification, that the
practice (as opposed to the rhetoric) of employee relations in different national and
organisational settings can move towards 'traditional' adversarial or 'standard modern'
opportunistic styles.

Whichever approach is taken, the focus is on improving organisational performance,
and this has increasingly been accepted by trade unions. Where the trade unions accept
the focus on increasing performance the opposition to efforts by organisations to
increase flexibility and productivity is likely to decline. HRM, although unitarist in origin,
does not prescribe a single approach to best practice when it comes to employee
relations. Pluralism does not seem to be ruled out, at least in practice, by a company
adopting a strategic approach to HRM. Rather the approach takes a contingency perspective, that is adopting an approach which is most likely to maximise performance. In
adopting a contingent view, however, it is important to maintain consistency between the
different strands of the employee relations approach – for example, on issues such as
employee involvement, and other areas of HRM policy such as selection, training and
reward management.

Emmott (2007) has argued that unions should make a positive impact on the psychological contract and hence on business performance. Reviewing previous research on
the WERS he notes that whilst a positive correlation between collective bargaining/joint
consultation and business performance has not been demonstrated, there is evidence
that informal relationships between employers and employee representatives, and a
combination of direct communication and joint consultation, does produce better
employee involvement and consequent business performance. The key to this positive
psychological contract, according to Emmot, is employee engagement, and this is
enhanced where employees believe that:

- they are listened to and can feed views up the organisation;
- they are well informed and understand what their contribution is;
- their managers are committed to the organisation and show respect to their workers.

Emmott argues that unions can assist in establishing these beliefs in the workforce
where there is a genuine joint approach with HR departments. This does, however, entail
a degree of trust and a willingness to step outside traditional adversarial roles on the
part of both unions and HR professionals.

The management of diversity is an emerging field of increasing importance. It has a
base in ethics and it can be understood through alternative ethical perspectives. In
addition, there are now strong arguments in business logic for encouraging diversity in

the workforce in order to match diversity in globalised markets, and to make the most of the available labour market.

While the health, safety and welfare function has been the 'Cinderella' of HRM it is clear that great care and attention should be paid to this field. There are both ethical and business-related arguments for this. On the ethical front it is important that people are properly treated in the workplace and that they are protected from dangers and excessive risks. On the business-related side, prevention is likely to be more cost effective than cure when it comes to accidents, injuries and illnesses that can occur as a result of unsafe processes and products. In addition, the workforce is unlikely to believe that the organisation is committed to them if it does not take care of their health and safety.

This chapter has covered a broad span of topics. It is important to bear in mind the link between the different areas. Although some models of HRM have emphasised individualism in employee relations this is not necessarily the HRM prescription. Rather the focus should be on finding the appropriate approach to communications, participation and general employee relations that enhances the connections and commitment between employees and the organisation.

Review and reflection questions

1. What is the distinction between industrial relations and employee relations?

2. What are the steps that can aid effective communication?

3. What are the relative advantages of face-to-face communications (such as team briefings) and remote communications (such as intranets)?

4. How can employee involvement be achieved?

5. What are the alternative roles of trade unions in modern organisations?

6. How would you typify the trends of trade unionism internationally?

7. How should HRM practitioners approach conflict in the workplace?

8. What can HRM do to 'manage' diversity?

9. How can HRM practices be used to minimise bulling in the workplace?

Activities

If you are in work:

1. To what extent is there employee participation in your organisation?

2. What participation techniques are used?

3. What, if any, changes in the amount and processes of participation are desirable?

If you are in full-time study:

1. Do you think that trade unions are still relevant in modern organisations?

2. To what extent does their relevance vary internationally?

Further reading and research

Within employee relations involvement and participation are issues that are always relevant. The following journal's special issue focuses on these issues:

Gollan, P.J., Poutsma, E. and Veersma, U. (2006) (guest eds) Special issue: Organizational participation, *Industrial Relations*, 45(4).

Diversity has been identified as a major challenge and opportunity for HRM and the following book provides insight into this subject:

Daniels, K. and MacDonald, L. (2005) *Equality, Diversity and Discrimination*, London: CIPD.

The following article explores the complementary area of work–life balance:

Fleetwood, S. (2007) (guest ed.) Special Issue: Work–Life Balance, *International Journal of Human Resource Management*, 18(3).

Over the past few years there has been an increasing emphasis on ethics and the following references will be helpful in further researching this topic:

Uhl-Bien, M. (2007) (ed.) Special Issue: Ethics and organizations, *Organizational Dynamics*, 36(2).

Fulmer, R.M. (2004) 'The challenge of ethical leadership', *Organizational Dynamics*, 33, 307–317.

McWilliams A., Siegel, D.S. and Wright, P.M. (2006) (guest eds) Special Issue: Corporate Social Responsibility: Strategic implications, *Journal of Management Studies*, 43(1).

We have also raised issues of leadership in this chapter, and references that could be used to follow up on this topic are:

Goffee, R. and Jones, G. (2007) 'Leading clever people. How do you manage people who don't want to be led and may be smarter than you?', *Harvard Business Review*, March, 72–79.

Tourish, D. and Pinnington, A. (2002) 'Transformational leadership, corporate cultism, and the spirituality paradigm: an unholy trinity in the workplace', *Human Relations*, 55, 147–172.

The TUC website (www.tuc.org.uk) provides a great deal of information on trade unions and related issues. These include member unions, worker rights, health and safety, international trade unions and work–life balance.

ACAS (www.acas.org.uk) also provide a wealth of information covering areas such as rights at work, briefings on employment law, equality and diversity and the model workplace.

References

Abrams, F. and Astill, J. (2001) 'Story of the blues', *The Guardian* (G2), 29 May, 2–4.

Bass, B.M. (1990) 'From transactional to transformational leadership', *Organizational Dynamics*, 18, 19–31.

Beardwell, I., Holden, L. and Claydon, T. (2004) *Human resource management: a contemporary approach*, Harlow, Essex: Pearson Education.

Beech, N. and Cairns, G. (2001) 'Coping with change: the contribution of postdichotomous ontologies', *Human Relations*, 54, 1303–1324.

Beer, M., Spector, B., Lawrence, P., Mills, Q. and Walton, R. (1984) *Managing Human Assets*, New York: Free Press.

Benwell, D. (2001) 'Range finders', *People Management*, 36, 36–37.

Berridge, J. and Cooper, C.L. (1993) 'Stress and coping in US organizations: the role of the Employee Assistance Programme', *Work and Stress*, 7, 89–102.

Bewley, H. (2006) 'Voice Recognition', *People Management*, 12, 40–43.

Blyton, P. and Turnbull, P. (2004) *The Dynamics of Employee Relations*, London: Macmillan.

Bright, D. (1993) 'Industrial relations, employment relations and strategic human resource management', in Harrison, R. (ed.), *Human Resource Management Issues and Strategies*, Wokingham: Addison Wesley.

Cartwright, S. and Cooper, C.L. (2007) 'Hazards to health: The problems of workplace bullying', *The Psychologist*, May, 284–287.

CIPD (2007a) *Managing Conflict and Work – survey report*, London: CIPD, www.cipd.co.uk.

CIPD (2007b) *Diversity in Business*, London: CIPD, www.cipd.co.uk.

Dessler, G. (2005) *Human Resource Management*, New Jersey: Pearson.

Dowling, P.J. and Welch, D.E. (2004) *International Human Resource Management*, London: Thomson Learning.

Dundon, T. and Wilkinson, A. (2006) 'Employee Participation', in Redman, T. and Wilkinson, A. (eds), *Contemporary Human Resource Management*, Harlow: FT/Prentice Hall.

Dundon, T., Grugulis, I. and Wilkinson, A. (2006) 'Employee Voice at Compucom', in Redman, T. and Wilkinson, A. (eds), *Contemporary Human Resource Management*, Harlow, Essex: FT/Prentice Hall.

Eccles, R.G., Hertz, R.H., Keegan, E.M. and Philips, D.M.H. (2001) *The Value Reporting Revolution*, New York: John Wiley.

Edwards, P. (1994) 'Discipline and the creation of order', in Sisson, K. (ed.), *Personnel Management*, Oxford: Blackwell.

Emmott, M. (2007) 'Unions and Business Performance', *Impact: Quarterly update on CIPD policy and research*, London: CIPD.

European Industrial Relations Observatory (2007) www.eurofound.europa.eu

Financial Times (2006) 'Bank bullying claim launched', 27 April, 4.

Financial Times (2007) 'Ethical path for Allchurches', in Companies and Markets Section, 7 August, 23.

Fox, A. (1974) *Beyond Contract, Power and Trust Relations*, London: Faber.

Geary, J.F. (1994) 'Task participation: employees' participation enabled or constrained?', in Sisson, K. (ed.), *Personnel Management*, Oxford: Blackwell.

Glendon, A.I., Clarke, S.G. and McKenna, E.F. (2006) *Human Safety and Risk Management*, Florida, USA: CRC Press (Taylor and Francis).

Gollan, P.J. (2006) 'Consultation and Non-Union Employee Representation', *Industrial Relations Journal*, 37, 428–437.

Granger, H. (2006) *Employment Market Analysis and Research*, National Statistics, www.dti.gov.ik.

Guest, D. and Hoque, K. (1994) 'The good, the bad and the ugly: employment relations in new non-union workplaces', *Human Resource Management Journal*, 5, 1–14.

Hall, L. (1995) 'More and more companies are using workplace counselling' (Health and Safety Executive sponsored Guide), *Financial Times*, November, 8–11.

Hardy, C. and Leiba-O'Sullivan, S. (1998) 'The power behind empowerment: implications for research and practice', *Human Relations*, 51, 451–483.

Hartley, R.F. (1993) *Business Ethics: Violations of the public trust*, New York: John Wiley.

Hendry, C. (1995) *Human Resource Management: A strategic approach to employment*, London: Butterworth-Heinemann.

Holden, L. (2001) 'Employee involvement and empowerment', in Beardwell, I. and Holden, I. (eds), *Human Resource Management: A contemporary approach*, Harlow: Pearson Education.

Hollinshead, G. and Leat, M. (1995) *Human Resource Management: An international and comparative perspective*, London: Pitman.

Legge, K. (1998) 'The Morality of HRM', in Mabey, C., Salaman, G. and Storey, J. (eds), *Strategic Human Resource Management: A reader*, London: Sage/The Open University.

Leopold, J. (2005) 'Employee Participation, Involvement and Communications', in Leopold, J., Harris, L. and Watson, T. (eds), *The Strategic Management of Human Resources*. Harlow: FT/Prentice Hall.

McAvoy, B.R. and Murtagh, J. (2003) 'Workplace bullying. The silent epidemic', *British Medical Journal*, 326, 776–777.

McKenna, E. (2006) *Business Psychology and Organizational Behaviour*, Hove: Psychology Press.

Marchington, M. (1987) 'Employee participation', in Towers, B. (ed.), *A Handbook of Industrial Relations Practice*, London: Kogan Page.

Marchington, M., Parker, P. and Prestwich, A. (1989) 'Problems with team briefings in practice', *Employee Relations*, 11, 21–30.

Marchington, M., Goodman, J., Wilkinson, A. and Ackers, P. (1992) *New Developments in Employee Involvement*, Employment Department Research Series No. 2, Manchester: Manchester School of Management.

Marsh, A. and Cox, B. (1992) *The Trade Union Movement in the UK 1992*, Oxford: Malthouse.

Millward, N., Stevens, M., Smart, D. and Hawes, W.R. (1992) *Workplace Industrial Relations in Transition*, Aldershot: Dartmouth Press.

Monks, J. (1994) 'The union response to HRM: fraud or opportunity?', *Personnel Management*, September, 42–47.

Montagnon, P. (1998) 'Public turning against the use of bribery', *Financial Times*, 14 October, 7.

Motzko, V. and Perkins, S.J. (2007) *All Talk but no Voice*, London: CIPD, www.cipd.co.uk.

OECD (2007) OECD Social Indicators, CO5, Strikes, http://caliban.sourceoecd.org

Pocock, P. (1989) 'Is business ethics a contradiction in terms?', *Personnel Management*, July/August, 244–247.

Poole, M. (1986) *Industrial Relations: Origins and patterns of national diversity*, London: Routledge & Kegan Paul.

Price, A. (2004) *Human Resource Management in a Business Context*, London: Thomson Learning.

Purcell, J. (1994) 'Human resource management: implications for teaching, research, and practice in industrial relations', in Niland, J., Verevis, C. and Lansbury, R. (eds), *The Future of Industrial Relations*, London: Sage.

Purcell, J. and Sisson, K. (1983) 'Strategies and practices in the management of industrial relations', in Bain, G.S. (ed.), *Industrial Relations in Britain*, Oxford: Blackwell.

Ramsay, H. (1996) 'Involvement, empowerment and commitment', in Towers, B. (ed.), *The Handbook of Human Resource Management*, Oxford: Blackwell.

Roche, W.K. (2000) 'The end of new industrial relations', *European Journal of Industrial Relations*, 6, 261–282.

Schneider, R. (2001) 'Variety performance', *People Management*, 26, 26–28.

Skypala, P. (2007) 'Socially responsible investment "better for the long term good"', FT Weekly Review of the Fund Management Industry, *Financial Times*, 6 August, 4.

Sparrow, P. and Hiltrop, J.M. (1994) *European Human Resource Management in Transition*, Hemel Hempstead: Prentice Hall.

Stace, D. and Dunphy, D. (2001) *Beyond the boundaries. Leading and creating the successful enterprise*, Sydney: McGraw-Hill.

Tailby, S., Richardson, M., Upchurch, M., Danford, A. and Stewart, P. (2007) 'Partnership with and without trade unions in the UK financial services: filling or fueling the representation gap?', *Industrial Relations Journal*, 38, 210–228.

Thatcher, M. (1998) 'Brewer and union agree national deal', *People Management*, 4, 13.

Trust News (2001) Chelsea and Westminster Healthcare NHS Trust internal newsletter, June.

Useem, M. (2000) 'How to groom leaders of the future', *Mastering Management Series*, *Financial Times*, Part 8, 20 November, 8–10.

Walsh, D. and Bott, D. (2005) 'Parting Company: the strategic responsibility of exit management', in Leopold, J., Harris, L. and Watson, T. (eds), *The Strategic Management of Human Resources*, Harlow: FT/Prentice Hall.

Welch, M. and Jackson, P.R. (2007) 'Rethinking internal communication: A stakeholder approach', *Corporate Communications: An International Journal*, 12, 177–198.

Wood, S. (1996) 'High commitment management and unionisation in the UK', *International Journal of Human Resource Management*, 7, 41–58.

Wolfe, R. (1995) 'Healthy workers, healthy office', *Financial Times*, 27 January, 13.

Workplace Employment Relations Survey (WERS) (2004) www.data-archive.ac.uk; www.wers2004.info.

Chapter 12

HRM: REVIEW, CRITIQUE AND DEVELOPMENTS

Introduction

HRM is a subject derived from a number of academic traditions, some more critical than others, and this has been instrumental in the shaping of the subject into an entity that can be seen as incorporating divergent views and even contradictions. Similarly, the practice of HRM has developed in different organisational, economic and cultural settings in such a way that it has created a range of practices that provide choice for managers and that need to be actively managed if they are to complement each other. Given the amount of criticism and debate HRM has generated it is important to be aware of some of the main trends and theories, and to understand how such critical engagement has assisted the development of both theory and practice.

Having read this chapter, you should:

- be aware of the theoretical criticisms of HRM;

- be aware of the research on the practice of HRM;

- know about the research on the implementation of HRM;

- be aware of the issues in the future development of HRM.

Traditions in HRM

Before examining the various criticisms of theory and practice, it would be wise to reflect for a moment on the different traditions in HRM. According to Bach and Sisson (2000), who use the term 'personnel management' most of the time, HRM has originated from a cross-breed of three perspectives, as follows:

1. *Prescriptive approach*: This is primarily concerned with providing managers with a bundle of techniques, which have been considered at length earlier in this book. The prescriptive approach has received heavy endorsement in the United Kingdom from a professional body – the Chartered Institute of Personnel and Development (CIPD) – with a strong vocational orientation, and it is considered the most popular approach. HRM offered personnel management a lifeline when it suggested that personnel management should react to the dictates of corporate strategy. In doing so it solved a dilemma for the CIPD by

offering the possibility of increased economic efficiency for the organisation coupled with an improved quality of working life for the employees. One could argue that the linking of the competitive advantage of the company to the implementation of HRM policies had some effect in silencing the critics of traditional personnel management.

2. *Labour process*: This sets out to identify the controlling aspect of personnel management and is critical of the prescriptive approach. Managers are seen as agents of those providing capital and they seek to maximise profits by not being averse to getting as much as they can from the workforce and systematically reducing labour costs; though it is acknowledged that managers in their role of employees are themselves subjected to an increased range of controls and new management practices. Personnel managers are viewed similarly, and are accused of using their battery of techniques to exploit the workforce (Braverman, 1974). The ideas of the contributors to the labour process debate could be considered a useful counterbalance to the strictures of the prescriptive school, and they certainly encouraged the emergence of more critical accounts of personnel management – see, for example, Legge, 1995a and Mabey *et al.*, 1998.

3. *Industrial relations approach*: This perspective, discussed in the previous chapter, views personnel management as a system geared to the regulation of employment practices where personnel techniques are mobilised to make a contribution to the continual negotiation of order within organisations.

While the above traditions evolved they drew on the contributions of the social and behavioural sciences and strategic management. There are inputs to the theoretical basis of HRM from academic disciplines or subject areas such as sociology, psychology, labour economics, marketing and strategy. As a result in HRM there is no one accepted body of theory. This should not be surprising, because HRM theory is seeking to explain the complex and multifarious behaviour of people at work. It is unlikely that any single theory or body of theories that share a single perspective would be fit for such a purpose. However, HRM goes beyond seeking to explain behaviour. It is also concerned with developing practical actions that will benefit employers, employees and more general stakeholders. Hence, the complexity of the task is further multiplied.

Review and critique of HRM

We have now reached the stage where it would be productive to examine briefly the criticisms levelled at HRM and to take note of developments likely to shape its future. HRM has attracted a considerable amount of critical comment and analysis. There has been criticism of both theory and practice.

CRITICISM OF THEORY

HRM takes on different manifestations in different situations, and some of the aspects of it can contradict each other (Legge, 1989). For example, elements of hard HRM such as performance appraisal linked to performance-related pay do not fit easily with the elements of soft HRM such as developmental and facilitating managerial behaviour. It is not just a matter of the different elements not fitting together in practice; it is that they are driven by different theoretical approaches. The set of assumptions about how people are motivated and managed under hard HRM is opposed to the set of assumptions governing motivation and management embedded in soft HRM. Such contradictions may arise in established subject areas, but they become the subject of intense debate. HRM seems to tolerate their presence, and some would argue that this points to a lack of rigour in the subject. On reflection, the above distinction between soft and hard HRM is not as fine as one has been led to believe. According to Morgan (2000), Storey's hard versus soft models of HRM dissolve into ambiguity when applied to Hewlett-Packard or Marks & Spencer, as both seemed to display qualities of both hard and soft at various stages of their development.

Keenoy (1999) argues that one way of understanding these apparent ambiguities and contradictions is to accept that HRM is a hologram, which when surveyed from different perspectives will be perceived as having divergent or even contradictory characteristics. As Martin (1992) has pointed out, while managers may believe that they have created an integrated culture in which there is shared vision it is possible that other stakeholders in the organisation view things differently. It is not uncommon to find different views of what the organisation is doing, and whether it is operating well or badly, subject to variation at different levels in the hierarchy and amongst different professional groups (Harris and Ogbonna, 1997; Watson, 2002). Similarly, critical analysts have expressed a number of divergent views of HRM, for example seeing it as a disguised way of exploiting workers, or as a way of apparently empowering employees while actually intensifying surveillance of their work. When observing from a Taylorist viewpoint one would be likely to see (soft) HRM as being a high cost/low performance option. Conversely, when looking at (hard) HRM from a labour process perspective, a view of organisational flexibility as exploitation through power inequity is likely to be arrived at. Such contradictions do not imply that HRM is meaningless. The implication is that it is not a singular object that is subject to one dominant theory, and often what is perceived says as much about the perspective from which the behaviour is being perceived as it does about the behaviour itself.

It has been suggested that HRM is merely a form of rhetoric that does not have a substantial theory behind it (Keenoy and Anthony, 1992). New phrases such as performance-related pay, the enterprise culture and so on do not represent new ideas about practice. It is said that the game plan is not the introduction of rigorously tested concepts but a ploy to solidify management control in organisations. This is also a theme considered by Legge (1995b). She is severely critical of HRM and views it as empty rhetoric serving to conceal the fact that the labour input to the organisation is increasingly treated as a commodity. She contends that HRM is simply promoting a hyped-up version of personnel management, and considers the response of management to the so-called enterprise culture as a ploy designed to justify changes to the employer–employee relationship under the umbrella of progressive HRM. This means that management can adopt a harsh regime in particular situations while pretending that they are subscribing to an inspired vision of the management of people. In addition to the theoretical traditions described by Bach and Sisson (2000) above, recent developments in postmodern theory have had a strong impact on critical theoretical thinking about HRM. Postmodernism has been referred to by some (e.g. Clegg, 1990) as a period in time that is characterised by fast, discontinuous change, and by a breakdown in traditional organisational structures in favour of flexible forms of organisation. The more radical (epistemological) form of postmodernism, exemplified by writers such as Lyotard (1984), maintains that the basis for our knowledge and understanding of the world of organisations has been fundamentally changed. In this sense, postmodernism is contrasted with modernism and 'the enlightenment project' (Alvesson and Deetz, 1999), which have been associated with the philosopher Kant. A belief fundamental to modernism is that knowledge is cumulative, and that it develops through scientific study in which ever-improved theories and getting hold of the facts leads us towards a more perfect knowledge of the truth. So, for example, our current understanding of motivation would be seen as more advanced and closer to the truth than those understandings that were prevalent a century ago.

Postmodernism rejects this general view of truth and knowledge in a number of ways. First, knowledge is not regarded as objective and progressive towards the truth. Rather, knowledge is strongly linked to power (Foucault, 1980) in that what counts as knowledge is determined by how it serves existing power structures. So, for example, the classification of a worker as either motivated or demotivated is a way of codifying knowledge of the individual which can subsequently be used in such a way that it influences reality for that person; for example, in the likelihood (or otherwise) of the future promotion of that individual. Thus a manager's perception of a worker and the worker's efforts to present certain facets of their behaviour (and hide others) to the manager are related to the power over distribution of rewards.

Secondly, doubt is raised over the existence of objective reality. Modernism seeks to uncover reality as it truly is. Postmodernism argues that we create 'reality', and that much of this creation is to do with image, perception and bias. People do not start their search for the truth with completely open minds, rather they gather representations of reality and fit them into dominant ways of seeing the world (Baudrillard, 1983). For example, from a modernist perspective a manager may have a perception of employees as being basically lazy (Theory X) and as a result will perceive their direct workers as not putting in as much effort as they could. Under a Theory X conception the remedy to this problem is greater control. In such a modernist analysis there is a dominant perspective and the facts of the case are linked through logical sequences (e.g. people in general are lazy, these people in particular are lazy, and the solution is to prevent them being their natural selves).

From a postmodern perspective the issues of motivation would be seen as more complicated and as specific to the context and meanings of the local situation. Workers may be regarded as lazy by this manager, but the workers may regard themselves as limited in the actions they can take by the fear they have of reprimand from their boss. Depending on the perspective adopted the workers may be thought of as lazy, hard working, or anything in between, and what you perceive may say as much about your presumptions as the actual activities of the workers. For critical and postmodern thinkers there is no single objective reality – rather there are multiple 'realities' created by the people in a particular setting and hence there is no single truth (or falsehood) and knowledge is regarded as relative. In a postmodern analysis there is no acceptance that there is a set of 'facts of the case' (e.g. it cannot be clearly determined that the people either are or are not lazy, in a sense they may be both simultaneously depending on the social construction of perceptions) and there is no expectation of uncovering single line logical sequences (e.g. by a manager the workers may be identified as lazy, the correct management techniques may be applied, but the workers may react in unpredicted ways) – rather one would expect multiple lines of reasoning (or rationalising) that may be contradictory.

In a conversation with a prominent organisation theorist (Professor John Child) in the United Kingdom in August 2001, reported in Box 12.1, it was suggested by him that there are two types of postmodernism.

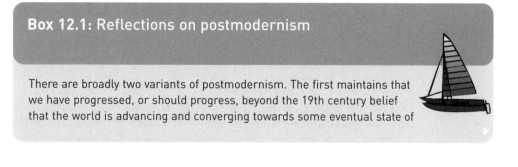

Box 12.1: Reflections on postmodernism

There are broadly two variants of postmodernism. The first maintains that we have progressed, or should progress, beyond the 19th century belief that the world is advancing and converging towards some eventual state of modern civilisation, underpinned by a bureaucracy in the Weberian mould that applies the same rules fairly and honestly to all and guarantees an acceptable order in society. While recognising that bureaucracy and the standardisation it represented had some virtues, adherents of this postmodern perspective argue that the modern approach fails to accommodate the huge variety of local cultural and material needs in society and the sheer speed at which these are evolving.

The second variant of postmodernism goes much further in the direction of seeking to deconstruct the institutions and organisations (and even the language associated with them) that we have taken more or less for granted in the recent past. It regards these as justifying and maintaining an essentially exploitative social order through the ways in which organisations are constituted and the ideology of corporate capitalism that lulls us into taking them for granted. This variant of postmodernism maintains that what each individual says and does is equally valid, and as such it is fundamentally opposed to any form of organisation except for the purely spontaneous and voluntary.

I find the first variant of postmodernism acceptable and constructive in helping us understand so-called new and evolving forms of organisation, as well as the wider cultural and other shifts in society they reflect. It is broadly the approach that Stewart Clegg adopts in his 1990 book on postmodern organisation. I don't find the second variant acceptable, either academically or in terms of the state of society to which it would lead us, for I believe it is likely to lead us to a kind of Hobbesian world in which everyone would be at war with everyone else. I view the first variant as espousing variety and creativity, and arguing for freedom, whereas I fear that the second espouses anarchy and threatens an eventual loss of freedom, which is ironic in view of its aspirations.

Question

Do you agree with John Child's view that the second variant – a radical deconstruction of the meaning of economic institutions – is likely to lead to a 'war of all against all' in Hobbesian terms?

These theoretical arguments raise certain questions for HRM and the study of organisations. First, they raise problems over seeking to gain objective knowledge of employees and using such knowledge as the basis for decision making. So, for example, in selection decision making, there would be scepticism about managers' ability to genuinely understand the candidates and choose the one who best fits the person specification. Secondly, people are not conceived as essentially rational beings and this has implications for, amongst other areas, performance management. An assumption which underlies typical performance management is that goals can be set for employees which they will understand and pursue in order to gain the rewards that follow from successful completion of their targets. However, from a postmodern perspective it may be expected that employees will not only pursue other goals, they will conceive their official goals in ways which diverge from the meaning intended by management, and will also indulge in behaviour that does not lead to any distinct goals, and from a Weberian perspective (Weber, 1962) would be irrational. Thirdly, one would expect fragmentation of organisational culture (Martin, 1992). Much of the rhetoric of HRM espouses an integrated culture in which there are shared meanings. A labour process view would expect opposition within the culture between managers and workers. A fragmentary view, however, maintains that different groups and individuals may not only disagree with each other on particular points, they may conceive what the point is differently, or not even be aware that they disagree. In a sense, groups will 'talk past each other' rather than disagreeing. This has an impact on many aspects of HRM. For example, in developing a strategy or managing change, the rhetoric of HRM often calls for clear goals and vision. For postmodernists, no matter how clear the manager is in setting a vision, there is always the possibility for 'reading' the situation differently, and the likelihood of really achieving a shared understanding is remote. This has an impact for the potential of achieving congruence and mutuality – two of the most fundamental concepts in models of HRM.

In an assessment of HRM Storey (2001a) acknowledges that HRM is no panacea for all corporate ills. However, he maintains that it has characteristics worthy of note, which should be considered in our quest for effective ways to manage organisations. He concludes that the HRM domain is lively and vibrant, where ideas are hotly contested. There are many new initiatives, and those who scrutinise the development of HRM are struggling to make sense of the changes and their significance. In a similar vein Bach and Sisson (2000) maintain that even though HRM may not have realised the optimistic expectations in store for it, nevertheless it is probably in a better state than it was previously, with the three traditions considered above – the prescriptive, the labour process, and the industrial relations approaches – continuing to make valuable contributions to our understanding of the field. We would maintain that the postmodern critique should be added to the stated traditions.

REVIEW AND CRITICISM OF PRACTICE

Early research studies into the practice of HRM found it wanting in a number of respects. For example, Storey and Sisson (1993) found that, apart from a few cases, the uptake of HRM was partial and fragmented. In some studies it was argued that there was little or no new practice to accompany the rhetoric that grew up in the mid-1980s to 1990s (Keenoy, 1990). It was argued that while there had been uptake of certain hard HRM practices (such as performance-related pay), soft HRM approaches to employee development were yet to be commonplace (Keep, 1990). In a similar vein, the results of the Workplace Employee Relations Surveys in the 1990s revealed that although there had been considerable 'employment relations' restructuring in the United Kingdom few organisations have redesigned these practices in line with the commitment models of HRM. Another difficulty is that, while HRM espouses valuing employees, there are aspects of it that have the effect of devaluing employees. With regard to the adoption of flexibility, the 'peripheral' workforce suffers instability and uncertain conditions of employment (Emmott and Hutchinson, 1998; Pollert, 1988). The management of culture can be seen as an attempt to manipulate the attitudes and activities of employees (du Gay, 1997; Willmott, 1993). Similarly, the adoption of customer-centred quality approaches can be seen as another managerial strategy to control the behaviour of the workforce through imposing new constraints and requirements (du Gay and Salaman, 1992). A snapshot of problems in practice brought about by the march of globalisation and technological change appears in Box 12.2 (Maitland, 2001).

Reflecting on Rajan and Chapple's (2001) criticism, it is fair to say that the CIPD's perspective on what it means to be a HR professional has developed since the context of the late 1990s and early 2000s. The concept and practice of being a business partner has been debated and is evolving in a positive way (Arkin, 2007). Of course, such a complex role will not be reducible to a simple 'one best way' and so those who seek simple answers to people issues will be disappointed, but the syllabus for trainee HR professionals now contains fundamental business

Box 12.2: Difficulties in implementing HRM

In a report prepared by Rajan and Chapple (2001), based on the views of 247 financial and business services companies mainly in the City of London, it is stated that change is being undermined by a lack of flexibility and dynamism amongst the very people who are asked to implement it, namely HR professionals and line managers. Both have experienced modifications to their roles in recent years, whereby managers are asked to handle people issues (e.g. recruitment and training) and HR professionals get involved in issues connected with corporate strategy. The HR function was also affected by outsourcing and by the application of software/intranets to routine activities.

The change in roles has been met with resistance. Some HR professionals feel that the changes have been detrimental to their professionalism. Many line managers, who are overloaded, are reluctant to take on HR functions. One glaring deficiency is that neither line managers nor HR professionals have been properly trained for their new roles and may not be the right people for the job. An HR director at a retail bank is quoted as saying that: 'HR people will have to be recruited from outside – we need people who have a blend of technical and business skills. Our HR people have been very old-fashioned.' Although senior HR executives are expected to work in partnership with the heads of business units on designing and implementing strategy, the report says that many HR executives do not have the necessary broader business qualifications or experience. Meanwhile line managers have little experience of HR and their priorities are different.

The authors of the report say that:

'more thought needs to be given to developing the appropriate skills of HR professionals and line managers. The majority of senior HR professionals – who work in partnership with line managers – and the line managers themselves, have rarely had any training in leadership skills or business awareness. Their understanding of the big picture is limited as is their ability to inspire trust and motivation.'

It is said that the emphasis placed on professional specialisation by the CIPD is not congruent with the new roles given to HR professionals. The latter are expected to become much more generalist and business oriented. An important conclusion is that both HR professionals and line managers require broad experience built through lateral moves in their early careers. Challenging assignments are likely to become the most significant form of training for HR professionals over the next few years, while line managers are expected to be exposed to a greater extent than before to coaching and learning by doing.

Source: based on Rajan and Chapple, 2001

Question

The CIPD now pays particular attention to business skills. Do you think it is right that HR managers should have such broad-based skills?

knowledge from across a broad range. The CIPD also offers training programmes on how to be a business partner and examples of good practice are growing. (Business partners were mentioned in Chapter 2 and will be discussed in the section below on developments in HRM.)

In addition to the problems discussed in Box 12.2, Pfeffer and Veiga (1999) have argued that it is difficult for organisations to implement HRM best practice for a number of reasons:

■ Managers may be enslaved by short-term pressures that divert them from being able to invest time in managing their people actively.

■ Macho norms about what constitutes good management (i.e. a control-oriented approach) are still pervasive in some organisations.

■ There may be a lack of trust between managers and workers, and hence a lack of delegation.

■ Organisations may fail to persist with the HRM strategies over a sufficient period of time to reap the full benefits.

In Case example 12.1, an SME leader rejects much of the thinking of HRM which he appears to associate with bureaucracy. However, he does adopt informal practices for motivating staff.

CASE EXAMPLE 12.1

MARRIS INTERIORS – MANAGING PEOPLE IN A SME

Michael Howard is Chairman of Marris Interiors, a successful office and refurbishment business in London, whose business has been helped by a boom in mergers and acquisitions that has led many companies to seek new premises or expand capacity in their existing space. He believes most HR practices are a waste of time. He has banned annual staff appraisals, believes management training is pointless, and hates team-building exercises. However, he seems to be concerned with efforts to motivate employees and cultivate their commitment to the organisation. He likes giving benefits in an informal way. The following are examples.

■ A senior female designer is allowed to work half days, so that she can spend more time with her young son.
■ An employee who lost three relatives in six months received a company allowance of £1,000 a month, which goes to his sister who lost her husband and is struggling to raise her two children.
■ Maverick incentive schemes were introduced, such as the free use of a company Porsche for the employee of the month, and flying the entire staff to Las Vegas for a Christmas office party.

Mr Howard and the two other shareholders changed the structure of the company, which employs 130 people, from that of a limited company to a partnership. The objective was to provide a direct reward structure for the top team without having to give equity to executives who might then leave the business. In the revised structure the partners receive a share of the profits and the share of capital has to be sold on exit from the company. It is said that the change in the legal structure of the company has encouraged more staff to seek senior positions, and this has motivational significance.

Mr Howard seems to dislike internal reports; they are banned because he finds them boring. His motto is if you want to know something, just ask. Given the informality, decisions are said to be made more quickly. Flexibility in response to business opportunities is endorsed. There is a heavy commitment to teamwork and a belief that teams control their own destiny, and practise self-management. Dressing down in the office is acceptable. The CEO hopes to expand the business organically and particular attention is given to the cost structure of the company, along with smarter use of IT systems.

Source: based on Moules, 2007

Question

What are the strengths and weaknesses of the approach to managing people at Marris Interiors?

In the case of Marris Interiors, HRM theory would approve of the link between activities and reward and the process of encouraging commitment to the organisational goals. However, HRM theory would not support removing appraisals and management training. In Chapters 8 and 10 we have considered these matters. Cases of good practice show that considerable benefit can be gained from appraisal and training where they are conducted effectively and reinforced by everyday practice. However, taken in isolation they are unlikely to be a positive experience.

In Chapters 1 and 2 we discussed the research evidence on the effectiveness of effective HRM implementation. There has long been evidence that the implementation of high-commitment work practices has shown positive results (Wood and Albanese, 1995; Wood and de Menezes, 1998), and case studies of top-performing UK companies (Tyson, 1995, 1997) has shown that these companies had a propensity to adopt HRM. Similarly, in broader-based studies that focused on performance, Huselid *et al.* (1997) in the United States and Patterson *et al.* (1997) in the United Kingdom have found telling evidence that soft HRM practices are strongly associated with heightened performance of the firm. Following this lead, there has been a considerable volume of research from around the world that has shown a correlation between HRM and business performance (Becker and Huselid, 2000). Thus, while it would still be reasonable to suppose that not all organisations that use the HRM rhetoric are carrying out the practice – and worse, that some are using the rhetoric as a cover for exploitative forms of management – it appears that there is a growing body of companies, particularly among the high-achieving firms, who are developing integrated and effective HRM strategies and practices. However, although the research evidence is as clear as it can be, communication of the findings to people outside the field is not easy, particularly where those people want simple answers, where they have had previous negative experiences of HR that lead them to be cynical, or where they are simply too busy to take the time to understand the debates and evidence. In Case example 12.2 the organisation's leader has sought to escape a bureaucratic approach and focus on organisational success through an ethical approach to managing people.

The Eden Project is an interesting example of good people-management practice. Not everything is labelled as HRM, but nonetheless there is a clear vision, ethical treatment of people and a consistently developmental approach to the management of people.

THE EDEN PROJECT

Tim Smit is co-founder and CEO of the Eden Project. The Eden Project is based in Cornwall in southern England and is a highly successful ecological regeneration project that is also a highly successful business. From a position in 1999 when the site of the Eden Project – a 60 metre deep ex-china clay pit – was a 'sterile wasteland', over £120 million of funding (from sources such as the Lottery Fund, the Regional Development Agency and European funding) has been raised and a transformation has taken place. It is now the site of three 'biomes' or climatic zones (The Eden Project, 2007). The first two are housed in giant conservatories (the largest in the world) and the third is outdoors. These include a humid tropical zone and a temperate zone in addition to the natural conditions of Cornwall.

The £121 million cost of building the project have reaped £700 million of economic benefit for the local area in the first five years following its opening in 2001. The Eden Project is regarded as a top international visitor attraction and was rated in the top five in the UK by the Consumers Association in 2004. It has attracted over eight million visitors and employs around 600 staff. This commercial success is mirrored by horticultural and ecological successes. For example, it is home to over 100,000 plants and 5,000 species. It has also been responsible for a 'soil creation' project in which a range of soils for different needs have been produced from recycled waste. The Eden Project is not only about the commerciality of tourism and the sustainability goals of horticulture, it is also about education and enabling people to think differently. In the region of 250 school children visit Eden every day, both from the United Kingdom and from overseas.

In 2006, the Eden Project was awarded the Quality in Construction Award by the construction industry. In accepting the award, Smit made a speech that chimed with the ethos of HRM:

'I wish everybody could have the opportunity just once in their lives of working with a large team, all of whom enjoy each other's company and admire each other's talent, and from this they build something that surpasses even their own imaginings.'

The Eden Project's staff are drawn from a range of fields including archaeology, botany, engineering and horticulture. The particular mix has not been undertaken before and Smit's approach has been to foster leadership. He seeks to avoid excessive bureaucracy and is sceptical about business jargon. But nonetheless his practice resonates with much that HRM as a subject does have jargon for! A lot of the work is arranged in project teams. The advantage of this, according to Smit, is that it allows a greater number of people to take on leadership responsibilities and this allows the natural leaders to rise to the surface (Edwards, 2005). Smit is opposed to 'creeping departmentalism' and encourages staff to challenge themselves by working in areas that are new for them. He stresses the importance of trusting people to run with their ideas. He is also opposed to the traditional vision statements. His argument is that what is needed is a shared attitude, but not adherence to a set of regulations that limit creativity. His basic philosophy is 'to dare to treat people as you would yourself like to be treated' (quoted in Edwards, 2005).

Smit is also a supporter of diversity: 'only idiots employ only the young'. His view is that healthy 'families' are a mix of people, which encourage a rounded understanding of people's needs and abilities.

Question

What lessons might be taken from this example and applied in other organisations?

The most important thing is how people are managed and how this is linked to organisational success. Sometimes good practice is labelled 'HRM' and overtly draws on research, sometimes not. Perhaps the quicker route is to be aware of good practice and adapt it to the situation, rather than having to (re)invent new ways of managing people. However, there is always an important aspect of managerial judgement in moulding and adapting theories and practices from other organisations to one's own situation.

Developments in HRM

HRM arose in a set of environmental conditions that included increases in competition, changes in technology and a series of economic recessions. HRM placed an emphasis on flexibility, high standards of performance and the development of employees so that the organisation can survive and flourish. As environmental conditions continue to impact on the organisation we can expect to see HRM developing. Speaking of development, particularly in the context of the study of strategic HRM, Mabey *et al.* (1998) distinguish between the first and second waves.

FIRST WAVE

The first wave was concerned with a number of central questions. First, did the emergence of HRM represent a substantive change, or was it merely a change in language (Keenoy, 1990)? Amongst the critics of HRM there was a perception that HRM did not bring with it changes in organisational practice, and that the rhetoric of HRM on such issues as employee involvement and development was, in reality, disguising the intention to cut costs and seek productivity increases from the workforce. Secondly, there was a question of to what extent HRM was of strategic importance (Sisson, 1990). HRM claimed to be central to the formulation of organisational strategy, but critics argued that while many directors of companies would claim that they were concerned for people, in reality the key strategic issues were those of markets, products and competition, and the workforce was only a matter of secondary interest. Thirdly, HRM claimed to be a cohesive set of policies, which were integrated (Hendry and Pettigrew, 1986). So, for example, the future direction of the organisation would be directly linked to recruitment and training policies and the approach to job design. Critics of personnel management had argued that it was a disparate collection of policies, which could even work against each other on occasions. Some believed that HRM, despite its claims, was little different to personnel management in this regard.

SECOND WAVE

However, subsequent research (e.g. Wood, 1996; Tyson, 1995) indicated that HRM was leading to changes in practice, which were both strategic and integrated. In particular, it has been shown that in the United Kingdom firms in the mid-1990s were increasingly following coherent strategies of 'high-commitment management' (Wood, 1996) that entailed enlarging/enriching jobs, introducing teamworking, involving employees in major decisions, and training and development to achieve functional flexibility amongst the workforce (Patterson *et al.*, 1997). Although this is not the only organisational model for financial success, these research findings have represented a significant shift to a second wave in the study of strategic HRM (Mabey *et al.*, 1998), which has the following focal points:

■ The significance of the social and economic context of HRM – for example, the attention that is paid to the needs and desires of a range of stakeholders.

■ The search for conclusive evidence that the best practice of HRM results in improved organisational performance.

■ The impact of changing organisational structures – for example, network arrangements between organisations or the use of contractors as part of the 'normal' workforce.

■ A focus on knowledge, organisational capability and learning as key themes in both general strategy and strategic HRM.

AFTER THE WAVES

Since these initial waves there has been a period of consolidation. There is now a more sophisticated understanding of strategy and clarity in the research on the impact of HRM on organisational performance. There is also an understanding that single solution 'best practice' models of HRM are not sufficient to work in all environments and contexts. Rather, a more developed approach to practice is being propounded. This incorporates various ongoing challenges, some of which are perpetual, others arising as societies and economies change. We will discuss briefly each of these points.

First, the 'strategy' issue has long been a live one for HRM. The aim has been for people matters to have greater strategic importance. These issues were discussed in Chapters 1 and 2, but it is worth summarising the current state of affairs. Much of the thinking in the early phases of HRM was in line with the 'design school' of strategy Johnson *et al.* (2005). Under this conception, strategy is made by the 'thinkers' at the top of the organisation and implemented by the 'doers' lower down the hierarchy. The purpose of management is to control what the doers do in order to maximise efficiency. This perspective is no longer accepted either in strategy (Johnson *et al.*, 2005) or strategic HRM (Watson, 2005). The view that is more broadly accepted now is that organisations are 'negotiated orders' in which different stakeholders have an interest and in which they will seek to exert influence. Stakeholder groups include customers and shareholders along with internal stakeholders such as managers and specific groups of employees such as professional and functional groups. Strategies are influenced by those at the top, but they are only effective if they take into account the views and needs of a variety of stakeholders. If they fail to do this, then conflict is likely to arise and this will be likely to slow systems down and harm business. In addition, the old view of the Design School, that strategies could be developed for the long term, has also been challenged. It is now accepted that with the pace of change, strategies need to be 'agile' and flexible to meet the realities of competition, customer demands and shifts in the internal and external environments.

Hence, strategies are seen as 'emergent', developing contingently by adopting a 'direction of travel' and constantly adjusting it by 'sensing the environment'. This conception of strategy fits well with HRM. It means that it is necessary to be able to consult with and involve stakeholders in an effective manner. This topic was discussed in Chapter 11. This means that the knowledge and expertise of the workforce can be fed up the organisation to improve strategic decisions. It is important, therefore, to ensure that employees are motivated to take participation seriously, and the example of John Lewis (Case example 9.2) shows one way of achieving this through tying employee and organisational interests together closely.

Secondly, there is now greater clarity in the research on the impact of HRM practice on organisational performance. This research was discussed in Chapters 1 and 2 but, in summary, large-scale surveys and a protracted programme of research (Becker and Huselid, 1998, 2000) has shown that successful companies have a strong tendency to have adopted developmental HRM practices including a strategic approach, training, teamworking, enriched job design, devolved decision making and a reward strategy that encourages mutuality. Initial criticisms of this research argued that it was US-centric and applicable only to large organisations. Subsequent research has shown that, with some adaptation, the broad approach applies to successful organisations around the globe, for example in Russia (Fuller, 2005), Taiwan (Huang, 2001) and China (Li and Putterill, 2007) amongst many international studies. Similarly, subsequent research (e.g. Brand and Bax, 2002) has indicated that HRM practices are applicable in successful SMEs, although often without full-scale systems that would be common in large organisations, and sometimes through outsourcing some specialist HR functions to external providers.

Thirdly, it is recognised that a combination of a more sophisticated understanding of strategy and strategic HRM and an awareness of the research on HRM's contribution to performance do not themselves guarantee that organisations will automatically adopt better people management practices, nor that such practices will unequivocally work on all occasions. It is possible to adopt, say, teamworking or appraisals, and for them not to impact positively on output or worker experience. In the example of Marris Interiors above (Case example 12.1) the ban on appraisals might represent such an experience. Appraisals might not work for a number of reasons, such as a lack of training for the appraiser, a reward structure that clashes with the purpose of the appraisal, a negative attitude towards the process by one or more of the participants, or a culture in which there is no follow-up to the appraisal (see Chapter 8 for a fuller discussion of appraisals).

What is required is a more sophisticated understanding of 'good practice' (Pfeffer and Sutton, 2006). As discussed in Chapter 2, this entails a different approach by HR managers – that of being a 'thinking performer' (Marchington and Wilkinson, 2005) or a 'business partner' (Ulrich and Brockbank, 2005). In this perspective there are certain transactional and administrative activities that have to be undertaken (either in-house or contracted out) but there are other functions of HR that add more value. These include specific areas of expertise (such as the application of employment law in the context of the organisation) and being fully involved in strategic decisions. The latter entails sufficiently understanding broader aspects of the organisation (its markets, financing, etc.) and also having knowledge of the people and professional expertise such as managing employee participation in decision making (Arkin, 2007).

A number of organisations have moved in this direction. In the public sector, the Ministry of Defence (MOD) has developed three types of business partner: single job-holders covering HR provision for a business unit; specialists, for example, in learning and development who provide advice and input across a broader area of the organisation on a narrower field of expertise; and strategic level input. Because the MOD is large and diverse, one approach does not work in all areas, and business partners need to have a good knowledge of the areas they are responsible for. However, the MOD's HR section has discovered that specific knowledge allied with HR skills need to be supplemented with a proactive attitude. According to the assistant director for HR, the most powerful business partners are those who do not wait for their customers to tell them what they want, they proactively go out and look for ways to make a difference (Arkin, 2007).

Similarly, in Reuters, the financial information providers, successful HR business partners are drawn from different backgrounds, including sales and general management. Reuters believes that these backgrounds enable them to build strong relationships with line management so that they can go into areas and give input without having to wait to be called in (Arkin, 2007). The title 'thinking performer' is also significant. This implies that the process of adding value is not merely knowing examples or case studies where a technique has worked before and copying it into a new situation. There is a need for thoughtful and critical appraisal of why a technique has previously worked, what organisational and contextual factors were important, and how these relate to the circumstances currently under consideration. Typically, it is the skills of critical appraisal and careful change management that enable the thinking performer to develop adaptations that will work in new situations. This calls for both analytical ability and creativity.

Therefore, when we reflect on the development of HRM, it has gone through waves which have entailed fairly extensive criticism and reform. It has now reached a position in which there are strong, research-based arguments for regarding it as strategically significant, and there are ongoing developments in the understanding of what it means to add practical value to organisations and people. It is acknowledged that these developments are not moving towards a set of 'one best way' practices that can be copied and pasted from one situation to another. Rather, there is a need for thoughtful critique and adaptation of inspiration for practice (which can be derived from cases, examples or theories) to fit with the requirements of the situation at hand.

On-going challenges

Certain challenges and areas of focus for HRM are perpetual, demanding continuous effort and innovative thinking over time. The requirement for flexibility and speed of response to market changes is likely to continue to increase. This has implications for the practice of HRM. If increases in flexibility create an increase in the peripheral workforce, the result may be that they are relatively untrained and deskilled, since most organisations are reluctant to invest in peripheral workers. If this is allowed to happen, it will be difficult for peripheral workers to be creative and to make a positive contribution to the organisation. There is a need, therefore, for HRM to be involved in seeking a way to invest in this section of the workforce and to ensure that its members have sufficient security. Similarly, many organisations have adopted quality approaches and a customer orientation. This is increasing in the public sector, which has been adopting HRM practices.

Organisational structuring is also a perpetual issue. Some organisations are entering into network arrangements where they link with others who may be their suppliers or their customers. Agreements are made that guarantee continuing relations between the companies, and the emphasis is on a high level of trust. In some cases companies have had an open approach to their accounts so that other members in the network will know the financial details and the implications of the deal. This is felt to be an effective way of operating, rather than trying to act competitively and maximise profit at every transaction. It should be pointed out, however, that some companies are not yet ready for this type of cooperation and collaboration.

The involvement of line managers in HR practice is an important tenet of HRM. But it is known that is a difficult process to handle. For example, Reddington *et al.* (2005) argue that line management involvement in HR work (e.g. absence management, grievance handling, management of discipline, and coaching/counselling of employees) is not without difficulty. On this theme Renwick (2003) points to the mixed results about the benefits of the devolution process and questions the competence of line managers in HR work generally. Renwick is inclined to the view that line managers may well lack the capability and the inclination or desire to assume responsibility for some HR work.

Obviously technology expresses itself in diverse forms. A computerised database recording various facets of the human resources is, if good, a technological development with a desirable impact on the practice of HRM. Likewise, the application of computer and telecommunications processes to psychometrics (e.g. in areas such as recruitment/selection and development) has facilitated certain economies as well as effectiveness. In recent times there has been an emphasis on the potential of what is called e-enabled HRM, which has the effect of helping to reduce costs of HR services and liberating HR practitioners from routine administration so that they can focus on strategic and change management issues (Martin, 2005). One manifestation of e-enabled HRM is the use of call centres for the giving of advice on HRM matters. It is not pleasant for innovative advisers to be dispensing advice without face-to-face contact with the users of the service. According to Hoobler and Johnson (2004), academics have neglected the technological determinants of HRM.

Managing organisational ethics is a significant area for HRM. There are many temptations towards unethical behaviour in business. For example, in a court room in the north of England in late 2003 former directors of SSL, the medical group that makes condoms, were charged with boosting the sales figures by £22 million over a 25-month period. The sales figures had been exaggerated by trade loading – selling retailers more products than they needed to make sales figures more attractive than was so in reality. An investigation by accountants and lawyers revealed that unfulfilled orders were at the centre of an elaborate attempt to overstate SSL's profits and sales through the use of fake invoices, which were then washed out of the accounts using inflated exceptional costs (Firn and Tait, 2003).

The greatest examples of unethical practice occurred in the United States in recent years (*Time*, 2002):

> 'Unlike Enron which fooled investors with esoteric and highly creative accounting tricks, WorldCom cooked its books with a scheme which a first-year accounting business student could devise. The company spent more than $3.8 billion on everyday expenses to run its business – just as you might pay your utility bills at home. But instead of reporting those expenses as costs of doing business, WorldCom treated them as money spent to buy assets, such as real estate or equipment. Over a period of 15 months, WorldCom shifted those expenses to its "capital expenditure" category, which allowed it to spread the cost over several years. That made WorldCom's profits (before taxes and other charges) appear $ 3.8 billion higher than they really were.'

A necessary first step in firmly tackling the type of behaviour described above is to acknowledge the importance of the ethical dimension in economic activity. One could say that the collapse of the Enron Corporation in late 2001 has made ethics, credibility of financial information, and conflicts of interest between companies and their auditors topics of concern for all executives. In the United States legislation was passed as a reaction to events such as those reported above in order to improve corporate governance. The Sarbanes–Oxley Act 2002 was passed in the wake of the Enron, WorldCom and other scandals. The passing of this Act was seen by many responsible business executives as a healthy reaction to the sins of the past. A number of listed companies now pay greater attention to internal control as a consequence of the corporate governance reforms and specific regulations to tackle the abuses of the past. However, in recent times there has been criticism of the Act because of the burden placed on corporations in order to comply.

For many within HRM, adopting an ethical stance towards business is a taken-for-granted. Recognising the ethical dimension of decisions from being objective in recruitment and selection to preventing bullying, to ensuring equality of opportunity and reward is part of what the profession is all about. There is an ongoing debate about whether we should promote ethical behaviour in these areas because it benefits the organisation (not just because it avoids being caught out like the examples above, but also because it increased the objectivity of decision making) or because it is a good thing in itself to act ethically.

The internationalisation of HRM leads to emergent trends. From a UK perspective Storey (2001b) says that the adoption of European-led social regulation suggests that US-style free market policies will not be acceptable in an unrestrained way. Neither would the adoption of a fully fledged social model, despite the attractiveness of the case made by its adherents. One of those adherents is Sisson (2000), who advocates the European social model as the way forward. Bach and Sisson (2000) see future trends in the field as following the European HRM model as distinct from the US model, but they accept that the old European social model is in the process of being eroded. For a definition of the old and new European and US models refer to Box 12.3.

Box 12.3: Models of HRM

The US model has, as its key features, relatively weak trade unions with little collective bargaining facility, which management influences heavily. The outcomes are job insecurity, relatively low pay, flexibility, competitiveness and high levels of employment.

The 'old' European model has, as its key features, strong trade unions and collective bargaining machinery founded on legal regulations based on assumptions about employee rights. The outcomes tended to be job security for those in employment with relatively high pay, but with the downside of inflexibility, lack of competitiveness and unemployment for others.

The new European model includes as its main ingredients flexibility, security, education and training, direct participation through empowerment and indirect participation through partnership. The outcome includes quality people, quality goods and services, competitiveness and good jobs.

Source: based on Bach and Sisson, 2000

In addition to the perpetuals, other challenges have been highlighted recently. It is often the case that these challenges have been considered before, sometimes under different names, but nonetheless it is difficult for organisations to ignore them as they arise anew or become fashionable.

CREATING LIGHT BUT EFFECTIVE SYSTEMS

The administrative systems involved in activities such as job evaluation, appraisal and recruitment and selection can become bureaucratic and paper-intensive. This has long been a source of criticism of HRM and professionals have been concerned to develop systems that are not overly time-consuming, but which maintain the aim of ensuring fairness in decision making.

Typically, there have been three allied approaches to this challenge. One is the use of IT to speed up document production storage and use. The second is to make sure that the right person is working on the system at any particular point and to prevent bottlenecks. For example, during recruitment some organisations enable potential candidates to undertake self-screening via the Web. This is not a foolproof system, but it does mean that people who might have been initially interested, but who realise that they would not be suited for the job withdraw themselves from the system before others have to take action. The third approach is to streamline system requirements. For example, many job evaluation and job description processes are being simplified with the result that information is more concise and quicker to produce and use.

FOSTERING EMPLOYEE ENGAGEMENT

The psychological contract has developed into a major topic area in HRM. It was discussed in Chapter 2 and subsequently referred to in many of the other chapters such as those on recruitment and selection and performance management. The reason that the topic recurs is that it is indicative of the relationship between the employee and the organisation. The concern with employee engagement is to bring the ideal of mutuality into reality. This means that the organisation needs to benefit not only from the employees' committed effort, but also their knowledge and insight for decision making and innovation, their creativity and their willingness to bring into being a culture that is productive. In return the organisation needs to pay attention to their views, give evidence that they are respected, provide a good basis for business success and reward and develop them appropriately. In short, there is a need to effectively manage the psychological contract such that employees become strongly engaged.

MANAGING PEOPLE IN A MORE 'HOLISTIC WAY'

There is increasing awareness of the need to engage with emotion at work (Redman and Wilkinson, 2006). Emotion is subsumed in positive outcomes such as commitment and negative ones such as aggression. It is also involved in the psychological contract which is not only a cognitive unwritten agreement, but is also fortified by feelings of attachment, or weakened by feelings of dissociation. Similarly, processes such as performance management are not emotionally neutral as they impact on people's hopes, aspirations and fears. In order to make these processes function, managers have to be able to judge how employees are perceiving what is going on and what impact it is having on them.

It is notable that Tim Smit's language in the Eden Project example (see Case example 12.2) has emotional content when he talks about 'enjoyment' and 'admiration'. However, whilst Smit's example is a positive one, it should be remembered that other factors can have less positive emotional impacts. For example, in many settings the traditional career structure has disappeared and so people can find themselves displaced or having to manage portfolio careers at a time in life when they would have expected to have seniority and respect from their peers. The constancy of change that typifies today's organisations can put a strain on people and add to frustrations, and global pressures can lead to downsizing and outsourcing of production to other countries. It is just as important for HR to be able to assist in managing the fears, worries and negative emotions that can arise in these situations. Further questions arise as to how HR can assist with such complex issues. In addition to providing advice for managers on how to deal with the emotional side of managing change, for example, it is possible to offer access to counselling services for employees.

CONTRIBUTING TO SUSTAINABILITY

Organisations are likely to continue seeking different ways of working. After the propensity for greed, which was evident in the 1980s with the emphasis on self, gain and competition, the 1990s saw pressures for organisations to act in an ethical way, and this is likely to continue in the present century. Pressures have included consumers becoming more environmentally aware and exerting influence on both political parties and companies to think carefully about the effect of their policies and practices on the environment. Nowadays it is common for organisations to claim 'green credentials'. However, it is clear that commercial pressures and individual greed are still present in the economy. Organisations that want their 'green credentials' to be more than rhetoric need a significant HR input to achieving such goals. The experience of Interface in seeking to be a pioneer in this area is discussed in Case example 12.3.

CASE EXAMPLE 12.3

INTERFACE'S GREEN APPROACH

InterfaceFLOR is the modular flooring division of the global company, Interface, based in the United States. It is a worldwide leader in the production of environmentally friendly floor coverings and other textiles. The carpet tile was invented 50 years ago at Interface, and it has continued to develop the market ever since.

InterfaceFLOR is committed to achieving environmental sustainability. Its aim, by 2020, is to 'put back more than [it] take[s] out' (Interface, 2007) and to show that it is sustainable in 'people, process, product, place and profits'. This target is being approached on 'seven fronts':

1. eliminate waste;
2. benign emissions (eliminating toxic substances from emissions);
3. operating facilities with renewable electricity sources;
4. redesigning processes to close the technical loop by using recovered and bio-based materials;
5. resource-efficient transportation;
6. sensitising stakeholders;
7. redesigning the business model to demonstrate the value of sustainably-based commerce.

As a result, the company has reduced unnecessary travel and waste, undertaken tree planting schemes, greatly reduced the use of paper and invested in on-site renewable generation of power.

However, laudable aims do not become reality unless they are embedded in action, and that is where HR have been particularly important in InterfaceFLOR. Firstly, sustainability has become a central plank of recruitment and retention. The 'green' aspect of the company has been made public and is used to ensure that potential applicants are aware of the sort of company they are applying to work for. The experience has been that many candidates come with a positive expectation of InterfaceFLOR and the environmental trailblazing is seen as a unique selling point. Equally, current employees have found involvement in a company with such green credentials to be meaningful and it has become part of the connection between employer and employee (Smedley, 2007).

Training has been another significant aspect of bringing the aspiration to life. A three-tiered training programme has been developed covering induction, functional specialism and critical analysis levels. All managers undertake the programme and other workers do so on a voluntary basis. The programme has been accompanied by support for initiatives and communications about what employees can do both within the workplace and at home.

The goal has been in place for 13 years, and it is claimed in that time £172 million worth of efficiency savings associated with sustainability have been achieved.

Question

What should HRM be doing in general to enhance ethical and sustainable approaches to business?

Conclusions

Although HRM has been strongly criticised over the past ten years its path appears to continue undaunted. This may be because it reflects a number of trends that have an impact on organisations – knowledge/learning as a distinctive competency, the need for flexibility, an acceptance of change, the provision of high-quality service and organisational performance through people. The speed and depth of change means that it is prudent to invest in training and development and produce a workforce that is adaptable and knowledgeable. Failure to do so can lead to ambitious employees being 'poached' by rival companies and to a lessened ability to compete. Flexibility of operation, whether in manufacturing or service industry, and increasingly in the public sector, has become a requirement of modern organisations. Satisfying the customer and delivering quality is vital to continued good performance. Of course it is always possible to seek change through restructuring the organisation, for example, to form alliances, outsource operations and flatten the hierarchy, but unless the people remain committed to the purpose of the company any such changes will be unlikely to reap their intended benefits.

There are no absolute guarantees that adopting HRM practices in order to gain commitment and performance will be effective. The direction of cause and effect, from individual motivation/commitment, to individual performance, to group and organisational performance, is convoluted and complex, and should not be oversimplified. Hence there is a need for thoughtful and reflective treatment of people in organisations, taking a contingent approach that does not fall into the trap of treating people in an unfair manner. Although the issues mentioned above are current for most organisations they are also reminiscent of the concerns that were of importance in HRM at its inception (e.g. Sisson, 1990). It may be that over time the issues remain broadly the same, but that circumstances change, and hence there is a requirement to develop in a way that addresses the core issues.

Review and reflection questions

1. What are three of the formative traditions in HRM?

2. What are the key barriers to implementing HRM?

3. To what extent is HRM applicable in entrepreneurial organisations such as Marris Interiors and the Eden Project?

4. What typifies the first and second waves of HRM?

5. What are the ongoing challenges for HRM?

6. How can HRM contribute to ethical management and sustainability?

Activities

If you are in work:

What should HRM and the management of people do to contribute to the following in your organisation:

(a) creating light but effective systems

(b) fostering employee engagement

(c) managing people in a 'holistic' way

(d) contributing to sustainability

(e) fostering ethical management of people?

If you are in full-time study:

Decision making and the treatment of people are central to both HRM and ethics. Identify the key practices of HRM (such as selection, rewards and participation) where ethical questions arise and describe the choices open to HRM professionals in these practice areas. (See further reading and research for more background on this issue.)

Further reading and research

In the following interview a prominent HRM thinker gives his views on the future of HRM:
Arkin, A. (2007) 'In the hot seat: HR guru Dave Urlich talks to Anat Arkin about the future of HR', *People Management*, 28 June, 28–32.

In the following article, Watson sets out an argument for the theoretical and research-based approach to HRM:

Watson, T.J. (2004) 'HRM and critical social science analysis', *Journal of Management Studies*, 41, 447–467.

The relationship between HRM and performance, which is a fundamental relationship, is discussed in:

Pauuwe, J. and Boselie, P. (2005) 'HRM and performance: What next?', *Human Resource Management Journal*, 15, 68–83.

Internationalism and globalisation continue to be significant topics in HRM and the following special issue and article offer academic insight into these topics:

Rowley, C. and Warner, M. (2007) (guest eds) Special Issue: Globalizing international human resource management, *International Journal of Human Resource Management*, 18(1).

Zheng, C., Morrison, M. and O'Neil, G. (2006) 'An empirical study of high performance HRM practices in Chinese SMEs', *International Journal of Human Resource Management*, 17, 1772–1803.

HRM and its applicability in SMEs is discussed in:

Brand, M.J. and Bax, E.H. (2002) 'Strategic HRM for SMEs', *Education and Training*, 44, 451–463, available at www.emeraldinsight.com.

Kasturi, P., Olov, A.G. and Roufagalas, J. (2006) 'HRM systems architecture and firm performance: evidence from SMEs in a developing country', *International Journal of Commerce and Management*, www.goliath.ecnext.com.

Ethics, HRM and decision making are discussed in some detail on the International Telecommunications Union website: www.itu.int/itudoc.

References

Alvesson, M. and Deetz, S. (1999) *Doing Critical Management Research*, London: Sage.

Arkin, A. (2007) 'Street Smart', *People Management*, 13, 24–28.

Bach, S. and Sisson, K. (2000) 'Personnel management in perspective', in Bach, S. and Sisson, K. (eds), *Personnel Management*, Oxford: Blackwell.

Baudrillard, J. (1983) *Simulations*, New York: Semiotext.

Becker, B.E. and Huselid, M.A. (1998) 'High performance work systems and firm performance: A synthesis of research and managerial implications', *Research in Personnel and Human Resource Management*, 16, 53–101.

Becker, B.E. and Huselid, M.A. (2000) 'Getting an Edge Through People', *Human Resource Management International Digest*, 8, 36–38.

Brand, M.J. and Bax, E.H. (2002) 'Strategic HRM for SMEs: implications for firms and policy', *Education and Training*, 44, 451–463.

Braverman, H. (1974) *Labour and Monopoly Capital*, New York: Monthly Review Press.

Clegg, S.R. (1990) *Modern Organizations: Organizations in the postmodern world*, London: Sage.

du Gay, P. (1997) 'Organizing identity: making up people at work', in du Gay, P. (ed.), *Production of Culture/Cultures of Production*, London: Sage.

du Gay, P. and Salaman, G. (1992) 'The culture of the customer', *Journal of Management Studies*, 29, 615–633.

Edwards, C. (2005) 'Paradise Found', *People Management*, 11, 30–32.

Emmott, M. and Hutchinson, S. (1998) 'Employment flexibility: threat or promise?', in Sparrow, P. and Marchington, M. (eds), *Human Resource Management: The new agenda*, London: Financial Times/Pitman.

Firn, D. and Tait, N. (2003) 'Former executives face fraud allegations', *Financial Times*, 6 November, 4.

Foucault, M. (1980) *Power/Knowledge: Selected interviews and other writings 1972–1977*, Brighton, Sussex: The Harvester Press.

Fuller, G. (2005) 'Come the Revolution', *People Management*, 11, 38–40.

Harris, L.C. and Ogbonna, E. (1997) 'A three-perspective approach to understanding culture in retail organizations', *Personnel Review*, 27, 104–23.

Hendry, C. and Pettigrew, A. (1986) 'The practice of strategic human resource management', *Personnel Review*, 15, 3–8.

Hoobler, J and Johnson, N.B (2004). 'An analysis of current human resource management publications', *Personnel Review*, 33, 665–676.

Huang, T.-C. (2001) 'The effects of linkage between business and human resource management strategies', *Personnel Review*, 30, 132–144.

Huselid, M.A., Jackson, S.E. and Schuler, R.S. (1997) 'Technical and strategic human resource management effectiveness as determinants of firm performance', *Academy of Management Journal*, 40, 171–188.

Interface (2007): www.interfaceeurope.com

Johnson, G., Scholes, K. and Whittington, R. (2005) *Exploring Corporate Strategy*, Harlow, Essex: FT/Prentice Hall.

Keenoy, T. (1990) 'HRM: rhetoric, reality and contradiction', *International Journal of Human Resource Management*, 1, 363–384.

Keenoy, T. (1999) 'HRM as hologram: a polemic', *Journal of Management Studies*, 36, 1–19.

Keenoy, T. and Anthony, P. (1992) 'HRM: metaphor, meaning and morality', in Blyton, P. and Turnbull, P. (eds), *Reassessing Human Resource Management*, London: Sage.

Keep, T. (1990) 'Corporate training strategies: the vital component?', in Salaman, G. (ed.), *Human Resource Strategies*, London: Sage.

Legge, K. (1989) 'Human resource management: a critical analysis', in Storey, J. (ed.), *New Perspectives on Human Resource Management*, London: Routledge.

Legge, K. (1995a) *Human Resource Management*, Basingstoke: Macmillan.

Legge, K. (1995b) 'HRM: rhetoric, reality, and hidden agendas', in Storey, J. (ed.), *Human Resource Management: A critical text*, London: Routledge.

Li, X. and Putterill, M. (2007) 'Strategy implications of business culture differences between Japan and China', *Business Strategy Series*, 8, 148–154.

Lyotard, J.-F. (1984) *The Postmodern Condition: A Report on Knowledge*, Manchester: Manchester University Press.

Mabey, C., Skinner, D. and Clark, T. (1998) *Experiencing Human Resource Management*, London: Sage.

Maitland, A. (2001) 'The thin, blurred line in personnel management', *Financial Times*, 25 January, 13.

Marchington, M. and Wilkinson, A. (2005). *Human Resource Management at Work*, London: CIPD.

Martin, G. (2005) 'Technology and People Management: the opportunity and the challenge', Research Report, London: CIPD.

Martin, J. (1992) *Cultures in Organizations: Three perspectives*, Oxford: Oxford University Press.

Morgan, P. (2000) 'Paradigms lost and paradigms regained? Recent developments and new directions for HRM/OB in the UK and USA', *International Journal of Human Resource Management*, 11, 853–866.

Moules, J. (2007) 'Drive to prove human resources are "all emperor's new clothes"', *Financial Times*, 31 March 31/1 April, 20.

Patterson, M., West, M., Lawthorn, R. and Nickell, S. (1997) *The Impact of People Management Practices on Business Performance*, London: IPD.

Pfeffer, J. and Sutton, R.I. (2006) 'A Matter of Fact', *People Management,* 12(19), 25–30.

Pfeffer, J. and Veiga, J.F. (1999) 'Putting People First for Organizational Success', *Academy of Management Executive*, 13, 37–50.

Pollert, A. (1988) 'The flexible firm: fixation or fact?', *Work, Employment and Society*, 2, 281–316.

Rajan, A. and Chapple, K. (2001) *Tomorrow's Organization: New mindsets, new skills*, Create Research Consultancy.

Reddington, M., Williamson, M. and Withers, M. (2005) *Transforming HR: Creating value through people*, Oxford: Butterworth-Heinemann/Elsevier.

Redman, T. and Wilkinson, A. (2006) 'Human Resource Management: A contemporary perspective', in Redman, T. and Wilkinson, A. (eds), *Contemporary Human Resource Management*, Harlow, Essex: FT/Prentice Hall.

Renwick, D. (2003) 'HR managers, guardians of employee well-being', *Personnel Review*, 32, 341–359.

Sisson, K. (1990) 'Introducing the *Human Resource Management Journal*', *Human Resource Management Journal*, 1, 1–11.

Sisson, K. (2000) 'The new European social model: the end of a search for an orthodoxy or another false dawn', *Employee Relations*, 21, 445–462.

Smedley, T. (2007) 'Tread Softly', *People Management*, 13, 30–32.

Storey, J. (2001a) 'Human resource management today: an assessment', in Storey, J. (ed.), *Human Resource Management: A critical text*, London: Thomson Learning.

Storey, J. (2001b) 'Looking to the future', in Storey, J. (ed.), *Human Resource Management: A critical text*, London: Thomson Learning.

Storey, J. and Sisson, K. (1993) *Managing Human Resources and Industrial Relations*, Buckingham: Open University Press.

The Eden Project (2007) www.edenproject.com

Time (2002) 'How to hide US$3,852,000,000', 8 July, 28.

Tyson, S. (1995) *Strategic Human Resource Management*, London: Pitman.

Tyson, S. (ed.) (1997) *The Practice of Human Resource Strategy*, London: Pitman.

Ulrich, D. and Brockbank, W. (2005) 'The HR value proposition', Boston, MA: Harvard Business School Press.

Watson, T. (2002) *Organising and Managing Work*, Harlow, Essex: FT/PrenticeHall.

Watson, T. (2005) 'Organisations, strategies and human resourcing', in Leopold, J., Harris, L. and Watson, T. (eds), *The Strategic Managing of Human Resources*, Harlow, Essex: FT/PrenticeHall.

Weber, M. (1962) *Basic Concepts in Sociology* (trans. H.P. Secher), London: Peter Owen.

Willmott, H. (1993) 'Strength is ignorance; slavery is freedom: managing culture in modern organisations', *Journal of Management Studies*, 30, 515–552.

Wood, S. (1996) 'High commitment management and organization in the UK', *International Journal of Human Resource Management*, 7, 41–58.

Wood, S. and Albanese, M.T. (1995) 'Can we speak of high commitment management on the shop floor?', *Journal of Management Studies*, 33, 53–77.

Wood, S. and de Menezes, L. (1998) 'High commitment management in the UK: evidence from the Workplace Industrial Relations Survey and Employers' Manpower and Skills Practices Survey', *Human Relations*, 51, 485–516.

INDEX